ADJUSTMENT
AND
MENTAL
HEALTH

pp. 396
" 248

ADJUSTMENT
AND
MENTAL HEALTH

ABE ARKOFF
UNIVERSITY OF HAWAII

McGRAW-HILL BOOK COMPANY

NEW YORK
ST. LOUIS
SAN FRANCISCO
TORONTO
LONDON
SYDNEY

**ADJUSTMENT
AND
MENTAL
HEALTH**

FOR
SUSIE,
AMY,
AND TY

The field of adjustment and mental health is filled with ferment and change. There are new insights into human behavior, a new appreciation for the individual—his problems and potential—and new approaches for helping him overcome his problems and achieve better ways of being and behaving. In this book I have tried to convey the excitement and promise of these developments, as well as their sense and substance.

In this rapidly evolving field workers of many levels and kinds of training—lay and professional—are making contributions. It is for all these individuals as well as for teachers and students of human behavior that this book is written.

The book is divided into four parts. The first presents an overview of the field and explores the meaning of adjustment. It attempts to answer some important questions. What is adjustment—a one-way process largely dictated by the environment or a two-way process with person and environment each influencing the other? Is adjustment a set and static process, or a dynamic, changing one?

The second part delineates the process of adjustment by pursuing a number of key concepts or ideas. What are the important motives which drive and direct the person? What frustrations, conflicts, and anxieties intrude? How does he defend himself against these anxieties? How does he learn to solve his problems and reach his goals?

The third examines the ways in which behavior can be evaluated and improved. How should we act? What should we be? What is *good* adjustment? What is mental health? How can we achieve good adjustment? How can we enhance mental health? Who can help us and how?

In the last part, the book focuses on adjustment in five important areas of living. What is meant by *good* family adjustment? *Good* school adjustment? *Good* college adjustment? *Good* marriage adjustment? *Good* vocational adjustment? And what makes for good adjustment or maladjustment in these areas?

In preparing this book, I have drawn material from many different persons and sources. I have also drawn upon my own clinical experience and upon the generous assistance of my colleagues and students. I am grateful to all those persons who have shared their experience with me during the past several decades and, in doing so, have helped me learn and grow.

Abe Arkoff

CONTENTS

PART ONE

INTRODUCING
ADJUSTMENT

CHAPTER ONE

THE
MEANING
OF ADJUSTMENT

In everyday life, frequent use is made of the word "adjustment." Are you aware of the many different meanings this term may have? For example, to some, adjustment connotes happiness and freedom from personal problems. To others it means an unhappy conformity to group demands and expectations. Psychologists, too, think and write about adjustment in different ways and do not always agree on which way is most meaningful.

This chapter, first of all, is concerned with defining adjustment. Then it provides an introduction to the study, evaluation, and improvement of adjustment—topics which later chapters will discuss more fully. Last, it illustrates what is meant by good adjustment in some important areas of living: family, school, college, vocation, and marriage.

DEFINING ADJUSTMENT

What is adjustment?

Adjustment can be defined as a person's interaction with his environment. Each person constantly strives to meet his needs and reach his goals. At the same time, he is under pressure from the environment to behave in certain ways. Adjustment involves the reconciliation of personal and environmental demands.

Interaction means mutual bearing or influence. Every person is influenced by his surroundings. And each has some effect on the particular environmental settings of which he is a part. The relative amount of influence varies from setting to setting and from time to time within a particular setting. Sometimes an individual is more influenced than influential, and sometimes it is the other way around.

Environment refers to everything external to the person with which he is in some relation. In the study of adjustment, the unit of study is frequently a social group. For example, the individual is studied in relation to his family or to the people with whom he works.

Information about adjustment often concerns an individual's performance in a stressful situation. The focus may be upon a person about to take his first parachute jump or undergo major surgery. It may be upon a man struggling to find purpose and meaning in his life.

Consider, as an example of effortful adjustment, a brief eternity—only four minutes—in the life of a seriously handicapped boy. Wally Wolfson was one of a number of children who were studied in their everyday environments. The following account shows his heroic accomplishment of what for al-most anyone else would be a task of no great consequence.

Wally Wolfson is a four-year-old boy, seriously crippled from poliomyelitis. Both legs are affected so that he has no control of them below the knees. He is able to crawl and to push himself about in his coaster wagon. The following account is a brief segment of a day-long record of Wally's behavior and situation made on July 9, 1951. The time is midmorning; Wally is engaged in free play in front of his home. He has been playing in some mud at the side of the road and, in this part of the record, goes from the road to the sidewalk. To do this he has to go up a low slope of approximately 20 degrees. This slope presents no difficulty at all to his two-year-old sister.

9:44 a.m. Using the wagon as a prop and holding onto it with both hands he pulled himself up off the ground from a sitting position. He put one knee in the wagon, and with the other knee began propelling himself up the short hill to the sidewalk. About halfway up, the weight seemed to be too much for him. He struggled hard. Then he rolled out of the wagon, sat down on the ground with a helpless air and held the wagon in place with both hands on the back end of the wagon. He sat behind the wagon with an expression of futility. He rolled over on his side till he was at the side of the wagon and held on. The wagon rolled back slightly.

9:45 With one hand he picked up a clod of dirt. He seemed to be angered at the difficulty he was now having with the wagon. He threw the clod into the ditch and shouted angrily, "Damned old mud!" He sat for a moment and glared at the muddy ditch. Wally rolled over and, using the wagon as a prop lifted himself up. With what seemed renewed determination, he put one knee in the wagon and with the other foot started to push the wagon up the hill. Since it was difficult for him to go directly up the hill, he tried to lessen the grade by taking a diagonal path up the hill. He turned the wagon to the left and pushed hard. He got caught in some weeds off the path along the side.

9:46 It was quite a struggle but he kept pushing strenuously. He rolled out of the wagon and tried to push the wagon with his hands. He pushed it up and tried to crawl up behind it but this was difficult because the wagon would not stay up; while he crawled, the wagon rolled back down. He had to block it with his body to prevent it from rolling all the way down the hill. Wally looked up at me (the observer). He was getting quite annoyed at the whole procedure. He asked hopefully, "Will you pull me up?" I asked him kindly, "Well, what would you do if I weren't here?"

9:47 He smiled quizzically and coaxed, "Pull me up." I said, "Well, would you pull up yourself if I weren't here?" Again he smiled. He turned around with what seemd a little more determination. He put one knee in the wagon and, with a great effort, strenuously pushed the wagon up. The wagon moved up the hill. He looked at me and said determinedly, "I'm getting up," as though he were showing me that he could do it himself if I weren't there. After a good deal of struggling he finally pushed the wagon up onto the cement sidewalk. When he got it up onto the cement sidewalk, he gave one final hard push.

9:48 The wagon suddenly moved forward on the sidewalk, and he fell flat on his stomach. He accepted this matter-of-factly. He crawled up to the wagon and got in it. Then he turned around, looked at me and said with pride in his voice, "I made it." There was also a note of criticism for not helping him, as if to say, "See, I can get along without you anyway" (Barker, Wright, Meyerson, & Gonick, 1953, pp. 3–4).

Although a few major adjustments may loom large in our lives, most of our adjusting is not of heroic or even semiheroic proportions. As a matter of fact, most of our adjustments occur almost automatically, almost without awareness. If we think back upon the events of a day—even a very average day—we may be surprised by the complexity of our interactions.

Consider a fairly ordinary day in the life of a fairly typical little girl in a small town in central United States. On a sunny, late spring day, Mary Ennis, eight years old, was observed by a relay of eight observers who recorded everything which occurred from 7 o'clock in the morning when she awakened to 9:27 in the evening when she fell asleep.

Mary kept busy. She moved in and out of twelve settings. She participated in 969 episodes of behavior, many of them overlapping and interwoven; on the average, she started a new action every fifty-three seconds. She used 571 different objects; on the average, a different object entered her psychological world every ninety seconds.

Most of the objects were people. During the day, Mary interacted with 97 people-objects: boys and girls, men and women. Sometimes she dominated them; sometimes they dominated her. Sometimes she helped them or appealed to them for help. These, in fact, were the most characteristic interactions. But attacking, resisting, and withdrawing behavior were also very much in evidence.

The nature of the interactions depended upon the nature of the other persons in the episode. In general, adults were more dominating and more nurturing, and with them, Mary was more submissive and solicited more help. But interaction varied from adult to adult. For example, Mary's

mother was more nurturant than dominating, while Mary's teacher was more dominating than nurturant, and Mary interacted
differently with each.

It took approximately 100,000 words
to record everything that happened in the
fourteen hours and twenty-seven minutes
Mary was awake. Even during this relatively
routine day in this relatively simple environment of this not too complicated little
girl, a good deal happened—a lot of adjusting took place (Barker, Schoggen, &
Barker, 1955).

In the study of adjustment, a micro-
scopic or a macroscopic view can be taken.
The focus may be the behavior of one
person in one situation at one moment of
time. The observation of Wally Wolfson
demonstrated this approach.

The focus may be broadened. A person
may be observed as he moves from setting
to setting. This was done in the case of
Mary Ennis. Or the individual may be
studied from time to time within the same
setting.

An even larger perspective may be
gained by including more time and more
space. Some scientists have studied an
individual or a number of individuals over
a period of years. An autobiography may
present a person's lifetime observation of
himself, and some biographies describe a
family's progress through a number of
generations.

Person or Environment?

Adjustment, as it was defined earlier, is the
interaction between a person and his environment. How we behave in a situation
depends on our personal characteristics.

And it depends on the characteristics of
the situation as well.

How much of our behavior can be attributed to persistent and enduring tendencies within ourselves? How much is dictated
by the situations of which we are a part?
Much more research needs to be done before these questions can be answered
(Sanford, 1963; Sundberg & Tyler, 1962).

In explaining human behavior, psychologists have tended to refer to the attributes
of the individual. Relatively little attention
has been given to the environment. For example, there are many tests of personality,
but there are few techniques for measuring
the dimensions of a situation (Bloom,
1964).

Like the psychologist, the man in the
street tends to ignore the contribution
which a situation makes to the behavior of
an individual. In trying to understand the
perplexing actions of a friend or acquaintance, we are more likely to wonder what
there was *in him* that made him behave as
he did rather than what there was *in the
situation* that triggered his behavior.

Sometimes a person is labeled "maladjusted" as if the maladjustment were something which resided in him, preventing him
from adjusting to any situation. However,
he is probably able to adjust to some parts
of his environment. In fact, he may handle
some situations quite well.

Even those who are considered well-
adjusted find some situations difficult to
manage. Certainly, no one is the master of
every part of his environment. Certainly,
everyone encounters situations which provoke fear or anger or which—for many
reasons—make it difficult to act effectively
and with composure.

In considering your own family, for illustration, you may note a large difference in various relationships. Perhaps there is a particular member of the family toward whom you feel very close. Your relationship with another may be quite strained. With a third you may continually fight and make up.

School adjustment may have involved a similar situational variation. You may have adjusted well to one school but badly to a second. And within each school, your adjustment varied depending upon who the teacher and other students were and upon many factors in the classroom.

If you went on to college, further situational influences may be noted. Perhaps you did very well in a small college near your home but floundered badly after transferring to a large and more impersonal university. Or maybe it was the other way around: you moved listlessly through a college in your community, but suddenly became alive when you reached a vibrant university setting.

In recent years, psychologists have been paying increased attention to the environment and its effect upon behavior. They have become more interested in observing the real-life situations in which people find themselves. Such environments are, of course, much more complex than laboratory situations, but ways are being devised to measure them and determine their influence on patterns of adjustment.

In evaluating and predicting behavior, psychologists are becoming increasingly aware of the necessity of taking into account environmental conditions. Instead of making general predictions about a person, they are more apt to make conditional ones. Instead of talking about a "maladjusted" person, they try to predict the situations in which he might do well and those in which he might not (Sundberg & Tyler, 1962).

In changing behavior, psychologists are also paying increased attention to the environment. In addition to changing the person to improve the situation, they are interested in changing the situation to improve the person. Rather than working with just one person at a time, they may work with a married couple or a whole family. Furthermore, there is increasing interest in working with and changing whole neighborhoods and entire communities to improve the mental health of the persons in them.

Perhaps, in order to give the environment its due, this discussion has overemphasized the part which it plays in adjustment. Certainly, a person's adjustment cannot be understood by simply considering the environment any more than it can be understood by simply focusing on personal characteristics. To understand behavior, both person and environment must be taken into account. As Sundberg and Tyler have succinctly stated, "It is the *interaction* between person and environment that is important" (1962, p. 165). (See Table 1.1.)

One-Way or Two-Way?

It is common to think of adjustment as a one-way process, a process in which the person—rather than the environment—must do the adjusting in order to ensure harmony. For example, we wonder how a child will adjust to his new school, rather than how the new school will adjust to the child. How will he adjust to a new house, a new neighborhood, a new set of playmates?

We may regard our own adjustments in the same way. We speak of having to adjust to a condition or situation or group of people in a way that implies that we have no say in the matter. In the abstract, at least, we may think of the environment as all-powerful and all-demanding.

One of the reasons for this one-sided view of adjustment is the one-sided concentration of scientific exploration. White, a psychologist, champions a broader view of adjustment, which he expresses in the following way:

The scientist has almost never studied ordinary people as they increase their mastery of the ordinary problems of daily life. Still less has he studied the investigatory activity of scientists, and he has thereby overlooked one of the most devoted, persistent, honest and selfless forms of human behavior. There are scarcely any systematic case records of great fortitude, rare heroism, unusual contribution to the arts, or special success in grasping and solving important social issues. The natural growth of personality and the higher flights of human achievement have been given almost no representation in man's current ideas about himself.

The consequences of these omissions are serious. The sciences of man have learned many things of great value to human welfare, but their partial view of human nature has added to the anxiety and pessimism of our times. We know a good deal about the ways in which conditions mould men, and this knowledge is important; we know very little about the ways in which men mould conditions, and this knowledge can hardly be called less important. It is grimly unfortunate that in a period when rationality, insight, and creative social invention are in such urgent demand, science is prepared to throw light mainly on man's irrationality and helplessness (1952, p. 4).

Writers and poets, frequently taking as their theme man caught in an all-powerful and all-demanding environment, have helped to dramatize and amplify this limited view of the adjustment process. Housman, the English poet, was able to mirror the feelings that many of us have had in the presence of seemingly inexorable environmental demands. In his *Last Poems*, he writes:

Table 1.1 Poverty: Person or environment? It has been estimated that about one-fifth of the people in the United States live in poverty. There are a number of opinions concerning the causes of poverty. One view is that the poor person is himself at fault, that his poverty is due to a lack of effort on his part. Another view is that the environment is to blame, that poverty is due to circumstances beyond the person's control. A third view holds that poverty is due to a combination of personal and environmental causes. In 1964, a nationwide Gallup Poll showed that about one-third of the pollees subscribed to each of these three views. However, further analysis showed that pollees with relatively high incomes ($10,000 and over) tended to blame poverty on the person more than on the environment, while respondents with very low incomes (under $3,000) tended to blame the environment more than the person.*

Question asked by Gallup Poll reporters: "In your opinion, which is more often to blame if a person is poor—lack of effort on his own part, or circumstances beyond his control?"

Answers of Pollees	Percent
Lack of effort	33
Circumstances	29
Equal	32
No opinion	6

* Gallup Poll Report (Spring, 1964).

And how am I to face the odds
Of man's bedevilment and God's?
I, a stranger and afraid
In a world I never made. [1]

Henley, another English poet, a critic and editor, was a man whose life was a constant struggle against sorrow, sickness, pain, and disappointment. His most famous poem *Invictus* reflects the courage with which he fought for life. Still, like Housman's protagonist, he is "master of his fate" only in his ability to *bear* the dreadful doings of his environment—not in his capacity to *change* them.

Out of the night that covers me,
Black as the Pit from pole to pole,
I thank whatever gods may be
For my unconquerable soul.

In the fell clutch of circumstance
I have not winced nor cried aloud.
Under the bludgeonings of chance
My head is bloody, but unbowed.

Beyond this place of wrath and tears
Looms but the horror of the shade,
And yet the menace of the years
Finds, and shall find, me unafraid.

It matters not how strait the gate,
How charged with punishments the
scroll,
I am the master of my fate:
I am the captain of my soul. [2]

This one-way view of adjustment has encouraged the equation of adjustment with conformity. "Adjusting," to some of us, means "conforming" to environmental de-

mands. In this way, adjustment may come to connote the loss of highly prized autonomy and individuality.

More recently the two-way nature of the adjustment process has been emphasized. White strongly urges this conception of adjustment. He writes:

> *The concept of adjustment implies a constant interaction between the person and his environment, each making demands on the other. Sometimes adjustment is accomplished when the person yields and accepts conditions which are beyond his power to change. Sometimes it is achieved when the environment yields to the person's constructive activities. In most cases adjustment is a compromise between these two extremes and maladjustment is a failure to achieve a satisfactory compromise.* [3]

This approach carries with it a greater optimism and hopefulness of man's fate and future. In this view, our environment influences us, but we also influence our environment. We not only *conform*, we are *conformed to*.

In speaking of environment, we sometimes lose track of the fact that it is largely composed of people, each of whom is engaged in his own adjustment processes. We, ourselves, are environment for many other people. And when we speak of environment, we may overlook that it is made up of many subenvironments or situations. Our living goes on in these relatively small units or settings.

We can divest ourselves of the one-way notion of adjustment by shifting our frame of reference from environment to environments—from the whole to the parts which make it up. The behavior of the child in the

[1] From "The laws of God, the laws of man" in *The Collected Poems of A. E. Housman,* Copyright 1922 by Holt, Rinehart and Winston, Inc. Copyright 1950 by Barclays Bank Ltd. Reprinted by permission of Holt, Rinehart and Winston, Inc.
[2] From *Poems by William Ernest Henley.* (6th ed.) New York: Scribner's, 1904.

[3] From Robert W. White—*The Abnormal Personality,* Second Edition. Copyright © 1956, The Ronald Press Company, New York. P. 103.

family has a bearing on the behavior of other members of the family; the behavior of the child in the classroom influences the behavior of others present; and so on.

In recent years, there has been a new appreciation of the individuality and power of the person. Rather than being simply "reactive," simply reacting to environmental stimulation, the infant is seen as "active," as an acting and interacting being. The mother influences the child but the child also influences the mother by sucking and clinging and crying and smiling. Kessen, who has emphasized this point, writes, "The shift in point-of-view—to set the antithesis sharply—has been from the child who is a passive receptacle, into which learning and maturation pour knowledge and skills and affects until he is full, to the child as a complex, competent organism who, by acting on the environment and being acted on in turn, develops more elaborated and balanced ways of dealing with discrepancy, conflict, and dis-equilibrium" (1963, p. 92).

Static or Dynamic?

Sometimes adjustment is spoken of as if it were a state or static condition. For example, a particular person is referred to as well adjusted (not well adjusting). Another is described as maladjusted (not maladjusting).

As has been indicated, a person's adjustment can be expected to change from situation to situation. And it can also be expected to change over a period of time in a particular situation.

All of life is change. We constantly change. Changes are especially obvious and rapid during our early life. But even during the relatively stable adult period, changes

are constantly taking place (Bayley, 1963).

At the same time, our environment is also constantly changing. Political, economic, and social circumstances alter. Family and friends change with age and experience. New people enter our social world and crucially influence it. People who were in it depart.

With this constant change in ourselves and in our environment, continual adjustment (or readjustment) is necessary. A satisfactory adjustment is not something which we achieve once and for all time. It is something that we must constantly achieve and reachieve.

Sometimes and in some areas of life our adjustment efforts may seem to be minimal. Sometimes they may appear to be of almost heroic proportions. But minimal or heroic, our efforts are never at an end.

Some interesting information concerning change in social adjustment has come out of the longitudinal studies of children at the University of California's Institute of Human Development. In studies of children as they develop from infancy through adolescence, evidence has been found for both consistency and change. Some patterns of behavior have shown continuity while others are very much in flux.

Very little could be predicted about a child's later adjustment from the behavior he showed the first and second year of life; these first two years had very little correlation with the quality of subsequent social adjustment. Adjustment patterns were more consistent during the middle childhood years. But at adolescence, again, there were considerable changes.

Many of the children's behaviors and behavior problems were found to be "age specific"—they occurred at some ages, but not at others. Children seemed to grow into certain problems at certain ages and then grow out of them. One set of problems was replaced by another set as a child developed. The fact that a child had a problem at one age did not necessarily indicate that he would continue to have the same problem—or even other problems—later on (Bayley, 1963; Macfarlane, Allen, & Honzik, 1954; Schaefer & Bayley, 1963).

We adults have our age-specific (and "situation-specific") problems too. Some of us are relatively problem-free. Some of us are relatively problem-prone. But most of us, regardless of a momentary calm, can expect a crisis or semicrisis around the corner. And, to look at the brighter side, regardless of a momentary crisis, we may look for a calm or at least a semicalm not too far away.

To give a few examples, the first year of college is often a critical time. Old patterns of adjustment may be rudely interrupted. The student may be away from home or on his own for the first time, and college may be completely unlike high school or anything he has known before. He may lack motivation or a sense of direction, and the competition may be intense. Considerable adjustment is necessary. A sizable proportion of students drop out the first year, and many never graduate (Summerskill, 1962).

For some people, the first years of marriage are a time of crisis. Divorce rates are particularly high during the initial years. Those who last out these early storms can expect less perilous weather ahead.

Some couples find adjusting to each other not as difficult as adjusting to the advent of their first child. The additional work and expense, as well as the changing roles, relationships, and routines, create critical problems. Most couples make a very satis-

factory recovery, but it may come only after a difficult few months (Dyer, 1963; LeMasters 1957).

The middle years bring crises for some people. A woman may find her valued homemaking role declining as her children grow up and depart, and she may have little skill or appetite for a new role. A man may find himself in a vocational blind alley and begin to doubt his worth, and there may be little chance or enthusiasm for a new start.

Retirement poses new problems. We may need to reduce our activities. We may leave a job which has given pattern and meaning to our life. Our social world changes as the people with whom our life has been interwoven move away or die.

These are only a few of the crises which lend a dynamic quality to life. Even less critical times present problems enough. To be well adjusted, we must adjust well and adjust continually.

STUDYING ADJUSTMENT

How do we adjust? What are the forces that drive us from within? What are the goals that draw us from without? How do we reach them? How can we understand the frustrations, conflicts, and anxieties that loom so large in our lives?

How do we adjust? Following are some concepts that have proved useful in understanding adjustment. They are key ideas. The present discussion is meant to serve as an overview of the adjustment process. In later chapters each concept will be reintroduced and discussed more fully.

Motive

We can begin our understanding of adjustment by observing our own behavior and the behavior of other people around us. We might note, for example, that we are hungry and look for food or that we are lonely and seek companionship. We would be able to identify a number of needs that prompt us to act and a number of goals toward which our acts are directed.

Our behavior seems to be fairly consistent or patterned. We tend to behave in the same way, reacting to the same needs and seeking the same goals. These patterns of need-impelled and goal-directed activity are called *motives*.

As this discussion indicates, the concept of motive includes the ideas of need, act, and goal. A *need* is a condition that prompts us to act. For example, we all need oxygen, food, and rest. Some of us need to be with people; others need to be apart from them. Many individuals have a strong need to achieve, and a few appear to have an unrelenting need to fail.

Act refers to the behavior that is stimulated by the need and directed toward a goal. It may be a simple reflex action such as a sneeze or a shiver or a quick withdrawal of the hand from a too hot surface. It may be a very complicated series of events. Consider, for example, the behavior involved in succeeding in college, estab-

lishing a business, or getting married and raising a family.

Goal is the end toward which an act is directed. Goals can be tangible things: food, shelter, money, a spouse, children. Other goals are intangible; for example, the end which is sought may be the approval of others or one's own self-respect.

In Figure 1.1 and those which follow, some important aspects of adjustment are represented diagrammatically. Although these diagrams cannot show the full complexity of the ideas involved, they should be helpful as a beginning.

Frustration

Stimulated by our needs, we act to reach our goals. Some of our goals are easily reached. In our society not everyone eats what he wants, but few are very hungry. And not everyone lives where or in what he would prefer, but almost no one lacks some shelter.

But many needs are poorly met or met only after a great struggle. Some goals seem unreachable or nearly so. Anything that interferes with need-impelled, goal-directed activity can be called a *frustration* (see Fig. 1.2). Frustration is a fact of life: we all have had many frustrations; we have

Figure 1.1 A *motive* is a pattern of need-impelled, goal-directed activity. Involved in each motive is a sequence of need, act, and goal. A *need* is a condition that prompts us to act. An *act* is the behavior prompted by the need and directed toward the goal. A *goal* is the end toward which the act is directed.

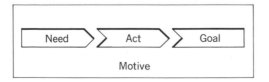

Figure 1.2 Anything that interferes with need-impelled, goal-directed activity can be called a *frustration*.

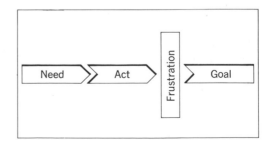

many now; and we must anticipate many more in the future.

Frustrations can be lacks or deficiencies. To lack enough time or enough money to do all the things we want to do is a common frustration. Or we may lack the intelligence or knowledge or skill that a particular situation requires.

Other frustrations are losses—things we possessed or conditions we enjoyed but have no more. Almost all of us have suffered the loss of someone whom we loved and needed very much. We may have lost our money in the stock market or in some other unsuccessful venture. An accident or sickness may have robbed us of our physical well-being.

Still other frustrations are obstacles—things that stand in our way. These things may be solid like stuck doors or high fences. More often they are social things like people who oppose us or intangible things like the feelings within us that serve to confuse or disrupt our actions.

Conflict

One of the most important forms of frustration—so important that it deserves special and separate consideration—is conflict. A *conflict* consists of the simultaneous op-

eration of mutually incompatible patterns of behavior (see Fig. 1.3). The individual must choose one pattern or the other (or make some compromise); until he does, he remains in a state of frustration.

Many conflicts are simple ones. They may involve several attractive choices, and no matter which we choose we get something we like. For example, should we vacation here or there? Should we buy this car or that one?

Other conflicts are not so easily resolved. We may be confronted by several courses of action, none of which is very attractive. For example, a small child may be told to eat all of a vegetable which he dislikes or else go to bed. Or an already hard-pressed student may find that he must study even longer and harder or else flunk out of school.

Probably most conflicts are between a number of alternatives, each of which has some desirable and undesirable features. We may be angry at someone and would like to get back at him or tell him off; to do so might give us great momentary satisfaction, but at the same time we may be afraid of the consequences. What to do? We may be eager to leave home and be free and independent, and yet we may be reluctant to abandon the emotional and fi-

Figure 1.3 A *conflict* consists of the simultaneous operation of mutually incompatible patterns of behavior. A conflict is a form of frustration; until the conflict is resolved in some way, the person is frustrated and unable to act.

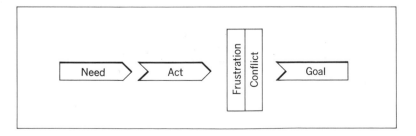

nancial support that our parents provide us. What to do?

Anxiety

Anxiety is a very important concept in adjustment, but it is complex, and writers in this area have formulated it in different ways. In everyday use, this word is also given different meanings: a person may say that he is anxious about a coming event, meaning that he dreads it, or that he is anxious to meet someone, meaning that he is eager to do so.

Anxiety, for this discussion, is defined as a state of arousal caused by threat to one's well-being (see Fig. 1.4). Anxious feelings can be objective in the sense that we, ourselves, and other people can understand and share them: we may be anxious about a speech that we must give or an examination that we must take. However, other feelings seem quite unobjective; we may, for example, be anxious without knowing why, or fearful about something that most people are not afraid of, or worried out of all proportion to a situation.

Some people are anxious almost all the time no matter where they are or what they are doing. Others are relatively free of anxiety except under special conditions or in certain situations. A few have great

bursts or attacks of anxiety that are exceedingly disconcerting and difficult to bear.

In the face of frustration and conflict and anxiety, we may still be able to forge ahead. We may continue our struggle to meet needs and reach goals. Goaded by anxiety, we may even intensify our effort.

Or we may be crippled by anxiety. Sometimes we are forced to abandon certain courses of action because of the anxiety they produce. Sometimes we must take measures to defend ourselves from anxiety. Some of us may become swamped by anxiety and seemingly fall apart or break down.

Defense

Certain patterns of behavior which are employed to protect oneself against threat or anxiety are called *defenses*. These patterns are also called "defense mechanisms" or "adjustment mechanisms." Occasionally, they are referred to as "ego defense mechanisms" since they protect the ego, or the self, against attack.

Defenses may be thought of as acts directed toward the goal of anxiety reduction. They are not necessarily special kinds of behavior. Almost any kind of act may be put to defensive or nondefensive uses.

Figure 1.4 *Anxiety* is a state of arousal caused by threat to one's well-being.

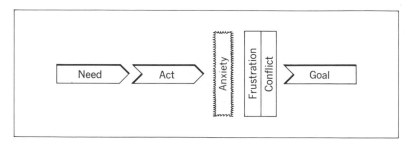

Defenses are rather special uses of common patterns of action.

Defensive behavior is not necessarily bad. How "bad" or "good" a defense is depends upon the consequences of its use in a particular situation. In one situation a particular defense might be thought to serve a person well by protecting him against disruptive anxiety. In another, it might serve him poorly by preventing him from facing and solving a soluble problem, or it might create a greater problem than it solves.

We all experience anxiety, and we all have to handle this anxiety in some way. Or, to put it differently, we all are called upon to defend ourselves against threat from our environment and from threatening or dangerous impulses arising within ourselves. Therefore, we all make some use of defensive behavior.

Learning

When we are very, very young, we are not expected to do very much for ourselves. Our environment adjusts to us. As we be- come older and able to do more, we are required to do more. We increasingly meet our own needs and reach our own goals.

We grow, and we learn. *Learning* refers to changes in behavior that come about through practice and experience (see Fig. 1.5). Deciding what is due to growth or maturation and what is the product of experience is not easy, but there is general agreement that human behavior is heavily influenced by learning.

A number of related questions are of particular interest in studying adjustment. How do we learn to overcome frustrations? How do we learn to resolve conflicts? How do we learn to deal with anxieties?

What do we do in a problem situation? Generally, we vary our behavior, trying one act or response, then another, and another. When we hit upon an act that is successful, it tends to be strengthened and used more frequently in the future. Acts that fail to solve problems are weakened and tend to be used less frequently in similar situations.

Sometimes, however, we are unable to abandon a response which serves us poorly. Sometimes we are unable to institute a new

Figure 1.5 *Learning* refers to changes in behavior that come about through practice and experience. Confronted by a problem situation, the person may try one act or response, then another, and another. Acts that are successful tend to be strengthened and used more and more. Acts that prove unsuccessful tend to be weakened and employed less in the future.

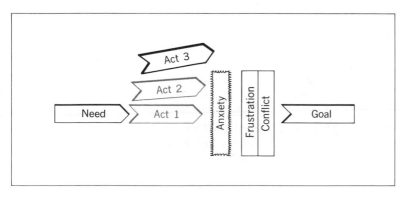

one which might serve us well. We need to unlearn ineffective responses or habits. We need to learn and strengthen better patterns of adjustment.

EVALUATING AND IMPROVING ADJUSTMENT

We frequently are called upon to evaluate or judge or state an opinion about the adjustment patterns of the people around us. Sometimes we try to evaluate our own adjustment. Occasionally, our evaluations lead us to seek professional assistance.

Evaluating Adjustment

Adjustment has been defined as the interaction between a person and his environment. But what is *good* adjustment? What do we mean when we say that a person is well adjusted? What is *poor* adjustment? What do we mean if we say that he is poorly adjusted or maladjusted?

In seeking answers to these questions, we will find it helpful to introduce some related sets of concepts. One such set is mental health and mental illness. Another is normality, neurosis, and psychosis. A third is sanity and insanity.

It should be explained at the offset that there is a good deal of confusion in the use of these terms. One reason for the confusion is that they are frequently used without being defined. A second reason is that each of the terms is used in different ways. And a third reason is that a number of the terms are used to convey the same meaning.

In a later chapter the matter of evaluation will be considered at length, but a brief preview of the later discussion will be helpful at this point.

"Good adjustment" and "mental health" are terms which are used by lay persons and professionals alike. Each term designates valued or desirable personal qualities or patterns of behavior. However, each has some special connotations which are worth considering.

Good adjustment generally indicates desirable or valued personal qualities or patterns of behavior. And this concept is typically spelled out in terms of the person *and* the environment. When we speak of adjusting, we speak of adjusting *to* something—perhaps to our family, or college, or our job. We can speak sensibly about a person who shows good adjustment or is well adjusted in one setting but not in another.

By contrast, the concept of mental health is not so closely linked to the environment. We would be unlikely to speak of a person as mentally healthy in one area of living but not in another. Mental health is generally thought of as a personal quality which, to some extent, transcends the settings of which the person is a part, although it will, of course, be affected by what goes on in these settings.

Like good adjustment, poor adjustment is generally spelled out in terms of the person and the environment. Like mental health, mental illness is more limited to the person himself. The maladjusted person is maladjusted to something or under some conditions. The mentally ill person is considered to have certain personal characteristics which are relatively independent of the individual settings in which he finds himself.

Mental health is sometimes reserved to identify *very desirable* personal qualities— perhaps qualities which only a few people show in any degree—and in this way mental health may connote something more than good adjustment. Similarly, mental illness may be used to identify *very undesirable* personal qualities—perhaps qualities which are associated with some underlying "disease" process—and as a result mental illness may connote something worse than just poor adjustment.

Normality, neurosis, and psychosis are terms which share meaning with adjustment and maladjustment as well as with mental health and mental illness. "Normality" is a term that has much in common with good adjustment and mental health. A norm is a usual value and to be normal means to be not too different from what is usual. Normality, then, strongly implies average or typical adjustment.

"Neurosis" is a term applied to adjustment conditions which deviate from normal and are of intermediate seriousness. Neurotics are generally handicapped in their pursuits, but they manage to get by. Professional help is considered desirable but not absolutely necessary. Prognosis or outcome is relatively hopeful for these persons.

"Psychosis" is a term applied to adjustment conditions which deviate considerably from normal—which are of considerable seriousness. Psychotics are unable to get along adequately in usual environments. Consequently, professional assistance is considered essential, and some form of hospitalization is frequently prescribed. Prognosis is poorer than with neurosis.

Other concepts used in evaluation are sanity and insanity. These terms crop up in ordinary conversation; however, they generally are not used by psychiatrists, psychologists, and other professionals except in legal proceedings.

"Sanity" denotes that a person is legally responsible or competent. He is considered to possess certain minimum qualifications, including mental or intellectual sufficiency, ability to tell right from wrong, and capacity for self-restraint. Such a person can be held accountable for his actions.

"Insanity" denotes that a person is not responsible or accountable for his behavior. If a defendant in a criminal action pleaded not guilty by reason of insanity, it would have to be shown that he suffered some mental condition *and* that his crime was a product of this condition. Were he ruled insane, he probably would be committed to a mental hospital.

Sometimes under the heading of "good adjustment," and sometimes labeled "mental health," much has been written about the qualities which are desirable in human beings and human behavior. As we might expect, there are varying opinions of what is or is not desirable. Still, there seems to be a core of agreement (see Table 1.2).

Two qualities which are highly valued are happiness and harmony. "Happiness" refers to a general sense of well-being. "Harmony" implies a balance between personal and environmental demands, with each receiving consideration.

A second set of valued qualities can be subsumed under the heading of "self-regard." Included here are self-insight (a knowledge of oneself), self-identity (a sharp and stable image of oneself), self-acceptance (a positive image of oneself), self-esteem (a pride in oneself), and self-disclosure (a willingness to let oneself be known to others).

A third set of valued qualities has to do with personal growth, maturity, and integration. "Personal growth" refers to the realization of one's potentialities. "Personal maturity" implies that one has realized or accomplished certain goals specific to one's age or stage of life. "Personal integration" refers to the achievement of unity and consistency in behavior—in short, integrity.

A final set of valued qualities includes *contact with* the environment, *effectiveness in* the environment, and *independence of* the environment. The first implies the ability to see the world as others do, the second, the ability to relate to others and be productive, and the third, the ability to be autonomous and not bound by group patterns of behavior.

Later, in the chapter on the evaluation of adjustment, more will be said about each of these qualities. Attention will be given to the way that each has been spelled out and to objections that each has raised.

The extent to which these qualities are consonant or dissonant with each other will also be considered.

Improving Adjustment

How can we improve our behavior? How can we develop the personal qualities which we want and value? What techniques can we use?

Literally hundreds of approaches have been made to changing or modifying patterns of behavior. Some of these approaches are medical or surgical and include such remedies as tranquilizers, electroshock treatments, and brain surgery. Some approaches are psychological or psychotherapeutic, including psychoanalysis and many other varieties of individual and group therapy. Still other approaches are sociological; they are designed to improve the adjustment or mental health of a person by changing the environment in which he finds himself—his family setting,

---

Table 1.2 What should we be? A good deal has been written about the qualities of good adjustment or mental health. Some writers mention one quality as desirable and some another, but there is a core of consensus. Below are some frequently mentioned qualities.*

Valued Quality	Brief Definition
Happiness	Overall sense of well-being or contentment
Harmony	Overall balance between personal and environmental demands
Self-regard:	
Self-insight	A knowledge of oneself
Self-identity	A sharp and stable image of oneself
Self-acceptance	A positive image of oneself
Self-esteem	A pride in oneself
Self-disclosure	A willingness to let oneself be known to others
Personal growth	The realization of one's potentialities
Personal maturity	The realization of age-specific goals
Personal integration	The realization of unity and consistency in behavior
Contact with the environment	Ability to see the world as others do
Effectiveness in the environment	Ability to relate to others and be productive
Independence of the environment	Ability to be autonomous and not bound by group patterns

* These qualities are described more fully in Chap. 8.

his neighborhood, his work milieu, and so on.

The whole area of behavior modification is filled with ferment and change. Old ideas and procedures are under examination. New approaches are being devised and applied. Later in the book these approaches will be presented in some detail, but now—as a preview and overview—six trends will be noted.

One trend has been the shift in focus from the person to the person-in-his-environment. In the past, the major task of improvement has been to deal with the person to alter the forces within him. Now the focus is beginning to be widened to include more and more of the social environment. Increasingly larger units are being brought into the improvement process—a marriage pair (rather than one spouse alone) or an entire family (rather than an individual member). Specific programs may be devised to encompass a whole neighborhood or an entire community.

A second trend concerns the shift from part to comprehensive planning in mental health. In a community of any size, a number of different services and agencies may play a role in the improvement of adjustment. Clinics, hospitals, and facilities of various kinds may be concerned. These facilities may duplicate each other's functions; at the same time, there may be no provision for other essential activities. Now there is a move toward greater coordination of efforts, and there is also an increasing determination to provide a full spectrum of services to communities beyond a minimum size.

A third trend has been the shift from professional to general public involvement. There is a growing belief that mental health is everyone's responsibility and right. Highly trained personnel such as psychiatrists, psychologists, and social workers are in very short supply, and there is a need for more help and more helpers. Lay persons are being encouraged to volunteer their services and also to assume paid part-time and full-time positions as mental health aides and counselors.

A fourth trend concerns the movement from custody to correction in the case of seriously troubled individuals. Rather than confining these persons to mental institutions which provide little more than custodial care, there are increasing efforts to help them toward better lives. If possible, these individuals are left in their usual living environments while they are being assisted. If it is felt necessary to remove them, there is an effort to return them as soon as possible and perhaps by progression through halfway houses or semihospitalization programs.

A fifth trend involves a movement beyond correction toward prevention. There is an increasing concern with the prevention of serious problems. Preventive procedures include reducing the conditions which cause the problems, reducing the severity of the problems through early diagnosis and treatment, and reducing the aftereffects of the problems by restoring the person quickly —but carefully—to his regular environment.

A sixth trend concerns the movement beyond prevention toward enhancement—beyond the prevention of mental illness toward enhancement of mental health. This trend, although barely under way, is of utmost importance. It aims not only to make us healthy and keep us healthy but to make us healthier than healthy. It aims to help us develop new potentialities—new ways of being and behaving.

ILLUSTRATING ADJUSTMENT

Human beings, with few exceptions, live among other human beings. They live in groups—in family, neighborhood, and community groups, in school and job groups, and so on. We sometimes speak of "personal adjustment" almost as if it could be considered apart from the social environment. But as has been indicated, the idea of adjustment implies an interaction between the individual and his surroundings. He doesn't just adjust, he adjusts to something. Or, to put it in another way, he interacts with it.

Later chapters will examine adjustments to a number of important areas. Good adjustment in each area will be described, and some factors correlated with valued and less valued adjustments will be noted. Attention will also be given to problems associated with these particular settings.

Here, to illustrate adjustment, are previews of later discussions concerning family, school, college, vocation, and marriage. First, there will be a very brief survey of adjustment qualities which are valued in the particular area. Then there will be an illustration of what one authority (or set of authorities) considers good adjustment.

Family Adjustment

Of all areas of adjustment, none is more important than the family. Much of our existence is spent in two family settings—

the family we grew up in and the family we have established or will establish for ourselves. The consequences of family experiences are reflected in every facet of our lives.

Families are complex. A single individual is complicated enough. And a family is a set of complicated individuals in complicated interaction. It is no wonder that families are not easily studied or understood. In the past, investigators have generally concentrated on segments of the family—especially on mother-child pairs—but now there is an increasing awareness of the need to study the family as a whole to understand the whole family.

Families are complex and changing. Each family has a life of its own. It is born, it lives, and it dies. The membership changes, each member changes, and the interaction between members changes. There have been relatively few longitudinal studies of families. The information from several studies suggests that there are systematic variations in a family's interaction over the years, but the evidence is still too scant to warrant conclusions (Yarrow & Yarrow, 1964).

What does it mean to identify a family as well adjusted? We frequently speak of individuals as well adjusted and maladjusted, but it is less frequent that we think of a whole family in these terms. What would a well-adjusted family be like? What would constitute a maladjusted family? Table 1.3 and the following discussion offer some definitions.

One way of defining family adjustment is in terms of physical coherence. Does the family stay together? Does it continue to exist as a physical entity? This is a simple definition, one that states an essential that can be easily and objectively determined.

On the other hand, the essential it states is a minimum one, and most of us would reserve the term "adjusted" for families who do much more than simply cohere.

A second definition of family adjustment is in terms of happiness. Many of us equate adjustment with happiness, and we may think of the well-adjusted family as one which is happy or has a general sense of well-being. The limitations of this approach to a definition are inherent in the subjective nature of happiness and in the considerable variation in happiness among family members and in any member from time to time.

A third definition is in terms of task achievement. There are certain tasks which a family is expected to perform. For example, it is expected to contribute to the support and socialization of its members. By this definition, the well-adjusted family is one which achieves the tasks the society has set for it.

A fourth definition is in terms of problem solving. Just as every individual struggles to deal with his problems, families attempt to work out solutions to the difficulties which face them. In this framework, the well-adjusted family is not one without problems (such families do not exist). It is one which is able to deal successfully with its problems.

Here is an example of a well-adjusted family:

The Rampion household represents a rather happy combination of those factors judged by the authors to be productive of a "good environment" for a child. The parents themselves are well-adjusted, vital, outgoing; they enjoy children as such, and their own children as individuals. They

Table 1.3 What is good family adjustment? Good school adjustment? What do we mean when we say that a person is making a good adjustment to college, to a job, or to marriage? Different definitions have been used. Some definitions are minimal—they state a bare essential—but they are easily pursued in research. Other definitions are more ambitious but sometimes harder to spell out. In essence each definition states a valued quality.*

Valued Quality	Brief Definition
Family adjustment	
Coherence	Family continues as a physical unit.
Happiness	Family has overall sense of well-being.
Task achievement	Family achieves the tasks which society has set for it.
Problem solving	Family deals successfully with its problems.
School adjustment	
Academic achievement	Pupil achieves what he is expected to achieve.
Social competence	Pupil forms satisfactory relationships with teachers and other children.
College adjustment	
Academic achievement	Student makes adequate grades, passes his courses, and graduates.
Personal growth	Student realizes his potentialities.
Vocational adjustment	
Vocational maturity	Vocational behavior is appropriate for one's chronological age.
Orderly progression	Vocational movement is through a succession of related and increasingly valued placements.
Job satisfaction	Individual experiences vocational contentment or happiness.
Marriage adjustment	
Permanence	Couple stays married.
Happiness	Couple achieves happiness in marriage.

* These qualities and some additional ones are discussed in the last part of this book.

show a healthy balance between the type of psychological detachment which allows them to appraise the child objectively and a warm emotionality that permits them to exhibit their devotion without embarrassment or artificiality. The child occupies his proportionate place in the household, is a full member of the family group, and is neither catered to nor ignored.

Mrs. Rampion herself is a healthy "farm-woman" type of person, sturdily built, stable, kindly and good-humored. She was a professional woman before her marriage, and possesses to a remarkable degree qualities of tolerance and patience. With a keen sense of humor she embellishes the most mundane situations, making life interesting and flavorful for her family. She is alert and interested in community life, contributes generously of her time and services for a variety of groups and causes. Liberal in her political philosophy, she is a genuinely democratic person in the home and in the community. . . .

The Rampions, more than any other family in the study, have explicit and formalized techniques for expressing their democratic philosophy of child care. Family council is traditional, with full and equal membership being accorded each child as soon as he can meet the requirement of repeating verbatim and explaining the motion before the group. The agenda may consist of matters ranging from the question of who shall wash and who shall wipe the dishes to the decision as to whether Mrs. R. should take a job offered her. The council convenes at the request of any member, and customarily handles the arbitration of all disputes. For example: "A situation has recently arisen in the Rampion family which is significant in that it shows the technique of settling difficulties among members of the family. While Bobby was combing his hair upstairs, Leonard 'dibbsed' on the wishbones from two chickens. Bobby was furious when he found what L. had done, said that it was unfair because one could never dibbs on more than his share, that he never had done it, etc. As a matter of fact, Bobby had done it more than any of the

others. The two argued about it far into the night. Both Mr. and Mrs. R. kept out of the argument, hoping, however, that Leonard would stick to his guns and that Bobby's fallacy in argument would be brought out by him. The night of my visit Bob had called a family council to settle the question, said that he would abide by the council's decision. Mrs. R. said that she was going to bring up the fact that Bobby was the prize dibbser unless the other children mentioned it first."

In spite of the formality of democratic government and in spite of the emotional distance which the Rampions maintain, the home atmosphere is not bleak or forbidding. The warm tone so evident in all the family's relationships characterizes their attitudes toward one another. Without a great deal of fondling or other overt symbols of affection the parents convey to the children their deep devotion (Baldwin, Kalhorn, & Breese, 1945, pp. 49–50).

The Rampions are one of a number of families which have been studied over a period of years by the Fels Research Institute. The Institute has been engaged in a long-term research program which has followed a group of children from before birth through maturity. As part of the program, the child's physical, intellectual, and social development was regularly evaluated, and his home was visited several times each year.

Although the Rampion home provides a good environment, the investigators do not claim that it is a perfect one. No home is without problems, and the Rampions have their share. But the family has more than its share of ability to deal with difficulties; as the investigators note, "Mrs. Rampion faces the usual run of disciplinary crises, feeding problems and general reversals that come to most mothers, though she handles such situations with more than average patience and understanding" (p. 50).

Leonard, the child who is in the focus of the study, also has his share of problems. Ironically, the very goodness of the family contributed to some of Leonard's adjustment difficulties both outside and inside the home. Leonard found his family so satisfying during his preschool years that, by comparison, the outside world seemed dull and in it Leonard appeared shy and withdrawn.

Within the home Leonard was the laziest and least responsible of the children, and the home's high standards (largely set by his siblings) caused him to feel inferior. However, these feelings were reduced by his subsequent success in school; here he proved to be highly popular and very much of a leader, and at the time of the report he was making a good adjustment.

It should be emphasized that the Rampions provide an example of only one pattern of good family adjustment. Other families achieve good adjustment in other ways. However, the family is high in a number of qualities which many authorities value and feel important: it is warm and democratic and also accepting and permissive. Furthermore, it meets the criteria of good family adjustment which were briefly stated above: it is physically close, it is generally happy, and performs its tasks and solves its problems.

School Adjustment

Much of our early life is spent in school. "Taught to the tune of a hickory stick" or any other way, our school experiences have a lasting effect.

Like families, schools are complex and changing environments. Each school system involves many people and forces—pupils,

teachers, guidance workers or counselors, curriculum specialists, principals, committees, boards, and other supervisory personnel, parent groups, teacher groups, parent-teacher groups, as well as many other groups and individuals.

What is meant by good adjustment as applied to a child's school life? One common way of defining school adjustment is to equate it with academic achievement. In this approach, the student who achieves what he is expected to achieve is considered adjusted. The student who does not learn, who is held back in grade, or who drops out of school before graduation would not meet this criterion of adjustment.

A second way of defining school adjustment is in terms of the relationships a child forms with his teachers and fellow students. By this definition, a child who gets along with his classmates and his teachers is considered adjusted. A child who is unable to form satisfactory relationships—one who is perhaps aggressive and unruly or overly shy and withdrawing—would be considered poorly adjusted.

Carla, a pupil in the fifth grade, is an example of good school adjustment:

> The teacher described her as a "lively, starry-eyed student who is perhaps the most outstanding student academically in the whole room." He was so impressed with her work that he recommended her for testing in the Gifted Child Program, which might result in grade acceleration. In this connection, he commented, "She suddenly is achieving to greater degree than her records show from previous years." He seemed to feel Carla was responding to some stimulus in his classroom; perhaps it was the older girls, whose attention-getting actions he said she tended to imitate. He felt she was seeking status academically; perhaps she was trying to impress these girls. Apparently,

superior ability and excellent work habits made this relatively easy for her; the teacher rated her as indicating little anxiety over achievement in the beginning of the year.

Much more seemed to be operating in Carla's case, however. Openness, intellectual curiosity, persistence, and intrinsic interest were facets of her personality which seemed to give her additional impetus in the school situation. At the beginning of the year she wrote, "I think that I should have learned some more things in my mind. I also think that I will learn more things by experience." She mentioned a desire to learn Spanish, expressed anticipatory enjoyment of the fifth-grade unit on Hawaii, and hoped that by the end of the school year she would learn a lot more than she knew then— not just in plain school work, but in all areas. Just before Christmas her wishes were for "a big history book and a record that will teach me all the different languages (Russian and Spanish, particularly)." She also had written, "In school I have a lot of fun. When I start to do something I hardly ever quit. I usually understand things easily and learn them pretty fast. I love to help other people with their school work. I like reading and spelling better than any of the other subjects, but I like arithmetic a lot, too." Aptitude tests indicated medium-high verbal and reasoning ability. She wrote, "I am really interested in science. I love discussions and when the teacher talks about something I usually am interested." . . .

But intellectual pursuits were not her only joy. She was active in Girl Scouts, busy early in the year in working for a community service badge. Music was an aesthetic interest. She played both the piano and the flute, which she loved, and was active in community musical groups; she had taken lessons from an early age. Sports also meant a great deal to her. In one writing assignment she said, "There isn't any sport that I don't like." And, like many children this age, she loved cats and dogs. The family had moved from a large urban area to this suburban community

before she started school; so, whatever her interests were, she had been able to pursue them in one setting without major moves interfering. All in all, her abilities and assets did not add up to just an "average person," even though she described herself as one. Although she wrote that she "liked practically everything," she did not seem to feel she was exceptionally good in these many endeavors. . . .

She indicated a healthy respect for her own feelings, good or bad. Her feelings, in fact, sometimes served as a guide to her behavior. She wrote, "I think that if you have won some kind of a game but you know that you had cheated in it, I don't think you would feel very good about it (at least, I wouldn't)." At the end of the year her comments indicated she had experienced considerable self-direction and that she was capable of objective self-evaluation. She wrote, "I wanted to be a little wiser in all subjects. I have accomplished this to my satisfaction. I think I have become a lot more mature, that I almost accomplished everything I set out to do." Earlier she had described herself as "sloppy," as not caring what she looked like, but at the end of the year she felt she was neater. Laziness and lack of poise, two traits she had chosen not to change, were not included in her summary of progress, although she did mention improvement in manners, which she had wanted to achieve. As she put it, "I could have manners even in football." There was no mention at the end of the year of improving her helpfulness at home or in controlling the short temper which she had mentioned having. She remarked earlier that she was helpful when she "wanted to be."

The fifth-grade teacher raised some doubt about her intrinsic motivation when he remarked that her parents probably had told her that she had been recommended for acceleration. He said, "She probably is attempting to prove to me that she is capable of this work because she has completed all assignments, even the advanced work in the sixth-grade books. At the time our notebooks were due, there was a 15-

page recommended maximum and Carla turned in a 35-page report. She spent very little time in the classroom, if any, playing around or wasting time socially." The teacher seemed delighted with her classroom behavior; he wrote in a midyear report-card comment, "It's a pleasure having such a good student in my room. Her work is very satisfactory. She has excellent study skills. I'm sure many of the students have learned a great deal about study habits from watching Carla."[4]

Carla was one of eight children who were intensively studied while they were in the fifth and sixth grades. The investigators were Pauline S. Sears, a clinically trained child psychologist, and Vivian Sherman, an elementary teacher and guidance worker. A variety of observations were made, and the impact of the child's classmates, teacher, and the school itself was noted.

All eight children under observation were considered "essentially normal," but Carla was identified as one who was particularly fortunate in her development. On the other hand, Carla was not without problems. And although she continued to do relatively well in school, her very good adjustment in the fifth grade could not guarantee the same high level of adjustment in the next grade with its changed configuration of teachers, pupils, and activities. However, in both grades Carla demonstrated the two valued qualities of school adjustment noted above: she achieved well and she related well to her teachers and classmates.

College Adjustment

For some of us, college is a high point in our lives—we look forward to it, enjoy it,

and carry pleasant memories along with us when we graduate. But many students find their college years filled with anxiety, doubt, and struggle. Some drop out along the way.

It has been estimated that about half of the students who enter college drop out (Summerskill, 1962). However, not all dropouts stay out. One investigator followed a group of students for ten years after they enrolled at a university; he found that about 32 percent graduated on schedule, about 17 percent more graduated not on schedule but after continuous attendance, about 25 percent dropped out but returned to some school and graduated or were potential graduates, another 11 percent dropped out and returned but seemed unlikely to graduate, and 15 percent never reentered (Eckland, 1964).

College environments and college populations vary considerably from institution to institution. Students who do poorly in one college environment may do better in another. Even within a campus, different programs may present very different demands.

What is meant by good college adjustment? One way of defining college adjustment is simply as academic achievement. (This is analogous to the first definition of school adjustment.) In this approach, the adjusted student is one who makes adequate grades, passes his courses, and graduates. Conversely, the maladjusted student is one whose grades are unsatisfactory, whose course work is marginal, or failing, and who drops out of school before graduation.

A fuller way of defining college adjustment involves the idea of personal growth. The first definition poses the questions: What does a student need to know? Does

[4] From *In Pursuit of Self-Esteem* by Sears and Sherman. © 1964 by Wadsworth Publishing Company, Inc., Belmont, California. Reprinted by permission of the publisher. Pp. 238–241.

he know it? The second poses a set of larger questions: What does a student need to become? Does he become it? These larger questions, of course, are more difficult to answer.

Here is a personality sketch of a college woman who was making a good adjustment:

"Hope" is the second oldest of six children in a family where both parents are college graduates, both have been active in politics, and both have been "fighting Liberals." In addition to maintaining a high academic record in high school, Hope was active in extracurricular affairs. She was elected president of her class in a large urban high school, was active in various kinds of public speaking, and in general was regarded as a "natural leader." She has continued this pattern in college, maintaining a high grade average, serving as one of the publication editors on campus, and as chairman of several committees. At the same time, she has worked part-time on campus during the week and assisted in church on weekends.

She is an extremely intelligent, observant young lady whose most striking characteristic, perhaps, is her precocious maturity in her interests and in her way of thinking. Equally impressive is her vigorous, action-oriented striving for creative self-realization. A sturdily independent individual she is actively and deliberately working to make the utmost use of all her various potentialities, intellectual, social, and esthetic.

This extremely busy pattern of life brings her considerable personal satisfaction. It is so demanding that on occasion she does get slightly weary and slightly cynical about it, but this mood rarely lasts long. She tends to do her major communicating and sharing with other people through the medium of ideas and words. She is just a little remote and restrained in her emotional relations with others. This does not at all reduce her deeply felt and firmly adhered to sense of responsi-

bility, both in work roles and in her interpersonal relationships.

She is genuinely creative in her use of her imagination. She is still youthfully vulnerable in this spot. If her ideas are rejected, she goes almost into a state of shock and mental immobility for a short time. She has not yet learned to divorce her ideas from her self, and from her personal pride. She is honest and unafraid, nonetheless, and almost defiantly asserts her views, whatever she may think their reception will be. She is not necessarily completely wise in her behavior, and there is enough evidence of underlying anxiety about emotional security to keep her from reaching the top of the scale in mental health (Peck, 1962, pp. 178–179).

Hope was one of a large group of coeds who were participating in a mental health research project. The investigator, psychologist Robert F. Peck, places her among those subjects who were high in mental health. Like the Rampions, who illustrated good family adjustment, and Carla, the example of good school adjustment, Hope was not without problems. In fact, anxiety and insecurity prevented her from getting a top score on mental health. Nevertheless, she demonstrated good academic achievement and good personal growth.

Vocational Adjustment

For many of us, work is more than a way to earn a living. It is a way of living. We pattern our lives around our work, and we look to our work to add pattern and meaning to our lives (Super, 1957).

Our work may be the most important source of our identity. The question, Who is he? is frequently assumed to mean, What does he do? We ask, Who is he? and the answer comes, He is a teacher, or he is in sales work, or he works in the shipping department down at the plant.

Knowing what a man's work is enables one to make some guesses about his educational background, his economic, social, and intellectual status, and, beyond this, his attitudes, values, and style of living (Wrenn, 1964).

The research evidence indicates that vocational adjustment is positively related to general adjustment. Those who are adjusted in work tend to be adjusted in home-life and in other social relationships (Super, 1957). The tensions arising in work environments have a considerable effect not only on psychological well-being but on physical health as well (Kasl & French, 1962; Mann & Williams, 1962; Wolfe & Snoek, 1962; Kahn & French, 1962).

What is good vocational adjustment? One way of defining vocational adjustment is in terms of vocational maturity. A person is said to be vocationally mature if his vocational behavior is appropriate to his chronological age, that is, if it has reached the level of development generally characteristic of his age peers. If vocational behavior is less fully developed than age warrants, he is considered vocationally immature or maladjusted. If vocational behavior is more advanced than is expected, he is considered precocious (just as he would be if his physical, intellectual, or social behavior showed accelerated development).

A second way of defining vocational adjustment makes use of the idea of orderly progression. Orderly progression means movement through a succession of related and increasingly desirable jobs or positions. By this definition, the well-adjusted worker is one who shows a meaningful succession of placements, with each serving as a stepping-stone to the next. The less well-adjusted person might be one who moves aimlessly from job to job or who is caught in a particular position beyond which he does not progress.

A third approach to a definition involves the notion of job satisfaction. In vocational research this has been the most widely used measure of adjustment. The well-adjusted person by this criterion is one who is satisfied or happy with his job. The maladjusted person is one who reports himself to be dissatisfied.

Here is an example of a good vocational adjustment:

Frank Congdon is a lawyer in his mid-forties. He lives and practices law in a small Midwestern city. He and his wife live in a private house which they own, in one of the more attractive parts of the city but not in its most expensive section. They have two children, a son aged 20 and a daughter aged 18; next year both of them will be in college. Congdon's practice is carried on as a partner in a suite of offices in the heart of the business section. He has a steady flow of clients, providing him with work that he likes and with a steady income. People in the community consider him moderately successful: he is a fairly high-ranking member of the Masonic Lodge, owns two cars, serves on several boards and committees, and eats his weekly lunch with his fellow Kiwanians. Congdon feels that he has made a good place for himself and for his family in the community, with a good practice, a good home, and popular children off at college with good futures in prospect. The son, he believes, will get an education which will enable him to earn a good living, and will make good contacts in the process. The daughter, he thinks, will no doubt meet an equally desirable young man while in college, and make a good wife and mother in due course. Congdon, in other words, is established. He has made his place in the world of work and in the community.

Occasionally, however, this middle-

aged lawyer has misgivings. He sees an occasional young lawyer getting started in his or in some other law firm, and his progress makes Congdon wonder whether he himself has done as well as he might have done. New types of legal problems emerge, relating to taxation, labor legislation, compensation, etc. Some of the younger lawyers, more recently out of law school, seem better posted on these subjects and better able to deal with related issues as they arise. His own greater experience gives him some advantages, but occasionally nearly trips him up when he finds that he has relied too heavily on his experience instead of poring over law journals, treatises, and similar materials. In fact, he finds that he is less interested in spending his evenings studying law at home than he used to be. Late hours are more wearing, and he feels he should be able to relax a bit now that he has made a place for himself and that his children are about ready to become independent. Then, too, occasional contacts with lawyers in larger, more dynamic cities make him wonder if he is stagnating.

A comfortable person, and rather secure in his achievements, Congdon does not let these occasional misgivings bother him much. He compromises spending some time studying new problems, but relying more on his ability to get one of the younger men to brief him when necessary. The system works, and Congdon feels generally secure in his place as a moderately successful lawyer. This being the case, he feels he can somewhat reduce his community service activities. Instead of accepting every committee or board appointment for which he thinks he can find time, he now accepts only those which he feels are particularly worth while, interesting, or honorific. He still functions as a leader in community affairs and civic service, but more selectively, more discriminatingly. Occasionally, but not often, he looks ahead to retirement. He will have an annuity, income from investments. The prospect of milder winters in California or Florida appeals to him; he'll have to ask

some of his older friends about the places to which they go. He wouldn't want to move there permanently; he feels too much a part of this community. And he can keep on practicing law, in a small way, rather than give it up entirely, if he feels so inclined. If it weren't for possible bad health, old age wouldn't seem so bad. As it is, middle age looks good to him. He enjoys driving across the high plateau of life with steep hills behind him, with pleasant and seemingly endless vistas ahead, before the eventual downward incline.[5]

Donald E. Super, the vocational expert who presents this illustration, notes that at the moment of the report the subject had reached the high point of his career and was poised there. He was on a plateau which proved relatively calm and satisfying, but there were qualms and dissatisfactions too. All in all, however, his vocational adjustment met the criteria briefly stated above in that it was appropriate to his stage of life, orderly in progression, and relatively satisfying.

Marriage Adjustment

Marriage has been much written about and much studied. Courses in marriage and family living, marriage manuals, and marriage counselors abound. In our culture, it is difficult to reach marriageable age without being aware of some of the pitfalls of marriage.

Nevertheless, marriage continues to be a troubled area. Attention is continually called to the high divorce rate. About three out of every ten marriages wind up in the divorce courts. Probably everyone knows of marriages which have failed.

Many of the marriages which do sur-

[5] From The Psychology of Careers by Donald E. Super. Copyright © 1957 by Donald E. Super. Reprinted by permission of Harper & Row, Publishers. Pp. 151–153.

vive have their stormy weather. In some marriages, the first few years are particularly touch and go. Other marriages run into stress at the time the first child is born, an event which changes the interaction of the household in crucial ways. It is not uncommon to see a marriage disintegrate with the passing years; the spouses develop in different directions and interact less and less.

What is good marriage adjustment? What is poor marriage adjustment? Two commonly used definitions are implied in what was just said; one involves the idea of permanence, the other, happiness.

Permanence is frequently used by researchers as a gross measure of marriage adjustment. For example, an investigator who is interested in the factors associated with success in marriage may contrast divorced couples with those who stay married. Permanence is relatively easy to measure and it states an essential. On the other hand, it is a minimum essential, and it attributes no measure of success to a marriage which, although abandoned, may have been a success or a partial success for a length of time.

A second definition of marriage adjustment is in terms of happiness. This is probably the first thing considered in evaluating a marriage. One wonders how the couple is getting along and if they are happy. Happiness—like permanence—has some limitations as a measure of marriage; it is, of course, subjective, and self-reports of happiness are vulnerable to falsification.

Here is an example of good marriage adjustment:

George and Ethel K. have what they consider—and their friends consider—a happy marriage. They live in a friendly, Middle Western city of 30,000 where George is in the insurance business. Ethel teaches in high school, though she did not teach while her children were small. Both George and Ethel are college graduates, and at present their son and daughter are in college. Both parents have always been active in the church; both are quite musical and have sung in the choir for many years. As might be expected, the children were brought up to participate actively in Sunday school and church and have found much good friendship in groups of young people sponsored by the church.

George was the oldest of three brothers and exercised some degree of dominance over them, though not excessively. Ethel was much younger than her two brothers and one sister and therefore rather spoiled by them. Also George is 16 years older than Ethel, though their children do not think of them as being that much different in age.

Although they are happy in their marriage, George and Ethel have their personality difficulties. Each likes his own way and at times tries hard to get it. Both lose their tempers at times, though Ethel shows less control than George, on the whole. Ethel considers George stubborn and "pigheaded" at times, while he sometimes considers her spoiled and unreasonable. She may want him to go shopping with her when he doesn't want to go, and the more she urges the more he objects. Sometimes the result is that she "blows up," and he consents to go along, obviously just to keep peace. But on a similar occasion she may suddenly give up the argument and go by herself, and without any anger toward him. Sometimes at a party or group affair George wants to go home before Ethel is ready. On these occasions she sometimes holds out and gets her own way, but sometimes she gives in and goes with very little protest. It almost appears that they are "taking turns."

The marriage is more equalitarian than otherwise. When Ethel again took up her teaching, George began to help with *the housework, and without protest. There is a joint checking account. There is agreement on matters pertaining to the children, and neither child can wheedle permission from one parent for something the other disapproves. George and Ethel came from much the same social and economic class and family backgrounds. They are both passionately fond of music and find it a great bond. They like the same kinds of books, entertainment, and friends, so they have a great deal in common. They have relatively few disputes, and even after a sharp clash they do not hold grudges. Their son and daughter quarrel with each other in the manner of all adolescents, but while this is a trial to the father and mother, they manage to pre-sent a unified front to their children and hold their love and respect in a very high degree (Baber, 1953, pp. 211–212).*

Roy E. Baber, a sociologist and an expert on marriage, presents this case. He calls this marriage a "successful" one. Once again, it can be noted that good adjustment is not a problemless state of affairs. George and Ethel K. have their differences and their difficulties, but the differences are accommodated and the difficulties are dealt with or weathered. Their marriage endures and provides them with satisfaction and happiness.

SUMMARY

Adjustment is defined as a person's interaction with his environment. Interaction implies a mutual bearing or influence. Environment includes everything external to the person with which he is in some relation.

How an individual behaves in a situation depends on his personal characteristics. It also depends on the characteristics of the situation. To understand behavior, we must take both the person and the environment into account, since it is the interaction between the two which is important. Adjustment is a two-way process—we influence our environment as well as being influenced by it. The one-way conception of adjustment has led some people to equate adjustment with conformity—we conform to environmental demands. The two-way view is a more accurate and optimistic one —we not only *conform* but we are *conformed to.*

Adjustment is dynamic rather than static in quality. We change. Our environment changes too. And our relation with the environment changes. Sometimes and in some areas of life, adjustment efforts may seem to be minimal. Sometimes they may be of heroic proportions. But minimal or heroic, our efforts are never at an end.

Some key ideas in understanding adjustment are motive, frustration, conflict, anxiety, defense, and learning. A motive is a pattern of need-impelled, goal-directed activity. Involved in this larger concept are three part-ideas: need which is a condition that prompts one to act; act which is the behavior stimulated by the need and directed toward a goal; and goal which is the end toward which the behavior is directed.

Frustration refers to anything which interferes with need-impelled, goal-directed activity. Some frustrations are lacks or deficiencies. Some are losses. Others are obstacles that interfere with behavior.

Conflict, a special kind of frustration, consists of simultaneous, but mutually incompatible, patterns of behavior. Conflicts may involve several alternatives, both attractive, or both unattractive, or a number of alternatives, each of which has some attractive and some unattractive features.

Anxiety refers to arousal caused by threat to one's well-being. Some anxieties may be objective and understandable, whereas others may appear to be unwarranted and baffling. The strength of anxiety varies from person to person and within any one person from time to time. Mild anxieties can act as helpful stimulants; very strong anxieties can serve to disrupt behavior.

Defenses include those patterns of behavior which are employed to protect oneself against threat. They are acts which are directed toward the goal of anxiety reduction. They are not necessarily special kinds of behavior. Neither are they necessarily bad—how bad or good they are depends upon their overall effect in a particular situation.

Learning refers to changes in behavior that come through practice and experience. In a problem situation a person may vary his responses, trying one, then another, and another. When he hits upon a response that is successful, it tends to be strengthened and repeated in similar situations. Less successful acts tend to be weakened and subsequently occur less often in similar contexts. As the individual grows and learns, he develops preferred or characteristic ways of dealing with his problems.

Good adjustment, mental health, and normality designate desirable or valued personal qualities or conduct, although each has special connotations. Good adjustment is typically spelled out in terms of the person and the environment. Mental health is more often considered a quality of the person himself. Normality implies average or typical personal qualities or patterns of behavior.

Like their cognates, poor adjustment is more environmental and mental illness is more personal in connotation. Mental illnesses of intermediate seriousness—conditions which are moderate deviations from normality—are sometimes referred to as neuroses. More deviant or serious conditions are called psychoses.

Sanity and insanity are terms in legal usage. Sanity denotes that a person is legally responsible or competent. Insanity denotes that the person is not accountable for his actions.

Sometimes under the heading of good adjustment, and sometimes labeled mental health, much has been written about the qualities which are desirable in human beings and human behavior. Not all writers agree, but there is a core of consensus. A pair of qualities frequently mentioned are happiness and harmony. A second set includes such components of self-regard as self-insight, self-identity, self-acceptance, self-esteem, and self-disclosure. A third set includes personal growth, maturity, and integration, and a fourth, adequate contact with the environment, effectiveness in the environment, and independence of the environment.

Many approaches have been made to the task of improving adjustment. Some current trends in behavior modification include the shift in focus from the person to the person-in-his-environment, from limited to more comprehensive community planning, and from professional to general public involvement. A further trend involves the progressive shift from custody to correction to prevention of mental illness and, beyond this, to the enhancement of mental health.

Finally, the chapter surveyed adjustment qualities which are valued in family, school, college, vocation, and marriage. An illustration of good adjustment was presented for each of these areas.

REFERENCES

Baber, R. E. *Marriage and the Family.* (2nd ed.) New York: McGraw-Hill, 1953.

Baldwin, A. L., Kalhorn, J., & Breese, F. H. Patterns of parent behavior. *Psychological Monographs,* 1945, **58**, No. 3 (Whole No. 268).

Barker, R. G., Schoggen, M. F., & Barker, L. S. Hemerography of Mary Ennis. In A. Burton & R. E. Harris (Eds.), *Clinical Studies of Personality.* New York: Harper & Row, 1955. Pp. 768–808.

———, Wright, B. A., Meyerson, L., & Gonick, M. R. *Adjustment to Physical Handicap and Illness: A Survey of the Social Psychology of Physique and Disability.* New York: Social Science Research Council, 1953.

Bayley, N. The life span as a frame of reference in psychological research. *Vita Humana,* 1963, **6**, 125–139.

Bloom, B. S. *Stability and Change in Human Characteristics.* New York: Wiley, 1964.

Dyer, E. D. Parenthood as crisis: A re-study. *Marriage and Family Living,* 1963, **25**(2), 196–201.

Eckland, B. K. College dropouts who came back. *Harvard Educational Review,* 1964, **34**, 402–420.

Gallup, G. Two basically different views held on causes of poverty. *American Institute of Public Opinion Report,* Spring, 1964.

Henley, W. E. *Poems by . . . .* (6th ed.) New York: Scribner, 1904.

Housman, A. E. *The Collected Poems of . . . .* New York: Holt, 1940.

Kahn, R. L., & French, J. R. P., Jr. A summary and some tentative conclusions. *Journal of Social Issues,* 1962, **18**(3), 122–127.

Kasl, S. V., & French, J. R. P., Jr. The effects of occupational status on physical and mental health. *Journal of Social Issues,* 1962, **18**(3), 67–89.

Kessen, W. Research in the psychological development of infants: An overview. *Merrill-Palmer Quarterly,* 1963, **9**(2), 83–94.

LeMasters, E. E. Parenthood as crisis. *Marriage and Family Living,* 1957, **19**(4), 352–355.

Macfarlane, J. W., Allen, L., & Honzik, M. P. *A Developmental Study of the Behavior Problems of Normal Children between Twenty-one Months and Fourteen Years.* Berkeley, Calif.: University of California Press, 1954.

Mann, F. C., & Williams, L. K. Some effects of the changing work environment in the office. *Journal of Social Issues,* 1962, **18**(3), 90–101.

Peck, R. F. Student mental health: The range of personality patterns in a college population. In R. L. Sutherland, W. H. Holtzman, E. A. Koile, & B. K. Smith (Eds.), *Personality Factors on the College Campus.* Austin, Tex.: Hogg Foundation for Mental Health, 1962. Pp. 161–199.

Sanford, N. Personality: Its place in psychology. In S. Koch (Ed.), *Psychology: A Study of a Science.* Vol. 5. New York: McGraw-Hill, 1963. Pp. 488–592.

Schaefer, E. S., & Bayley, N. Maternal behavior, child behavior, and their intercorrelations from infancy through adolescence. *Monographs of the Society for Research in Child Development,* 1963, **28**, No. 3 (Whole No. 87).

Sears, P. S., & Sherman, V. S. *In Pursuit of Self-esteem.* Belmont, Calif.: Wadsworth, 1964.

Summerskill, J. Dropouts from college. In N. Sanford (Ed.), *The American College.* New York: Wiley, 1962. Pp. 627–657.

Sundberg, N. D., & Tyler, L. E. *Clinical Psychology.* New York: Appleton-Century-Crofts, 1962.

Super, D. E. *The Psychology of Careers.* New York: Harper & Row, 1957.

White, R. W. *Lives in Progress.* New York: Holt, 1952.

———. *The Abnormal Personality.* (2nd ed.) New York: Ronald, 1956.

Wolfe, D. M., & Snoek, J. D. A study of tensions and adjustment under role conflict. *Journal of Social Issues,* 1962, **18**(3), 102–121.

Wrenn, C. G. Human values and work in American life. In H. Borow (Ed.), *Man in a World at Work.* Boston: Houghton Mifflin, 1964. Pp. 24–44.

Yarrow, L. J., & Yarrow, M. R. Personality continuity and change in the family context. In P. Worchel & D. Byrne (Eds.), *Personality Change.* New York: Wiley, 1964. Pp. 489–523.

PART TWO

STUDYING
ADJUSTMENT

CHAPTER TWO

MOTIVE

We differ. One of us enjoys positions of leadership while another is comfortable only in the role of follower. Someone likes to be independent and free to come and go as he pleases while another is happy only when he is with people. One person constantly finds fault with others; another invariably finds fault with himself. One person seeks variety and change; another clings to old familiar patterns.

We differ—yet we are alike. We all need food and warmth and activity and rest. Most of us need people to be with, to dominate and be dominated by, to care for and be cared for in return. Most of us struggle for recognition: we seek to win our own approval and the respect of others around us. We are not as alike as peas in a pod, but, considered broadly, the patterns of our lives are similar to those of many other people.

What do we do? And why do we do what we do? Sometimes those around us are easy to understand. But sometimes their behavior seems senseless. Sometimes, too, our own thoughts and feelings and actions are puzzling. *Why* do I have such thoughts? *Why* do I feel this way? *Why* did I do such a thing? The search for answers to these questions begins with the study of motives. This study will help us understand people and the things they do. And it will help us understand ourselves better.

DEFINING MOTIVE

As we observe ourselves and watch the people around us, we see that our behavior takes certain patterns. We appear to have certain needs that drive and push us. We seem to have certain goals that pull and draw us. Pushed by our needs and pulled by our goals, we act in certain ways. And each of us could be described in terms of the needs he has, the actions he performs, and the goals he seeks.

Our patterns of need-pushed and goal-pulled behavior may be referred to as *motives*. Various sorts of motive patterns can be identified. Our effort to be somebody and accomplish something is spoken of as the "achievement motive." Our sex needs, acts, and goals are referred to as the "sex motive." These motives and a number of others will be discussed later in this chapter.

"Motive" is sometimes used in a more limited way. For example, a detective called in to solve a crime may search for the motive. He asks himself, "Why was this crime committed?" He hopes that "why" will lead to "who." "Why" is part of the broader definition of motive, but "what" and "where" are included as well. *What*

Figure 2.1 A *motive* is a pattern of need-impelled, goal-directed activity. Involved in each motive is a sequence of need, act, and goal. *Need* is a condition that prompts us to act. *Act* refers to the behavior prompted by the need and directed toward the goal. *Goal* is the end toward which the act is directed.

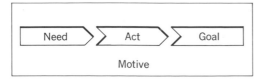

do we do? *Why* do we do it? *Where* does our behavior seem to lead us?

As the definition indicates, each motive involves a patterned sequence of behavior. This sequence includes the idea of need, act, and goal (see Fig. 2.1).

Need

When we think and talk about our behavior, we frequently make use of the concept or idea of "need." We need to eat or to stop eating so much. We need to get out of the sun or to get into it. We need to take a rest or to get busy and do something. *Need*, as most of us use the word and as it will be defined here, refers to a condition that prompts us to act.

Not only simple behavior, but complex patterns as well may be talked about in terms of need. A five-year-old suddenly "forgets" how to walk and wash and feed himself; he demands to be treated like his newborn sister, and his mother tells us he has a need for attention. A friend refuses to change jobs or spend his money or try anything new, and we say he has a need for security.

Needs are generally regarded as stimulus conditions. Hunger pains and sensations of thirst, for example, are stimuli that prompt us to act in certain ways. In one view of motivation, these stimuli serve to upset our equilibrium. When we act to reduce the stimuli, our equilibrium is restored.

A number of psychologists have pointed out, however, that men (and animals too) are "stimuli-seeking" as well as "stimuli-reducing" organisms (Hunt, 1960). For example, we can be tempted to eat our favorite food or a novel tidbit even when we are not hungry. We may seek sexual stimulation even when there is little opportunity for it to be reduced or satisfied. And some of us deliberately seek change, excitement, and danger.

It has been suggested that there may be optimal levels of stimulation. Above a certain level, the individual may be prompted to reduce stimulation. Below a certain level, he may act to increase it (Hebb, 1955; Hunt, 1960).

Some psychologists object to the idea of "need" because it implies that man is essentially inert unless he is stimulated or enlivened in some way. They point out that activity is inherent in living tissue. To be alive is to be active, and, in this view, the role of need stimuli is not to initiate action; rather it is to modify, modulate, and direct our movements (Hunt, 1960; Kelly, 1958).

Act

What do we do in a particular situation? How do we "behave"? The study of behavior depends upon the careful observation of our responses in a variety of circumstances.

Responses are defined and described in various ways. Relatively large units or smaller ones can be employed. A psychologist, for example, may be interested in responses involving a single muscle group or a single gland or limb.

In the study of adjustment, larger response units will be emphasized, particularly those pertinent to needs and goals. A response of this kind may be called an act and defined as behavior prompted by a need and directed toward a goal. Of special interest are those responses or acts

which are employed in problem situations— situations involving frustration, conflict, and anxiety.

Acts of adjustment may be simple or very complex. A psychologist, for example, might be concerned with the response of a preschooler who is denied access to some attractive toys. Or he might be interested in the much more complicated maneuvers of a man defending himself against nearly overwhelming anxiety.

Although the word "act" may seem to imply only overt or visible processes, covert processes are meant to be included as well. Thoughts and feelings as well as external actions are an important part of behavior in an adjustment situation.

Goal

A third idea involved in motive is that of "goal." A goal can be defined as the end result toward which behavior is directed. Food, money, prestige, a good job, a nice home, and people to love and be loved by are common goals.

Some goals are explicit and clear, and our behavior is very obviously directed toward them. Sometimes goals are rather ambiguous; we may not be too sure where we are headed or what we seek. Occasionally behavior may seem to be without a goal; it appears aimless or purposeless.

Some goals are immediate whereas others are relatively distant. To some extent, we must sacrifice immediate goals or satisfactions in order to reach important but distant ones. For example, we save money in order to buy something important in the future, or we delay getting married until we have finished our schooling.

Psychologists speak of "positive"

goals and "negative" goals. A positive goal is something that attracts the individual, something he acts to get. A negative goal describes something to be avoided. Pain, fear, and guilt as well as a case of mumps are negative goals.

STUDYING MOTIVE

Psychologists disagree about motivational ideas. In fact, some of their most interesting arguments have concerned this area. The discussion which follows briefly presents the major points of controversy.

Few or Many Motives?

Behavior is rich and varied. How many patterns is it useful to separate and identify? Or to put it another way, how many motives should be described? If a psychologist tried to capture and name every minute difference in behavior, he would have a list of motive patterns running into the billions (Krech & Crutchfield, 1958). Or one might attempt, as some psychologists have, to sum up the essence of all human behavior in a single master motive or a pair or trinity of motives (Lindzey, 1958).

Murray (1938, 1958) is a psychologist who believes that it is useful to describe a large number of motives. He notes that even a simple bit of behavior may be complex in origin. He and his research associates formulated an elaborate system of needs that has proved useful in the study of adjustment. Ten of these needs will be discussed later in the chapter.

By contrast, White (1959) and Combs and Snygg (1959) feel that a good deal of human behavior can be understood in terms of a single motivational concept. White believes that all human behavior reflects a need to deal competently or effectively with the environment. Similarly, Combs and Snygg feel that all behavior can be understood as part of a fundamental and never-ending quest for personal adequacy. They say:

> We can define man's basic need, then, as a need for adequacy. *It represents in man the expression of a universal tendency of all things. It is expressed in man's every behavior at every instant of his existence. Asleep or awake, each of us is engaged in an insatiable quest for personal adequacy. This quest may find its expression in a wide variety of behavior aimed, in one form or another, at the maintenance or enhancement of our perceptions of personal worth and value. Other authors have spoken of this need as a need for self-actualization, or self-realization. In the field of psychotherapy this need has been described as a need for growth. In this book, whenever we refer to man's basic need, we mean that great driving, striving force in each of us by which we are continually seeking to make ourselves ever more adequate to cope with life (1959, p. 46).*

Learned or Unlearned Motives?

Behavior is rich and varied. Where does it all come from? How much of it is learned? How much is innate or inherited? To what extent is behavior affected by experience and environment? To what extent is behavior fixed and unchanging?

Sigmund Freud, the founder of psychoanalysis, emphasized the role of innate biological factors in the development of behavior. He placed relatively little weight on social factors. A number of Freud's followers broke with him on this issue, feeling that he neglected the influence of learning and the social environment.

American psychologists in general have stressed the importance of learning (Hall & Lindzey, 1957). Valued patterns of motives are typically attributed to favorable learning experiences, and the modification of less-valued patterns is characteristically seen as a learning, unlearning, or relearning task. Almost everyone has heard the saying, "You can't change human nature." But it has been pointed out that human nature is not nearly as set as we may think it is. As Szasz says, "Both man and society change, and as they do, 'human nature' changes with them" (1961, p. 7).

A number of psychologists have pointed out that the old controversy of heredity versus environment is not very meaningful since the two are so interwoven (Kluckhohn & Murray, 1955). Murphy points out that we never really acquire something new; everything is a modification of something that was already there. He writes:

> Of all the verbal quagmires into which man has fallen in his attempt to tell what he is, none has caused more damage than the uncritical use of the opposing terms "heredity" and "environment." Our folklore is saturated with the belief that we inherit certain full-fledged traits and that we acquire other traits by virtue of environmental forces. For three-quarters of a century the literature on "nature and nurture" seemed to support such a belief, and authorities are still quoted to show that some traits are truly hereditary, others truly acquired. The toughness of this form of thinking, its resistance to evidence, is shown by the fact that modern geneticists, embryologists, comparative psychologists, and students of the infant and small child, though perfectly aware of the fallacies in this type of language,

find themselves forced, if they are to make contact with their readers or hearers, to employ these question-begging terms.

> But if the organism is a tissue system undergoing changes partly because of its own dynamics, partly because of interaction with the outer world, it is "acquiring" new characteristics all the time, never by accretion but always by modification of what it is. No organism differently constituted could acquire in the same way or acquire the same tendencies. What is acquired is just as completely an expression of the inherited make-up of the organism as it is an expression of the outer forces. Nothing meaningful can be said about our acquisition of tendencies, or about the effects of the environment, except in terms of a specific knowledge of the dispositions of the living system. New tendencies, habits, traits are not acquired, plastered on, or stuck on as one affixes a postage stamp to a letter. The organism grows into new phases of behavior, under one form of pressure or another, as long as life continues. Similarly, to use the term "acquired traits" is to talk redundantly, for all traits are acquired by some kind of reaction with environmental forces. There was a time when any given trait was not there; and if one speaks precisely, no trait that is there will remain long in its present apparent form. As Heraclitus said, no man can step twice into the same river; it is a different man, a different river. The way a man talks, or even his attitude toward himself, basic as it may be, is a function both of past tissue changes and of present environing pressures (1947, pp. 50–51).

Conscious or Unconscious Motives?

Behavior is rich and varied. How much is accompanied by insight? "Unconscious" and "repression" are words that are in most of our vocabularies. A friend appears to work hard at everything he attempts but never seems to get anywhere, and we conclude that he has an unconscious need to fail. The name of an old adversary escapes us, and someone says that we must have repressed it.

Most of us do not understand ourselves as much as we would like. We do things without knowing fully why we do them. We think thoughts that annoy and pain us. We have feelings that are mystifying and confusing.

How can we explain our thoughts and feelings and actions? For any bit of behavior we might think up a dozen reasons. Some psychologists lean heavily on the concept of unconscious motivation as they set about explaining behavior. Others emphasize conscious motives and the immediate experience of the behaving individual.

This is a complicated matter. An adaptation of an illustration used by Phillips (1956) will make it clearer. Suppose we know somebody who is "accident-prone"— someone who seems to be always having accidents and hurting himself. He doesn't seem to know why he is so unlucky, but we might attempt to understand his behavior, using the idea of unconscious motivation. We might hypothesize, for example, that he has an unconscious need to punish himself and that he meets this need by having accidents.

But there are other possible explanations for his behavior which do not involve the concept of unconscious motivation. Perhaps it seems to us that this man overestimates himself, that he is always running around trying to do too much too fast. Then we might hypothesize that his numerous accidents are the by-products of his efforts to play a role that doesn't fit him.

Freud pointed out the effects of unconscious motives on everyday behavior. He saw the task of psychoanalysis as making the unconscious conscious through the use of free association techniques. Describing "Freud's attack on the traditional psychology of consciousness," Hall and Lindzey state:

> [Freud] likened the mind to an iceberg in which the smaller part showing above the surface of the water represents the region of consciousness while the much larger mass below the water level represents the region of unconsciousness. In this vast domain of the unconscious are to be found the urges, the passions, the repressed ideas and feelings—a great underworld of vital, unseen forces which exercise an imperious control over the conscious thoughts and deeds of man. From this point of view, a psychology which limits itself to the analysis of consciousness is wholly inadequate for understanding the underlying motives of man's behavior (1957, p. 30).

Freud emphasized the importance of distant, buried determinants of behavior, but other psychologists have emphasized immediate, conscious determinants. Phillips (1956), for example, feels that behavior can be better understood if one deals with "perceptually present events, than if one assumes that dark, inaccessible forces account for the observable events." Similarly, Snygg and Combs hold that it is better to pursue immediate experience than remote antecedents. They present the following case to illustrate their position:

> A young man had a severe phobia for flying birds. A sparrow alighting on his window sill would throw him into such a panic that he would attempt to retreat by any available means. In his perceptual field a bird was an extraordinarily threatening object. What is more, his perceptions were highly differentiated and his behavior extremely precise. Now his objective psychologist, knowing that he had

*been most insecure as a child and know-
ing that his nurse had been accustomed to
control him by threats of feeding him to
"the wild geese in the attic" sees these
events as the causes of his present behavior. Indeed, the young man himself may,
at other times, ascribe his present behavior
to those events because in describing his
behavior he is making an external observation, just as the psychologist does. At
the instant of his panic, however, he is
not behaving in terms of unconscious
causes but in terms of sharply differentiated present perceptions that birds are
vicious, dangerous, and immediate threats
to himself. Thus it appears that behavior
described from an external point of view
as unconscious, from a [personal] point
of view is not unconscious at all but, on
the contrary, may be very highly "conscious" (1950, p. 525).*

The controversy concerning conscious
and unconscious motivation has changed
in recent decades. Hall and Lindzey (1957)
feel that there has been increasing acknowl-
edgment of the existence of unconscious
motivation. There is, however, considerable
difference of opinion on how strong or
important such motives are and how useful
it is to search for them.

SOME IMPORTANT NEEDS

The remainder of the chapter describes some
important patterns of behavior. For sim-
plicity, the discussion is focused on needs
rather than motives. However, each need
description will note or imply the acts that
are prompted by the need and the goals
toward which the acts are directed.

Everyone, of course, needs oxygen,
food, and water. We would not live very
long without them. But in the study of adjustment most of the physiological needs
are not of the greatest interest in them-

selves because they are comparatively easy
to satisfy. Oxygen needs are automatically
met except under unusual circumstances,
and although we do not always eat and
drink what we prefer, not many go hungry
or thirsty for very long in our society.

As was indicated earlier, some needs
that are of considerable concern in the
study of adjustment have been described
by Murray and his associates (1938). Murray brought together a group of investigators of varied backgrounds who made an
intensive personality study of a number of
subjects and formulated a system of needs
that has proved to be of value in understanding behavior. Recent research has
given us additional information. The discussion which follows presents ten of the
most important of these needs. (See Fig.
2.2.)

Achievement Needs

The need for achievement is manifested in
the desire to overcome obstacles, accom-

Figure 2.2 In order to better understand the
needs which are described and to give them
personal meaning, think about each need in
relation to yourself. After each need is discussed ask yourself two questions: How
strong is this need in me? How well satisfied
is this need in me? Consider the scale below
as you attempt to decide.

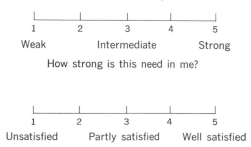

plish difficult things, and surpass others. People with strong achievement needs like to set hard goals for themselves, and they strive to reach them. Their aspirations are high; they want to accomplish something important, something which will be notable. They attack problems with zest and energy. They enjoy competing with others in work and play.[1]

Why are some of us so highly motivated to achieve? Many factors and combinations of factors may play a part. The general culture to which we belong, the social class of which we are a member, and the family setting in which we grew up—all have an important influence.

In the American culture there is considerable emphasis on achievement. We are under pressure to improve ourselves and get ahead. We struggle for a better job and then a better job than that. We struggle for a better house in a better neighborhood. As soon as we reach one goal, another appears.

The need for achievement is especially high in the middle class (Douvan, 1958; Rosen, 1958; Strodtbeck, 1958). There is competition for grades and scholarships, medals and badges, and awards of all sorts. Immediate satisfactions are often put aside in favor of long-range goals.

Family environments can have an important and lasting effect on achievement patterns. The need for achievement tends to be high in those whose parents set high standards of performance and who were rewarding when these standards were met (Child, 1954; McClelland, Atkinson, Clark, & Lowell, 1953; Winterbottom, 1958). Other things being equal, the highest

achievement patterns may be found in those whose parents demand as much as can be expected, neither more nor less (Child, 1954). (See Case Study 2.1.)

Case study 2.1 A strong need for achievement. (This material was freely adapted from a paper written by a man, twenty-two years old.)*

Achievement has always been very important in our family. My father was a small shop owner who worked day and night, Sundays, and holidays to make a go of things. He had practically no formal education himself, but he seemed to live in the academic achievements of his children. Much of the time there was not even enough cash in the till of the cash register for change, but if money was needed for school books or supplies, somehow that money was produced.

I will never forget the day that my oldest brother graduated from college. I was only in the sixth grade at the time, but my father's pride is still vivid in my memory. The newspaper article concerning the ceremonies listed the names of hundreds of graduates, but my father cut it out and hung it up in our store. It was as if my brother was the only one to graduate. It must have been on that day that I resolved to go to college and make my father proud of me.

I have never been a brilliant student. My grades have always been good, but every A was hard earned. When other kids were out playing ball, I was burrowing in my books. When I was tending my father's store and there were no customers around (this was unfortunately too often the case), I would be studying behind the counter. So much of my spare time was spent in the library that in my family it was a standing joke to ask me how my love affair with the librarian was coming along.

Last year my father died suddenly of a heart attack while he was at work. It was a severe blow to all of us. I'm sorry that my father will not see me graduate, but I'm glad that he lived to see me win two scholarships and be elected to the presidency of my college class. Even with my father gone, I continue to work hard. I want to be somebody and get someplace. It is as if my

---

[1] This need description and those which follow are based on Murray et al. (1938), and Edwards (1954, 1959).

father is still alive. It is as if my father were part of me. Everything I do, I do for both of us.

---

* This case study and others throughout the book are taken from student papers and used by permission. All have been condensed and reworked, and identifying matter has been omitted or altered.

Affiliation Needs

The need for affiliation is manifested in the desire to associate with, cooperate with, and form friendships with others. People with strong affiliation needs enjoy being with others; they would much rather spend their time with others than by themselves. They like to work and play in groups; they join clubs, fraternities, political parties, and organizations of all kinds. They form close relationships, become very much attached to friends, and are loyal to them.

In the American culture there is considerable emphasis on doing things with others and getting along with them. The individual starts life in a group—the family—and he soon belongs to a number of other neighborhood, school, and community organizations. Even at elementary school age, a child may be a member of five or six groups, including, perhaps, a gang, a playground, a scouting organization, and a hobby club. As he grows older, he may continue to join, moving to groups that are appropriate to his age and interests.

Middle-class individuals generally show a higher need for affiliation than those lower in social status. They tend to be joiners. By the time a middle-class adult reaches middle-age, he is likely to be thoroughly affiliated with social and professional organizations. His children, in turn, are likely to belong to more groups than do children in the lower class (Stendler, 1949).

The need for affiliation is closely related to the experiences one has had with people in the past. If these experiences have been rewarding, people are valued and sought out. But if people have proved unrewarding or punishing, the need to be with others may be slight; even more than that, there may be desire to avoid them.

The matter, however, is not so simple, because almost no one has a social environment made up entirely of friendly or hostile people. Some associates are rewarding; others, less so. A complicating fact is that even the most rewarding ones are punishing sometimes, and even the most punishing may be occasionally rewarding.

Evidence suggests that early relationships have an abiding influence on affiliative behavior. Individuals from families in which parent-child relationships have been positive tend to have high needs for affiliation (Child, 1954; Sanford et al., 1943). In such settings one is more likely to develop the identifications, attitudes, and skills that are important in personal relationships. (See Case Study 2.2.)

Case study 2.2 A strong need for affiliation. (This material was freely adapted from a paper written by a woman, eighteen years old.)

Ever since I can remember I've enjoyed being with people. In fact, it's gotten so that I can scarcely stand being alone. Solitary card games, crossword puzzles, and quiet evenings of reading are my idea of nothing to do. However, I don't mind doing nothing as long as there are a lot of people to do it with.

Even the things that I ordinarily find enjoyable are dull unless there is someone around to share them. For example, I love to eat. My idea of a pleasant evening is to have dinner with a group of friends. With food, conversation, jokes, and laughter, dinner may go on for two or three hours. But I hate to eat alone, and if there is nobody around to eat with, I will just wolf down a sandwich to get it over with.

It doesn't matter if there is no real social interaction. I just like having people about. I'm living in a dormitory now with a roommate. In the evening if my roommate sits down to study, I can study too. But if she leaves, I feel lonely and go wandering about the dormitory looking for someone else to be with.

Some of my friends will go to see a movie alone. Even if I want to see a movie very much, I hate to go by myself. In fact, I hate to have nice things happen unless there is someone around to share them. A beautiful rainbow, a play, good music—all seem wasted unless other people are around to enjoy them with you.

I am a great joiner. I belong to more organizations than anyone else I know. Sometimes I find myself going to two club meetings the same evening. Even at gatherings and parties that other people find dull, I have fun. I find myself trying to keep parties together as long as possible, and I'm usually the last to poop out.

Ever since I started dating, I've always gone steady. As soon as I break up with one boy I become attached to another. Sometimes when a boyfriend is away somewhere, I somehow find myself going steady with two boys. I know that I should be true to one or the other, but I don't seem to want to break either friendship so I make everyone happy—especially myself—by going steady with both of them. Perhaps this is carrying affiliation too far.

Autonomy Needs

The need for autonomy is manifested in the desire to be free and independent. People with strong autonomy needs like to be free to come and go as they please and do what they want to do without restrictions. They avoid routines, responsibilities, and obligations. They refuse to conform; they ignore convention, disregarding the opinions and demands of others, defying authority. They wish to remain unattached and free of restraint or confinement.

Writers in this area define autonomy differently and regard it differently, some in positive and others in negative terms. Maslow (1954) and Riesman (1950), for example, both emphasize the importance of autonomy. The autonomists they describe, however, are not fiery rebels; rather they are strong and independent people who are free to be autonomous or nonautonomous as individual circumstances warrant.

Maslow notes that autonomy is a characteristic of self-actualizing people—people who make the most of themselves. Such people are relatively free of their physical and social surroundings. Although they are dependent upon their environment for the satisfaction of basic needs, once these needs have been met, they are free to go their own way and develop their potentialities. These people are "self-contained" and not easily upset by environmental adversities.

Riesman's autonomous man is free to conform or not as he sees fit. He is under no compulsion to act in one way or another, and he stands in sharp contrast to those who must conform and to those who have no capacity to do so. Riesman observes that "men are created different" and should be allowed freedom from coercion to conformity.

Is autonomous behavior sufficiently emphasized in the American culture? Writers on this topic disagree. Many have criticized our culture for discouraging the independent actions of its members and for putting undue pressure on them to conform. Others have pointed to the cultural forces which promote independence. For example, Martin and Stendler state:

Every American dreams of some day being "independent." By that term, he most often means financial security—a home paid for, a new car in the garage, paid-up annuities, money in the bank. He looks forward to the time when he doesn't have to take orders from anybody. A man wants to own his business or his farm. The unconditional possession of material things is a clear sign of independence. The strength of these aspirations lies in the fact that they have so often been realized throughout American history. That the gaining of such "independence" brings with it many responsibilities, that many who achieve it do not know what to do with it—these do nothing to dispel the dream (1959, p. 180).

Erikson (1955) points out that the transition from dependence to autonomy is a critical one in the early life of the child. If childhood experiences are appropriate, the individual gradually relinquishes dependency and becomes increasingly autonomous. Few individuals remain completely dependent and almost no one achieves complete autonomy; most effect some sort of balance between the two extremes.

The person with high autonomy needs may be from a family which started independence training early and which rewarded his early efforts to do things for himself (McClelland, Atkinson, Clark, & Lowell, 1953; Winterbottom, 1958). Or such an individual may be from a family that left him on his own to sink or swim (Burgum, 1940). Some persons with low autonomy needs have had parents who stressed the family group rather than the individual; as a consequence, they may be quite subordinate to the group and feel guilty when they oppose group decisions (McClelland et al., 1953). (See Case Study 2.3.)

Case study 2.3   A strong need for autonomy.
(This material was freely adapted from a paper written by a woman, twenty-one years old.)

I have always been a rebel. I remember one summer when I was nine years old, I was repeatedly warned not to go swimming in a stream near where we were staying. Nevertheless, I continued to go. Finally, my parents took my swimming suit away, but this didn't stop me. I waited until no one was around and then dashed down for a swim in the nude. I stayed in until the coast looked clear, and then I dashed back.

I remember too that I used to like to climb trees, and I would remain up in them for long periods of time. It gave me a feeling of being free and away from everything. One day after a scolding from my mother concerning the negative aspects of feminine tree climbing, I ran angrily out of the house and shinnied up the first tree I could find. Unfortunately, both the tree and I proved to be a little shaky. I lost my grip, collided with the ground, and acquired a broken leg in the process. But as soon as it mended, I went back to climbing trees.

Since beginning college I have worked each summer in the cannery in order to get enough money to see me through the school year. My parents could easily afford to send me, and they would if I would allow them to, but now that I'm able to earn my own way I wouldn't feel right about taking their money. I need to feel independent. The work is back-breaking, but it makes me happy to feel that I'm self-supporting and indebted to no one.

Last year when I was living farther from college, a fellow student offered me a lift in her car each morning. Even without thinking it over, I declined. The ride would have saved me time, money, and the inconvenience of catching the bus, but I didn't want to feel obligated to her. And I didn't want to be tied down to a schedule.

In the dormitory where I am staying this year, the girls do everything in a group. They eat together, study together, and when they go out, they double and triple date. They have long group discussions to make decisions of no importance. For example, before going to a movie they may spend ten or fifteen minutes discussing whether or not they should all wear jeans. By the time they are all assembled and in proper costume, the evening is half over.

I like to be free to come and go and do and don't do as I please. I mingle with the other girls but not to the point of becoming attached to them or bound by group decisions. I guess they think I'm an odd one or a snob because I don't attach any value to things they think are pretty important. I guess if I were an animal, I would be a hermit crab. But better a crab than a sheep.

Dominance Needs

The need for dominance is manifested in the desire to influence, direct, and control the behavior of others. People with strong dominance needs enjoy arguing for their own point of view and persuading others to adopt it. They enjoy guiding and supervising the activities of others. They derive satisfaction from having power, giving orders, and being in charge of situations. They like to lead groups, be the presidents of clubs, chairmen of committees, or officers of a class.

It is important to note that the need for dominance and the capacity for leadership are not synonymous. Some of us with high dominance needs have continually sought and filled leadership positions, and we may show considerable skill as leaders. Krech and Crutchfield point out that "other things being equal, those persons who have insistent needs for dominance, power, and prestige may be expected to have higher potentiality for leadership" (1948, p. 437).

But some people with high dominance needs fail as leaders. They lack the qualities that are important in achieving and executing leadership roles. Continued failure may cause them to give up or modify attempts at domination or, in some, it may lead to even greater efforts in this direction.

Even though an individual fails in one leadership position, he may succeed in another. Leadership is a complex phenomenon. No consistent pattern of qualities seems to characterize all leaders. The leadership qualities that are important in a particular situation depend on the group itself, its members, its goals, and other factors (Gibb, 1954).

Why are some people more dominant than others? Sex typing influences dominance patterns. In general, men show greater needs for dominance than women, but in both sex groups there are considerable differences (Edwards, 1954, 1959). It is not uncommon for a man to show little dominance behavior or for a woman to show a good deal.

Family patterns affect our dominance behavior, but the relationship is very complex. A child with dominating parents may as a consequence become quite submissive. Or through identification, he may take over his parents' dominating ways. Or he may be submissive and dominating by turns. The situation is even more complex if one parent has been highly dominating and the other much less so or if each parent has shown inconsistent and varying behavior.

Some evidence indicates that individuals from warm, permissive, and democratic homes show a lot of assertive behavior quite early in life. Furthermore, this assertion is patterned in such a way that it is generally acceptable to others. By contrast, the early assertive behavior shown by those from coercive, punishing, and autocratic homes is more likely to be offensive and generally unacceptable to others (Mummery, 1954). (See Case Study 2.4.)

Case study 2.4   A strong need for dominance.
(This material was freely adapted from a paper written by a woman, twenty-one years old.)

Although I know that in our culture the male is supposed to be dominant—not the female—I happen to be a dominant female. On occasions I have tried to play the clinging vine role, but it doesn't work. I'm more suited to be the sturdy oak. I enjoy directing the lives of others, making suggestions, offering guidance, and even giving orders.

I like being head of things and often find myself in leadership positions. I have been president of a number of organizations and chairman of committees and discussion groups many times. Sometimes I run very active campaigns to get these positions. But even when I don't, I usually wind up getting elected anyway.

Sometimes I am afraid of appearing too dominant, and I try to put myself in the background with the thought of giving others a chance. But if the discussion seems to be getting nowhere or the leader seems incompetent, I just can't keep myself from stepping in. No matter what happens I usually contribute more than my two cents' worth.

People think of me as a fairly strong person. My friends frequently consult me with their problems. I try to help them find their own solutions without telling them point blank what to do. However, sometimes what they ought to do seems so clear to me that I have a hard time keeping myself from giving direct advice.

I find that I am also dominant in my relationships with the opposite sex. I've been warned, "Oh! Oh! Watch out! Men don't like dominant women." Yet I've never had any trouble getting dates. A lot of college men—nice as they are—don't seem to have much orientation. When I get interested in a fellow, I like to have an active share in his life. Of course some of them don't like it. But some do.

I know that when I get married, I don't want to wear the pants in my family. I don't want a husband who is henpecked. He ought to be head of the house in both theory and practice. Incidentally, I have already found one that fits the bill. He is a dominant person

too but in a quiet and gentle way. Since knowing him I have learned an important lesson: one can be dominant without being domineering.

Deference Needs

The need for deference is manifested in the desire to admire, follow, and be guided by others. People with strong deference needs enjoy praising and applauding outstanding individuals. They like to pick out a person whom they respect and follow his suggestions, his patterns of behavior, or his goals. They derive satisfaction from following the advice of others, conforming to their wishes, or being led by them. In groups, they prefer to be followers; they cooperate and are comfortable in subordinate positions.

The relationship of deference to the role of the follower appears to be analogous to that between dominance and the role of the leader. Although leadership has been given a good deal of study, the role of follower has received little attention.

Leadership brings with it prestige, power, and privilege, but the satisfactions of the follower role are less well understood. Sometimes the follower is seen as a would-be leader who failed to make the grade. In this view, the follower is not truly submissive or deferent; he is a person who has been subordinated.

Gibb (1954) has described some of the more positive satisfactions of the follower's role. The follower benefits from the assistance of the leader in solving individual and group problems. He is able to transfer early attitudes of dependency to the leader and in doing so to rely upon the leader as he once did upon his parents. Furthermore, in close identification with the leader, he vicariously shares in the leader's achievements.

What environmental factors play a part in producing deference behavior? Certainly cultural determinants are important; some cultures place more emphasis on deference than others. The Japanese, for example, have been noted for their highly developed deference patterns. Japanese who come to the United States have shown relatively high deference behavior, but this appears less true of third-generation Japanese-Americans than of earlier generations (Arkoff, 1959).

Sex typing influences deferent behavior. As previously indicated, men are generally more dominant than women, and, as might be expected, women generally prove to be more deferent than men. Again, there are wide differences in each group; men high in deference and women high in dominance are not unusual (Edwards, 1954, 1959).

What family experiences cause high deference needs? Again, as in the production of dominance needs, the matter is very complicated. Deference patterns may be learned through identification with deferent parents or because one is rewarded for deference and not rewarded for dominance. An investigator has suggested that dominating parents may produce deferent or submissive children, but that these children grow up to become dominating parents, in turn to produce another generation of submissive offspring (Symonds, 1939).

Crandall and his associates (1958) have thrown some light on the development of deference behavior in children. This group was interested in studying "face-to-face compliance," that is, the extent to which children deferred or yielded to the suggestions and demands of other people.

Older children (six-, seven-, and eight-year-olds) prove to be more consistent in their compliance behavior than nursery schoolers.

The amount of compliance behavior shown by the older children outside the home was found to be related to the amount of reward and punishment administered by their mothers in the home situation. The more compliant children tended to receive more reward for compliance and more punishment for noncompliance. And there was some suggestion that the reward for compliance was more effective in producing this behavior than was the punishment for noncompliance. (See Case Study 2.5.)

Case study 2.5   A strong need for deference. (This material was freely adapted from a paper written by a woman, twenty-eight years old.)

Everyone in the world can't be a captain. I'm one of those people who don't mind being crew; in fact, I prefer it that way. Some people hate to follow orders. I have one friend who frequently makes a point of doing the exact opposite of what she's told to do. But when I respect a person, I happily follow his or her suggestions. There is a comfort in having someone to rely on.

In this world a good deal of fuss is made over things which aren't really important. Even when I feel that I'm right and others are wrong, I don't argue very vigorously. I usually ask myself, "Will this decision make any difference a year from now?" If the answer is "no"—and you'd be surprised how often the answer is "no"—I go along without protest.

Sometimes, however, when something seems extremely important, I do try to make a stand. This is very difficult for me to do. I begin to overreact. I feel myself getting tense and shaky. I become extremely uncomfortable about the whole thing and wish that I hadn't made an issue out of it in the first place.

None of the women in my immediate family have been what you would call career women. Dad was a sort of benevolent despot, and everyone did pretty much what he said.

Even so, there were plenty of times when my mother, employing quiet but effective methods, got her own way. In important matters she made herself felt.

In my own married life I find that deference is an expedient policy. My husband is a dominant individual and a rather opinionated one. Fortunately, I share most of his opinions, so I defer to him a great deal. This keeps him happy and the household running smoothly. Some of my friends who are constantly battling with their husbands get irritated with me for not asserting myself more in my marriage. But to me a happy home and a happy husband are more important than empty verbal victories.

Aggression Needs

The need for aggression is manifested in the desire to overpower opposition and to criticize, attack, and punish others. People with strong aggression needs display their anger; they express themselves and blow off steam. They are ready to do battle, and they enjoy a good fight or a hot argument. They stick up for their rights, and they openly find fault with others, blaming and denouncing them. When they have been harmed by others, they seek to even the score.

An individual with high aggressive needs may find himself at an advantage in certain situations and at a disadvantage in others. Sheer hostility, of course, serves to alienate others and causes them to retaliate. But a fighting attitude may be of value in some situations, and aggressive persons are in demand in a number of positions and occupations. Much depends on the ability to express aggressiveness in socially approved patterns.

Although psychologists have given a good deal of attention to the study of aggression, not much is known about the conditions which produce certain patterns of this behavior (Sears, 1958). In general, the evidence suggests that the amount of aggression is related (1) to the amount of frustration that has been experienced and (2) to the ways in which parents and other socializing agents have reacted to this aggression.

Frustration leads to aggression (Dollard, Doob, Miller, Mowrer, & Sears, 1939). Persons with strong aggression needs have probably undergone a good deal of frustration. For example, it has been found that cold, rejecting, and autocratic homes tend to produce highly aggressive children.[2]

Sears, Maccoby, and Levin (1957) have pointed out some important and interesting facts concerning the effect of certain parental actions on children's aggression patterns. Where parents permit aggression, children are likely to show a good deal of this behavior. But where parents are not permissive, the amount of aggression produced in the child depends on methods of control.

Nonpunitive control methods are likely to result in lowered levels of aggression; punitive methods are likely to have the opposite effect. Parents who vigorously punish aggression in their children tend to make them more rather than less aggressive. In discussing this point, Sears and his associates write:

> Our findings suggest that the way for parents to produce a non-aggressive child is to make abundantly clear that aggression is frowned upon, and to stop aggression when it occurs, but to avoid punishing the child for his aggression. Punishment seems to have complex effects. While undoubtedly it often stops a particular form of aggression, at least momentarily,

[2] This is discussed at greater length in Chap. 12.

it appears to generate more hostility in the child and lead to further aggressive outbursts at some other time or place. Furthermore, when the parents punish— particularly when they employ physical punishment—they are providing a living example of the use of aggression at the very moment they are trying to teach the child not to be aggressive. The child, who copies his parents in many ways, is likely to learn as much from this example of successful aggression on his parents' part as he is from the pain of punishment. Thus, the most peaceful home is one in which the mother believes aggression is not desirable and under no circumstances is ever to be expressed toward her, but who relies mainly on non-punitive forms of control. The homes where the children show angry, aggressive outbursts frequently are likely to be homes in which the mother has a relatively tolerant (or careless!) attitude toward such behavior, or where she administers severe punishment for it, or both (1957, p. 266).

(See Case Study 2.6.)

Case study 2.6 A high need for aggression. (This material was freely adapted from a paper written by a man, twenty-two years old.)

Sometimes my aggressiveness worries me. My temper seems to come to a boil in a minute. I frequently have the desire to beat up somebody that gets in my way. And too many times this desire has been fulfilled to my own disadvantage. However, even when I go down for the count, I find some pleasure in being beaten by a tougher man. Figure that out!

I'm always ready to stick up for what I think is right. Last month a policeman stopped me and accused me of doing 55 m.p.h. in a 45 m.p.h. zone. He looked so cocky that it took all my will power to keep from hitting him. Anyway, I emphatically denied that I had been going faster than the speed limit. I must have become a little too emphatic because I soon found myself being escorted to the police station.

My friends—I do have some—say that I argue just for the sake of arguing. The trouble is that even mild discussions become arguments after I get into them. And I never give up. I hate to be wrong, and I usually won't admit that I am, even though the fallacies in my position become obvious to everyone else and even to me.

The army was very rough on me. There wasn't much room for discussion. You were told what to do and that was it. I couldn't even venture an opinion. Unfortunately there were too many men like me in the service and, to make matters worse, most of them outranked me.

Sometimes my sense of fight is useful in

Presentation 2.1 Aggression, war, and peace.

Is war inevitable? Is man inevitably warlike? Social scientists who have pursued these questions have generally answered them in the negative. During World War II a "Psychologists' Manifesto" signed by more than two thousand members of the American Psychological Association stated in part: "War can be avoided. War is not born in men; it is built into men. No race, nation, or social group is inevitably warlike" (Murphy, 1945). Several years later eight eminent scientists who were assembled by the United Nations Educational, Scientific, and Cultural Organization to consider international aggression and understanding stated: "To the best of our knowledge, there is no evidence to indicate that wars are necessary and inevitable consequences of 'human nature' as such" (Allport, Freyre, Gurvitch, Horkheimer, Naess, Rickman, Sullivan, & Szalai, 1948). In 1966 an appeal was made by the International Union of Psychological Science requesting psychologists everywhere to direct their energies toward world peace; various actions were suggested, including further emphasis of the generally accepted conclusion that there are no unchangeable human characteristics making war unavoidable or cooperation impossible (Fraisse, Klineberg, & Leontiev, 1966).

a more constructive way. For example, when we received the bill for repairs to our house, the amount was considerably more than the estimate. Even though it would have been quite a hardship, my family would have paid the bill except for my opposition. The contractor argued that the job required more expensive material than he originally thought, and I argued that he should have let us know before going ahead. Finally, he gave in and accepted the amount of the original estimate.

This year I have gone out for debating. Although I haven't been good enough to make the team, I find that this is a good outlet for my aggressiveness. Sometimes, however, when the opposition starts twisting my arguments around, I have a hard time waiting until my rebuttal to set the record straight. But little by little I am slowly learning to control my mouth and my fists. Maybe I'm growing up.

Abasement Needs

The abasement need is manifested in a desire to admit inadequacy, to accept blame, and to suffer punishment. People with strong abasement needs feel humble and inferior. When something goes wrong, they are quick to accept the blame, quick to apologize. They frequently feel guilty for things they have done or are tempted to do, and they accept criticism and punishment and sometimes even seem to seek it. They allow themselves to be ordered about and taken advantage of without fighting back.

The need for abasement is closely related to the need for aggression. Both needs are, in essence, attacking behavior. In aggression, as it has been defined, the attack is directed outward onto environmental objects. In abasement, the attack is turned inward onto oneself.

An act which is ostensibly self-punishing can, nevertheless, serve to inflict punishment on others. By hurting ourselves, we sometimes hurt others who are near us. An example is the girl who contracted pneumonia by exposing herself to winter weather in order to gain revenge on her parents (Murray, 1938).

Many daydreams follow this patterning. The daydreamer may fantasy that all sorts of terrible things are happening to him. He is poor, hungry, ill, in great pain, dying. However, the intent of the daydream is not self-punishment, but rather to draw the sympathy of others, to make them sorry for having treated him so badly in the past, and to make them resolve to do better in the future.

Abasive actions serve a number of other functions. By submitting to punishment of various sorts, the abasive individual rids himself through a kind of atonement of guilt for his actions, real or imagined, past, present, and future. Sometimes, too, abasive actions serve to disarm an adversary or secure the support, reassurance, or assistance of a friend. Soliciting compliments by being ostentatiously self-critical or modest is a common maneuver.

Very little is known about the ways in which abasement patterns are learned. Dollard and his associates have suggested that self-aggression or abasement tends to occur when other forms of expression are not possible. For example, if there is severe discipline and if outward forms of aggression are severely punished, the individual may turn his aggressive acts back upon himself. The following case study is an illustration of this process:

A small boy in an institution displayed unusually strong aggression against adults. This took the form of biting, pinching, and hair-pulling. Under the severe discipline of the institution, this overt aggression was soon inhibited by expectation of punishment. Then the child began running after other children, biting them, pinching them, and pulling their hair. These manifestations of aggression were in turn eliminated, in fact so thoroughly that the child ceased biting altogether, even refusing to bite into solid food. Then the child commenced to pinch himself, bang his head, and to pull out his own hair. These actions were so injurious that he created bad sores on his body and two large bald spots on his head, and he finally had to be sent to another institution for treatment. Therapy consisted of removing frustrations, particularly those centering around toilet training and eating, and of attempting, by complete absence of threats, to remove the anticipations of punishment which were inhibiting direct aggression against adults. Under this treatment the child first expressed more aggression against adults and less against himself. Then, as the frustrations which seemed to have been the root of his trouble were lessened, his manifestations of aggression against adults began to weaken. The case appears to present a picture of frustration imposed by adults, aggression against adults, inhibition of this aggression and displacement of it to other children, inhibition of the aggression against other children and turning of it, still with much the same responses, against the self. During treatment this picture was reversed. As aggression against adults became possible, self-aggression disappeared, and as frustrations were lessened, all aggression waned (Dollard et al., 1939, pp. 49–50).

Dollard has also suggested that self-aggression tends to be high when one perceives himself as the cause of his frustrations. If the individual sees himself as to blame for his own or others' misfortunes, he may feel the need of self-criticism or punishment. Persons with low estimations of themselves regard themselves as more

blameworthy. And those with an overly strong superego or conscience structure frequently feel guilty because of what they did or did not do, or are tempted to do; as a consequence, they may show a good deal of self-aggression.

It has been noted that in addition to being highly aggressive, rejected children show marked abasive patterns (Symonds, 1939; Wolberg, 1944). Rejecting parents are frequently punitive, simultaneously serving as identification models, instigators, and punishers of aggression. In this situation, a rejected child may feel a heightening of aggressive impulses and a necessity to displace these impulses onto safe objects. At the same time his parents' treatment may make him feel unloved and unlovable, unworthy and blameworthy, and some of his aggression may be directed back onto himself. (See Case Study 2.7.)

Case study 2.7 A high need for abasement. (This material was freely adapted from a paper written by a woman, twenty-two years old.)

I wish that I could get rid of my feeling of inferiority. I've tried hard to overcome it but with little success. People who have great confidence in themselves fill me with envy and make me feel all the less adequate by comparison. In fact, I am constantly comparing myself with others and constantly convincing myself that I don't stack up so well.

Even in areas where I am competent, I am afraid to trust my own abilities. Recently I took some driving lessons and had no trouble at all until I went down to pass the test. Then I seemed to fall to pieces. I couldn't park, couldn't hold the car on a hill, and once even went into reverse instead of forward. The policeman was sympathetic and kept telling me to take it easy, and I kept criticizing myself and making new mistakes. As a result I didn't get a license. Looking back now, I see that I behaved stupidly.

My feelings of inadequacy have always

interfered with my social life. Although I am more at ease around much older and younger men, I am uncomfortable with fellows my own age. For one thing, I am sensitive about my appearance. Blind dates were always torture because I was sure that my date would be disappointed in me. I seemed to find comfort in hiding behind my dark glasses—as if they covered all of me!

The funny thing about it is that I'm considered quite attractive. Yet when people compliment me on my appearance, I think they are just saying it for formality's sake. I have a difficult time just saying "thank you" and leaving it at that. Either I am brusque or protest or else I get very flustered.

Since I have become engaged, things have gotten a little better. When my fiancé first proposed, I couldn't believe he really loved me. He is a very nice guy who could have the pick of the crop, and I couldn't understand why he picked me. Even now when we go out together, I project this feeling onto others. I keep thinking that they are sizing us up as a couple and thinking, "What does he ever see in her?"

My fiancé is not at all like me, and he is good for me in many ways. He keeps picking on me to quit picking on myself. Sometimes when I rush in to apologize for something that he thinks isn't my fault, he jokingly accuses me of trying to hog all the blame. Last week when we were out driving, we went through an area that had been hit by a freak wind. As we were inspecting a house that had been blown over and deposited on its side, my fiancé glanced over at me, smiled, and said, "A lot of damage. A lot of damage. Aren't you going to apologize?"

Nurturance Needs

The nurturance need is manifested in the desire to sympathize with, assist, and protect others. People with strong nurturance needs commiserate with the illnesses and misfortunes of others. They are affectionate and kindly, and others are drawn to them

and feel able to confide in them. They enjoy helping others by doing favors and by giving of themselves, their time, and their energies. They like to take care of pets, children, sick people, and those who are weaker or less fortunate than themselves.

One way of obtaining information concerning the need for nurturance is to examine its expression in parenthood. The relationship between parent and child is the foremost example of nurturance and succorance. The child draws succor from the nurturing parent.

The patterns of nurturance in mothers have been found to vary a great deal. They range from the complete absence of nurturance shown in maternal rejection or desertion to the exaggerated expression of nurturance in maternal overprotection. Through the use of interviews Levy (1955) classified mothers into high, low, and intermediate groupings according to the degree of maternal behavior that was shown. Here is Levy's description of a highly nurturant mother of four children:

As a young child, her favorite game was taking care of dolls, dressing them, putting them to bed. She played with dolls until the age of fourteen or fifteen. She used to make visits among her mother's friends to take care of their babies. When she thought of being a mother, she hoped to have six children, and have them as soon as possible. When she saw a pretty baby on the street, she had a strong urge to take it in her arms and hug it. She was a "baby-carriage peeker" before, as after, marriage. In her relations with men she was always maternal; much more, she said, than they liked.

Actually, she had four children and is now pregnant with her fifth. She had a nurse for her first child and was miserable, she said, because she couldn't take full care of it. She hated the hospital rule of not having the baby in her room. She fed all her children at the breast, and with ease. She had a copious supply of milk.

Her husband stated that she really spoiled the children; that every so often she fought against this tendency and became severe, to protect them from her spoiling. But the children "see through it" (p. 106).

By contrast, consider Levy's description of a mother of two children who was considered in the low nurturant group:

(She) never played any "maternal" games in childhood, nor played a maternal role to another child. She had very little interest in dolls and stopped playing with them when about age six. When she saw a pretty baby on the street, she was not at all interested. As an adolescent, she never indulged in the fantasy of being a mother and having children. She was ambitious to get married, but never thought about having children. As a mother she has felt quite incompetent. She took her children off the breast after two weeks, because she didn't like it; she felt like a cow, she said. She still hates the physical care of children, though she is a dutiful mother and rather affectionate. She never was maternal towards men. Her interests have always been feminine, and she has been quite popular with men (p. 106).

Although women in general have higher nurturance patterns than men (Edwards, 1954, 1959), males of all ages may show high nurturance patterns. An older brother may nurture a younger one. In dealing with their children some men are more nurturant than their wives. In many positions in business and industry and in the professions, nurturant qualities may prove to be a definite asset. It has been suggested that the best supervisors are those with some "motherly" or nurturant

feelings toward the men in their charge (Guilford & Zimmerman, 1949).

What learning experiences play a part in the production of nurturance motivation? There is almost no evidence that bears on this matter. Levy (1955) noted that psychological experiences tending to make maternal women more maternal (for example, infidelity of the husband, difficulties in conception, illnesses in the child) have the opposite effect on nonmaternal women. He felt that the relevant factors could not be entirely psychological and found some evidence suggesting that part of causation might be organic in nature, but not much more is known about this matter. (See Case Study 2.8.)

Case study 2.8 A high need for nurturance. (This material was freely adapted from a paper written by a woman, twenty-six years old.)

When I was fourteen, my mother died, leaving behind my father, myself, and three younger brothers. From that day until this one I have never stopped being a mother. Many people might pity me for not really having had any adolescence or being able to participate in any teen-age activities. But I have never felt any regret. The truth is that I enjoy the role of mother.

During the months that my mother was ill, my family remarked on the great tenderness with which I cared for her. When she died, I guess I transferred this feeling to my three brothers. My father has never been a very strong person, and over the years I seem to have become the adult of the family, taking care of the rest and making the important decisions.

It wasn't just my father and brothers that got mothered. Anything that could walk, crawl, or drag itself into our house was guaranteed loving care. At one time we had five cats, all bedraggled specimens, who had just wandered in and decided they liked the layout. We have also had a continuous assortment of dogs, fish, birds, mice, and turtles.

Now that my brothers have all grown up

and left home I continue to keep house for my father. Last year I began school with the idea of becoming an elementary teacher. At the present time I teach Sunday school. The thought of having about thirty youngsters to teach and take care of is very appealing to me.

Why haven't I had some children of my own? Well, it takes two. Until recently there hasn't been too much time for dates, and to be perfectly frank about it, with my big bones and ample proportions I am not exactly the college boy's dream. However, recently to my very pleasant surprise a young man has got interested in me. He isn't very much to look at either, but he is very considerate and gentle. I must admit that when I look at him, I think, "Now there's a man who would make a very good husband and father." If he ever gets up enough courage to ask me, I plan to say "yes." Poor guy, before he knows what has happened, he'll have a house full of kids. But I think he'll like it. I know I will too.

Succorance Needs

The succorance need is manifested in the desire to seek sympathy, assistance, and protection from others. People with strong succorance needs tell others about their problems and look for commiseration and understanding. They like to be the subject of a good deal of love and attention. They solicit advice and guidance from others, and they enjoy having an older person or a parental figure on whom they can rely. They tend to feel helpless and insecure when they are alone or left to depend on their own resources.

Succorant, we come into the world. As we grow, we change from a dependent child who must be succored into an independent adult who can nurture others.

Even among young children, however, there are wide differences in succorant needs. Sears and his associates studied patterns of dependence or succorance in a group of five-year-olds; some of the children seemed to require a lot of attention while others needed almost none at all. Here in the mother's own words is a description of a child with little need for attention:

> Well, we're kind of a funny family. I mean we don't show too much affection towards one another. I mean affection is there but we just, we're not the very sloppy kind. She comes in from school, she kisses me good-bye in the morning, and, of course, I go to the door with her, and I watch her down the street. She's not a child that you would say would fall all over you. She'll kiss you and all that, but I mean she's not a child that you would say was exceptionally affectionate (Sears et al., 1957, p. 147).

By contrast, this mother reports that her child seeks a good deal of attention:

> He wants a lot of attention. He wants all my attention. . . . He doesn't let me talk on the telephone—he is climbing all over me, interrupting me, and if I were talking to anyone—even here now—he would resent it terribly. He would have to be climbing all over me and want my attention, and if he can't get it he does something very naughty to get it (p. 148).

The studies of Sears and his associates are an important source of information concerning the origin of succorance or dependency behavior. Their findings indicated, first, that the mother's tendency to permit dependency behavior and to reward it was unrelated to the amount of child dependency that was shown; in other words, mothers who dropped what they were doing and responded to their children's dependency demands did not seem to have children who were more dependent because of this. Second, punishment for dependency did not make children any less dependent; just the opposite, it made them more dependent than ever. Third, the greatest dependency was found in children whose mothers were high in *both* reward and punishment; this situation was felt to produce a conflict of expectations which served to energize dependency behavior.

Strong succorance needs are seen in adults as well as in children. Some adults may retain strong dependency ties with parents or establish new dependency relationships with friends, teachers, employers, or a marriage partner. They arrange their lives so that there are people around who are kind and helpful.

It is important to note that the individual can be succorant or dependent in some ways but quite independent in others. He can be dependent on some people while other people are dependent upon him. Or one can exchange succorance for succorance. A mother, for example, can succor her children while she in turn is succored by her husband. Or a married couple may baby each other. Women in general are more nurturant than men, and they are also more succorant (Edwards, 1954, 1959). (See Case Study 2.9.)

Case study 2.9 A high need for succorance. (This material was freely adapted from a paper written by a man, eighteen years old.)

An only child, I was born to my parents when they were both in their forties. By the time I arrived on the scene they had been married and wanting a child for nearly twenty years. To say that my welcome was royal is to put it mildly.

Both of my parents are very warm people. They tend to mother each other and to overprotect me. Any time that I was ill, it was a major emergency. Whenever I was away at camp for a week or two, there was a flood of telephone calls, and my parents heaved a tremendous sigh of relief when I returned. As I grew up and began to stay out later at night, there was literally a light left burning in the window.

Sometimes I rebelled against this heavy dose of mothering, but to be frank I guess I really liked it too. I never realized how protected I had been until this year when I left home to come to the university. For the first time too I have begun to get a little worried about my dependence on my folks and about my ability to stand on my own two feet.

My need for mothering seems to follow me wherever I go and into whatever I do. Last semester I took German from a very motherly teacher. I took an instant liking for her and soon was going to her with all my problems, language and otherwise. She has been very kind to me, but I know that the time has come for me to go it on my own.

On dates I have the same problem. I find that I am attracted to older women. My first dates this year were with a student about ten years older than I am. Recently I have become interested in a freshman girl. She was quick to spot my dependent ways, and now she gets after me when I try to get her to make the decisions on our dates together. Little by little I'm growing up, but it isn't always easy.

Sex Needs

The need for sex is usually manifested in the desire to think about, associate with, fall in love with, and have sexual relations with members of the opposite sex. People with strong needs of this sort enjoy reading about and discussing love and sex. They enjoy the company of the opposite sex at dances, parties, and other social activities. They fall in love quite easily and enjoy love relationships. They feel a strong physical attraction to members of the opposite sex.

Patterns of sexual motivation vary considerably. Some of us have much stronger sex needs than others, and we differ in the extent to which we accept these needs and satisfy them. We differ, too, in the ways that we meet these needs.

Even though the origins of sexual motivation are physiological, both sex strength and patterning are heavily influenced by learning (Child, 1954; Sears, 1958). There is a good deal of evidence to indicate that the learning experiences provided by culture (Ford & Beach, 1951), social class (Kinsey, Pomeroy, & Martin, 1948), and family relationships (Maccoby & Gibbs, 1954; Sears, 1958) play an important part in the determination of sexual behavior.

Cultures vary widely in the patterns of sexual behavior that are allowed or prohibited. Behavior that is quite acceptable in one culture may be highly punished in another (Ford & Beach, 1951). There are also wide variations in child-training practices concerning sex (Whiting & Child, 1953).

Available evidence suggests that sexual adjustment presents fewer problems in those cultures with comparatively permissive practices. After reviewing the findings of a number of studies Kluckhohn (1954) concludes that impotence and frigidity are rare in cultures which are tolerant of childhood sexuality and which accept sexual behavior as "one of the good things of life."

The American culture places comparatively severe restrictions on sexual behavior (Sears, 1958; Whiting & Child, 1953). Early explorations are commonly discouraged or punished, and this treatment may serve to inhibit sexual activity or cause it to be hidden. Shame, fear, and anxiety can become attached to sexual behavior and persist to interfere with sexual adjustment in adulthood.

The middle class is generally more permissive and less severe in sex training of children than the lower class. For example, an investigation of upper-middle-class and upper-lower-class mothers of kindergarten children showed that sex training was clearly more severe in the lower group. Upper-middle mothers were more permissive toward nudity, masturbation, and sex play among children, and they began modesty training at a later age (Maccoby & Gibbs, 1954).

Although early family experiences have an important effect on adult sex behavior, little has been established about the exact relationships involved (Child, 1954). Available evidence suggests that where there has been a lot of sexual stimulation in childhood and also a good deal of gratification, the amount of sex motivation in adolescence and adulthood is increased (Sears, 1958).

It is generally agreed that a fairly permissive, informative, and matter-of-fact handling of early sexual behavior is favorable to the production of healthy patterns of response later in life. Where early sexual behavior has been heavily suppressed and punished, sex impulses may cause a good deal of anxiety all through life, and deviant sex patterning is more likely (Sears, 1958). (See Case Study 2.10.)

Case study 2.10 A strong need for sex. (This material was freely adapted from a paper written by a man, nineteen years old.)

Even for a young male in the prime of life, perhaps I spend too much time dwelling on sex. No matter where or what the circumstances, the stimulus I respond to most is a pretty girl. Sitting in class I find that my attention wanders away from the lecturer to the various blondes, brunettes, and redheads. In one of my classes I sit between two pretty girls (I had nothing to do with this—it is just a fortunate alphabetical circumstance), and my notes in this class are in chaos.

When I go to the library to study, I arrange all my books and notes around me and attempt to burrow in. Yet I am conscious of every coed moving about. Sometimes in order to eliminate distractions I seat myself in the corner facing two blank walls, but then I begin to daydream. The young ladies in my daydreams are even nicer than those in real life, and they are much more easily impressed.

The fact of the matter is that my daydreams and my days are considerably different. Maybe one of the reasons that I'm *preoccupied* with sex is that I am not very *occupied* with it. I don't date very often, and asking a girl to go out is something of a chore. Usually I won't approach a girl for a date unless I am pretty sure that she is going to accept.

Once out on a date, I am usually not my natural self. If the girl is not too attractive, I can relax and have a good time. But if the girl is really pretty, I get all shook up. I feel

Figure 2.3 How do men and women differ in need patterns? Here are some of the personality test results on 760 college men and 749 college women who were enrolled at a number of American colleges and universities. The instrument was the Edwards Personal Preference Schedule which is widely used in research and counseling. For each individual, the maximum possible score on a need is 28, and the minimum is 0 (Data from Edwards, 1954, 1959).

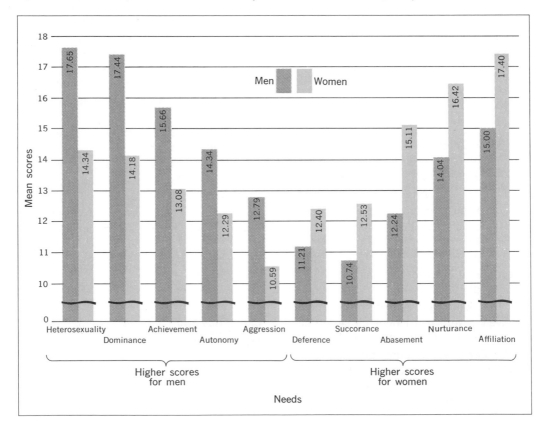

that I have to make a big impression on her and usually wind up making a fool of myself and spending too much money. Afterward I could kick myself.

I spend a lot of my "recreational" time lounging around with the boys. Of course, the subject for conversation is usually girls. Sometimes we're worse than a bunch of old women. We gossip about this girl and gossip about that one. We criticize. We disparage. But we aren't kidding anyone, least of all ourselves. It's the old sour peach mechanism. If you can't reach the peaches, you say they're sour. But you don't take your eyes off of them—not for a moment.

How do men and women differ in need patterns? Figure 2.3 shows the test results of an investigation among American college students.

SUMMARY

Motive refers to a pattern of need-pushed and goal-pulled behavior. Each motive is a sequence of need, act, and goal. Need is a condition that prompts us to act. Act refers to the behavior impelled by a need and directed toward a goal. Goal is anything that can satisfy the need and terminate the act.

Psychologists disagree about motivational ideas. Some major controversies concern (1) the number of motives it is useful to describe—whether few or many, (2) the relative roles that heredity and learning play, and (3) the usefulness and importance of the concept of unconscious motivation. Ten motives or needs which are important in the study of adjustment are achievement, affiliation, autonomy, dominance, deference, aggression, abasement, nurturance, succorance, and sex.

The achievement need is manifested in the desire to overcome obstacles, accomplish difficult things, and surpass others. This need is generally strong in the American culture and especially high in the middle class. Family relationships have an important effect on achievement patterns.

The affiliation need is demonstrated in efforts to associate with, cooperate with, and form friendships with others. Like the achievement need, it appears to be relatively high in the American culture and specifically in the middle class. The need for affiliation is considerably affected by earlier social experiences, especially by those within the family circle.

The autonomy need is manifested in the wish to be free and independent. Different writers describe autonomy in different ways, and they differ on their evaluation of autonomous behavior in the American culture. Autonomy needs seem particularly high in those individuals whose families emphasized and rewarded independence and in those whose families left them on their own.

The dominance need is reflected in impulses to influence, direct, and control the behavior of others. The need for dominance and the capacity for leadership are not synonymous; some individuals with high dominance needs fail as leaders. In general, men are more dominant than women. Family patterns affect dominance behavior but the relationship is complex.

The deference need is shown in the desire to admire, follow, and be guided by others. Like the leadership role, the role of follower brings with it a number of satisfactions. Cultural, familial, and sex factors all appear to affect the strength of deference needs.

The aggression need is revealed in the desire to overpower opposition and to criticize, attack, and punish others. The amount of aggression seems to be related to the amount of frustration that has been experienced and to the ways that parents and others have reacted to aggressive behavior. Punishing aggression in children tends to make them more rather than less aggressive.

The abasement need includes the desire to admit inadequacy, to accept blame, and to suffer punishment. Although abasement patterns are ostensibly self-attacking, they can serve indirectly to attack and control the behavior of others. Abasive behavior may occur when the individual sees himself as the source of his own frustrations or when outward forms of aggression are denied him.

The nurturance need is shown in the desire to sympathize with, assist, and protect others. Males as well as females and children as well as adults may be high in this need. Mothering is the foremost expression of nurturance, but mothers vary widely in the strength of their nurturance needs.

The succorance need is manifested in impulses to seek sympathy, assistance, and protection from others. The individual's succorance behavior is strongly influenced by the way his family met his early dependency and independency demands. Strong succorance needs are seen in adults as well as in children.

The sex need is usually demonstrated in impulses to think about, associate with, fall in love with, and have sexual relations with members of the opposite sex. The patterning and strength of sex needs vary widely. So does the ability to express and meet these needs. Culture, class, and family factors play an important part in the determination of sexual behavior. The American culture places comparatively severe restrictions on sexual expression.

REFERENCES

Allport, G. W., Freyre, G., Gurvitch, G., Horkheimer, M., Naess, A., Rickman, J., Sullivan, H. S., & Szalai, A. Tensions affecting international understanding. *AAUP Bulletin,* 1948, **34,** 546–549.

Arkoff, A. Need patterns in two generations of Japanese Americans in Hawaii. *Journal of Social Psychology,* 1959, **50,** 75–79.

Burgum, M. Constructive values associated with rejection. *American Journal of Orthopsychiatry,* 1940, **10,** 312–326.

Child, I. L. Socialization. In G. Lindzey (Ed.), *Handbook of Social Psychology.* Vol. 2. *Special Fields and Applications.* Reading, Mass.: Addison-Wesley, 1954. Pp. 655–692.

Combs, A. W., & Snygg, D. *Individual Behavior.* (2nd ed.) New York: Harper & Row, 1959.

Crandall, V. J., Orleans, S., Preston, A., & Rabson, A. The development of social compliance in young children. *Child Development,* 1958, **29,** 429–443.

Dollard, J., Doob, L. W., Miller, N. E., Mowrer, O. H., & Sears, R. R. *Frustration and Aggression.* New Haven, Conn.: Yale, 1939.

Douvan, E. Social status and success strivings. In J. W. Atkinson (Ed.), *Motives in Fantasy, Action, and Society.* Princeton, N.J.: Van Nostrand, 1958. Pp. 509–517.

Edwards, A. L. *Edwards Personal Preference Schedule.* New York: Psychological Corporation, 1954, 1959.

Erikson, E. H. Growth and crises of the "healthy personality." In C. Kluckhohn, H. A. Murray, & D. M. Schneider (Eds.), *Personality in Nature, Society, and Culture.* (2nd ed.) New York: Knopf, 1955. Pp. 185–225.

Ford, C. S., & Beach, F. A. *Patterns of Sexual Behavior.* New York: Harper & Row, 1951.

Fraisse, P., Klineberg, O., & Leontiev, A. An appeal to psychologists. *International Journal of Psychology,* 1966, **1**(2), 165–167.

Gibb, C. A. Leadership. In G. Lindzey (Ed.), *Handbook of Social Psychology.* Vol. 2. *Special Fields and Applications.* Reading, Mass.: Addison-Wesley, 1954. Pp. 877–920.

Guilford, J. P., & Zimmerman, W. S. *The Guilford-Zimmerman Temperament Survey.* Beverly Hills, Calif.: Sheridan Supply Company, 1949.

Hall, C. S., & Lindzey, G. *Theories of Personality.* New York: Wiley, 1957.

Hebb, D. O. Drives and the C.N.S. (conceptual nervous system). *Psychological Review,* 1955, **62,** 243–254.

Hunt, J. McV. Experience and the development of motivation: Some reinterpretations. *Child Development,* 1960, **31,** 489–504.

Kelly, G. A. Man's construction of his alternatives. In G. Lindzey (Ed.), *Assessment of Human Motives.* New York: Holt, 1958. Pp. 33–64.

Kinsey, A. C., Pomeroy, W. B., & Martin, C. E. *Sexual Behavior in the Human Male.* Philadelphia: Saunders, 1948.

Kluckhohn, C. Culture and behavior. In G. Lindzey (Ed.), *Handbook of Social Psychology.* Vol. 2. *Special Fields and Applications.* Reading, Mass.: Addison-Wesley, 1954. Pp. 921–976.

────── **& Murray, H. A.** Personality formation: The determinants. In C. Kluckhohn, H. A. Murray, & D. M. Schneider (Eds.), *Personality in Nature, Society, and Culture.* (2nd ed.) New York: Knopf, 1955. Pp. 53–67.

Krech, D., & Crutchfield, R. S. *Theory and Problems of Social Psychology.* New York: McGraw-Hill, 1948.

────── & ──────. *Elements of Psychology.* New York: Knopf, 1958.

Levy, D. M. Psychosomatic studies of some aspects of maternal behavior. In C. Kluckhohn, H. A. Murray, & D. M. Schneider (Eds.), *Personality in Nature, Society, and Culture.* (2nd ed.) New York: Knopf, 1955. Pp. 104–110.

Lindzey, G. The assessment of human motives. In G. Lindzey (Ed.), *The Assessment of Human Motives.* New York: Holt, 1958. Pp. 3–32.

McClelland, D. C., Atkinson, J. W., Clark, R. A., & Lowell, E. L. *The Achievement Motive.* New York: Appleton-Century-Crofts, 1953.

Maccoby, E. E., & Gibbs, P. K. Methods of child-rearing in two social classes. In W. E. Martin & C. B. Stendler (Eds.), *Readings in Child Development.* New York: Harcourt, Brace, 1954. Pp. 380–396.

Martin, W. E., & Stendler, C. B. *Child Behavior and Development.* New York: Harcourt, Brace, 1959.

Maslow, A. H. *Motivation and Personality.* New York: Harper & Row, 1954.

Mummery, D. V. Family backgrounds of assertive and non-assertive children. *Child Development,* 1954, **25,** 61–80.

Murphy, G. The psychologists' manifesto. In G. Murphy (Ed.), *Human Nature and Enduring Peace.* Boston: Houghton Mifflin, 1945. Pp. 454–460.

———. *Personality: A Biosocial Approach to Origins and Structure.* New York: Harper & Row, 1947.

Murray, H. A. Drive, time, strategy, measurement, and our way of life. In G. Lindzey (Ed.), *Assessment of Human Motives.* New York: Holt, 1958. Pp. 183–196.

——— et al. *Explorations in Personality.* Fair Lawn, N.J.: Oxford, 1938.

Phillips, E. L. *Psychotherapy: A Modern Theory and Practice.* Englewood Cliffs, N.J.: Prentice-Hall, 1956.

Riesman, D. *The Lonely Crowd.* New Haven, Conn.: Yale, 1950.

Rosen, B. C. The achievement syndrome: A psychocultural dimension of social stratification. In J. W. Atkinson (Ed.), *Motives in Fantasy, Action, and Society.* Princeton, N.J.: Van Nostrand, 1958. Pp. 495–508.

Sanford, R. N., et al. Physique, personality and scholarship. *Monographs of the Society for Research in Child Development,* 1943, **8,** No. 1 (Serial No. 34).

Sears, R. R. Personality development in the family. In J. M. Seidman (Ed.), *The Child: A Book of Readings.* New York: Holt, 1958. Pp. 117–137.

———, Maccoby, E. E., & Levin, H. *Patterns of Child Rearing.* New York: Harper & Row, 1957.

Snygg, D., & Combs, A. W. The phenomenological approach and the problem of "unconscious" behavior: A reply to Dr. Smith. *Journal of Abnormal and Social Psychology,* 1950, **45,** 523–528.

Stendler, C. B. *Children of Brasstown.* Urbana, Ill.: University of Illinois Press, 1949.

Strodtbeck, F. L. Family interaction, values, and achievement. In D. C. McClelland, A. L. Baldwin, U. Bronfenbrenner, & F. L. Strodtbeck. *Talent and Society.* Princeton, N.J.: Van Nostrand, 1958. Pp. 135–194.

Symonds, P. M. *The Psychology of Parent-Child Relationships.* New York: Appleton-Century-Crofts, 1939.

Szasz, T. S. *The Myth of Mental Illness.* New York: Hoeber-Harper, 1961.

White, R. W. Motivation reconsidered: The concept of competence. *Psychological Review,* 1959, **66,** 297–333.

Whiting, J. W. M., & Child, I. L. *Child Training and Personality: A Cross-cultural Study.* New Haven, Conn.: Yale, 1953.

Winterbottom, M. R. The relation of need for achievement to learning experiences in independence and mastery. In J. W. Atkinson (Ed.), *Motives in Fantasy, Action, and Society.* Princeton, N.J.: Van Nostrand, 1958. Pp. 453–478.

Wolberg, L. R. The character structure of the rejected child. *The Nervous Child,* 1944, **3,** 74–88.

CHAPTER THREE

FRUSTRATION

Aroused by our needs, we act to reach our goals. Some needs may be satisfied immediately or with little effort. Oxygen requirements are filled automatically except in unusual circumstances. Water is almost always available, and although we cannot always have the food of our choice, few of us go hungry for very long.

But many, many times during our lives we find that our needs cannot be satisfied. Sometimes important goals are not obtainable. Sometimes goal objects that we have come to depend on are withdrawn or disappear. And sometimes formidable obstacles stand between us and our goals.

A life without frustration is difficult to imagine. And such a state might not be a very desirable one. Living is problem solving, and much of life's zest as well as its pain stems from the problems it presents for solution. Anyway, we have no choice in the matter: frustrations are inevitable, and in this chapter we will set out to learn more about them.

DEFINING FRUSTRATION

Frustrations are frequent and "frustration" is a frequently used word. Psychologists define and use this term in very different ways (Lawson & Marx, 1958; Yates, 1962). In this discussion *frustration* is simply defined as interference with goal-directed behavior. The material which follows describes frustration both as a process of blocking and as a state of feeling (see Fig. 3.1).

Frustration as a Process of Blocking

One way of describing frustration is as a process in which our behavior is blocked. This description focuses on the frustrating situation itself. Any situation in which we are thwarted and prevented from expressing a need, carrying out an act, or reaching a goal would be considered a frustration.

We may, for example, apply for admission to a particular college and be turned down. The situation is a frustrating one. We are blocked from meeting the achievement, affiliation, or other needs that, for us, may be involved in attending and graduating from the college.

Or perhaps we are admitted to the col-

Figure 3.1 Interference with goal-directed behavior is referred to as *frustration*. This term is used to identify both the process of interference or blocking itself and the state of feeling which accompanies this process.

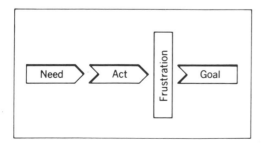

lege but find the courses uninteresting or the work too difficult or the entire environment a complex and intimidating one. We end the first semester with failing or nearly failing grades. We're blocked in the pursuit of our goals. We're frustrated.

Frustration as a State of Feeling

A second way of describing frustration is as the state of feeling which accompanies the thwarting process. This description focuses on the frustrated individual rather than on the frustrating situation. It considers his experience as he finds himself blocked and unable to reach his goals.

An important distinction can be made between these several ways of describing frustration. Two persons placed in seemingly the same frustrating situation may experience quite different amounts of frustration, and their subsequent behavior may also be quite different (Yates, 1962).

If, for example, we have been blocked in our attempts to be admitted to a particular college, we may feel frustrated. We're disappointed, maybe embarrassed and discouraged. Perhaps we're angry. Or maybe we just tell ourselves, "Oh, well, better luck next time."

And if we are admitted and flunk out or nearly flunk out before we really get started, some of us might be nearly overwhelmed by our feelings of frustration. But others might experience considerably less frustration, and a few could seem scarcely concerned.

Feelings of frustration vary in quality and strength. They range from expressions of deep discouragement and despair or from violent anger and rage to affective states that are even pleasant. Mild frustrations may be actually sought out; they can be enjoyable and serve as a tonic and stimulus.

Feelings of frustration also vary in duration. Some dissipate quickly, but others linger for a long time. There are persons in whom feelings of frustration appear to be rather general and permanent; these individuals nearly always seem to feel frustrated and unhappy.

Sometimes the terms "feelings of anxiety" and "feelings of frustration" are used interchangeably. In a later chapter "anxiety" will be defined as arousal caused by threat to well-being. Many frustrations pose threats but not all of them do. The idea of "threat" is an important one in adjustment, and it will be considered more fully in the discussion which follows.

STUDYING FRUSTRATION

Psychologists have spent a considerable amount of time studying frustration, and they have found it to be a very complex phenomenon (Lawson & Marx, 1958). In the study of adjustment some of the most significant issues are these: Is frustration inevitable? When is frustration threatening? And when is it intolerable?

Frustrations: Avoidable or Inevitable?

Many people seem to view frustration only in a negative light. For example, they may say that children should never be frustrated. Sometimes, moreover, *they say* that *psychologists say* this.

It has been pointed out, however, that all learning involves some degree of frustration (Melton, 1941). Brown and Farber (1951) note that frustration serves as an important source of new patterns of response. And May (1961) adds that ". . . the thwarting of a goal response is precisely a prime condition that gives rise to thinking."

The socialization process itself is a process of frustration. As Murray (1938) notes, through ". . . suggestion, persuasion, example, rewards, promises, punishment, threats, physical coercion and restraints" the child is directed to behave in certain ways and prevented (frustrated) from behaving in certain others. The child is taught to meet his needs according to what Murray calls the "time-place-mode-object" formula:

> A child is allowed to play during the day but not at night (time). He may defecate in the toilet but not on the floor (place). He may push other children but not hit them with a mallet (mode). He may ask his father but not a stranger in the street for money (object). No need has to be inhibited permanently. If the individual is of the right age and chooses the permitted time, the permitted place, the permitted mode and the permitted object, he can objectify any one of his needs (1938, p. 136).

Frustration is inevitable, but not all frustration is inevitable. Some frustration can be avoided or prevented and ought to be. Extended frustration of important needs is of serious consequence.

Vaughan (1952), a psychologist, criticizes the fairly typical American idea: "Hitch your wagon to a star!" "Americans," he says, "are inclined to be over-ambitious. . . . Setting one's sights toward unattainable goals is responsible for much of the frustration which affects us Americans."

Frustrations: Benign or Threatening?

Whether in the psychological laboratory or in the laboratory of everyday life, people are affected very differently by frustration. A situation which swamps one person, scarcely moves another. Why?

Maslow suggests that frustrations are important or unimportant depending on the amount of "threat" they pose to important needs and goals. He points out, for example, that if we are criticized by a friend, we may listen and even be grateful, but if the criticism is interpreted as an attack on our worth as a person, we may respond very differently.

Maslow notes that a single goal object can have several meanings: an intrinsic one and a symbolic one.

> Thus a certain child deprived of an ice-cream cone that he wanted may have lost simply an ice-cream cone. A second child, however, deprived of an ice-cream cone, may have lost not only a sensory gratification, but may feel deprived of the love of his mother because she refused to buy it for him. For the second boy the ice-cream cone not only has an intrinsic value, but may also be the carrier of psychological values. Being deprived merely of ice cream qua ice cream probably means little for a healthy individual, and it is questionable whether it should even be called by the same name, i.e., frustration, that characterizes other more threatening deprivations. It is only when a goal object represents love, prestige, respect, or other basic needs, that being deprived of it will have the bad effects ordinarily attributed to frustration in general (1954, p. 156).

Maslow feels that when a child is generally secure—when he feels loved and respected—he is much less threatened by his frustrations and much less likely to show unfavorable effects. Says Maslow, "Observations of children who are completely assured of the love and respect of their parents have shown that deprivations can sometimes be borne with astonishing ease."

Frustrations: Tolerable or Intolerable?

It has just been noted that the same frustrating situation may affect several persons differently. It can also be noted that some people, generally, are able to tolerate more frustration than others. *Frustration tolerance* and *frustration threshold* are two ideas that have been proposed in this connection.

Frustration tolerance is defined by Rosenzweig (1944) as the ability to "withstand frustration . . . without resorting to inadequate modes of response." He likens it to the medical concept of resistance to disease. Rosenzweig suggests that individuals differ in their ability to tolerate frustration and that for any one person there may be adjustment areas of relatively high or low frustration tolerance.

Maier and Ellen note that qualitatively different sorts of behavior are shown in frustrating and nonfrustrating situations. They suggest that there is a *frustration threshold* which is a level or point below which behavior is "constructive" and above which it is "nonconstructive." They say:

> Frustration theory postulates that behavior that is constructive, motivated, problem solving, or goal oriented in nature may suddenly be replaced by behavior that is hostile (aggression), immature (regression), stubborn (fixation), apathetic (resignation), or some combination of these symptoms whenever the frustration thresh-

old of the individual is exceeded. It is also assumed that individuals will show either constructive or nonconstructive type of behavior in a stressful situation, depending on the height of their frustration thresholds (1959, pp. 196–197).

What accounts for wide individual differences in the ability to bear frustration? Rosenzweig (1944) reviews the evidence and concludes that very little is known about this. He suggests that the amount of childhood frustration may play a part. Too little frustration spoils us so that we do not learn how to meet and deal with it when it occurs. Too much frustration overwhelms us, and we are forced to adopt defensive adjustment patterns that interfere with our later development.

CLASSIFYING FRUSTRATIONS

Frustrations are many and varied, and a number of systems have been proposed for classifying them. The systems are neat and simple, much more so than the frustrations, so that pigeonholing a particular instance of frustration isn't very easy. The following discussion describes several systems which are useful in classifying a number of frustrations.

Need, Act, and Goal Frustrations

One system of classification that has been proposed focuses on the ideas of need, act, and goal (Sappenfield, 1954). If we are unable to meet a need through any act or in relation to any goal, we are said to experience a *need frustration*. If we are unable to meet a need through a particular

act that we are trying, we are undergoing *act frustration*. If we are unable to meet our need in relation to a particular goal, the interference is called *goal frustration.*

Need Frustrations

Need frustration is a broad category; it subsumes all interferences. If a particular act is frustrated, we will suffer need frustration as well until we find a more successful pattern of activity. If a particular goal object is unattainable, our need will go unmet until a substitute goal is found.

Some need frustration is self-imposed. If our earlier experience in trying to meet a need has been unhappy and painful, we may tend to inhibit this need, blocking its impulses as they arise. Sex and aggression, for example, are needs that many of us have difficulty in expressing because of earlier repressive and punitive experiences. In a later section of this chapter, the frustrations that beset sex and aggression will be discussed as well as those that affect some other important needs.

Act Frustrations

Act frustrations are a feature of everyday living. In a new and unfamiliar situation we may try and fail and try and fail until we hit upon a successful response. In upsetting situations and those for which we have a habitual solution, it can be very difficult for us to abandon a response even though it continues to be frustrated.

Here are some examples of act frustration. A young man, smoldering with anger, learns that the people he attacks strike back at him, leaving him worse off than before. A student who scarcely cracked a book in high school tries the same approach in college with unhappy results. A dominating mother finds that her children increasingly resent and resist her control as they grow up.

Goal Frustrations

Goal frustrations, too, are part of everyday life. We frequently can't get our preferred goal. We have to compromise. We settle for second best, sometimes even for third and fourth best, sometimes for nothing at all.

Some of our frustrations do not concern the goals we didn't get—they concern the "goals" we did. Our actions are directed toward certain things and away from others. Sometimes we are unable to avoid the latter things or conditions. For example, we receive the flunk which we crammed to avoid, or we wind up with our roommate's case of mumps (see Fig. 3.2).

Lacks, Losses, and Obstacles

A second system of classification makes use of three categories into which many of our common frustrations can be grouped (Rosenzweig, 1938). Sometimes we are frustrated because we *lack* something, or because of the *loss* of something, or because of some *obstacle* that blocks our behavior.

Lacks

All of us have been frustrated because we lacked things that were important to our well-being. Some of us have known great poverty and lived in environments that scarcely provided us with the bare necessities of life. Even in the United States, one of the richest countries of the world, a sizable minority live in poverty (Chilman & Sussman, 1964). Jacqueline Cochran, now prominent in aviation and business,

was raised in impoverished circumstances, and in her autobiography she sharply recalls some of the frustration of her early years (compare this with a similar recollection in Case Study 3.1):

> *Until I was eight years old, I had no shoes. My bed was usually a pallet on the floor and sometimes just the floor. Food at best consisted of the barest essentials—sometimes nothing except what I foraged for myself in the woods or in the waters of the nearby bayou or the running "branch." Mullet and beans were the staples, with a bit of sowbelly added when we were in clover, with some black-eyed peas thrown in if and when we were on the crest. No butter, no sugar. My dresses in the first seven years of my life were usually made from cast-off flour sacks.*[1]

The lack of physical necessities has been noted, but the social environment can be generally impoverished too. We may have been raised in a broken home scarcely knowing one of our parents. Even if our family were intact, it may have lacked important qualities, for example, warmth, security, and guidance.

Many important lacks might be thought of as personal ones, as existing within ourselves. Deficiencies or defects that we have had since birth or for as long as we can remember might be considered in this connection. Perhaps we lack the physical qualities necessary to reach our goals: we are too tall or too short, too ugly or too attractive, too lacking in strength or coordination. Perhaps we lack the intelligence, or knowledge, or skill necessary to satisfy a particular need or reach a particular goal.

[1] From *The Stars at Noon* by Jacqueline Cochran. Copyright 1954, by Jacqueline Cochran. Reprinted by permission of Atlantic-Little, Brown and Company, Publishers. P. 3.

Figure 3.2 Diagramming Frustration (Based on Brown, 1957; Lewin, 1935; Miller, 1964).

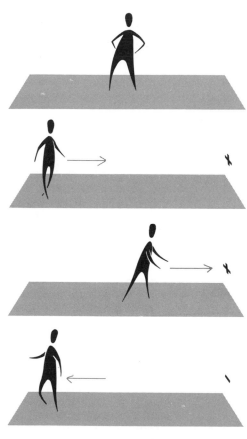

Here in diagram form are some ideas concerning frustration. The rectangle includes the individual and the significant features of a situation.

The person moves toward certain goals which are said to have positive valence (+).

The nearer he is to a goal with positive valence, the stronger are his tendencies to approach it.

The person moves away from certain goals which are said to have negative valence (−).

The nearer he is to a goal with negative valence, the stronger are his tendencies to avoid it.

Anything that interferes with the approach toward a positive goal or the avoidance of a negative one can be considered a frustration.

Case study 3.1 Lack. (This material was taken from a paper written by a woman, twenty years old.)

In these days of rising standards of living, I wonder if you can imagine what it was like to be from a family that was desperately poor. For me the pain of poverty was not so much in the lack of money and of the things that money buys. It came from having to pretend before others. You see, although we were poor, we were proud.

Dad kept a store—it was about 12 feet square—and mother worked with him from morning to night. On the school forms we always put "merchant" for father's occupation and "housewife" for mother's since she wasn't paid help. These euphemisms gave the impression that we were much better off than we actually were. When money was required for something in school, it was hard to admit that there was none, and to teachers who didn't understand the pride of the poor, it must have appeared that I was simply being negativistic.

It was in the third grade that being poor first became a distasteful thing. My teacher began a campaign to get every child to buy a hot school lunch. During the noon period she made a point of examining everyone's lunch sack. She would invariably point out the inadequacies of my sandwiches, but I insisted I preferred them to the school lunches. The truth was that in our family there were eight children, all of school age, and eight hot lunches were out of the question.

Things that are made into pleasant games for most children can be pretty hard on poor ones. I remember getting a D in cooperation for not contributing to the March of Dimes, Red Cross, and Community Chest. I couldn't attend the class party because it cost 25 cents. Each year every child would get a purple seal by his name if he had an O.K. card signed by a dentist. We couldn't afford dental work, and my teacher would get very upset because I kept the class from being 100 percent.

When I visited the homes of my school friends, I would marvel at the things they had. One home actually had two telephones in it; this to me was unimaginable luxury.

But I would go to great lengths to prevent my chums from visiting my house. Its barren poverty seemed shameful to me.

Being poor isn't the worst thing that could happen to a person, but when I was younger it seemed to be. Our financial position is better now, and it is easier to look back at those old experiences. But when I hear people talk about the good old days and the joys of their youth, I envy them their memories. I, for one, would not care to live my childhood over again.

Losses

Some frustrations are losses. Having something and losing it is a different kind of problem from having always lacked it. Sappenfield (1954) suggests that losses are more frustrating than lacks because "the loss of something that was once possessed may require radical readjustments, whereas the continued lack . . . may require little more than the continuation of habitual adjustments."

Although modern society helps us to guard against losses, our lives are touched by calamity. Tornadoes, floods, earthquakes, and other disasters can deprive us of our property, our lives, or our peace of mind. Some of us have lost money in the stock market or in money-making ventures that made no money. Recessions, automation, and changing conditions cost some of us our jobs, perhaps forcing us to sharply change our patterns of living.

Divorce, sickness, death, and warfare all serve to disrupt the security of the family. Losing or being separated from a loved one can be a source of serious frustration. Sometimes the separation is affectional rather than spatial as, for example, when a child perceives that his parents have removed their affection to a newborn sibling or when a spouse no longer seems attentive.

Illnesses, accidents, and the process of aging all serve to impair bodily functioning. Illnesses prevent us from the usual pursuit of our goals; we may be left weakened or permanently impaired. Accidents also may disrupt regular patterns of living, causing temporary or permanent readjustment. Aging serves to reduce physical efficiency; sight and hearing may be impaired, and activities may have to be modified.

Obstacles

Many of our frustrations seem most easily described as obstacles or barriers that stand in our way. Some obstacles are sim-

---

Presentation 3.1 Aging and Loss.

The number of older people has been increasing, and it has been estimated that about 9 percent of the population are beyond sixty-five years of age. There has also been greater scientific interest in the adjustment problems of older people and a growing literature on this subject. Research indicates that for many of the aged the later years of life are a period of heightened frustration. Some of the sources of frustration are loss of health, companionship, income, prestige, and self-esteem.

1 Loss of health. Advancing age is frequently associated with a reduction in physical vigor and diminished sensory acuity. Older people are ill more often, and they take longer to recover. They also suffer more chronic disease. It should be noted, however, that many people feel better after retirement than before. Partly it is a matter of attitude; in some older people the fear of illness can be as frustrating as illness itself, and many of the aged appear to fear disability more than death.
2 Loss of companionship. With advancing age, one's mate may die, leaving one very much alone. Old friends and acquaintances may also die or move away, and the circle of relationships built around work activities may disappear with retirement. Children grow up, marry, form their own families, develop their own interests, and perhaps scatter to far parts of the country. Impaired health may also be a factor in reducing social activities. Many older people express deep feelings of loneliness and isolation.
3 Loss of income. With age may come a reduction in income-producing activities, and many older people find themselves in very modest circumstances. In 1964, the President's Council on Aging gathered evidence that nearly one-half of the families headed by a person over sixty-five had annual incomes of less than $3,000. About two-thirds of the persons over sixty-five who were living alone had annual incomes below $1,500, and one-third had annual incomes of less than $1,000. And these older persons were also found to have very little in the way of savings.
4 Loss of status. In the past, older people have been respected and honored, and they have been sought out for advice and counsel. The present society tends to idealize youth; there is emphasis on being young and staying young. Old people may be ignored or depreciated and treated with condescension and pity. Furthermore, with age a person may need to step down from various posts and positions to which a certain degree of prestige has been attached.
5 Loss of self-esteem. With diminishing health, companionship, and income, and with loss of status in the eyes of others, may come self-depreciation. An aged person may come to share some of the public's negative stereotypes of age or, at least, he may find it difficult not to be affected by them. He may begin to think of himself as less adequate and less worthy. Feeling less worthy, he may attempt less and be less, and thus fulfill his own evaluation.

ple physical ones. The Great Wall of China built to keep the non-Chinese out and the Berlin Wall used (among other things) to keep the East Berliners in are examples of this sort. A child stuck in a playpen, a motorist stuck in the mud, and a prisoner stuck in a cell are frustrated and prevented from reaching their goals.

But important environmental obstacles are usually social ones. They are not *things;* they are *people.* We continually run up against people who stand in the way of our goals. A woman may be prevented from accepting a job by her husband, who desires her to remain at home. A man may be kept from entering a business venture by his wife, who considers the undertaking too risky. For the child, parents are external obstacles who constantly interfere with his activities.

An important obstacle for each person is himself. Many times every day we prevent ourselves from acting on an impulse. We may suppress a bothersome thought, block a feeling that might prove painful, or prevent ourselves from doing something that we feel would be wrong. For example, we stop ourselves from saying something that we might be sorry for later or doing something that would make us feel guilty.

Those of us who are said to be "overly conscientious" or to have "rigid consciences" might be described as people who undergo considerable self-frustration. We have elaborate systems of "shoulds" and "should nots" and feel guilty when we think we're not living up to them. Others of us might be described as quite the opposite; we frustrate ourselves relatively little, but this doesn't mean that we suffer relatively little frustration—our frustrations come as we meet head on with the people around us.

SOME IMPORTANT FRUSTRATIONS

What is an *important* frustration? One definition could be in terms of the importance of the need that is being interfered with. We may be willing to tolerate considerable frustration of relatively unimportant needs. But if the satisfaction of a need is central to our well-being, a seemingly small frustration may produce surprisingly vigorous repercussions. The following discussion considers some frustrations that affect important needs (see Fig. 3.3).

Achievement Frustrations

The desire to get ahead, to be a success, to become somebody is strong in many of us. In school we struggle to make good grades. At work we strive to be promoted. We endeavor to win at bridge, tennis, or Scrabble. Sometimes we fail. We may lack a number of qualities that are essential to successful goal seeking. Modest ability, inadequate education, physical limitations, and personal maladjustment are some of the things that may hold us back.

Figure 3.3 (right) Mental illness and frustration. After preliminary research with a large number of questions having to do with childhood frustration or deprivation, twenty items which appeared to differentiate psychiatric patients and nonpatients were made into a questionnaire and administered to a new group of inpatients, outpatients, and nonpatients. It was found that psychiatric patients reported more deprivation than nonpatients, although inpatients and outpatients were not significantly different. Items concerned with the *fact* of deprivation (questions 1 through 13) differentiated patients and nonpatients less well than did those dealing with *feelings* of deprivation (questions 14 through 20). Responses indicating deprivation are in bolder type (Banks & Cappon, 1963).

	Questionnaire item	Response	Reporting deprivation
			Patients ▨ Nonpatients ▨
1.	As an infant I spent some time in hospital.	**Yes** No	19% 4
2.	When under five I was ill a great deal or for a long time in hospital.	**Yes** No	9 2
3.	My parents brought me up through my childhood. . . .	Yes **No**	13 6
4.	My parents were divorced or separated before I grew up. .	**Yes** No	17 8
5.	As I grew up I usually had to share my bedroom and some-times I had to share my bed with someone else. . . .	**Yes** No	55 58
6.	In my home I was exposed to alcoholism **or** frequent fights **or** separations between my parents or parent substitutes. .	**Yes** No	30 18
7.	In my early life, I moved often.	**Yes** No	27 26
8.	As I grew up we were very poor **or** very rich.	**Yes** No	33 18
9.	I had my mother during my growing-up period.	Yes **No**	14 4
10.	I had my father during my growing-up period.	Yes **No**	23 14
11.	I have experienced the loss of several people (other than my parents) who were important to me.	**Yes** No	27 36
12.	I have experienced the loss of wealth or home or social standing.	**Yes** No	22 10
13.	I feel that my mother or the person who acted as my mother loved me genuinely and deeply.	Yes **No**	26 4
14.	I feel that my father or the person who acted as my father loved me genuinely and deeply.	Yes **No**	24 12
15.	I feel that my love for my mother or the person who acted as my mother was genuine and deep.	Yes **No**	29 6
16.	I feel that my love for my father or the person who acted as my father was genuine and deep.	Yes **No**	35 16
17.	One or both of my parents smothered me with love. . . .	Yes **No**	20 10
18.	As a child I often felt unwanted by my parents or the people who acted as my parents or not accepted for what I was.	**Yes** No	31 10
19.	My parents, or the people who brought me up, loved one another.	Yes **No**	25 10
20.	I have been **deeply** and **continuously** affected by the loss of people or things I loved or valued.	**Yes** No	33 14

The amount of frustration we suffer depends to some extent upon the discrepancy between our level of aspiration and our level of competence. Johnson (1946) identified a pattern of achievement frustration

Figure 3.4 Reacting to frustration. How do we react to frustration? One common view holds that the natural or dominant reaction to frustration is aggression. However, in the belief of various authorities not all frustration stimulates aggression and not all aggression stems from frustration.*

Rosenzweig (1934, 1960) provides a comprehensive system for classifying reaction to frustration. One aspect of the system is concerned with three kinds of blameworthiness which are identified as extrapunitive, intropunitive, and impunitive. In the first mode of responding, we blame others; in the second, we blame ourselves; in the third, there is no blame.

The Rosenzweig P-F Study was devised to study frustration behavior. It consists of twenty-four cartoon situations, two of which are presented below (size reduced). Each cartoon depicts a frustration, and the subject is instructed to write in the first response which occurs to him. An extrapunitive response to the first cartoon might be: "If you hadn't rushed me, this wouldn't have happened." An intropunitive response: "I seem to be getting more and more forgetful." An impunitive response: "Let me take another look." (Reproduced with permission from the Rosenzweig P-F Study, Copyright 1948).

* Some interesting discussions of this problem are contained in Bandura and Walters (1963); Berkowitz (1962); Lawson (1965); and Yates (1962).

that he called the "IFD Disease." This pattern is made up of a sequence of idealism, frustration, and demoralization. It begins with a struggle toward an ideal that is highly valued but unrealistic. Failing to attain the impossible ideal, we feel frustrated, and continued frustration brings personal demoralization.

We may set our level of aspiration too low as well as too high. In doing so, we protect ourselves against defeat. If we don't try, we can't fail. If we don't expect anything, we can't be disappointed. Some of us apply ourselves to small tasks, and we do each one of them perfectly. But we shy away from important work because we might not do it well.

Affiliation Frustrations

The need for affiliation may be frustrated in many ways. Although we solicit the company of others, we find that others do not always wish to associate with us. We are unable to break into a clique, denied membership in a club or fraternity, or blackballed by a lodge. We can be ignored, snubbed, or rejected. This rejection may be due to our race, religion, national origin, social class, economic status, associates, education, standards, values, appearance, or personality patterns.

Without realizing it, we may serve to frustrate our own affiliative needs. This sometimes happens when we hold a low opinion of ourselves. Consider the case of a young man who feels worthless and believes that others share this view. When people seek his company, he is suspicious of their motives. Asked to a party, he thinks the host only did it to be nice so he refuses to go. He doesn't try to get a date because he is certain he will be turned down.

Autonomy Frustrations

As the child grows and learns, he is able to do more and more things for himself— and do them in his own way. His parents frequently step in to frustrate his autonomy. The mother or father who finds the child's dependence rewarding may discourage even the healthful impulses to independence that accompany normal development.

To a large extent our society is made up of mixers and joiners. A person with a high need for autonomy may prefer his own company, or, at least, he may be most comfortable by himself. Other people may neither understand nor respect his need; they may consider him standoffish or snobbish.

Every group has its schedule of approved and disapproved behavior. Conformity to the group's way of doing things may be the price of membership in the group. Not many of us want to go it completely on our own, yet we may find our ties a bit binding.

Dominance Frustrations

Since many people resist domination, frustration of this need is common. The parent who dominates his children, the teacher who dominates his students, the employer who dominates his employees, and marriage partners who seek to dominate each other frequently encounter resistance. In fact, dominance behavior in one individual may induce dominance behavior in others, creating a vicious circle of dominance (Anderson & Brewer, 1945).

Ordinarily, leadership positions should provide suitable goals for dominance needs.

But exaggerated needs for dominance can lead to actions that are repugnant to others. The desire for dominance is only a small part of successful leadership. Would-be leaders may find themselves frustrated by the lack of a number of qualities that are important to leadership in a particular situation.

Deference Frustrations

The need for deference would not seem to suffer the same degree of frustration as some of the other needs. But this need is thwarted when leadership is not available and when there is no one to turn to for advice and guidance. In some cases the guide is suddenly lost, as in the death of a parent or the loss of a commander in battle. Sometimes, too, the person we turn to rejects our deference or proves to be inadequate and undeserving.

As we progress in many areas, we must advance from follower to leadership roles. Success in our vocation may mean moving into an executive position. In various organizations we are expected to advance through the chairs and serve as chairmen of various committees. To the person with pronounced deference needs, these changes in the expectations and demands of others can be extremely frustrating.

Aggression Frustrations

Aggression is a primitive and satisfying response to frustration, but aggression, itself, is frequently frustrated (see Figs. 3.4 and 3.5). As children, we learn that aggressive actions result in punishment and retaliation. The pommeled parent spanks. The boy next door returns blow for blow. The bitten dog bites back. As adults, too, we find that many of the people who frustrate us cannot be assaulted with impunity. Teachers can flunk us; employers can fire us; the police officer can give us a ticket or haul us into court.

Many of us learn to escape retaliation and punishment by expressing our aggression in subtle ways. We cannot attack our teacher in class, but we can spread some rumors to damage him on the campus. We cannot tell our employer off, but the monkey wrench we drop into the works can cause him some expensive repairs. We sit tight-lipped while the traffic officer delivers his sermon, but once out of earshot we have some devastating things to say about a police force that spends its time enforcing the speed limits while murderers and hoodlums roam the city.

Abasement Frustrations

Since it is much more acceptable in our society to attack oneself than others, the need for abasement suffers less frustration than aggression and other needs. But sometimes people step in to frustrate our abasement needs. "Stop picking on yourself!" they tell us. "Quit being a doormat!" Others accuse us of enjoying our suffering.

Sometimes the abasive individual attacks others who are identified with him as well as himself. For example, a mother with strong abasement needs may depreciate not only herself but her husband and her children too. In many instances, these assaulted parties may resist inclusion in the abasement circle. Their unwillingness to share in her humble patterning may be a source of some frustration to her.

Nurturance Frustrations

Nurturance needs are frequently frustrated because of the lack of suitable goals. Many couples who want very much to have children find themselves unable to; sometimes they have difficulty in adopting a child. A single person or one who is separated or divorced may very much miss the opportunities for nurturance that exist in warm and close family situations.

Even in familial settings nurturance needs can undergo a good deal of frustration. For example, a young wife finds that her husband resists her attempts to mother him. And although she enjoys nurturing her children, they soon grow up and become frustratingly independent.

Sometimes strong nurturance needs exist in combination with a need for dominance. The people we attempt to nurture and control frequently don't appreciate our efforts. Children, for example, can feel more smothered than mothered. Employees, too, may resent this treatment and accuse us of being paternalistic.

Succorance Frustrations

Children raised in institutions receive less mothering than those reared in normal

Figure 3.5 Aggression frustration (© United Feature Syndicate, Inc., 1956).

family constellations. But there is some evidence to indicate that institutionalized children are not particularly high in succorant behavior (Spitz & Wolf, 1946; Wittenborn, 1954). Apparently their succorant needs do not develop because they have lacked experience with nurturant adults. Greatest frustration may be felt by the child who has known the satisfaction of affectional bonds and then finds that these bonds are in danger of disruption (Sears, Maccoby, & Levin, 1957).

As we grow older we are usually expected to become less succorant. But some of us have difficulty in emancipating ourselves from our homes, in going away to college, or in securing employment. Anywhere along the line, we may be frustrated by others who taunt us for being a crybaby, momma's boy. They insist that we grow up, stand on our own two feet, and be a man.

A person with high succorant needs looks for nurturance everywhere. At school he may respond best to a fatherly instructor. At work he enjoys the security of a protecting employer. In marriage he seeks a warm and motherly mate. But not all teachers, employers, and spouses are nurturant—some of them make a point of not being so—and succorant needs undergo a good deal of frustration.

Sex Frustrations

Sex cannot be considered the strongest of the primary drives. Hunger, pain, and fatigue, at their peak levels, are more potent (Dollard & Miller, 1950). Furthermore, a number of secondary drives also can outrank sex. But in our culture no human need is more frustrated or occasions more conflict than the sex need.

From the very beginning the child shows an active curiosity in the world around him. He begins to ask questions, to investigate and experiment. His sex explorations usually encounter considerable frustration. Simple questions are hushed up or go unanswered. Masturbation is punished. Almost any sort of sex talk or sex play may result in a flood of parental threats or worse.

We are physiologically prepared for mature heterosexual functioning long before appropriate goals are available. Marriage provides a convenient and meaningful way of meeting adult sex needs, but marriage may be delayed for economic, academic, familial, or a number of other reasons. Even in marriage, sex needs may be frustrated because of the incompatibility or shortcomings of the partners.

FRUSTRATIONS IN THE SOCIALIZATION PROCESS[2]

In the process of becoming an adult we must learn to perform more and more difficult tasks. This process involves frustration. There is no getting around it.

Children cannot and should not be shielded from all frustration. Neither should they be exposed to too much stress. The child who is kept a baby too long will never be able to grow up. The child who is turned into an adult too soon forms a reliance on a pattern of defenses which serve him poorly later on.

As we pass through infancy, childhood, adolescence, and into adulthood, we are progressively able to learn more things.

[2] This discussion follows Dollard et al. (1939) and Symonds (1946).

If the tasks set for us in each stage of development are congruent with its level of competence, we grow up well able to face adult frustrations and deal with adult problems.

Feeding Frustrations

At birth we move from our protected state in the womb into an environment that has its own ideas about how our needs will be met. Almost at once we confront the food and feeding practices of our society. The food we are given may not be fully agreeable to us, and the times when it is offered may not coincide with the times that we are hungry. After a while, our sucking behavior must be interrupted, and we must learn to give up the breast and bottle and begin to chew our food.

Exploratory Frustrations

As small children, we see the world as a wonderful place filled with shiny, colorful, and curious objects to be examined. But we must be taught that many of these objects cannot be scratched or touched, or pulled or pushed, or beaten or walked on, or put in the mouth. Sometimes the toys which we are allowed seem little compensation for the objects of the world that we must renounce. Sometimes areas for exploration are sharply reduced as we are plopped in a playpen or led on a leash.

Cleanliness Frustrations

Elimination, when we are very small, is a simple matter. Tension accumulates in the bowel or bladder, by reflex action a sphincter is released, and excretion occurs without regard for social convention. We must be taught to gain mastery over eliminative processes. This may involve long periods of immobilization on the toilet-training seat, punishment for wet pants and wet beds, and rewards for dry pants and dry beds. This process may be especially frustrating if parents become impatient with the state of progress and expect faster and better control than the developing body is able to command.

Sex Frustrations

In our society many frustrations attend our sexual development. As small children, we may find an intriguing mystery surrounding the entire subject of sex. Yet our pursuit of the subject may be constantly impeded as we are distracted, enjoined, admonished, or punished for being too immodest or too curious, for masturbating, or for other sexual explorations. During much of childhood, adolescence, and even adulthood, our efforts to achieve adequate sexual expression may run into considerable frustration.

Sex-role Frustrations

As we grow, we learn that there is a definite way in which each sex is expected to act. Boys must behave in one way, girls in another. Boys must not play with dolls, cry, or be overly dependent on their mothers. Girls must not spit, fight, or climb trees or, if they insist on doing so, they must not hang by their knees. A boy who acts like a girl may be accused of being a sissy. A girl who acts like a boy may be reproached for her tomboy activities.

Sex typing aims to produce a personality to match our biology, but it may cause frustration if we find the limitations of our sex too confining. Individuals who seek to

Figure 3.6 Sex-role frustration.

Swinging his children on the shore of a lake in Washington state, the slender young man moved with a panther's grace. Jacques d'Amboise was displaying the same power that has made him America's first great male ballet dancer. D'Amboise, the leading dancer of the New York City Ballet, recoils from the popular notion—which he admits—that to be a ballet star is to be "flitty." He is anything but that. A rugged family man and natural athlete, he could easily have won his fame in bigtime sports. Instead, he is a dancer with a mission: "I hope I can encourage youngsters to take up dancing as naturally as they would baseball."

"I have fun when I meet people and tell them I'm a ballet dancer," says D'Amboise, who speaks almost as boundingly as he leaps. "They look at me, and in their eyes I see the inevitable doubt, the nagging question: Is he a man?"

As D'Amboise sees it, this attitude—which is not without justification—endangers ballet in the U.S. despite its soaring popularity on TV, Broadway and in the movies. "Grace, beauty, quickness—these are what a great dancer needs," Jacques says. "Some people think of them as being feminine attributes, but they're dead wrong. A great dancer is like a great cat that you know could tear you to bits, but the miracle is how softly and beautifully it leaps."

Such is the ill fame of male ballet dancers that few American boys want to take up ballet, even if their dads would encourage them. Says D'Amboise, who at 28 is already an elder statesman: "They're afraid of being thought of as sissies. Heaven knows how many great male dancers we may have lost because of the prejudice against studying it as kids." Peter Bunzel, Let's Make Ballet a Manly Art. (LIFE Magazine © Time Inc., 1963, **54**(25), 63–68). Photograph by John Dominis.

reverse traditional sex roles, for example, men who become nurses and women who become doctors, may have to put up with a number of frustrations along the way (see Fig. 3.6).

Age-role Frustrations

Each new developmental stage revokes old privileges which still may be desired and presents new responsibilities which must be assumed. After a certain time, we cannot expect to be picked up and cuddled, to have things done for us, to run to our parents with our problems. We are expected to grow up and do more and more things for ourselves. We must learn to feed, wash, and dress ourselves and solve our own problems.

It is a source of frustration for us as children to see our older brothers and sisters as well as our parents indulging in behavior that we are not allowed. It may be equally frustrating to see younger children, perhaps a newborn brother or sister, receiving care and attention that we still might like. Too little for some things and too big for others, the child can find any particular age a frustrating one (see Fig. 3.7).

School Frustrations

When we begin school, we are confronted by more restrictions, prohibitions, and demands. We must leave our parents and familiar home environments. We must sit still, we must be quiet, we must attend, we must study, we must make good grades. We may find that the academic demands made of us are frustrating because they are so difficult or, sometimes, because they are too easy. And, especially if we are of a different social class or culture from our teachers, we may find that behavior which is rewarded and punished at home is quite different from that which is rewarded and punished at school.

Adolescent Frustrations

Adolescence can be a very difficult transitional period. Sexual impulses become intensified, and new patterns of social skills and codes of behavior must be adopted toward the opposite sex. The value systems of our contemporaries may be quite different from those of our parents, and we may feel considerable strain trying to be accepted in our age group while still at peace with our families. Then, too, we must begin

Figure 3.7 Age-role frustration.

to emancipate ourselves from our families and make decisions about work, college, marriage, or military service.

Adult Frustrations

Frustrations continue through adulthood. Marriage brings with it constant demands for readjustment. Children arrive and must be socialized (they may be as completely unaware and unappreciative of the ultimate rewards of the process as we once were). We must secure a job, retain it, be promoted, make as much money as our brother-in-law. We must move in the right circles, acquire status, be somebody. There is the threat of natural and man-made catastrophes and sickness and death.

SUMMARY

A frustration is an interference with goal-directed behavior. In describing frustration one can focus on the frustrating situation itself and picture it as a process of blocking, or one can focus on the frustrated individual and describe his state of feeling.

All learning involves some frustration, and frustration is inevitable. But not all frustration is inevitable; some of it can and should be avoided or prevented. Frustrations can be thought of as threatening when they involve important needs and present a challenge to our worth as a person. Frustration tolerance and frustration threshold are important ideas pertaining to the amount of frustration that we can undergo without behaving inadequately or nonconstructively.

Frustrations are complicated phenomena and difficult to classify. Several classification systems that have been proposed sort frustrations into need, act, and goal frustrations and into lacks, losses, and obstacles.

Some of the most important frustrations are those affecting our needs for achievement, affiliation, autonomy, dominance, deference, aggression, abasement, nurturance, succorance, and sex. There are many frustrations involved in the socialization process and in every phase and stage of life.

REFERENCES

Anderson, H. H., & Brewer, H. M. Studies of teachers' classroom personalities. I. Dominative and socially integrative behavior of kindergarten teachers. *Applied Psychology Monographs,* 1945, No. 6.

Bandura, A., & Walters, R. H. *Social Learning and Personality Development.* New York: Holt, 1963.

Banks, R. K., & Cappon, D. Developmental deprivation and mental illness: "A study of 20 questions." *Child Development,* 1963, **34,** 709–718.

Berkowitz, L. *Aggression: A social psychological analysis.* New York: McGraw-Hill, 1962.

Brown, J. S. Principles of intrapersonal conflict. *Journal of Conflict Resolution*, 1957, 1(2), 135–154.

———— & Farber, I. E. Emotions conceptualized as intervening variables—with suggestions toward a theory of frustration. *Psychological Bulletin*, 1951, **48**, 465–495.

Bunzel, P. Let's make ballet a manly art. *Life*, 1963, **54**(25), 64–67.

Chilman, C., & Sussman, M. B. Poverty in the United States in the mid-sixties. *Journal of Marriage and the Family*, 1964, **26**(4), 391–395.

Cochran, J. *The Stars at Noon*. Boston: Little, Brown, 1954.

Dollard, J., Doob, L. W., Miller, N. E., Mowrer, O. H., & Sears, R. R. *Frustration and Aggression*. New Haven, Conn.: Yale, 1939.

———— & Miller, N. E. *Personality and Psychotherapy*. New York: McGraw-Hill, 1950.

Johnson, W. *People in Quandries*. New York: Harper & Row, 1946.

Lawson, R. *Frustration: The Development of a Scientific Concept*. New York: Macmillan, 1965.

———— & Marx, M. H. Frustration: Theory and experiment. *Genetic Psychology Monographs*, 1958, **57**, 393–464.

Lewin, K. *A Dynamic Theory of Personality*. New York: McGraw-Hill, 1935.

Maier, N. R. F., & Ellen, P. The integrative value of concepts in frustration theory. *Journal of Consulting Psychology*, 1959, **23**, 195–206.

Maslow, A. H. *Motivation and Personality*. New York: Harper & Row, 1954.

May, M. A. Foreword. In J. Dollard, L. W. Doob, N. E. Miller, O. H. Mowrer, & R. R. Sears, *Frustration and Aggression*. (Paperback ed.) New Haven, Conn.: Yale, 1961.

Melton, A. W. Learning. In W. S. Monroe (Ed.), *Encyclopedia of Educational Research*. New York: Macmillan, 1941.

Miller, N. E. Some implications of modern behavior theory for personality change and psychotherapy. In P. Worchel & D. Byrne (Eds.), *Personality Change*. New York: Wiley, 1964. Pp. 149–175.

Murray, H. A. Proposals for a theory of personality. In H. A. Murray et al., *Explorations in Personality*. Fair Lawn, N.J.: Oxford, 1938. Pp. 37–141.

————. Types of reactions to frustration: A heuristic classification. *Journal of Abnormal and Social Psychology*, 1934, **29**, 298–300.

Rosenzweig, S. VI. A general outline of frustration. *Character and Personality*, 1938, **7**, 151–160.

————. An outline of frustration theory. In J. McV. Hunt (Ed.), *Personality and the Behavior Disorders*. Vol. 1. New York: Ronald, 1944. Pp. 379–388.

————. *The Rosenzweig P-F Study*, 1948. Published by Saul Rosenzweig.

————. The Rosenzweig Picture-Frustration Study, Children's Form. In A. I. Rabin & M. R. Haworth (Eds.), *Projective Techniques with Children*, New York: Grune & Stratton, 1960. Pp. 149–176.

Sappenfield, B. R. *Personality Dynamics*. New York: Knopf, 1954.

Sears, R. R., Maccoby, E. E., & Levin, H. *Patterns of Child Rearing*. New York: Harper & Row, 1957.

Spitz, R. A., & Wolf, K. M. Anaclitic depression. In A. Freud et al. (Eds.), *The Psychoanalytic Study of the Child*. Vol. 2. New York: International Universities Press, 1946. Pp. 313–342.

Symonds, P. M. *The Dynamics of Human Adjustment*. New York: Appleton-Century-Crofts, 1946.

Vaughan, W. F. *Personal and Social Adjustment*. New York: Odyssey, 1952.

Wittenborn, J. R. *The Development of Adoptive Children*. New York: Russell Sage, 1954.

Yates, A. J. *Frustration and Conflict*. New York: Wiley, 1962.

CHAPTER FOUR

CONFLICT

In everyday life we are constantly bombarded by stimuli. Environmental demands and impulses arising within ourselves compete for attention and expression. We cannot, of course, act upon every demand or express every impulse. We must decide among various patterns of actions.

Many everyday decisions are relatively simple, and they are simply and easily made. But when there are a number of competing tendencies—all strong and seemingly equal in strength—we may experience serious difficulty. Sometimes, too, we feel ourselves pulled apart by forces that we scarcely understand and are scarcely able to deal with.

This chapter will describe the role that conflict plays in the adjustment process. Conflict will be defined and some ways of classifying and dealing with conflicts will be discussed. A close look will be taken at ten important conflict areas.

DEFINING CONFLICT

A *conflict* involves competition among several patterns of behavior. Conflict is a form of frustration. Like other forms of frustration, it serves to interfere with goal-directed activity (see Fig. 4.1). Until a conflict is dealt with in some way, our goals go unreached and our needs go unmet. In brief, we're frustrated.

Like frustration, conflict can be described in two ways: as a process of competing tendencies or as a state of experience or feeling.

Conflict as a Process of Competing Tendencies

What happens in conflict? Caught up in competing tendencies, we may be momentarily or indefinitely blocked. We hesitate. We vacillate, moving from one alternative to another.

If, for example, we have applied to a number of colleges for admission and find that we have been accepted by all, we may be in conflict. One college looks good in some ways, but it has some real drawbacks. Another college doesn't have some things that we consider desirable, but it has other important advantages. We can't

decide which to select, and perhaps the more we try to decide, the more confused we become.

Or, perhaps, all the colleges have turned us down. What should we do? Apply to others? Would there be any use? Get a job? Could we get one that would be worthwhile? Get a job and take evening courses somewhere? Or not think about it at all for a while?

The conflict process may be conscious, partly conscious, or unconscious. Sometimes we are aware of the forces working upon us; sometimes, however, they are poorly understood or misunderstood. We may be indecisive or have mixed feelings about a particular situation without knowing why. Or, perhaps, we think we know why, but others do not agree that our reason is the real reason.

The process may be an easy and even pleasant one, or it may be very difficult and unpleasant. When the process is relatively easy, we are more likely to use words such as "choice" or "choosing" to describe the decision making. For some of us, the word "conflict" captures the dynamic qualities which seem characteristic of more difficult or dramatic situations.

Figure 4.1 A *conflict* involves a competition among several patterns of behavior. Conflict is a form of frustration; like other frustrations, it serves to block or interfere with goal-directed activity.

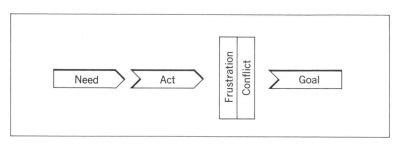

Brown (1957) notes, however, that conflict is not a special kind of process. He points out that when we speak of "conflict" behavior, we generally refer to situations involving two or more competing tendencies which are relatively equal in strength; "nonconflict" situations involve a tendency which is much stronger than any other. But every instance of decision making can be thought of as falling at some point along a continuum which ranges between these two end points.

Choices and the conflict between choices are constant features of living. Tyler (1959) points out that at each step of life we confront "an incredibly complex assortment of stimulating conditions and behavior possibilities." She adds, "in order to function at all, each of us must choose from this plethora of possibilities. . . ." Brown (1957) emphasizes the conflict built into such situations. He writes that "conflict is an inevitable consequence of an inherent capacity to act in any manner and especially of the ability to perform a multiplicity of acts."

Conflict as a State of Feeling

A second way of describing conflict is as a state of feeling accompanying the process of conflict. This approach focuses on the individual in conflict rather than on the conflict situation. It considers what we experience when we are "in conflict."

If, for example, we are trying to decide which of several colleges to choose, we may feel intrigued by the situation and interested in weighing the merits of each. Or we may feel mixed-up, confused, and torn in all directions.

If we have been turned down by all the colleges, we may be in even more con-

flict. None of the alternatives may be very much to our liking. We may be at a loss and feel helpless and unable to make a decision.

Shakespeare, a master at portraying emotions, captured the mood of intense conflict in Hamlet's famous soliloquy.

To be, or not to be: that is the question:
Whether 'tis nobler in the mind to suffer
The slings and arrows of outrageous fortune,
Or to take arms against a sea of troubles,
And by opposing end them? To die: to sleep:
No more; and by a sleep to say we end
The heartache and the thousand natural shocks
That flesh is heir to, 'tis a consummation
Devoutly to be wish'd. To die, to sleep;
To sleep: perchance to dream: ay, there's the rub:
For in that sleep of death what dreams may come,
When we have shuffled off this mortal coil,
Must give us pause. There's the respect
That makes calamity of so long life;
For who would bear the whips and scorns of time,
The oppressor's wrong, the proud man's contumely,
The pangs of despriz'd love, the law's delay,
The insolence of office and the spurns
That patient merit of the unworthy takes,
When he himself might his quietus make
With a bare bodkin? who would fardels bear,
To grunt and sweat under a weary life,
But that the dread of something after death,
The undiscover'd country from whose bourn
No traveller returns, puzzles the will
And makes us rather bear those ills we have
Than fly to others that we know not of?
Thus conscience does make cowards of us all;
And thus the native hue of resolution

*Is sicklied o'er with the pale cast of
   thought,
And enterprises of great pith and moment
With this regard their currents turn awry,
And lose the name of action (Hamlet.* Act
III, Scene 1, Lines 56–88).

As in all frustrations, reactions to
conflict vary. We differ in our ability to
confront and resolve conflicts. Some of us
have considerable difficulty in making decisions. Even in matters of seemingly little
importance we may have trouble in electing
a course of action and sticking to it.

CLASSIFYING CONFLICTS

Generally speaking, conflicts are complex
phenomena. A number of classification systems have been proposed, but important
human conflicts are not easily sorted out
into one category or another. Viewed in a
particular light, a conflict may seem to be
of one sort, but further examination may
lead to its reclassification.

The material which follows describes
two classification systems which seem helpful in the study of adjustment. In the first,
conflicts are classified according to what
part of a motive seems most affected: need,
act, or goal. In the second, conflicts are
classified according to the combination of
approach and avoidance tendencies that
are involved in the situation.

Need, Act, and Goal Conflicts

One way of classifying or sorting out conflicts is in terms of the part of the motivational sequence that is most affected (Sappenfield, 1954). *Need conflicts* involve
either the competition of several needs or
the simultaneous operation of impulses to

express and inhibit a single need. *Act conflicts* involve competition among several
modes of meeting a need and reaching a
goal. *Goal conflicts* involve competition
among several goals.

Need Conflicts

Some conflict situations seem to involve
competition among several need patterns.
Many adolescents, for example, get caught
up in a battle which might be described as
a conflict between autonomy and succorance. They appear to want to be on their
own, almost divorcing themselves from
family proceedings, and at the same time
they want to retain their family's emotional support and guidance.

Other situations appear to involve a
battle between impulses to express and
inhibit a particular need. A young unmarried couple, for example, may be very much
attracted to and sexually stimulated by
each other. They may want to express their
sexual impulses, but at the same time they
may feel considerable guilt, fear, or anxiety
arising out of the situation.

In a later section of this chapter more
attention will be given to some examples
of need conflict. The ten important needs
which were introduced in the second chapter and considered from the standpoint of
frustration in the third chapter will be discussed in terms of the conflicts that serve
to interfere with their expression.

Act Conflicts

How should we go about reaching our goals
and meeting our needs? Some situations
present us with little or no freedom. Others
offer many possibilities for action.

What should we do in a particular
situation? Try an old response that's not

been completely successful? Try a new one that might fail? Plan ahead? Wait and play it by ear?

Here are some situations that might be considered examples of act conflicts. An overweight little girl is troubled by the taunts of her schoolmates. ("Tub of lard. Tub of lard. Big around as a St. Bernard.") Should she throw something at them? Insult them instead? Or frame a reply. ("Sticks and stones can break my bones, but words can never hurt me.")

A young woman is nearly overwhelmed by her feelings for a young man. She is tempted to tell him how she feels. She is tempted to love him extravagantly. Would this be wise? Would he be frightened away? Would he take advantage of her? Should she control herself, and play it cool?

A controlling mother would like to lay down the law and make her children toe the line. At the same time she feels that this wouldn't be right, and maybe she should "use psychology" on them. What to do? How to act?

Goal Conflicts

There may be no goal available to satisfy a particular need. Or there may be a number of goals, and we have to choose between them. Perhaps, in order to gain one we must give up another, or in order to avoid one we cannot escape from another which is almost equally bad. Maybe none of the goal objects is fully attractive or completely unattractive.

Consider, for example, a highly nurturant but childless couple. Should they simply nurture each other? Or adopt a child? Spend time with the children of their relatives or friends? Be active in

youth work? Raise a household full of pets? All of these might be goals for their nurturance needs.

Or consider affiliation patterns. We may want to affiliate with two groups of people, both congenial to us but incompatible with each other. We may have to choose between them even though we would like to enjoy the company of both.

Our parents, to extend the example, may expect us to behave in one way; our peer group in quite another. If we behave in ways that are acceptable to one we may alienate the other. Both groups may be very important to us, and we may experience considerable conflict.

Or, to develop the example differently, perhaps our parents are in conflict with each other, openly or subtly. Although they don't actually say so, they seem to call on us to take sides. But if we ally with one, we make an enemy of the other. What should we do? Which one should we choose?

Approach, Avoidance, and Approach-Avoidance Conflicts

A second way of classifying conflicts is in terms of the combination of approach and avoidance tendencies that they involve (Lewin, 1935). On this basis three kinds of conflicts can be identified.

Approach-Approach Conflicts

Sometimes we seem simultaneously attracted to several courses of action, but to carry out one we must abandon the other. Such a situation is called an *approach-approach conflict*. We are pulled in two different directions at the same time, or, sometimes, in more than two directions, since in a particular situation we might have three (or even more) attractive courses of action.

Many everyday decisions appear to involve a choice between several attractive (or at least acceptable) but mutually incompatible alternatives. Which job should I take? Both are promising. Which house should we buy? Each has some advantages. Where should we go on vacation? There are at least five places we would like to see.

An old saying that describes the approach-approach conflict is, "You can't have your cake and eat it too." We can't have everything we want. Frequently to get one thing we have to give up something else.

Some major sources of approach-approach conflicts have been pointed out by Sappenfield (1954). First of all, time is limited; there aren't enough hours in the day to do everything we would like to do. Second, energy is limited; we can't keep on the go all the time; we have to take time off to rest, nap, and sleep. Third, resources are limited; we can window-shop all we like, but once the money is spent, it's gone. Fourth, the number of places we can be at one time is limited; although a mother may give a good approximation, she can't be everywhere at once. And fifth, the number of things that we can do at one time is limited; it isn't easy to watch television, eat dinner, feed the baby, and hold a conversation at the same time (but some of us almost manage to do it).

Animals and human beings appear to resolve approach-approach conflicts with little difficulty. Donkeys do not starve to death midway between two piles of fragrant hay. A child with a single penny does not remain immobilized in front of the candy counter despite the many attractive choices. Why should this be so?

One reason that approach-approach conflicts cause little trouble has to do with a property of approach situations. Theory and research generally support the idea that our tendency to approach a desirable goal is stronger the nearer we are to it (Miller, 1964). If, for example, we are very hungry and having trouble making a choice between two items on the menu, we may select the one that can be served the soonest.

In an approach-approach situation we find ourselves between two attractive alternatives. As has been indicated, the attractiveness of each depends upon our nearness to it. As we begin to make tentative approaches toward one alternative, its attractiveness increases with proximity while that of the other decreases with distance. Hence, once movement is begun toward one alternative or the other, the conflict is settled without difficulty.

Another reason for the easy resolution of approach-approach conflicts is that there will be reward no matter which of the alternatives is selected. At the ball game a small boy may want both popcorn and soda pop, but if he is required to choose between them, it is unlikely that he will take much time to make a decision. And it is also unlikely that he will risk the strategy of insisting on both of the alternatives or none at all.

A third reason for the lack of distress in this type of conflict is that the alternatives may sometimes be achieved in turn. Although we cannot have the incompatible alternative this minute, perhaps it can be achieved later in the day or month or maybe next year. We come home both hungry and tired, help ourselves to a sandwich, take a nap, and then have dinner.

The little boy at the ball game may decide upon the hot, salty popcorn, and later on use this as a basis to renew his plea for the cold, wet soda pop.

Avoidance-Avoidance Conflicts

Sometimes we appear to be simultaneously repelled by two courses of action, but to escape one we must carry out the other. This is called an *avoidance-avoidance conflict* (see Fig. 4.2). A situation of this sort might involve more than two unattractive alternatives; we might be confronted by three or four alternatives each as repellent as the other.

Here are some situations that might (at least on preliminary inspection) be considered avoidance-avoidance situations. Home from the ball game and filled with popcorn and soda pop, the little boy is told to finish all of his dinner (avoidance) or be sent to bed (avoidance). He must wash (avoidance) or wipe (avoidance) the dishes. He must finish his homework (avoidance) or face a bawling out (avoidance).

Your instructor warns you to study harder (not an appealing prospect) or flunk the course (avoidance). Your employer insists that you work harder (avoidance) or take a cut in salary (avoidance). The judge bangs down his gavel and announces: "Thirty days (avoidance) or one hundred dollars" (avoidance).

A number of common expressions describe avoidance-avoidance conflicts. We speak, for example, of "being on the horns of a dilemma" when we are confronted by two equally unsatisfactory ways of getting out of a predicament. "Being between the devil and the deep blue sea" or "having a choice between the head or the tail of the herring" are metaphors referring to avoidance-avoidance situations.

Avoidance-avoidance conflicts are difficult to deal with. It was said earlier that the tendency *to approach an attractive object* is stronger the nearer we are to it; now it can be noted that the tendency *to avoid an unattractive object* is also stronger the nearer we come (Miller, 1964). Consider the example of a baseball player caught in a rundown between two basemen. He turns to run away from the baseman with the ball but finds that the ball has exchanged hands; he turns again, again, and again (while his luck holds out) always away from the more immediate danger (Morgan, 1961).

In avoidance-avoidance conflicts we find ourselves faced with unattractive al-

Figure 4.2 Avoidance-avoidance conflict.

FREDDY

ternatives. Since the strength of a tendency to avoid an unattractive object increases with nearness, as one object is approached it becomes increasingly repellent while the alternative, because of its greater distance, becomes less so. We reverse our fields only to find the same process occurring again; an alternative that does not appear to be so bad from a distance becomes increasingly worse with proximity. Consequently, we continue to move between the alternatives, trying hard to maintain a distance from each of them.

In avoidance-avoidance conflicts we are faced with the prospect of unpleasant alternatives as well as with the unpleasant and distressing process of vacillating back and forth among them. If it seems at all possible, we will try to avoid or escape all the alternatives. Lewin (1935) called this act of breaking out of the conflict situation "leaving the field."

Our freedom to leave the field or conflict situation will depend upon the strength of the physical, social, and personal forces that serve to restrain us. The little boy faced with the necessity of finishing his dinner or going to bed can, if his mother leaves the room, dash out of the back door to play. Confronted with the choice of studying or flunking out of school, you may sit down, open your text, and idly turn the pages while daydreaming of pleasanter activity.

Sometimes, however, the restraining forces are of sufficient strength to hold us in the situation. Thus, while his mother is present at the dinner table, the little boy may dawdle at his food and delay a decision, but he will not be able to escape. Ultimately, his mother's patience will near the breaking point, and the decision will have to be made. With maturity, we prevent ourselves from avoiding unpleasant decisions. We make ourselves face the music.

Approach-Avoidance Conflicts

Sometimes we are simultaneously attracted to and repelled by a single course of action. This sort of situation is called an *approach-avoidance conflict*. Some situations seem to involve a number of courses of action, each with attractive and unattractive features.

Many everyday conflicts take this form. In fact, when we stop to think of our alternatives in a particular situation, we may find that they are neither fully desirable nor fully undesirable. Even the most unattractive course of action may have some compensating features.

We speak of the bittersweet qualities of life, of having to take the bad with the good. Several thousand years ago the chief pandit of an Indian prince said, "There is no gathering the rose without being pricked by the thorns." And much more recently Emerson wrote, "For every thing you have missed, you have gained something else; and for every thing you gain, you lose something." These words express the combination of attractive and unattractive qualities inherent in many of life's situations.

Consider some examples. This job pays well (approach), but there's little security (avoidance). This vacation sounds like a lot of fun (approach), but it also would cost a lot of money (avoidance). This house is nice (approach), but its location is awful (avoidance).

I'd like to try that (approach), but I'm afraid I'd fail (avoidance). I'm tempted to do that (approach), but I wouldn't be able to live with myself if I did (avoidance). If I told you my troubles (approach), would you laugh at me (avoidance)?

Like avoidance-avoidance conflicts, approach-avoidance ones are difficult to deal with. The attractive features of the situation draw us forward, but its unattractive ones bounce us back. Brown states:

> Because of this self-balancing aspect, an approach-avoidance conflict can never be resolved unless the values of the tendencies are markedly altered. Perhaps this self-regulatory feature of behavior in ambivalent situations accounts for the relative inescapability of such conflicts and for their stubborn resistance to therapeutic amelioration (1957, pp. 142–143).

Multiple Approach, Avoidance, and Approach-Avoidance Conflicts

Approach-approach, avoidance-avoidance, and approach-avoidance situations are basic forms of conflict behavior, but not many of our problems fit neatly into one of these three categories. The choices we must make are seldom between simple pairs of incompatible reactions. Even the most ordinary decisions of everyday living may be more complex.

As was indicated earlier a particular conflict may present more than two attractive alternatives. Such a situation, existing when there is simultaneous attraction to a number of incompatible patterns of behavior, can be referred to as a *multiple approach conflict*. Furthermore, a choice may have to be made between one major attraction and a combination of several minor ones (Sappenfield, 1954). For example, that vacation tour sounds fine, but on the other hand, we might buy a new set of clubs and spend the time golfing, loafing, and catching up on loose ends.

In a similar fashion, a particular predicament may present more than two alternatives, each as unpleasant as the other.

A situation in which it is necessary to carry out one of a number of repellent patterns of behavior can be referred to as a *multiple avoidance conflict*. As members of an organization we may be unable to avoid serving on at least one of its committees. On a lazy afternoon we are routed out of the hammock and given our choice of trimming the hedge, washing the windows, or painting the back steps.

Under certain circumstances we may be confronted by two or more goals, each with positive and negative features. A situation in which we are simultaneously attracted and repelled by a number of incompatible alternatives can be referred to as a *multiple approach-avoidance conflict*. As will be seen shortly, on fullest examination many of our important conflicts can best be described in this way.

Conflicts that seem quite simple in form frequently prove to be much more complicated. Although a situation appears to involve only approach or avoidance tendencies, further analysis may show a subtle interweaving of both. In this connection, several experiments have recorded what appeared to be an unwarranted vacillation between desirable goals. In theory such approach-approach conflicts should be resolved without difficulty. It was felt that the goals actually had negative features that were concealed by the stronger positive ones (Miller, 1944).

If both goals are highly valued, even simple approach-approach situations may develop complications. In these conflicts it is necessary to give up one goal in order to get the other, but we may be quite unwilling to relinquish either goal. Thus, we may tend to approach and avoid both alternatives (Godbeer, 1940).

Avoidance-avoidance situations may be

complicated in the same way. If by accepting one of two unpleasant alternatives, the other may be avoided and the distressing conflict situation terminated, the situation may be described in both approach and avoidance terms.

When they are most fully considered, then, many human conflict situations seem best described as multiple approach-avoidance ones. To illustrate this point, consider how an approach-approach situation might prove to be a more complicated multiple approach-avoidance conflict. A young man is torn between his desires to get a job (approach) and to go to college (approach). Further scrutiny, however, reveals that he is attracted to work because of the immediate financial reward (approach) but repelled by the prospect of winding up in a blind alley because of the lack of advanced training (avoidance). He is attracted to college because of the brighter future it ensures (approach) but repelled by the hard work it will require (avoidance).

In similar fashion, a conflict that is ostensibly avoidance-avoidance may turn out to be more complex. Consider a soldier who fears both battle (avoidance) and cowardice (avoidance). He is repelled by the thought of being a coward (avoidance) but attracted to the physical safety that would be involved (approach). He is repelled by the hazards of combat (avoidance), but this course would protect and enhance his self-esteem (approach).

Even single approach-avoidance conflicts may often be better described as multiple approach-avoidance ones. An adolescent both desires and fears emancipation from his parents (approach-avoidance). He wants the freedom of independence (approach) but isn't ready to assume its responsibilities (avoidance). On the other hand, dependence is desirable because of the emotional and financial support it provides (approach) but unattractive because of the restrictions it entails (avoidance) (see Fig. 4.3).

RESOLVING CONFLICTS

What do we do about our conflicts? Some indication has already been given of how we behave in certain conflict situations. Now these patterns of response will be categorized and discussed more fully. In connection with the discussion, see Figures 4.4 – 4.6.

Blocking

Every conflict involves some degree of blocking as opposing impulses compete for expression. There may be a very brief hesitation or pause pending a decision. Or there may be prolonged vacillation or wavering.

As has been said, conflict situations involving only approach tendencies appear to occasion little blocking. But when avoidance tendencies are involved, considerable blocking may occur. Brown (1957) calls these latter situations "self-perpetuating," and he contrasts them with situations involving only approach tendencies, which he terms "self-resolving."

In some situations we may appear to be indefinitely blocked and unable to effect some course of action. Perhaps we move back and forth between alternatives, unwilling or unable to make a choice. Sometimes we are caught up in situations into which we have little insight; we scarcely understand the forces pulling at us and

Figure 4.3 Diagramming conflicts.

In approach-approach conflicts, we must choose between two attractive alternatives.

In multiple approach conflicts, we must choose between a number of attractive alternatives.

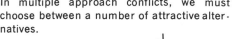

In avoidance-avoidance conflicts, the alternatives are both repelling, but to withdraw from one we move toward the other.

In multiple avoidance conflicts, we are confronted by a number of alternatives, all repelling.

In approach-avoidance conflicts, we are simultaneously attracted to and repelled by a single course of action.

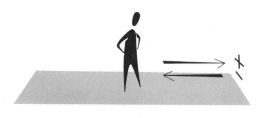

In multiple approach-avoidance conflicts, we face a number of courses of action, each with its attractive and unattractive features.

Figure 4.4 Resolving conflicts.

What happens in a conflict situation? Here a person is depicted in an approach-approach conflict. He is simultaneoulsy attracted toward several courses of action.

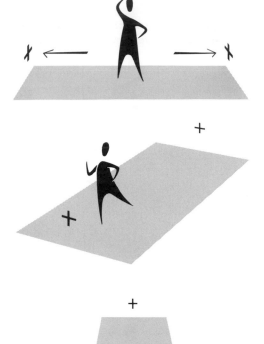

He makes tentative approaches toward each. Theory and research support the idea that the nearer a person is to an attractive object or condition, the more strongly he tends to approach it.

In approach-approach conflicts both alternatives are attractive, and as the individual moves toward one or the other, he is increasingly drawn toward it. Therefore, such conflicts may be resolved with little difficulty.

In avoidance-avoidance conflicts a person is confronted by two alternatives, each unattractive or repelling.

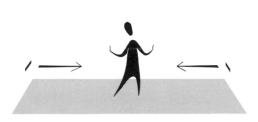

The nearer a person is to a repellent object or condition, the more he tends to avoid it. As he moves toward on alternative, it becomes increasingly repelling while the other, because of its greater distance, becomes less so.

He reverses his field only to find that the same process is occurring again. Alternatives that do not appear so bad from a distance, seem increasingly worse with proximity.

The person is blocked. He moves back and forth, trying to maintain his distance from each alternative. Unless he is forced to do so, he may attempt to delay making a decision. Or, if physical, social, or personal restraints are of insufficient strength, he may seek to escape from the conflict situation.

Here are people depicted in approach-avoidance conflicts. Whether the situation contains one or two or even more courses of action, each course is simultaneously attractive and repelling. The attractive features draw the person forward. The repellent features push him back. He is caught up in these opposing forces until the situation is restructured in some way which makes a solution possible or necessary.

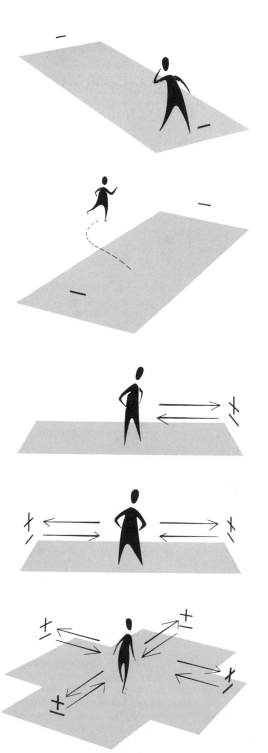

The conflict board (shown in *a*) devised by Hovland and Sears presented a surface of paper 6 inches square in a metal frame. A nick in the middle of the border nearest the subject provided a place for him to rest his pencil at the beginning of each trial. At the two corners of the opposite side varying combinations of lights were placed

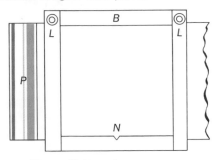

Diagram of the conflict board.
    (*P* = roll of stylograph paper; *B* = brass border; *N* = nick in which stylus rests and from which reactions start; *L* = lights.)

(*a*)

To produce approach-approach conflicts two uncolored bulbs, one at each corner, were flashed separately and in a random order. The subject was instructed to draw a line toward the flashing light. After a number of non-conflict trials both lights were flashed simultaneously to create a conflict.

To produce avoidance-avoidance conflicts, the same procedure was followed except that the subject was instructed to draw a line away from the flashing light; after a number of trials both lights were flashed simultaneously to produce a conflict.

To produce approach-avoidance conflicts two bulbs, one red and one green, were placed together at one corner. The subject was instructed to approach the flashing green light and avoid the flashing red one. After a number of separate presentations, both lights were flashed simultaneously to cause the conflict.

To produce a double approach-avoidance conflict, green and red bulbs were placed at both corners. The four lights were flashed separately and in random order for a number of trials after which all four lights were flashed simultaneously creating the conflict.

The investigators classified the reactions of subjects into four categories. *Single responses* referred to approaches to one corner or set of lights. *Double responses* referred to approaches to both corners (shown in *b*). *Compromise responses* referred to movements up the center of the paper half way between the two corners (as shown in *c*). *Blocked responses* referred to no response or a very slight or negligible one.

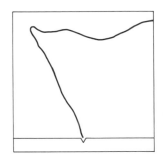

One form of the *Double* mode of resolution.

(*b*)

It was found that approach-approach conflicts were resolved with little difficulty. They usually prompted a single response to one goal or the other. Some double responses were observed, but there were relatively few compromise responses or blocking.

Avoidance-avoidance and approach-avoidance conflicts caused more difficulty than approach-approach conflicts. These former kinds of conflicts produced more compromise responses and more blocking.

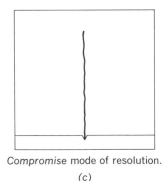

Compromise mode of resolution.

(*c*)

Figure 4.5 (left) How can conflict behavior be studied? Hovland and Sears (1938) devised a conflict board and observed the behavior of subjects as they were confronted with various kinds of conflicts. Consistent with theory, approach-approach conflicts proved to be the most easily resolved.

Figure 4.6 (below) How can conflict behavior be studied? The author (Arkoff, 1956–1957, 1957) devised a set of cards in which conflicts were created by pairing seven personal characteristics: adjustment, attractiveness, health, intelligence, popularity, talent, and wealth. Each of the characteristics was paired with every other one in both of two types of pairings, one in which the subject was required to designate the alternative which he would rather have in greater degree than he had at present (approach-approach conflict), and a second in which he was required to designate the alternative which he would elect to have in lesser degree than he had at present (avoidance-avoidance conflict).

The results of the experiment showed the approach-approach conflicts to be more easily resolved than the avoidance-avoidance conflicts. Approach-approach conflicts required a significantly less time to resolve than did avoidance-avoidance conflicts, and significantly more approach-approach conflicts were judged easier to resolve than were avoidance-avoidance conflicts.

In a modified procedure, subjects were allowed to resolve the conflicts or leave them unresolved. Subjects who elected the latter course with reference to any particular conflict were in effect escaping the conflict situation. As was predicted, the subjects left the conflict situation more often when confronted by avoidance-avoidance conflicts than when faced by approach-approach ones (Photograph by Masao Miyamoto, University of Hawaii).

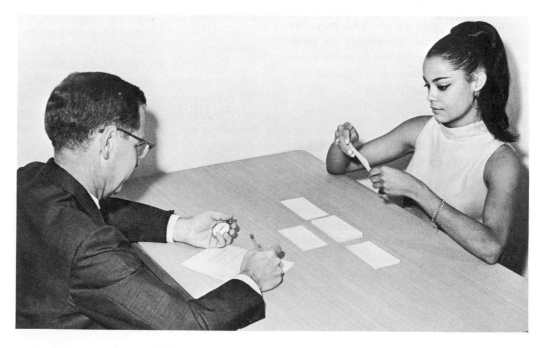

are scarcely able to do anything about them. Not all, but some conditions that are called nervous breakdowns seem to be the result of intense, prolonged, and seemingly insoluble conflicts.

Escaping

When all the alternatives confronting us are unattractive, we may attempt to escape from the situation and avoid all of them (Lewin, 1935). As was already noted, this is one of the ways that we deal with avoidance-avoidance conflicts.

Perhaps the president of an organization to which we belong insists that we choose some committee to serve on, but we would like to wriggle out of doing so if possible. We might not go to meetings, or if we do, we stay away from him. If he gets us cornered, we say that we've been thinking about it, and we need more time to decide which committee it will be.

We won't be able to escape from every unattractive situation. Sometimes other people prevent our escape and make us come to a decision. Sometimes we serve to frustrate our own desire to escape; our conscience keeps us in the situation and forces a decision.

Restructuring

For a conflict to be resolved, the situation must be restructured in some way so that the alternatives are changed in strength. This restructuring may occur within ourselves as our perception of the situation changes. External forces, too, can cause a change.

As we explore a conflict situation, we may begin to perceive it in somewhat different light. Perhaps the situation involves a number of attractive possibilities, and we tell ourselves that one of the alternatives is really better than the others. Or in a generally unhappy predicament, we begin to feel that one of the solutions is really not so bad after all (Levinger, 1957).

After being caught up in a conflict for awhile, we may feel that any solution is better than none at all. Being hung up can itself become intolerable, and impulsively we elect one alternative or another.

Forces within us may change. An adolescent, for example, who is in conflict about masturbation may find it increasingly difficult to restrain himself. In the same way, a young couple who have mixed feelings about their lovemaking may find themselves increasingly stimulated and drawn toward greater sexual expression.

The social environment has a bearing upon the restructuring process. Other people pressure us to behave in certain ways, or they may relax the pressure they have been exerting. In talking the situation over with others and receiving their help and guidance, we may come to see the situation differently.

Even after we have made a decision, the restructuring may need to continue. We may be unhappy about having to give up the rejected alternative, and this unhappiness will have to be dealt with in some way (Adams, 1954).

Festinger (1957) has suggested a number of ways that are used to resolve postdecision unpleasantness. The person, for example, might convince himself that the alternative he chose was even more attractive than he thought or that the alternative he abandoned really wasn't so attractive after all. Or maybe he could persuade himself that, after all, the alternatives were really very similar. Or he could discount the whole decision as really not a very important one.

Festinger and Bramel write:

> Imagine, for example, a student who, after considerable conflict, decides to go out on a date rather than study on the night before an examination. After having made his decision he may be expected to try to convince himself that studying more would not have helped him; that, in fact, last-minute cramming might be positively harmful; that the girl is really extremely attractive; and that the movie he will take her to is one that he very much wants to see. The net effect of all this, whatever the specific form of the dissonance reduction, would be to increase the attractiveness of the chosen alternative and/or to decrease the attractiveness of the rejected alternative after a decision has been made.[1]

Electing

The simplest (not necessarily the easiest) way of resolving a conflict is to elect one alternative and inhibit competing ones. For example, we decide that we will continue in college and forget about dropping out and getting a job. We decide that we will do this (and no dilly-dallying), or we won't do that (and no more monkey business).

Electing a solution to a conflict is more likely when the situation is well understood and the alternatives are clear-cut and clearly incompatible. It is difficult to be decisive about a conflict into which we have little insight. And if the alternatives may be compromised in some way, a decisive solution may not be necessary.

[1] From "The reaction of humans to cognitive dissonance," by L. Festinger & D. Bramel, Chapter 8 of *Experimental Foundations of Clinical Psychology*, edited by Arthur J. Bachrach, Basic Books, Inc., Publishers, New York, 1962. P. 259.

Electing a solution is also more likely when the alternatives are not overly important. If a rejected alternative is strong or of great value, it may not stay rejected; we may find ourselves precipitated back into the conflict or into some sort of compromise solution.

Alternating

One way of responding in a conflict situation is to express the tendencies or impulses in alternation. Sometimes approach-approach conflicts may be dealt with in this way. We achieve one goal and then work toward the other.

Occasionally the alternation is a more complicated "doing" and "undoing" process. Shall we be good or bad? Sometimes we misbehave, then repent and reform, only to misbehave again. Shall we be generous or stingy? Sometimes we may be very generous (perhaps overly so, so much that we can withhold nothing), and then we tighten up, become miserly, and want to keep everything for ourself.

Shall I be neat or disorderly? Shall I be kind or cruel? Shall I love you or hate you? The conflicts that these and many similar questions pose are not uncommonly dealt with by expressing one alternative and then its opposite.

Compromising

Another way of meeting a conflict situation is to compromise. Shall we eat out tonight or stay home and save money? Well, let's eat out but at an inexpensive place. Shall I go to the opera with my wife? Well, I'll go but I won't listen.

Compromise solutions are possible when the alternatives are not wholly incompatible. Often several tendencies may serve to modify or modulate but not block one another. Torn between being good and bad, we may be in between—not bad, but no angel either. In the same way we may affect a middle position between opposing tendencies to be neat or disorderly, kind or cruel, and loving or hateful.

Some compromise solutions are much more subtle and complicated than the above examples indicate, and many come about without our full awareness. Moved by both duty and hate, we give someone a present but not one that they are likely to want very much. Moved by opposing impulses, we may be nasty nice—so nice that we aren't nice—or nasty clean—so clean that we're worse than dirty.

Many conflict situations allow for compromise solutions. And the choices that we make in our everyday lives are frequently compromises. Dramatic conflicts necessitating dramatic solutions are the exception rather than the rule.

SOME IMPORTANT CONFLICTS

How important is a conflict? This would be difficult to determine without knowing the meaning that a conflict situation has for a particular individual. This section will reintroduce the ten needs that were discussed previously and show how each may run into conflicts that might be of considerable importance to many of us.

Achievement Conflicts

Our society encourages us to get ahead, but in order to achieve we may have to sacrifice other satisfactions. We are tempted to settle for the limited goal that is immediately accessible rather than struggle to the distant, more worthwhile one. Sometimes there is a tug between the need for achievement and another need that seems equally worthy. Shall I get married and have a family now or wait until I have completed school and my future is assured? Shall I take a chance and go into business for myself or keep the secure job I have?

As we struggle to achieve, we suffer continual conflict. The competition for goals may be fierce. The methods we must use are not always acceptable to ourselves or others. Those we have bested and others who are envious criticize and disparage us. The higher we go, the more we are liable to attack and the farther we have to fall.

Success is both desired and feared. The good student has been known to conceal his achievements from his associates. He may be marked as a "brain," a person who does all his living above the neck. He is subject to censure as a "grind" or a "curve raiser" and looked upon with disfavor by some of the other students. Through his response in class, he may make himself liable to the accusation that he is currying favor with the instructor.

Achievement may run afoul of strong abasive or dependency needs. Success may make us feel guilty or threaten our dependency status. As soon as we begin to get too successful at anything or too competent or too worthy, we feel uncomfortable. Then, we arrange for ourselves to fail. Some of us have a lifetime of this patterning. We almost but never quite allow ourselves to make the grade.

Affiliation Conflicts

For those who have had consistently satisfying interpersonal experiences, the desire to associate with others is strong and occasions little conflict. Some of us, however, have had deeply distressing relationships. In us the impulse to associate with others brings with it the fear of rejection and humiliation. Are we acceptable to others? Sometimes we seek to prove that we are by forcing ourselves into social situations. Sometimes we seek to avoid the answer by keeping as much to ourselves as possible. But when the anticipated rewards of affiliation are closely balanced by the anticipated punishments, we find ourselves in an approach-avoidance conflict.

To make ourselves acceptable to others we must in some degree accept their standards and modes of behavior. This may interfere with the expression of our other needs. Invited to a formal party you are expected to dress properly and make polite conversation. The host may usurp the conversation, the hostess may insist on explaining the art of making salad (a topic on which you are the expert), or another guest may be insulting, but it may be necessary for you to keep your peace. In this situation your need for affiliation might run into conflict with autonomy, dominance, achievement, aggression, and perhaps a number of other needs.

Autonomy Conflicts

The freedom of autonomy is an important one, but responsibility and obligation, rankling as they might seem, bring with them compensatory privileges and pleasures. For example, the autonomous individual may assiduously avoid the "bonds" of matrimony. Gradually, however, most of his friends marry and when he visits them the pleasures of family living, the warm affectional ties, the children are not lost on him. He enjoys his freedom, but. . . .

As we have noted before, society makes certain demands of all of us. The autonomous individual finds many of these demands impossible to accept. He resists them as much as possible. But to those who conform, society offers a number of things: explicit codes for living, ready-made standards and values, financial security, and cadenced, comfortable daily life. The conflict between holding out and giving in can be strong. In many cases the pull to conformity is irresistible, and it is not uncommon for the rebellious youth to mellow with age and adopt increasingly conservative habits.

Dominance Conflicts

Dominance activities bring us into conflict with others who do not wish to be dominated, especially when our behavior is more domineering than masterful. Although our need for dominance pushes us on, it may soon become painfully apparent that we are not winning friends and influencing people.

Sometimes we appear to have captive groups for domination. The parent may dominate his children, the employer his employees, the commanding officer his men. However, even in these instances the dominated individuals may find many subtle ways of resisting and retaliating.

No one can be a leader all the time. Many good leaders also have the capacity to be good followers. This is a difficult lesson for some of us to learn. Our need keeps driving us into dominating actions even in situations where neutral or deferent behavior might seem more advisable.

Deference Conflicts

The individual with strong deference needs may not be fully reconciled to this behavior in himself. To some extent the society's rewards and approbations are reserved for those who are successfully dominant. Although he would like to be dominant, he has little capacity for and little comfort in this role. He may feel forcibly subordinated rather than truly submissive.

This conflict may be resolved in a patterning that includes simultaneous dominance and deference. The foreman defers to the superintendent but dominates the men under him. The deferent employee goes home to dominate his family. Once out on the playground, the teacher-dominated dunce becomes a bully. If we find a small enough pool, any one of us may become the largest fish.

Aggression Conflicts

The impulse to aggression is strong, but we know from sad experience the repercussions which may follow. The people who frustrate us and toward whom we feel aggressive are usually important to us. Frequently, therefore, aggression is a luxury which we cannot afford. For example, our parents may impose annoying restrictions, but if we speak out, they further restrict our activities or withdraw love or financial support. Even if they make no threats at all, we may feel guilty about our actions and provide our own censure.

So well do some of us learn our lesson that we not only inhibit overt aggression, we withdraw as soon as we sense aggressive impulses in ourselves. People and situations that stimulate such impulses are avoided. As a further measure of control, we may assume a facade of extreme mildness. Sometimes, too, we fail to differentiate between acceptable assertion and hostile aggression, and we fear to express ourselves at all because of the possibility of triggering more violent actions.

Abasement Conflicts

When outwardly directed aggressive acts are inhibited, they may be turned back upon the individual himself. Other-aggression becomes self-abasement. Freud (1917) noted that the depressed patient may accuse himself of things that he has not done. However, these accusations do fit some person close to the patient. In criticizing himself the patient is actually indicting someone else who he feels has wronged him.

These patterns sometimes prove to be unstable. The self-abasement breaks down and the impulses again are directed toward the original source. Individuals who are known to be mild and inhibited suddenly lash out and astound others with their violence. Later on they may become doubly abasive; they apologize profusely and rebuke themselves mercilessly for their outbreak. This alternation of patterns illustrates the conflict a number of us have in managing hostility.

Nurturance Conflicts

The need for nurturance may run into conflict with a number of other patterns of behavior. A man may be very much attracted to children but afraid of the responsibilities of marriage. He would like to have children, but he has difficulty imagining himself competent to be a father. A young business woman may be very nurturant and desire to have a family of her own. At the same time she is bound up with her career and fearful of the effect marriage might have on it.

Sometimes nurturance and succorance needs conflict with each other. Although a person may desire children, he may, without realizing it fully, think of himself as a child who must be taken care of. If he marries, he expects his wife to take care of him. Children are resented as competitors for the nurturance that he seeks for himself. However, the needs for nurturance and succorance are not necessarily incompatible; in family, in business, and in almost every other situation, the individual may participate in both roles and interchange them.

Succorance Conflicts

Some of us find it extremely pleasant to be watched over by others. The world is after all a large and uncertain place, and it is comforting to be protected. The people upon whom we depend, however, exercise control over us. This can be irritating. What we might really like is the security of dependence with the freedom of independence. But this is scarcely possible. If the conflict is to be dealt with at all, it must be settled in one direction or the other or through some sort of compromise.

Conflict may be further increased by the inconsistent demands made of us. In some quarters we are treated like a child;

in others we are expected to act adult. For example, our family may reward dependency behavior and discourage attempts at independence. However, our friends are becoming increasingly independent, and if we do not progress with them, we are subject to their criticism and perhaps to our own as well. At school and work, too, we are expected to demonstrate greater and greater self-reliance.

The conflict between dependence and independence is especially dramatic in the adolescent. In the process of emancipation from his family, he frequently rebels against restrictions that he considers inappropriate to his new status. At the same time, he is not at all sure that he is ready to be on his own; he looks to his family for both affectional and economic support. To complicate the matter more, his parents may not be consistent in their actions; they may encourage his emancipation in some ways and discourage it in others. Or one parent may encourage the adolescent to grow up while the other is unhappy about the prospect. Succorance conflicts may be a long time in resolution; some of us never settle them satisfactorily.

Sex Conflicts

No area of functioning occasions more conflict than that involving sex. The urge to sexual activity is powerful, but the inhibitions placed on it are powerful too. The child's curiosity about sexual matters is seldom met calmly and with the simple information that is sought. Early attempts at masturbation and other forms of sex play are frequently punished. The sexual functioning of those around him, as nearly as he understands it, can seem violent and anything but desirable. Many people grow up with the idea that sex is wrong, forbidden, dirty, harmful, or dangerous.

As we mature, the sex need begins to assert itself with increasing force. We are strongly tempted to masturbate, to neck and pet, or to have intercourse. However, these impulses may bring with them a wave of anxiety. We are both attracted and repelled. We waver back and forth. If we give in to our impulses, we are assailed by other waves of guilt and remorse. Even in marriage, sexual functioning can be disrupted by unfavorable attitudes stemming from early training.

The sex need occasions conflict in numerous other ways. For example, considering the female role in intercourse as a submissive one, a woman with strong dominance needs may be unable to attain sexual satisfaction. A man with strong succorant needs may seek out maternal women; however, his conception of his partner as a mother figure may invoke the incest taboo and make sexual relations impossible. An individual with a great need for autonomy may fear anything but the most casual sexual relationships. Conflicts in this area are frequently complex and difficult to understand.

SUMMARY

A conflict involves competition among several patterns of behavior. Conflict can be described as a process or as a state of feeling accompanying this process.

Conflicts can be classified in terms of the part of a motive that seems most affected. Need conflicts involve either the competition of several needs or the simultaneous operation of impulses to express and inhibit a single need. Act conflicts involve competition among several modes of meeting a need and reaching a goal. Goal conflicts involve competition among several goals.

A second way of classifying conflicts is in terms of the combination of approach and avoidance tendencies they include. Approach-approach conflicts involve simultaneous attraction to several incompatible patterns of action. In avoidance-avoidance conflicts we are simultaneously repelled by several courses of action, but to escape one we must carry out another. In approach-avoidance conflicts we are simultaneously attracted and repelled by a single course of action or by several such courses of action. Many human conflict situations seem most fully described as multiple approach-avoidance conflicts.

All conflicts involve a certain amount of blocking as we work toward some solution. Approach-approach conflicts are relatively easy to resolve, but conflicts involving both approach and avoidance tendencies may be very difficult to deal with. If only avoidance tendencies are involved in a conflict situation, we may try to escape from it and avoid making any decision.

For a conflict to be resolved, the situation must be restructured in some way. Sometimes in dealing with a conflict we are able to elect one alternative and inhibit the others. At other times we alternate between two courses of action or hit upon some compromise solution.

Some of the most important conflicts are those which affect our needs for achievement, affiliation, autonomy, dominance, deference, aggression, abasement, nurturance, succorance, and sex.

REFERENCES

Adams, D. K. Conflict and integration. *Journal of Personality,* 1954, **22,** 548–556.

Arkoff, A. Resolution of approach-approach and avoidance-avoidance conflicts. *Journal of Abnormal and Social Psychology,* 1957, **55,** 402–404.

———. Resolving conflicts. *Proceedings of the Hawaiian Academy of Science,* 1956–1957, 29. (Abstract).

Brown, J. S. Principles of intrapersonal conflict. *Journal of Conflict Resolution,* 1957, **1,** 135–154.

Festinger, L. *A Theory of Cognitive Dissonance.* New York: Harper & Row, 1957.

Festinger, L., & Bramel, D. The reaction of humans to cognitive dissonance. In A. J. Bachrach (Ed.), *Experimental Foundations of Clinical Psychology.* New York: Basic Books, 1962. Pp. 254–279.

Freud, S. Mourning and melancholia (1917). Reprinted in *Collected Papers.* Vol. 4. London: Hogarth, 1925.

Godbeer, E. Factors introducing conflict in the choice behavior of children. Unpublished master's thesis, Yale University, 1940. Cited by N. E. Miller, Experimental studies of conflict. In J. McV. Hunt (Ed.), *Personality and the Behavior Disorders.* Vol. 1. New York: Ronald, 1944. Pp. 431–465.

Hovland, C. I., & Sears, R. R. Experiments on motor conflict. I. Types of conflict and their modes of resolution. *Journal of Experimental Psychology,* 1938, **23,** 477–493.

Levinger, G. Kurt Lewin's approach to conflict and its resolution: A review with some extensions. *Journal of Conflict Resolution,* 1957, **1,** 329–339.

Lewin, K. *A Dynamic Theory of Personality.* New York: McGraw-Hill, 1935.

Miller, N. E. Experimental studies of conflict. In J. McV. Hunt (Ed.), *Personality and the Behavior Disorders.* Vol. 1. New York: Ronald, 1944. Pp. 431–465.

———. Some implications of modern behavior theory for personality change and psychotherapy. In P. Worchel and D. Byrne (Eds.), *Personality Change.* New York: Wiley, 1964. Pp. 149–175.

Morgan, C. T. *Introduction to Psychology.* (2nd ed.) New York: McGraw-Hill, 1961.

Sappenfield, B. R. *Personality Dynamics.* New York: Knopf, 1954.

Tyler, L. E. Toward a workable psychology of individuality. *American Psychologist,* 1959, **14,** 75–81.

CHAPTER FIVE

ANXIETY

The times we live in have been called the "age of anxiety," but probably every age or era of human history could be designated in the same way. Anxiety, fear, and worry seem to be permanent parts of the human condition.

Anxiety has been of central concern in the study of the individual. Three decades ago Freud wrote, "The problem of anxiety is a nodal point, linking up all kinds of most important questions; a riddle, of which the solution must cast a flood of light upon our whole mental life."

Today scientists are hard at work on this riddle. This chapter will present some things which have been found out about anxiety and its role in the adjustment process.

DEFINING ANXIETY

What is anxiety? Workers in this area do not agree. Various theories of anxiety have been proposed, a number of descriptions have been formulated, and dozens of measures of anxiety have been devised.

What is anxiety? In this discussion *anxiety* will be defined as a state of arousal caused by threat to well-being (see Fig. 5.1). "State" means a condition involving the entire organism. "Arousal" means a condition of tension, unrest, or uneasiness, and a readiness to act and respond. "Threat" means anticipation of pain or danger or serious interference with goal-seeking activities.

Frustrations and conflicts, of course, interfere with goal-seeking activities, but not all frustrations and conflicts are perceived as threatening and anxiety arousing. However, the difference between a "non-threatening" and a "threatening" frustration is not an either-or distinction. It is one of degree or amount. All frustrations and conflicts could be placed along a continuum with the most nonthreatening or benign at one end and the most threatening or anxiety arousing at the other.

The man in the street has his own terms for anxiety. Some of these are fear,

worry, and nervousness. Nervous tension and emotional tension, having the jitters, and being shaken up also are used to describe anxious conditions.

Stressor *and* Stress

Some writers make use of the terms "stress" and "stressor." *Stress* is used to refer to the state of a person in a threatening or difficult situation. *Stressor* refers to a condition which is potentially threatening or difficult. In this usage, the term "stress" is interchangeable with "anxiety," and "stressor" designates a process of frustration or conflict.

It has been widely noted that a situation which is very threatening for one person is not necessarily so for another. Under seemingly similar conditions, one person may appear to be quite upset, while another may be quite composed. For example, two middle-aged males who have suffered a heart attack or two students facing an important examination may report considerably different amounts of stress or anxiety.

In the psychological laboratory, subjects are found to vary widely in their re-

Figure 5.1 *Anxiety* is defined as a state of arousal caused by a threat to well-being. Many, but not all, frustrations and conflicts involve threat and anxiety.

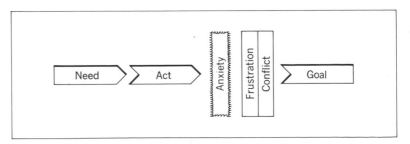

sponses to a controlled application of stressors. A single subject's reaction cannot be predicted from a simple description of the situation itself. As Lazarus, Deese, and Osler (1952) note, "One person may tremble, sweat, experience discomfort, and show signs of behavioral disorganization. Another may show an impairment in performance with no other subjective concomitants. Still others may show no measurable effects from the situation."

The discrepancy between the ostensible force of the stressors (or frustration and conflict) a person is subjected to and the amount of stress (or anxiety) he demonstrates is an important psychological problem. What could account for this discrepancy? In the section which follows we will consider some possible explanations.

Stressor *into* Stress

"By what means does a stressor (event) become transformed into stress for any given individual?" This is a question posed by Cowen (1960), and although he finds that scientists have not yet arrived at much of an answer, he suggests some hypotheses which seem well worth examining.

First, Cowen hypothesizes that "to the extent that a given stressor (event) blocks the gratification of a need, to that extent it is likely that the stressor will eventuate in the internal stress state." He presents the case of two students, one with a strong need for achievement who is planning to apply for medical school, the other who is in college to delay going to work in his father's store. Both fail an examination in chordate anatomy. The former may experience much stress while the latter, if his college standing is not immediately jeopardized, may feel little or none.

Second, Cowen proposes that "the stronger the need which is being thwarted by a particular stressor event, the more intense is the state of stress likely to be." In some of us, for example, the need for affiliation is very strong, and meeting the need is central to our well-being; anything that serves to frustrate affiliation activities may produce considerable anxiety. However, by contrast, our dominance needs may be of only minor or peripheral importance to us, and failure to be recognized as a leader or to be elected to positions of power may not be very bothersome.

Third, Cowen suggests that "a need-blocking event is more likely to be followed by a stress state to the extent that alternative gratifications are unavailable." When substitute goals are available, inability to obtain a particular goal (even though it is very much preferred) will not be so threatening. Or failure in meeting certain needs may be ameliorated by success and gratification in other areas. By way of illustration Cowen writes:

> An orthopedic impairment, for example, may thwart an adolescent's need for affiliation which, prior to that time was fulfilled largely through athletic participation and Boy Scout camping activities with peers. In that sense it will be stress-producing. However, to the extent that substitute gratifications, e.g., stamp collecting or any number of intellectual activities can fulfill the blocked affiliative needs, to that extent will the stress be reduced (1960, pp. 144–145).

Fourth, Cowen says, "A given stressor is more likely to be followed by stress, if the prior and/or concurrent stress characteristics of the organism are elevated." He calls this a "straw-that-breaks-the-camel's-back" principle. How we respond to a new stressful event depends on how much stress we are already undergoing and how much stress we can handle. If we are already sorely tried or near the breaking point, the addition of one more stressor (even one that we ordinarily could take in our stride) may be sufficient to precipitate a powerful state of stress.

DESCRIBING ANXIETY

Some of the best descriptions of anxiety have been made by psychiatrists, psychoanalysts, psychologists, and other workers who have considerable experience in dealing with anxious people. The language of the clinicians seems to imply that there are different kinds of anxiety, and indeed research suggests that there may be a number of different dimensions of anxiety which have little relationship to one another (Jackson & Bloomberg, 1958; Sarason, 1960). Some of the differences in anxiety which clinicians have identified and described relate to its objectiveness, its specificity or generality, its acuteness or chronicity, and its degree of consciousness.

Objective versus Nonobjective Anxiety

If you asked a group of people to write down their anxieties or worries, you would probably find a great difference in their responses. Some of their concerns might seem well defined while others would be quite vague and ambiguous. And some of their concerns might strike you as worth worrying about while others might appear ill-founded, even ridiculous.

Anxiety is said to be "objective" if it seems commensurate with the threat posed by a situation. This implies that the danger is actually known (it is not something obscure or mysterious) and that the arousal is proportional to this explicit danger. For example, it is objective to be somewhat anxious about a child who has contracted the measles or mumps and considerably anxious about one who has polio or must undergo a major operation. A number of writers prefer calling feelings of this sort "fear" rather than anxiety. Sometimes, rather than being designated as objective, this kind of anxiety is called "normal," "rational," or "realistic."

By contrast, anxiety is considered "nonobjective" if it is not commensurate with the threat involved in a situation or if the threat is vague or unknown. For example, many of us are apprehensive about high places; driving along a precipitous mountain road, we begin to sweat and feel uneasy; a few of us, however, are absolutely terrified by such experiences and avoid them at all costs. There are also some situations which seem to involve little danger at all but which for no clearly discernible reason make us feel anxious. For example, we may be extremely apprehensive about being seated in the middle of an audience, or riding in an elevator, or being around cats or dogs or certain other

Figure 5.2 What are college students afraid of? A group of students were asked to indicate how fearful they were of fifty-one things. From the results the investigators concluded that "unrealistic fears" were quite common in this group. Nearly 40 percent of the subjects listed one or more of their fears as severe, and women had higher fear scores than men. Here are the mean scores for 161 men and 109 women (Data from Greer, 1965).

Degree of fear

	Men		Women

Degree of fear scale:	None 0	Very little 1	A little 2	Some 3	Much 4	Very much 5	Terror 6

	Men	Women
1. Sharp objects	1.6	1.9
2. Being a passenger in a car	0.6	0.9
3. Dead bodies	1.7	2.0
4. Suffocating	2.1	2.0
5. Failing a test	3.3	3.3
6. Looking foolish	2.8	2.9
7. Being a passenger in an airplane	1.3	1.8
8. Worms	0.3	1.3
9. Arguing with parents	1.3	1.4
10. Rats and mice	1.0	2.3
11. Life after death	0.9	1.2
12. Hypodermic needles	1.5	1.1
13. Being criticized	2.0	2.3
14. Meeting someone for the first time	1.3	1.5
15. Roller coasters	1.3	2.0
16. Being alone	0.7	1.2
17. Making mistakes	2.2	2.5

Degree of fear

	Men	Women
18. Being misunderstood	1.7	1.9
19. Death	2.0	2.4
20. Being in a fight	1.8	1.8
21. Crowded places	0.7	0.8
22. Blood	0.8	0.8
23. Heights	1.8	1.7
24. Being a leader	1.0	1.5
25. Swimming alone	1.0	1.4
26. Illness	1.3	1.9
27. Being with drunks	1.2	2.6
28. Illness or injury to loved ones	3.1	4.1
29. Being selfconscious	2.2	2.4
30. Driving a car	0.5	1.1
31. Meeting authority	1.3	1.7
32. Mental illness	1.3	2.0
33. Closed places	0.8	1.2
34. Boating	0.5	1.9

Scale: None 0 — Very little 1 — A little 2 — Some 3 — Much 4 — Very much 5 — Terror 6

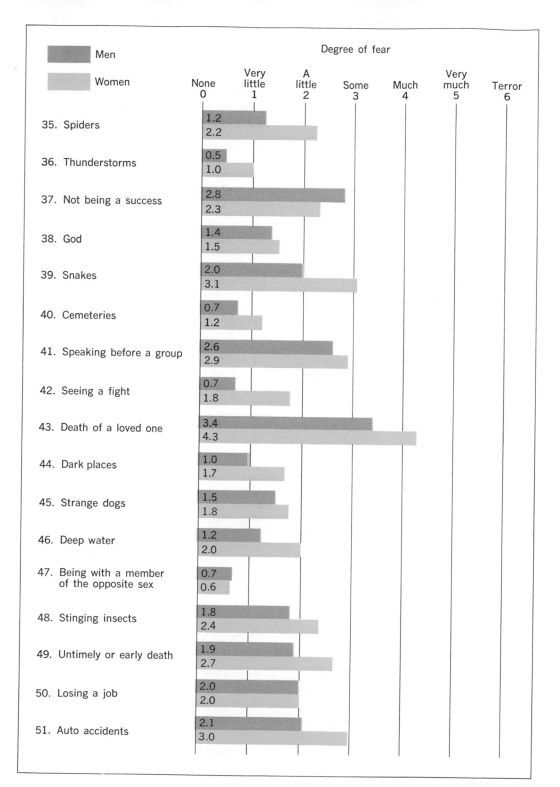

Degree of fear

Men
Women

	None 0	Very little 1	A little 2	Some 3	Much 4	Very much 5	Terror 6

35. Spiders
1.2
2.2

36. Thunderstorms
0.5
1.0

37. Not being a success
2.8
2.3

38. God
1.4
1.5

39. Snakes
2.0
3.1

40. Cemeteries
0.7
1.2

41. Speaking before a group
2.6
2.9

42. Seeing a fight
0.7
1.8

43. Death of a loved one
3.4
4.3

44. Dark places
1.0
1.7

45. Strange dogs
1.5
1.8

46. Deep water
1.2
2.0

47. Being with a member of the opposite sex
0.7
0.6

48. Stinging insects
1.8
2.4

49. Untimely or early death
1.9
2.7

50. Losing a job
2.0
2.0

51. Auto accidents
2.1
3.0

animals. This kind of anxiety is sometimes called "neurotic," "irrational," and "unrealistic" (see Fig. 5.2).

Situational versus General Anxiety

Nobody feels at ease in every situation. Each of us has some situations which we find particularly trying. And some of us may feel generally or continually anxious.

Anxiety that occurs only under particular circumstances is called "situational" anxiety. We may learn to recognize and avoid anxiety-provoking situations; as long as we can do so, we remain relatively free of anxiety. For example, some of us find contact with the opposite sex upsetting, and when we are drawn into such situations, we experience considerable anxiety. This kind of anxiety is sometimes called "bound" because it is tied to certain situations and can be controlled as long as these situations are avoided (see Case Study 5.1).

"General" anxiety describes anxiety that pervades the activities of the individual. Rather than being tied or bound to one situation, it is experienced in many different ones; the person may be unable to relax and unable to feel at ease under any circumstances. This kind of anxiety is sometimes referred to as "free-floating" because it is unattached to specific circumstances or as "characterological" because it is considered a part of the more permanent character makeup of the individual.

Case study 5.1 Situational anxiety. (This material was taken from a paper written by a man, twenty-two years old.)

My problem is one of anxiety or nervousness which exhibits itself in the form of tremors in my hands when I find myself the object of attention. Since I am a pianist, this condition is a serious one. Of course, there are other situations which sometimes make me feel rather nervous or excited, but I seem to be able to function well enough in them so no harm is done. But when I am performing publicly my nervousness sometimes amounts almost to paralysis.

During a concert I simply cannot control my fingers, and my major concern is how to keep them from shaking. This inhibits my ease in playing and makes certain passages and technical feats nearly impossible. I cannot concentrate on the music, and I try to cover my extreme nervousness and give the impression of being relaxed and composed. If one cannot see the keyboard, he may imagine that all is well—unless attentive ears tell him otherwise.

I have given many recitals besides having played concertos with orchestras. I never break down completely, yet it is very seldom that I am able to play with ease and give a performance that approaches what I can do when I play privately.

The intensity of my nervousness varies. I never know beforehand just how severe it will be. Sometimes it is not so severe, and occasionally, very occasionally, it is absent entirely. I have played often enough to know what conditions I like during recitals. I prefer to be somewhat distant from the audience. If the audience is very close, I am extremely ill at ease.

Why I have this anxiety I do not know. For a while I thought I might outgrow it or conquer it. However, now I feel that it is here to stay, and I must learn to live with it.

Acute versus Chronic Anxiety

We all experience anxiety, but the amount of anxiety we feel from time to time varies. Sometimes we may feel relatively calm, at other times quite anxious. Probably all of us have had moments when we were very nearly overwhelmed by anxiety, when we were very near panic.

"Acute" anxiety is sharp and intense. It is relatively sudden in onset or recent in appearance. After a period of relative calm, we may suddenly begin to feel extremely anxious. Some of us suffer from "anxiety attacks" which are sudden bursts of anxiety that rapidly mount to a peak and then fade away.

"Chronic" anxiety refers to elevated states of anxiety which have persisted over a long period. Some of us have long histories of heightened anxiety; it may be difficult for us to recall any period of our life that was calm and tranquil.

Conscious versus Unconscious Anxiety

When we speak of being anxious or feeling anxious, we imply that we are very much aware of our feelings. We feel what we feel even though we may not know why we feel it. In other words, our anxiety is conscious even though our reasons for it may not be.

Yet workers in the area speak of "unconscious anxiety." For example, Frieda Fromm-Reichmann (1955) writes, "We observe both healthy and mentally disturbed people doing everything possible to ward off anxiety or to keep it from awareness."

With varying degrees of success, we learn certain ways to deal with anxiety. These are sometimes called "defenses" since we use them to defend ourselves against stress. But if these patterns of behavior are interfered with in some way, we are again assaulted by anxiety. Anxiety that is adequately defended against is sometimes called "unconscious" anxiety. Anxiety that is not controlled in some way is called "conscious."

Not all writers and workers in this area are happy with the idea of uncon-scious anxiety and with the notion that anxiety can somehow exist even though it is not within awareness. Cattell and Scheier (1961) think the concept is a useful one, and Rosenwald writes:

> It is well known that anxiety is in certain instances further characterized by conscious experiences of distress and by physiological stress symptoms. However, these additional conditions are of secondary importance in the definition of anxiety and may be completely lacking. Thus the term anxiety may be applied regardless of whether subjective experiential factors and physiological stress symptoms play a minimal role or assume spectacular importance, as they do, for instance in anxiety attacks. Only its traceable origin in past experience, which has rendered the drive dangerous, and the automatic elicitation of defenses are central to the definition of anxiety (1961, p. 667).

Some authorities, however, prefer to restrict the use of the term "anxiety" to feelings that are present and experienced. This is the position of Martin, who writes:

> There exists a possible source of confusion with respect to the responses that have been learned to reduce anxiety in that clinicians frequently infer anxiety on the basis of these "defenses" against anxiety as much as from direct expression of anxiety itself. Again, from the point of view of theory as well as measurement it is preferable to keep these two variables distinct if possible. In fact, it would seem likely that when a person is making a successful "defensive" response, no anxiety is present. To the extent that this is so it would be misleading to infer the strength of the momentary anxiety level from the presence of learned anxiety reducing responses (1961, p. 235).

ASSESSING ANXIETY

We speak of people who are very anxious and people who have very little anxiety, of a person who is very anxious in one situation but not in another. But how do we know how anxious a person is? How do we go about assessing this "state of arousal"?

One of the chief ways of evaluating anxiety or stress has been to infer it from the stressor stimuli which were involved in a situation. If a situation appeared to be a stressful one, it has been assumed that a person in it was suffering from stress. But, as has already been indicated, this supposition is hardly a safe one because people vary in their responses to similar stressors.

Another procedure has been to infer anxiety from the responses that are employed to reduce or avoid it. If a person shows a lot of "defensive" behavior, it is assumed that he is considerably affected by anxiety which he is struggling to control, "bind," or keep "unconscious." This method of evaluating anxiety has been subjected to criticism by those writers who prefer to keep separate the ideas of anxiety and defense.

Recently, an increasing amount of study has been made of a number of observable response patterns which might be considered reflections of anxiety. Many specific measures have been used. Most of these measures fall within three broad classes of expression: affect, motor, and visceral (Lazarus, 1961).

Affect Expression

Affect expression refers to a person's state of feeling. States of feeling in frustration and conflict have already been discussed. In anxiety there is the added element of threat, or, it might be more accurate to say, this element is heightened or accentuated.

Threat may be challenging or intimidating. We so frequently focus on the negative aspects of anxiety that we may forget to take note of the aliveness—even zest— we can feel when a situation involves more than the usual amount of risk, when the

---

Presentation 5.1. Anxiety scales.

Psychologists have devised a number of scales to measure anxiety. Many of the items which make up these scales are self-reports of affect or feeling. One widely used instrument is the Manifest Anxiety Scale (Taylor, 1953). The scale is composed of 225 items, 50 of which are included because they were judged to be anxiety indicators. In the test score, 1 point is added for every answer that indicates anxiety, so a subject's score can vary from 50 (high anxiety) to 0 (low anxiety).

Here are some sample items which, if answered "true," are scored 1 point:

Life is often a strain for me.
I am a very nervous person.
At times I have been worried beyond reason about something that did not really matter.

Here are some sample items which are scored 1 point if answered "false":

I am usually calm and not easily upset.
I am happy most of the time.
I am very confident of myself.

chips are down, the stakes are high, and there is something important to be lost or won.

But when a threat is poorly defined or even misinterpreted and when the course of action is uncertain or continually ineffective, we feel quite differently. There may be a heavy and unshakable sense of apprehension, a feeling of uneasiness and foreboding. We may feel that we cannot allow ourselves to relax, that we must be continually on our guard, that we are inadequate, helpless, and surrounded by a hostile environment.

As was said earlier, the things we fear may be vague or unknown. We aren't aware of what is going to happen, when it is going to happen, or why it should happen. Sometimes we may be concerned about things which present little danger or, if dangerous, could hardly occur. Yet, we tell ourselves, they just might be dangerous, and they just might happen. When? Well, maybe sometime—you can't tell about these things.

Sometimes our anxious feelings become suddenly heightened. Apprehensions turn into terror and even panic. It seems as if the anxiety will be too much to bear. We feel that we are reaching the breaking point, that we are about to go to pieces or become insane. Something horrible is about to happen or we, ourselves, are about to do something unforgivable. These feelings quickly reach their crest and then gradually subside.

Just as we all have demonstrated the overt characteristics of anxiety, we all have experienced the feelings that accompany these signs. We may know that there is nothing to be afraid of or, even if there is, that it is ridiculous to feel as frightened as we do. Perhaps powerless to act, per-

haps powerless to even understand the cause of our apprehension, we feel all the more powerless. Sometimes we feel that if we weren't so frightened, we wouldn't be so frightened.[1] Feelings of anxiety can be much more difficult to bear than physical pain.

Motor Expression

Motor expression refers to the muscular activity of the body. In anxiety we are roused and ready for action. We are keyed up and ready to go. Our motor expression depends on how keyed up we are and where, if any place at all, we are going.

Roused, we are ready for fight or flight, but there may be only a sense of threat without insight into what the threat is all about or what is to be fought or fled from, overcome or resolved. In such cases we can present a picture of diffuse and useless activity. We may be unable to remain in any posture for very long. Standing, we shift from foot to foot and pace about. Seated, we are apt to perch on the edge of our chair, jiggling our legs, crossing them, uncrossing them, and crossing them again. Lying down, we turn, pitch, and toss, continually changing our position.

Our fingers, hands, and arms may be constantly active. Perhaps we drum our fingers, crack our knuckles, bite our nails, pull at our ears, twist, rumple, and smooth our hair. We rub our hands together, clench them into fists, open them, inspect them, and close them again. We move our arms about, fold them in front of us, in back of us, and then unfold them again. We fidget, writhe, and wriggle.

Sometimes we show little activity, but

[1] Some of us may be reminded of a pertinent phrase of Franklin Delano Roosevelt's first inaugural address: "The only thing we have to fear is fear itself."

our entire bearing seems strained. Our posture is rigid, our muscles tense, our arms and legs stiff. We seem to be effortfully inhibiting all motion. Our appearance is similar to that of a man in the dentist's chair who, feeling the warm friction and dull pain of the drill, half expects it to slip from the tooth onto the tender gum at any moment.

Generally, there is a heightened response to stimuli. A small noise startles us. A gentle touch on our shoulder may cause us to jump. A slight movement behind us causes us to whirl about. Every new stimulus captures our attention and, therefore, no stimulus is able to hold it for very long. We have difficulty in concentrating our attention and applying ourselves.

Since all of us have periods of anxiety, all of us have demonstrated some or even many of these signs. While making a speech, before going onstage, waiting in the doctor's office, on our first airplane ride, during our wedding, waiting for the test results, and in many other situations (including some in which there was little objective reason for apprehension) we have appeared this way. Our voices may have wavered, changed pitch, and squeaked. We may have felt ourselves flush or blanch, turn hot or ice cold. Our hands may have shaken, our knees knocked together, or perhaps we trembled all over.

Visceral Expression

Visceral expression refers to physiological changes occurring within the body. What physiological events take place when we "feel" anxious or "look" anxious? There has been progress (Martin, 1961), but researchers have not yet been too successful in distinguishing one emotional state

from another on the basis of physiological indexes. As Morgan (1961) states, "Although we can distinguish mild from severe emotional states, we have so far not been able to distinguish different emotions in this way with any degree of success."

Autonomic Reactions in Stress

The physiological changes that take place in emotional states are primarily produced by the autonomic nervous system. The two divisions of the system supply innervation to the glands and the smooth muscles of the various organs of the body. The parasympathetic division is in charge in the quiescent states of the individual, that is, during the calm, relaxed, vegetative activities of everyday living. The sympathetic division takes over during excited, mobilized, emergency states.

The two divisions of the system tend to work in opposition. If the effect of one is to facilitate the activity of an organ, the effect of the other is to inhibit it. To use some broad examples, the parasympathetic division serves to augment digestive activities while the sympathetic division retards them. The sympathetic division raises the blood pressure and accelerates the pulse rate while the parasympathetic division lowers the blood pressure and retards pulsation.

During the quiet processes of everyday living, the parasympathetic division is in charge. For example, consider yourself seated in a pleasant meadow in front of an excellent picnic lunch. The pupil of each eye is constricted to protect it from the bright light, and the lens is adjusted for near vision. Your salivary glands are secreting saliva. Your stomach is active, and the digestive juices flow. Your heart is beating quietly, your pulse is even, and your blood pressure is moderate. Your perspiration is limited. You breathe evenly.

In this state of parasympathetic activity, digestion is facilitated. There is no competing skeletal muscle activity. The body is prepared to receive food, digest it, and eliminate the waste products. There is saliva in the mouth to begin digestion. The contractions and secretions of the stomach further the process. The bladder and bowel are relaxed to permit the ultimate elimination of waste products. There is an abundant supply of blood in the stomach and intestines to assist in the process.

Suddenly you notice a very unfriendly looking bull approaching you. The sympathetic division takes over. The pupil of each eye is dilated to admit more light, and the lens is adjusted for more distant vision. Your salivary glands stop secreting saliva; your mouth and lips feel dry, and you have difficulty swallowing. Your digestive processes stop. Your heart begins to pound, your pulse races, and your blood pressure rises. You break out into a cold sweat. You breathe more rapidly.

In this state of sympathetic activity, digestion is inhibited, but large muscle activity is facilitated. With increasing heart beat and blood pressure and with the diversion of blood from the viscera to the skeletal muscles, the body is prepared for strenuous activity. In addition, the adrenal glands secrete adrenalin into the blood accentuating the sympathetic process and particularly making more energy available by inducing the liver to release sugar.

In preparing us for fight or flight the internal changes produced by the sympathetic division of the autonomic nervous system can have considerable survival value (Cannon, 1953). If we are confronted by an unfriendly bull, it is more important to run than to eat. The sympathetic division prepares us to run by inhibiting the digestive processes and facilitating skeletal muscle activity.

Although primitive man could react to emergency situations by running or fighting, modern man finds himself in different circumstances. Sometimes we may wish to fight but when our adversary is an employer, a teacher, a parent, or someone else in authority, we may find it impossible to do so. Facing the prospect of a difficult course, a serious operation, or a trying evening, we may wish to run away but be unable to. And when we do not fully understand the cause of our apprehension, as is often the case, we are able neither to fight nor run. In this event the sympathetic nervous system mobilizes the body for activity which it cannot perform (see Fig. 5.3).

Psychophysiologic Reactions in Stress

When frustrations and conflicts are serious and of long duration and when the anxiety produced by them is not controlled in some way, the body remains in a constant state of mobilization. After a time this strain may result in certain physiological dysfunctions or changes (Alexander, 1948). Physiological disorders due to chronic and exaggerated emotional states are referred to as *psychophysiologic reactions* or *psychosomatic disorders.*

The body responds as a whole to stress, but the work of Lacey and his associates (1953, 1958) suggests that each of us may have our own individual pattern of autonomic response, and Alexander (1948, 1962) has postulated that some persons have organ systems which are particularly vulnerable to certain kinds of emotional stress. Among the most important and most studied stress patterns are those involving the cardiovascular, gastrointestinal, respiratory, and skin systems.

Cardiovascular Reactions   Of the various organ systems of the body the heart is probably the most sensitive recorder of emotional stimuli (Kraines & Thetford, 1943). During calm states, heart beat is quiet and regular, pulse is even, blood pressure is relatively low, and visceral organs are well supplied with blood to facilitate their operation. With excitement, important changes occur in the heart rate, pulse, blood pressure, and in the distribution of blood in the body.

In excited states, the heart begins to pump blood faster and with greater force.

Figure 5.3 The sympathetic and parasympathetic divisions of the autonomic nervous system tend to work in opposition to each other. If the effect of one division is to facilitate the activity of an organ, the effect of the other is to inhibit it. The parasympathetic division predominates when we are calm and relaxed. The sympathetic division takes over when we are angry or fearful.

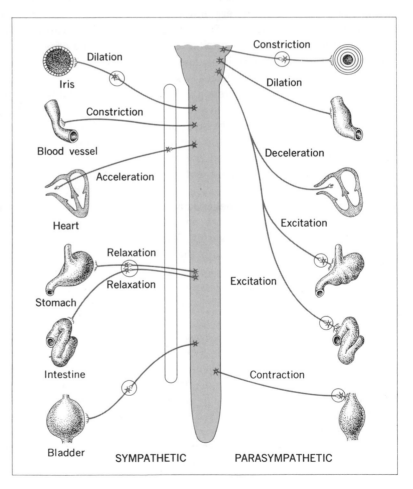

Pulse quickens, and blood pressure mounts. The vessels of the visceral organs constrict, and blood is forced back to the heart to be sent in greater quantity to the muscles of the trunk and limbs. The digestive processes of the body are inhibited while large muscle activities are facilitated by this redistribution of blood.

More than any other organ, the heart is used to symbolize emotion. People are described as warmhearted or coldhearted, softhearted or hardhearted. A person may feel lighthearted or heavyhearted. Sometimes the heart may appear to move about, leaping with joy or sinking with despair. Upon meeting an attractive female, a young man may find that his heart stands still. He gives his heart away, and if it is not handled with care, heartache or even heartbreak results. Afterward he may decide to lock his heart and throw away the key.

Weiss and English (1957) state, "In spite of the enormous incidence of cardiovascular disease, *the majority of patients who have symptoms referred to the heart region do not have evidence of organic heart disease.*" Since the heart has traditionally been the center of emotion, it easily becomes the center of concern. Among the best studied clinical syndromes in which emotional stress may play an important part are migraine, hypertension, syncope, cardiac arythmias, and neurocirculatory asthenia (Ham, 1962).

The role of stress in the production of migraine headaches, in particular, has been fairly well established. These headaches are severe, usually unilateral and frequently accompanied by nausea, vomiting, constipation, or diarrhea. One bit of clinical evidence concerned a patient whose almost daily headaches were related to her relationship to her daughter. On the first clinic visit the physician was very sympathetic, and no headaches occurred in the week which followed. During the second visit, however, the physician did a complete about-face, sternly criticizing the patient for her behavior. She appeared contrite and showed no resentment, but shortly after the inerview ended she developed a severe headache (Marcussen, 1950).

Gastrointestinal Reactions The gastrointestinal system is second only to the heart in its sensitivity to emotional stimuli (Kraines & Thetford, 1943). Pleasant emotions facilitate the digestive activities of the body. Joy, laughter, and other states of well-being are compatible with the heightened abdominal and intestinal functioning involved in food assimilation.

Unpleasant emotional states tend to interfere with digestive activity. Fear serves to diminish the production of salivary and digestive juices and to decrease the stomach's motility and blood supply. Anger may have an opposite effect; in some cases of hostility and resentment, for example, gastric hyperfunction has been found with increased acid secretion, motility, and blood flow.

The effects of emotion on your own gastrointestinal system can be easily observed. For example, before making a speech at a banquet you may notice that salivary action has stopped; your mouth feels dry, as though it were full of cotton, and you lick your lips to increase the moisture. There is difficulty in swallowing because of the lump in your throat. Although the food is sumptuous, you have little appetite; your stomach feels as if it were tied in knots or filled with butterflies.

In summing up the evidence presented by a number of investigators, Weiss and English (1957) conclude that "emotional factors are the *chief* cause of gastrointestinal complaints." In two-thirds of the cases gastrointestinal symptoms are partly or fully psychological in origin.

Among the gastrointestinal effects of emotion are undereating and overeating. During periods of tension and unhappiness we may lose our appetite completely, or we may gorge ourselves with food. Related disturbances in which emotional factors may be prominent include chronic gastritis, peptic ulcer, colitis, constipation, and diarrhea.

The influence of emotion upon gastric activity has been demonstrated in a number of ways. A representative study (Mittelmann & Wolff, 1942) involved two groups of subjects, one suffering from gastroduodenal disturbances and another which was free of them. Emotional stress was induced in both groups through the discussion of upsetting experiences. It was noted that the stress tended to increase gastric activity. Furthermore, the increased activity was greater among the subjects with gastroduodenal disturbances than among those of the control group. A related study is shown in Figure 5.4.

Respiratory Reactions   The respiratory system is very sensitive to emotional changes. During quiet states, breathing is even and inconspicuous. During activity and excitement, patterns of breathing demonstrate changes in depth, rate, and rhythm.

Boredom makes us yawn. Sudden stimuli inhibit breathing. In talking about a particular experience, we may say that it was breathtaking. Afterward, we may breathe a sigh of relief. Sometimes, too, we sigh with despair or longing.

In anger, fear, and anxiety, we tend to breathe more rapidly. Breathing may be

Figure 5.4
Effect of emotion on the stomach is spectacularly demonstrated by a man whose stomach was exposed in an unusual accident years ago. Using a cord inserted into the man's stomach, Dr. Stewart Wolf at the University of Oklahoma records the organ's muscular contractions on the chart behind the bed. Result shows what happened when one question made the man angry: formerly quiet stomach suddenly reacted with violent motion (Carter, 1958). (Photographs from the medical motion picture "Human Gastric Function," produced and distributed by Smith, Kline and French Laboratories.)

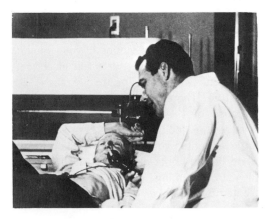
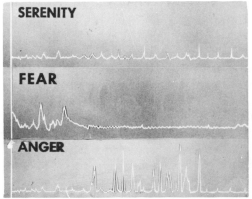

quite shallow, or it may be deeper than usual. In addition, the pattern of inspiration and expiration may demonstrate an irregular rhythm.

Emotional factors have been held to play a role in a number of respiratory disorders. Persistent coughing, clearing the throat, and hiccoughs are frequently intensified if not actually caused by emotional tension (Kraines & Thetford, 1943). Emotional patterns leading to undernourishment, fatigue, and anxiety are of importance in the etiology of pulmonary tuberculosis (Weiss & English, 1957).

Asthma is a disorder in which the importance of emotional factors has been well established. This disorder is manifested in a wheezing and straining for breath caused by spasm of the muscles which line the tiny air passages of the lungs. With the narrowing of these air passages, breathing becomes difficult. Clinical evidence shows that this spasm may be due to allergens or emotional factors or to both in combination. In the latter case it is usually sufficient to remove one set of factors or the other to free the patient from further attacks (Alexander, 1950).

Skin Reactions   All of us are familiar with various ways in which emotion is reflected in the skin. In addition to being an elastic container the skin has many functions and is filled with innumerable nerve fibers, blood vessels, and sweat glands. During emotional states the functioning of these and other components of the skin is altered, producing changes in sensation, color, temperature, perspiration, and texture.

In anger, for example, we flush or show a pallor. We demonstrate changes in temperature. Our language shows how well

the relationship between emotion and skin functioning has been observed. The angry individual is said to be hot under the collar, and the responsible party is rubbing him the wrong way or getting under his skin. Angrier still, he becomes purple with rage or threatens to boil over.

In fear and anxiety we turn pale. Our hands and feet may become cold, and we may perspire profusely. The combination of coldness and moisture produces a clammy feeling. In sudden fright gooseflesh may appear. Again, our speech reflects these phenomena. We may sweat out a particular situation or develop cold feet and leave. We turn pale as a ghost or white as a sheet. A situation may be enough to make our hair stand on end or to curl it.

Beyond these transient manifestations of feeling, emotional states which are intense and enduring may play a part in the production of a number of skin disorders. Nearly half of the more than seventeen thousand patients studied at a dermatological teaching hospital were suffering from conditions in which emotional factors were believed to be important (Wittkower & Russell, 1953). Acne, eczema, neurodermatitis, psoriasis, and urticaria are among the skin disorders which are sometimes found to have emotional causation. And Schoenberg and Carr (1963) report some success in treating neurodermatitis patients with psychotherapy designed to help them express their emotions.

The relationship between emotion and skin symptoms was dramatically seen in a young woman who was undergoing psychoanalysis. The patient had an intense but unsatisfied longing for affection. When she felt most frustrated, she sometimes released her feelings in fits of weeping. However, when her weeping was suppressed, she developed urticaria, especially manifested by a swelling of the skin about the face and eyes. With renewed weeping, the urticaria often disappeared (Saul & Bernstein, 1948). An effect of stress on the skin is diagrammed in Figure 5.5.

STUDYING ANXIETY

Anxiety is one of the most important problems in psychology, and it is becoming one of the most studied and written about. The material which follows describes some approaches to the study of anxiety and presents some of the findings these approaches have revealed.

Some Approaches

Some of the earliest information about anxiety was gathered by professionals who treated adjustment problems and described the individuals who came to them for help. More recently, knowledge about anxiety has been acquired through the use of specially devised tests and experimental situations.

Figure 5.5 An effect of stress on the skin is shown here in the record of a woman with urticaria which is a disorder characterized by hives or rash and itching. She was under observation for eighteen months. During this period, her skin condition was found to be related to stress stemming from her interactions with other people, especially her mother-in-law. The major episodes of urticaria coincided with stressful events in which she suppressed her anger. The severity of urticaria is indicated on the vertical axis and ranges from 0 to 4+ (Stevenson & Graham, 1963).

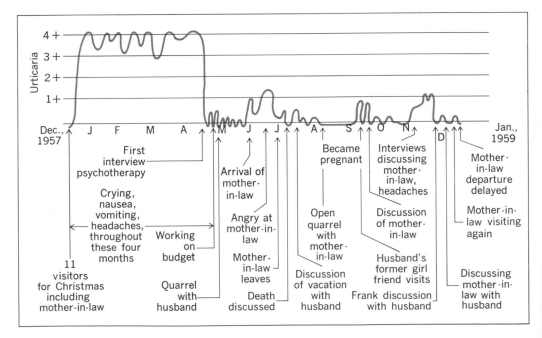

Descriptive Approaches

One way to learn about anxiety is to observe and describe people who say they feel anxious or who are designated as anxious on some other basis. Since none of us is free of anxiety and most of us have some very anxious moments, information about anxiety can come from simply noting our own behavior in threatening situations.

People who have adjustment problems and seek help generally have a heightened level of anxiety, and the therapist is in a good position to study this phenomenon. There are many descriptions of anxious people in the psychological literature. Here is a case history of an anxiety reaction presented by a psychiatrist who describes the patient's anxiety, traces its cause and course, and shows its treatment and outcome.

A twenty-two-year-old married woman was referred to the psychiatrist by a friend of hers. She was an attractive, intelligent young woman who, athough very anxious, was quite sincere in her efforts to find a solution to her problems. She had for some time recognized that her difficulties were on an emotional basis. She said that she feared insanity and that she had become increasingly nervous and disturbed about a multitude of things for the previous six months. Her final decision to seek psychiatric consultation had been precipitated by an anxiety attack which had lasted for about five days. She had been forced to quit her work because of this anxiety and had become increasingly fearful about everything which she had to do. She was apprehensive about such simple things as leaving her home, meeting people, going to bed, greeting her husband, or even answering the doorbell.

She was accompanied to her initial interview by her husband, a merchant.

Because of her anxiety, she had been unable to come to this interview alone. Her repeated anxiety attacks during the previous week had frequently necessitated her calling her husband from his work. She had been able to achieve some measure of comfort only when he was sitting near her. She had often awakened him during the night when she had been unable to sleep and on numerous occasions had called the family physician at all hours of both day and night.

This patient's history, which she herself gave, revealed that she had been married for about six months and felt that her marriage was a successful [and] proper one. Her husband was the head of a thriving business and was obviously quite attached to her and interested in her well-being. She had been a laboratory technician prior to marriage and had graduated some two years previously. She said that she had always performed her work adequately and had left her job only because of the gradual increase in her apprehensiveness. Her family history revealed that she had one sister, three years her senior, who apparently had no emotional problems of consequence. Her parents were living and, as she stated in the initial interview, were happy and well-adjusted people.

The patient spontaneously went on to say that she had always been a moody person who had either been "way up or way down." She said that she had also been inhibited and made friends rather slowly, but got along with them quite well after she established good relationships. She had always been timid in her initial contacts with people for fear of possible resentment or rejection. She was unable to say why they might resent or reject her, but she always refrained from thoroughly accepting others until she had convinced herself that they were truly friendly toward her and that there was no chance that she might be snubbed or ignored.

As the patient described her childhood and adolescence, it soon became evident that in addition to being the youngest child she had also been the favorite, particularly of her father. He had showered many gifts upon her and had never hesitated to show his preference for her. Her mother had been more of the disciplinarian in the family, and in spite of the patient's occasional attempts to be friendly with the mother, the relationship had always been distant and cool. Further elucidation of this area showed that the mother had never been excessively demanding, but had certainly been less permissive than the father. The patient had been able, in the majority of situations, to obtain whatever she wanted and had rarely denied herself anything. If she was unable to obtain whatever she wanted from her mother, it was usualy possible for her to get it from her father. As a result, whenever she had run into frustration, she had always turned to her father. He had constantly praised her and had frequently been her ally against her mother.

This patient said that the majority of her complaints had begun soon after her marriage. As she talked, it became evident that she felt that her husband was not as understanding as she had hoped that he would be. She had discovered, soon after marriage, that their financial status, though adequate, was certainly not unlimited. At times it became necessary for her to deny herself things and such a deprivation had rarely occurred to her prior to marriage. She had also begun to discover that there were many responsibilities which fell to her after marriage that were of a type she had never experienced or expected. Actually these responsibilities stemmed from her husband's normal tendency to expect her to share their marital responsibilities. There had been numerous occasions when the patient had become extremely angry at her husband, stamped her feet, and screamed at him, as she had previously done at her own parents. However, she soon found that her husband did not respond to this in the same "understanding" way as her parents had.

As succeeding interviews passed, it became increasingly evident that she was an extremely narcissistic, selfish, and immature woman, who had never been given the opportunity to learn to carry responsibilities herself. From childhood onward, she had always been able to turn toward her father in times of difficulty and he, in turn, had always provided her with an easy solution, often removing the difficulties of the situation in which she was involved. She had expected the same sort of treatment from her husband, and when it was not forthcoming, had found him wanting in good qualities. She had become increasingly angry at him and, at the same time, entertained some doubts as to the wisdom of choosing him as her marital partner. She had always assumed, unrealistically, that marriage would be a utopian type of existence, and she had fantasied that there would be few responsibilities. Actually, without realizing it, she had expected to get the same kind of treatment from her husband as she had from her father. When reality was presented to her in the form of her husband's reasonable demands, she had become extremely hostile. Much of this hostility remained within her, with only portions of it being expressed in occasional temper outbursts and the remainder of it remaining within her on an unconscious level. It gradually came into conflict with her conscience's demands, and thus she began to feel guilty. The result was that instead of feeling the resentment itself, she began to suffer acute anxiety attacks which, without psychotherapy, might have merged into a true chronic anxiety reaction.

After approximately a dozen interviews, the patient began to recognize her immature strivings and to improve her adjustment in marriage. She could accept her husband's demands more and was willing to attempt to fulfill at least some of them. As her understanding of her own immaturities and unrealistic expectations increased, her anxiety symptoms diminished. She ceased hating and began to use her aggression constructively and to receive the strengthening benefits of love and approval which a healthy environment always gives to maturely behaving people.

In summary, then, this patient had reached adult life and marriage with an immature and unrealistic outlook. Because of her childishness she made excessive demands upon her environment. These had always been sufficiently satisfied in the past, particularly by her father, so that there had been no great reason for the weaknesses of her personality to reveal themselves in the form of anxiety. However, when she married and had to face additional responsibilities, she became chronically dissatisfied and frustrated. This stirred up a great deal of inner resentment, some of which appeared in explosive outbursts, but much of which remained within her, stirring up considerable guilt. Her anxiety appeared as a warning signal to keep the true extent of her inner resentment from becoming evident to her. As is true of many neurotic con-

flicts her anxiety gradually spread to involve new areas of her life until she became almost totally immobilized. However, and this is also typical in many such cases, as her understanding of her own personality and her relationships increased, her anxiety diminished. Her symptoms disappeared and her own desire to mature became more prominent as well as more gratifying.[2]

Relational Approaches

Another way that anxiety has been studied is by relating it to other phenomena. For example, we might be interested in the relationship between anxiety and age. (Are children more anxious than adults?) Or we might be curious about the relationship between anxiety and occupation. (Are

[2] (Reprinted from *Introduction to Psychiatry* by O. Spurgeon English and Stuart M. Finch. By permission of W. W. Norton & Company, Inc. Copyright © 1954, 1957, 1964 by W. W. Norton & Company, Inc. Pp. 155–157 (1957 ed.).)

Figure 5.6 How anxious are Americans? An anxiety questionnaire was adapted and administered in six countries. Mean anxiety scores are shown in the bars. The possible range of scores was from a low of 6 to a high of 30. Numbers in parentheses indicate the size of the group tested in each country. As the bars indicate, Americans had the lowest anxiety scores of any group (Data from Cattell, 1963).

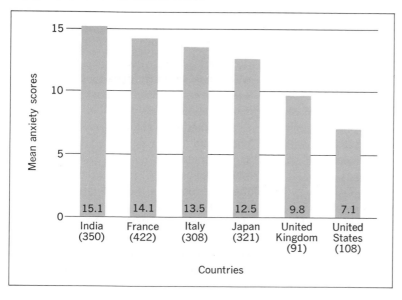

artists more anxious than policemen?) Or we could pursue the relationship between anxiety and culture. (Are Americans more anxious than Frenchmen?)

Some modest information concerning these several questions has been provided by anxiety questionnaires which have been administered to large groups of people. For the relationship between anxiety and age, results indicate that anxiety fluctuates in early childhood. It rises consistently in adolescence and declines through early and middle adulthood. After age sixty or sixty-five, it rises again.

Concerning the relationship between anxiety and occupation, the results do not support Gilbert and Sullivan's operatic claim that "a policeman's lot is not a happy one!" Policemen, engineers, and clerical workers were among those with lower anxiety scores. Occupational groups with higher levels of anxiety included artists, newspaper editors, and air cadets in training.

Concerning the relationship between anxiety and culture, the results did not indicate that Americans were anxiety ridden (see Fig. 5.6). When compared with the subjects of five other countries, Americans proved to have the lowest anxiety scores. The investigator notes, "National comparisons are invidious and notoriously tricky, but these results may possibly fit a theory that low anxiety is associated with better economic level and closer political integration" (Cattell, 1963, p. 104).

Experimental Approaches

In descriptive and relational approaches, people are observed, described, and measured, but no attempt is made to manipulate them or change their behavior. In the experimental approach, subjects are observed under certain controlled conditions to see the effect of these conditions. Such conditions may be created in the laboratory or they may exist in real life.

In the laboratory it is not easy to devise meaningful situations in which anxiety can be elicited and its effects studied. For one thing, there is a limit to the amount of stress to which human subjects can be exposed. Furthermore, as was noted, subjects react differently to stress; a situation which will prove stressful for one person may scarcely affect another.

Many methods have been used to induce stress or anxiety in laboratory situations; just a few examples will be presented here. Some experimenters have devised generally frustrating environments. In one experiment subjects were forced to remain awake all night while they were exposed to a number of other irritating circumstances (Sears, Hovland, & Miller, 1940). Another investigator surreptitiously locked groups of subjects in a room into which smoke was allowed to seep to give the appearance of an outbreak of fire (French, 1944). In a study involving children, the subjects were placed in a room with some very attractive toys which, however, were inaccessible (Barker, Dembo, & Lewin, 1943).

Sometimes subjects are aroused by being told that they are taking an important personality or intelligence test on which they would want to do well, and their performance is compared with that of control subjects given neutral instructions (Sarason & Palola, 1960). After they have been aroused, they may be given very difficult tasks, and they may be arbitrarily failed and criticized (Sarason, 1957).

Some investigators have used the threat of physical pain to induce stress. In one experiment, electrodes were attached to the arm of the subject and he was led to anticipate a series of painful electrical shocks (Sarnoff & Zimbardo, 1961). In another, the subjects were led to believe that the apparatus to which they were affixed was faulty and that they were liable to receive a dangerous charge of electricity (Ax, 1960).

Motion pictures have also been used as sources of threat. In one study, "Wages of Fear," a film depicting the perilous journey of men driving trucks loaded with nitroglycerin, was used to produce stress (Alexander, Flagg, Foster, Clemens, & Blahd, 1961). Another group of experimenters has made wide use of an anthropological film showing painful puberty rites in the Arunta, a Stone Age culture of Australia (Lazarus & Opton, 1966).

The situations described above are not real life, of course. Furthermore, there are some problems inherent in the laboratory use of deception and stress. Psychologists conducting research are expected to follow the code of ethical standards set forth by the American Psychological Association. This code puts restrictions on the experimental use of stress and requires that harmful aftereffects be avoided or removed as soon as possible (Ethical Standards of Psychologists, 1963).

Many stress situations can be observed in real life, but they are usually more difficult to study than those in the laboratory. One set of investigators studied young men who were experiencing the real stress of paratroop training (Basowitz, Persky, Korchin, & Grinker, 1955). Another made an intensive study of the behavior of patients who were undergoing major surgery (Janis, 1958). A third investigated the effect of stress on learning and conditioning by using people (undergraduates, graduates, and staff members of the University of Illinois) who were undergoing real-life events which might be considered anxiety provoking; these included giving oral reports which were part of course requirements, taking preliminary examinations for the doctoral degree, and appearing in a drama before a large audience on opening night (Beam, 1955).

Some Findings

What effect does anxiety have on behavior? Anxiety has been defined as a state of arousal, and the discussion will first consider the effects of arousal in general. We know that in order to get anything done we must rouse ourselves or be aroused to some extent. In such situations we probably would not use the word "arousal," but we might talk about being motivated or getting a move on.

How aroused we need to be depends on the task which confronts us. If we seem too little activated or energized for what is in store, we may give ourselves a pep talk, or somebody else with an interest in the matter may prod us a bit. Sometimes, however, we get so highly aroused that we are unable to act effectively in a particular situation, and we may need to stop racing our motor, simmer down, and cool it.

The idea that there is an optimal level of arousal for a particular task situation has been explored by a number of psychologists. In this connection Woodworth and Schlosberg write:

In a sense, all behavior is organized or patterned; when we say it is disorganized, we are evaluating it in terms of its efficiency in attaining some specific objective that confronts the organism. It is a safe bet that there is an optimum level of activation for each task; it would be low for reading a light novel, higher for working a math problem, and still higher for playing football. Below the optimum level the organism lacks energy, persistence, and concentration, but above this level his performance lacks precision; it is disorganized as far as the task is concerned (1954, p. 111).

A similar idea has been developed by Malmo (1962), who theorizes that there may be an optimal level of activation for a specific individual on a specific task (but this level is not necessarily optimal for another person or on another task). Relatively more or less than this optimal amount leads to a poorer performance. Malmo schematizes his idea in this way:

Activation level	Low	Moderate	High
Expected performance level	Low	Optimal	Low

In an analogous fashion, a number of psychologists have written about the usefulness, even the necessity and attractiveness, of mild or moderate levels of anxiety. Hebb (1955) calls attention to the "positive attraction of risk taking." He says, "When you stop to think of it, it is nothing short of extraordinary what trouble people will go to in order to get into more trouble at the bridge table, or on the golf course. . . ." Mowrer (1953) puts the matter in even stronger terms; he writes that "normal anxiety is the force that keeps driving the personality toward wholeness, toward unity, and toward maximal effectiveness.

It is the force which helps the personality achieve ever higher levels of synthesis, new integrations, and a more stable and durable organization."

Margaret Mead develops the idea that there is an optimal ("right") amount of anxiety for our society as well as for the individuals that make it up. She writes:

It is clear that we have developed a society which depends on having the right amount of anxiety to make it work. Psychiatrists have been heard to say, "He didn't have enough anxiety to get well," indicating that, while we agree that too much anxiety is inimical to mental health, we have come to rely on anxiety to push and prod us into seeing a doctor about a symptom which may indicate cancer, into checking up on that old life insurance policy which may have out-of-date clauses in it, into having a conference with Billy's teacher even though his report card looks all right.

People who are anxious enough keep their car insurance up, have the brakes checked, don't take a second drink when they have to drive, are careful where they go and with whom they drive on holidays. People who are too anxious either refuse to go into cars at all—and so complicate the ordinary course of life—or drive so tensely and overcautiously that they help cause accidents. People who aren't anxious enough take chance after chance, which increases the terrible death toll of the roads.[3]

What does the experimental evidence indicate? First, it tends to support the idea that stress, up to a point, may be helpful in learning and performing certain tasks. Martin (1961) reviews the evidence on this point which has come out of the psychological laboratory. Comparing the

[3] Mead, M. One vote for this age of anxiety. New York Times Magazine, May 20, 1956, p. 13+. © 1956 by The New York Times Company. Reprinted by permission. Pp. 13, 56.

results of many investigators, he notes that the findings are not clear-cut but that they tend to support the generalization that "increasing stress results in improved performance up to a point and impairment thereafter."

Second, the evidence suggests that the characteristic or general anxiety level of the individual must be considered. Reviewing the evidence, Sarason (1960) concludes that, more often than not, subjects with high scores on anxiety scales do more poorly under laboratory stress conditions than subjects with lower scores. Sarason also notes that, compared with low anxious subjects, high anxious ones "have been found to be more self-deprecatory, more self-preoccupied, and generally less content with themselves."

Third, the evidence indicates that the complexity of the task or situation must be considered; performance of more complex tasks is more likely to be impaired by high anxiety than the performance of simpler ones. In situations, for example, where there is only one response, anxious sub-

jects may perform at higher levels than less anxious ones, but in complex situations involving a number of strong, competing responses low anxious subjects may be at an advantage (Martin, 1961; Sarason, 1960).

In this connection it has been observed that individuals of certain characteristic anxiety levels may be at an advantage in a number of situations and at a disadvantage in others. One set of investigators devised a test to measure anxiety specific to testing situations. Using it in a study involving college students, they found that subjects with high anxiety levels did better on course examinations than did less anxious students. In this type of situation the instructor and his demands were known to the class, and the anxious students in particular could alleviate stress by making the necessary preparation. However, in novel test situations, those for which no preparation was possible, the less anxious students did better than the more anxious ones (Sarason & Mandler, 1952).

SUMMARY

Anxiety is a state of arousal caused by a threat to well-being. Stress is a term used interchangeably with anxiety, and a stressor is a condition which may produce threat. People respond with varying amounts of stress to seemingly similar stressors; it has been hypothesized that the amount of stress that a stressor produces is related to the extent to which it interferes with the satisfaction of a need, the strength of the need that is interfered with, whether alternative goals are avail-

able, and the general stress level of the individual.

Anxiety is said to be objective when it is commensurate with the threat posed by a situation and nonobjective when it is not proportional to the threat or when the threat is vague or unknown. Anxiety is considered situational when it occurs only under certain circumstances and general if it pervades the activities of an individual. Anxiety is called acute when it is sharp and intense and also when it is sudden in onset; chronic anxiety describes long-standing elevated states of arousal. Anxiety is referred to as conscious when it is within one's awareness; it is unconscious if it is controlled or defended against in such a way that it is not experienced.

In assessing anxiety, we may utilize patterns of affect, motor, or visceral expression. The visceral changes that take place in stress are primarily produced by the autonomic nervous system; of its two divisions, the parasympathetic is in charge in quiescent states and the sympathetic division takes over during excited states. Some of the most important and most studied stress patterns involve the cardiovascular, gastrointestinal, respiratory, and skin systems.

A number of approaches are used in studying anxiety. In the descriptive approach, anxiety in various people is observed and described. In the relational approach, anxiety is studied by relating it to other phenomena. In the experimental approach, subjects are observed under certain stressful conditions to see what effect these conditions have upon their behavior. The evidence to date tends to support the idea that increasing stress, up to a certain point, produces improvement in the learning and performance of certain tasks, but beyond this point impairment results. Highly anxious subjects tend to do more poorly under laboratory stress conditions than do less anxious subjects. The performance of complex tasks is more likely to be impaired by anxiety than is the performance of simpler ones.

REFERENCES

Alexander, F. Introduction. In F. Alexander, T. M. French, et al. (Eds.), *Studies in Psychosomatic Medicine*. New York: Ronald, 1948. Pp. v–viii.

——. *Psychosomatic Medicine*. New York: Norton, 1950.

——. The development of psychosomatic medicine. *Psychosomatic Medicine,* 1962, **24,** 13–24.

——, Flagg, G. W., Foster, S., Clemens, T., & Blahd, W. Experimental studies of emotional stress. I. Hyperthyroidism. *Psychosomatic Medicine,* 1961, **23,** 104–114.

Ax, A. F. Psychophysiology of fear and anger. *Psychiatric Research Reports,* 1960, **12,** 167–175.

Barker, R. G., Dembo, T., & Lewin, K. Frustration and regression. In R. G. Barker, J. S. Kounin, & H. F. Wright (Eds.), *Child Behavior and Development.* New York: McGraw-Hill, 1943. Pp. 441–458.

Basowitz, H., Persky, H., Korchin, S. J., & Grinker, R. R. *Anxiety and Stress.* New York: McGraw-Hill, 1955.

Beam, J. C. Serial learning and conditioning under real-life stress. *Journal of Abnormal and Social Psychology,* 1955, **51,** 543–551.

Cannon, W. B. *Bodily Changes in Pain, Hunger, Fear and Rage.* (2nd ed.) Newton, Mass.: Branford, 1953.

Carter, R. Mysterious stomach: Always in trouble. *Life,* Nov. 15, 1958. Pp. 148–160.

Cattell, R. B. The nature and measurement of anxiety. *Scientific American,* 1963, **208**(3), 96–104.

—— & Scheier, I. H. *The Meaning and Measurement of Neuroticism and Anxiety.* New York: Ronald, 1961.

Cowen, E. L. Personality, motivation, and clinical phenomena. In L. H. Lofquist (Ed.), *Psychological Research and Rehabilitation*. Washington, D.C.: American Psychological Association, 1960. Pp. 112–171.

English, O. S., & Finch, S. M. *Introduction to Psychiatry*. (2nd ed.) New York: Norton, 1957.

Ethical standards of psychologists. *American Psychologist*, 1963, **18**, 56–60.

French, J. R. P. Authority and frustration. Studies in topological and vector psychology. III. Organized and unorganized groups under fear and frustration. *University of Iowa Studies in Child Welfare*, 1944, **20**, 231–308.

Freud, S. *A General Introduction to Psycho-analysis*. New York: Liveright, 1935.

Fromm-Reichmann, F. Psychiatric aspects of anxiety (1955). Reprinted in D. M. Bullard & E. V. Weigert (Eds.), *Psychoanalysis and Psychotherapy: Selected Papers from Freida Fromm-Reichmann*. Chicago: University of Chicago Press, 1959. Pp. 306–321.

Geer, J. H. The development of a scale to measure fear. *Behavior Research and Therapy*, 1965, **3**, 44–53.

Ham, G. C. Psychosomatic perspectives: The cardiovascular system. *Psychosomatic Medicine*, 1962, **24**, 31–36.

Hebb, D. O. Drives and the C.N.S. (conceptual nervous system). *Psychological Review*, 1955, **62**, 243–254.

Jackson, D. N., & Bloomberg, R. Anxiety: Unitas or multiplex? *Journal of Consulting Psychology*, 1958, **22**, 225–227.

Janis, I. L. *Psychological Stress*. New York: Wiley, 1958.

Kraines, S. H., & Thetford, E. S. *Managing Your Mind*. New York: Macmillan, 1943.

Lacey, J. I., Bateman, D. E., & Van Lehn, R. Autonomic response specificity: An experimental study. *Psychosomatic Medicine*, 1953, **15**, 8–21.

——— & Lacey, B. C. Verification and extension of the principle of autonomic response-stereotypy. *American Journal of Psychology*, 1958, **71**, 50–73.

Lazarus, R. S. *Adjustment and Personality*. New York: McGraw-Hill, 1961.

———, Deese, J., & Osler, S. F. The effects of psychological stress upon performance. *Psychological Bulletin*, 1952, **49**, 293–317.

———, & Opton, E. M., Jr. The study of psychological stress: A summary of theoretical formulations and experimental findings. In C. D. Spielberger (Ed.), *Anxiety and Behavior*. New York: Academic, 1966. Pp. 225–262.

Malmo, R. B. Activation. In A. J. Bachrach (Ed.), *Experimental Foundations of Clinical Psychology*. New York: Basic Books, 1962. Pp. 386–422.

Marcussen, R. M. Vascular headache experimentally induced by presentation of pertinent life experiences: Modification of the course of vascular headache by alterations of situations and reactions. In Association for Research in Nervous and Mental Diseases, *Life Stress and Bodily Disease*. Baltimore: Williams & Wilkins, 1950. Pp. 609–614.

Martin, B. The assessment of anxiety by physiological behavioral measures. *Psychological Bulletin*, 1961, **58**, 234–255.

Mead, M. One vote for this age of anxiety. *New York Times Magazine*, May 20, 1956, pp. 13f.

Mittelmann, B., & Wolff, H. G. Emotions and gastroduodenal function: Experimental study on patients with gastritis, duodenitis and peptic ulcer. *Psychosomatic Medicine*, 1942, **4**, 5–61.

Morgan, C. T. *Introduction to Psychology*. (2nd ed.) New York: McGraw-Hill, 1961.

Mowrer, O. H. Neurosis and psychotherapy as interpersonal process: A synopsis. In O. H. Mowrer (Ed.), *Psychotherapy: Theory and Research*. New York: Ronald, 1953.

Rosenwald, G. C. The assessment of anxiety in psychological experimentation: A theoretical reformulation and test. *Journal of Abnormal and Social Psychology*, 1961, **62**, 666–673.

Sarason, I. G. The effect of anxiety and two kinds of failure on serial learning. *Journal of Personality*, 1957, **25**, 383–392.

———. Empirical findings and theoretical problems in the use of anxiety scales. *Psychological Bulletin*, 1960, **57**, 403–415.

———, & Palola, E. G. The relationship of test and general anxiety, difficulty of task, and experimental instructions to performance. *Journal of Experimental Psychology*, 1960, **59**, 185–191.

Sarason, S. B., & Mandler, G. Some correlates of test anxiety. *Journal of Abnormal and Social Psychology*, 1952, **47**, 810–817.

Sarnoff, I., & Zimbardo, P. G. Anxiety, fear, and social affiliation. *Journal of Abnormal and Social Psychology*, 1961, **62**, 356–363.

Saul, L. J., & Bernstein, C., Jr. The emotional settings of some attacks of urticaria. In F. Alexander, T. M. French, et al. (Eds.), *Studies in Psychosomatic Medicine*, New York: Ronald, 1948. Pp. 424–451.

Schoenberg, B., & Carr, A. C. An investigation of criteria for brief psychotherapy of neurodermatitis. *Psychosomatic Medicine*, 1963, **25**, 253–263.

Sears, R. R., Hovland, C. I., & Miller, N. E. Minor studies of aggression. I. Measurement of aggressive behavior. *Journal of Psychology*, 1940, **9**, 275–295.

Stevenson, I., & Graham, D. T. Disease as response to life stress. II. Obtaining the evidence clinically. In H. Lief, V. Lief, & N. Lief (Eds.), *The Psychological Basis of Medical Practice*. New York: Harper & Row, 1963.

Taylor, J. A. A personality scale of manifest anxiety. *Journal of Abnormal and Social Psychology*, 1953, **48**, 285–290.

Weiss, E., & English, O. S. *Psychosomatic Medicine*. (3rd ed.) Philadelphia: Saunders, 1957.

Weisz, B. *Biology*. New York: McGraw-Hill, 1954.

Wittkower, E., & Russell, B. *Emotional Factors in Skin Disease*. New York: Hoeber-Harper, 1953.

Woodworth, R. S., & Schlosberg, H. *Experimental Psychology*. (2nd ed.) New York: Holt, 1954.

CHAPTER SIX

DEFENSE

We have all felt the necessity of defending ourselves from the criticisms of others. Some people or situations make us especially "defensive." And there are some things about ourselves that we may be especially "sensitive" about.

We can be defensive without even knowing it. A friend may ask us why we're being so defensive, and we may claim we're not. "Who's defensive? I'm not defensive!" we insist. But like Shakespeare's Lady Macbeth, we give ourselves away by protesting too much.

Sometimes, too, we feel the necessity of defending ourselves from ourselves. We may need to justify to ourselves what we have thought or felt or done. Or we may need to protect ourselves against impulses arising within us that could prove disturbing and disrupting.

Defensive operations play an important part in the adjustment process. This chapter will discuss defenses, what they are, how they work, and the ways they help and hamper us.

DEFINING DEFENSE

We are constantly flooded by stimuli arising in our environment and from within ourselves. Of course, we cannot respond to every stimulus. We cannot express every impulse.

We find some of the stimuli in the environment unpleasant, painful, and threatening. If these stimuli are too threatening, we may attempt to defend ourselves against them. Perhaps we avoid them or ignore them or reinterpret them so that we no longer find them so bothersome.

Impulses arising in ourselves also can prove threatening. We may have worrisome thoughts and distressing feelings that we seek to inhibit or modify. We may seek to get a grip on ourselves so that we will not do something we are tempted to do.

Or perhaps we have already done something which has filled us with guilt and remorse. We may seek to atone for it or make some restitution. Or we may attempt to alter the memory of it in some way and see it differently so that we can live with ourselves.

Certain patterns of behavior that are employed for protection against threat or anxiety are called *defenses*. These patterns are sometimes called "defense mechanisms" or "adjustment mechanisms," and they do tend to operate in a machinelike or automatic way (Kroeber, 1963; Murphy et al., 1962). Sometimes they are referred to as "ego defense mechanisms" since they serve to defend the ego or the self from threat.

Patterns which have been identified as defenses are sometimes very simple. For example, Menninger and his colleagues (1963) include such simple expedients as laughing it off and crying it out as "coping devices of everyday living." As this chapter will show, however, many defenses are much more complicated.

As individuals, we vary in the patterns of defense that we show. Fairly early in life each of us develops a repertoire of defenses that characterizes our own individual adjustment (Murphy et al., 1962). Still we may show a preference for certain defenses in certain situations or at certain times (Swanson, 1961).

To the extent that defenses are successful, there will be relief from anxiety. However, our defensive behavior serves us better at some times than at others, and we have relatively unanxious periods interspersed with those in which anxiety is accentuated.

Psychologists, psychiatrists, and other workers in this area sometimes speak of the "strength" of a person's defenses. A person with "strong defenses" is one whose defensive behavior is generally adequate to shield him from debilitating anxieties. A person whose defenses are "weak" or "brittle" tends to be instable and highly vulnerable to stress. "Failing defenses" describes the condition of a person who after a relatively more stable period seems increasingly less able to keep himself free of severe and disrupting anxiety (see Fig. 6.1).

Figure 6.1 Human behavior is complexly determined. A particular response or act may be the result of a number of forces and serve a number of purposes. Almost any bit of behavior may have defensive and nondefensive aspects. However, here for the purposes of illustration, the defensive and nondefensive components of behavior have been separately indicated.

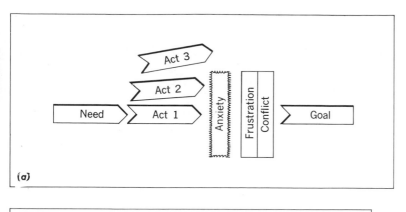

(a)

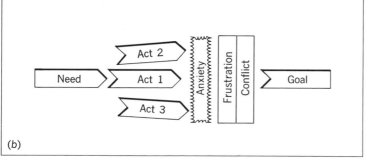

(b)

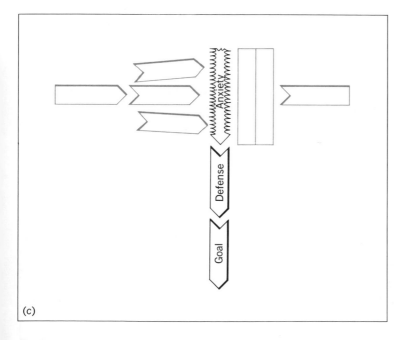

(c)

Figure 6.1 (Continued)

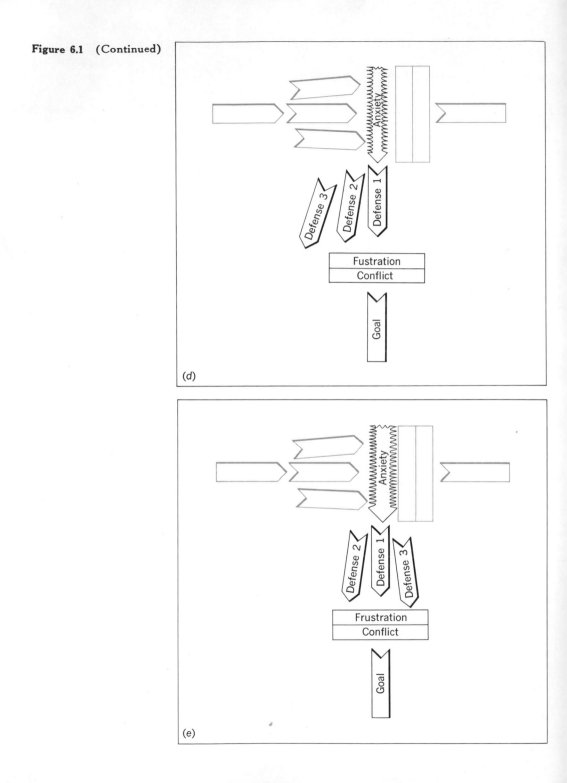

(d)

(e)

STUDYING DEFENSE

Defense is an important concept in adjustment and much has been written about it. But authorities have approached this idea in somewhat different ways. For one thing, there is no agreement on how many sorts of defensive behavior it is useful to describe. Second, it is questioned whether defenses are special sorts of behavior or simply special uses of common processes. Third, there is some difference of opinion about the extent to which defensive actions may be conscious and deliberate. Fourth, there is some disagreement about how pathological defense behavior should be considered.

How Many?

How many separate sorts of defense is it useful to identify? Sigmund Freud, the founder of psychoanalysis and the originator of the concept of defense as we are using it here, first described and emphasized the importance of a single defensive behavior (repression), but later came to believe that this was only one of a number of ways that the person defends himself (S. Freud, 1915, 1936). Throughout the years the list of defenses has grown, and in 1936 Freud's daughter, Anna, who continued her father's work, listed ten defenses (A. Freud, 1936).

Since that time the list has grown longer and longer. In 1952 Hilgard, a prominent psychologist, wrote that the length of the list of defenses that an elementary psychology student knows "depends upon who his teacher is and which textbook he reads." And indeed a survey of eight books on adjustment revealed mention of thirty-two different defenses

with different lists from book to book; only two defenses—repression and rationalization—were noted in all the books, three more were included in seven of the eight books, four in six of the books, and the remaining twenty-three were mentioned by four books or less (Shaffer & Shoben, 1956).

How Special?

How special is defense behavior? Are there certain patterns of behavior that come into operation when we need to defend ourselves from threat and other patterns which operate when we are relatively free from anxiety?

Certain patterns of behavior have been traditionally regarded as defenses, but almost any sort of behavior can be put to defensive and nondefensive uses. Identification, for example, usually finds a place in lists of defense mechanisms, yet identification plays an important role in the development of every human being. Earlier, aggression was described as an important motive, and its use is not necessarily defensive; however, a person may use aggression to protect himself from threat. (The best defense is a good offense.)

Some writers have suggested that defenses should not be considered special mechanisms; rather they should be thought of as special uses of common patterns of behavior (Kroeber, 1963; Lampl-De Groot, 1957). Used in one way, a pattern might be considered defensive; used in another it might not. And in some situations it might serve both defensive and nondefensive purposes.

Other writers have noted that human behavior is the result of many forces and may serve a number of purposes. Almost nothing one does is simply defensive or nondefensive. Almost any bit of behavior may have its defensive and nondefensive aspect.

Schafer expresses this viewpoint well when he writes:

> The conceptual separation of the defensive aspects of behavior from its impulse (nondefensive) aspects, while useful and justifiable, should not be misunderstood to imply that there is such a thing as defense in itself. All human behavior must be thought of as multiply determined, as being the resultant of a number of psychological forces. In the case of any psychological phenomenon, defensive efforts may constitute some of the forces behind it but certainly not all of them. Consequently, we cannot say of any behavior item or trend simply that it is a "defense" —except as a shorthand way of saying that its defensive aspect is particularly striking, relevant or crucial. . . . Defenses or defensive operations are therefore abstractions we make from total, multiply determined behavior. Of any piece of behavior we may ask: In what ways, to what extent, and how well does it serve a defensive function?[1]

Kubie (1952) points out that defensive patterns themselves are hardly separable from one another; rather they are highly interrelated and interdependent processes. Where one defense process is emphasized but proves inadequate, another or several others may be accentuated to bolster and supplement it. In many situations a person's defensive operations are so involved that they are not easily described in terms of individual patterns at all; they appear to be complex mixtures or amalgamations of a number of patterns.

[1] Schafer, R. Psychoanalytic Interpretation in Rorschach Testing. New York: Grune & Stratton, 1954. By permission. Pp. 162–163.

How Unconscious?

Defensive operations are traditionally described as taking place automatically and without the person's insight or awareness. In fact, it is generally believed that the purpose of the defense is to keep an impulse or set of impulses from consciousness and open expression. Only when a defense failed would the person become aware of the impulse.

In this scheme of things, operations that are more conscious (or deliberate) are classified separately. Such operations are sometimes called "coping," "adaptive," or "task oriented." Operations of this nature are supposedly designed not to block an impulse but to discharge it—usually in a modulated or tempered form.

However, much of a person's behavior does not seem either conscious or unconscious in motivation, either deliberate or nondeliberate, either voluntary or involuntary. There may be varying degrees of insight and conscious control. In the same way, much of one's impulse life does not seem either completely blocked or completely spontaneous. There are varying degrees of blockage and modulation. The discussion which follows includes operations of varying degrees of consciousness and modulation.

How Pathological?

In many accounts, the impression can easily be gained that defense patterns are signs of maladjustment. Anxiety itself is frequently pictured as "bad," and since defenses come into operation to protect us from too much anxiety, defensive processes themselves can be considered bad, pathological, or at least an indicator of pathology.

We know, too, from our everyday experience that some sorts of defensive behavior are widely regarded as signs of weakness or poor adjustment. They may be considered "symptoms" of certain underlying pathological conditions.

However, everyone experiences anxiety and somehow has to handle it. In other words, we are all called upon to defend ourselves from threats in the environment and from certain impulses arising within ourselves. All of us make some use of defensive behavior.

It has already been suggested that defenses should not be considered special mechanisms but, rather, special uses of common patterns of behavior. And the use of defensive behavior is not necessarily pathological or bad; badness or goodness depends on its overall effect in a particular situation. In one situation a particular defense might be thought to serve a person well by protecting him against anxiety which might overwhelm him and disrupt his functioning; in another it might be held to serve him poorly by preventing him from facing and solving a soluble problem.

SOME IMPORTANT DEFENSES

This section will discuss a number of defenses or defensive aspects of behavior that seem particularly common or particularly important in the adjustment process.

Suppression

We cannot respond to every stimulus or express every impulse to which we are subject. For one thing, we do not have enough time or energy to do so. For another, some of our impulses may be unacceptable to us or threatening to our general well-being.

One of the ways that we have of dealing with threatening impulses is to make a deliberate effort to inhibit them. We may, for example, be occupied with a bothersome thought or obsessed with some worry, and we attempt to put it out of mind. We may feel that we are about to break down and cry, but we struggle to hold back our tears because we don't want to give the appearance of weakness. Or, perhaps, we are about to lash out at someone but we count to ten to give ourselves time to cool off.

Behaving in this way, that is, effortfully inhibiting the expression of a threatening impulse, is called *suppression*. As the definition implies, suppression is a relatively conscious or voluntary process. The person is aware of the threatening impulse and makes an effort to control or suppress it.

Suppressive efforts, of course, are not always successful. Despite attempts to achieve peace of mind, we find ourselves occupied with threatening thoughts and feelings. Despite the struggle for self-control, we indulge in actions which cause us trouble and regret.

Sometimes suppression works or continues to work only if it is combined with other efforts. We may be able to suppress a particularly bothersome thought only if we keep ourself busily occupied with other thoughts and activities. And we may be able to suppress a particular action only if we avoid environments which seem to stimulate it; for example, we get along with some people only by keeping out of their way and seeing them as little as possible.

We use suppression a great deal in everyday life. We close our eyes to unpleasant sights. We deafen our ears to criticism. In conversations, we sometimes deliberately choose pleasant topics, and when we hit upon material which provokes anxiety, we change the subject by tacit or explicit agreement. For example, at a party the conversation may get around to the subject of cancer, or heart attacks, or nuclear destruction, and somebody will ask that the subject be changed to something more pleasant (Dollard & Miller, 1950).

Suppression is a useful and necessary mechanism. Every society requires its individuals to inhibit or modify their impulses in some way. Some people run into difficulty because they lack the ability to make certain suppressions.

All of us have had troublesome thoughts or worries which have kept us from working effectively. It has been suggested that suppression is a defense that can be perfected and used to give us "mental freedom" (Dollard & Miller, 1950). Through practice we can learn to remove our attention from one thing and focus it on something else. Appropriate use of suppression occurs when there is a task that must be done and when other matters competing for attention are insoluble or may be postponed. Freed, at least for awhile from other problems, we can become absorbed in the more urgent activity.

Of course, not all uses of suppression are beneficial. Some people seem overly inhibited or overly suppressed in one or more areas of living. Suppressions can be detrimental when their effect is to push away a problem that should be faced. Constantly shunted aside, many adjustment problems grow less manageable, and the momentary relief that suppression brings can be purchased at considerable cost to future happiness.

Repression

The process of inhibition is not always conscious and deliberate. Sometimes it appears to occur automatically, without the individual's awareness. The automatic inhibition of a threatening impulse is called *repression*.

Although automatic, noninsightful inhibitions are classified as repressions while deliberate, insightful ones are called suppressions, actual behavior is seldom so neatly dichotomous. Frequently, there is partial insight or semiawareness of defense processes. Sometimes, too, an impulse which is usually well repressed becomes bothersome, and one needs to take more deliberate actions to contain it.

Suppression is easily understood, but the concept of repression is more difficult to grasp and accept; indeed, many psychologists have challenged the usefulness or validity of this idea (MacKinnon & Dukes, 1962). Dollard and Miller have suggested that repression can be understood as a process in which the person prevents himself from *thinking* about something which would be painful or threatening just as in some instances he prevents himself from *doing* something which might cause pain or embarrassment. They state:

Repression is somewhat harder to understand than other symptoms because we are not used to considering the stopping of thinking as a response. We cannot point to it and study it in the same way that we can examine overt responses.

Yet to stop talking is obviously a response. Everyone has had the experience of catching himself just in time before blurting out something he would have regretted saying. It is possible to learn either to stop talking about certain limited subjects or to stop talking altogether in some situations. According to our hypothesis, stopping thinking is a similar response (1950, p. 203).

A pattern of behavior may have been so heavily punished in the past or so associated with unhappy experience that the person prevents himself from expressing it in any way. Aggressive behavior, for example, is frequently severely disciplined and, as a consequence, can be severely repressed. In a similar way, early sex behavior may have been the occasion of considerable unhappiness and punishment, with considerable subsequent repression.

Like attempts at suppression, repressive efforts are not always successful. Heightened anxiety levels and bursts of anxiety are commonly interpreted by clinicians as evidence of failing repressions. In the same way, some individuals who suffer from chronically elevated anxiety are thought to have considerable but precarious repressions.

Some sudden changes in behavior are also interpreted as failures in repression (and, as will be seen later, as failing reaction formations). For example, a generally meek individual may show a sudden and violent outburst of anger that may surprise others and himself as well. Or a relatively kind and gentle person may do something that seems very cruel and very much out of character.

Slips of the tongue and pen, lapses in memory, and certain mishaps or accidents have also been attributed to the workings of (and weakenings in) repression. Such occurrences have been held by Freud (1904) and others to be evidence of incomplete repressions. Brenner writes:

A slip of the tongue or a slip of the pen is often the consequence of a failure to repress completely some unconscious thought or wish. In such cases the speaker or writer expresses what he would have unconsciously liked to say or write, despite his attempt to keep it hidden. Sometimes the hidden meaning is openly expressed in the slip, that is to say, it is clearly intelligible to the listener or reader. On other occasions the result of the lapse is not intelligible and the hidden meaning can only be discovered from the associations of the person who made the slip (1955, p. 146).

Everyone has probably caught himself saying something he did not consciously mean to say. A student who flunked a course wrote to his teacher as follows: "I could register for the *curse* in Summer School if I had to" (Vaughan, 1952). Perhaps we "forget" to check essential materials out of the library, thereby neatly resolving the conflict between studying or not studying over the weekend. Or maybe we do something "accidentally" which somebody else may claim was accidentally on purpose.

Like suppression, repression serves us by defending us from threatening impulses. It prevents us from thinking distressing thoughts, from feeling distressing feelings, and from engaging in certain actions which might prove dangerous or painful. It helps us hide our thoughts and feelings and actions from ourselves just as we sometimes more consciously attempt to conceal certain things from others.

Repression can prove detrimental in

the long run for a number of reasons. Problems that are kept out of awareness cannot be faced and solved. In addition to the use of this mechanism, we may have to restrict our lives in various ways and use other defenses to prevent the inhibited impulses from finding expression. Energy consumed in the process might otherwise be available for the activities of everyday living. Repression brings some relief from anxiety, but it can also restrict, impoverish, and distort behavior (Cameron & Magaret, 1951).

Whether repression is good or bad depends upon the uses that are made of it. Hall notes what happens when there is a considerable reliance on this defense:

> Although repression is necessary for normal personality development and is used to some extent by everyone, there are people who depend upon it to the exclusion of other ways of adjusting to threats. These people are said to be repressed. Their contacts with the world are limited and they give the impression of being withdrawn, tense, rigid, and guarded. Their lips are set and their movements are wooden. They use so much of their energy in maintaining their far-flung repressions that they do not have very much left over for pleasurable and productive interactions with the environment and with other people (1954, p. 88).

Lying

Throughout life we constantly struggle to understand ourselves. The reasons for our behavior are often unknown or unclear. For a particular bit of behavior there may be a dozen plausible reasons.

At the same time we are constantly called upon to explain our actions to others: Why did you do that? How could you do such a thing? Why do you feel that way? Where did you ever get such an idea?

How much of the truth do we know? How much of the truth do we tell others? How much of the truth do we tell ourselves? And how much do we need to lie?

Lying, as a defense, refers to the deliberate use of falsehood to prevent threat to one's well-being. The liar attempts to bring about a false belief which would be to his own benefit. Like suppression, lying is generally thought of as a conscious process; the liar knows that he is lying; although he attempts to deceive another person, he himself is not deceived.

The very young child does not make a sharp distinction between reality and fantasy, between truth and untruth. Stone and Church write:

> It is because the preschool child's world is a mélange of what to the adult are fact and fiction, shot through with magical potentialities, that the child may seem to adults uninstructed in his ways to be playing free and easy with the truth. During most of this period, however, the very notion of an untruth is inconceivable to the child. A preschool child will have a very hard time complying with an adult's request that he repeat a statement such as "the snow is black," although he could enjoy pretending that snow is black. When, however, the child's own wishes conflict with reality, reality is likely to yield. If the child can make things so merely by thinking or saying them, then his claim that he has performed an assigned task or his denial that he has committed a misdeed is sufficient to do or undo the action in question. The young child can create past history—not to mention a present and a future—by waving the wand of his tongue. But he is not lying, in the sense of thinking one thing and saying another (1957, pp. 158–159).

As the child grows older he becomes better able to tell the difference between what is true and what is not. Demands are placed upon him to always tell the truth and never lie. But, paradoxically enough, demands are also placed upon him to recognize situations in which he should not tell the truth since certain sorts of lies are a prominent part of our life. Woolf (1949) writes, "What education really demands and teaches the child is to know when not to lie, when not to tell the truth and when a lie is necessary." He presents the following example:

> *A mother told me the following story of her four-year-old son. The family were expecting a young girl and her fiancé to call. The child overheard the comment that while the fiancé was nice, he had an ugly long nose which spoiled his looks. In the evening, when the couple was sitting in the drawing room with the family, the child approached the fiancé with a stick in his hand and said as he touched the young man's nose with it: "This has to be cut off." The little boy behaved with calm and assurance and without the slightest awareness of the embarrassment caused by his unsuitable veracity. He was later enlightened, in rather an awkward manner, about the possible negative consequences of truthfulness in real life. His veracity was described to him as insolence and terrible rudeness, and this new point of view was confirmed by suitable "educational measures" (1949, p. 266).*

George Washington is reputed to have never told a lie. Probably nobody (except a liar) would claim to have equaled that record. Many of us have never stopped to consider what part falsehood plays in our general adjustment. If we do think about it, we will probably admit to having made some use of lying as a defense against threat.

Even those of us who pride ourselves on our honesty may confess to an occasional benign or white lie, that is, one which we feel is trivial, not harmful, or even for someone else's benefit. Even so, we might have to admit that such a lie was for our own benefit as well, that it served our purposes to tell it.

Much of our lying is accomplished by omission rather than by commission. We may justify omitting the truth by saying that what people don't know won't hurt them. Karpman calls this "implied lying." He writes:

> *This is a form of lying which consists of merely maintaining silence, of refraining from telling the truth rather than the actual telling of an untruth. It is more correctly called dissembling or dissimulation. A person may say, "I didn't tell you about this before, but—" and then proceed to confess some past action, the absence of your knowledge of which had led you to form an entirely different impression of his behavior than that which is now disclosed by his retarded admission of this or that reprehensible action (1949, p. 147).*

A similar way of lying is by telling a half-truth. This is usually a statement that is not really false in itself, but which is designed to be interpreted or misinterpreted in a way that will be beneficial to the teller. For example, suppose there is an important book which we should be conversant with; we did buy a copy, but we have never opened it. A colleague asks us if we have read it, and we answer that we have a copy of it at home. We hope that he will assume that we have read it and let the matter rest there.

Telling the truth, the whole truth, and nothing but the truth is not easy. Honesty is valued by our culture, but so are other qualities with which honesty sometimes conflicts. So, for example, is politeness, and it is sometimes impossible to be both polite and completely honest.

From the standpoint of adjustment it is useful to try to understand the push behind a lie. To what extent is it simply a polite convention? To what extent is it benevolent and designed to help another? To what extent is it defensive and used to get oneself out of a difficult or threatening situation?

Rationalization

Not all misrepresentations can be considered conscious and deliberate. The reason for a particular bit of behavior may be unknown or unclear. Or there may be a number of possible explanations. In such situations it is perhaps only natural that the person leans toward explanations which are socially and personally acceptable.

Interpreting behavior in an acceptable way in order to prevent a threat to one's sense of well-being is called *rationalization*. Unlike lying, which is a conscious process, rationalization is usually considered to operate without the individual's full insight or awareness. The liar attempts to deceive others, but he himself is not deceived. By contrast, the rationalizer deceives others and himself as well.

It is frequently difficult to classify a bit of behavior as either a lie or a rationalization. Sometimes we seem to half deceive ourselves. We may not be completely satisfied with the way we have explained things. Are we fooling ourselves? Maybe we are. But, then again, maybe we're not.

How do we know if we are rationalizing? If there are two or four or eight possible reasons, how can we know whether a particular one is real or rationalized. Jourard (1963) suggests that a person may be rationalizing if his announced aim and the consequences of his behavior do not agree, if there are other possible explanations for his behavior, and if he refuses to consider them. For example, a parent may steadfastly maintain that his severe and arbitrary disciplinary policies are for his child's own good even though there is considerable evidence that the child is suffering because of them.

Consider the numerous opportunities that you have to employ rationalization in the course of a single day. Although you have vaguely decided to go on a diet, you sit down to a large breakfast of fried ham and hot cakes dripping with syrup and melted butter because, as you tell yourself, everyone needs a good breakfast to start the day right. In your first class you decide not to take notes because you never seem to get very much out of them anyway. Between classes you go to the snack bar rather than the reserve room because the book you need will probably be checked out already. The waitress forgets to add the price of dessert to your lunch check, but you decide not to call this to her attention because it wasn't very good anyway.

In the afternoon you get into a bridge game with some other students, and when your partner criticizes you for making a couple of stupid mistakes, you announce that you're glad that you don't take the game as seriously as all that. In the evening you sit down to study for a test on the following day, but you can't concentrate. Well, you tell yourself, it's too late to cram now. If you don't know it now, you never will. Besides it would be better to take it easy this evening, relax, and go into the test with a clear head. So off you go to a movie.

Malingering

All or almost all of us have been sick, but our experience with illness has doubtless varied. It would appear to go without saying that a person would rather be well than sick. On reflection, though, such a preference would seem to depend in part on how ill we're treated when we're well and how well we're treated when we're ill. For some individuals, sicknesses are not a completely unrewarding state of affairs.

One of the ways that we have of adjusting to difficult situations and protecting ourselves from threat is by pretending to be ill. Removal of a threat or anxiety by feigning illness is called *malingering*. Like suppression and lying, this defense is usually thought of as a conscious one; the person is not deceived himself, but he attempts to deceive others.

Samuel Clemens (Mark Twain) clearly and vividly describes this defense in Tom Sawyer:

Monday morning found Tom Sawyer miserable. Monday morning always found him so—because it began another week's slow suffering in school. He generally began that day with wishing he had had no intervening holiday, it made the going into captivity and fetters again so much more odious.

Tom lay thinking. Presently it occurred to him that he wished he was sick; then he could stay home from school. Here was a vague possibility. He canvassed his system. No ailment was found, and he investigated again. This time he

thought he could detect colicky symptoms, and he began to encourage them with considerable hope. But they soon grew feeble, and presently died wholly away. He reflected further. Suddenly he discovered something. One of his upper front teeth was loose. This was lucky; he was about to begin to groan, as a "starter," as he called it, when it occurred to him that if he came into court with that argument, his aunt would pull it out, and that would hurt. So he thought he would hold the tooth in reserve for the present, and seek further. Nothing offered for some little time, and then he remembered hearing the doctor tell about a certain thing that laid up a patient for two or three weeks and threatened to make him lose a finger. So the boy eagerly drew his sore toe from under the sheet and held it up for inspection. But now he did not know the necessary symptoms. However, it seemed well worth while to chance it, so he fell to groaning with considerable spirit.

But Sid slept on unconscious.

Tom groaned louder, and fancied that he began to feel pain in the toe.

No result from Sid.

Tom was panting with his exertions by this time. He took a rest and then swelled himself up and fetched a succession of admirable groans.

Sid snored on.

Tom was aggravated. He said, "Sid, Sid!" and shook him. This course worked well, and Tom began to groan again. Sid yawned, stretched, then brought himself up on his elbow with a snort, and began to stare at Tom. Tom went on groaning. Sid said:

"Tom! Say, Tom!" [No response.] "Here, Tom! Tom! What is the matter, Tom?" And he shook him and looked in his face anxiously.

Tom moaned out:

"Oh, don't, Sid. Don't joggle me."

"Why, what's the matter, Tom? I must call auntie."

"No—never mind. It'll be over by and by, maybe. Don't call anybody."

"But I must! Don't groan so, Tom, it's awful. How long you been this way?"

"Hours. Ouch! Oh, don't stir so, Sid, you'll kill me."

"Tom, why didn't you wake me sooner? Oh, Tom, don't! It makes my flesh crawl to hear you. Tom, what is the matter?"

"I forgive you everything, Sid. [Groan.] Everything you've ever done to me. When I'm gone——"

"Oh, Tom, you ain't dying, are you? Don't, Tom——oh, don't. Maybe——"

"I forgive everybody, Sid. [Groan.] Tell 'em so, Sid. And Sid, you give my window-sash and my cat with one eye to that new girl that's come to town, and tell her——"

But Sid had snatched his clothes and gone. Tom was suffering in reality, now, so handsomely was his imagination working, and so his groans had gathered quite a genuine tone.

Sid flew down-stairs and said:

"Oh, Aunt Polly, come! Tom's dying!"

"Dying!"

"Yes'm. Don't wait——come quick!"

"Rubbage! I don't believe it!"

But she fled up-stairs, nevertheless, with Sid and Mary at her heels. And her face grew white, too, and her lip trembled. When she reached the bedside she gasped out:

"You, Tom! Tom, what's the matter with you?"

"Oh, auntie, I'm——"

"What's the matter with you——what is the matter with you, child?"

"Oh, auntie, my sore toe's mortified!"

The old lady sank down into a chair and laughed a little, then cried a little, then did both together. This restored her and she said:

"Tom, what a turn you did give me. Now you shut up that nonsense and climb out of this."

The groans ceased and the pain vanished from the toe. The boy felt a little foolish, and he said:

"Aunt Polly, it seemed mortified, and it hurt so I never minded my tooth at all."

"Your tooth, indeed! What's the matter with your tooth?"

"One of them's loose, and it aches perfectly awful."

"There, there, now, don't begin that groaning again. Open your mouth. Well—— your tooth is loose, but you're not going to die about that. Mary, get me a silk thread, and a chunk of fire out of the kitchen."

Tom said:

"Oh, please auntie, don't pull it out. It don't hurt any more. I wish I may never stir if it does. Please don't, auntie. I don't want to stay home from school" (1929, pp. 50–53).

In the same way, many of us have pretended to have a headache in order to avoid a situation that may be boring or threatening, or, once we are in the situation, the "headache" conveniently furnishes us with an excuse to leave. A "backache" has been used by more than one soldier (but not always successfully) as an excuse to get out of a hike or a run through the obstacle course.

Pretending to be ill may serve to get us the attention, sympathy, or nurturance that we might not otherwise receive. Like Tom Sawyer, we can overdo this defense and tax the patience and credulity of those who are exposed to it, but it is difficult to disprove an ache or pain or some other such vaguely defined malady. In fact, the malingerer himself may become half convinced of the validity of his complaints.

Adjustment by Ailment

Sometimes, without any conscious pretense, we may feel ill even though the doctor can find nothing physically wrong. Or perhaps we feel more ill or more incapacitated than we should from a particular ailment. Or we get well more slowly than we should.

The relatively noninsightful use of illness, imaginary or real, as a way of averting anxiety is called *adjustment by ailment.* Unlike malingered conditions which are deliberate pretenses, adjustments by ailment imply no conscious deceit. In this latter defense the individual is unaware of the psychological implications of his behavior.

In actual practice, however, it may be difficult to distinguish between malingering and adjustment by ailment. Some situations appear to contain elements of both, and an act of malingering may gradually shade into adjustment by ailment as we slowly convince ourselves that we are indeed as ill as we were pretending to be. For example, we may be searching for an excuse to avoid attending a trying social or professional function. If we were ill, we tell ourselves, we wouldn't have to go. Well, we already feel a little upset. The more we think about it, the more upset we become. Finally, we decide that we really are sick; we thus spare ourselves the pain of going to the function as well as the pain of admitting that we didn't want to go.

In anxious states the body's functioning is upset, and it is easy to imagine illness. An upset cardiovascular system may convince us that we have heart disease or at least a severe headache. An upset digestive tract may lead us to believe that we have a stomachache or indigestion. Overwhelmed by problems, we indeed feel tired, worn out, and sick. Describing a trying experience, we may say, "I was just sick about it," and mean it both figuratively and literally.

This defense protects us from threat in various ways. We may use an imaginary ailment to take our attention away from an anxiety-provoking problem. We may use the "ailment" as an excuse to avoid an unpleasant situation or once in the situation, to get out of it with no loss of face. Sometimes an imaginary ailment serves to attract the attention and sympathy of others. And occasionally we employ it to punish ourselves and rid ourselves of feelings of guilt.

Simulated ailments may help us to handle difficult situations but, to the extent that they are successful in doing so, they make it unnecessary for us to face our real problems and attempt to solve them. With extensive reliance on this defense, we may become a chronic "psychological" invalid. Not only psychological problems but real medical problems as well may go unattended because of the masking effect of imaginary ones.

Fixation

In the process of growing up we move through a number of stages: infancy, childhood, adolescence, and adulthood. Each succeeding stage offers new opportunities and carries additional responsibilities. Some individuals move continually forward, enjoying the opportunities and accepting the responsibilities afforded by each stage. Others, caught up in frustrations, conflicts, and anxieties, become arrested at a particular stage. And a few, under the pressure of problems, may move backward into earlier, more manageable stages.

Fixation refers to the continuation of a pattern of behavior which has become immature or inappropriate. A person who uses fixation as a defense responds to threat by adhering to old ways of doing things rather than trying out those which would be more suited to the situation at hand. In the face of threat the fixated person is unable or unwilling to vary his behavior, and the greater the threat the more fixated he may appear.

People vary in the extent and duration of their fixations. Some appear to be fixated in many ways or in a number of areas of adjustment, while others show a very few fixated patterns. Furthermore, fixations may be relatively enduring, or they may be quite temporary and transient.

If a person has made extensive use of fixation, he will appear to be generally immature. You may know someone who is chronologically an adult, but who acts more like an adolescent. Or someone who, although not immature in his behavior, rigidly adheres to the same habits of living and is relatively closed to new experience. As one grows older, he tends to get more fixed or set in his ways.

Fixations can occur at any level of development. Those which date from early development, of course, will appear less age appropriate than those which take place later on. Some of us may have been told: Grow up and act your age! But the charge (or insult) is more serious if we're accused of acting like a baby than if we are said to be behaving like a child.

Most fixations are relatively limited and affect only part of one's life. For example, consider the situation of a young man who has completed college, has a responsible and well-paid position, and participates widely in community activities. But he lives at home, has quite a close relationship with his mother, shows very little interest in young women of his own age, and on the few occasions on which he does date, he feels awkward and uncomfortable. Although he is immature in his heterosexual relationships, he is able to function adequately in a number of other areas of daily life.

An instructor who defined fixation as "arrested development" received the following test response from a student: "Fixation is a rest in development" (Vaughan, 1952). And this is a positive value of fixation. One cannot always make steady progress in every area of adjustment. Sometimes there is a need to combine partial progress with partial fixation. Sappenfield sums this up very nicely:

> Continued fixation at a particular level of adjustment in some areas of behavior may provide the feeling of security that is required as a basis for the individual's progression to a higher level of adjustment in some other area of behavior. The individual may progress in certain respects while remaining fixated in other respects; after a particular progressive adjustment has been "consolidated," so that he feels secure in this adjustment, he may then progress in other respects (1954, p. 265).

Of course, fixations are a serious matter if they are relatively widespread and enduring or if they affect important areas of functioning. Persons fixated at immature levels do not become adults in the complete psychological sense of this word. They may be unable to fully accept the responsibilities of adult status and unable to fully participate in its rewards.

Regression

Sometimes we progress but find ourselves threatened by our new experiences. When we encounter frustration, conflict, and anxiety, perhaps we tend to withdraw or retreat. Since present patterns of behavior seem inadequate, responses which were rewarding in the past may be renewed and relied on.

Regression refers to the recovery of a pattern of behavior which was characteristic of an earlier level of development. Used as a defense, regression implies that the individual finds his present behavior threatening and reinstates responses which had seemingly been outgrown. The regressed person appears, then, to be functioning in an age-inappropriate way (see Fig. 6.2).

It is not uncommon for a child to show some regression upon the birth of a sibling. A considerable amount of the parents' attention may be given over to the new baby, leaving the older child with feelings of deprivation. Although he has been walking for several years, suddenly he may insist that he is unable to do so, that he is too little and must be carried.

Baby talk which has been largely outgrown crops up again, and toilet habits may be abandoned. Such regressions may be interpreted as attempts to regain lost attention or status.

Fixation and regression are somewhat similar; both imply the use of behavior which is relatively immature or inappropriate. In fixation, however, the individual has not progressed beyond a certain level, while in regression he has advanced beyond the level but then retreats. The young man who never formed age-appropriate relations with young women was said to be fixated. Contrast this example with that of a young woman who tries but finds it impossible to meet the demands of marriage and regresses by returning home to her parents.

Regression is encouraged by the human tendency to selectively repress un-

Figure 6.2 Frustration and regression (© United Feature Syndicate, Inc., 1956).

pleasant memories while allowing pleasant ones free expression. People frequently long for the good old days. Old graduates at class reunions grow nostalgic for their college days. They talk about the football games, parties, and the night of the raid on the girl's dormitory, but fail to recall the examinations, term papers, and financial privation.

Like fixations, regressions may be relatively permanent and widespread or considerably more momentary and limited in their effects. All of us make some use of temporary, partial, or limited regressions. In recreation we retreat from the responsibilities and cares of everyday living and regress to play activities, to games and sports and hobbies. At a convention or party we may let down our hair and engage in unadult antics. And almost anyone in extreme provocation may indulge in a childish display of anger, tears, or other feelings.

It has been suggested that the healthy, mature, and creative adult has the ability to be childlike when he wants to be; that is, he has the ability to voluntarily regress and recapture the qualities of childhood (Kris, 1952; Maslow, 1958; Schafer, 1958). He can be completely spontaneous, vigorously emotional, and uncritically enthusiastic; he can engage in great nonsense and wild fantasy. Then he can become controlled, rational, critical, sensical, and realistic again (in short, grown-up) (Maslow, 1958).

When regressions are involuntary, they are of more dangerous consequence. Regression may become relatively permanent. It may encompass a number of areas of adjustment. It may involve a retreat to very early patterns of behavior. Adjustments have been noted in which there is a general regression to childish or even infantile levels of functioning. In extreme cases, the regressed individual may be completely unable to take care of himself.

Identification

Our lives are bound up with the lives of others. We share in the lives of the people close to us and these people, in turn, share in our lives. To some extent, their successes are our successes, their failures are our failures, and our successes and failures are theirs.

Identification is a general term which refers to the various ways in which we establish a oneness with another person, group, or object. We are said to "identify" with another person when we model our behavior after him and become like him. We also identify when we regard another person as an extension of ourselves so that, in a sense, what happens to this person also happens to us.

Used as a defense, identification implies that we feel threatened and respond by drawing upon the valued qualities of others. We may copy their patterns in order to enhance ourselves. Or we may establish or emphasize a mutual identity which in some way leads to our own enhancement.

Just as we grow physically by ingesting food, our personality grows by taking in or introjecting the forms of behavior that we are exposed to (Szasz, 1957). Small children model their behavior after their parents, their siblings, and other people with whom they come in contact. Behavior that is seen as having successful consequences and models who are highly rewarding and highly regarded are especially apt to be copied (Bandura & Walters, 1963).

Probably all of us have seen some little girl enacting the identity of her mother. She makes up with her mother's lipstick, dresses in her mother's clothes, and totters about in her mother's high heels. She cares for her dolls as her mother cares for her, addressing them with the same words and in the same tones. She sets the table, pours the "tea," and even gossips with the imaginary guests (perhaps in a way that mother may find a little too identical).

Boys frequently express the desire to be like their fathers. They wish to be as big as their fathers and have their fathers' strength or privileges or material possessions. Boys copy, share in, and draw on their fathers' accomplishments. ("*My* dad can lick *your* dad!" "Oh yeah, my dad can lick the whole world with one finger!")

Parents identify with their children and share in their children's accomplishments. The father who was unable to complete school may pride himself on his children's education. Their diplomas can mean more to him than his own ever could. A mother whose own career or marriage has been a failure may identify closely with her daughter; the mother may direct her daughter's progress and share in her success.

We identify with groups as well as with other people. We may identify with our neighborhood or school, our gang or club, our race or religious designation, and our state or country. Sometimes such identifications are painful or embarrassing for us, and we struggle to disidentify ourselves and form new, more acceptable identifications.

Identification can be a very open and conscious process or it can be a very subtle one into which we have only a limited insight. And we may identify with someone or something only in part or seemingly completely. For example, the enthusiastic fan at a football game is more than a spectator; with ten seconds left and goal to go, he is as poised and ready as any man on the field to get that ball over the goal line.

We pattern ourselves after prestigious and accomplished models, those who are successful in reaching the goals that we may be struggling for. In effecting a model's behavior, we may be able to attain his successes. Or, at least, he may reward us for our efforts (or punish us less) or love us more (or hate us less).

In establishing a common identity with another person, we participate in this person's life. We vicariously share in his status or achievement and feel more worthy and fulfilled ourselves. Identifying with a prestigious group of people or a powerful or successful organization may bring similar feelings of worth and satisfaction.

Difficulty occurs when models for identification are absent, inadequate, or harmful. A boy whose father is bumbling and ineffectual may take over these qualities for himself. Or, at least, he may be very threatened by his identity with his father. A girl whose mother is antagonistic toward males may introject her mother's unfortunate attitudes. When the parent of the same sex is missing, unsympathetic, or hostile, the child may pattern himself after the parent of the opposite sex and develop behavior inappropriate to his own sex role.

Sometimes damage is done when a number of important models have conflicting patterns of behavior. A husband and wife, for example, may have important differences in standards and values; their children through identification with both parents can take over these incompatible systems and experience considerable conflict. Or an adolescent or young adult may find that his parents, his teachers, and his age-mates, all of whom he is identified with to some extent, present very different examples.

Projection

A feature of some identifications is the taking in or introjection of something from the external environment. Not everything that we take in or everything that we become will serve us well or be valued by us. Just as we strive to acquire and accentuate prized patterns of behavior, we struggle to avoid, inhibit, or disassociate ourselves from those which we hold in low esteem.

Projection refers to our tendency to attribute our own thoughts, feelings, and actions to others. We tend to regard other people as somewhat like ourselves. If, for example, we feel bored in a particular situation, we imagine that others are bored too. If we hold a particular belief very strongly, it may be difficult for us to understand how anyone else could not feel as we do.

Both positive and negative qualities can be projected. It has been suggested that we project acceptable and positively valued characteristics to people whom we like and identify with. Unacceptable, negatively valued qualities are projected to people whom we dislike, to people whom we feel we could not possibly be like (but, of course, are) (Zimmer, 1955).

If we sense good in ourselves, we may tend to see good in others. To the pure, all things are pure, goes an old saying. If we sense bad, we may see other people in the same unfavorable light; for example, we may see ourselves and others too as hostile and self-seeking: "It's all dog-eat-dog," we say, "so I better get in the first bite."

Used as a defense, projection implies that a person has certain thoughts or feelings or actions which are threatening to him, which he then denies are his, and instead attributes to others. As is indicated, three steps are involved: (1) a sense of some unacceptable motive operating in oneself; (2) a repression of this motive; and (3) an attribution of this motive to others.

Those of us who use projection as a defense may be especially hostile to other people who seem to share our unacceptable impulses (Cohen, 1956). "That's like the pot calling the kettle black," we sometimes say when one person criticizes another for a fault he has himself. Sometimes the projector has some insight into what he is doing, and occasionally an individual suggests that maybe the reason he cannot get along with another person is that this person is too like himself.

In our own culture aggressive impulses frequently undergo repression and projection. Those of us who sense unacceptable feelings of hostility in ourselves may attribute these feelings to others, most commonly to the person for whom the hostility was originally felt. We may start off with the thought: I hate you, and I'd like to hurt you. Through projection, we wind up with the thought: You hate me, and you'd like to hurt me.

Sexual urges are also frequently repressed and projected. A young woman who senses a strong but unacceptable sexual motivation in herself may deny this and instead see others as overly interested in sex. A man who is tempted to be unfaithful to his wife may be considerably concerned about his wife's "flirtations." An individual who has homosexual impulses may react against them and accuse others of making indecent advances.

Most frequently people are the objects of projection, but in some cases animals, natural and supernatural forces, or even inanimate articles may serve as objects. Primitives project human motives onto their gods, sometimes perceiving them as angry and at other times content. Sometimes a tennis player will conduct an ostentatious investigation of his racket after he has completely missed the ball—as if there were a hole in it big enough for the ball to go through. The person who stumbles on a chair may go back and kick the chair for tripping him.

Jourard (1963) suggests a number of guideposts for establishing whether or not a person is using projection as a defense. He says that we may suspect such is the case if bad things are imputed to others with little justification, while these same things are denied in oneself but with some evidence to the contrary.

In projecting threatening qualities we are able to accomplish a number of things. First, we can disclaim responsibility for these qualities. (*I* don't have dirty thoughts, but *they* do.) Second, we can attack these qualities, thereby establishing distance from them. (I can't stand people who have dirty thoughts.) Third, we may feel that we are not so blameworthy since these qualities are widely shared. (So what if I have a dirty thought now and then? Everybody does.) And, fourth, we may gain some vicarious satisfaction from seeing these

qualities indulged in by others. (I'd better keep my eye on these people and see what sort of dirty things they're up to.)

Insofar as we project positive qualities, our relationships with others may be facilitated. For example, a person who is genuinely friendly may project this feeling and expect that other people are friendly too. Whether the people he comes in contact with are friendly or not, his attitudes and behavior increase the possibility of their being so. To some extent people respond in kind, and just as aggression is frequently met with aggression, one friendly overture may prompt another.

In projecting negative qualities we protect ourselves from seeing ourselves in an unfavorable light. In the long run, however, this negative projection can be seriously detrimental to adjustment. It prevents us from facing problems and dealing with them effectively. Furthermore, as we project negative qualities onto others and then act in accordance with this projection, relationships with others will suffer. The projection mechanism carried to an extreme is seen in certain paranoid processes.

Displacement

Some of our behavior is threatening because of the people that it is directed toward or because of the particular form that it takes. Assuming that we express an impulse only in certain ways and only toward certain people, we may escape anxiety.

In *displacement* there is a shift of thought, feeling, or action from one person or situation to another. Displacement occurs because the original impulse causes or would cause considerable anxiety. Consequently, there is a shift to a neutral object or to one that is more vulnerable or less dangerous than the original (see Fig. 6.3).

Sometimes the new object is similar to the original; the two may stand for each other or be identified with each other in some way, and the new object symbolizes the old one. For example, the little boy who is angry with his mother may trample her flower bed instead of attacking her directly. Or he may take his feelings out on his teacher if she in some way reminds him of his mother and is more vulnerable to attack.

Sometimes, however, the similarity between the new object and the old one is quite subtle and can be understood only by a person with a good deal of psychological training. Occasionally, on the surface at least, there appears to be no relationship. Occasionally, too, displacement seems to be a diffuse process in which the troublesome impulse is channeled to many new objects with little apparent rhyme or reason.

It has already been noted that the aggressive impulse is one that is frequently diverted or displaced. Other processes that commonly undergo displacement are fear, love, and attention.

Fears may be displaced in the same way that aggressive impulses are. People who are constantly worried about little things which appear to constitute no danger may actually be concerned about something more important which has been repressed. A child who fears his father, a person with whom he must be in constant association, may displace this fear to animals. A woman who hates her husband and fears that she may do him violence may instead express a fear of knives and other sharp instruments.

The people whom we wish to love and be loved by do not always respond. In this event, we may displace our love and affection to someone else. For example, a boy who is unable to establish a satisfactory relationship with his father may turn his affection to a teacher, a scoutmaster, or some other adult male. Sometimes a person who has been jilted by a lover finds and quickly marries someone else on the rebound. Some forms of self-love appear to be displacements: constantly rebuffed by others, a person may remove all of his affection to himself (Symonds, 1946).

Sometimes we make doubly sure that upsetting problems stay out of the focus of attention by keeping ourselves busy with other activities. A man who is having difficulty with his homelife may displace his attention to his work; in fact, he may throw himself into his job with such vigor

Figure 6.3 Displacement (© Bell-McClure Syndicate, 1957).

that his friends mistakenly attribute his adjustment difficulties to overwork. In the same way, a woman who is having trouble with her roles of wife and mother may busy herself in social or professional activities. Many people look forward to their vacation as the time when attention can be diverted from the bothersome problems of the everyday environment.

Through the use of displacement we are able to discharge our feelings in acceptable directions. Positive feelings may be displaced to objects that will accept and respond to these feelings. Negative feelings may be diverted from important and dangerous objects onto those which are unimportant and vulnerable. Positive and negative feelings may be separated and applied to separate objects. In this way, we may love some things, hate others, and not be torn by ambivalence (Isaacs, 1937; Symonds, 1946).

Unfortunately, insofar as displacement involves negative feelings, one relationship may be improved at the cost of another. Although the second object is more vulnerable than the first, it may be an important one nevertheless. For example, the employee who displaces feelings of hostility from his office to the home environment ensures the safety of his job at the expense of vital family relationships (Sappenfield, 1954).

Reaction Formation

When we sense things in ourselves that are threatening to our self-esteem and general welfare, we may attempt to convince ourselves and others that these things are not so. One way that we can accomplish this is by accentuating opposite qualities. We strive to feel, think, and act in ways that are sharply in contrast to the ways that we tend to feel, think, and act.

Reaction formation refers to efforts to inhibit, mask, or overcome certain impulses by emphasizing opposite ones. Using such behavior as a defense against threat is very common. Sensing fear, we may attempt to act very brave. Sensing weakness, we may attempt to be tough and hard-boiled. Sensing unacceptable dependence, we may make a great show of rebellion. Sensing anxiety-provoking affectionate feelings, we may react by being very cynical and take a cool and jaundiced view of human beings (Sarnoff, 1960).

A person who is strongly tempted by unacceptable sex needs can react against them by being extremely puritanical. He may prevent any sexual expression in himself and avoid almost all association with the opposite sex. Furthermore, he may criticize others who engage in any sexual activity no matter how mild; sometimes he may even attempt to prevent them from doing so. Whether his activities are ostensibly on his own behalf or seemingly on the behalf of others, they are designed to help him keep his own forbidden impulses in check.

Sensing unacceptable aggressive urges in himself, a person can react against them by being very kind. Such a person will appear to be extremely polite, deferent, and solicitous about the welfare of others. He may be unable to be aggressive even when aggressive actions appear to be quite appropriate. His behavior is dedicated to keeping his hostile impulses under control.

A reaction formation toward selfish tendencies may be manifested in extreme generosity. Stinginess and avarice may be repressed and replaced by magnanimous

Figure 6.4 How do we defend ourselves against threat or anxiety? Some information concerning this question has been provided through the use of a stressful film showing subincision rites in an Australian Stone Age tribe; these rites involve a series of crude operations performed on the genitals of the tribal boys at puberty.

The film is a disturbing one, and as the individual subject views it, continuous recordings are made of such stress indices as skin conductance, heart rate, respiration, and motor activity. In the figure, the lines show the mean skin conductance rates for three groups of male college subjects. The high points in skin conductance signify threat arousal. The peaks occur when the operations take place (the first three are most disturbing), and the low point in the middle coincides with a relatively innocuous postoperative ceremony in which the tribal boys have their hair dressed.

One group of subjects saw the film without any introduction or commentary. The second group had a running commentary which, following reaction formation and denial defenses, suggested positive aspects of the ceremony (for example, the pleasure the boys had from participating in a significant ceremony) and denied the painful and harmful aspects. For the third group, the commentary preceded the film.

As the graph indicates, the reaction formation and denial commentary served to reduce the stress of the film in both defense and predefense groups. Furthermore, the predefense condition was more effective than defense. The investigators reasoned that the predefense condition allowed the subjects to get prepared or "innoculated" against the potential threat while the first defense condition did not (Lazarus, 1964; Lazarus & Alfert, 1964).

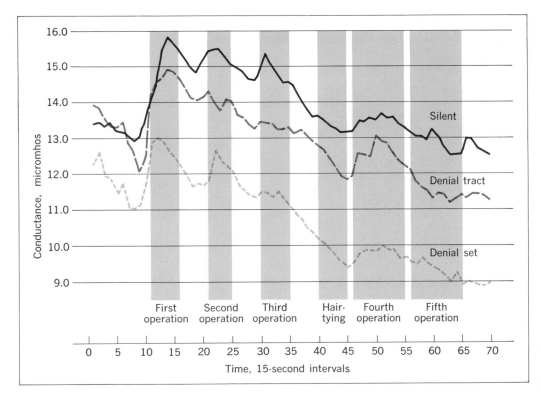

actions. In this patterning the person will feel compelled to give and be generous; he must constantly demonstrate to himself and others that he is not the self-seeking person he inwardly suspects himself to be.

Reaction formations are characterized by their extreme and compelling strength. As was noted, reaction formations to sex may be manifested in very puritanical behavior, those to aggression may produce excessively mild and gentle actions, and those counteracting selfishness may compel great generosity. In each case the individual will be unwilling and unable to modify his position. The force of the reaction is necessary to prevent the original impulse from breaking out of control into open expression.

Reaction formations may show inconsistencies and imperfections. Sometimes the forbidden behavior and the reaction behavior exist side by side. For example, a person who has reacted strongly against a tendency to be dirty and disorderly may still engage in certain activities or have certain places in which he is very messy.

Sometimes, too, a reaction formation will break down, allowing the original impulse free expression. A child who has always been extremely polite and well behaved may be caught in acts of extreme cruelty toward animals. A man who has always seemed extremely mild in his actions may suddenly lash out in some verbal or physical aggression. A woman who has spent a good deal of her life attacking certain patterns of behavior may suddenly be found to be engaging in this very behavior.

Reaction formation plays an important part in the socialization process. Gen-erosity, kindliness, orderliness, and many other personal qualities that are valued in our society are not natural expressions of the child; they are partly formed in reaction to earlier, diametrically opposite patterns of behavior. The small child, for example, has little concept of cleanliness; it is through constant training that he develops a dislike for dirt, a disgust for filth, and a loathing for his bodily wastes.

It is interesting to observe reaction formations in the process of development. One might note, for example, a sudden shift in a child from attraction to dirt to aversion to dirt. A little girl who formerly played in her dress until it was filthy suddenly becomes sensitive to the smallest spot. Any garment that is the slightest bit dirty must be immediately removed. Little by little, her actions may become modulated so that she learns to be clean but not excessively so.

Severe, unmodulated reaction formations distort our lives. We need to be clean, of course, but we should not need to be always immaculate. We should be generous, but we should not feel compelled to give. We need to be kind, but we should be able to express hostility when the occasion seems to warrant it. In general, we should not be strangers to any of our impulses; instead of attempting to seal them off, we should learn to know them and express them in the ways we value (see Fig. 6.4).

Fantasy

The world we live in, reality, leaves much to be desired. Our efforts may help to change it. Or we may change our perceptions of it and somehow see it as a more desirable place. Or we may be able to escape it for awhile by constructing a private and more satisfying world.

Fantasy refers to imaginary constructions. It includes make-believe play, reveries, and daydreams. Novels, movies, plays, and similar literary and dramatic works might be considered to provide the individual with ready-made fantasy experiences.

As a defense, our fantasy life provides us with an escape from the dangers, threats, and boredom of the real world. In our fantasies we can meet our unmet needs and reach our unreached goals. We can picture ourselves as a different sort of person and the world as a different sort of world.

Freud (1900) and others have pointed out the strong element of wish fulfillment in fantasies. Holt notes a number of reasons why, in daydreams, wishes may be expressed in very direct, crude, and primitive ways. He writes:

> The fact that the daydream is private and uncommunicated, that it is a regressive and often not recalled kind of thinking, makes it possible for the fulfillment of wishes to be relatively direct and for the wishes themselves to be unsublimated and close to the hypothetical state of original drives. If someone has annoyed us, we can easily imagine killing him or inflicting on him tortures we would not even consider witnessing in reality, much less carrying them out ourselves.[2]

Fantasy is a very common pursuit at every age. The child acts out his fantasies. His play is filled with make-believe. He pretends that he is the person he would like to be, living in a world he would like to live in. He becomes his father, a cowboy, a spaceman, or a ferocious animal. He finds himself on the Western plains, high above the earth, or deep in the jungle. In his play he escapes the limitations of being young and weak and small and under the domination of adults.

As we grow older we increasingly daydream our fantasies rather than act them out. We not only create new experiences, we also relive old ones that have been enjoyable. Sometimes our fantasies are previews of events which are to occur in the future; certainly part of the pleasure of a vacation, a trip, or a party is in its anticipation.

In later maturity, many daydreams tend to be re-creative ones. In his fantasies the elderly person may live again happy experiences out of his past. Even these daydreams have elements of creativeness; in memory some old experiences become more satisfying than they were in actuality.

"Conquering hero" and "suffering hero" are two common types of fantasies. In conquering-hero fantasies the individual imagines that he is the master of some situation. He is a famous athlete, a brilliant student, a great lover, or a fascinating conversationalist. He is applauded, acclaimed, and sought after. In fantasy he may reenact an old experience but this time he says and does all the things that he failed to say and do during the actual experience.

In conquering-hero fantasies a person may have the experiences that are not forthcoming in real life. For example, a youth who is hungry for heterosexual experience may imagine a relationship with some girl who has caught his eye. He may

[2] From Holt, R. R. The nature of TAT stories as cognitive products: A psychoanalytic approach. In J. Kagan (Ed.), *Contemporary Issues in Thematic Apperceptive Methods*. Springfield, Ill.: Charles C Thomas, 1961. Pp. 3–43. Courtesy of the publisher. P. 29.

daydream about asking her for a date and then conjure up the conversations they would have, the dances and parties they would attend, and the affection they would share. In the same fashion, a single woman may daydream that she is married, has a handsome and considerate husband, attractive children, and a nice home.

In suffering-hero fantasies the individual imagines himself to be the victim of some situation. He sees himself as undergoing great hardship or suffering adversity. He is cold and hungry, unloved and unwanted, or destitute and outcast. He may be wounded, dying, or dead.

In fantasying oneself in such pitiful circumstances, a person becomes a figure who is deserving of the sympathy and commiseration of others. At the same time, he is worthy of their admiration for carrying on so well in the face of such circumstances. Elements of revenge may also be

present since now certain people will be very sorry that they did not treat the person better in the past. Suffering-hero daydreams are common in children who are having difficulties with their parents.

When life is uninteresting and frustrating, fantasy permits us to escape into a dream world where exciting things occur and difficult goals are reached. In fantasy we can relive the pleasant experiences of the past (sometimes making them even more pleasant than they really were), and we can live in advance the anticipated pleasures of the future. Creative thinking and fantasy are closely related; representing our needs, activities, and goals in fantasy may be the first step to instituting them in reality (Hartmann, 1958; Varendonck, 1921).

Fantasy becomes detrimental when it becomes a substitute for reality achievements. Compared with the ideal goals

Table 6.1 Many patterns of behavior may be put to defensive use. Here, in addition to those more fully discussed in this chapter, are some common defenses.

Name	Definition	Example
Denial	Refusing to admit some threatening external reality	A mother refuses to accept the fact that her child is seriously handicapped.
Undoing	Making amends or atoning for guilt-producing thoughts, feelings, and actions	A rejecting parent lavishes material things on a child.
Sublimation	Expression of frustrated motives in socially sanctioned ways	A teacher, frustrated in the desire for a family of her own, lavishes affection on her pupils.
Compensation	Substitution of achievement in one area to make up for failure in another	A classroom dunce becomes the playground bully.
Overcompensation	Turning an area of weakness into one of great strength	A polio-crippled person develops himself into a great athlete.
Physical withdrawal	Staying away from threatening situations	An adolescent boy, uncomfortable around girls, avoids dances and similar social activities.
Emotional withdrawal	Restricting emotional involvement to guard against pain and disappointment	A young woman, disillusioned by earlier love affairs, refuses to take her dates seriously.

available in fantasy, the small rewards possible in the real world may seem hardly worth the effort. Fantasy can rob a person of large amounts of time which otherwise might be applied to real-life pursuits. In some serious adjustments the individual tends to be unable to distinguish completely between the worlds of fantasy and reality.

Table 6.1 outlines a number of common defenses, and Table 6.2 summarizes this discussion of defenses.

Table 6.2 Here is a summary of the defenses discussed in this chapter.

Name	Definition	Example
Suppression	Deliberate inhibition of threatening stimuli	A cigarette smoker quickly turns the page when he sees an article about lung cancer.
Repression	Automatic inhibition of threatening stimuli	A student has trouble remembering the name of an instructor who failed him last year.
Lying	Deliberate use of falsehood to prevent a threat to well-being	A man tells everyone that he is doing well in his business although he knows he is going broke.
Rationalization	Interpreting behavior in personally and socially acceptable ways	A parent convinces himself that his severe disciplinary policies are for his child's "own good."
Malingering	Removal of a threat by feigning illness	A boy pretends he is ill to keep from going to school.
Adjustment by ailment	Noninsightful use of illness, imaginary or real, as a way of avoiding anxiety	A woman develops a severe headache whenever she is confronted by an unpleasant task.
Fixation	Continuation of patterns of behavior which have become immature or inappropriate	A young man remains tied to his mother's apron strings.
Regression	Return to patterns of behavior which have become immature or inappropriate	A young wife runs home to mother at the first sign of marital discord.
Identification	Establishing a oneness with a valued person, group, or thing and drawing on its qualities	A little boy refuses to fight another boy, but insists, "My father can lick your father!"
Projection	Attributing one's own qualities to others	A man who is tempted to be unfaithful shows unwarranted concern about his wife's flirtations.
Displacement	Shifting a thought, feeling, or action from one object to another	A little boy, mad at his mother, tramples her flower beds.
Reaction formation	Inhibiting, masking, or overcoming threatening impulses by emphasizing opposite ones	A man who feels weak and inadequate affects a tough, hard-boiled stance.
Fantasy	Finding satisfaction in make-believe play, reveries, and daydreams	An unpopular boy has daydreams in which he is the center of everyone's attention.

Presentation 6.1 Delinquency and defense. In 1967 the President's Commission on Law Enforcement and Administration of Justice reported that a majority of the persons apprehended for serious crimes were under twenty-one years of age. Of all age groups, fifteen-year-olds had the highest rate of arrest. Boys were much more likely to get into trouble than girls; before reaching adulthood, one male in every six is referred to juvenile court. Redl and Wineman have recorded the defense patterns of a group of young delinquents with whom they were working. The delinquents used a number of "alibi tricks" or "guilt evasion tricks" to avoid feeling bad about their behavior. Here is a partial list of these tricks along with illustrations of how they were employed. Do you detect any of the defenses discussed in this chapter?

"He did it first"

For a long time, at camp, we were fooled by considering the youngsters with the most patent trend to accuse others, as the more "delinquent ones." For some of them that is still correct. We had to learn, though, that sometimes this actually works the other way around. The great need to find somebody who did it first need not come from a need to be revengeful or accusatory, but may, on the contrary, point to the very intact part of the youngster's superego. Only because he would really have to feel guilty for what he did, does a child sometimes seek so hard to find somebody else to blame.

"Everybody else does such things anyway"

Lefty, a twelve-year-old boy in one of our Detroit Group Project Clubs, stole two watches and a ring from counselors. After it was finally established that he had committed the thefts, following a long and stubborn "holdout," he and his caseworker discussed the situation. Lefty admitted almost proudly to the caseworker that he had been stealing for a long time. When the caseworker asked how he felt about this, whether he was bothered at all, he replied, "The only thing that bothers me is if I get caught." Did he believe it

was right to go around "swiping stuff," asked the caseworker. To this he replied, heatedly, "There isn't a single boy in my neighborhood who doesn't steal. Everybody steals sometime in their life, even you, I'll bet. Even preachers steal." Nor was this an expediency of the moment. In interview after interview, Lefty used the same argument, thus showing how deeply imbedded it was.

"We were all in on it"

On one occasion the whole Pioneer group had been involved in a very dangerous and destructive episode of throwing bricks from the top of the garage. We decided to have individual interviews with each of the boys to "rub-in" the total unacceptability of such behavior. Andy, especially, was fascinating in his real indignation at even being approached on the subject. Tearfully he shouted at the Director who was doing the interviewing, "Yeah, everybody was doing it and you talk to me. Why is it my fault?" When it was pointed out to him that we were not saying it was all his fault but that he was responsible for his individual share in the matter, he was still unable to admit the point: "But we were all in on it. Why talk to me?"

"But somebody else did that same thing to me before"

Following the closure of Pioneer House, Danny eventualy went back to live with his own family, since he was not able to make an adjustment in a foster home because of the unavoidably premature release from treatment. Slowly he began to acquire a stealing pattern. Eventually he stole twenty dollars from a staff member at the School of Social Work with whom he had a very positive relationship during the Pioneer House period, when she had been involved in much of the programming at the Home. In interview, when confronted with this and asked if he really felt comfortable in stealing from this person who had always been so nice to him, he said, "Hell, my stepfather wrecked my

---

Presentation 6.1 (Continued)

---

cowboy gun two weeks ago. Threw it in the stove. I had to get another one." Even after he admitted that this wasn't the staff member's fault, he still clung to the feeling that it wasn't wrong for him to take the money if his stepfather had been so mean to him.

"He had it coming to him"
This reminds us of a rather sadistic child we had at camp who yet was obsessed by a strict self-imposed code of not "hurting anybody who is weaker than you." Placed with a group, all of whom happened to be weaker than he, he was soon in desperate straits. He finally found the way out—all he had to do was wait for the chance that one of the children did something that he felt unjustified, like disarranging his blanket when climbing up to his upper bunk, and he could afford a really vicious and dangerous attack on his intended victim. The superego-directed argument that this child now "deserved" what he got, took care of any potential guilt feelings to which his own behavior code might otherwise have made him vulnerable.

"I had to do it, or I would have lost face"
We have seen many children in dire predicaments like this: Exposed to a delinquent gang, the cozy group atmosphere of which appealed to them, they were caught in a conflict between their individual superego and the delinquency-immune code of the group. Soon they would be drifting into a great deal of behavior which would be quite unacceptable to their own value system, but they realized that noncompliance with the group demand would be accompanied by a total loss of face. As soon as the first battle was lost in favor of this issue as a "guilt-assuaging" factor, they would extinguish, or at least reduce, their individual feeling of guilt, by the inner argument that they "couldn't have avoided it without being called a sissy."

"I didn't use the proceeds anyway"
At camp, one season, Whitey broke into the staff quarters and stole several cartons of cigarets. Many of these were used to buy his way into the favor of some of the tough addict smokers who had high prestige in his group. A few, curiously enough, he threw into the lake. He, himself, didn't smoke any. In interviews concerning this behavior this last point became his strongest argument. "What the hell! I didn't smoke a damn one, did I?"

"But I made up with him afterwards"
We had quite a time once at camp with a youngster who had been apprehended just when he had tried a particularly vicious attempt at homosexual rape. The child was an habitual pervert, and of course the sexual side of the picture wouldn't have aroused any guilt feeling in him at that time. He was, however, strongly identified with a group code of "fairness toward those who are weak," so we tackled him on the brutality side of the issue. He put up quite a struggle though, trying to avoid admitting that what he did was wrong. His argument, of all things, was that the particular child bore him no grudge, and he "had made up with him" afterwards. In a similar vein, it was hard to squeeze even a drop of guilt feeling out of our sneak thieves if their victim seemed to be careless about his possessions to begin with, took inadequate precautions against theft, or left them lying around. The slogan "never give a sucker a break" can apparently also be applied for internal use.

"He is a no good so-and-so himself"
Dick, who stole a fountain pen from the director's lodge at camp, was subsequently a victim of some of his cabin mates who stole his fountain pen and jacknife. In our discussions with the culprits, they tried to side-issue the interview with the argument, "Yeah, what are you talking to us for? You know what a dirty

---

---

crook that guy is. Why he came in here and stole a fountain pen last week. What right does he have to complain?" "Did he steal from you?" we asked. Even after they had to admit that he hadn't, it still did not detract from the vehemence or tenacity of their plea. He was still a "lousy crook" and had it coming.

"They are all against me, nobody likes me, they are always picking on me"

In addition to justifying his stealing on the basis that "everybody steals," Lefty also argued that his mother never got him "nothin' that he wanted," that she was nicer to his step-siblings than to him, and that his step-father was cruel and stingy. In reality these things were all true to a certain extent, as the family story proved. Thus, "if she ain't gonna buy me that Bulova watch I want, I'm gonna steal one, just wait and see." And he did. The fact that his mother, who did reject him, was still not financially able to buy him a watch anyway made no difference. His feeling of rejection from her and the step-father was still enough of an argu-

ment so that he could go out and steal valuable items on a guilt-free basis. "How about the guy from whom you swiped it? What did he do to you?" we asked. This made no difference to Lefty who continued to argue in the same vein.

"I couldn't have gotten it any other way"

During the initial phase of treatment at Pioneer House, Sam stole the Director's cigarette lighter. In an interview with him we tried to get at some of his motivation for the theft. His only defense seemed to be, "Well, I wanted a lighter." When further challenged, "Yes, you wanted a lighter but how about going to such lengths as to steal it from someone?" he grew quite irritated. "How the hell do you expect me to get one if I don't swipe it? Do I have enough money to buy one?" There was no question that, having logically narrowed down his chances of getting a lighter to stealing it, the act itself was quite justifiable to him on a "closed issue" basis: "I want it, there is no other way, so I swipe it—just because I want it. (Reprinted by permission of the publisher from *The Aggressive Child* by F. Redl & D. Wineman. Pp. 147–155. Copyright 1951, 1957 by The Free Press, a corporation.)

SUMMARY

Certain patterns of behavior which are employed for protection against anxiety are called defenses. Although sometimes conceived of as special sorts of automatic behavior, defenses can also be thought of as special uses of common processes which may operate with varying degrees of insight and control. Almost any bit of behavior may have a defensive and a nondefensive aspect, and whether a particular use is bad (or pathological) or good de-

pends upon its overall effect in a particular situation.

As defenses, suppression and repression pertain to the inhibition of threatening impulses; suppression refers to conscious and deliberate efforts to inhibit such impulses; repression includes relatively automatic and noninsightful inhibition.

We are constantly called upon to justify ourselves. Lying, used as a defense, refers to the deliberate use of falsehood to prevent a threat to our well-being. When, without conscious intent, we explain circumstances in personally and socially acceptable ways, we are said to use rationalization.

Illness, real or pretended, is frequently used as a defense. Malingering refers to our efforts to protect ourselves from threat by feigning illness. In contrast, adjustment by ailment includes the non-insightful use of illness (imaginary or real) to avert anxiety.

When we are threatened by change or new experience, we may defend ourselves by adhering to present patterns of response or by retreating to earlier ones. Fixation refers to the continuation of a pattern of behavior which has become immature or inappropriate. Regression refers to the recovery of a pattern which has been outgrown.

Identification is a general term which refers to the various ways in which we establish a oneness with another person, group, or object. Used as a defense, identification implies that the person feels threatened and responds by drawing upon the valued qualities of others.

Projection refers to the tendency to attribute one's own thoughts, feelings, and actions to others. When personal impulses are threatening, we may project or impute them to others whom we then see as blameworthy rather than ourselves.

Some of our behavior is threatening because of the people toward whom it is directed or because of the particular form it takes. Displacement refers to the shift of a thought, feeling, or action from one person or situation to another that is less threatening.

One way to convince ourselves and others that we do not have negative and threatening qualities is to emphasize contrary characteristics. Reaction formation refers to efforts to inhibit, mask, or overcome certain impulses by emphasizing opposite ones.

If the world we live in leaves much to be desired, we may be able to defend ourselves against it by constructing a private and more satisfying world. Fantasy refers to imaginary constructions including make-believe play, reveries, and daydreams; in his fantasies a person may meet unmet needs and reach unreached goals.

REFERENCES

Bandura, A., & Walters, R. H. *Social Learning and Personality Development*. New York: Holt, 1963.

Brenner, C. *An Elementary Textbook of Psychoanalysis*. New York: International Universities Press, 1957.

Cameron, N., & Magaret, A. *Behavior Pathology*. Boston: Houghton Mifflin, 1951.

Cohen, A. R. Experimental effects of ego-defense preference on interpersonal relations. *Journal of Abnormal and Social Psychology*, 1956, **52**, 19–27.

Dollard, J., & Miller, N. E. *Personality and Psychotherapy*. New York: McGraw-Hill, 1950.

Freud, A. *The Ego and the Mechanisms of Defense* (1936). New York: International Universities Press, 1946.

Freud, S. *The Interpretation of Dreams* (1900). London: Hogarth, 1953.

————. *The Psychopathology of Everyday Life* (1904). In *Basic Writings of Sigmund Freud*. New York: Vintage Books, Random House, 1938.

————. Repression (1915). In *Collected Papers*. Vol. 4. London: Hogarth, 1946. Pp. 84–97.

————. *The Problem of Anxiety*. New York: Norton, 1936.

Hall, C. S. *A Primer of Freudian Psychology*. Cleveland: World Publishing, 1954.

Hartmann, H. *Ego Psychology and the Problem of Adaptation*. New York: International Universities Press, 1958.

Hilgard, E. R. Experimental approaches to psychoanalysis. In E. Pumpian-Mindlin (Ed.), *Psychoanalysis as Science*. New York: Basic Books, 1952. Pp. 3–45.

Holt, R. R. The nature of TAT stories as cognitive products: A psychoanalytic approach. In J. Kagan (Ed.), *Contemporary Issues in Thematic Apperceptive Methods*. Springfield, Ill.: Charles C Thomas, 1961. Pp. 3–43.

Isaacs, S. *Social Development in Young Children*. New York: Harcourt, Brace, 1937.

Jourard, S. M. *Personal Adjustment*. (2nd ed.) New York: Macmillan, 1963.

Karpman, B. Lying: A minor inquiry into the ethics of neurotic and psychopathic behavior. *Journal of Criminal Law and Criminology*, 1949, **40**, 135–157.

Kris, E. *Psychoanalytic Explorations in Art*. New York: International Universities Press, 1952.

Kroeber, T. C. The coping functions of the ego mechanisms. In R. W. White (Ed.), *The Study of Lives*. New York: Atherton, 1963. Pp. 178–198.

Kubie, L. S. Problems of techniques of psychoanalytic validation and progress. In E. Pumpian-Mindlin (Ed.), *Psychoanalysis as Science*. New York: Basic Books, 1952. Pp. 46–124.

Lampl-De Groot, J. On defense and development: Normal and pathological. In *The Psychoanalytic Study of the Child*. Vol. 12. New York: International Universities Press, 1957. Pp. 114–126.

Lazarus, R. S. A laboratory approach to the dynamics of psychological stress. *American Psychologist*, 1964, **19**, 400–411.

————, & Alfert, E. The short-circuiting of threat by experimentally altering cognitive appraisal. *Journal of Abnormal and Social Psychology*, 1964, **69**, 195–205.

MacKinnon, D. W., & Dukes, W. F. Repression. In L. Postman (Ed.), *Psychology in the Making*. New York: Knopf, 1962. Pp. 662–744.

Maslow, A. H. Emotional blocks to creativity. *Journal of Individual Psychology*, 1958, **14**, 51–56.

Menninger, K., Mayman, M., & Pruyser, P. *The Vital Balance*. New York: Viking, 1963.

Murphy, L. B., et al. *The Widening World of Childhood*. New York: Basic Books, 1962.

Redl, F., & Wineman, D. *The Aggressive Child*. New York: Free Press, 1957.

Sappenfield, B. R. *Personality Dynamics*. New York: Knopf, 1954.

Sarnoff, I. Reaction formation and cynicism. *Journal of Personality*, 1960, **28**, 129–143.

Schafer, R. *Psychoanalytic Interpretation in Rorschach Testing*. New York: Grune & Stratton, 1954.

————. Regression in the service of the ego: The relevance of a psychoanalytic concept for personality assessment. In G. Lindzey (Ed.), *Assessment of Human Motives*. New York: Holt, 1958. Pp. 119–148.

Shaffer, L. F., & Shoben, E. J., Jr. *The Psychology of Adjustment.* (2nd ed.) Boston: Houghton Mifflin, 1956.

Stone, L. J., & Church, J. *Childhood and Adolescence.* New York: Random House, 1957.

Swanson, G. E. Determinants of the individual's defenses against inner conflict: Review and reformation. In J. C. Glidewell (Ed.), *Parental Attitudes and Child Behavior.* Springfield, Ill.: Charles C Thomas, 1961. Pp. 5–41.

Symonds, P. M. *The Dynamics of Human Adjustment.* New York: Appleton-Century-Crofts, 1946.

Szasz, T. S. A contribution to the psychology of schizophrenia. *A.M.A. Archives of Neurology and Psychiatry,* 1957, **77,** 420–436.

Twain, Mark (Samuel L. Clemens). *The Adventures of Tom Sawyer* (1875). New York: Harper, 1929.

Varendonck, J. *The Psychology of Daydreams.* New York: Macmillan, 1921.

Vaughan, W. F. *Personal and Social Adjustment.* New York: Odyssey, 1952.

Woolf, M. The child's moral development. In K. R. Eissler (Ed.), *Searchlights on Delinquency.* New York: International Universities Press, 1949. Pp. 263–272.

Zimmer, H. The roles of conflict and internalized demands in projection. *Journal of Abnormal and Social Psychology,* 1955, **50,** 188–192.

CHAPTER SEVEN

LEARNING

Satisfying our needs is not always an easy matter. Sometimes we move forward only to find that obstructions prevent us from reaching our goals. Sometimes we find ourselves torn between several incompatible tendencies to act. At other times we are assailed by fear and anger and painful apprehension.

Living, simply defined, is problem solving. To meet our needs we must *learn* to overcome our frustrations. We must *learn* to resolve our conflicts. We must *learn* to control our anxieties. In brief, we must *learn* to adjust to our environment and to make our environment adjust to us.

This chapter discusses learning and the part that learning plays in the adjustment process. Included in the discussion are some important principles which help explain how adjustment patterns are learned and unlearned.

DEFINING LEARNING

Everything we are and everything we do is the result of a complicated interaction between heredity and environment. We begin life with what we have inherited, but at birth (and even before) our environment molds and modifies and changes us.

We become what we are partly through growth: we mature and unfold. We sometimes say that a child has "learned" to sit up (or stand or walk), but it would be as accurate to say that he has "grown" to sit up, since this behavior appears when the body has reached a certain level of development. A good deal of our behavior appears when the time is ripe. Or, to put it another way, it comes naturally.

But human behavior is heavily influenced by learning. For example, consider speech. Do we speak English or Hindustani? Do we speak up when we're called on? Speak down to our audience? Speak out when the occasion calls for it? We "grow" to make sounds, but we "learn" what to say and how and when to say it. In speech, as in other patterns of behavior, the role of learning is readily apparent.

It is not always easy to determine the relative influence of heredity, growth, and learning in a particular pattern of behavior. Bugelski describes the difficulty well when he writes:

What kinds of things are learned and what kinds come naturally? In order to find out what learning is, we have to know where to look for it. Do we have to learn to talk, ride a bicycle, fly an airplane, do algebra, play a piano, read? Are you sure about any of these things? Some children seem to be able to ride bicycles with little or no instruction. They get on one, in one way or another, and while there may be a little trouble, in a little while they are off riding

with passable grace. Did they learn quickly? Or did they "get the idea"? Is "getting the idea" learning or is it the natural use of a native intelligence or other equipment? But algebra, that's different, that you have to learn. Do you? Somebody had to invent the stuff—he did not learn it, it was not there to learn. Does the student in an algebra course repeat this process of invention for himself, to some extent at least, or does he learn algebra? Some students never learn to handle algebra in any reasonable fashion even if they manage to attain a passing mark. Others continually find fault with what has been "taught" and find new ways of handling the assigned problems. Are they learning? We would be a lot better off if we could describe the characteristics of learned behavior and discriminate it from other, nonlearned behavior. Our trouble is that we do not know the characteristics of either in any unequivocal fashion (1961, pp. 198–199).

Yet there is no doubt that learning is of major importance in the acquisition of human adjustment patterns. Deese (1958) puts the matter tersely when he says, "Most human behavior is learned." And Hilgard (1962) adds, "While modification through learning is a rule throughout the animal kingdom, the higher organisms, with prolonged infancy, depend more upon learning for their adjustment to their environment than do those lower in the evolutionary scale. Man is a learner *par excellence.*"

What is learning? *Learning* refers to a relatively enduring change in behavior which results from past experience. This includes the changes which come about as we act on our environment and it acts upon us. Not included are changes due to growth or aging, to fatigue or illness, or to bodily injury.

ANALYZING LEARNING

Psychologists have learned a lot about learning, but they still have a lot to learn. There is a good deal of controversy about what actually takes place in learning. This discussion is largely based on the formulations of Dollard and Miller (1941, 1950, 1959), an important pair of workers in this area, and it is limited to a consideration of some principles of learning which seem most relevant to the study of adjustment. To begin with, here is an illustration of learning, along with a brief analysis.

An Illustration of Learning[1]

A small boy is out on a hand-in-hand stroll with his mother. After awhile he decides that he wants to go it on his own. He attempts to pull away but finds that his mother's grip is firm. " 'Go, mommy, 'go," he pleads, but his mother refuses to let go. He grows angry. "Bad mommy. Bad mommy. Bad mommy," he says. However, his mother seems invulnerable to censure. He begins to whimper, then wail, then howl. His mother finally begins to show signs of weakening. He gains momentum, begins screaming, kicking, and skyrocketing around in this mother's grasp. Exhausted and overcome, she lets go, and her son toddles off to explore the world on his own.

The next day the scene is repeated. First, there is the tugging, then the verbal pleading and rebuke, and finally the accelerating tantrum which accomplishes the job. In the days that follow, the unsuccessful responses begin to drop out, and the successful one occurs earlier. The little boy no longer expends much of his energy

[1] This illustration was suggested by a similar presentation by Morgan (1956).

tugging, pleading, and rebuking. Almost as soon as he encounters resistance, he goes into the full-fledged tantrum without the useless preliminaries.

Since the tantrum is successful in one situation, it can be put to work in similar situations. It may force his mother to relinquish a cookie even though it is almost time for lunch. It may gain him access to the out-of-doors even though the afternoon is rainy. Although bedtime has come and gone, the tantrum may be his ticket to more play, more television, or another glass of water. Since his mother is vulnerable to tantrums, displays of temper become the order of the day—and night.

Because the tantrum is so useful in dealing with his mother, it can be tried out on others who similarly serve to frustrate him. His father, grandmother, and the baby-sitter are all fair game. However, the tantrum may not prove successful with all of them. Although this tactic devastates his grandmother, the baby-sitter is scarcely moved. Furthermore, in trying out the tantrum on his father, the child finds that he places the security and comfort of his bottom in jeopardy.

The Illustration under Analysis

Consider again the toddler in the illustration. He is beginning to feel the need for a little autonomy. He tries one response, then another, and another until he finally hits upon one that is successful: the tantrum. Since the tantrum gets him to his goal, it is *reinforced* or strengthened, and there will be a tendency to repeat this response in the future.

At the same time, the little fellow was trying out a number of responses that were not successful. The pleading and verbal attack, for example, served little purpose. These responses were not reinforced. Responses that do not lead to reinforcement are *extinguished* or weakened, and there will be a tendency for these responses to drop out in the future.

As was said, the tantrum has been reinforced and will tend to be used again. It will be tried not only in the same situation but also in many similar ones. The more similar a second situation is to the first, the greater will be the tendency for

Figure 7.1 Learning by imitation. Where do our acts or responses originate? The responses we show in a particular situation may be carried over from an earlier one. Sometimes a response is derived from earlier bits of behavior; just as we perfect our skill at a sport, social behavior may be shaped and modified until it serves our purposes. Another important source of behavior is imitation: we acquire new responses by modeling our behavior after that of other people. Imitation may also serve to facilitate or inhibit behavior which is already in our repertoire.

The way that reactions to frustration may be shaped through imitation was demonstrated in an experiment involving several groups of preschool children. An experimental group witnessed real-life aggressive models or filmed portrayals of aggression; the control group did not. Then both groups were mildly frustrated (their play with highly attractive toys was interrupted), and they were removed to another room which contained some toys which could be used for aggressive or nonaggressive behavior. The results indicated that the experimental group expressed nearly twice as much aggression as the control group, and as the photographs show, some of the children in the experimental group showed aggressive behavior which was nearly a carbon copy of their models (Bandura, Ross, & Ross, 1963).

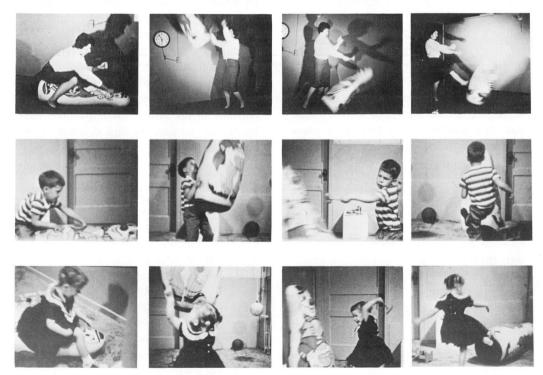

the tantrum to recur. When a response which has proved successful in one situation is employed in a similar one, the response is said to be *generalized.*

The little boy finds, however, that the tantrum is not always successful in the other situations to which it is applied. It works fine on his grandmother, not very well on the baby-sitter, and not at all on his father. Where the tantrum is rewarded, it tends to be repeated. Where it is not rewarded, it tends not to be used again. This process of distinguishing between situations in which a generalized response is successful and those in which it is not is called *discrimination.*

Certain responses which have been found to be useful in a number of situations tend to become a prominent part of a person's behavior. They form a pattern of adjustment, a typical or characteristic way of reacting to both old and novel situations. In this way, to extend the illustration, a tantrum may become a lifelong mode of response. If early tantrums have been successful, a person may continue to display childish fits of temper even as an adult. By contrast, another individual whose tantrums have not been rewarded

will abandon this response early in childhood. (See Fig. 7.1)

SOME IMPORTANT PRINCIPLES OF LEARNING

In the foregoing analysis a number of basic learning principles were briefly identified. These principles are central to the present discussion since they throw light on how a person learns new acts and new needs and new goals as well. Each principle is reintroduced and amplified in the material that follows.

Reinforcement

When we are driven by a need and encounter frustration, conflict, or anxiety, we may try one act or response, then another, then another. If we hit upon a response that helps us solve our problem, this response is *reinforced* or strengthened. With recurrence of the problem in the future, the response that has proved successful in the past tends to be used again (see Fig. 7.2).

Figure 7.2 Confronted by a problem we may try one act or response, then another, and another. A response that helps us get to our goal is *reinforced* or strengthened and tends to be used again in similar situations.

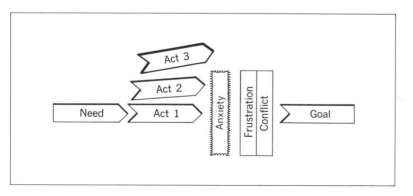

Primary and Secondary Reinforcement

Goal objects whose reward value does not have to be learned are called *primary reinforcers* and are said to provide *primary reinforcement*. Water and food are examples of primary reinforcers; each of these is originally and inherently satisfying and provides reward value without any necessity of prior experience.

Goal objects whose reward value is learned are called *secondary reinforcers* and are said to provide *secondary reinforcement*. Money is an example of a secondary reinforcer. Babies and people in barter societies do not value money. Even in our own culture the value placed on having money varies widely. Some of us are little interested in money and wealth, and a few of us seem to be little interested in anything else.

Secondary reinforcers acquire their reward value through association with primary reinforcers or with other secondary reinforcers which have already attained such value. Money has reward value because of the rewarding things that money can provide (food, power, and so on). But, as Dollard and Miller (1950) point out, in runaway inflation, money may no longer provide these things, and it can lose its power as a reinforcer.

Secondary reinforcement plays an important role in the adjustment process. Consider, for example, the need for affiliation. In the chapter on motives this need was said to be manifested in the desire to associate with, cooperate with, and form friendships with others. People differ considerably in the strength of their affiliation needs and in the ways they manifest them.

The newborn infant shows little need for affiliation. However, it does demonstrate a number of physiological needs. It needs nourishment, rest, and comfort, and its mother or a mother substitute usually provides the goals (or primary reinforcers) for these requirements. Thirsty, hungry, tired, hot, cold, wet, or in pain, the infant cries, and the mother comes to attend its wants. In this way, hour after hour, day after day, the mother becomes associated with the satisfaction of important needs.

Now a progressive change occurs in the infant's behavior. Although it may be in need and crying lustily, it becomes increasingly quiet as its mother approaches. Sometimes, without apparent physiological need, it cries but appears silent and content as soon as it is within its mother's arms. Sometimes, too, it is quiet until it sees or hears its mother; then it begins to cry and continues to do so until it is picked up and held.

At this point one could say that the infant demonstrates a need for its mother. Through her association with primary reinforcers, the mother has acquired reward value herself. She is a secondary or learned reinforcer.

The matter is not this simple, for there is some possibility that the intimate physical contact provided by the mother is itself inherently satisfying (Bowlby, 1961; Harlow, 1958). But it is true that as the baby develops, it shows a decided preference for its mother or whoever has been caring for it even though other people can and may upon occasion provide it with nourishment and physical comfort.

As the individual grows, his social environment expands rapidly. His needs are largely met in association with other people. If early social relationships are happy ones, that is, if they are associated with successful goal seeking, people come to be desired for themselves. The individual will want to be with others, and he enters new relationships with the expectation, based on previous experience, that these will also be rewarding.

Sometimes early social relationships are unhappy ones. Early needs may have been met irregularly, without affection, even with hostility. If so, the individual may be extremely reluctant to form new relationships. He regards people as irritating, dangerous, or at best useless objects.

In this way needs are learned or modified, and the things that can satisfy them acquire reward value. If people have been associated with satisfying experiences, we learn to need them and seek them. If experiences with others have been unrewarding or punishing, our need for affiliation may be minimal. In fact, we may seek to avoid others and to be by ourselves as much as possible.

Continuous and Partial Reinforcement

Continuous reinforcement exists when a particular response is always followed by reward. In *partial reinforcement,* reward sometimes but not always follows the response. In the laboratory, learning conditions may be controlled so that reinforcement occurs always or never or any specified amount of the time. Outside the laboratory, however, reinforcement is seldom continuous.

In real life few responses are so successful that they are always rewarded. Some responses prove successful only occasionally. And a response that on one occasion leads to reward may on another result in punishment.

Consider a little girl who is showing off. On one occasion her parents may think she is funny, and their laughter, attention, and approval are highly rewarding. But on a second occasion they may be too busy to take notice, and if she persists in her behavior, they may become annoyed, decide that she is acting too smart, and send her off to bed.

A child's eight-o'clock headaches may sometimes (but not always) convince her mother that there should be no school that day. And when the headaches fail, her nine-o'clock vomiting may sometimes (but not always) convince her teacher that she should be allowed to return home. Since the stratagems are sometimes successful and sometimes not, they can be said to be partially reinforced.

We know from personal experience that old habits are hard to break. Some adjustment patterns that seem seldom rewarded—even some that appear to do us more harm than good—are resistant to change and modification. Our rationalizations, for example, may only half deceive ourselves, yet they may go on endlessly. Our lies may almost never deceive others, yet we may seem unable to stick to the truth.

Using both animal and human subjects, laboratory scientists have discovered some important differences in the effects of continuous and partial reinforcement. Their findings have some important practical implications. (But, of course, caution must be used in generalizing from carefully controlled laboratory behavior to the behavior which occurs under natural conditions.)

First, it has been found that subjects can learn under continuous or partial reinforcement. Generally speaking, however, continuous reinforcement is more effective than partial reinforcement in establishing the desired behavior in a subject. Acquisition of a new response, a new act, or a new adjustment pattern proceeds more quickly if it is rewarded each time it occurs (Jenkins & Stanley, 1950).

Second, once established, behavior is adequately maintained with partial reinforcement (Jenkins & Stanley, 1950). That is to say, once a particular bit of behavior has been learned or acquired, it does not need to be rewarded each time it occurs. It will persist even if it is rewarded only occasionally.

Third, responses which have been built up under partial reinforcement generally prove to be more resistant to extinction than do those which are acquired under continuous reinforcement (Bijou, 1957; Jenkins & Stanley, 1950). In the absence of further reward, habits which were learned under continuous reinforcement die out or fade away more quickly than do those which were only occasionally reinforced during the acquisition process. Deese (1958) suggests that the reason most habits are so resistant to extinction is that they are built up under partial reinforcement; parents, he points out, are inconsistent in their use of rewards and "inconsistency in the application of reinforcement is the stuff of which persistent behavior is made."

Immediate and Delayed Reinforcement

Rewards that coincide with or immediately follow a particular response are said to provide *immediate reinforcement* for that response. If a reward occurs some time after the response, it is said to provide *delayed reinforcement*. The difference between the two is a simple matter of degree. The nearer the response and reward are to each other in time the more *immediate* and less *delayed* the reinforcement.

Immediate reinforcements are more effective than delayed reinforcements (Bijou & Baer, 1961; Dollard & Miller, 1950). The more closely a reward follows a response the more it will serve to strengthen this response. Conversely, the more delay there is between response and reward, the less effective the reward.

For a reward to be most effective, then, it must be presented quickly. Those of us who have taught or trained children have probably made practical use of this principle. Given a choice between one nickel today and two nickels tomorrow, the small child will almost invariably take the former. Asking a youngster to be good in January so that Santa Claus will bring him something nice next Christmas is not apt to be very successful. However, on December 24, the technique may work wonders.

This principle also applies to the administration of punishment. For a punishment to be most effective it must quickly follow the response that we want to eliminate. The young child who is punished long after committing a prohibited response has difficulty in associating the two events. Punishments that are delayed for hours (You just wait until Daddy comes home!) frequently fail to produce the desired effects.

One of the difficulties in training children is that the responses we attempt to discourage through punishment have already been rewarded. A boy may be punished for playing hookey from school but he already has had a wonderful afternoon at the movies or down at the creek.

The hookey response is more closely associated with the pleasurable matinee than with the tearful evening.

If we attempt to increase the amount of punishment in order to compensate for its delay, we may produce other unhappy consequences. And anyway it may not work, because an immediate reward—even a small one—may prove more powerful than a punishment that is delayed. "Why did I do it?" we ask ourselves when we wake up with a splitting headache the morning after. "Never again!" we insist. But how many of us manage to keep our resolution?

However, the matter is not so hopeless as it might seem, because we can learn to respond to symbolic punishments and rewards (Dollard & Miller, 1950). The threat of punishment may be as painful or even more painful than the punishment itself. In the same way, the promise of reward may be as reinforcing as immediate reward, and a good deal of the pleasure of a reward may be in its anticipation.

Society teaches us to forego small immediate rewards in order to gain more important rewards in the future. Rather than settling for a bird in hand, we work for the two in the bush. We may scrimp and slave and struggle through four or six or eight years of college. The thought of future rewards—more than anything else—may be the thing that keeps us going.

Positive and Negative Reinforcement

Our actions are directed toward certain objects and away from others. For example, we may be attracted to money, a sex partner, good food or drink, a medal, or praise. We avoid disease, extreme temperatures, and situations that made us unhappy or anxious. The contrast made here is between positive and negative reinforcement (Skinner, 1953). A *positive reinforcer* is something which strengthens a response when it is presented. A *negative reinforcer* is something which strengthens a response when it is withdrawn.

The relative merits of reward and punishment in promoting learning and controlling behavior have been a matter of controversy for years both among laymen and psychologists. Postman writes:

> Many of our educational, social, and legal practices are based on the assumption that rewards and punishments are effective and reliable tools for the modification of behavior. The general belief is that actions which are followed by rewards are strengthened, while actions which are followed by punishments are weakened or eliminated. These assumptions of common sense have not received undivided support from the experimental study of behavior. In fact, the role played by rewards and punishments has become one of the most controversial issues in contemporary learning theory (1962, p. 331).

Ordinarily what is meant by "reward" is the presentation of a positive reinforcer (food, money, praise, a good grade, a gold medal, and so on) in order to ensure and strengthen a response. It is also rewarding to have a negative reinforcer removed; for example, a person may work hard so that he won't be criticized or punished. "Punishment" generally refers to the presentation of a negative reinforcer such as a spanking, a fine, or imprisonment. But having a positive reinforcer removed is also punishing as, for example, when a child is prevented from watching television or sent to bed without dinner.

Since the beginning of time, punishment has been the most common technique for controlling behavior. As Skinner states:

> The pattern is familiar: if a man does not behave as you wish, knock him down; if a child misbehaves, spank him; if the people of a country misbehave, bomb them. Legal and police systems are based upon such punishments as fines, flogging, incarceration, and hard labor. Religious control is exerted through penances, threats of excommunication, and consignment to hellfire. Education has not wholly abandoned the birch rod. In everyday personal contact we control through censure, snubbing, disapproval, or banishment. In short, the degree to which we use punishment as a technique of control seems to be limited only by the degree to which we can gain the necessary power. All of this is done with the intention of reducing tendencies to behave in certain ways. Reinforcement builds up these tendencies; punishment is designed to tear them down (1953, p. 182).

More recently there has been an increasing emphasis on reward. Part of this change has been due to heightened humanitarian concern. Much of it has been influenced by a number of psychological investigations which have raised doubt that punishment was accomplishing all it was supposed to. Some of the more important arguments against the use of punishment are these:

1 Punishment may inhibit a response without destroying it (Estes, 1944). If the response were made without reinforcement, ultimately it would suffer extinction. However, if the response is simply suppressed, it may continue to exist in the individual's repertoire. It may appear in disguised ways or, where punishment is not imminent, it may crop out in its original form.

2 Punishment may result in entrenching the very behavior that it was designed to eliminate (Hilgard, 1962). In their study of child-rearing patterns Sears, Maccoby, and Levin, for example, found that punishment was ineffectual and had unwanted consequences. They write:

> The evidence for this conclusion is overwhelming. The unhappy effects of punishment have run like a dismal thread through our findings. Mothers who punished toilet accidents severely ended up with bed-wetting children. Mothers who punished dependency to get rid of it had more dependent children than mothers who did not punish. Mothers who punished aggressive behavior severely had more aggressive children than mothers who punished lightly. They also had more dependent children. Harsh physical punishment was associated with high childhood aggressiveness and with the development of feeding problems.[2]

3 Punishment may tell the individual what not to do but not what to do (Hilgard, 1962). When a person is punished for a response, he may not know what to do instead. Sometimes it must seem to the child that he is acceptable only when he is completely inactive. However, he can hardly meet his needs by doing nothing at all. He should be helped to find ways of responding which are satisfactory both to himself and to others.

4 Punishment may cause emotional arousal which is not conducive to changing be-

[2] From *Patterns of Child Rearing* by R. R. Sears, E. E. Maccoby and H. Levin. Copyright © 1957 by Harper & Row, Publishers, Inc. Reprinted by permission of Harper & Row, Publishers. P. 484.

havior. Everyone involved in the punish-ment situation may be highly aroused. In a family setting, for example, both the punishing adult and the punished child may be extremely angry and in-dignant. There may be little attempt to explain to the child why he was wrong. Do what you're told and don't ask ques-tions! The child may become extremely resentful and more determined than ever to repeat his response, although em-ploying greater care not to get caught.

5 Punishment may produce considerable hostility in the person being disciplined. Since hostility is frequently punished and since punishment itself may cause considerable hostility in the punished person, aggressive discipline may only intensify the very behavior that it is in-tended to eliminate (Bandura, 1961; Sears et al., 1957). Furthermore, when a parent punishes a child in an aggressive way, he is furnishing his child with a model for aggression which the child may then emulate (Sears et al., 1957).

6 Punishment may produce unfortunate attitudes toward the punisher and to-ward authority figures in general (Estes, 1944; Hilgard, 1962). Any adult who administers severe punishment may be regarded with considerable anger and fear by the child. Since this same adult may also reward as well as punish, strongly ambivalent feelings may be pro-duced. The child is caught between con-flicting tendencies to love and to hate, to approach and to withdraw.

7 Punishment may be more an expres-sion of the punisher's need for aggres-sion than of the victim's need for change (Hilgard, 1962). The aggressive adult, for example, frequently victimizes his children since they are "safe" objects

for his displeasure. He rationalizes his actions, perhaps claiming that he is doing it for his children's good, but punishment administered in this way can scarcely do anyone good. Any upset par-ent is likely to displace aggression at some time or other, and his children may sense these times and modify their own behavior accordingly.

8 Punishment may take place too long after a forbidden response has occurred to have any effect (Estes, 1944). Im-mediate consequences are more effective than delayed ones, and in many cases reward is immediate while punishment is delayed. Consider again the example of the little boy who has spent the after-noon at the movies or elsewhere instead of in school. He may be punished that evening when he gets home, true, but he has been rewarded all afternoon.

9 Punishment may lead to a reliance on external restraints rather than on more desirable internal controls (Bandura, 1961; Bandura & Walters, 1959). Re-ferring to the treatment of antisocial adolescents, Bandura writes:

The threat of punishment is very likely to elicit conformity; indeed, the patient may obligingly do whatever he is told to do in order to avoid immediate difficulties. This does not mean, however, that he has acquired a set of sanctions that will be of service to him once he is outside the treatment situation. In fact, rather than leading to the development of internal con-trols, such methods are likely only to in-crease the patient's reliance on external restraints. Moreover, under these condi-tions, the majority of patients will develop the attitude that they will do only what they are told to do—and then often only half-heartedly—and that they will do as they please once they are free from the therapist's supervision (1961, p. 151).

Presentation 7.1 Crime and punishment. In 1967, the President's Commission on Law Enforcement and Administration of Justice estimated that 7 million persons would get into some trouble with the law that year and that 400,000 persons were behind bars and another 900,000 were on parole or probation. Among the reforms the Commission called for were changes in the treatment of criminals. In the past, a heavy reliance has been placed on punishment. Today this emphasis is changing, since punishment has not proved to be a very effective device in modifying the behavior of lawbreakers. Below is a review of some of the limitations of punishment in the treatment of criminals (compare these arguments with the more general arguments against the use of punishment noted on pages 180–181).

1 *Punishment often isolates the individual who is punished and makes him a confirmed enemy of society, and his influence may extend to other individuals. When the sole reaction is punitive, criminals are isolated from law-abiding groups, and neither understand nor are understood by these groups. Hatred of the criminal by society results in hatred of society by the criminal. In this respect, the behavior is much like war, which produces a relatively complete isolation and dissociation of warring nations. When he is effectively ostracized, the criminal has only two alternatives: he may associate with other criminals, among whom he can find recognition, prestige, and means of further criminality; or he may become disorganized, psychopathic, or unstable. Our actual practice is to permit almost all criminals to return to society, in a physical sense, but to hold them off, make them keep their distance, segregate them in the midst of the ordinary community. Thus they are kept isolated from law-abiding groups. If they are to be turned into law-abiding citizens, they must be assimilated into society and treated as persons with the potential to be law-abiding citizens.*

2 *Punishment develops caution. Probably a painful experience, such as being punished or being stung by bees, will* make the actor "think twice" before he repeats the behavior. But, in the case of the bees, "thinking twice" may be a means of securing immunity from the bees while molesting them. The actor has been made cautious by the previous suffering, but not "reformed." Similarly, an unanticipated consequence of current systems for punishing criminals might be cautiousness, not reformation. For example, professional and organized criminals have great skill in the execution of their crimes and in addition take many precautions to provide in advance for immunity in case they are caught. The result is that twenty-five amateur shoplifters who have stolen little articles in stores are likely to be convicted in a court while one professional shoplifter who steals hundreds of times as much as all of these amateurs escapes conviction. The amateur criminal, however, in the course of a few punishments of this nature acquires skill, largely in the penal institutions.

3 *Punishment creates other unanticipated attitudes. Even if some acts were known to be preventable by punishment, this prevention would not necessarily prove that punishment has promoted the social welfare. Whatever is accomplished by preventing that specific act may be more than off-set by general attitudes produced by it. For instance, a child's practice of lying might be stopped by punishment. But as a result, the child might come to fear the parent who inflicted the punishment, and be estranged or alienated. If the parent is to have great influence over the child, he must keep the confidence of the child, and the relation between them must be very intimate and friendly, especially at the time when the child begins to be away from home many hours a day. Similarly, if the prevention of a particular delinquency results in loss of general control of the child, it is a doubtful gain. And thus the punitive reaction frequently creates other attitudes in criminals or in the public even when a particular crime*

is successfully forestalled—lack of respect for law, lack of patriotism, lack of willingness to sacrifice for the state, and lack of initiative. Perhaps the most serious consequence of punishment to the offender is loss of self-respect. Real efficiency in dealing with criminals involves not only the stopping of specific violations of law but the accomplishment of this result without the loss of other social values.

4 *Punishment often gives an offender high status.* Among criminals, one's standing is frequently promoted by punishment. In states whose prisons are scaled from tough maximum-security institutions down to minimum-security institutions, youthful offenders frequently request assignment to the maximum-security institutions, because such assignment will result in high status among their friends when they are released. They attempt to avoid assignment to reformatories and minimum-security institutions, because incarceration there does not bring the desired prestige. [It has been] shown that within prisons positions of leadership go to men convicted of serious offenses, such as robbery, and to men with long punitive sentences.

5 *Punishment generally stops constructive efforts.* If the group, in a spirit of hatred, inflicts punishment upon the offender, it generally sits back, after the penalty is inflicted, with a sigh of relief and with a feeling that the matter is now settled. But the situation remains, in general, just as it was before the punishment was inflicted. Such a punitive reaction may produce fear in the offender, but more than fear is required for an alteration of character, personality, and behavior. Reformation involves not only a determination to change one's behavior, but a constructive process of organizing or reorganizing behavior. One must have stimulations, patterns, suggestions, sentiments, and ideals presented to him. And the individual must develop his definitions and attitudes by practice, generally in a slow and gradual manner. One must have an appreciation of the values which are conserved by the law, and this can be produced only by assimilating the culture of the group which passed the law, or, stated otherwise, only if the group which passed the law assimilates the criminal. The negative act of prohibiting a thing is not sufficient because it is not constructive and does not promote assimilation. (Reprinted by permission from *Principles of Criminology* by Edwin H. Sutherland and Donald R. Cressey, published by J. B. Lippincott Company. Copyright © 1924, 1960, 1966 by J. B. Lippincott Company.)

The information that is accumulating on this subject should lead us to be very cautious in our use of punishment. This does not mean, however, that punishment is never warranted. Sometimes it is unavoidable. And under certain conditions it may be a useful technique. Some of these conditions are as follows:

1 Punishment may be used to temporarily suppress a response. As has been already noted, punishment serves to inhibit rather than destroy a response. However, in some circumstances it may be necessary to interrupt a response so that a new one may be elicited and reinforced (Deese, 1958; Estes, 1944). Thus, we might punish a child who persistently eats with his fingers in order to get him to try to use his spoon.

2 Punishment may be used when alternative responses are available. If a need is strong and only one response is available to meet it, punishment will not be very effective. The most it may do is inhibit the response for awhile. However,

if alternative responses are available, punishment of the original response may elicit the alternative actions. We cannot, for example, allow our little son to molest the baby, and our concern may lead us to punish him or threaten punishment. At the same time, we encourage him to express his feelings in other ways, perhaps verbally or in aggressive play with his toys.

3 Punishment may be used to supply information (Hilgard, 1962). This assumes that the punishment is more of a signal than anything else and that it is mild enough not to cause very much pain, fear, or anger. The child who teases the cat and is scratched or who eats too many green apples and has a stomachache is being administered some informative punishment. No! Bad boy! Don't do that! These and similar parental expressions of displeasure also may serve as mild punishments. The student who receives a low mark on a test also feels punished; however, at the same time he has an opportunity to correct and supplement his inadequate information and learn how he stands with reference to the rest of the class.

4 Punishment may be used to direct behavior. Some punishments have the effect of eliciting a desired response. For example, removing the blanket from an oversleeping child may administer a punishing draft of chilly air and encourage him to get up, get dressed, and go off to school. In this connection, Sears and his associates write:

It must be remembered that punishment is not only an impelling force, but also a directive one. A slap on the hand will not only make a child jerk: it will make him jerk away from the forbidden object. If the punishment is of a kind that produces

(directs) action of a kind the mother wants, the punishment is likely to have a salutary effect—just as an offered reward would have.[3]

In evaluating punishment we must consider the effect it has on the child's long-term adjustment as well as on his immediate behavior. Many authorities agree that for the best overall results, if punishment is to be administered, it should be mild, prompt, and consistent. Hilgard, a psychologist prominent in the field of learning, sums up this position as follows:

Parents are often puzzled about how much they should punish their children and yet most of them find that they resort to some sorts of deprivation if not to the actual inflicting of pain. The best advised use of punishment is the informative one, so that the child will know what is and is not allowed. Children occasionally "test the limits" to see what degree of unpermitted behavior they will be able to get by with. When they do, it is advisable to use discipline that is firm but not harsh, and to administer it promptly and consistently. Nagging at the child for his non-conforming behavior may in the end be less humane than an immediate spanking. The child who is threatened with some kind of vague but postponed punishment ("What kind of person do you think you will grow up to be?") may be punished more severely than one who is taught what is expected, who pays a consistent penalty for infringement, but who then is welcomed back into the family circle as a good citizen (1962, pp. 330–331).

Extinction

In a problem situation we may vary our

[3] From *Patterns of Child Rearing* by R. R. Sears, E. E. Maccoby and H. Levin. Copyright © 1957 by Harper & Row, Publishers, Inc. Reprinted by permission of Harper & Row, Publishers. Pp. 485–486.

behavior, trying first one response and then another. Those responses that do not help us solve our problems tend to be *extinguished* or weakened. In similar situations in the future such responses tend not to be used again (see Fig. 7.3).

Once a response has become habitual it may be very difficult to extinguish. Many of our habits resist change even though they are clearly detrimental in the long run. A number of methods have been proposed for breaking habits. The discussion of punishment was concerned with one such method, and the material that follows presents additional approaches. Some of these methods are focused directly on the offending response itself, others on encouraging an alternative response, and still others on altering the stimulus situation.

The Unrewarded Response Method

In the *unrewarded response method* an unwanted response is extinguished by withholding reward or reinforcement. We can think of many examples of this method applied to everyday problems. In fact, a good deal of our behavior is "shaped" by other people who reward us if we behave in certain ways and withhold reward when we "misbehave."

Here are some examples of this method applied to specific problems. To stop our dog from hounding the table, we decide to quit giving it snacks and scraps from our plates. To discourage procrastination in completing assignments, a teacher announces that effective at once he no longer will accept late papers. To put an end to the nightly ritual of carrying water to her bedded youngster, a mother deafens herself to his pleas (see Fig. 7.4).

A person can apply this method to himself as well as to others. When you go to the library to study, you may find the assignment boring and you feel sleepy. After all there is no point in wasting time trying to study when you are tired. However, fifteen minutes after this strategem has been rewarded, you find yourself at the bowling alley full of pep. If you refuse to reward the feigned sleep response and stay on the job, something may be accomplished. At least, the next time in the library there will be a diminished tendency to try this deception, although, of course, you may discover other ways to outwit yourself.

Figure 7.3 Confronted by a problem we may vary our acts or responses. Responses that do not help us solve our problems or reach our goals tend to be *extinguished* or weakened, and they are less likely to be used in the future.

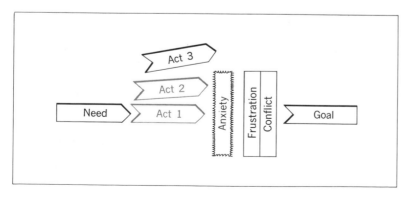

Figure 7.4 What can be done about the delaying tactics shown by children at bedtime? The unrewarded response method was applied in the case of a small boy, twenty-one months old. Although recovered from a serious illness, he demanded the same care as before. When put to bed, he threw a tantrum unless an adult attended him while he fell asleep.

When there was medical reassurance that the boy was well, it was decided to try to put a stop to this behavior. The extinction began with the boy being put to bed in a relaxed and leisurely way. Then the adult left the bedroom, closed the door, and did not return despite the tantrum behavior.

The results are shown in the figure. The first bedtime under this method, the boy cried for forty-five minutes; the second time he did not cry at all, perhaps because he was worn out by his earlier tantrums. By the tenth time, crying had stopped. However, about a week later the tantrum behavior flared up again, and it was reinforced by an aunt who remained in the bedroom until the boy fell asleep. A second process of extinction was begun with results similar to the first. By the ninth time, all crying had stopped and did not recur. No unfortunate aftereffects were noted in the two-year follow-up period (Williams, 1959).

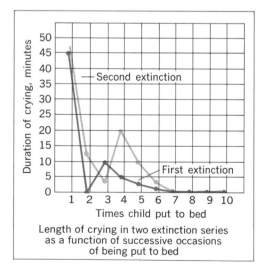

Length of crying in two extinction series as a function of successive occasions of being put to bed

Some professional psychotherapies make important use of this method. In the therapy situation the client may show the same unfortunate defensive behavior that has added to his difficulties in everyday life, and the therapist attempts to extinguish this behavior by showing the client that it is unnecessary and unrewarding. In this connection, Shaffer and Shoben write:

> The therapist's behavior brings about an extinction of the client's defenses in the therapeutic situation. The client's defensive behavior is unrewarded because it does not work. The therapist does not "fall for it." The defensive behavior may even be considered to be mildly punished because the therapist gently calls the client's attention to his evasions and to the functions they serve. As therapy proceeds, defensive and evasive tactics tend to occur with decreasing frequency, giving the client an opportunity to think more straightforwardly about his anxieties and nonintegrative adjustments (1956, p. 531).

This method is a simple one, but it is not necessarily an easy or quick way to break unwanted habits. If a habit has been built up over a long time, it may be quite resistant to extinction procedures. Furthermore, this method is effective only when it is rigidly observed. As was noted before, a response that has received partial reinforcement may be extremely resistant to extinction. In the process of extinguishing a response, we must be careful never to reward it. If we lapse and reward the response just one more time, we may not only undo everything we have done, we may make our job much harder than before.

The Exhausted Response Method

In the *exhausted response method* there

is an attempt to facilitate the production of the unacceptable response while withholding reward so that it may be extinguished more rapidly. This is sometimes felt to be necessary since the situation in which the response occurs may be relatively infrequent, and between several trials the response may recover much of its original vigor. Laboratory studies generally show that extinction is more easily accomplished under continuous or nearly continuous practice than under practice which is distributed over a long period (Bandura, 1961).

Broncobusting is a simple example of the exhausted response method. The broncobuster attempts to stay on the horse until it is too worn out to buck. The buster further encourages the bucking response by shouting at and goading the horse. After a while, assuming that the buster has been able to maintain his seat, the horse becomes too fatigued to respond, and it is less likely to do any bucking in the future.

Ungentle as this method seems, it is not infrequently used by parents. Some of them appear to facilitate unacceptable behavior in their children. The crying child, for example, may be encouraged in this response. Sometimes he may be swatted so that he will have something to cry about. The philosophy behind this treatment seems to be that the sooner the child has it out the better.

Sometimes this method is used with responses that, when overpracticed, provide their own punishment. The small boy who is caught smoking is made to continue until he is thoroughly ill and averse to the whole business. Parents may allow a child on some occasion to eat all the candy or pie or green apples that he can

hold, with the hope, frequently futile, that the ensuing abdominal distress will teach him a lesson the hard way.

Some professional psychotherapies make use of a nearly identical technique called "negative practice." In this technique a person who has some unwanted (negative) behavior voluntarily practices this behavior. In effect, the negative behavior is extinguished by practicing it without reinforcement.

Negative practice has been applied to a wide variety of behavior with varying degrees of success (Bandura, 1961; Lehner, 1954). For example, it has been shown to be of some benefit in correcting errors in spelling, typing, and piano playing. There are indications that it may be of use in the treatment of speech disorders, such as stuttering (Sheehan, 1951; Sheehan & Voas, 1957), and in the alleviation of tics (Abi Rafi, 1962; Yates, 1958).

The Impossible Response Method

In the *impossible response method* we attempt to break a habit by making it impossible or at least extremely difficult for the response to occur. Even though the response is prevented, the stimulation is continued and perhaps intensified. Thus, it is hoped that the unacceptable response will be extinguished and that some other more acceptable behavior will be learned.

It was noted earlier that one of the effects of punishment is to temporarily interrupt or inhibit a response. In such a situation our behavior may become more variable. We try other responses, and when one of these (hopefully, a better one) is reinforced it may substitute for the unwanted and punished response (Postman, 1962).

This method is frequently used in

rearing children. For example, parents are concerned about making certain approach responses impossible: hence, the cookie jar on the top shelf, the pills and medicines locked away, the fence around the swimming pool. Two squabbling youngsters may be placed in separate rooms to make friction less possible and necessary.

At the same time, a parent may be concerned about making certain avoidance responses impossible. When all else seems to fail, a child may be literally dragged to the doctor or dentist or barber. Sad to say, more than one child has been forced into a fearful situation (locked in a dark room, dunked in the swimming pool, etc.) by a parent who was determined to show that there was nothing there to be afraid of.

This method is also used by adults to modify their own behavior. They may commit themselves to a course of action from which they are not able to deviate later. One savings plan makes it necessary for the person to save since once the money is deposited it cannot be withdrawn for a certain length of time. One type of therapy for alcoholics makes use of a drug with which alcohol is incompatible; once the drug is administered, alcohol cannot be consumed, since in combination the two cause almost immediate and violent physical distress.

The Rewarded Alternative Method

In the *rewarded alternative method* the learner is taught an acceptable response to the situation. This response is rewarded while the unacceptable response is not. The method is structured more as a learning task than as an extinction one. It emphasizes what *is* to be done rather than what *is not* to be done (see Fig. 7.5, pp. 190–191).

To the small child parents must sometimes appear to be people who "don't" you. Don't do this. Don't do that. To be good you have to be something that doesn't do anything at all. You must be as inactive as possible. The rewarded alternative method, by contrast, aims to put the "do" back into behavior.

Distraction sometimes plays an important part in this method. The baby's fingers are guided away from his medicated bandage and to the interesting toy. The mother who is concerned about her son's absorption in television buys him some colorful books, airplane kits, or a chemistry set and rewards the attention that he gives these items.

We may use this method to show children how to meet their needs in acceptable ways. Children who seem to be going through aggressive phases, for example, can be helped to discharge their feelings in activities which the society does not frown on. For example, they can be encouraged to express themselves in certain forms of aggressive play. All sorts of toy weapons may help serve the purpose, and in addition, children may be turned loose with materials (*not* people) that can be assaulted, beaten, pounded, and torn apart.

The Incompatible Alternative Method

In the *incompatible alternative method* the situation is altered so that an acceptable response which is incompatible with the unacceptable response is called forth (see Fig. 7.6). When two antagonistic responses are aroused simultaneously, both cannot gain full expression. In this method there is an attempt to make the bond between the stimulus and the acceptable response stronger so that it will always be elicited.

A good deal of practical use is made of this method. Some dentists show movies when they are working on a small child. The movies not only serve as a distraction, but they help elicit an acceptable response. Other people who deal with children use similar methods. A barber, for example, may silence a protesting child by plopping a sucker into his mouth.

Sometimes we attempt to apply this method to ourselves. A person who feels himself driven toward unacceptable sexual behavior may indulge in some strenuous athletic activity in order to make himself too tired to respond. One "cure" for smoking directs the person to chew gum or suck on a mint whenever he feels the impulse to smoke.

This method of breaking habits can backfire if it is not used carefully. The mother who attempts to get her youngster to take a distasteful medicine by putting it in his orange juice may not only fail to get the child to take the medicine but also cause him to develop an aversion to orange juice. A further example is provided by a child psychiatrist who reports that when a mother attempted to break her child of sucking his fingers by smearing them with quinine, the child not only continued the sucking, he developed a taste for the drug. Once when the drug was temporarily unavailable, "the mother was driven frantic by her child's persistent demand for more quinine to be smeared on his fingers, which he sucked as lustily as ever" (Kanner, 1948).

This method of altering behavior is a prominent aspect of many psychotherapies. Most people entering therapy suffer from considerable anxiety. Confronting their problems makes them all the more anxious, and they frequently seek to avoid really disturbing areas. At the same time, the warmth, support, and permissiveness provided by the therapist helps a client to feel more secure and comfortable. Through a skillful pairing of these two sets of stimuli (the problem confrontation which triggers anxiety and the therapeutic relationship which evokes comfort), problems may be approached with greater comfort, and this greater ability to deal with problems may generalize to life outside the therapy sessions (Shaffer & Shoben, 1956; Shoben, 1949, 1953).

A psychotherapeutic approach which makes central use of this method has been elaborated by Wolpe (1958). It has been called "psychotherapy by reciprocal inhibi-

Figure 7.5 (pp. 190–191) The rewarded alternative method. A group of research workers have made successful use of the rewarded alternative method in changing the behavior of socially withdrawn children in nursery school. Such children show an excessive amount of solitary play or interact only with the teacher. Interestingly enough, it has been observed that a teacher may unintentionally reinforce solitary behavior since she may be more concerned about the child and give him much more attention when he is alone than when he is with other children.

A plan was devised in which the teacher was to withhold attention from the child when he was alone and give attention whenever he made approaches to other children. First the child was attended if he merely approached another child, then if he played beside another, and finally only if there was definite interaction.

Under these new reward conditions, solitary play was greatly reduced and social play was greatly increased. Furthermore, once social play was well established it was found to persist, and the teacher did not need to continue to give more than usual amounts of attention (Resource: Donald M. Baer. Based on Baer, 1967; Harris, Wolf, & Baer, 1964.)

The teacher is inadvertently reinforcing isolate behavior; she wants the boy to interact with other children but rewards him with her attention only when she sees him by himself.

Here she notices that he is not relating to the other children.

She is concerned and goes over to give him some attention.

She persuades him to join several other boys, and then she goes off to attend some other children.

Without the teacher's attention, the boy is not attracted to the group activity. In fact, if he stays with the group, he loses the teacher's attention.

He hangs back or goes to solicit the attention of the teacher.

The teacher is again concerned and again gives her attention to the boy.

Once more she tries to persuade him to join the group, but if he does so, she takes her attention elsewhere. The boy is rewarded by the teacher's attention when he is alone but not when he is with others.

To attract the boy to social play, the teacher decides to withhold attention from him when he is alone and give attention quickly and consistently when he is with other children. To facilitate matters she prompts interaction whenever she can.

Here she notices that he is not relating to the other children.

She is concerned and goes over to the group to tell them that the little boy might know a good game with a truck.

She encourages one of them to invite the boy to join in the play.

And she helps the boy become a valued member of the group.

She rewards the boy and the group with her attention and approval.

Sometimes, of course, she leaves the group to pay attention to other children.

But she is careful to return to reward the boy and the group for their interaction. Once social play has been well-established, it persists and does not require more than usual amounts of attention. However, if the teacher consistently withdraws her attention from social activity and again rewards solitary play, the latter quickly reappears.

tion" since one response is employed to inhibit or interfere with another response which is simultaneously occurring. For example, the client is helped to relax (usually through the use of hypnosis) and then asked to imagine events that are ordinarily anxiety provoking. In the following example Wolpe discusses a case in which he uses assertive responses to inhibit anxious ones.

A university student of 19 came for treatment in a most unhappy state. For years he had been almost continuously tense and depressed, could make no friends, and although highly intelligent, had been unable to pass his examinations. I want to show you how, by expressing anti-anxiety feelings in his relationship with his stepmother he overcame some important fears. She was a most domineering woman who constantly criticized him. In a typical outburst she might say: "Why can't you pass your exams? Johnny Jones next door always passes." To this the patient would react in one of three ways—he would try to defend himself, or sulk, or have an outburst of impotent rage—for example, he once smashed the dinner plates on the floor and on another occasion pulled the electric bell out of the dining room ceiling. These three patterns of behavior, although widely different in themselves, are all expressive of the anxious, helpless feeling that this woman aroused in him. In any situation where a person is unjustly attacked, he feels anger and resentment, no matter what other reactions he may be having at the same time. My young patient had no difficulty in recognizing this to be true of himself in his encounters with his stepmother.

I told him that by giving outward expression to this anger, he would on each occasion simultaneously suppress some of the anxiety that she aroused in him. He soon became well able to express his anger against her, so that, for example, if he were now attacked on the theme of "Johnny Jones next door" his response might be "You say this sort of thing because you are jealous of Mrs. Jones. Isn't that so?" This was hitting back, expressing his resentment at the stepmother's attack. Practice of appropriate counterattack against her gradually led to a complete removal of all his fears of her, an increase in confidence with other people, a diminishing general level of anxiety. He became a very well-adjusted person, and mainly on the basis of this kind of direct action (1958, pp. 116–117).

The Increasing Stimulus Method

In the *increasing stimulus method* the stimulus for an unacceptable response is introduced at a strength insufficient to elicit this response, that is, at a level which can be accommodated. As adaptation occurs to the stimulus at one level, it is increased slightly, and this procedure is continued until considerable amounts of stimulation can be presented without triggering the unacceptable response. This approach is sometimes called the "toleration"

Figure 7.6 The incompatible alternative method. (© 1958 King Features Syndicate, Inc.)

method since at any particular time the subject is exposed to only the amount of stimulation that he can tolerate or stand without resorting to unacceptable behavior. Another term that is used is "systematic desensitization" (Wolpe, 1958).

This method is sometimes used for treating children's fears. For example, a child who is afraid of the dark is first allowed to sleep with the full light on. Gradually the wattage of the light is diminished and perhaps, too, the light is moved to a distant location. Ultimately the child may be able to tolerate complete darkness or, at most, a small light in the hall may be sufficient. In the same way, a child may be encouraged to gradually approach a dog that he fears or some other frightening object or situation.

Adults may also attack their problems in this fashion. If, for example, we are uncomfortable in social gatherings to the point of avoiding them, we may first limit ourselves to very small and intimate groups. As we gain skill and confidence in these groups, we attend increasingly larger gatherings. Finally, we may be at ease in very large groups, even in those where we are almost completely surrounded by strangers.

We may try to stop smoking by gradually cutting down, perhaps from two packs to one pack each day and then to half a pack or to one cigarette after each meal and finally to none at all (or maybe back to two packs a day). Some diets proceed in the same way; we cut down gradually, hopefully shrinking our stomachs and our appetites. These graduated or tapering-off procedures can be contrasted with crash regimens which attempt to institute immediate and drastic alterations in behavior. Wolpe (1958) has devised a systematic desensitization technique based on

relaxation. First, a client is taught to relax. An anxiety hierarchy is composed that lists in order of their potence the stimuli which cause the client to feel anxious. Then the subject is hypnotized, deeply relaxed, and asked to imagine the weakest item on the list. If there is no undue disturbance, the next weakest item is presented and so on. Usually two to four items are presented at each session, and in time it is possible for the client to calmly visualize all the formerly upsetting stimuli. This ability then is generalized to situations outside the therapy.

Clark (1963) reports a case of phobia treated by systematic desensitization. The patient was a young woman who was specifically afraid of birds and feathers. She was so fearful that she could not go for walks out of doors or to parks or zoos. She avoided pillows and cushions that had feathers in them, and she nearly fainted on one occasion when she was given a feathered hat to try on. Except for this incapacitating phobia, however, the woman appeared to be quite adequately adjusted. After twenty sessions in which relaxation was hypnotically induced and the patient was progressively introduced to feathered stimuli (first a single feather at a distance, then closer, then larger feathers and more of them, a bundle of feathers with a solid feel, stuffed birds borrowed from a museum, and so on including visits to aviaries and public parks), the patient became largely free of her original fears.

The Withheld Stimulus Method

In the *withheld stimulus method* the stimulus is prevented from occurring so that the unacceptable response is not elicited. It is hoped that the response will decay through disuse and that it will not be triggered when the stimulus appears again. Sometimes, too, during the period of withholding, the individual gains new competence to deal with the situation, making the unacceptable response no longer necessary.

Many situations which are overwhelming to small children can be managed successfully by older ones. As a child develops he is able to manage increasingly greater frustrations and conflicts. If he is exposed to undue stress, the child may take refuge in patterns of response which are detrimental to his long-term adjustment. Although a child should not be overprotected, it seems advisable to shield him from situations which provoke considerable fear, anger, and other unpleasant emotions.

As adults we may keep ourselves out of situations which provoke unacceptable responses. We avoid, for example, situations that cause us to feel anxious and people that irritate us and cause us to lose our tempers. Sometimes we leave a situation until we are sufficiently composed and organized to handle it in a way that is satisfactory to us.

For some of us, vacations may serve as an example of this method of extinguishing unacceptable responses. Sometimes we may be almost overwhelmed by problems and unable to help ourselves. The doctor may tell us that we should get away from it all. On vacation we attempt (not always successfully) to leave old stimuli behind with the hope of returning refreshed and ready for more appropriate action.

Generalization

Once we learn to handle a problem in a certain way, we tend to respond in the same way whenever the problem recurs. Furthermore, we tend to *generalize* or transfer this response to similar problem situations. Therefore, not only the original situation but any other that bears a resemblance to it will tend to trigger the response.

In the controlled environment of the laboratory the same stimulus situation can be presented again and again, but in real life almost no situation seems exactly like any other. Nevertheless, in confronting a problem we are seldom at a complete loss for response. The new situation may contain a number of stimulus elements similar to those encountered in the past. These elements tend to trigger the responses with which they have been connected.

The more similar one stimulus is to another, the more it tends to elicit responses which have been tied to the other. To say it in another way, the more two situations resemble each other, the more the transfer that will occur between them. For example, a child who has been scratched by his aunt's prize Siamese cat may as a consequence avoid all animals. However, he will probably be less wary of dogs than of cats and less concerned about the alley cats of the neighborhood than by his aunt's pet.

Consider again the little boy who is making use of tantrums to control his social environment. Since the tantrum is rewarded for its use on his mother, it is elicited in other situations that present the same stimulus elements. To greatly oversimplify the matter, these elements may be identified as female-relative-adult stimuli. The more these elements are present, the more vigorously the tantrum will be triggered. It may be elicited with great force by his grandmother (female-relative-adult), with lesser strength by his father (relative-adult) and only weakly by the adolescent baby-sitter (female).

Responses learned in one environment are transferred to many other environments. The child's earliest patterns of behavior develop in the home setting. Here in interaction with his parents, siblings, and others who may be present the child begins to form a reliance on certain sorts of rewarded behavior. As he moves into new environments he carries these ways of responding with him. Thus, to the extent that they resemble the home environment, his neighborhood, school, and other situations will elicit the same behavior he demonstrates within his family.

The school as well as the home is considered an important training ground for patterns of response. Once the child has learned something in school he is expected to be able to apply this to many other situations. Indeed, if generalization failed to occur, there would be little practical use in going to school. The student who is taught to add and subtract in the classroom is expected to be able to use this knowledge when he makes purchases for his family and himself. In the same way other academic achievements are applied to the world at large.

Failure to Generalize

Sometimes desirable generalizations fail to occur. This may be a function of limited intellectual capacity. Although the small child demonstrates an increasing capacity to form appropriate generalizations as he develops, he tends to think in specific terms (Jersild, 1960). To use an example, the little boy who has been trained to keep his hands away from the household bric-a-brac may have to be constantly disentangled from the merchandise at the supermarket.

The similarities of several situations may be too subtle even for adults to detect. Even a person who is alert to the similarities and differences involved in a situation may fail to form a necessary generalization. The gross differences may mask or call attention away from the more tenuous similarities.

Sometimes intended generalizations fail because training situations are too unlike those which are encountered later. For example, many correctional institutions present highly controlled environments which are in considerable contrast to the larger society. Inmates who adjust well to institutional stimuli (model inmates) frequently fail to respond successfully to the very different patterns of stimuli which confront them upon release (Arkoff, 1957). To remedy this situation, some institutions have been attempting to make their environments more nearly similar to those in which their inmates must later function.

Enhancing Generalization

Innate similarities in several situations may be made more explicit through appropriate labeling. By attaching the same meaningful label to several things we increase the amount of generalization. Thus, once the child has learned the meaning of "hot" we may keep him away from the stove, the radiator, a candle, and other items by specifically labeling them "hot" (Dollard & Miller, 1950).

In order to enhance generalization from training situations to practical ones, the former should be made to resemble the latter as much as possible. Noted earlier was the attempt to make correctional institutions more nearly like outside environments. As a further example, consider the soldier who is being trained for battle. He is subjected to stimuli which approximate combat conditions. He is put through obstacle courses which make use of live ammunition. He participates in battle games which are conducted almost as if they were real campaigns. These training methods take their toll of casualties, but the responses which are learned to these stimuli are appropriate to survival and victory later on.

Generalizing Emotional Response

All of us have at some time or other met a person whom we instantly liked or disliked. All of us, too, have been in some situation to which our response seemed senseless or entirely out of proportion. How can we demonstrate such full-blown emotional responses with so little apparent cause?

It was already noted that no situation is completely like another. But it is also true that no situation is completely *unlike* any other. If certain stimulus elements in the new situation have been tied to responses in the past, they will tend to trigger these responses anew. This can occur even when the general setting is quite different.

Sometimes we have insight into the transferred response. We realize, for example, that we like A because A reminds us of B whom we have always liked. Or we dislike C because C is too much like D whom we never could stand. Or we are all confused about E because E is like A and B in some ways but reminiscent of C and D in others.

It is important to note, however, that generalization may occur without our awareness of it. The new situation triggers responses which have been tied to similar old ones without producing insight. This may be the case even when the similarity in the several situations is quite gross and

obvious to others. This does not mean that we always feel mystified by our response under these circumstances. Commonly we rationalize our response, giving "good" reasons for our feelings and actions; this tends to mask our lack of insight into the "real" reason.

Love and affection are prime examples of positive emotions that can be transferred from one person to another. Other feeling states such as dependency, confidence, and admiration may also be involved.

Consider, for example, an adolescent whose father has managed the paternal role in the family effectively and with considerable fairness and warmth. Over the years the adolescent may have developed a positive response to his father, relishing his affection, respecting his authority, and learning to have confidence in it. As the adolescent goes out into the world he transfers this response to other figures who consciously or unconsciously remind him of his father. His teachers and employers are some of the people who may elicit this positive transference.

Consider as well a young woman who has grown up in the same setting. She may develop a repertoire of positive response which generalizes to other males. Since her father provided her with a good deal of reward, she expects other males to do likewise, and she responds to them in the expectation that they will. She may be especially responsive to males who have a number of her father's esteemed qualities and may seek such a man to marry.

Anger, fear, and anxiety are examples of unpleasant emotions which may be generalized from one situation to another. Other negative feeling states that are commonly transferred include jealousy, suspicion, and negativism.

Some of us grow up in families whose authority figures are punitive, hostile, and unrewarding. Feelings of antagonism and rebellion aroused by these figures are easily generalized to other persons in authority with whom we come in contact. Even authority figures who are quite benevolent may trigger the old response, leading us to resist and attack. As a result, we may be unable to get along with our teachers and employers. We may reject any sort of direction from others, railing against social, religious, and political leadership.

Rival family members can form a basis for negative transference. Consider the case of a young woman who has long felt at a disadvantage in comparison with a much prettier sister. As a girl, she struggled to get her share of love and attention. In high school she fought to outdistance her sister in popularity and academic achievement. Although her sister married and moved to another part of the country, this did not end the matter. The young woman went on to college where it became necessary for her to have more dates than her sorority sisters and better grades than the girls in her classes. Whenever she met a very pretty woman, old feelings of tension and hostility returned.

Generalized emotions may involve elements of both pleasant and unpleasant emotion. As was noted before, parents can arouse love and hate simultaneously in their children because they provide both reward and punishment. Other family figures also stimulate simultaneous positive and negative feelings. Later on, people in the social environment who remind one of these important figures trigger the same mixed or ambivalent emotions.

In this way, we may reenact all through life childhood's unresolved conflicts. Our response to authority figures may be an alternation of submission and rebellion, mirroring an earlier struggle with one or both parents. If early figures have been inconsistent in their love or failed us at crucial times, as adults we may find it impossible to love or trust anyone completely.

Discrimination

In meeting a problem we may try a number of solutions which have been successful in similar situations in the past. Rewarded solutions gain strength and are increasingly used in the future. Unrewarded solutions are weakened and tend not to be used further in this situation. Little by little, we *discriminate* or distinguish between situations in which a particular response is or is not successful.

Consider again the tantrum-prone boy. He finds that his fits of temper serve him well in manipulating his mother and grandmother. However, the tantrum has little effect on his baby-sitter, so he will tend not to use it again on her. And its application to his father proves to be actually dangerous. Little by little, the boy learns to discriminate between the stimuli or situations in which the response is and is not effective. Where it has been rewarded, it will be used again; where it has produced nonreward or punishment, it will tend to be replaced by other modes of response.

Failure to Discriminate

Useful discriminations may fail to be established for a number of reasons. It has already been said that the small child's failure to generalize may be a function of his limited intellectual capacity; paradoxically, he may fail to discriminate for the same reason. The little babbler, for example, who suddenly masters the word "dada" or "daddy" may apply it not only to his father but to all vaguely similar stimuli, including the milkman, the bus driver, and the family doctor. And once the family canine has been titled "doggy," any quadruped may elicit this response.

The essential difference in several similar situations is difficult for the youngster to detect. If one wooly object bites, all wooly objects bite. If the liquid in one container is drinkable, the liquid in all containers is drinkable. If you can take your clothes off in the house, why can't you undress in the front yard?

No discrimination between several similar objects can be made as long as the individual is unwilling to approach any of them. If a stimulus has been sufficiently fearful, for example, transfer of the avoidance response may be made to many similar objects. The little girl who has been very badly scratched by the Siamese cat avoids all animals. If we could get her to approach one animal, perhaps a friendly puppy, she could begin to discriminate harmless from harmful animals. However, she cries and pulls back whenever we bring the puppy near and the discrimination process is stymied.

In the same way, a young man whose father has been punitive and hostile may transfer feelings of antagonism from his father to all authority figures. If he kept an open mind, he would soon learn that all authority figures do not have his father's negative traits. However, the antagonism response is firmly tied to the authority stimulus no matter what the setting in which it appears. In demonstrating his antagonism for these figures he indeed may arouse hostility in them. So he sees what

he expects to see and proves to himself all over again that he is right.

Even with considerable insight into an inappropriate generalization, the individual may fail to discriminate. Consider the young woman whose sex training has been an extremely repressive one. As a child, she found her questions concerning simple sex functions met with stony silence. Attempts at masturbation brought severe threats. Occasional ventures into the neighborhood "father and mother" sex play resulted in furious punishment. She grew up feeling that sex was dirty and dangerous. In her marriage she is cold and frigid. She knows that she is permitted and expected to enjoy sex relations with her husband, but she is unable to do so. Avoidance and anxiety responses remain firmly tied to all sex stimuli.

Enhancing Discrimination

Just as we enhance generalization through labeling the similarities in several situations, we can promote discrimination by labeling differences and making them more explicit (Dollard & Miller, 1950). We see a simple illustration of this process in the beginnings of speech. When our little speaker addresses every animal as "doggy," we reinforce this response for dogs but give him different labels for other animals. When he calls the dog "doggy," we say, "Yes, doggy, doggy." But when he makes a similar response to a horse, we say, "Not doggy. Horsie."

We sometimes extend the process when the child has had a frightening experience with a dog or other animal. The "good" label and the "bad" label may be employed if these have become familiar to the child. The offending dog is labeled "*bad doggy*" and the child is allowed to withdraw from it. But other dogs are labeled "good doggy" and approach responses are encouraged. In this way we attempt to prevent the child from transferring the avoidance response to all dogs and perhaps to all animals. The difference in labels points up the difference in animals and facilitates a difference in response.

Dollard and Miller (1950) point out the common failure of the maladjusted adult to discriminate between past and present conditions. Adult neurotics continue to respond to certain stimulus elements in the ways that they learned as children even though the stimulus context has changed and their responses are no longer appropriate. In therapy the labels "past" and "present" are applied, and a careful differentiation is made between them. For example, if sex stimuli are tied to avoidance responses because of repressive parental training methods, a sharp contrast is made between *past* sex to which avoidance was an appropriate response because of the possibility of punishment and *present* sex to which avoidance is not appropriate since instead of punishment, there is permission and encouragement.

The use of discrimination in psychotherapy is dramatically illustrated in the case presented below. The patient was suffering from a neurosis precipitated by a traumatic war experience. Pentothal, a drug, was administered to facilitate the expression of repressed material.

A patient under the influence of pentothal was discussing the alarming and horrifying circumstances of a combat mission. As he proceeded, his description had evoked in him a very intense fear response which was evident in facial expression, writhing, gestures, and all relevant signs. He was apparently reacting only to the sentences he was making and not at all to his safe situation in a hospital. Suddenly the therapist asked him, "Where are you?" The patient turned with a blank look to see his hospital bed and room, his American doctor, the sunlight of the Florida afternoon. He began to react to these stimuli and as he did so his anxiety rapidly faded. The therapist said, "I'm not Duke, the pilot. I'm your doctor." The patient who had given his doctor a role in the drama of the flight looked first with incredulity and then with dawning recognition. In this case, the doctor had forced him to make a discrimination between the fantasy of the flight which was producing intense anxiety and the secure conditions of his present life, thus sharply discriminating the circumstances of origin of the anxiety from the stimuli of the current situation. The discrimination operated to prevent generalization of anxiety responses from past to present cues and also gave the "safe" cues of the present situation a chance to inhibit anxiety. Our conviction is that it might have taken months of slow extinction practice in civilian life to produce so marked a reduction of anxiety (Dollard & Miller, 1950, pp. 307–308).

SUMMARY

Learning refers to a relatively enduring change in behavior which results from past experience. Human behavior is heavily influenced by learning. Some principles of learning highly relevant to the study of adjustment are reinforcement, extinction, generalization, and discrimination.

Reinforcement refers to the strengthening of a response. When a response has been rewarded in a particular situation, it is reinforced or strengthened, and the person tends to use it again in the future. Goal objects whose reward value does not have to be learned are called primary reinforcers and are said to provide primary reinforcement; goal objects with learned reward value are called secondary reinforcers and are said to provide secondary reinforcement.

Continuous reinforcement exists when a particular response is always followed by reward; in partial reinforcement, reward sometimes but not always follows the response. Continuous reinforcement is generally more effective than partial reinforcement in promoting learning, but once a particular behavior has been learned, it is adequately maintained with partial reinforcement; furthermore, responses which have been built up under partial reinforcement generally prove to be more resistant to extinction than do those acquired under continuous reinforcement.

Rewards that coincide with or immediately follow a particular response are said to provide immediate reinforcement for that response. If a reward occurs some time after the response, it is said to provide delayed reinforcement. Immediate reinforcements are generally more effective than delayed ones; the more closely a reward follows a response the more it will serve to strengthen this response.

Positive reinforcers (or rewards) are things which strengthen a response when they are presented. Negative reinforcers (or punishments) are things which strengthen a response when they are withdrawn. Psychological investigations have raised doubt that punishment is very effective in promoting learning. There are some important arguments against the use of punishment, but under certain conditions punishment may be a useful technique.

Extinction refers to the weakening of a response. When a response has been unsuccessful in a particular situation, it tends to be extinguished or weakened, and the person is less likely to use it in similar situations in the future. A number of techniques have been devised to extinguish unwanted responses or habits. In the unrewarded response method an unwanted response is extinguished by simply withholding reward. A similar method is the exhausted response method in which there is facilitation of the unacceptable response (while withholding reward) so that it may be extinguished more rapidly. The impossible response method attempts to make it impossible or at least very difficult for a response to occur.

In the rewarded alternative method the learner is taught an acceptable response to the situation, and this response is rewarded while the unacceptable one is not. The incompatible alternative method involves alteration of a situation so that a strong acceptable response which is antagonistic to the unacceptable response is called forth.

In the increasing stimulus method the

stimulus for an unacceptable response is introduced at a strength insufficient to elicit this response; then it is gradually increased until considerable amounts of stimulation can be presented without triggering the unacceptable response. Finally, in the withheld stimulus method a stimulus is prevented from occurring so that an unacceptable response which is linked to it is not elicited.

Generalization refers to the transfer of a response from one situation to similar ones. The more similar one stimulus is to another, the more it will tend to elicit the response which has been tied to the other. Sometimes desired generalizations fail to occur because of the limited capacity of the individual, the subtleties of a situation, or the dissimilarity of the training situation to those encountered later. Generalizations can be enhanced through appropriate labeling and more effective training procedures.

Discrimination refers to the process of distinguishing between situations in which a particular response is and is not successful. As in generalization, desired discriminations may fail to occur because of the limitations of the individual as well as because of the complexities or emotional nature of a situation. Discrimination can be enhanced through appropriate labeling and through effective training procedures including psychotherapy.

REFERENCES

Abi Rafi, A. Learning theory and the treatment of tics. *Journal of Psychosomatic Research*, 1962, **6**, 71–76.

Arkoff, A. Prison adjustment as an index of ability to adjust on the outside. *Journal of Correctional Education*, 1957, **9**, 1–2.

Baer, D. M. Some remedial uses of the reinforcement contingency. In J. Schlein (Ed.), *The Third Conference on Research in Psychotherapy*. Washington, D.C.: American Psychological Association, in press.

Bandura, A. Psychotherapy as a learning process. *Psychological Bulletin*, 1961, **58**, 143–159.

———, **Ross, D., & Ross, S. A.** Imitation of film-mediated aggressive models. *Journal of Abnormal and Social Psychology*, 1963, **66**(1), 3–11.

———, **& Walters, R. H.** *Adolescent Aggression*. New York: Ronald, 1959.

Bijou, S. W. Patterns of reinforcement and resistance to extinction in young children. *Child Development*, 1957, **28**, 47–54.

———, **& Baer, D. M.** *Child Development*. Vol. 1. *A Systematic and Empirical Theory.* New York: Appleton-Century-Crofts, 1961.

Bowlby, J. Separation anxiety: A critical review of the literature. *Journal of Child Psychology and Psychiatry*, 1961, **1**, 251–269.

Bugelski, B. R. *An Introduction to the Principles of Psychology*. New York: Holt, 1961.

Clark, D. F. The treatment of monosymptomatic phobia by systematic desensitization. *Behaviour Research and Therapy*, 1963, **1**, 63–68.

Deese, J. *The Psychology of Learning*. (2nd ed.) New York: McGraw-Hill, 1958.

Dollard, J., & Miller, N. E. *Personality and Psychotherapy*. New York: McGraw-Hill, 1950.

Estes, W. K. An experimental study of punishment. *Psychological Monographs,* 1944, **57,** No. 3 (Whole No. 263).

Harlow, H. F. The nature of love. *American Psychologist,* 1958, **13,** 673–685.

Harris, F. R., Wolf, M. M., & Baer, D. M. Effects of adult social reinforcement on child behavior. *Young Children,* 1964, **20**(1), 8–17.

Hilgard, E. R. *Introduction to Psychology.* (3rd ed.) New York: Harcourt, Brace, 1962.

Jenkins, W. O., & Stanley, J. C., Jr., Partial reinforcement: A review and critique. *Psychological Bulletin,* 1950, **47,** 193–234.

Jersild, A. T. *Child Psychology.* (5th ed.) Englewood Cliffs, N.J.: Prentice-Hall, 1960.

Kanner, L. *Child Psychiatry.* (2nd ed.) Springfield, Ill.: Charles C Thomas, 1948.

Lehner, G. F. J. Negative practice as a psychotherapeutic technique. *Journal of General Psychology,* 1954, **51,** 69–82.

Miller, N. E. Liberalization of basic S-R concepts: Extensions to conflict behavior, motivation and social learning. In S. Koch (Ed.), *Psychology: A Study of a Science.* Vol. II. *General Systematic Formulations, Learning, and Special Processes.* New York: McGraw-Hill, 1959. Pp. 196–292.

———, & Dollard, J. *Social Learning and Imitation.* New Haven, Conn.: Yale, 1941.

Morgan, C. T. *Introduction to Psychology.* New York: McGraw-Hill, 1956.

Postman, L. Rewards and punishments in human learning. In L. Postman (Ed.), *Psychology in the Making.* New York: Knopf, 1962. Pp. 331–401.

Sears, R. R., Maccoby, E. E., & Levin, H. *Patterns of Child Rearing.* New York: Harper & Row, 1957.

Shaffer, L. R., & Shoben, E. J., Jr., *The Psychology of Adjustment.* (2nd ed.) Boston: Houghton Mifflin, 1956.

Sheehan, J. G. The modification of stuttering through nonreinforcement. *Journal of Abnormal and Social Psychology,* 1951, **46,** 51–63.

———, & Voas, R. B. Stuttering as conflict. I. Comparison of therapy techniques involving approach and avoidance. *Journal of Speech Disorders,* 1957, **22,** 714–723.

Shoben, E. J., Jr. Psychotherapy as a problem in learning theory. *Psychological Bulletin,* 1949, **46,** 366–392.

———. A theoretical approach to psychotherapy as personality modification. *Harvard Educational Review,* 1953, **23,** 128–142.

Skinner, B. F. *Science and Human Behavior.* New York: Macmillan, 1953.

Sutherland, E. H., & Cressey, D. R. *Principles of Criminology.* (7th ed.) Philadelphia: Lippincott, 1966.

Williams, C. D. The elimination of tantrum behavior by extinction procedures. *Journal of Abnormal and Social Psychology,* 1959, **59,** 269.

Wolpe, J. *Psychotherapy by Reciprocal Inhibition.* Stanford, Calif.: Stanford, 1958.

Yates, A. J. The application of learning theory to the treatment of tics. *Journal of Abnormal and Social Psychology,* 1958, **56,** 175–182.

PART THREE

EVALUATING
AND
IMPROVING
ADJUSTMENT

CHAPTER EIGHT

EVALUATING ADJUSTMENT

What is good adjustment? What does it mean to be well-adjusted or maladjusted? To be mentally healthy or mentally ill? Or normal or neurotic or psychotic?

This chapter will present a number of concepts or ideas which are used in the evaluation of behavior. Then it will describe some personal qualities or patterns of behavior which have been held highly desirable in human beings.

SOME CURRENT CONCEPTS

In evaluating or judging the quality of a person's adjustment, we can use a number of terms. One set of such terms is "good adjustment" and "poor adjustment" or "maladjustment." Another set is "mental health" and "mental illness." A third is "normality," "neurosis," and "psychosis." And a fourth is "sanity" and "insanity."

Good Adjustment and Mental Health

"Good adjustment" and "mental health" are almost synonymous these days. Each term refers to a valued way of living. A person who has made a good adjustment or one who is called mentally healthy demonstrates patterns of behavior or personal characteristics which are valued or considered desirable. However, these terms have some differences in connotation which are worth elaborating.

First, the concept of adjustment is somewhat more environmental while mental health is more personal in connotation. We can speak sensibly of a person who is well adjusted in one area of life but not in another. We would be much less likely to think of him as mentally healthy in one sphere but not in another. Mental health is more often conceptualized as a personal quality which transcends the settings of which a person is a part, although, of course, it will be affected by what goes on in these settings.

Second, the concept of adjustment is somewhat more dynamic, while mental health is somewhat more static in connotation. Just as a person's mental health is thought to be somewhat independent of

the environment, it is also less variable in time. Mental health is considered a relatively enduring personal quality. Even though a person is having great difficulty in adjusting to a particular situation, he might be considered sufficiently healthy to weather his troubles and overcome them.

Third, the concept of mental health is sometimes reserved to designate very desirable personal characteristics. These may be qualities which only a few people show in any degree. Sometimes the qualities are stated as goals toward which each of us or the society as a whole should work. Used in this way, mental health is more than just good adjustment—it is superior adjustment.

Fourth, unlike the concept of adjustment, mental health implies a physical or medical condition. The term "health" is borrowed from medicine, and an analogy is made between physical health and mental health. This is an important difference in connotation between adjustment and mental health, and it will be pursued shortly in connection with the discussion of mental illness.

Maladjustment and Mental Illness

"Maladjustment" and "mental illness" share meaning, but these two concepts are not so interchangeable as good adjustment and mental health. Both maladjustment and mental illness refer to undesirable or poorly regarded patterns of behavior or characteristics. Like adjustment, maladjustment has environmental and dynamic implications. Like mental health, mental illness is more personal and static in meaning. And just as mental health is sometimes used to designate something better than just good adjustment, mental illness is used to designate something worse than poor adjustment. Up to a point we may be considered maladjusted, but when this point is passed, we may be considered mentally ill or "sick."

A Medical Approach

A very important difference between maladjustment and mental illness has to do with the medical connotation of the latter term. Most commonly, mental illness is regarded as a disease analogous to physical disease. If we feel ill and consult a physician, he may check our symptoms, diagnose our condition, and prescribe a treatment. He assumes that there is some cause underlying our symptoms—perhaps some germ or virus or lesion—toward which treatment should be directed.

In a similar way, the behavior which mentally ill persons show may be considered symptomatic of an underlying condition. This condition or pathology may be psychological (for example, deep and pervasive conflicts) or neurophysiological (for example, an endocrine malfunction) or an interaction of both (such as a condition compounded from certain neural defects and learning experiences). The task of the therapist is to diagnose the pathology or categorize the disease and carry out a remedy.

One reason that some patterns of behavior tend to be thought of as disease or illness is that until recently there were no other satisfactory explanations for them (Albee, 1966). Some responses such as those which seem highly exaggerated or nonsensical or involuntary invite ex-

planation in terms of disease (Bandura, in press). For example, a hostile boy may be thought of as bad or maladjusted, while an extremely hostile one calls forth the label of ill or sick. Murder with a motive is a punishable crime but a "senseless" murder raises the question of mental illness or insanity and so does one committed by a person who is assumed to have been unable to control himself.

A second reason for this medical or disease conception is that certain kinds of behavior are related to organic pathology. Neurosyphilis and brain deterioration in senility, for example, may trigger important behavioral changes. There is the assumption on the part of some physicians, psychiatrists, and other workers that many or even all kinds of mental illness may be attributed to neurophysiological processes which sooner or later will be discovered by medical research (Szasz, 1960, 1961).

A third reason for this conception is the central role which medicine has played in this area. Psychiatrists are "doctors," and this gives a medical connotation to their activities. Many of the terms used in this field are borrowed from medicine, as, for example, the words illness and disease themselves (Adams, 1964). The use of various medical procedures such as drugs, electroshock, and hospitalization also adds to the notion, although, of course, medical remedies may be used for psychological conditions while psychological remedies may be applied to medical ones.

A fourth reason for this conception is that it has supported the abandonment of responsibility both by the person and the public. The person is not held accountable for his actions—after all, "he's sick." It allows the relatives of the person to absolve themselves of guilt and responsibility. Furthermore, it permits the public to avoid facing some distressing possibilities. In this regard, Albee (a proponent of the psychosocial approach which will be presented shortly) states:

> If mental disorder is indeed a disease, then funds can be spent in good conscience for research seeking the neurological, biological, and chemical causes and society can convince itself that it is doing its best to eliminate mental disease. If, on the other hand, mental disorder is eventually acknowledged to be largely social and cultural in origin, the consequences for action will be very serious if not downright dangerous to the status quo. It may be necessary to direct our efforts at prevention to the modification of social institutions which now enjoy strong support from those favoring the status quo. To choose one example, if it is acknowledged that discrimination, with associated unemployment, poverty, broken families and poor housing, is a major cause of emotional disorder then social action to insure employment, decent housing, and equal social participation, is indicated as a remedy for mental disorder, rather than more biological research. Understandably, this solution may be more threatening than a sickness model (1966, pp. 5–6).

A Psychosocial Approach

A small but rapidly growing group of workers feel that it is misleading to draw an analogy between physical and mental illness. In fact, some of them deplore the use of the term mental illness. They believe that almost all of what we call mental disease or mental illness is simply maladaptive or maladjustive behavior (Adams, 1964; Albee, in press; Szasz, 1960; Ullmann & Krasner, 1965).

These workers regard all behavior as important in its own right. No behavior is considered simply a symptom of some underlying condition. We behave in a certain way because we have learned to behave in this way. And if our ways of behaving or adjusting are not satisfactory, we can unlearn them and learn better patterns to take their place.

In this view, there are no disease entities involved in most people who are called mentally ill. Each has simply learned patterns of behavior which society (or the person himself) does not want or value. And it is important to remember that what is not valued and not wanted varies from society to society and within a society from time to time (Ullmann & Krasner, 1965).

Workers who share this view have shown how even the most bizarre behavior —behavior which invites the label of disease or illness—can be learned. When fully studied, this behavior proves to be not so senseless.

Ullmann and Krasner (1965) are psychologists who have made a strong case for this approach. In their opinion, all behavior—regardless of label—is of the same origin. They write, "Maladaptive behaviors are learned behaviors, and the development and maintenance of maladaptive behavior is no different than the development and maintenance of any behavior." And they add for emphasis, "There is no discontinuity between desirable and undesirable models of adjustment or between 'healthy' and 'sick' behavior" (p. 20).

A leading opponent of the disease conception, Thomas Szasz, has called mental illness a "myth." He believes that the conditions called mental illness are simply "problems in living"—problems which are inherent in the complexities of our lives. He writes:

> The notion of mental illness . . . serves mainly to obscure the everyday fact that life for most people is a continuous struggle, not for biological survival, but for a "place in the sun," "peace of mind," or some other human value. For man aware of himself and of the world about him, once the needs for preserving the body (and perhaps the race) are more or less satisfied, the problem arises as to what he should do with himself. Sustained adherence to the myth of mental illness allows people to avoid facing this problem, believing that mental health, conceived as the absence of mental illness, automatically insures the making of right and safe choices in one's conduct of life. But the facts are all the other way. It is the making of good choices in life that others regard, retrospectively, as good mental health!
>
> The myth of mental illness encourages us, moreover, to believe in its logical corollary: that social intercourse would be harmonious, satisfying, and the secure basis of a "good life" were it not for the disrupting influences of mental illness or "psychopathology." The potentiality for universal human happiness, in this form at least, seems to me but another example of the I-wish-it-were-true type of fantasy. I do not believe that human happiness or well-being on a hitherto unimaginably large scale, and not just for a select few, is possible. This goal could be achieved, however, only at the cost of many men, and not just a few, being willing and able to tackle their personal, social, and ethical conflicts. This means having the courage and integrity to forego waging battles on false fronts, finding solutions for substitute problems—for instance, fighting the battle of stomach acid and chronic fatigue instead of facing up to a marital conflict.
>
> Our adversaries are not demons, witches, fate, or mental illness. We have no enemy whom we can fight, exorcise, or dispel by "cure." What we do have are problems in living—whether these be biologic, economic, political, or sociopsychological (1960, p. 118).

Normality, Neurosis, and Psychosis

Normality, neurosis, and psychosis are terms which are in common usage. "Normality," to some extent, is used interchangeably with good adjustment and mental health. "Neurosis" and "psychosis" are designations which are given to certain states of maladjustment or mental illness.

What is normality? To be normal, strictly speaking, means to conform to a norm or usual value. To be normal means to be average. The more a person departs from average, the more unaverage or abnormal he is considered.

For a number of personal characteristics to be average or not too deviant from average is considered a good thing. For example, consider height. To be average in height for one's age and sex is generally considered good. For a boy or man to be rather tall and for a girl or woman to be rather small or petite may be looked upon with favor, but it is not so desirable to be extremely tall or extremely short.

The same attitude is common toward patterns of behavior. For example, someone may complain about a child who is "overly aggressive." Perhaps the person goes on to say that it can't be normal to be so aggressive and that something must be wrong with the child. And—although not so frequently—someone may complain about a child at the other extreme, one who is unable to express any aggression, one who cannot assert himself at all or stand up for his own rights.

There is no doubt that many of us feel *uncomfortable* in being *unaverage*. We may wonder sometimes if we are normal and worry if we think that we are not. We wonder if it is normal to feel and think and act as we do.

We worry about the normality of our children—we say that we want to provide them with a normal childhood so that they can grow up and lead normal lives. We worry about the normality of the people around us—we become uncomfortable if they seem too different from ourselves.

There is no doubt that many of us feel comfortable in being average. Since we share the patterns of the people around us, we may get along more harmoniously with them. In short, our interaction may be less effortful.

Still, as a criterion of behavior, normality has many limitations. For one thing, we have little information concerning the frequency or commonness of many kinds of behavior. As information accumulates, we are sometimes surprised to find how statistically normal certain attitudes and actions are.

Second, we have little information concerning the behavior of certain groups of people and, therefore, little knowledge of what is normal for such groups. There is considerable information concerning college students since they are readily available to college-based investigators. And we know quite a bit about the middle-class child. Judged by middle-class norms (as is frequently the case), lower-class children may not get high marks for normality—but then neither would middle-class children who were judged by lower-class norms.

A third bothersome aspect of this approach is the implication that usual qualities or behaviors are the most desirable ones. On a moment's reflection, we can see that they may not be. Some personal qualities which are unusual or even rare may be highly valued by the society, and other characteristics which are usual may be criticized by some segments of the society or by other societies.

A fourth criticism of this approach is the possible inference that we should all be alike. Such a state is hardly conceivable, nor is it a very enchanting prospect. If we think of the persons we greatly like or admire, we may be struck by the unaverageness of their qualities.

Now let us contrast normality with neurosis and psychosis. All of us—normal or not—have problems. But some of us have greater problems than others, and "neurosis" is a term frequently applied to conditions of intermediate seriousness. The dividing point between what could be considered a normal problem or set of characteristics or behavior and a neurotic one is difficult to establish. The differences between the two are generally considered quantitative rather than qualitative—they are differences in degree rather than kind. A person who is labeled neurotic is like the rest of us but maybe more so or less so.

The term "psychosis" is applied to very serious conditions. Generally speaking, such conditions are considered both quantitatively and qualitatively different from normality—they differ both in degree and kind. For example, people labeled psychotic are generally higher in anxiety than persons called neurotic and much higher in anxiety than persons called normal, and this is a difference in degree. But psychotics sometimes show a thought disorder which is not considered a feature of normal and neurotic conditions.

Other distinctions that are made between normal, neurotic, and psychotic conditions are in terms of prescription and prognosis. A person considered normal requires no help. A person considered neurotic can benefit from assistance, but it is not absolutely necessary, and the outlook for his improvement is favorable. By contrast, the psychotic definitely needs help, and the outlook is more guarded (Hollender & Szasz, 1957).[1]

The concepts of neurosis and psychosis tend to be avoided by workers who take the psychosocial approach. Rather than neurosis, psychosis, or for that matter, mental illness, they prefer concepts which do not imply disease entities or discontinuities between what is "sick" and what is "healthy." They tend to speak of "maladaptive behavior," "maladjustive behavior," "deviant behavior," "disturbed behavior," and "behavior disorders."

Sanity and Insanity

Sanity and insanity are words in legal usage. They are seldom used by psychiatrists and psychologists except in a court action. These terms and the concepts they designate have occasioned considerable criticism and confusion.

"Sanity," as the term is now used, denotes that a person can be held accountable for his actions. It means that he is legally responsible. If he is accused of a crime, he can be brought to trial, and if he is convicted, he can be punished or otherwise dealt with.

"Insanity," by contrast, denotes a condition that makes a person not accountable for his behavior. If a person is adjudged insane, he is not treated as a regular defendant. Instead he is probably committed to a mental hospital.

Probably most of us have read about murder trials in which the defense maintains that the defendant is not guilty by reason of insanity. Acquittal in such cases may depend upon the answers to two questions, each of which must be answered in the affirmative and beyond a reasonable doubt. These questions are: "Is the defendant suffering from a mental disease or defect? If so, was his crime a product of the mental disease or defect?" (Graham, 1964).

As the public knows, psychiatrists frequently disagree in their testimony. Each side may produce a battery of psychiatrists to bolster its own case. These battles of psychiatric experts point up some of the problems in this area. Thomas Szasz, who as noted earlier suggests abandoning the concept of mental illness, holds further that we should not use mental illness as an "excusing condition" in legal proceedings. He writes (also see Fig. 8.1):

> To the extent that a person acts involuntarily, he cannot be regarded, in the social sense of the term, as a human being. This, then, leads to the dilemma typical of contemporary forensic psychiatry. Either we regard offenders as sane, and punish them; or we regard them as insane, and though excusing them of the crimes officially, punish them by treating them as beings who are less than human. It seems to me that there is a more promising alternative. Let us not consider mental illness an excusing condition. By treating offenders as responsible human beings, we offer them the only chance, as I see it, to remain human (1963a, p. 137).

[1] For a further description of neurosis and how it may be dealt with, see pp. 254–256.

Psychiatrist Questions Criminal Law

Was Oswald's Killer Temporarily Insane?

The forthcoming trial of Jack Ruby, slayer of Harvey Lee Oswald, the President's assassin, will project the question of insanity before the law into public view as no other case in recent history. A prominent authority in this field highlights the crucial aspects of this controversial subject. The author, trained in Europe and the United States, is professor of psychiatry at the Upstate Medical Center, State University of New York, Syracuse, N.Y. He also wrote the recently published book "Law, Liberty and Psychiatry."

By THOMAS S. SZASZ, M.D.
North American Newspaper Alliance
Special to The Advertiser

SYRACUSE, N. Y.—Never before have so many people witnessed a murder as when Jack Ruby shot Lee Harvey Oswald in the Dallas police station. That Ruby caused Oswald's death is an incontestable fact. However, this does not mean that Ruby committed a crime. Only through the judicial process can a man be defined as guilty of a crime.

In our culture, few acts are prohibited unconditionally. Take killing, for example. It is not a crime to kill the enemy in wartime; rather, it is encouraged as a patriotic duty. It is not a crime to kill in self-defense: rather, it is excused as a necessary act. Similarly, it is not a crime to kill if the killer is "insane": this, too, is excused as an act for which the killer is not legally responsible.

⋆

WE ALL KNOW what warfare is, and what self-defense is. But what is insanity?

The plea of insanity is a legal tactic for beating the murder-rap. The notion of insanity has served this function in American courts for decades. It will continue to do so until we put an end to it.

The charge of insanity is a legal tactic for incriminating as insane a presumably innocent person and imprisoning him in a psychiatric hospital.

In brief, insanity is a cruel legal-psychiatric hoax in which defense and prosecution alternately deceive each other. In the end, however, we are all deceived and victimized by it.

Ruby's attorney has announced that he plans to plead temporary insanity. Why was this defense chosen? What does it mean? How is it justified? And what are its consequences?

Typically, a defendant pleads insanity only when the deed is murder, and when his responsibility for the deed is incontestable. For example, when a jealous husband shoots his wife's lover in a public place; or when a man, like Ruby, kills Oswald before a television audience.

How can such a person defend himself in court? He cannot claim that he didn't cause harm or that he acted in self-defense. But he can plead another excuse: insanity. Thus, I believe the insanity plea was chosen because, under the circumstances, it is not only the best

ple of psychiatric-legal reasoning: The accused killed his victim because he was insane, and he was insane because he killed him.

If the plea of temporary insanity is successful, its consequence is that the accused is acquitted "by reason of insanity." His deed is excused and is not considered a crime.

⋆

IF WE BELIEVE in our system of criminal law, Ruby must be tried in a court of law, not in the newspapers. I believe in our system of criminal law. Therefore I do not want to add my voice to the chorus that has not only tried both him and Oswald but has also explained their actions.

I do not wish to argue either for or against Ruby's guilt. But I do wish to call into question the credibility of certain statements whose meaning hinges on the term "insanity."

Why is Ruby's act attributed to insanity? Other explanations are possible and have been suggested.

For example, on Dec. 5, The Syracuse Herald-Journal reported that, after talking to Ruby, Rabbi Hillel E. Silverman stated: "All he (Ruby) remembers is seeing a crowd of people and Oswald; and Oswald was just leering, there was a smirk on his face, and he lost his head . . . as an American he just had to shoot the man that shot the President."

However, apparently it is not considered enough to attribute Ruby's act to his wish to avenge the President's assassination, or to some other "rational" motive. He must have also been "insane." But if we attribute Ruby's conduct to insanity, do we clarify or obscure his particular act and the larger tragedy in Dallas?

⋆

THIS IDEA of two-people-in-one lingers on because it provides a convenient excuse not only for men accused of crimes, but for many others as well.

If the accused acted from unconventional motives—as Oswald might have—insanity helps to explain his motive. If he acted from conventional ones—as Ruby might have—insanity helps to disguise it.

Thus, sometimes we use insanity to explain conduct, and sometimes to explain it away. It all depends on how we feel about the crime, the criminal and the victim.

⋆

How is Ruby's insanity plea justified? By statements about his "mind." On Dec. 4 The New York Times reported: "His sister and his friends said they believed Ruby was so overwrought by Mr. Kennedy's death that his mind snapped."

But how do we know that his "mind snapped"? This cannot be an inference from his being "overwrought," for millions of Americans were also overwrought. It must, therefore, be an inference from Ruby's act—that is, from his having shot Oswald.

Thus, we are asked to believe that the "snapped mind" automatically transforms its owner into a killer. This myth, if repeated often enough, may become the official "explanation" of Ruby's act. It is a typical exam-

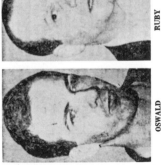

OSWALD   RUBY

defense, but the only defense possible.

In effect, the plea of insanity means that the accused claims that he was "not himself" at the time of the alleged crime. Therefore, he did not commit the act; his "temporarily insane self" did!

Absurd? Of course it is. It is a fairy story for adults, dressed up as psychiatric theory. It asks us to believe in a Jekyll-and-Hyde conception of the personality. If we do, we cannot punish Jekyll for a crime committed by Hyde.

⋆

own impulsiveness and be required to avoid situations that might inflame his temper?

Of course, nothing that I have said depends in any way on Ruby's actual mental condition. On the contrary, I suggest that we ask ourselves why we are interested in his mental condition.

In my opinion, the insanity defense is a hoax. In effect, the defendant is saying: "Excuse me, please. I committed the crime but don't punish me for it, because I was 'crazy' when I did it." By accepting the excuse, we corrupt the administration of justice.

⋆

TWO CAN PLAY at this game as well as one. If the defendant can plead insanity, the district attorney can charge him with it. He can request a pre-trial psychiatric examination, to determine whether the accused is fit to stand trial.

What happens if the psychiatrists—representing the court, not the defendant—declare him unfit? He will be deprived of his constitutional right to trial, guaranteed by the Sixth Amendment, and will be incarcerated in a hospital for the criminally insane, possibly for life.

I consider this a cruel and dishonest tactic. But it is no more dishonest, and only slightly more cruel, than the tactic of the insanity plea.

To the defendant charged with insanity, the prosecutor says in effect: "Although you are presumed innocent of the crime with which you are charged, we really don't care about that. You are a 'sick man'—you are crazy—so we'll take care of you by locking you up in an insane asylum."

Far-fetched? On the contrary. It is now alleged that Oswald had also tried to kill Gen. Edwin Walker. It's a small world, indeed: When Walker was accused of insurrection in Oxford, Miss., last fall, he was not brought to trial, but was ordered, against his will, to submit to pretrial psychiatric examination. He managed to foil this tactic.

But one of our greatest poets, Ezra Pound, was less fortunate; he was never tried for his alleged offense and served 14 years in an insane asylum—a sentence well in excess of that meted out to many convicted Nazi war criminals.

⋆

WHEN THE ORDINARY man-on-the-street is accused of insanity, he can never rebut the charge and invariably becomes a victim of this legal-psychiatric strategy.

The law is, or ought to be, color-blind. But is this enough? No, I believe the law should also be psychiatry-blind. Why should people be treated unequally before the law because of their mental state?

If a person is sane enough to engage in prohibited conduct, why should we not consider him sane enough to be legally responsible for it?

Just as we cannot have a free society with one set of laws for the white man and another for the black man, so we cannot have a free society with one set of laws for the "sane" and another for the "insane."

⋆

IF "TEMPORARY INSANITY" means anything at all, it means that Ruby did not plan to kill Oswald, but did so in a fit of sudden passion.

However, if Ruby was upset by the President's assassination, and if he knew that he was an impulsive man —why didn't he stay away from the accused assassin? Why did he go to the police station? And why did he have a gun in his pocket? On the chance that he might do something rash, Ruby could have at least gone to the jail without his gun. After all, the ideal that Oswald might be killed before coming to trial occurred to many people.

My point is that if "temporary insanity" is some sort of disability, it must be comparable to other disabilities. A person subject to epileptic seizures is responsible for his own epilepsy: he must avoid driving, lest he kill someone with his car while having a fit. Thus, if a man is impulsive, why should he not be responsible for his

Figure 8.1 Thomas S. Szasz, a prominent psychiatrist and psychoanalyst, has been highly critical of some of the concepts and practices in the fields of mental health and mental illness. Here, in connection with the then forthcoming trial of Jack Ruby (the slayer of the accused slayer of President Kennedy), Szasz critically examines the concept of insanity (Used by permission of North American Newspaper Alliance and the Honolulu Advertiser).

SOME VALUED QUALITIES

A good deal has been written about the personal qualities or patterns of behavior which are desirable in human beings. Many lists of these qualities have been drawn up. And there are even some lists of lists.

There is considerable similarity and overlap in these lists. Some qualities appear in almost every list. Each writer may spell out the qualities to suit himself, but there is a common core of agreement.

There are also some important differences. A quality noted and emphasized by one writer may be ignored or subordinated by another. Everyone, of course, will not agree on values. Each of us will have our own ideas on what is good, desirable, or ideal.

The differences become especially apparent when we stop speaking in generalities and start speaking in specifics. For example, we may agree that it is good to be autonomous. But we may find that the more exactly we spell out what we mean by autonomy, the more we part company.

It should be noted that there may be some incompatibilities between certain characteristics or patterns of behavior which are valued. What if research shows that better-behaved children are less creative? What if, in becoming more sensitive and sympathetic human beings, we find ourselves also less sturdy and less resistant to upset? (Sanford, 1965)

It should also be noted that there will be incompatibilities between the lists of characteristics which are valued by differ-

ent groups of people. To some extent, we participate in the value systems of our sex and age group, our class and culture, and our era. There are few personal qualities or patterns of behavior which are universally or eternally valued.

The present discussion builds on the work of Jahoda (1958), who found that many ideas in this area could be sorted into a number of categories. Nine major categories are utilized in the material which follows, but the sorting job is far from perfect. Some categories overlap, and some ideas cut across categories and make several appearances. Even so, the material offers the substance of present thinking concerning desirable human qualities.

Happiness

A most highly valued quality is happiness. In asking about another person, we are likely to make our inquiry in terms of happiness. How happy is he? Is his marriage a happy one? Does he have a happy home life? How happy is he at his new job?

A number of terms are used interchangeably with happiness. "Satisfaction" and "contentment" are frequently used. Other terms include "peace of mind," "feelings of security," and "a sense of well-being."

Happiness is frequently studied by students of human behavior (see Table 8.1 and Fig. 8.2). For example, this quality is an important criterion or index of marriage and vocational adjustment. There have been literally hundreds of studies concerning happiness or satisfaction in these areas.

Happiness research, unhappily, is not without its problems. Happiness is a complex subjective state. How well can we measure it? The alternatives used in questionnaire studies of happiness—alternatives such as "very happy" and "pretty

Table 8.1 "Taking things all together, how would you say things are these days—would you say you're *very happy, pretty happy,* or *not too happy* these days?"

This question was included in interviews held throughout the United States to find out about the nation's mental health. As the authors point out, answers to a question of this sort must be interpreted with great caution. Here's how 2,460 adults—a cross-section of the country's population—responded:*

Response	Percent
Very happy	35
Pretty happy	54
Not too happy	11

* *Americans View Their Mental Health* by G. Gurin, J. Veroff and S. Feld, Basic Books, Inc., Publishers, New York, 1960.

Figure 8.2 "What would your life have to be like for you to be completely happy?" "What is missing for you to be happy?" "What are your hopes for the future?"

These are some of the questions which native interviewers asked samples of the adult population in thirteen countries to determine the pattern of human concerns. The countries represented a variety of economic and political conditions, and altogether nearly twenty thousand persons served as subjects.

One of the features of the study was a pictorial device, "the ladder of life," whose top represented the best possible life and whose bottom represented the worst possible life. The subject was asked to indicate where he stood on the ladder at that time, five years before, and where he would be five years in the future.

Highest mean position on the ladder was achieved by members of Israeli kibbutzim (small collective agricultural communities); the general Israeli sample scored lower. People of all countries except the Dominican Republic and the Philippines felt that they had come up the ladder in the preceding five years, and people of all countries without exception expected their situation to improve in the future. (Compare these findings with the cross-cultural study of anxiety which appears on pp. 129–130 (Cantril, 1965).)

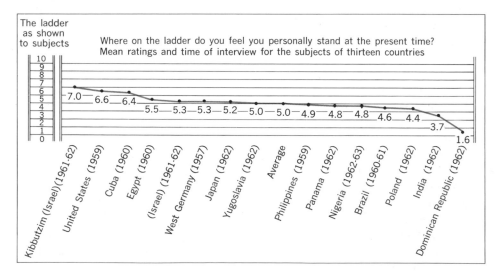

The ladder as shown to subjects

Where on the ladder do you feel you personally stand at the present time? Mean ratings and time of interview for the subjects of thirteen countries

7.0 — 6.6 — 6.4 — 5.5 — 5.3 — 5.3 — 5.2 — 5.0 — 5.0 — 4.9 — 4.8 — 4.8 — 4.6 — 4.4 — 3.7 — 1.6

Kibbutzim (Israel) (1961-62)
United States (1959)
Cuba (1960)
Egypt (1960)
(Israel) (1961-62)
West Germany (1957)
Japan (1962)
Yugoslavia (1962)
Average
Philippines (1959)
Panama (1962)
Nigeria (1962-63)
Brazil (1960-61)
Poland (1962)
India (1962)
Dominican Republic (1962)

happy" and "not too happy"—are rather nebulous and mean different things to different people.

Furthermore, in studies of happiness, the question of honesty arises. Many people try to appear happier than they are. They may try to conceal their unhappiness even from themselves. Others are candid about their feelings. Some may even make a to-do about unhappiness, letting the world know that they could use a little tender loving care and understanding.

It should also be noted that happiness frequently comes into conflict with other valued qualities. What if we achieve happiness at the expense of others' happiness? What if we purchase happiness (or immediate pleasure) at the cost of our own personal growth?

How happy or satisfied or contented should we be? The goal of some people, it seems (we may be among them), is to be without problems. To them, adjustment implies an absence of frustration and conflict and anxiety. To them, adjustment is an ideal state in which one is always or almost always happy.

How many of us are always happy? No one seems to be. To be unhappy sometimes and deeply unhappy occasionally appears to be the human condition. If we are not content with our present state, we may struggle—not for complete happiness —but to be more happy than we are. We seek—not to be free of problems—but to be better able to handle the problems we have.

Robert F. Peck, a psychologist, set out to study the lives of fairly typical adults. His subjects were a representative group of middle-aged men and women in the Middle West. In summing up his evidence,

he presents a picture of average happiness as he sees it:

There are times, in studying case after case, when one sadly muses that perhaps Thoreau was literally right. Perhaps most men—and women—do lead lives of quiet desperation. Certainly, the chaos of bewilderment, the tempest of unreasoning passion, the whine of years-long unhappiness, the tremendous sorrow of engulfing tragedy—these are not strange to the typical American. He, or she, has lived with them and is living with their echoes.

The joy of utter mastery of life? This is a rare experience, encountered by few people. More typical is a quiet, slightly puzzled sense of some things lacking, some spots of grey where colors ought to be; and all beyond one's comprehension to identify, or one's skill to remedy.

For more than half of us, life is a matter of settling for a good deal less than we want. We know it; we've known it for years; and we are decidedly not happy at the many moments when we think about our losses, our disappointments, and our never-will-be's. For such of us, life is never brilliantly happy. Unalloyed joy is an unknown or forgotten sensation. Too many hurts, big and little, have chipped the bright colors away.

Yet for this "almost average" American, life is not really a matter for despair. On the contrary, he and she pride themselves on "making out," and "getting along"; and what is more, they do get along, and make their way. If they don't have nearly the love, or stature, or pleasure, or security their hearts hunger for, they don't sink into self-pity. If bright happiness is out of reach, a more shaded kind is still attainable. Above all, there is the self-respect, dimly but proudly felt, of the person who makes his own way in life.

Are there completely happy people? No. We find no one whose life is and has been, without some hard-hitting frustration or some profound sorrow. When a *beloved parent dies, or a just-grown child —what door of escape is there? There is no way out of the grief except to live through it. . . .*

Sometimes it seems as if we ask too much of life and of ourselves. We want "perfect" happiness, "perfect" peace of mind, "perfect" mental health. As far as all experience indicates, along with the present data, the best one can reasonably ask for is good health, mental and physical, with which to meet each day (1959, pp. 251–252).

Harmony

A second highly valued quality is harmony. This quality is frequently noted by writers whether they write of adjustment or mental health. For example, English and English in their psychological dictionary define adjustment as "a condition of harmonious relation to the environment wherein one is able to obtain satisfaction for one's needs and to meet fairly well the demands, physical and social, put upon one" (1958, p. 13). The same harmony between the person and the environment is implied in Boehm's definition of mental health, which he describes as "a condition and level of social functioning which is socially acceptable and personally satisfying" (1955, p. 537).

There is a pattern of interdependence and interdependability that characterizes human life (Shoben, 1957). We depend on other people to help us meet our needs. And others depend on us. This mutual resourcefulness and responsibility implies a certain degree of harmony.

In everyday life we do not use the word "harmony" very much in describing adjustment. "Getting along," however, is a common phrase which conveys much the same idea. Harmony and getting along

both imply a several-sided adjustment process with each side having some say-so.

When we say that life is a give-and-take proposition, we also state the case for harmony as a criterion of adjustment. Live and let live is a similar phrase. Dog eat dog expresses the contrary view.

Harmony and other valued qualities frequently come into conflict with each other. How much should we sacrifice for harmony? How much should we yield to our environment? How much should our environment yield to us?

Some of the motives which move us—achievement, for example—may put us into disharmony with certain segments of our social environment. A man may be eager to move to a new community where a better position awaits him. His wife and teen-age children are dead set against uprooting themselves. What should he do?

Our social and political ideas may put us into sharp opposition to broad swaths of society. Should we live in harmony with a society we dislike? Or should we try to make it into a society with which we can live in harmony?

Consensus and compromise are harmonious ways of achieving group goals. There is a lot to be said for them. But there are those persons who earn our admiration—unabashed or begrudged, depending on our valuation of their ideas—by living out of harmony with patterns which they feel it important to live out of harmony with.

Family beginnings can set the stage for later harmony or cacophony. Large families have been seen as good training grounds for learning how to get along with others. Bossard and Boll studied 100 large families (six or more children) and found that 97 provided good training for harmony. As you can see, harmony figures prominently on this list of things attributed to large families by some of the children who grew up in them:

Teaches fair play
You learn to share
Getting along with people
Cooperating with others
Tolerance of other people
Learn to listen as well as to talk
Learn to like people
Self-control and self-discipline
Respect for the property and rights of others
Responsibility for other people
Learn to participate in group activities
Life is not a bed of roses
Learn how to keep from annoying other people
Frees children from parental smothering
Less tendency to become selfish
Learn to take stresses and strains of life in stride
Rubs rough edges off
Wears you smooth
Learn to live with both sexes and assorted ages
Accustoms one to having people around
Enriches one's experience
Gives feeling of courage and security
Gives a proper perspective of one's place in life (1956, pp. 194–195)

In the excerpts which follow, two alumni of large families present in a little fuller detail the socializing and harmony-enhancing effect of their family experiences:

Living in a large family socializes a child to an appreciable extent. . . . In general, living and being reared in a large family teaches one that life is not a "bed of roses" and that there are other people in the world all with "equal rights" to the pursuit of happiness in life. . . . A child in a large family has brothers and sisters of contemporary age who understand him as

a child and in the "give and take" of their everyday life each learns to control emotions, think in terms of "we" and not "me," "to live and let live," to look out for oneself and yet to consider the rights of others, and a host of similar terms all meaning to live as a real human being should and not as an animal.

It is my conviction that living in a large family has a great socializing influence on a child. . . . In the large family a child has to become adjusted to other people for there is no retreating from their presence. These continual and reinforced relationships by necessity have to assume a character of workability in order for the family to operate as an integrated group. The things that a large family impart to a child better prepare him for living in a large group. The multiplicity of the relationships in a large family form the potential for an easy transition of the child into other group situations. The child of a large family usually learns responsibility toward his fellows by growing up in an environment where such considerations are the rule . . . also tends to give a child a more certain basis on which to meet and interact with other people. . . . In summary, by virtue of the large number of individuals living in close and intimate contact, as in a large family, a child is more easily and less consciously equipped to take his place in adult society (Bossard & Boll, 1956, p. 196).

Self-regard

A third quality—a set of related qualities really—is subsumed under the label "self-regard." The idea of "self" frequently occurs in discussions of adjustment and mental health. In criticizing a person, we may say that he doesn't understand himself. Or accept himself. Or respect himself.

Some Self-concepts
Each of us has a number of self-concepts or self-pictures. Each concept or picture is

a particular view. We have a view of ourselves as we think we really are, another as we think others see us, and still another as we would like to be.

The Subjective Self   The term *subjective self* refers to our own private view of ourselves. It is the way we see ourselves. It is what we think ourselves to be.

The subjective self is built up of all the ideas that we have concerning our own characteristics. Some of these ideas have been heavily influenced by our parents. Others have been hammered out in interaction with our peers and our larger social environment.

There is some evidence that children tend to see themselves as they assume their parents see them. In short, their view of themselves is influenced by what they believe is their parents' view. When they perceive that their parents are not in accord—when they assume that their father sees them in one way and their mother in another—their adjustment suffers (Wylie, 1961).

We tend to perceive greater similarity between ourselves and our friends than we do between ourselves and nonfriends or nonpreferred people. We tend to see our friends as we see ourselves or, maybe it is the other way around, we tend to see ourselves as we see our friends. But, interestingly enough, there is no substantial evidence that we are actually more similar to our friends than to our nonfriends (Izard, 1963; Wylie, 1961).

The Objective Self   The *objective self* refers to others' views of us. It is the self that others see. It is the person they think us to be.

The objective self also includes the data provided by various tests and mea-surements. Height as measured by a yard-stick, weight as measured by a scale, intelligence as measured by an IQ test, academic ability as measured by an aptitude or achievement test—all are germane to the objective self.

Of course, not all people or all measurements will picture us in the same light. Nor are we the same in the light of every situation. We may behave one way at home, another at school, yet another at work, and the people in each of these environments may have varying perceptions of us.

The Social Self   The term *social self* is used to describe the picture that we think other people have of us. It is the way we think we look to others. It is our view of others' views of us.

How others see us (or how we think they see us) influences our own view. If others value us, it is easier for us to value ourselves. If others depreciate us, our self-estimation may suffer. In such a case, we may defend ourselves by depreciating them (Goldfried, 1963).

Some of us need to be liked by almost everyone; if anyone seems to dislike us or appears indifferent, we are bothered and uncomfortable. A few of us seem little concerned with the opinions of others. Almost all of us, however, are sensitive to the approval and disapproval of certain people who play important parts in our lives.

The Ideal Self   The *ideal self* is our concept of the person we would like to be. It is our ultimate goal. It is the self we would like to become.

It would be hard to imagine a person who was perfectly content with himself. Almost all of us would admit to wishing that we were different in some respects from what we are. Some of us might like to have a nearly whole new self.

A certain amount of idealization is necessary. Our ideals set the guidelines and form the goals of our self-development. Some of us, however, set extremely high goals for ourselves. In the struggle to reach them, we wear ourselves out. Or in contemplation of the wearing struggle, we give up.

Some Self-qualities

Many self-qualities have been valued and considered desirable. These self-qualities incorporate the basic concepts which were just introduced. The following discussion presents a number of these qualities, including self-insight, self-identity, self-acceptance, self-esteem, and self-disclosure.

Self-insight *Self-insight* means possession of knowledge or understanding of oneself. Self-insight is frequently mentioned as a quality of good adjustment or mental health. A commonly stated goal of psychotherapy is to assist the person who comes for help toward a fuller and more accurate self-insight.

How do we know if we have full and accurate self-insight? How do we know if we are as we think we are? In research, a person's self-insight is commonly assessed by comparing his view of himself (the subjective self) with the views that others have of him (the objective self). For example, the person may be asked to rate himself on certain personal qualities, and friends or acquaintances or trained observers also rate him. The smaller the discrepancy between the two sets of ratings, the more self-insight the person is credited with.

A second approach is to have the person report how he thinks others see him

(the social self). This may or may not be how he actually sees himself (the subjective self). Then an assessment is made of how he actually appears to others or to a trained observer. Again, a small discrepancy between the two views is considered evidence of self-insight.

How good is our self-insight? Apparently pretty good if we do say so ourselves. One psychology professor reports that 96 percent of the students whom he asked claimed that their self-insight was average or better; only 4 percent expressed some doubts about their self-insightfulness (Allport, 1961).

How good is our self-insight? Apparently not so good according to the bulk of research that has been done (but some of the research is not so good either so we must be careful about accepting it at face value). Wylie (1961), who reviewed and qualified the evidence, found that the correlations between self-ratings and ratings by others were generally quite low. There was usually some agreement, but it was far from perfect.

How good is our self-insight? Are we as good as we think we are? A considerable amount of evidence suggests that we're not. Self-overestimation is more common than self-underestimation (Wylie, 1961). In general, we don't take a dim view of ourselves—at least not for publication.

Self-identity *Self-identity* refers to the clearness and stability that mark a set of images concerning a person. A sharp sense of self-identity has generally been considered a desirable quality. A person with a clear and stable identity knows who he is and what he values and what he is likely to do under a particular set of circumstances. Other people, too, know what the person stands for and what to expect of him.

A well-developed self-identity seems to presume a well-formulated self-knowledge. There is some evidence that persons who do not maintain stable conceptions of their subjective, social, and ideal selves also do poorly on self-insight measures (Smith, 1958). Other evidence suggests that unstable self-images are associated with heightened anxiety (Rosenberg, 1962).

Block hypothesizes that the optimal condition is one in which our identity is neither too rigidly nor too diffusely defined. He speaks of an aspect of identity called "role variability" which is characterized at one extreme by "role diffusion" and at the other by "role rigidity." He writes:

> The meaning of role variability is perhaps most readily indicated by describing its extremes. At one end of this dimension, there is "role diffusion," where an individual is an interpersonal chameleon, with no inner core of identity, fitfully reacting in all ways to all people. This kind of person is highly variable in his behaviors and is plagued by self-doubts and despairs for he has no internal reference which can affirm his continuity and self-integrity. At the other extreme, there is what might be called "role rigidity," where an individual behaves uniformly in all situations, disregarding the different responsibilities different circumstances may impose. Here the core of identity is hollow, based not on a genuine and unquestioned sense of personal integrity but rather upon deep seated fear of any amount of self-abandon. Somewhere in between, presumably, a proper balance can be struck in the struggle both for identity and the capacity for intimacy (1961, p. 392).

Similarly, Erikson (1959) writes of "identity diffusion" which is a danger in late adolescence. No longer a child but not an adult, the adolescent may flounder about, trying on one identity, then another. Identity diffusion is well-illustrated in White's case of Joseph Kidd. At the time that Joseph Kidd wrote the following description of himself he was eighteen years old and at "the lowest point" of his life:

> I began trying to fit a personality to my make-up. I began "acting" out personalities and tried observing people and copying them, but I realized what I was doing and so carried that "how'm I doing attitude," that is, continually looking at and thinking about what I'd said or done, what impression I had made. But these personalities were all short-lived because they pleased some and not others and because they didn't produce that underlying purpose of making people like me; and every time unconsciously I would resort to my childish attitude to make myself noticeable. Examples of these "personalities" are independence (but I couldn't keep it up); arrogance (but people were only arrogant back at me); big shot in sex (but people weren't so much in love with it as I thought); hatefulness (people paid no attention to me); extreme niceness (people took advantage of it, kidded me about it because I did it to an ultra degree); humorous nature (but I was only being childish, silly); quiet and studious (but people were only passing me by and I kept feeling I was missing something). I became a day-dreamer so intensively that up to the present I find I'm day-dreaming almost all the time. I became conscious of a person's approach and would become fluttered, flustered, would try to make a friend of him no matter who he was but I overdid it (1952, p. 154).

Erikson has also written of "positive" and "negative" identities. Unlike positive identities, negative ones are built up of patterns of behavior which others have held out as wrong or perverse. Negative identities may stem from the conviction that one cannot amount to much, and rather than being "not quite somebody" it is better to be nobody or somebody bad.

As was already indicated, a frequent goal of psychotherapy is to help the person gain self-insight. Another common aim is to help the person establish or clarify his self-identity. He is helped to discover him-

---

Presentation 8.1 Heroin addiction and negative identity. The Federal Narcotics Bureau has estimated that there are about sixty thousand heroin addicts in this country, but unofficial estimates run much higher. Far from leading disorderly lives, many heroin addicts or "junkies" in the metropolitan areas of the United States have well-structured careers. They exist as members of a deviant subculture—one with its own behavior and language—and they take on a deviant or negative identity.

The subculture defines the symbolic meaning and behavior which attends the definition, "junkie." Not only does it make plain what it means to be hooked, but it makes clear how people who meet this criterion go about coping with a dilemma which it defines as drug-induced. Along with this, of course, there goes an additional set of ideas about one's self as junkie and how to sustain that image. Use of drugs induces a state of being at ease with the world. This experience of transcending reality by means of an almost other-worldly though all-knowing detachment is, of course, the state of being "cool." Drug users, perhaps in inverse relation to their ability to cope with the terrors and pitfalls of social interaction, affect a stance of poise, the scarcest, therefore highest, value they know. All addicts, whether using or not, strive to "keep their cool." Needless to say, it is easier to maintain this self-image on rather than off drugs. . . .

Addict culture endorses skills for procuring drugs, administering them, obtaining one's high, and simultaneously avoiding exposure. All the informal learning that goes with "scoring," "making a connection," testing the quality of the "stuff,"

stashing the "works," using the "outfit," "snorting," "sniffing," "skin-popping," "main-lining," "tieing up," in short, getting one's "kicks," is acquired during the detached intimacy of addict social relations. In time, skills for practicing deceit are learned as the need to obtain an illicit supply of drugs mounts. . . .

Addict culture also prescribes a casual set of norms for governing interaction betwen junkies as well as interactions with the various kinds of "squares" who make up the world of those who are not "hip." Squares, of course, as is now so very well known, do not "dig," that is, understand, the existential meaning of the drug experience. Being in their company is a "drag," it "brings one down." Consequently, the only way to manage interaction with squares is to "put them on," "work them," or "score for drugs" off them. One may share his "works" or "good stuff" with a fellow user, one may send a trusted fellow-addict out to "make the run" but one must avoid all contact or dealings with "rats," "finks," "stools," all of whom play informer with narcotics agents in exchange for drugs. Such men have only a "fifty-cent habit" and are, of course, the lowest of the low. . . .

Minimal conformity to these casual and drug-centered norms guarantees a fairly stable and orderly world view. Outsiders are square and meant to be worked, no set of obligations must take precedence over supporting one's habit, and insiders alone can be counted on to understand the drug mystique. Proof positive of this black-and-white image of the world is afforded once and for all when its content is expressed in the symbolic forms of the addict's argot (Rubington, 1967, pp. 15–16).

self or to discover how the many fragments of his identity may be fitted together to make a self.

This statement, written by a woman in therapy, illustrates, to use the therapist's words, "the discovery of self":

> You know, it seems as if all the energy that went into holding the arbitrary pattern together was quite unnecessary—a waste. You think you have to make the pattern yourself; but there are so many pieces, and it's so hard to see where they fit. Sometimes you put them in the wrong place, and the more pieces mis-fitted, the more effort it takes to hold them in place, until at last you are so tired that even that awful confusion is better than holding on any longer. Then you discover that left to themselves the jumbled pieces fall quite naturally into their own places, and a living pattern emerges without any effort at all on your part. Your job is just to discover it, and in the course of that, you will find yourself and your own place. You must even let your own experience tell you its own meaning; the minute you tell it what it means, you are at war with yourself (Rogers, 1961, p. 114).

Self-acceptance   *Self-acceptance* refers to a generally favorable or positive attitude toward one's own personal qualities. Self-acceptance generally implies some self-insight and self-identity. If we are self-accepting, we have some knowledge of our personal assets and our personal liabilities, and there is not undue pride in the former or undue shame or guilt about the latter (English & English, 1958).

Self-acceptance is considered a very important quality, and the concept has been studied and written about a great deal. In research, a frequent approach has been to obtain two measures, one assessing the person's subjective self, the other

his ideal self. If there is little difference between the two—if the person sees himself as not too different from what he wants to be—he is considered self-accepting (Wylie, 1961).

Extreme self-dissatisfaction is generally considered an undesirable condition. However, not all who are esteemed by others show self-acceptance. In some people, very high disparity between subjective and ideal selves accompanies a high degree of social competence as evidenced by their educational, occupational, and marital histories (Achenbach & Zigler, 1963).

Self-satisfaction is generally considered a desirable quality, but not all of us who have a lot to be modest about show a discrepancy between our subjective and ideal selves. There is, of course, the possibility that we may be well-satisfied with ourselves without sufficient cause—because we haven't faced the facts or because we have distorted them (Block & Thomas, 1955). Or we may be well satisfied because we are very undemanding of ourselves; in this regard, some writers have suggested that a small discrepancy between objective and ideal selves is better than no discrepancy at all (Wylie, 1961).

Many writers have suggested that people who accept themselves are also more accepting of others. There is some research evidence to support this contention (Wylie, 1961). Those of us who accept and respect ourselves tend to respect others. Those of us who depreciate and reject ourselves reject and depreciate others as well.

It has been suggested that there may be an element of projection in the relationship between the acceptance of self and the acceptance of others. If we depreciate ourselves, we may assume that others depreciate us too. In retaliation, we reject and depreciate them in order to bolster our own feelings (Goldfried, 1963).

The proper acceptance of ourselves seems to be vital to our acceptance of others and to our getting along with them. In psychotherapy there is frequently an attempt to get the person to be more accepting of himself. As therapy progresses, the person may see himself as more worthy and closer to his ideal self. And he may revise his ideal self, making it more congruent with his objective self (see Fig. 8.3).

Self-esteem   Self-esteem denotes that a person has pride in himself. The difference between self-acceptance and self-esteem is one of degree. Both terms imply a sense of worthiness, but self-esteem connotes a greater degree.

Just as self-acceptance and acceptance of others go together, self-esteem and esteem for others appear to be related. Fromm speaks of "self-love" which he feels is closely related to love for others. He says, "The idea expressed in the Biblical 'Love thy neighbor as thyself!' implies that respect for one's own integrity and uniqueness, love for and understanding of one's own self, cannot be separated from respect and love and understanding for another individual. The love for my own self is inseparably connected with the love for any other being" (1956, pp. 58–59).

The whole idea of self-esteem or self-love is a bothersome one for many of us. We have been taught to be modest about our own qualities. We have been taught not to be conceited or infatuated with ourselves.

It is readily apparent in the writings on this subject that self-esteem and self-love have little in common with self-conceit and self-infatuation. The two sets of terms are poles apart in their implications. Fromm illustrates this point nicely in his contrast of selfishness and self-love. He writes:

> *Selfishness and self-love, far from being identical, are actually opposites. The selfish person does not love himself too much but too little; in fact he hates himself. This lack of fondness and care for himself, which is only one expression of his lack of productiveness, leaves him empty and frustrated. He is necessarily unhappy and anxiously concerned to snatch from life the satisfactions which he blocks himself from attaining. He seems to care too much for himself, but actually he only makes an unsuccessful attempt to cover up and compensate for his failure to care for his real self. Freud holds that the selfish person is narcissistic, as if he had withdrawn his love from others and turned it toward his own person. It is true that selfish persons are incapable of loving others, but they are not capable of loving themselves either (1956, pp. 60–61).*

Self-disclosure   Self-disclosure refers to the process of making oneself known to other people (Jourard, 1964). It refers to our ability and willingness to let others know us as we are—to share our thoughts and feelings with them. Are we able to leave ourselves unconcealed and undefended?

Jourard holds that self-disclosure is an important aspect of mental health. Mentally healthy persons, he says, have the ability to make themselves known to at least one significant other. In disclosing himself to another, the person comes to know himself better and he becomes a better self.

By contrast, the less healthy person is unable or unwilling to drop his guard. He is alienated from others and from his

Figure 8.3 Physical disability, the self, and the environment. It has been estimated that there are more than ten million persons in the United States who are physically disabled. This includes the blind and partially sighted, the deaf and hard of hearing, and those with cerebral palsy, epilepsy, and orthopedic impairments. One task in the rehabilitation of the severely disabled is helping them see themselves as worthy. This can be done by increasing their competence to deal with the environment and at the same time perhaps modifying the environment to increase their competence. Dorothy Liston who decided to make a career as a homemaker instead as a "polio" writes of her own experience:

Polio had struck like a runaway truck and I was trying to get back on my feet and pick up the pieces. That was back in 1949. At the time I didn't know that I wasn't going to walk away from it. It was just as well.

After months in the hospital I had a 12-hour pass and an invitation to Sunday dinner from friends who were as unaware as I of how thoroughly the disease had flattened me. When my husband, Jim, drove me home from the hospital I wore a dressing gown and slippers. Everything else was at home.

It was a joy to be home—if only for a few hours—and the excitement of it kept me from realizing not everything was just the same. I chose a dress and Jim helped me. I couldn't raise my arms to slip it over my head, so he tried putting one arm into a sleeve, then the other. My muscles were stiff and sore and I cried out in pain. We tried putting the dress over my head and then working the arms into the sleeves. Again I couldn't make it.

"Let's try all three," said Jim, slipping my hands through the sleeves. He stooped over, joined my hands behind his neck, and told me to "hold on and bend your head toward me." As he drew back he straightened my arms and slipped the dress over my head. Success. But he still had to put on my nylons. His forehead was beaded with perspiration. I hadn't foreseen all this; just getting me dressed took an hour.

While Jim went out to get the car I picked up my gloves. Fumbling and struggling, I couldn't get them on. The fingers of the gloves drooped limply like the hands of a scarecrow. That did it. I was kidding myself. I couldn't hold back the tears.

"Will you please tell me what's the matter?" asked Jim.

"What's the use?" I countered. "I can't even put on my gloves without help. Who am I kidding? I have no business accepting an invitation. Why don't I put on my robe and admit that I'm just a cripple."

Finally, Jim broke the long silence: "Do you want to go as a polio, or as yourself?"

"What do you mean?"

"Just what I said."

"Help me get these gloves on," I finally managed through the tears.

"Now you're talking," Jim beamed.

I went as myself that day. It wasn't easy, but I suppose it restored my self-respect because I felt a sense of satisfaction as great as if I had walked.

"Remind me of that often, will you—to go as myself?" I asked my husband when it was over. "I'm glad I didn't go as a polio."

It was an incident that has affected my outlook ever since. The doctors and the therapists did the best they could, but there just wasn't enough left to build a vertical housewife. When they started telling me that many homemakers managed very nicely from a wheel chair I got the message: There are some things you can't change and must accept. If you can't see, you wear glasses; if you can't walk, you wear wheels. It's a lot better than mooning about what you used to be able to do.

So I studied all the hints, techniques, and gadgets the therapist had to offer for the handicapped housewife's home, rejecting some of them. At the same time I resolved that if we had to make changes in our home, it was going to look as little as possible like a *"home for the handicapped housewife." Then, as now, I was well past the stage of being unrealistic about my limitations. A handicapped person—yes, but equally determined not to make a career of it* (Narrative and photos from *Today's Health* published by the American Medical Association).

HOMEMAKERS ON WHEELS

THE THIRD-FLOOR "APARTMENT" at the Rehabilitation Institute of Chicago fills daily with a determined group of women—all physically handicapped as a result of illness or injury and all with a singular resolve not to make a career of it.

A casual look at the "living quarters"— living room, combination kitchen and dinette, bathroom, and bedroom—reveals very little of the special character of this "home." But the subtleties are there for the disabled home-makers to explore. Kitchen sink and encased cooking elements, for example, are lowered slightly. And the under-counter storage bins are missing, permitting the homemaker to wheel up to her tasks. Hand rails line corridor walls and grab bars are found in the bath-room. Beds are slightly lower than average. Many such features might be added to advantage to any home.

Having already begun a systematic regime of physical therapy, women of every age and every degree of disability come into these environs. They may manage perfectly with commercially marketed housekeeping aids or they may require special appliances, including custom-made devices—many of which have been researched and developed at the Institute which will aid them in resuming activities of daily living.

Since a basement laundry was out of the question and room was lacking elsewhere, the Listons installed appliances in a spare bedroom and concealed them in a cabinet. Mrs. Liston (shown in the picture) writes, "After months of feeling useless, nothing restored my self-respect like the first small load of laundry I ran through the washer and dryer myself."

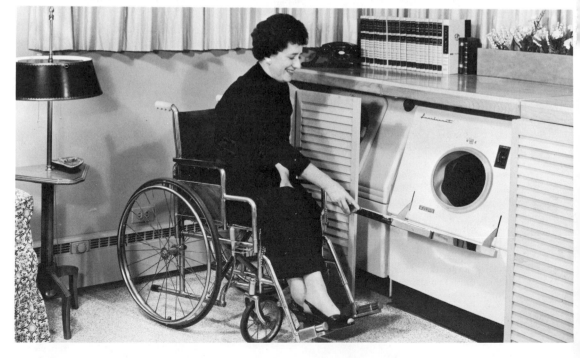

Figure 8.3 (continued)

Rehabilitation Institute of Chicago has installed a complete kitchen incorporating many modifications particularly suited to the disabled housewife's needs, such as the lowered knee-hole sink with touch controls and peg board for handy storage of frequently used wares. The kitchen is available to all homemakers, regardless of disability, where they regain agility in performance of most routine tasks, such as opening can, to preparation of complex meals.

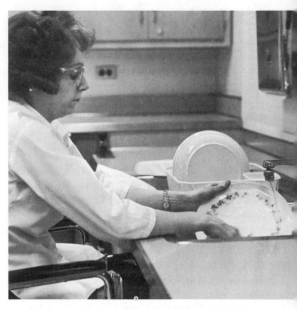

Occupational therapist works with a convalescing homemaker on kitchen replica which enables the latter to visualize adjustments in design and arrangement she may be able to make in her own kitchen, rendering it much more convenient.

Sometimes all it takes is the simplest gadget, such as the fetch stick (below), to restore the disabled homemaker to her efficient self. Others may regain independence with use of custom devices.

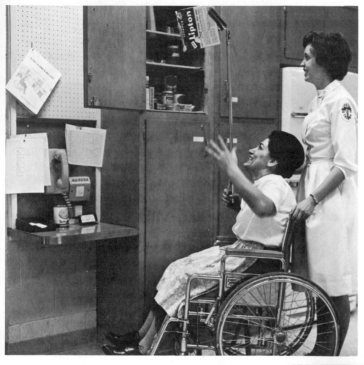

own self as well. Jourard (1964, p. 26) writes, "Every maladjusted person is a person who has not made himself known to another human being, and in consequence does not know himself. Nor can he be himself. More than that, *he struggles actively to avoid becoming known by another human being.* He works at it ceaselessly, 24 hours daily, and it is work!"

None of us is completely transparent or completely opaque, nor should we be. Too much disclosure, like too little, is undesirable. Disclosure requires the appropriate time and place and person (Jourard, 1963). The important thing is to have a person or persons with whom we can be ourselves, see ourselves, and become ourselves.

One way of measuring self-disclosure is to compare the subjective self with the social self. Do we see ourselves as we see others see us? Do we struggle to construct public selves incongruent with our private images?

People can learn to disclose themselves. In the warmth and security of certain relationships, we can dare to be ourselves. We let down our guard and let others see us and we see ourselves. In the material below, a woman in psychotherapy describes her struggle to know herself and to let her therapist know her:

As I look at it now, I was peeling off layer after layer of defenses. I'd build them up, try them, and then discard them when you remained the same. I didn't know what was at the bottom and I was very much afraid to find out, but I had to keep on trying. At first I felt there was nothing within me—just a great emptiness where I needed and wanted a solid core. Then I began to feel that I was facing a solid brick wall, too high to get over and too thick to go through. One day the wall became translucent, rather than solid. After this, the wall seemed to disappear but beyond it I discovered a dam holding back violent, churning waters. I felt as if I were holding back the force of these waters and if I opened even a tiny hole I and all about me would be destroyed in the ensuing torrent of feelings represented by the water. Finally I could stand the strain no longer and I let go. All I did, actually, was to succumb to complete and utter self pity, then hate, then love. After this experience, I felt as if I had leaped a brink and was safely on the other side, though still tottering a bit on the edge. I don't know what I was searching for or where I was going, but I felt then as I have always felt whenever I really lived, that I was moving forward (Rogers, 1961, pp. 110–111).

Personal Growth

A fourth valued quality is personal growth. Personal growth refers to the realization of our potentialities. We should, we are told, try to make the most of ourselves. We should become the best and fullest persons we can.

Such a notion is both bothersome and provocative. It is bothersome because it is so nebulous. It is almost mystical. How can we know what our potentialities are? How do we know if we have realized them? What is the best and fullest person we can become?

Still the notion is a provocative one. We all desire to be more than we are. How much more can we aspire to? We all set goals—some we will reach, some we might reach, and some perhaps are beyond any possibility of attainment.

We probably all know people who, in our opinion, failed to fulfill their potentialities. We may be acquainted with a person who showed considerable promise in high school who then—somehow—was unable to make anything of himself. Perhaps, in referring to him, we say he wasted his life.

On the other hand, we know some people whose lives were very much fulfilled. They may have been individuals of great promise or fairly modest promise. But we think of them as having made something of themselves.

Many psychologists have been intrigued with the idea of growth as a measure of man. One of the most eloquent has been Abraham Maslow (1954, 1956). He suggests that within each of us there are several sets of forces. One set impels us toward immediate safety and security, the other toward growth and change.

Maslow holds that human needs may be arranged in a hierarchy according to their power or prepotence. The hierarchy contains five levels of needs: physiological, safety, love, esteem, and self-actualization. Ordinarily, the lower, more basic needs

must be satisfied before higher ones can emerge and find expression (see Fig. 8.4).

Most prepotent of all requirements are those involving physiological needs. Until these needs are met, we are seldom free to pursue higher ones. As Maslow points out, when we are dangerously hungry, nothing is important except food.

As physiological needs are met, safety needs, which are at the next level of the hierarchy, can emerge. We begin our search for an orderly environment, one in which unpredictable events cannot happen. We employ safeguards and take precautions against danger. We attempt to make ourselves stronger than any adversary, present or potential. Maslow indicates that in our culture most adults feel relatively safe, but needs at this level are expressed in such activities as seeking jobs with tenure, opening savings accounts, and taking out insurance of all kinds.

Figure 8.4 Maslow's hierarchy of motivation includes five levels of needs. As we meet our more basic needs, we may proceed up the hierarchy to express and satisfy higher ones including the need to actualize the self.

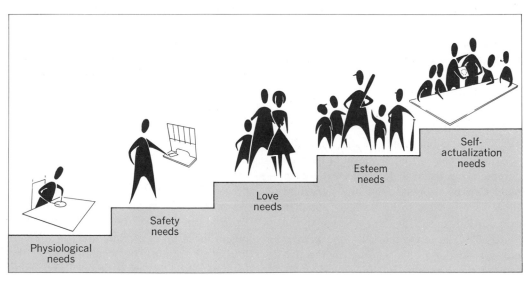

Following the satisfaction of physiological and safety needs, love needs may be expressed and attended. Almost everyone wants to give and to receive affection. We want to be a member of an affectional group and to know and be assured of our place in this group. We need people around us who are important to us and to whom we are important: parents and friends, sweethearts, and then a family of our own.

Esteem needs can emerge when physiological, safety, and love needs have achieved some satisfaction. Esteem needs involve our desire to respect ourselves and to have the respect of others around us. Each of us needs to feel that he is a worthy person, one who is well thought of by others. In part, our self-appraisal is based on the opinions of others; it is difficult to respect ourselves if others refuse to take us seriously, laugh at us, or hold us in contempt.

Finally, with the satisfaction of our more basic requirements, the need for self-actualization can find expression. This refers to our desire to actualize or fulfill ourselves, to make the most of our potentialities. The patterning of this need varies, depending upon the potentialities that each of us has. We may strive for fulfillment in education, athletics, parenthood, art or music, or many other areas.

Generally, as we satisfy our needs at one level of the hierarchy we may move up and attend to our needs at the next. But it is not necessary that one level of need be completely satisfied before the next higher need can be expressed. At any particular time we are likely to be partially satisfied and partially unsatisfied at each level of the hierarchy. The lower the level, the greater our satisfaction is likely to be: at the bottom of the hierarchy our physiological requirements are comparatively well met, but at the top our need for self-actualization is seldom well realized.

As Maslow notes, there are a number of important exceptions to the hierarchy. For example, if early personal relationships are painful, we may attempt to insulate ourselves against love needs. One who has suffered a good deal of deprivation may attempt to live safely and according to minimum essentials. Another person may give little attention to more basic needs as he assiduously pursues higher ones. History notes a number of individuals who have sacrificed comfort and safety and even life itself for a particular cause or for other people who were important to them.

Personal Maturity

A fifth valued quality is personal maturity. This term may be used in a number of ways. A person can be considered mature if he is functioning like an adult. He also may be said to be mature if he shows behavior which is appropriate to his chronological age. Sometimes we call a person mature when he is somewhat accelerated in his development.

The concept of maturity is frequently used in evaluation. It is common to hear someone compliment a child or adolescent by saying, "He's very mature for his age." It is also common for someone to insult another person by calling him immature and telling him to grow up.

Two conceptions of maturity will be presented. The first introduces the idea of "developmental tasks" and posits that the "successful human being" is one who meets these tasks as they arise in the various stages of life. The second presents the idea of "developmental crises" and holds that the "healthy personality" is one which resolves the crisis of each stage of life and builds on it.

Developmental Tasks

Havighurst identifies six stages in the developmental sequence of our lives. These stages are (1) infancy and early childhood, (2) middle childhood, (3) adolescence, (4) early adulthood, (5) middle age, and (6) later maturity.

Each stage is characterized by a number of developmental responsibilities or tasks. According to Havighurst, "A developmental task is a task which arises at or about a certain period in the life of the individual, successful achievement of which leads to his happiness and to success within later tasks, while failure leads to unhappiness in the individual, disapproval by the society, and difficulty with later tasks" (1952, p. 2).

The successful human being, to use Havighurst's term, is able to master the developmental tasks of each stage of life. He moves through life, building upon the accomplishments of the stage just past, confronting the tasks of the current stage, and preparing for the future. Unsuccessful human beings, by this criterion, fail to master their developmental tasks, and this leads to difficulty with subsequent responsibilities.

Developmental tasks may vary from culture to culture and from class to class within a culture. Havighurst, for example, notes that vocational preparation is relatively simple in primitive societies, but it is a difficult and anxiety-laden task for middle-class American adolescents.

Although developmental tasks are placed at a particular period of life, many of them have their forerunners in earlier periods, and many of them—after having their day (and stage)—recur in later stages. Although they peak during a particular time, some tasks persist throughout almost all of life.

Havighurst describes six to ten broadly defined developmental tasks for each of the six age periods. He spells out the tasks in some detail, noting their nature, their biological, psychological, and cultural basis, and their educational implications. The titles of the tasks for each stage are presented below:

Infancy and early childhood (Birth–6 Years)

1 *Learning to walk*
2 *Learning to take solid foods*
3 *Learning to talk*
4 *Learning to control the elimination of body wastes*
5 *Learning sex differences and sexual modesty*
6 *Achieving physiological stability*
7 *Forming simple concepts of social and physical reality*
8 *Learning to relate oneself emotionally to parents, siblings, and other people*
9 *Learning to distinguish right and wrong and developing a conscience*

Middle childhood (6–12 Years)

1 *Learning physical skills necessary for ordinary games*
2 *Building wholesome attitudes toward oneself as a growing organism*
3 *Learning to get along with age-mates*
4 *Learning an appropriate masculine or feminine social role*
5 *Developing fundamental skills in reading, writing, and calculating*
6 *Developing concepts necessary for everyday living*
7 *Developing conscience, morality, and a scale of values*
8 *Achieving personal independence*
9 *Developing attitudes toward social groups and institutions*

Adolescence (12–18 Years)

1 Achieving new and more mature relations with age-mates of both sexes
2 Achieving a masculine or feminine social role
3 Accepting one's physique and using the body effectively
4 Achieving emotional independence of parents and other adults
5 Achieving assurance of economic independence
6 Selecting and preparing for an occupation
7 Preparing for marriage and family life
8 Developing intellectual skills and concepts necessary for civic competence
9 Desiring and achieving socially responsible behavior
10 Acquiring a set of values and an ethical system as a guide to behavior.

Early Adulthood (18–30 Years)

1 Selecting a mate
2 Learning to live with a marriage partner
3 Starting a family
4 Rearing children
5 Managing a home
6 Getting started in an occupation
7 Taking on civic responsibility
8 Finding a congenial social group

Middle Age (30–55 Years)

1 Achieving adult civic and social responsibility
2 Establishing and maintaining an economic standard of living
3 Assisting teen-age children to become responsible and happy adults
4 Developing leisure-time activities
5 Relating oneself to one's spouse as a person
6 Accepting and adjusting to the physiological changes of middle age
7 Adjusting to aging parents

Later Maturity (55 on)

1 Adjusting to decreasing physical strength and health

2 Adjusting to retirement and reduced income
3 Adjusting to death of spouse
4 Establishing an explicit affiliation with one's age group
5 Meeting social and civic obligations
6 Establishing satisfactory physical living arrangements[2]

Developmental Crises

Erikson (1959, 1963) identifies "eight ages of man." These include (1) infancy, (2) early childhood, (3) play age, (4) school age, (5) adolescence, (6) young adult, (7) adulthood, and (8) mature age. These ages or stages are similar to those posited by Havighurst except that there are four rather than two preadolescent periods.

Each stage is marked by a developmental crisis—a critical psychological conflict. Each crisis is a conflict between two qualities of personalities, one positive, the other negative.

The healthy personality weathers the crisis, resolves the conflict, and emphasizes the positive quality. The less healthy personality fails to resolve the conflict or is caught up in the negative pattern.

Erikson points out that even in the healthy personality the negative qualities are never permanently conquered. In each crisis, the positive prevails over the negative, but the negative remains in some degree and must be continuously reconquered.

The healthy personality is built up of the positive qualities emerging from each conflict. These qualities—the components of a healthy personality—are trust, autonomy, initiative, industry, identity, intimacy, generativity, and integrity.

[2] From Havighurst, R. J. Developmental Tasks and Education. (2nd ed.) New York: Longmans, Green, 1952. Used by permission of David McKay Company.

Infancy: Trust versus Mistrust According to Erikson, the first component of a healthy personality is trust. By *trust* he means a confidence in the environment and in oneself. The trusting person has confidence that the environment is a safe and pleasant place to be in. And he has confidence in his own adequacy and worth.

The opposite of trust is mistrust. The mistrusting person does not have confidence in himself or in his world. Under stress, he may attempt to withdraw from the environment. Or he may, in a sense, withdraw from himself by erecting elaborate defenses.

Erikson places the crisis and ascendancy of this component at the very beginning of life—within the first year after birth. Therefore, the relationship between the infant and the mother (or mother substitute) is all important. It is in the ways the mother meets or fails to meet the infant's needs that trust or mistrust is established.

Early Childhood: Autonomy versus Shame and Doubt The second component of a

---

Presentation 8.2 Havighurst suggests that the "successful" human being is one who completes a number of developmental tasks as they arise through various stages of life from infancy to late maturity. Here is an example of a developmental task placed at middle childhood.

Learning an appropriate masculine or feminine social role

Nature of the Task. *To learn to be a boy or a girl—to act the role that is expected and rewarded.*

Biological Basis. *The actual anatomical differences between boys and girls do not require a difference in sex role during middle childhood. Girls' bodies are as well built for physical activities as are boys' bodies, and girls are nearly as large and strong as boys. It is not until adolescence that the anatomical differences between the sexes makes girls actually inferior to boys in certain physical activities. Toward the end of middle childhood, about age nine or ten, the body chemistry of boys and girls becomes differentiated.*

Psychological Basis. *The psychological basis for this task is laid in the family, where boy babies are taught to behave like boys, and girl babies like girls. These teachings are re-enforced by the psychological identification which the child usually makes with the parent of the same sex in early childhood.*

Cultural Basis. *The American culture expects differences in the behavior of boys and girls, and lays these expectations on the child early, through the agency of the family. Through the peer culture these same expectations are enforced during middle childhood.*

There are differences in the acceptable sex role in different social classes. For instance, the lower-class boy is expected to be a good fighter, while the middle-class boy is not expected to be openly aggressive, though he is taught to fight "in self-defense."

Educational Implications. *The sex role is taught so vigorously by so many agencies that the school probably has little more than a remedial function, which is to assist boys and girls who are having difficulty with the task. However, there have been some criticisms of American manhood, coming from representatives of other societies, to the effect that the American male grows up too much under the domination of women to learn most successfully a male role. In any case, it is generally conceded that more male teachers for children in middle childhood would have a good influence on boys, by giving them a closer relationship with male models at a time when they are engaged in learning how to behave like men.* (From Havighurst, R. J. *Developmental Tasks and Education.* (2nd ed.) New York: Longmans, Green, 1952. P. 19. Used by permission of David McKay Company.)

healthy personality is autonomy. Erikson's *autonomy* includes the wish to do things for oneself and be independent. In the first year of life the infant is to a large extent helpless and dependent, but by the end of his second year he can do many things for himself.

The opposite of autonomy is dependence, which for the child occasions shame and doubt. The child may become ashamed of his failure to do things for himself and to meet environmental demands. He can come to doubt himself and his capacity to be adequate.

Erikson places the crisis involving this component at the second year of life. As was just said, during this year the child is far less helpless than before. The timing of parental demands is important. If the parents prevent the child from making use of his growing capacities, or if they expect too much too soon, they interfere with the healthy development of autonomy. Parental example, guidance, and support plus freedom to practice provide the child with the opportunity to develop respect and confidence in his own abilities and readiness to approach the responsibilities that lie ahead of him.

Play Age: Initiative versus Guilt   The third component of a healthy personality is initiative. Erikson uses *initiative* to mean the intrusion of oneself into the social environment. In speaking of the activities characteristic of this stage, Erikson writes, "These include the intrusion into other bodies by physical attack; the intrusion into other people's ears and minds by aggressive talking; the intrusion into space by vigorous locomotion; the intrusion into the unknown by consuming curiosity" (1959, p. 76).

During this stage the child is "on the make." There is pleasure in attack and conquest. There is rivalry with one's own siblings and with other children. There is rivalry with one's parents.

During this stage, conscience shows rapid development. The sense of initiative can be hamstrung by the guilt produced by an overly critical and overly punitive conscience. As a child and as an adult, an "overly conscientious" person is prevented from exercising his full initiative and from making full use of his abilities.

Parents can help their children through this stage by proper understanding and guidance. Instead of manipulating people, the child can learn to cooperate with them. With an adequate relationship between parent and child, the latter can learn to identify with rather than rival the former. The child learns to "make" things, not to "make" or take advantage of people. He exercises his initiative without guilt because his achievements are not at the expense of others.

School Age: Industry versus Inferiority   By *industry*, Erikson means pleasure in work. As the child grows, there is increasing desire to leave the land of make-believe—of fantasy and play—and accomplish things in the larger world. He wants to learn things and make things and accomplish things, and to participate more fully in the adult environment.

At this stage there is danger that the child will feel inferior. Family life may not have prepared him adequately for school life. Early conflicts may not have been resolved. There may be mistrust of the world. Attempts at autonomy may have caused him to doubt himself, and attempts at initiative may have produced guilt.

The teacher plays an important part

in this stage of development. Erikson writes that there must be good teachers with whom the child can identify—teachers "who *know* things and know how to *do* things." The school can help the child to develop industry and avoid a sense of inferiority by seeing that he makes the most of his assets and the least of his liabilities.

Adolescence: Identity versus Identity Diffusion   By *identity*, Erikson refers to a knowledge of who one is, what one's role is, and how people react to one. The child is exposed to many identities: male and female, good and bad, real and fictitious. Mental health requires that he ingest and disgorge bits (and bites) of identity until he arrives at one that has unity—an "inner sameness and continuity."

The danger of this stage is that there will be diffusion rather than integration. In this case, the person does not know who he is or what he stands for. He may be unable to accept himself or the role that others expect him to play. He may be unsure of himself—unsure whether he is a child or an adult, male or female, delinquent or law-abiding, real or phony.

Some of the most striking behavior shown by teen-agers stems from their search for identity. In speaking of this phenomenon in adolescents, Erikson writes:

To keep themselves together they temporarily overidentify, to the point of apparent complete loss of identity, with the heroes of cliques and crowds. On the other hand, they become remarkably clannish, intolerant, and cruel in their exclusion of others who are "different," in skin color or cultural background, in tastes and gifts, and often in entirely petty aspects of dress and gesture arbitrarily selected as the signs of an in-grouper or out-grouper. It is important to understand (which does not mean condone or participate in) such intolerance as the necessary defense against a sense of identity diffusion, which is unavoidable at a time of life when the body changes its proportions radically, when genital maturity floods body and imagination with all manners of drives, when intimacy with the other sex approaches and is, on occasion, forced on the youngster, and when life lies before one with a variety of conflicting possibilities and choices. Adolescents help one another temporarily through such discomfort by forming cliques and by stereotyping themselves, their ideals, and their enemies (1959, p. 92).

Young Adulthood: Intimacy versus Isolation After the person has achieved an identity he is ready for closer personal relationships or *intimacy*. Sure of his own identity, the person can risk close personal relationships and unions that combine sex and love. The youth who cannot establish his own identity cannot establish intimate and enduring relations with others. Erikson notes before "true twoness . . . one must first become oneself."

Failure to accomplish identity and intimacy leads to *isolation* in which the person avoids close relationships with others. He may establish formal, limited relationships which lack the warmth, spontaneity, and closeness of real intimacy. Some persons make continued attempts to establish close relationships, only to meet with continued failure.

Adulthood: Generativity versus Self-absorption This stage is closely related to the preceding one. *Generativity*, a term coined by Erikson, means commitment to the new generation and to the future. It includes the willingness to be a parent. But it also involves the larger willingness to transfer one's attention and energies from oneself and the present to one's children, the new generation, and the future.

Erikson emphasizes that adults need children as much as children need adults. Each generation depends on the other. Absorption in others enhances oneself. Self-absorption leads to stagnation and impoverishment.

Mature Age: Integrity versus Despair   As Erikson points out, *integrity* is difficult to define. He spells it out as the acceptance of one's life as it has been and is. Integrity implies that the person has achieved a style of living that protects him against threat. It implies a certain dignity.

When integrity is not achieved or when it is lost, there is *despair*. The despairing person finds little meaning or satisfaction in life. He feels that his life is running out and that there is no time to start anew and make sense of both life and death.

Personal Integration

A sixth valued quality is personal integration. Integration means that the personality has unity and consistency. An integrated person is free of disrupting and paralyzing conflicts.

Allport (1961) points out that in wholesome development we become differentiated but not disintegrated. We learn special behaviors for special situations. We learn specific adjustments for specific environments. But we form a relatively coherent whole.

This idea has been discussed by many writers. Psychoanalysts have been especially interested in it. Integration, from a psychoanalytic point of view, depends on the adequacy of ego functioning. The inte-

grated person is one who has a "strong ego" or "ego strength." Before this idea can be fully understood, however, one must know something about the imaginative psychoanalytic conception of personality.

Freud identified three important parts of personality which he termed the *id*, the *ego*, and the *superego*. Although these are elaborate and complex concepts, in greatly simplified form they can be thought of as three patterns of impulses or actions. Each pattern has an identity of its own, but all three are highly interrelated. A person's behavior at any particular moment is the result of interaction between these three patterns.

The id symbolizes the earliest and most primitive pattern of behavior. Freud said, "In popular language, we may say that . . . the id stands for the untamed passions" (1933, p. 107). It is the spoiled brat of the personality, the part that wants to do what it wants to do when it wants to do it. It is the caveman in us who wishes to act without inhibition and without concern for social conventions and niceties.

The id patterns are said to operate on the *pleasure principle*. This describes the tendency of such impulses to maximize pleasure and minimize pain. Id patterns seek to avoid tension at all costs. As tension mounts from any source, these patterns are designed to discharge the tension or to reduce it as much as possible.

Id patterns may be said to make up the behavior of the young infant. In general, the infant is able to meet his needs only through reflex activities or wish fulfillment. Within the limits of his small repertoire of responses, the infant responds quickly to tension by sneezing, crying, belching, urinating, defecating, wriggling, and so on.

As we mature, id patterns become modified through interaction with those symbolized by the ego and superego. Even in adults, however, fairly uninhibited id actions can occasionally be seen. Hall writes:

We can see the id in action whenever a person does something impulsive. A person, for example, who acts on an impulse to throw a rock through a window or trip someone up or commit rape is under the domination of the id. Similarly, a person who spends a lot of time daydreaming and building castles in the air is being controlled by his id. The id does not think. It only wishes or acts (1954, p. 21).

The next set of patterns to achieve prominence are symbolized by the ego. Freud writes, "In popular language, we may say that the ego stands for reason and circumspection" (1933, p. 107). More specifically, the ego can be thought of as the knower, thinker, and doer of the personality. In short, it is the problem solver (Mowrer, 1950; Symonds, 1951).

The ego is said to operate on the reality principle. In contrast to the id, which has no concern beyond its own immediate pleasure, ego patterns take into account the demands of the external environment or reality. The ego serves as a mediator between the id and reality conditions. It must adjust the demands of one to the other. In the process the ego may delay id impulses, modify them, or prevent them completely. In the same way, the ego may manipulate the world of reality to allow for the discharge of id impulses.

The last personality pattern to show itself is the superego. Freud says, "For us the super-ego is the representative of all moral restrictions, the advocate of the impulse towards perfection, in short it is as much as we have been able to apprehend psychologically of what people call the 'higher' things in human life" (1933, p. 95). Another word for superego is conscience. Our superego or conscience tells us what we must do and what we must not do. It tells us what we must be and what we must not be.

To coin a term, it might be said that the superego operates on the idealism principle. Unlike the id which strives for pleasure and the ego which observes reality, the superego seeks perfection or the ideal. The superego struggles to prevent the id from discharging its impulses, and it attempts to make the ego give up its realistic goals and adopt more moral or idealistic ones.

Freud noted that the ego has a difficult task: it must coordinate the demands of the id, the superego, and the external world. These demands are frequently in conflict. It is necessary for the ego to weigh all the demands, resolve the conflict, and institute some action.

The strong ego is able to handle the conflicting demands of the id, superego, and the external world. Id expression is allowed but only in patterning acceptable to the rest of the personality. Superego demands are attended to but they are not given tyrannical power. And there is awareness and response to the requirements of the external environment.

When the ego is strong, the person feels competent to cope with both the forces within himself and those in the external environment. He has the capacity to meet problems without being overwhelmed and to endure adversity without foundering (Barron, 1963). He is more at ease, and there is less need for defense. Consequently his behavior is more spontaneous and flexible.

If the ego is weak, the personality may be at the mercy of id or superego demands, or it may be a battleground on which first one patterning is supreme and then the other. When id forces predominate, the individual may be given to rash, impulsive, and intemperate actions. When superego forces are supreme, the personality may be flooded with feelings of anxiety and guilt.

When the ego is weak, the individual may take considerable measures to defend it. As he becomes more defensive, his behavior becomes more rigid and compelled. He shows an increasing amount of subterfuge and is less open and spontaneous (Kroeber, 1963).

In the well-integrated personality, the id, ego, and superego operate in balance with one another (Krapf, 1961). This balance allows the individual to go about the business of living with a minimum amount of stress. In the poorly integrated person, the three patterns are in conflict. Much energy may be tied up in this struggle, leaving less free for more constructive pursuits (see Fig. 8.5).

Figure 8.5 Superego versus Id (Drawing by Frascino; © 1967 The *New Yorker Magazine, Inc.*).

Contact with the Environment

A seventh valued quality is contact with the environment. It has already been said that we should know ourselves. But we need to know our world too.

In order to live effectively in the world, we must have an adequate perception of it. Our actions are based on our perceptions. If our perceptions are wrong, our actions are apt to be wrong as well.

Of course, there is not just one correct way of perceiving the world. When we say that a friend or acquaintance of ours is being unrealistic or living in a world of his own, we may just be saying that his perceptions do not agree with ours. There is not just one reality; there are many, a different one for every perceiver. There is, however, concern when a person's perception of reality becomes grossly deviant.

Accurate perception of the world requires that a person have the ability to empathize with others. He must be able to put himself in another person's shoes or psyche, so to speak, and share this person's frame of reference. Because he knows both himself and others, his behavior is likely to make more sense.

Accurate perception of the world also implies the ability to rise above personal needs. When our needs are very strong, we may distort the world to fit them. We may not see what is there to be seen. Or we may see what is not there.

Jahoda points out that the mentally healthy person tests reality or verifies his perceptions to make sure that they are not distorted by his wishes and fears, while a less healthy person does not do so. She writes, "Parents, for example, ordinarily wish that their children will do well in school or fear they may fail. A mentally healthy parent will seek objective evidence and accept it, even it goes against his wishes. One lacking in health will not seek evidence, or will reject it if it is presented to him and it does not suit him" (1958, p. 52).

In some serious maladjustments a person may be confused or remote and out of contact with his environment. He may have delusions—false but firmly held beliefs—which strongly color his interactions with others. Or he may have hallucinations—false sensations—hearing, seeing, smelling, tasting, and feeling things which are not there to be sensed.

In making evaluations, psychologists, psychiatrists, and other clinical workers concern themselves with what they call the person's "reality testing." Does the person see the world as others see it? Does he misperceive it enough to make himself ineffective in dealing with it? Enough to make him a danger to himself or others?

Effectiveness in the Environment

An eighth valued quality concerns a person's effectiveness in his environment. Various names have been used in descriptions of this quality. Some of these include "competence" (White, 1959), "interpersonal competence" (White, 1963), "social competence" (Zigler & Phillips, 1961, 1962), "psychological effectiveness" (Levine & Kantor, 1960), and "human effectiveness" (Brayfield, 1965).

We should not only perceive our world correctly, we should be able to participate in it effectively. We should be able to move around in it freely and securely, enjoying it, and making the most of it. We should be able to play prescribed roles and meet social expectancies.

One of the simplest but most meaningful definitions of effectiveness was given by Freud. He was once asked what a person should be able to do well. It is a question to ponder, and a ponderous answer might have been expected. But Freud's response was brief. *"Lieben und arbeiten,"* he answered. What should a person be able to do well? He should be able to love and to work (Erikson, 1963).

To Love

What does it mean to love? Sometimes love is spoken of as sexual intimacy, sometimes in terms of warm and affectionate relations, and sometimes in a broader social sense. Writers have included all these aspects of love in their conceptions of mental health.

Psychoanalytic writings have emphasized the role of sex in human experience. They underscore the importance of satisfying sexual relations. Erikson writes that sexual "health" involves the "mutuality of genital orgasm" and that sexual "utopia" goes beyond sex in isolation to include:

1 *mutuality of orgasm*
2 *with a loved partner*
3 *of the other sex*
4 *with whom one is able and willing to share a mutual trust*
5 *and with whom one is able and willing to regulate the cycles of*
   a *work*
   b *procreation*
   c *recreation*
6 *so as to secure to the offspring, too, all the stages of a satisfactory development*[3]

Love involves a broad spectrum of relationships. It includes the establishment of suitable relationships with parents,

[3] Reprinted from *Childhood and Society*, Second Edition, Revised and Enlarged, by Erik H. Erikson. By permission of W. W. Norton & Company, Inc. Copyright © 1950, 1963 by W. W. Norton & Company, Inc. P. 266.

spouse and children, relatives and friends, neighbors and associates, and other people. It implies a bond and a concern with all people.

Love relationships might be charted within the framework of a series of ever-widening concentric circles. The small, center circle would include the closest and most intimate relationships, likely those involving members of one's family. The next circle might include close friends and relatives; the one next to that, social acquaintances and work associates, and so on.

Some individuals seem able to relate well to persons of the innermost circle but have little empathy or regard for those beyond it. Conversely, others appear unable to establish or maintain intimate relationships—they do better in those which allow for a certain social distance. The most effective persons have the ability to relate well in every circle of their human environment.

To Work

Work, in the sense the term is used here, encompasses a wide variety of activities. It includes vocation and avocation. It includes school and college pursuits. It includes all sorts of productive and creative endeavor.

For many of us, work and study give purpose and pattern to our lives. We have the need to learn something, produce something, and contribute something. We would work whether we had to or not. In fact, not to work may seem almost unthinkable.

Although many people look to work to add meaning to their lives, some have jobs which are not very meaningful. One writer has pointed out that there are not enough meaningful opportunities for the employment of youth in our society (Goodman,

1960). And in this increasingly automated world, jobs may become less and less satisfying and also less and less numerous (Wrenn, 1964).

Fortunately many of us can work at our avocations. It may be in our off-work work that we find satisfaction and fulfillment. In the interests we pursue, in the committees we serve on, in the causes we promote, we find meaningful occupation.

To Love and to Work

Loving is only part of our effectiveness in our environment. Working is also only part. And it is only one part or the other that some of us achieve (Shoben, 1956).

Some of us sacrifice our love relationships to our work. We become increasingly occupied with jobs and ambitions and increasingly less occupied with our families. Sometimes the pursuit of financial success is rationalized as being for the family's welfare, but economic privation may be less serious than the emotional neglect which supplants it.

Some of us sacrifice our careers to love relationships. Feminists have lamented the lack of opportunity for women to develop themselves in American society. Some writers, however, have pointed out that there are many unseized opportunities and that many women do not seek fulfillment outside their families.

"Love and work," said Freud. Both, not one or the other. Erikson (1963), who recalls the story also explains it: when Freud said "love" he meant sex and affection, and when he said "love and work" he meant work that enhances a person and does not rob him of his loving quality. It is, says Erikson, a formula that cannot be improved on.

Independence of the Environment

It was said that a person should be in contact with his environment and be effective in it. A number of writers have felt that the individual should be independent of his environment. Some have posed independence as a prime quality.

At first glance, there may seem to be some conflict among these several criteria. How can one be in contact with his environment and independent of it at the same time? How can one be effective in his environment and still stand apart from it?

Of course, there is no need that each quality be compatible with every other. Several qualities may be suggested by different writers with differing sets of values. Each authority may state and argue his opinion.

However, in a more exact delineation of independence, it becomes apparent that there is less incompatibility between this quality and the previous one than might at first glance appear. This can be seen in the two descriptions of independence or autonomy which follow.

Maslow's Autonomy

Maslow (1954) made a study of a number of "self-actualizing" people. These were individuals who had made or were making the most of their potentialities. They were, in Maslow's opinion, people who had achieved "psychological health."

Among the qualities which Maslow noted in these people were detachment and autonomy. They were a part of their environment, but they were also apart from it. More than the average person, they enjoyed privacy and independence.

Maslow described these people as "self-contained." He writes, "This inde-

pendence of environment means a relative stability in the face of hard knocks, blows, deprivations, frustrations, and the like. These people can maintain a relative serenity and happiness in the midst of circumstances that would drive other people to suicide" (p. 214).

At the same time, these people maintained profound interpersonal relationships. However, their deep relationships were few, and their circle of friends was small. They showed regard and respect for all people, but they were in intimate association with a very limited number.

Riesman's Autonomy

In his provocative book, *The Lonely Crowd*, Riesman describes three contrasting types of character structure. Each person, he hypothesizes, is predominantly one of these types.

The first character type is one which Riesman, somewhat idiosyncratically, calls "adjusted." This category includes those people whose character suits and fits the demands and expectancies of their society. These people, therefore, adjust with relatively little effort.

The second character type is the "anomic" or the maladjusted. In this category Riesman places both the "underadjusted" and the "overadjusted." The former are unable to conform to society's patterns, and the latter conform too much.

The third character type is that of the "autonomous." This category includes those individuals who have the capacity for both conformity and deviation. They are not compelled to conform, but they are able to. And they are not compelled to go their own way, but they can. In short, they are free to choose.

Riesman values autonomy, and he explores the ways in which a more autonomous character might be developed in our society. He is not satisfied with his search, but he is generally hopeful and ends his book in this way:

> But while I have said many things in this book of which I am unsure, of one thing I am sure: the enormous potentialities for

diversity in nature's bounty and men's capacity to differentiate their experience can become valued by the individual himself, so that he will not be tempted and coerced into adjustment or, failing adjustment, into anomie. The idea that men are created free and equal is both true and misleading: men are created different; they lose their social freedom and their individual autonomy in seeking to become like each other (1961, p. 307).

SUMMARY

Good adjustment and mental health are almost synonymous concepts these days. Each refers to a valued way of living, but there are some important differences in connotation. Adjustment is more environmental and dynamic in connotation, while mental health is more personal and static and implies a physical or medical condition. Mental health is sometimes reserved to designate very desirable personal characteristics.

Maladjustment and mental illness also share meaning. Both refer to undesirable or poorly regarded patterns of behavior. Maladjustment has environmental and dynamic implications while mental illness is more personal, static, and pejorative.

There are two different ways of regarding mental illness. The medical approach considers mental illness a disease analogous to physical disease. The psychosocial approach regards mental illness simply as learned but undesirable patterns of behavior.

Normality, neurosis, and psychosis are related concepts. Normality refers to average or typical characteristics or patterns of behavior. Neurosis designates more deviant and less desirable characteristics or patterns. Psychosis denotes very deviant and very undesirable characteristics or patterns which may be qualitatively as well as quantitatively different from normality and neurosis.

Sanity and insanity are terms or concepts in legal usage. Sanity denotes that a person can be held accountable for his actions. Insanity indicates that the person is not legally responsible because of a mental disease or defect.

Some highly valued human qualities include happiness and harmony. Happiness refers to an overall sense of well-being. Harmony implies an overall balance between personal and environmental demands.

A second set of valued qualities includes such components of self-regard as self-insight (a knowledge of oneself), self-identity (a sharp and stable image of oneself), self-acceptance (a positive image of oneself), self-esteem (a pride in oneself), and self-disclosure (a willingness to let oneself be known to others).

A third set of valued qualities includes personal growth (the realization of one's potentialities), personal maturity (the realization of age-specific goals), and personal integration (the realization of unity and consistency in behavior).

A last set of qualities includes contact with the environment, effectiveness in the environment, and independence of the environment. The first refers to the ability to see the world as others do, the second, the ability to relate to others and be productive, and the third, the ability to deviate (and conform) to group patterns.

REFERENCES

Achenbach, T., & Zigler, E. Social competence and self-image disparity in psychiatric and nonpsychiatric patients. *Journal of Abnormal and Social Psychology,* 1963, **67**(3), 197–205.

Adams, H. B. "Mental illness" or interpersonal behavior? *American Psychologist,* 1964, **19**(3), 191–197.

Albee, G. W. Needed: A conceptual breakthrough. Unpublished manuscript, 1966.

Allport, G. W. *Pattern and Growth in Personality.* New York: Holt, 1961.

Bandura, A. *Behavioristic Psychotherapy.* New York: Holt, in press.

Barron, F. *Creativity and Psychological Health.* Princeton, N.J.: Van Nostrand, 1963.

Block, J. Ego identity, role variability, and adjustment. *Journal of Consulting Psychology,* 1961, **25**(5), 392–397.

————, & Thomas, H. Is satisfaction with self a measure of adjustment? *Journal of Abnormal and Social Psychology,* 1955, **51**(2), 254–259.

Boehm, W. W. The role of psychiatric social work in mental health. In A. M. Rose (Ed.), *Mental Health and Mental Disorder.* New York: Norton, 1955. Pp. 536–555.

Bossard, J. H. S., & Boll, E. S. *The Large Family System.* Philadelphia: University of Pennsylvania Press, 1956.

Brayfield, A. H. Human effectiveness. *American Psychologist,* 1965, **20**(8), 645–651.

Cantril, H. *The Pattern of Human Concerns.* New Brunswick, N.J.: Rutgers, 1965.

English, H. B., & English, A. C. *A Comprehensive Dictionary of Psychological and Psychoanalytical Terms.* New York: Longmans, 1958.

Erikson, E. H. Identity and the life cycle. *Psychological Issues,* 1959, **1**(1), Monograph 1.

————. *Childhood and Society.* (2nd ed.) New York: Norton, 1963.

Freud, S. *New Introductory Lectures on Psycho-analysis.* New York: Norton, 1933.

Fromm, E. *The Art of Loving.* New York: Harper & Row, 1956.

Goldfried, M. R. Feelings of inferiority and the depreciation of others. A research review and theoretical reformulation. *Journal of Individual Psychology,* 1963, **19**, 27–48.

Goodman, P. Youth in organized society. *Commentary,* 1960, **29**(2), 95–107. (February, 1960).

Graham, T. F. McNaghten to Jenkins. *Insight: Quarterly Review of Religion and Mental Health,* 1964, **2**(4), 10–19.

Gurin, G., Veroff, J., & Feld, S. *Americans View Their Mental Health.* New York: Basic Books, 1960.

Hall, C. S. *A Primer of Freudian Psychology.* Cleveland: World Publishing, 1954.

Havighurst, R. J. *Developmental Tasks and Education.* (2nd ed.) New York: Longmans, 1952.

Hollender, M. H., & Szasz, T. S. Normality, neurosis and psychosis. *Journal of Nervous and Mental Disease,* 1957, **125**(4), 599–607.

Izard, C. E. Personality similarity and friendship: A follow-up study. *Journal of Abnormal and Social Psychology,* 1963, **66**(6), 598–600.

Jahoda, M. *Current Concepts of Positive Mental Health.* New York: Basic Books, 1958.

Jourard, S. M. *Personal Adjustment.* (2nd ed.) New York: Macmillan, 1963.

———. *The Transparent Self.* Princeton, N.J.: Van Nostrand, 1964.

Krapf, E. E. The concepts of normality and mental health in psychoanalysis. *International Journal of Psycho-analysis,* 1961, **42**, 439–446.

Kroeber, T. C. The coping functions of the ego mechanisms. In R. W. White (Ed.), *The Study of Lives.* New York: Atherton, 1963. Pp. 178–198.

Levine, L. S., & Kantor, R. E. Psychological effectiveness and imposed social position: A descriptive framework. Paper read at American Psychological Association, Chicago, September, 1960.

Liston, D. Housekeeping on wheels. *Today's Health,* 1965, **43**(5), 62–66, 86–87.

Maslow, A. H. *Motivation and Personality.* New York: Harper & Row, 1954.

———. Defense and growth. *Merrill-Palmer Quarterly,* 1956, **3**, 36–47.

Mowrer, O. H. *Learning Theory and Personality Dynamics.* New York: Ronald, 1950.

Peck, R. F. Measuring the mental health of normal adults. *Genetic Psychology Monographs,* 1959, **60**, 197–255.

Riesman, D., Glazer, N., & Denney, R. *The Lonely Crowd.* (new ed.) New Haven, Conn.: Yale, 1961.

Rogers, C. R. *On Becoming a Person.* Boston: Houghton Mifflin, 1961.

Rosenberg, M. The association between self-esteem and anxiety. *Journal of Psychiatric Research,* 1962, **1**(2), 135–152.

Rubington, E. Drug addiction as a deviant career. *International Journal of the Addictions,* 1967, **2**(1), 3–20.

Sanford, N. The prevention of mental illness. In Benjamin B. Wolman (Ed.), *Handbook of Clinical Psychology.* New York: McGraw-Hill, 1965. Pp. 1378–1400.

Shoben, E. J., Jr. Work, love, and maturity. *Personnel & Guidance Journal,* 1956, **34**, 326–332.

———. Toward a concept of the normal personality. *American Psychologist,* 1957, **12**, 183–189.

Smith, G. M. Six measures of self-concept discrepancy and instability: Their interrelations, reliability, and relations to other personality measures. *Journal of Consulting Psychology,* 1958, **22**(2), 101–112.

Symonds, P. M. *The Ego and the Self.* New York: Appleton-Century-Crofts, 1951.

Szasz, T. S. The myth of mental illness. *American Psychologist,* 1960, **15**(2), 113–118.

———. *The Myth of Mental Illness.* New York: Hoeber-Harper, 1961.

———. *Law, Liberty, and Psychiatry.* New York: Macmillan, 1963. (a)

———. Psychiatrist questions criminal law: Was Oswald's killer temporarily insane? *The Sunday Star-Bulletin & Advertiser,* Dec. 29, 1963, p. B4. (b)

Ullmann, L. P., & Krasner, L. What is behavior modification? In L. P. Ullmann & L. Krasner (Eds.), *Case Studies in Behavior Modification.* New York: Holt, 1965. Pp. 1–63.

White, R. W. *Lives in Progress.* New York: Holt, 1952.

———. Motivation reconsidered: The concept of competence. *Psychological Review,* 1959, **66**(5), 297–333.

———. Sense of interpersonal competence: Two case studies and some reflections on origins. In R. W. White (Ed.), *The Study of Lives*. New York: Atherton, 1963. Pp. 72–93.

Wrenn, C. G. Human values and work in American life. In H. Borow (Ed.), *Man in a World at Work*. Boston: Houghton Mifflin, 1964. Pp. 24–44.

Wylie, R. C. *The Self Concept*. Lincoln, Nebr.: University of Nebraska Press, 1961.

Zigler, E., & Phillips, L. Social competence and outcome in psychiatric disorder. *Journal of Abnormal and Social Psychology*, 1961, **63**, 264–271.

——, & ——. Social competence and the process-reactive distinction in psychopathology. *Journal of Abnormal and Social Psychology*, 1962, **65**, 215–222.

CHAPTER NINE

IMPROVING ADJUSTMENT

Our adjustment is not static. We constantly change. The environment constantly changes. Constant readjustment is necessary.

The quality of our adjustment changes too. Adjustment in a particular area of life—once adequate—may falter. Occasionally everything of importance seems to go wrong, and we are precipitated into a major personal crisis.

Generally speaking, when we get worse, we get better. Each life is a series of ups and downs. There is a tendency among some of us to make too much of the downs. And there is a tendency to make too little of our ability to help ourselves. Most of us are able to get ourselves upright and back on our feet even after a major personal disaster.

In times of trouble and crisis, we may have the help of friends and family. Sometimes we get assistance from our minister or physician. Occasionally, a psychiatrist or psychologist or someone else specially trained in helping people may be needed.

This chapter will describe three general ways in which adjustment may be changed. Then, since this whole area is rapidly growing and changing, some current trends will be noted. The next chapter will present some workers and facilities that play important parts in improving adjustment.

SOME APPROACHES TO IMPROVEMENT

We are physical, psychological, and social beings. Our adjustment is affected by each of these aspects of ourselves and by all of them in combination. In order to change adjustment, we may attempt to modify our physical or psychological nature or the nature of the environment in which we find ourselves. Approaches of the first kind may be called somatotherapy; the second kind, psychotherapy; and the third, sociotherapy.

Somatotherapy

The term *somatotherapy* subsumes a variety of medical and surgical techniques which are designed to change a person's adjustment by altering his physical being. Therapy of this kind has had a prominent place in psychiatric history. Many techniques—once promising or prominent—have fallen into disuse and others have risen to take their place. For example, psychosurgery (operations performed on the brain) had some vogue in the 1940s and 1950s but now has been largely replaced by less drastic methods (Greenblatt & Levinson, 1965). Hydrotherapy (prolonged baths and wet packs) is one of the oldest somatotherapies but is increasingly less used (McGraw & Oliven, 1959). Today the most frequently prescribed somatotherapies are electroshock and drugs.

Shock Therapy

Shock has been used in the treatment of mental illness for the past thirty years or so. This approach employs electric current or a chemical agent to induce a sudden and profound alteration of bodily functioning. Generally, the shock state is accompanied by convulsions and loss of consciousness or coma.

The most common present use of this technique is the administration of electroshock to depressed individuals. It is especially likely to be prescribed where the depression is severe. In some cases shock may be considered necessary to alleviate the threat of suicide.

How does electroshock work? Many different hypotheses have been formulated. Some writers suggest that the therapeutic effect of shock is essentially psychological; others offer physiological explanations. However, no single hypothesis has been well substantiated or proved generally acceptable (Campbell, 1961; Wolman, 1965).

How effective is electroshock? Reaction to this treatment appears to vary greatly from person to person (Wittenborn, 1965). Some patients seem to respond quickly, but relapses are not uncommon. A comprehensive review of experimental studies of electroshock found that the evidence was inconclusive and that further research was necessary (Riddell, 1963).

Whatever its effectiveness, shock therapy is becoming less used. Drugs have supplanted shock to a considerable extent; they are more convenient to administer as well as less drastic in action. Improvement in psychological approaches to mental illness has also lessened the need for shock techniques.

Drug Therapy

Drugs are the chief form of somatotherapy used in mental illness. In fact, drugs have largely replaced other somatic treatments. It has been stated that in current practice the "typical psychiatric patient" is taking some kind of psychopharmaceutical preparation (Wortis, 1965).

Many different drugs have been used in the treatment of mental illness. New chemical compounds are being developed, explored, and put on the market. Considerable excitement has been raised by the promise of wonder drugs.

There is a limit to what may be expected of drugs. Generally speaking, the drugs used in therapy may be thought of as chemical stimuli which serve to modify patterns of response. One authority writes, "We cannot expect drugs to introduce anything new into the mind or into behavior, but merely to accentuate or to suppress functions in behavior which are already present" (Kety, 1961, p. 79).

It is to accentuate or suppress certain impulses or responses that most drugs are employed in therapy. For example, the tranquilizing drugs are used to calm and relax a person and make him less anxious, agitated, excited, or aggressive. Stimulant drugs are used to energize or activate a depressed individual and to make him more responsive to his environment.

How effective are drugs in the treatment of mental illness? Their effects are not easy to assess. Much of the research on drugs has been poorly conceived and executed (Holliday, 1965). Changing attitudes as well as new psychotherapeutic and sociotherapeutic approaches may be responsible for some of the success attributed to drugs.

The most widely acclaimed psychopharmaceuticals have been the tranquilizing drugs. There is little rigorous evidence that tranquilizers are very effective in the treatment of most office patients (Trouton & Eysenck, 1961), but drugs of this kind

have shown promise in the management of extremely troubled persons (Waggoner & Holmes, 1961).

A major claim made for tranquilizing drugs is that they reduce the length of hospitalization or make it unnecessary. Wortis reviewed this use of tranquilizers. The "chlorpromazine" he mentions below is a commonly used tranquilizer; "schizophrenia" is a common diagnosis of hospitalized patients; and "placebos" are inactive substances which, for control purposes, are administered as if they were medicines.

How useful do the tranquilizers appear after ten years? Two thorough and careful recent studies . . . leave no doubt that chlorpromazine relieves a number of specific symptoms in schizophrenic patients. Hospitalization is often delayed or averted, the behavior of hospitalized cases is improved and discharge rates increase; but there is a distressingly high readmission rate, and in the ambulatory cases sooner or later the hospitalization rate matches that of patients on placebos. . . . One recent large scale study . . . reports that the tranquilizers hardly affected hospital stay, discharge, readmission, or death rate, though [other investigators] believe that readmission rates can be kept low if the patients are adequately maintained on drugs (1965, p. 648).

A number of cautions must be noted concerning the use of drugs in the treatment of adjustment problems and mental illness. First, drugs may produce unwanted effects (side effects) that may be worse than the original behavior itself (Paredes, Gogerty, & West, 1961). Second, some drugs may have hidden toxic effects (Waggoner & Holmes, 1961; Wortis, 1965). Third, resorting to drug treatment may prevent a person from accepting responsibility for and coming to grips with his adjustment problems.

Psychotherapy

Psychotherapy refers to efforts to change adjustment patterns through psychological means. Many different techniques have been employed. For example, use has been made of support and reassurance, advice and persuasion, suggestion and hypnosis, rest and relaxation, books, art, dancing, music, and so on (Watkins, 1965).

Some people think of psychotherapy as an art. Others regard it as a science. And there is considerable controversy over how helpful current approaches are and which approaches may be most helpful or most promising. The view has been expressed that the American public may have been oversold on the need for professional psychotherapy and undersold on the ability of the individual to weather his troubles or find help from friends and other people (Schofield, 1964). Evaluating the effectiveness of therapeutic procedures is a complex and difficult task, but some important and promising research is currently in progress (Matarazzo, 1965).

Many people think of psychotherapy as a mysterious process, but it is becoming less and less so. Some of the newer and more promising approaches are relatively straightforward applications of well-known and well-established psychological principles (Grossberg, 1964). Under scrutiny, a good deal of psychotherapy seems not too different from the behavior which anyone of us might show as we seek to help a friend or acquaintance.

Many psychotherapies—different as they appear—share certain features. The discussion which follows describes some of these common elements. Then some differences or special techniques will be presented.

Some Common Features

Most psychotherapies emphasize the importance of the relationship between the therapist and the person coming for help. Many therapies encourage catharsis, that is, the relief of anxiety through thinking out, feeling out, and talking out a problem. Many strive for insight or self-understanding. And many, explicitly or implicitly, make use of learning principles.

Relationship   An important feature of many psychotherapies is the relationship between the therapist and the person seeking help. This relationship is characterized by a number of qualities less prominent in ordinary human interaction. Specifically, it is accepting, permissive, and supportive.

The Relationship Is Accepting. By word and action, the therapist demonstrates that he accepts the person and accepts him unconditionally. No matter what the person thinks or feels, no matter what he has done or is tempted to do, he is acceptable to the therapist.

There is a difference between the unconditional acceptance of the therapist and the more qualified acceptance of other people. With others, our acceptance may be contingent upon our thinking in certain ways, feeling in certain ways, and acting in certain ways. Furthermore, for others to merit our acceptance they must perform in the ways that are acceptable to us.

In maladjustment we frequently are overwhelmed by thoughts and feelings and actions that are socially undesirable. For example, there may be hostile or sexual impulses which are culturally forbidden. We are overcome with anxiety and guilt. We feel unacceptable to others and, indeed, unacceptable to ourselves.

The behavior of the therapist makes it clear that the person coming for help is worthy. It is not the purpose of the therapy to assign fault or blame. The person is "change-worthy" not "blame-worthy." He is worth working with and worth helping.

The Relationship Is Permissive. Although the person coming for help cannot be permitted to *do* anything he wishes in the therapy situation, he is allowed to *feel* anything and to *say* anything. No matter what is expressed, the therapist does not judge or criticize; he is neither shocked nor repelled. The person may even lash out— perhaps demonstrating in therapy the behavior which has troubled his relationship with others—but the therapist does not retaliate.

Outside the therapy situation, our environment may not be very permissive. We have been taught not to think certain thoughts, not to feel certain feelings, not to act certain actions. To avoid punishment we learn to make extensive use of suppression and repression.

In therapy the person learns that he is not punished for what he thinks or feels. He can say what he thinks; he can display his feelings; he does not need to maintain a facade. Perhaps for the first time in his life he is permitted to be himself. At first it is difficult to grasp the full freedom and permissiveness of this new situation. But little by little, in the calm, understanding, and noncritical environment provided by the therapist, the person can relax old defenses and go to work on his problems.

The Relationship Is Supportive. The person usually enters therapy under considerable stress. He is beyond the help of friends and relatives, and he is unable to help himself. Listening attentively and sympathetically, the therapist, an individual with prestige and training, demonstrates a concern and desire to help.

Outside the psychotherapy situation, this support may be largely absent. Friends and relatives and teachers and employers may have tried to help the person and have given him up as hopeless. Or he may have been dismissed with the homespun diagnosis that he was just born that way. Or it may have been suggested that he go see a "head shrinker," with the strong implication that one would have to be pretty far gone to take this step.

There may, indeed, be no realization that the individual has a problem at all. He may be accused of malingering or seeking sympathy. He may be enjoined to get a hold of himself, to straighten up, or to use some will power. He may, in fact, begin to make these accusations of himself, and when he comes into the therapy situation, he may be apologetic for taking up the therapist's time with so trivial a problem or with so worthless a person.

The psychotherapist provides the support that is lacking elsewhere. The person is shown that his feelings are understood and that his concerns are important. More than this, the person is made to feel that he is not hopeless; the therapist indicates the steps which are to be taken and stands ready to help the person begin.

Catharsis   A second feature of many psychotherapies is *catharsis*, which refers to the open expression of pent-up thoughts and feelings. Catharsis is a cleansing or purging process. It may also be thought of as a process of reliving in which old problems are verbalized and reexperienced.

The professional use of catharsis is similar to the everyday experience of blowing off steam or crying it out.

The person brings to the psychotherapy situation the same troublesome defenses that he has employed on the outside. Several things in therapy serve to weaken these defenses and to facilitate catharsis. First, the accepting, permissive, and supportive atmosphere makes defensive maneuvering less necessary. Second, the defenses prove not to be very useful because the therapist is not mislead by them; he gently but persistently identifies the defenses as they occur, and he unmasks them and explains them to the person (Shaffer & Shoben, 1956).

With the relaxation of defenses, the person can see himself in broader perspective. He can verbalize his problems more openly and more accurately. He brings to life his deep frustrations and hidden conflicts. He talks about painful experiences of the past and of his fears for the future. He talks of the forbidden things that he has done or is tempted to do, of the essential things that he must do but cannot.

Accompanying this verbal catharsis may be an important emotional one—a release of feelings. Before, the person may have had difficulty in expressing strong emotions; in fact, he may have denied that his problems were serious and that he felt deeply about them. But now, as he explores his problems and brings them into sharper focus, they come to life with all the emotional expression appropriate to them: anger and hate, envy and jealousy, fear and terror.

Why is catharsis beneficial? Used by itself, catharsis may have little permanent effect. Under certain conditions, however, it may provide important benefits.

First of all, catharsis brings relief from tension. The person has brought his problems into the open, looked at them himself, and allowed another to see them. Now it is not so necessary to be on guard against this painful material. Psychologically speaking, he has unburdened himself, and he may feel—almost literally—that a huge weight has been taken off his shoulders.

Second, the person may become less sensitive to his problems. As he brings his problems into verbal expression, he may experience again the emotional distress that caused them to be inhibited. The more he expresses his problems, the more he dissipates their emotional charge.

Third, present in the psychotherapy situation is comfort and security created by the therapist's acceptance, permissiveness, and support. The positive cues of the situation supplant the negative emotional stimuli formerly associated with the problems. Thus, through a process of conditioning, the person's problems may be divested of their pain and viewed calmly and securely (Shaffer & Shoben, 1956).

Insight A third aspect of many psychotherapies is *insight* or self-understanding. As the person explores himself in therapy he forms a new and fuller understanding. He understands why he has the thoughts he has, why he feels as he does, and what motives lie behind his behavior.

Many of us seem to be strangers to ourselves. Some of us are acutely aware of this lack of insight. We enter therapy sorely troubled and mystified by our own behavior.

Many of us, however, seem unaware that we lack insight. We lack insight that we lack insight. Or at least we do not see ourselves as others see us. The insight we have may be false or rationalized.

Some insights occur dramatically, with the person suddenly seeing himself in a new light or grasping an important connection. More frequently the process of self-understanding is long and laborious. The same insights are arrived at again and again, often in relationship to different life situations. For example, a very succorant or dependent person may bit by bit acquire insight into how this salient need affects his relationship with his parents, his wife, his employer, his friends, and other people in his life.

Change in behavior, either for better or for worse, may occur without insight. Just as we can learn ineffective adjustments without much awareness, we can learn better patterns without full understanding. Children and adults in therapy may make important gains without being able to verbalize the reasons for the change.

Change in behavior may occur without insight, and insight may occur without change in behavior. Many of us know what we should do to make a bad situation better, but we find ourselves unable to act on our knowledge. Somehow we are blocked, and one purpose of therapy may be to free us to act on our insights.

Generally, it is felt that insight expedites improvement. Being willing and able to explore oneself are signs of strength. Knowing oneself—the good and bad—means knowing the assets there are to work with and the deficits there are to work on.

Learning A fourth common feature is *learning*. Sometimes the therapy is explicitly designed as a learning task. Some-

times the learning is more implicit. But whether it is explicit or implicit, the person learns in therapy to see himself and his world differently; he learns new attitudes, values, and patterns of behavior.

An earlier chapter of this book described the part that learning plays in the adjustment process. It may be helpful here to review the principles which were introduced at that time and to consider them in relation to psychotherapy.

Within this framework, the person coming for help is considered to have learned certain patterns of adjustment which should be extinguished. He has failed to learn or to implement certain more desirable patterns which should be reinforced. And he needs help in forming certain discriminations and generalizations.

In therapy the person is helped to extinguish unwanted patterns of response. The more secure he feels in the accepting, permissive, and supporting situation, the more he is able to discuss his fearful and anxiety-provoking problems. And the more he discusses these problems, the less fearful and anxiety provoking they become. In this way, fear and anxiety gradually decrease.

The behavior which the person brings to the therapy situation is grist for the therapeutic mill. To some extent, it mirrors behavior on the outside. But on the inside, evasive and defensive tactics do not work. The therapist identifies these tactics and leaves them unrewarded (Shaffer & Shoben, 1956). Like fear and anxiety, unwanted behavior tends to diminish.

In therapy the person is helped to extinguish unwanted behavior and to institute or strengthen desirable patterns of response. Some of these desired responses may have been tried in the past but abandoned when they were punished or went unrewarded. Some may be present but only infrequently used. Some may be completely missing from the person's response repertoire (Rotter, 1954).

Where a wanted response pattern is inhibited, the task of therapy is to free it for use. Antagonistic or conflicting patterns may need to be extinguished. The person can be encouraged to try out the wanted behavior in situations where it is apt to be successful and, therefore, reinforced. For example, a person who can assert himself only with great difficulty and anxiety can be helped to assert and express himself in the therapy situation, and then in other relatively safe situations, and then in any situation.

When a pattern of wanted behavior is absent, the task of therapy is to teach or inculcate the pattern. Sometimes the therapist serves as a model for the person to imitate or emulate, or the therapist may suggest ways of approaching a problem and help the person practice them. Conditioning procedures may also be employed.

In therapy unwanted patterns are extinguished, wanted patterns are reinforced, and these latter patterns are generalized to the outside environment. The therapy situation might be thought of as a laboratory of social learning. It is a place arranged so that certain sorts of patterns can occur and be strengthened. But it must also be arranged so that these patterns will be carried over into the larger society.

The person generalizes his new attitudes toward himself and others. He generalizes more effective patterns of response. In this way behavior which has been tried out in the relatively protective and supportive confines of the therapist's office, the therapy group, the mental hospital, and other therapeutic environments is transferred to the larger world.

The person generalizes. However, he learns to make necessary discriminations too. He learns why his old behavior was unsuccessful in some situations. He learns to which situations his new behavior can be usefully applied. He learns to think more flexibly and behave more flexibly—to tailor his behavior to the situations in which he finds himself.

The goal of therapy is not to solve all the person's problems. Rather, it is to help him learn to behave in ways which make problems less likely. And it is to help him learn to deal effectively with present and future problems (Rotter, 1954).

The following presentation is a good description of the learning factors involved in psychotherapy of neurotic individuals:

What is psychotherapy? To answer this question one must first pose a prior question: What is neurosis? The facts about neurosis seem to be these. Some people come out of childhood with an impairment of mental life and an inhibition of power to act in critical life areas. In early years neurotic persons had been frightened out of their capacity to think, love, and work at a high level. Subjected to adverse conditions, they learned bad habits of not thinking straight and not acting effectively. Consequently they are unable to relate themselves in a cooperative way to other persons. Both the mental impairment and inhibition of action of neurotics are due to emotional conflict.

The inability to think about important problems makes the neurotic seem stupid. The pressure of conflicting drives makes him miserable. Symptomatic acts somewhat, but only partly, reduce his misery. The neurotic is thus strangely incapacitated, unable to describe his past, unable to cure himself, and unable to act effectively in the real world.

The business of psychotherapy is to correct the bad mental and emotional habits the neurotic has learned. Since new habits can be learned only under new conditions, a new learning situation must be created. This the therapist proceeds to do. To begin with, he has the prestige of a specialist. He sets up a warm, permissive atmosphere, different from that to which the patient has formerly been exposed. The therapist encourages free expression on the part of the patient. He does not judge or condemn. Temporarily the therapist becomes an important person in the patient's life. The patient's tendencies to love and hate are transferred to the therapist and are clearly exhibited in the relations between the two. The study of this relationship gives the therapist essential information. Throughout the relationship the therapist stands for reason and reality. The therapist thus gives the patient an experience more benign than any he had had before.

The therapist is more than permissive about free speech. Indeed he urges the patient to say everything that comes to mind. He pits this urgent requirement against the patient's reluctance to speak his thoughts.

As the work proceeds, the patient fearfully recites his thoughts and intentions and awaits the thunderclap of disapproval which he has learned to expect. When it does not come in the course of repeated trials, his fear is extinguished, and the once frightening sentences lose their power to create alarm. As fear is reduced, new thoughts can occur especially those which have formerly been opposed by anxiety. . . .

When the patient cannot find words for the strong tensions which beset him the therapist offers them. We call it "labeling." Thus words and sentences are attached to emotions formerly repressed. It comes as a great relief to the patient to have a complete and correct account of his own inner experience. Through the provision of new labeling the patient can be said to become emotionally intelligent. He is made capable of dealing with his conflicts at the mental level. For the first time he can anticipate problem situations and act with foresight in important areas of his life.

The neurotic person lives in a fog of confusion. He still anticipates punishments which could only be imposed in childhood. Here the therapist can help by aiding the patient to make discriminations. He separates imaginary fears from real ones. Emotions and courses of action for which the patient was once punished can be shown to be no longer punishable. By contrasting life conditions of the past with the present, the therapist can show that courses of action which would once have been dangerous can now be not only not dangerous but positively rewarding and essential to life. The patient can be reminded that though once small and mentally helpless he is now grown and mentally capable.

As fear is reduced by extinction and discrimination, as new labeling units become available, the patient in therapy tries out new solutions at the mental level. Extinction of anxiety and discrimination between dangerous and benign situations generalize quietly to the persons and situations of daily life. As this occurs, responses formerly inhibited can be tried out. . . .

The result of the new learning in the therapy sessions should be a change in the real-life behavior, a fresh try, as it were. We hold that successful experience involving other people is essential to therapeutic effect. If the real-life situation is favorable, the responses newly tried out are strongly rewarded. Thus new habits are formed in the critical spheres of sex and love, self-assertion, independence, and self-confidence. If the real-life situation is unfavorable such benevolent results cannot occur.

Moreover, the effect of strong rewards is much more general. Reward effects extend backward from the successful goal acts and strengthen the labeling habits and action tendencies which led to reward. The indirect but important result is an intensification of mental life and increased ability to work out his own solu-

tions to problematic situations. The neurotic comes to seem less stupid and unpredictable to other people. The reduction of basic drives, formerly inhibited, reduces misery and develops hopeful attitudes. The minor escape provided by symptoms is no longer needed as the capacity to love and work is restored. In short, when these effects occur repeatedly the neurotic becomes no longer neurotic.[1]

Some Special Features

As was just indicated, a number of common elements run through many approaches to psychotherapy. However, as might be expected in such a complex and rapidly evolving activity, there are important dif-

---

[1] Reprinted by permission of the publisher from *Steps in Psychotherapy* by J. Dollard, F. Auld, Jr., and A. M. White. Copyright 1953, The Macmillan Company. Pp. 3–6.

ferences. The material which follows briefly presents several special approaches.

Group Therapy   Traditionally, psychotherapy has been a one-to-one relationship. It has involved one helping person and one person coming for help. This image of therapy is implicit in much of the preceding discussion.

Another approach is *group therapy* in which two or more persons are seen simultaneously by a therapist (see Fig. 9.1). Six or eight persons meeting with a single therapist is a fairly usual pattern. Some groups are smaller and some larger. Some have more than one therapist and others none at all. In one approach several therapists meet with a single client.

Some groups are composed of chil-

Figure 9.1 Stuttering, group therapy, and catharsis. It has been estimated that there are nearly two million stutterers in the United States. Many stutterers feel anxious and inadequate, and therapy commonly attempts to reduce the anxiety-provoking elements of the environments while building up the individual's self-esteem and confidence. According to the National Hospital for Speech Disorders in New York, a central problem is the stutterer's inability to express his feelings. These pictures taken at the hospital show psychologist Murry Snyder conducting therapy with a group of young stutterers. In therapy, Snyder works to establish an atmosphere of warmth and affection, and he encourages the children to express their pent-up thoughts and feelings—to speak up and to stand up for themselves (Rx for stutterers: Get mad. *Life*, 1961, **50** (23), 65-67). (Photographs courtesy Ted Russell.)

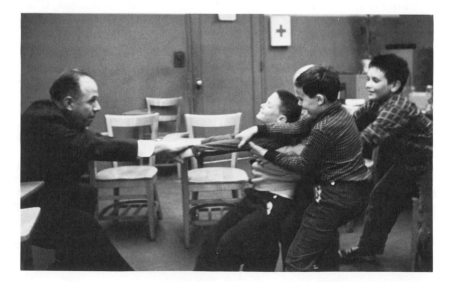

dren and oriented largely around play activities. Other groups involve adolescents or adults. A particular group may be composed of the members of a family, the people of a particular work setting, or persons who are or have been in individual therapy.

Some groups are conducted in the format of individual therapy. Others are essentially educational, featuring the presentation of certain materials which the members discuss and apply to themselves. A few groups are largely inspirational, banding together persons who share common experiences or problems.

One of the advantages of group therapy is that it makes more efficient use of the limited supply of therapists; it provides assistance for persons who otherwise might not be able to afford or obtain it. Beyond this, the group situation provides an environment in which social skills can be shaped and tested. It also permits persons with common problems to support and help one another.

Group therapy is not without limitations. For example, some people find it impossible to talk about themselves and their problems in a group. And, for that matter, some groups find it impossible to make progress in the presence of certain members. Considerable skill is required on the part of the group therapist.

Sometimes group therapy is combined with individual therapy. A person may begin in individual therapy and then enter a group when he is ready for this experience and when a suitable group becomes available. The group may be conducted by his individual therapist, but this is not always the case. Once in the group, the person may terminate individual therapy, or he may reduce the frequency of individual sessions.

Family Therapy   As was noted, therapy has traditionally been a one-to-one relationship. When several members of a family are being helped, it is not uncommon for them to be seen by different therapists. For example, at a guidance center a troubled child may be seen by one staff member and the mother or perhaps both parents by a second.

Family therapy is a relatively new approach in which two or more members of a family are seen together. The group in therapy may consist of a troubled married pair. Or it may be a set of parents and one or more of their children. Sometimes it is the whole family. One variation involves the whole family (or most of it) in its natural habitat—the home (Speck, 1964).

Each member of a family is influenced by every other member. In order to understand a member, we need to understand his relationship with the rest of the family. In order to change him, we may need to change the others as well. If we attempt to change him without changing the others, we may find family circumstance conspiring to keep him as he is. There may be a

---

Presentation 9.1   Alcoholism, group therapy, and Alcoholics Anonymous. It has been estimated that there are about 4,500,000 problem drinkers in the United States. The majority of these are males in their middle years whose drinking may have considerable effect on their marriage, family, and vocational life. Various kinds of somatotherapy and individual and group psychotherapy have been used with alcoholics. One important group approach is Alcoholics Anonymous.

Among the numerous kinds of group therapy used in treating alcoholics, the voluntary fellowship of Alcoholics Anonymous occupies a prominent position. Lacking any professional standing, it has appealed to alcoholics to join with others of their kind in mutual support against the uncontrollable need to drink. In short, it is an unguided, self-help, alcoholic-treat-alcoholic movement, in which alcoholics themselves assume responsibility for arresting their disorder. AA grew spontaneously, without guidance from professionals such as psychiatrists, psychologists, or sociologists.

At both open meetings to which the public is invited and the closed meetings for alcoholics only, AA members frankly narrate their drinking histories and explain how the program enabled them to gain sobriety. Members travel in small groups to adjacent towns to tell their stories and to share their program for sobriety at AA meetings there. Often two or three members will hold meetings in prisons or hospitals where they explain the AA program to alcoholic inmates.

The fellowship of AA, however, is more than this. Local groups sponsor dances, parties, and picnics. Families of the members often form family auxiliaries, such as "Al-Anon" and "Al-Ateen," for spouses and children. Individual members often go together to eat lunch or drink coffee; they meet after work to bowl, to fish, to play cards. These informal contacts extend the fellowship beyond the more formal meetings. In this network of interpersonal relationships, the fellowship's "Twelve Steps" to sobriety make up the core of the effort to remain sober. For example, the first step strikes at the constant denial of a drinking problem: "We admitted we were powerless over alcohol—that our lives had become unmanageable."

Membership in AA depends solely upon whether or not an alcoholic says he is a member. Current members carry their personal histories to other alcoholics and "sponsor" them as novices. This is called "Twelfth Step" work. According to the fellowship's definition, an AA group exists whenever two drunks join together to practice the AA program for sobriety. There are no officers, no hierarchy, no dues.

Although AA is not organized in the usual sense, a common body of tradition underlies the movement. The "Twelve Traditions" set forth the policies that have been effective guides for the fellowship in the past. One of them is a statement of AA's single, explicit purpose: to help alcoholics remain sober. Another is to refrain from embracing any cause, religious, political, or social, except the one of helping alcoholics.

Thus AA is a group endeavor on the part of alcoholics themselves to find a solution to their crippling problem. Out of their face-to-face associations with one another a network of group controls for sobriety emerges that is not present in the usual doctor-patient relationship. Members frequently refer to their experience in AA as a "way of life," since for them it is an emotionally satisfying alternative to chronic drinking. Why does AA work for those alcoholics who do affiliate? Prominent among the reasons is AA's effect on self-concepts. Thus through "Twelfth Step" work the AA member continues to see himself as he used to be. At the same time membership promotes an abstaining, acceptable image of the self. In addition, his role permits him to recapture a respectable social position in the community: AA is truly a "way back."

Another important reason why AA works, once affiliation takes place, is that it sets up a network of social controls, for example, an "in-group" atmosphere that serves as a potent sobriety guide. Furthermore, the primary group flavor of AA, a gemeinschaft [fellowship] in a secular, anomic society, gives a member an opportunity to satisfy his need for warmth, reassurance, and dependency (Trice, 1966, pp. 98–100).

"pathological family equilibrium" which is difficult to interrupt (Ackerman, 1958).

It has been noted that the person who first seeks help or is referred for help is not necessarily the most maladjusted or destructive member of the family. He may, in fact, be the weakest or most defenseless or most docile. He may be a scapegoat or someone sent on ahead to test the therapeutic climate (Ackerman, 1958).

The advantages of family therapy can be inferred from this discussion. For one thing, this approach brings all or a large portion of the family under study and thereby makes the behavior of each person more understandable. It makes changes in the whole family interaction, ensuring that change in one person will not be counteracted by the behavior of another. Furthermore, it allows the family to work on its problems as they occur.

Family therapy is a challenging and promising approach. It may, however, be quite difficult and demanding for the family and therapist alike. It is possible to combine arrangements and to see the members of a family in a flexible assortment of individual and group contacts during the course of therapy (Ackerman, 1958).

Here is an illustration of family therapy involving an adolescent girl and her parents. Spread over a five-month period, the therapy program involved six sessions with Sally and her parents together, one with Sally alone, and one with her mother alone.

Sally, age thirteen, the oldest of five children in the family, was constantly stealing within the house, the school, and from stores. She was known to the police and was on probation from Children's Court. She was almost totally beyond the control of her parents because of her defiance, lack of cooperation, constant fighting with the younger sister, and staying out late with boys. Despite good intelligence, she was failing in her schoolwork. In addition, she was defiant to the teachers, fooled around with the boys, would send "nasty" notes, and so forth. The school was about to suspend her. The stealing began eight months ago. The difficulties at home and in school were reported as evident for five years.

Developmental and medical history was normal. Although the parents have been together throughout and there has been no unusual family instability and disorganization, the father's role was almost entirely confined to providing financial support. He worked long hours in a factory, from mid-afternoon to early morning, six or seven days a week, and on holidays. He was usually asleep when the children were awake and at home. The marital relationship naturally lacked depth under these circumstances. Frustrated and angry about it for the first several years, the mother had long since become resigned and adjusted to the limited and constricted relationship with her husband, and to raising the children with little assistance from him. The vicious-cycle kind of breakdown in the parent-child relationships seemed to get started with Sally's upset, acting-out behavioral reactions to the birth of the second daughter five years ago, and the inability of the parents to help her over this difficult period so that at the time of referral there was overwhelming mutual hostility.

In the first interview with the parents and Sally, all three interactively gave significant information about the present problems; when and how their problems and other symptoms originated, the past and present family life, developmental and medical history, and so forth. The therapist then said: "Such troubles as Sally's usually come from a deep unhappiness within the family. I suggest we talk about this openly and don't be afraid to tell how you really feel." The parents started by expressing more fully their disappointment and resentment about Sally's behavior. "I don't know why she does those things. We always get her most everything she needs and wants. She doesn't appreciate what we do for her." Sally tightened up noticeably and would not talk when the therapist turned to her. The therapist commented that getting things from her parents has not given Sally the feeling that they truly love her. There still was no verbal response from Sally, but tears welled up in her eyes. Pressing her a bit further, the therapist said: "Sally, you mentioned that your sister is always getting into your things and you get mad at her. Could you tell me more about this?" (Youngsters need something specific like this as a vehicle to let go of their feelings.) Sally blurted out: "Whenever Joyce and I have a fight, I always get blamed even if she started it. I am the one who always gets punished. You never punish her."

Sally described several other incidents, apart from Joyce, wherein she felt the parents were unfair. The parents questioned the facts and were generally defensive. The therapist commented: "It doesn't matter much whether or not the incidents were as Sally described them. What I see is that Sally has been feeling for many years, probably since Joyce was born, that you don't love her. I'm sure that deep down you do love her, but this has been difficult for you to show." The mother now cried. The father seemed deeply moved. The mother said to Sally: "Sure, I've been very angry with you and even sometimes felt like putting you in a home. I'm partly to blame, but you have done many things to make me angry. Your father and I don't like to feel this way. We love you very much. You're just as dear to us as Joyce and the other kids."

Asked about his feelings, the father spoke about having had little contact with Sally and the whole family because of his work. His eyes reddened. The therapist commented: "I know you feel badly. Sally, the other kids, and your wife needed you more, but maybe you could not help yourself because of your job. Yet, you have done a lot in earning a livelihood for your

family." Sally's and the mother's facial expressions saddened even more. They did not have to verbalize their feelings in this regard. As though in answer to these feelings, the father thought he might try to get on a different shift so that he could be home more with his family.

By the end of the second interview, it was possible for the therapist to show that Sally's behavior was an expression of her unhappiness and also her way of punishing her parents, without being fully aware of this. He then proceeded to discuss in down-to-earth terms the vital necessity of Sally taking herself in hand even though he knew this would be hard for her to do—"cutting out" the stealing, "buckling down" in school, taking her share of responsibility at home, and so forth. With Sally's and the parents' permission, he conferred with the probation officer and the teacher, giving them an understanding of Sally's problems and encouraging consistent supervision and realistic controls as a help to the youngster in her efforts to learn self-control. Marked change for the better in all areas occurred after this interview.

There was an isolated stealing episode two months later, precipitating a crisis. The parents became extremely angry, told Sally she was no good and maybe ought to be put away, and wanted to withdraw from the clinic. The therapist talked on the phone with both parents, explaining that the recent stealing incident did not wipe out the progress made and that it would be a great mistake to give up because of this. They agreed to come in again with Sally. In an intensely dramatic and dynamic session lasting two hours, the parents and Sally first vented their terrifically angry feelings toward each other and then settled down to look at what actually had happened. Sally was made to stay in one night because she had not been keeping her room in order, refused to wash the dishes and had been generally "nasty" and disagreeable about carrying out her responsibilities. The stealing was a conscious act of retaliation. The therapist underscored the importance of

Sally learning to take responsibilities as part of growing up, and pointed out that her retaliatory act hurt not only her parents but also herself. The therapist was able to support Sally by showing the parents that Sally's disobedience in regard to responsibilities stemmed from their drifting back into preferential treatment of Sally's sister. By the end of the session, positive feelings between the parents and Sally were restored. The feelings of resentment and discouragement on the part of the parents toward the therapist were also dissipated.

Thereafter, Sally made steady progress at home and in school. The father actually arranged to work a different shift and became more a part of the family life. Sally and the mother were quite happy about this. . . . Periodic telephone follow-up contact with the mother, Sally, and the school revealed that the gains have been sustained—for eight months, thus far (Cutter & Hallowitz, 1962, pp. 613–616).

Dramatic Therapy   Traditionally therapy has involved the talking out of problems, but problems may be acted out as well. Potential solutions may be acted out, too, as a dress rehearsal to their performance in everyday life. Psychotherapy which makes use of the enactment of roles and incidents may be called *dramatic therapy.* Role playing and psychodrama are examples of this approach.

In *role playing* the person acts out the behavior of a certain individual in a certain situation. He may act as he himself did on a particular occasion or perhaps as he should have acted. He may try on another person's role. Role playing gives the therapist and the person the opportunity to gain an understanding of the person's conception of himself and others. It also permits the person to achieve catharsis and to practice new ways of behaving which can

be generalized beyond the therapy situation.

In *psychodrama* the person acts out or improvises a role in a theater setting. This procedure is more elaborate than role playing and generally involves five elements: a stage, the director (the therapist), a central character (the person seeking help), auxiliary characters (other persons or therapists), and the audience. The person acts out his problems with the assistance of the auxiliary characters and the audience. The director guides and interprets the dramatic activity.

In this approach an attempt is made to draw every person into the psychodrama. Some participate directly and some vicariously. It is hoped that each will achieve some catharsis and insight as well as greater creativeness and spontaneity in approaching life's problems.

Play Therapy   We can talk out problems or act them out. We can play them out too. Play is a natural medium of expression for children, and therapists working with children frequently make use of play activities.

Play therapy is the name given to changes in behavior which are accomplished through play activities. Generally speaking, this approach provides the child with a highly permissive, accepting, and supportive relationship. The child is encouraged to unburden himself and play out his problems. In doing so he achieves catharsis and becomes free to explore new ways of feeling and acting.

The setting for play therapy is usually a room with a variety of materials which the child may use to play out his problems and express his feelings. Generally there is running water, a sandbox, building, painting, drawing, and modeling materials, a doll house and family of dolls, toy knives and guns, and other equipment. Old clothes, play clothes, or other protective clothing may be worn.

Play therapy has been adapted to both individual and group approaches. It has been used for children exhibiting different kinds and degrees of problems. For example, it has been applied to children with problems of family or school adjustment and for those with mental or physical handicaps.

Here is an illustration of play therapy. The child, Burt, is a nine-year-old boy, pleasant in appearance and from a home of above-average means and status. However, as the therapist notes, "His parents live on the verge of separation, and their conflict is reflected in Burt's anxious and demanding behavior. As he discovers that the sessions are places of freedom, he releases much pent-up hostility."

This is the fifth therapy session with Burt. He comes into the room and stands a moment hesitantly near the door. The therapist follows him and gently closes the door. Burt stalks to the sand box and begins to dig vigorously. Taking a bucket of water, he pours this into the sandbox and then digs. He looks up at the therapist and begins the conversation in a petulant and demanding voice: "Help me! Help me!"

Therapist: "All right, I'll help." The therapist saw this as a bid for attention and comfort rather an indication of any warmth of feeling for the therapist.

Burt: Stops digging and looks up at the therapist. "What can I do? What can I do?"

Therapist: "Today, it's hard to decide what to do!"

Burt: "I want to break some things!" Burt wanders over to the doll house and takes the mother doll of the doll family from the house. He holds her close to his face and speaks to the doll in a harsh voice. "I am going to tear you up." He places the doll on the table and with quick, clumsy movements begins to pound the doll with a building block. He stops for a moment and pulls the doll's dress up and peeks underneath. He turns to the therapist and smirks. Quickly he turns and begins to pound with great force so that in a moment he tears off an arm, then a leg, and furiously dismembers the doll. At last the head rolls from the table and falls to the floor. He picks up the remainder of the doll and hurls it with all his might against the wall. Then with his mouth drawn down at one corner in an angry grimace, he moves about the room stamping on toys. As he comes to a shovel, he picks it up and hurls it against the wall in a frenzy of feeling. He returns to the sandpile and after filling the bucket with sand, throws it on the floor. Turning to a nearby shelf and taking from it a toy pistol, he points it at the therapist. "I'm gonna kill you." He fires imaginary bullets at the therapist. He screams "Zing, zing, zing." Throwing the pistol to the floor, he spies a full-sized nursing bottle filled with water on the shelf. "Can I drink from this, is it clean?"

Therapist: "Yes, you can drink from it."

Burt: Drinks from the bottle and leans against the wall while sucking vigorously. "Fill it up again!" He hands the bottle to the therapist who fills the bottle for him. Burt again leans against the wall with his whole body relaxing and sagging a little. Jerking the nipple from the bottle, he drinks most of the water. Replacing the nipple, he brings the bottle to the therapist, speaks demandingly. "Here, you drink the rest of it."

Therapist: "I should drink some of it, too?"

Burt: "Yeah!" But, turning, he tosses the bottle to the floor and looks out of the window. His hostile outburst has quieted him and he again faces the therapist. "Is my time up?"

Therapist: "Your time is up for today, Burt. We can go back to your mother in the waiting room." Without waiting further, Burt runs to the door and races down the hall to the waiting room.

Burt shows none of this violent behavior either at home or at school, only at the clinic where he thinks it is safe. It is clear that he has intense hostile feelings. How much of it is in reality directed toward the mother is yet to be seen. Burt does not yet have a clear perception of the therapist. He is not sure whether or not the therapist could be included in his fantasy and frenzied release of feeling. His threat to kill the therapist may well indicate that his hostility is generalized—all adults are not to be trusted and are to be hated. His offer of the nursing bottle to the therapist was interpreted as a genuine offer to share the contentment he had received as well as an effort to obtain approval of his infantile behavior.

As week after week passed, Burt's hostility lessened and he no longer felt the need to break things. His play became more cooperative with the therapist and he began to take great delight in building blocks. He would build a structure higher than his head and then knock it to the floor with a great crash. Then one day after working diligently and quietly building the structure, he turned at the end of the hour and said, "I like it." He smiled at the therapist over his shoulder as he left the room, his building still intact.

The remarkable change in Burt as the result of psychotherapy was reflected in part by some change in his mother. She had seen more clearly Burt's needs as well as the importance of improved relationships with her husband. Because, however, her husband had been unwilling to be involved, the relationship of Burt's parents was only partly changed. It is not unlikely that, in spite of this negative factor, Burt can hold the gains he has made if his mother retains her new attitudes and if his home community is of assistance. Perhaps it will be an understanding teacher who helps him find satisfying emotional exchange outside his family and thereby lessens the traumatic effects of family discord (Alexander, 1963, pp. 64–66).

Sociotherapy

Sociotherapy includes a variety of efforts designed to improve the adjustment or mental health of an individual by altering his environment. Somatotherapy and psychotherapy focus on the person. Sociotherapy shifts the focus to the person's physical and social milieu.

We all know that our surroundings have a considerable bearing on our happiness and well-being. When our environment starts to get us down, we begin to think about getting away from it all or promoting a change of scene. Or if we are stuck with it, we begin to think about modifying it. "Something," we say, "has got to give."

As in these common remedies, sociotherapy is directed toward modifying an environment or providing a new and more favorable one. Such approaches frequently go beyond the single person to include groups of people, perhaps all those involved in a particular setting. And such approaches are frequently preventive rather than corrective in nature, aiming at forestalling mental illness or enhancing mental health.

Family Environments

Family environments are frequently the targets of improvement approaches. Parents themselves realize the importance of the family climate and may hit upon their own bits of sociotherapy. For example, a set of parents may wait until their children are in bed or out of earshot to thrash out a difference of opinion.

Family therapy was described earlier.

This approach assumes that the unwanted behavior of one or more of the members is the result of whole family interaction. Disturbed families are not necessarily fragile. Quite the contrary, such families may be quite homeostatic, operating to maintain the *status quo* and to hinder the change of any of its members. Family therapists recognize this and attempt to change the whole family environment or climate so that individual members may improve (Haley, 1963; Parloff, 1961).

If the family is beyond repair or if there is no family, a new environment may be provided. This new environment may be a foster family or a residential setting which serves as a semifamily. The next chapter will discuss foster homes and residential houses as important facilities in the improvement of adjustment.

Neighborhood Environments

Just as a family member may be locked into a family interaction, a member of a neighborhood may be a captive of surrounding forces. His behavior, troublesome as it may be for the larger society, may represent a nearly unavoidable adjustment to his immediate milieu. In this case, it may be necessary to remove the person from the neighborhood or to modify the neighborhood around the person.

There has been growing concern about neighborhood forces. Increasing attempts are being made to improve marginal neighborhoods by providing better housing, better schools, and better recreational areas and programs. New youth and service activities are being put into operation. Recently attempts have been made to mobilize the members of such neighborhoods to organize, to set their own goals, and to work toward them.

One very interesting approach is called "area youth work." Workers in this program spend time with neighborhood gangs wherever they can be contacted—at street corners, candy stores, and pool halls. The worker establishes a relationship with the members of the gang. He works to overcome their suspiciousness and hostility and to obtain their confidence. He helps them get jobs, plan social functions, and make use of neighborhood facilities. He encourages them to modify antisocial activities and to participate constructively in the community (Fink, Wilson, & Conover, 1963).

School and College Environments

In recent years increasing attention has been given to the environments in which learning takes place. The social and physical milieu as well as the educational program are major forces in the student's development. What goes on outside the elementary, secondary, and college classroom may be as influential as the formal activity in it (Danskin, Kennedy, & Friesen, 1965; Rice, 1965).

College environments are composed of things and people in complex interaction. The things—architecture and settings—reflect and influence educational processes. The people—students, teachers, administrators, and staff of various sorts—all contribute to the educational climate. And the climate or special atmosphere is the resultant interaction of personal and nonpersonal elements (Rice, 1965).

Recent research on college environments has shown that there are considerable differences between campuses. This research has also demonstrated the importance of environmental factors in the survival and success of the student. A review of recent studies of campus climates suggests three generalizations:

1 *An educational institution does have its own distinctive climate or atmosphere. This climate remains fairly constant from year to year. It attracts with startling consistency the same kinds of students and has the same kind of impact on them.*
2 *Peer-group interaction and faculty-student interaction outside the classroom are important elements in the campus climate;* these have a stronger and more significant impact on student attitudes and values than the things that go on in the classroom. *Even narrowly defined academic achievement is affected by the environment on the campus.*
3 *Many of the activities that go on outside the classroom—the advising program, the extraclass program, counseling services, a dormitory system and residence program, and a campus program of cultural events—enhance the motivation to learn and increase the perceived relevance of learning. They not only encourage but also facilitate the mastery of specific subject matter (Rice, 1965, p. 307).*

Work Environments

Currently, considerable attention is given to the study of work settings and the effects they have on productivity and adjustment. Both physical and mental health have been found to be related to vocational satisfaction. For example, foremen who are caught between employee and administrative forces frequently show signs of maladjustment (Cobb, French, Kahn, & Mann, 1963).

Environmental improvements have been directed at both the physical and social structures of the work setting. Physical improvements include better lighting, soundproofing, and more cheerful surroundings. Social improvements have been directed at such vital processes as the communication (or lack of it) between employees at various levels of the administrative hierarchy.

One considerable source of maladjustment has been low status in the company hierarchy. This is felt to be especially true in our achievement-oriented culture (Cobb et al., 1963). It has been suggested that work settings be changed to increase the power and prestige of low-status workers by decentralizing and delegating authority and by widening participation in decision-making processes (French, 1963).

Institutional Environments

Studies by sociologists and other social scientists have shown the vital part that an institution's physical and social environment plays in its therapeutic mission. Such institutions are miniature societies in which staff, inmates, and settings have important effects upon one another. These studies have pointed the way to the modification of institutional environments.

Penal programs generally have made provisions to upgrade their staffs and provide better environments for rehabilitation. Where possible, inmates are placed in minimum security settings which more closely simulate external environments to which they must later adapt. More liberal and elaborate probationary and parole programs have been designed to keep the person in the community or return him to it as soon as possible.

Mental hospitals have undergone considerable change, moving from isolated, custodial units to therapeutic ones. Modifications have been made in both the physical and social milieu, and efforts are exerted to make the hospital an integral part of the larger community. These changes will be discussed at some length in the next chapter.

SOME TRENDS IN IMPROVEMENT

The whole area of mental health is filled with ferment and change. Old ideas and procedures are under examination. New approaches are being devised and applied.

This section will describe some current trends. Several are barely underway but point the direction of things to come. The presentation will overlap and extend some of the material which was just discussed. It also introduces a number of ideas which will be elaborated later in the book.

From Person to Person-in-the-Environment

In the field of mental health, the major focus has been on the individual and his personality (Cobb et al., 1963). The determinants of mental illness have been thought to be primarily in the individual and perhaps laid down very early in his life (Sanford, 1965). Consequently, the major task has been to deal with the person to alter the forces within him.

With the changing conception of mental illness from a disease to a disturbance in interpersonal relationships, the focus in improvement is being broadened from the person to the person-in-his-environment. Increasingly larger social units are being brought into the improvement process. Such units may include a marriage pair (rather than just one spouse) or an entire family (rather than just one or two troubled members).

Improvement efforts are being further enlarged to include whole neighborhoods and communities. Such efforts are typically environment-centered rather than focused on individuals. These efforts are aimed at improving mental health by improving the environments in which people live and work and play.

Some of the things done in the name of mental health seem far removed from traditional concerns. Some lay people and professionals, too, are becoming concerned about the presumptions and breadth of programs in this area. Whether done in the name of mental health or human welfare, there is no doubt that the programs which have been set in motion will influence the psychological well-being of large segments of the nation.

Addressing himself to fellow psychologists, Nevitt Sanford has made some predictions which seem applicable to all workers in this area. He writes, "It seems not unlikely that the present generation of psychotherapists will be the last to devote themselves primarily to the private practice of psychotherapy." And he notes that "although in the foreseeable future there will be a place for individual diagnosis and treatment, the clinical psychologist who would be maximally useful socially and constantly challenged intellectually must broaden his horizons and must be prepared to utilize his special knowledge of people in various settings where actions for human welfare are carried out" (1965, p. 1395).

From Part to Comprehensive Planning

Many different services and agencies play a part in the improvement of adjustment. There are hospitals, clinics, workshops, and residential facilities of various descriptions. There are rehabilitation, welfare, health, and other social agencies.

Many communities are very limited in their mental health facilities. Some offer almost nothing at all. A small and poor rural community may provide little more than the services of a general practitioner or a minister, and sometimes not even these are available (Robinson, DeMarche, & Wagle, 1960).

Larger communities generally offer a variety of services. Many of the facilities are privately established and independent of each other. If there is little overall planning and coordination, some services may be duplicated, others may be lacking, and there may be difficulty in moving persons between facilities.

At present there is a trend toward greater planning and coordination of a community's mental health resources. There is an increasing determination to provide a full spectrum of services to communities beyond a minimum size. There is also an increasing desire and effort to coordinate the activities of these services to heighten their usefulness to the individual and the community.

Beyond the community, there is the necessity of planning at state and national levels. Addressing the 88th Congress, President Kennedy said, "I propose a national mental health program to assist in the inauguration of a wholly new emphasis and approach to care for the mentally ill. . . . Governments at every level—Federal, state, and local—private foundations and individual citizens must all face up to their responsibilities in this area" (1963, p. 2). Concern about mental health has clearly become a matter of national concern and responsibility (Caplan, 1964).

From Professional to Lay Involvement

With the growing concern about mental health, there is a growing effort to make available more help and more helpers. The hope is to provide help for everyone who needs it regardless of personal circumstance. And a recent direction is to make helpers of many people regardless of professional status.

Psychiatrists, psychologists, social workers, and other mental health personnel are in very short supply. Group therapy represents one attempt to spread out available resources. Short-term, limited-goal techniques can also be employed in this direction.

One promising approach to the problem is the enlistment and training of lay persons as volunteer workers, mental health aides, and counselors. This movement has paralleled the changing conception of mental illness from disease to psychological distress. The less esoteric ideas about mental illness have become, the more nonprofessionals have been enfranchised to deal with it.

For years, lay persons have been active in mental health organizations and activities. Volunteers, for example, have been of considerable service in mental hospitals. Recently such activities have been expanded and upgraded. With some training and supervision, volunteers now play central roles in therapy programs. This will be discussed at greater length in the next chapter.

Consideration is being given to training nonprofessionals to assume full-time mental health roles. In one project, a small group of college-educated housewives have been trained to be "mental health coun-

selors." With two years of study and training they have been able to assume therapy
positions in schools and clinics. Another
group of women have been trained to
counsel mothers of preschool children
(Pines, 1965; Rioch, 1965).

Neighborhood mental health service
centers—really first-aid stations—have
been set up in problem areas of a large
Eastern city. These stations are manned
by "mental health aides" who are people
recruited from the neighborhood and
given only a few weeks of training. With
the assistance and supervision of professional workers, these aides provide help to
troubled people of the neighborhood. Problems which are beyond their competence
are referred to other facilities (Pines,
1965).

From Custody to Correction

Another trend in mental health concerns
the handling of seriously troubled persons.
Customarily, these individuals have been
removed from their homes and communities and committed to mental institutions,
some of which provided little more than
minimum physical care.

The custodial treatment of troubled
persons has been based on a number of
ideas or rationalizations (Williams, 1964).
For one thing, not much was known about
mental illness. People who were seriously
troubled were viewed with suspicion and
distrust.

Second, the mentally ill were considered dangerous to themselves or to others.
At best, they were bothersome and a source
of embarrassment. Therefore, it was considered best for everyone that they be removed from their community.

Third, such persons were considered

seriously and perhaps irreversibly ill. Very
little could be done to help them. Consequently, it was thought best to put them
away and use the resources of the community in more hopeful enterprises.

Fourth, it was felt that mentally ill
persons were relatively insensitive to their
environments. Since they were "crazy,"
it did not matter how they were treated. In
fact, it was thought relatively harsh treatment might even be beneficial.

More recently, changing ideas about
mental illness have helped bring about a
major shift in the handling of these persons (see Table 9.1). Much more is known
about mental illness, and persons classified
as mentally ill are viewed with less suspicion and fear. Although more burdened
with problems, such persons are considered not so different from other people.
They have learned inadequate and faulty
patterns of behavior, and they can be
helped to develop better patterns.

From Correction to Prevention

As was just indicated, there is a move from
custody to correction. And movement has
been made beyond correction toward the
prevention of conditions which lead to mental illness.

Nobody will argue against the value
of prevention. But mental health resources
are limited, and the question of priorities
arises. How much of the resources should
be given over to correction? How much to
prevention? And to what kind of prevention?

Primary Prevention
Primary prevention refers to programs designed to ward off mental illness by reducing the conditions which produce it. Such

Table 9.1 Two contrasting types of mental health programs are depicted in this table. The direction today is from custody to correction. And there is also some movement beyond correction toward the prevention of mental illness and toward the enhancement of mental health.*

Number of facilities or units in the system:

Custodial Program: A single, isolated facility—an "all or none" situation—no alternatives for patients— the single unit is sharply cut off from the rest of the community.

Correctional Program: Several facilities, conceived as alternatives to meet different needs of patients and to provide comprehensive care—private practitioners, clinics, acute and emergency outpatient treatment services, longer term treatment facilities (but resembling community as closely as possible), day hospital, night hospital, halfway houses, clinic services for postacute treatment and rehabilitation, special facilities for children, the aged, and special problems (juvenile delinquency, epileptics, alcoholics, mentally retarded), provision for consultation, inservice training and education, research and vital statistics.

Paths in and out of mental health facilities:

Custodial Program: Via courts, and sometimes jails—paths out not clearly marked.

Correctional Program: Alternative paths, well marked in relation to needs of patients, and well marked toward rehabilitation all along the way.

Movement through the system:

Custodial Program: Accumulation of a core of chronic patients—little movement in this group, except by relatively high death rates.

Correctional Program: Shorter stay in inpatient services—greater movement and flow through the entire system.

Social organization:

Custodial Program: Authoritarian and feudal—superintendent has many of the attributes of the "lord of the manor" particularism, employees have personal loyalty to superintendents and are oriented toward security.

Correctional Program: Democratic and "universalistic" system as a whole has high degree of functional differentiation but units within it are kept small and follow a relatively "undifferentiated" type of structure.

Social definitions of mental illness:

Custodial Program: The mentally ill are radically different, dangerous, unpredictable—mental illness is generally irreversible—marked by stigma attached to the mentally ill.

Correctional Program: Mental and emotional disorders are simply the more extreme forms of problems of living faced by everyone—they can be helped—seeking help is no disgrace.

Philosophies and practices of treatment in rehabilitation:

Custodial Program: Nothing can be done except give patients relatively decent custodial care, and even that is difficult—if it looks gruesome, after all, these people are crazy and probably don't know the difference anyway.

Correctional Program: The etiology of mental disorders is complex, and includes biological, psychological and social factors, in varying proportions—similarly, there are various treatment procedures—some of these disorders have manifest physiological components and require, in significant measure, physiologically based treatment procedures—in other disorders the primary emphasis in treatment is on change in the personality of the patient, and in the social situation in which he lives—a reduction in doctrinaire approaches—use of patient participation—a growing conviction that in many instances the locus of the difficulty lies in primary social units, notably the family, and that these units must be treated as a whole—growing realization that the treatment of many of these disorders is affected by the social characteristics of the total treatment setting, as a community, that the larger community outside of the treatment setting must be understood, and that various modes of transition between treatment settings and the wider community must be provided.

---

* Modified from Williams, R. H. Trends in community psychiatry: Indirect services and the problem of balance in mental health programs. In L. Bellak (Ed.), *Handbook of Community Psychiatry and Community Mental Health*. New York: Grune & Stratton, 1964. Pp. 343–356. By permission.

programs are directed at large groups of people, perhaps the entire population of a community or larger area. They may be specifically designed for groups of people who seem especially vulnerable, such as those in locations of high delinquency, crime, or mental illness (Caplan, 1964).

Secondary Prevention

Secondary prevention refers to programs designed to lower the rate of mental illness by preventing mild or moderate conditions from dragging on and worsening. Secondary prevention is accomplished through early diagnosis and prompt treatment. Problems which are detected and brought to treatment early require less complicated and less expensive procedures and have more favorable prognosis (Caplan, 1964).

Tertiary Prevention

Tertiary prevention refers to programs designed to avert the residual effects or after-effects of mental illness. Such programs aim to restore the person as quickly as possible to a full-functioning role in his community. Efforts of this kind are frequently identified as rehabilitation programs (Caplan, 1964).

From Prevention to Enhancement

This discussion has been primarily concerned with the correction and prevention of mental illness. What about mental health? What about those valued qualities which were presented at some length in the last chapter?

It was said earlier that there was a question of how scarce resources in mental health should be allocated. How much for correction? How much for prevention? And now, how much for enhancement?

Some workers in the area of mental health have cautioned against attempting too much or hoping for too much. One of them, Eisenberg, argues against aiming for "total mental health" or "universal happiness." Says he, "Unless we specify our goals in restricted terms, we condemn ourselves to repeat the self-defeating cycle of grand promise and paltry accomplishment that breeds doubt and despair" (1962, p. 783).

Other workers feel that we should not and cannot be modest in our aims. Some— with a perspective that goes beyond the conventional confines of mental health— believe that simple survival requires that we enhance man's nature. Murphy speaks of the need to help man evolve a capacity for positive social relations. He writes:

> The realization of human potentialities lies in studying the directions in which human needs may be guided, with equal attention to the learning powers of the individual and the feasible directions of cultural evolution. The last thousand years have created a level of scientific and esthetic satisfaction which has already made human nature different today from what it was in the middle ages; yet this is merely a beginning. Even this much of an evolution has hardly commenced in the area of interpersonal relations, where modern psychology, including psychoanalysis, has shown us more about the roots of conflict and destructiveness among people than about the development of positive social feeling. If we cannot make rapid gains in the control of conflict, there will be no human future. But if we can, the future extension of scientific and esthetic interest, together with the evolution of greater capacity for satisfaction in relations between people, will not constitute a goal or a Utopia, but will define a widening theater for the development of new potentialities.[2]

[2] From *Human Potentialities* by Gardner Murphy, Basic Books, Inc., Publishers, New York, 1958. P. 329. Also by permission of George Allen & Unwin Ltd., Publishers, London.

SUMMARY

Three approaches to improving adjustment and mental health include somatotherapy, psychotherapy, and sociotherapy. Somatotherapy subsumes a variety of medical and surgical techniques which are designed to modify a person's adjustment by altering his physical being. Two of the most common somatotherapies today are electroshock and drugs.

Psychotherapy refers to efforts to change adjustment patterns through psychological means. Many different techniques have been employed. Many psychotherapies attach importance to the relationship between the therapist and the person coming for help, to catharsis or emotional release, to insight, and to learning procedures. Some special kinds of psychotherapy include group therapy in which several persons are seen simultaneously, family therapy in which several or more members are seen together, dramatic therapy which features the enactment of roles and incidents, and play therapy.

Sociotherapy includes various techniques designed to change the adjustment or mental health of an individual by altering his environment. Some environments which are targets of sociotherapeutic approaches are the family, neighborhood, schools and colleges, and work settings. Institutional environments, such as mental hospitals and prisons, also figure prominently in this approach.

The whole area involved with the improvement of adjustment is filled with ferment and change. One trend is the shift in focus from the person to the person-in-the-environment. With the changing conception of mental illness from a disease to a disturbance in interpersonal relationships, increasingly larger social units are being considered in behavior modification —a marriage pair (rather than just one spouse) or an entire family (rather than just one or two troubled members)—even a whole neighborhood or community.

A second trend concerns the movement from part to comprehensive planning. There is an increasing effort to plan and provide a full spectrum of adjustment services to communities beyond a minimum size. There is also an increasing effort to coordinate the activities of all these services in order to heighten their usefulness to the individual and the community.

A third trend concerns the movement from limited professional involvement to general public involvement with adjustment and mental health matters. Mental health has become a matter of general public concern, and important roles are being assumed by the general public. To supplement the work of scarce trained professional workers, lay persons are serving as volunteer workers, mental health aides, and counselors.

A fourth trend concerns the movement from custody to correction in the treatment of seriously troubled individuals. In the past, many of these individuals were considered incurable (or nearly so), and they were removed from their homes and communities to institutions which provided little more than physical care. Now, such persons are regarded more optimistically, and a determined effort is being made to help them and return them to their homes and communities.

A fifth trend concerns the movement from correction to prevention. There is an increasing effort to prevent mental illness by reducing the conditions which produce it, by keeping mild conditions from dragging on and worsening, and by averting the residual effects or aftereffects of mental illness.

A sixth trend concerns the movement beyond custody, correction, and prevention—all concerned with mental illness—to the enhancement of mental health. The aim is not only to make us well and keep us well but to make us "weller than well" —that is, to augment our valued qualities.

REFERENCES

Ackerman, N. W. *The Psychodynamics of Family Life.* New York: Basic Books, 1958.

Alexander, T. *Psychotherapy in Our Society.* Englewood Cliffs, N.J.: Prentice-Hall, 1963.

Campbell, D. The psychological effects of cerebral electroshock. In H. J. Eysenck (Ed.), *Handbook of Abnormal Psychology.* New York: Basic Books, 1961. Pp. 611–633.

Caplan, G. *Principles of Preventive Psychiatry.* New York: Basic Books, 1964.

Cobb, S., French, J. R. P., Jr., Kahn, R. L., & Mann, F. C. An environmental approach to mental health. *Annals of the New York Academy of Sciences,* 1963, **107**, 596–606.

Cutter, A. V., & Hallowitz, D. Diagnosis and treatment of the family unit with respect to the character-disordered youngster. *Journal of the American Academy of Child Psychiatry,* 1962, **1**(4), 605–618.

Danskin, D. G., Kennedy, C. E., Jr., & Friesen, W. S. Guidance: The ecology of students. *Personnel and Guidance Journal,* 1965, **44**(2), 130–135.

Dollard, J., Auld, F., Jr., & White, A. M. *Steps in Psychotherapy.* New York: Macmillan, 1953.

Eisenberg, L. If not now, when? *American Journal of Orthopsychiatry,* 1962, **32**(5), 781–791.

Fink, A. E., Wilson, E. E., & Conover, M. B. *The Field of Social Work.* (4th ed.) New York: Holt, 1963.

French, J. R. P. The social environment and mental health. *Journal of Social Issues,* 1963, **19**(4), 39–56.

Greenblatt, M., & Levinson, D. Mental hospitals. In B. B. Wolman (Ed.), *Handbook of Clinical Psychology.* New York: McGraw-Hill, 1965. Pp. 1343–1359.

Grossberg, J. M. Behavior therapy: A review. *Psychological Bulletin,* 1964, **62**(2), 73–88.

Haley, J. Marriage therapy. *Archives of General Psychiatry,* 1963, **8**, 213–234.

Holliday, A. R. A review of psychopharmacology. In B. B. Wolman (Ed.), *Handbook of Clinical Psychology,* New York: McGraw-Hill, 1965. Pp. 1296–1322.

Kennedy, J. F. Message from the President of the United States relative to mental illness and mental retardation. 88th Cong., 1st Sess., Feb. 5, 1963, House of Representatives, Document No. 58. *American Psychologist,* 1963, **18**, 280–289.

Kety, S. S. Chemical boundaries of psychopharmacology. In S. M. Farber & R. H. L. Wilson (Eds.), *Control of the Mind.* New York: McGraw-Hill, 1961. Pp. 79–91.

McGraw, R. B., & Oliven, J. F. Miscellaneous therapies. In S. Arieti (Ed.), *American Handbook of Psychiatry.* Vol. 2. New York: Basic Books, 1959. Pp. 1552–1582.

Matarazzo, J. D. Psychotherapeutic processes. In P. R. Farnsworth, O. McNemar, & Q. McNemar (Eds.), *Annual Review of Psychology.* Vol. 16. Palo Alto, Calif.: Annual Reviews, 1965. Pp. 181–224.

Murphy, G. *Human Potentialities.* New York: Basic Books, 1958.

Paredes, A., Gogerty, J. H., & West, L. J. Psychopharmacology. In J. H. Masserman (Ed.), *Current Psychiatric Therapies.* Vol. 1. New York: Grune & Stratton, 1961. Pp. 54–85.

Parloff, M. B. The family in psychotherapy. *Archives of General Psychiatry,* 1961, **4**, 445–451.

Pines, M. The coming upheaval in psychiatry. *Harper's Magazine,* October, 1965. Pp. 54–60.

Rice, J. G. The campus climate: A reminder. In S. Baskin (Ed.), *Higher Education: Some Newer Developments.* New York: McGraw-Hill, 1965. Pp. 304–317.

Riddell, S. A. The therapeutic efficacy of ECT. *Archives of General Psychiatry,* 1963, **8**(6), 42–52.

Rioch, M. J. *Pilot Project in Training Mental Health Counselors.* Washington, D.C.: National Institute of Mental Health, 1965.

Robinson, R., DeMarche, D. F., & Wagle, M. K. *Community Resources in Mental Health.* New York: Basic Books, 1960.

Rotter, J. B. *Social Learning and Clinical Psychology.* Englewood Cliffs, N.J.: Prentice-Hall, 1954.

Rx for stutterers: Get mad. *Life,* June 9, 1961. Pp. 65–67.

Sanford, N. The prevention of mental illness. In B. B. Wolman (Ed.), *Handbook of Clinical Psychology.* New York: McGraw-Hill, 1965. Pp. 1378–1400.

Schofield, W. *Psychotherapy: The Purchase of Friendship.* Englewood Cliffs, N.J.: Prentice-Hall, 1964.

Shaffer, L. F., & Shoben, E. J., Jr. *The Psychology of Adjustment.* (2nd ed.) Boston: Houghton Mifflin, 1956.

Speck, R. V. Family therapy in the home. *Journal of Marriage and the Family,* 1964, **26**(1), 72–76.

Trice, H. M. *Alcoholism in America.* New York: McGraw-Hill, 1966.

Trouton, D., & Eysenck, H. J. The effects of drugs on behavior. In H. J. Eysenck (Ed.), *Handbook of Abnormal Psychology.* New York: Basic Books, 1961. Pp. 634–696.

Waggoner, R. W., & Holmes, D. J. Drugs and psychotherapy. In J. H. Masserman (Ed.), *Current Psychiatric Therapies.* Vol. 1. New York: Grune & Stratton, 1961. Pp. 86–99.

Watkins, J. G. Psychotherapeutic methods. In B. B. Wolman (Ed.), *Handbook of Clinical Psychology.* New York: McGraw-Hill, 1965. Pp. 1143–1167.

Williams, R. H. Trends in community psychiatry: Indirect services and the problem of balance in mental health programs. In L. Bellak (Ed.), *Handbook of Community Psychiatry and Community Mental Health.* New York: Grune & Stratton, 1964. Pp. 343–356.

Wittenborn, J. R. Depression. In B. B. Wolman (Ed.), *Handbook of Clinical Psychology.* New York: McGraw-Hill, 1965. Pp. 1030–1057.

Wolman, B. B. Schizophrenia and related disorders. In B. B. Wolman (Ed.), *Handbook of Clinical Psychology.* New York: McGraw-Hill, 1965. Pp. 976–1029.

Wortis, J. Psychopharmacology and physiological treatment. *American Journal of Psychiatry,* 1965, **121**(7), 648–652.

CHAPTER TEN
IMPROVING ADJUSTMENT, CONTINUED

The last chapter discussed three important ways in which adjustment may be changed and noted some new trends in this area. This chapter will describe the work of mental hospitals and other related facilities. It will also describe a number of key workers whose job it is to help us improve our patterns of adjustment.

SOME FACILITIES IN IMPROVEMENT

New ideas concerning mental illness and new approaches in dealing with it have led to changes in treatment facilities. This section will discuss what is happening to the mental hospital. It will also discuss some other facilities—proved and promising.

The Mental Hospital

Mental hospitals are of many kinds. They range from those which are custodial and isolated to an increasing number which are therapeutic and community-oriented. Most mental hospitals have been undergoing extensive and dramatic changes.

Greenblatt and Levinson (1965), whose writing forms a basis for this discussion, have noted three discernible trends. One has concerned the change in mental hospitals from primarily custodial facilities to therapeutic institutions—"therapeutic communities." A second trend concerns their change from fairly isolated institutions to community-based centers—"a community in the community." A third trend has concerned efforts to change the society outside the hospital so that it will facilitate the recovery of troubled persons —"therapeutic society."

A Therapeutic Community

The first group of changes concerns the conversion of mental hospitals into therapeutic communities. In such communities, patients are brought into interaction with one another, with the members of the hospital staff, and with the larger society outside the hospital. Greenblatt and Levinson

have enumerated nine developments which characterize this trend:

1 There has been a reduction of restraint and seclusion. Force and isolation are inappropriate and seldom required in a therapeutically oriented environment. As staff and patients interact and understand each other better, the morale of each and the atmosphere of the hospital improves.

2 There has been an improvement of the physical environment. The patients are seen as supersensitive (rather than insensitive) persons for whom surroundings are important. Attempts are made to make the hospital environment pleasant and homelike.

3 There has been an improvement in the social environment. Social interaction in the hospital has been increased, bringing into contact patients of both sexes, the staff, and people from the outside community. Social activities have been expanded and include competitive sports, music and dancing, arts and crafts, and various other kinds of recreational activities.

4 There has been increased patient participation in the activities of the hospital. Patient groups have been organized to help set hospital policies and to participate in the government of the hospital. Patient self-help organizations have also come into being.

5 There has been an attempt to increase the competence and performance of the hospital staff. The morale of the staff, of course, has an important bearing on

the morale of the patients. Therefore, there are increasing efforts to obtain the best possible workers and to provide them with the best possible working conditions.

6 Increasing attention has been paid to the philosophy governing the operation of the mental hospital. Certain ideas, explicitly stated or understood, underlie the hospital's general structure and function. Currently there is greater responsiveness to new ideas and new approaches and greater efforts to evaluate the old and the new.

7 There has been a reduction in the size of hospitals. This has been accomplished in several ways. New hospitals have been built to a smaller scale. Old hospitals have been divided into smaller units or generally reduced in size. These changes have been facilitated by improved programs which have shortened or obviated the need for hospitalization.

8 There has been an increased continuity of patient care. It is felt important that the patient have secure and substantial relationships in the hospital rather than being transferred from worker to worker. Insofar as possible, the patient continues with the same personnel from the time of admission to discharge and during the aftercare period as well.

9 There has been increasing reliance on therapeutic teams composed of a variety of specialists. Such teams may include a psychiatrist, psychologist, nurse, social worker, and occupational therapist, as well as the ward attendant, hospital volunteers, and others. The work of such teams is coordinated by a person who takes primary responsibility for the patient.

A Community in the Community

The second group of changes has concerned the relationship of the mental hospital to the larger community. Increasing efforts are being made to bring the hospital out of isolation and to put it squarely in the community. The intention is to keep the patient in his usual environment or return him to it as soon as possible. Greenblatt and Levinson note six developments which delineate this trend:

1 There has been movement toward an "open-door" policy. Rather than being locked or confined in their rooms or wards, patients are permitted freer movement within the hospital and in the community. This policy, coming with other improvements in hospital environment and programming, has not precipitated more suicides, escapes, or problems of management.

2 Increasingly, the staff lives away from the institution and serves to represent the hospital to the community. From this position, they are better able to act as ambassadors of good will for the hospital and its programs. And, as part of the community, the staff is more familiar with the general environment from which the patients come and to which they return.

3 Volunteers from the community are used to supplement the hospital staff. Such volunteers provide a useful link between the hospital and the community. Volunteers are being used to help various staff members in the conduct of their duties and to offer special courses and programs. Some of the volunteers assist in raising funds and pressing for new legislative programs. In recent years, an in-

creasing number of high school and college students have joined the volunteer ranks in central therapeutic roles.

4 A number of transitional facilities have been established to bridge the gap between the hospital and the community. For example, there are a number of partial-hospitalization programs, such as the day hospital, the night hospital, and the weekend hospital. These and a number of similar facilities will be described later in this chapter.

5 Increasingly, the patients' families are being involved in the programs of the hospital. Close contact is maintained with the family. Therapy may be performed with the whole family or selected members. Occasionally, other members of the family are admitted to the hospital along with the patient.

6 An attempt is being made to provide and extend emergency services. These services are designed to deal with crises quickly and in the environmental context in which they arise. Assistance of this sort makes hospitalization unnecessary in many cases.

A Therapeutic Society

In addition to the increasing conversion of custodial institutions to therapeutic communities and the increasing incorporation of these therapeutic communities into the larger community, attention has been focused on changing the larger community or society itself. Summing up this trend, Greenblatt and Levinson write:

It is difficult to appreciate how much societal attitudes have changed toward the mentally ill unless one has had the opportunity to observe, firsthand, the reduction of fear and stigmatization attending mental illness over the last few decades. While prejudice and suspiciousness are still rampant in most segments of society, the gains have been remarkable. Those who have practiced over a span of years have witnessed earlier referrals of sick individuals for help, earlier discharges to family and community, voluntary participation in the mental health movement by citizens everywhere, and increasingly wider responsibility for improving the lot of the mentally ill.

To an extent, the mental hospital has actually fostered these changes by direct efforts to involve the community in its program, recognizing that severe limitations are imposed upon it by a standoff attitude on the part of the public. Public relations work in the family, factory, school, and church has therefore become a necessary function of the modern mental hospital. The goal of a therapeutic society, which only a few years ago appeared to be an unattainable dream, now looms as a significant end in itself, an end that will also serve to facilitate and simplify the work of the mental hospital (1965, p. 1356).

The Semihospital

As we have indicated, it is desirable to keep the troubled person within or as near his usual environment as possible. Hospitalization—although deemed necessary in some cases—has its drawbacks. The hospitalized patient may come to think of himself as helpless and hopeless. He may give up the struggle and abandon responsibility for himself. Hospitalization can also result in the severance of community ties, which may be difficult to reestablish, and in a stigma which may be difficult to erase (Kramer, 1962).

Partial-hospitalization programs—in effect, semihospitals—have been established for persons who need less than around-the-clock care but more than one or two or three hours a week of outpatient service. Since these programs do not detach the patient completely from his community, they sidestep some of the pitfalls of full hospitalization. Such programs are also less expensive and allow limited facilities and personnel to be shared by more people.

Partial-hospitalization programs provide much of the same service offered by conventional hospitalization. They serve as links between the hospital and the community, expediting, easing, and ensuring the patient's transition from one to the other. They also make full hospitalization unnecessary in some cases.

Partial-hospitalization programs are usually set up within or in connection with a mental hospital, general hospital, health center, or some similar facility. Some partial programs which have been tried with success include the day hospital, the night hospital, and the weekend hospital.

The Day Hospital

The day hospital generally provides an array of diagnostic and therapeutic services. During the day, the person participates in the hospital program, and in the evening he returns to his family. A person may participate in the program every day, or on certain designated days, or only when he feels the need, and the hospital may be alternated with a work assignment (Kramer, 1962).

The Night Hospital

Night programs provide hospital services and a home base for patients who function in the community during the daytime. Such patients may have jobs, attend school, or participate in other activities beyond the hospital. In the evenings, they return to the institution where they again can avail themselves of the special resources and a protective environment (Moll, 1957).

The Weekend Hospital

A relatively new idea is to make weekend programs available. These programs, extending from Saturday morning to Monday morning, may be made up of group therapy sessions, group living and socialization, and activities of various sorts. This plan has the advantage of permitting persons to hold down their jobs, be with their families, and participate in usual living routines during the week. It also permits fuller use of the hospital facilities on weekends when inpatients may be on home visits (Vernallis & Reinert, 1963).

Residential Facilities

In addition to partial-hospitalization programs, a number of other facilities have been established for persons who do not require twenty-four-hour care. Some of these facilities have been designated as "halfway" or "pathway" organizations. However, these terms are not always appropriate since some persons who make use of these facilities have never been hospitalized. Two kinds of residential facilities will be noted: the residential house and the foster home.

The Residential House

The residential or halfway house provides a home for persons who are not ready or able to be full members of their families or the community. Some of these persons do not have homes to which they can go. Others may have homes which are not suitable, at least for the while.

Generally speaking, residents of such places work and find some of their social life and recreation in the community. The residential house provides them with a protective environment in which and from which they can operate. In the house are peers and professional consultants who offer help, support, and understanding.

The house is usually a large dwelling in a residential part of the community. There is generally a director in residence and perhaps seven to twelve residents. The length of stay may vary from a few weeks up to a year or so (Wechsler, 1960b).

An example of a halfway house organization is Woodley House. Unlike a hospital, it is small and homelike, simple in structure, and an anonymous part of its environment. Woodley has a board of directors (including both psychiatrists and laymen), a staff (a director, an associate director, an occasional staff assistant, a part-time secretary, and a part-time maid), and a consultant who is visited for weekly conferences.

Woodley House is located in an old-fashioned town house, twin to an adjoining private home, on a busy main street in Washington, D.C. On the well-kept street apartment buildings, town houses, hotels, and shops are mixed. The house, which was formerly used as a boardinghouse and judging from its appearance might still be one, has seven bedrooms and space enough for ten or eleven people to live comfortably. It is furnished like a middle-class home. Each resident has a key and comes and goes as he wishes.

The director and her associate were trained as occupational therapists and worked in hospitals for many years. They take turns being in charge of Woodley House, usually alternating days and nights at the house and at their own homes. Each is fully responsible while she is working. The range of responsibilities includes such disparate tasks as deciding what to prepare for dinner and cooking it, choosing a resident from among several applicants, and determining when a resident's acute psychotic state requires emergency measures. For the most part, like mothers or housemothers, they have no fixed on- or off-duty hours.

The only continuing group activity for residents of Woodley House is eating dinner together. Everyone gets up at a different time and makes his own breakfast and almost everyone is away at midday. Other than the fixed dining hour, group activities wax and wane as residents come and go and change the atmosphere of the house. For example, when the temporary and part-time staff assistant changed—from a group worker to a history major—the atmosphere changed, too. About a year ago there was a very cohesive resident group and strong house spirit, with the residents sharing many activities—trips, picnics, swimming, concerts, movies, bowling. They formed a French class and brought a teacher into the house. Now residents do less together and many find friendships outside the house.

The criteria for admission are: That the person wants to come; that he be under the supervision or treatment of a private therapist, accredited agency, or hospital that will assume responsibility for him while he is living at Woodley House; and that he be able to care for himself and show some willingness and ability to plan his own life. Age, sex, and diagnosis are not specific criteria for admission to Woodley House but are considered in terms of making the group of residents heterogeneous and reasonably congenial. Most of the residents who have lived there have been diagnosed as schizophrenic and have been hospitalized at some time before coming to Woodley House.

There is no admission procedure beyond an informal three-way discussion with the therapist, patient, and either the director or her associate, in which mutual expectations and obligations are discussed, and in which the staff member emphasizes the lack of controls and the lack of the protection that such controls might have offered the residents in prior institutions.

Woodley House receives no case histories. The referring therapist is asked only what he thinks is the best and the worst thing which might happen to the patient who is moving to the house.

The fee scale is set to encourage residents to work outside the house. Fees are highest for the unemployed, lower for those employed part-time, and lowest for persons employed full-time. Volunteer jobs or school are counted as work and lowering rent for these activities is equivalent to paying residents for engaging in them.

Just as there is no intake, so there is no discharge procedure. People stay as long as they and their therapists think it is a good idea. This has ranged from a few hours to almost four years but the average stay is about nine months.

There is nothing equivalent to formal patient government, but at one time a group worker who was on the staff held a series of scheduled house meetings at which grievances were aired and resolutions passed. Currently little seems to excite, interest, or anger the residents as a group. As individuals they complain or make suggestions at the dinner table, write additions to the grocery list, put notices on the bulletin board, and participate in house affairs.

Having extremely limited control over and responsibility for residents' lives, the staff has available none of the usual institutional disciplinary or punitive measures. If anyone does something which annoys a staff member, she tells him to stop, and may threaten with a vague "or else!" But there really is no "or else" and the residents know it. Any ability to correct behavior comes from the residents' respect for the staff member or for her point of view. Beyond this the only recourse is to the resident's therapist, and only rarely has a therapist been convinced that Woodley House could not handle the difficulties his patient presented.

Particular rules come and go as they are needed, but they are never written down or codified for fear they will act as challenges and force staff members into police roles. When a problem arises, some temporary rule may help to deal with it, but once the issue is resolved or some of the people involved in the conflict have left Woodley House, the rule is forgotten. Thus, at various times there have been announced rules against wearing pajamas downstairs during the day, against making noise after 10:30 at night, against keeping liquor in bedrooms, and against hitting a staff member.

Although they are also unwritten, the standards by which rules have been created are the common middle-class American standards of society. When there is any question about sanctioning or censuring particular behavior, these middle-class standards of propriety are applied.

Socially acceptable behavior is emphasized even while there is awareness that such behavior is not consistent with the residents' impulses or desires. Pressure is put on the residents to act as if they were less sick than they may be and to repress signs of illness. The staff also discourages the acting-out of anger, hostility, aggression, and other emotions but tolerates bizarre or unusual behavior which does not interfere socially. Much staff attention is devoted to the here and now and little is given to consideration of the historical or the dynamics. Residents are encouraged to save analytic material for their therapy sessions.[1]

The Foster Home

The foster home, or family-care program, provides a home for a person within a private family. Foster placement for children from distressed or broken homes is an old idea. Foster homes or family care for the mentally ill also has a long history (Padula, 1964).

[1] Rothwell, N. D., & Doniger, J. Halfway house and mental hospital—some comparisons. Psychiatry, 1963, 26, 281–288. Reprinted by special permission of The William Alanson White Psychiatric Foundation, Inc. Pp. 282–283.

Foster homes for mental patients are generally selected and supervised by the hospital or some social agency. An agency worker helps prepare the patient and the foster family for their new relationship. There may be regularly scheduled meetings of the heads of the foster families.

In contrast to the residential house, the foster home provides the person with a traditional family unit, and placement is usually longer and may be permanent. It is a conventional setting, and fairly conventional behavior may be encouraged and expected of the person; the residential house provides a less conventional environment and perhaps a greater tolerance of unusual behavior (Wechsler, 1960b).

The Sheltered Workshop

The sheltered workshop is a resource for training people who have been disabled by injury or illness. The aim of such installations is not so much to teach specific job skills as to produce work attitudes and habits that will generalize to future placements. The person is helped to become increasingly self-confident and self-sufficient so that he may ultimately enter the regular labor market.

The workshops themselves are of various sizes and descriptions. They provide training to a variety of persons, such as the blind, the mentally retarded, and so on. A limited number of mental hospital expatients have been accommodated in such settings.

Like the residential house, the sheltered workshop can be of value to persons who are in transition between an institution and the larger society. Such settings offer a protected environment in which to try out social and vocational skills. Here are a number of helpful effects which sheltered workshops have been held to have for a participant:

1 He has the opportunity to earn money and thus feel that he is useful to self and family; furthermore, the "secondary gain" in acting out his conflicts in the work situation decreases when the pay decreases.
2 He learns a work skill that he might use after leaving the shop.
3 Even if he does not use the specific skill learned at the shop, he does learn elements of a "work personality": time patterns; cooperation patterns; authority patterns; attitude toward job, bosses, fellow workers and earnings. Though these patterns are habitual for the regular worker, they have been impaired, lost or were never learned by the post-psychotic. In the workshop he has the opportunity to relearn those patterns by being in a situation where they are operating, and where he can see their operation concretely.
4 Structures of time, space and relationships are given to him. Some psychiatric expatients are not yet ready to develop such structures for themselves.
5 He has the opportunity to begin to learn about values that exist in the community, outside of his home. Thus, he is brought in touch with social reality.
6 He gets the feeling of belonging to, and of acceptance in, a real work community (Olshansky, 1960, p. 34).

The Social Club

A number of social clubs have been established for individuals who share common adjustment problems. There are, for example, organizations made up of former drug addicts and alcoholics. Clubs for expatients have increased considerably in the past ten years.

There are various types of expatient

clubs. Some are run by the expatients themselves, but most are sponsored by professional agencies. Even in the latter, the members may assume considerable responsibility for activities.

Most of these organizations are social in nature, and their activities include parties, dances, and other recreational functions. Some clubs have educational or group therapy programs. Other services may be provided for the members, such as help in finding jobs and residences.

Some of the assumptions which underlie expatient clubs are as follows:

1 *The mental patient on return to the community may find difficulty in reestablishing satisfactory interpersonal relations.*

2 *Re-establishment and maintenance of adequate social relationships are of vital importance to the former mental patient, as failures in the social sphere may serve as contributing factors in relapse and rehospitalization.*

3 *Opportunities should be provided for the expatient to meet with other individuals who would accept him, despite the stigma often associated with mental illness, and present him with necessary social supports.*

4 *Individuals who share the common experience of hospitalization for mental illness may tend to be more understanding, self-accepting, and supportive of each other.*

5 *One way of meeting these objectives is to form social groups composed primarily of former mental patients.*

6 *As a consequence, the expatient group may produce a milieu relatively freer from stress than other community organizations or ordinary community life.*

7 *Within this sheltered social environment, the expatient may be able to establish interpersonal relationships more easily, and develop and test various adaptive patterns of behavior.*

8 *As the expatient gains confidence from acceptance within the group, and more experience in forming interpersonal relationships, it is hoped that he eventually will be able to relate to other persons outside of the protected setting (Wechsler, 1960a, p. 48).*

The Community Mental Health Center

As was indicated, the range and supply of mental health resources varies widely from community to community. Many—especially smaller agricultural communities—are very short on personnel and facilities. Some larger communities offer a wide array of services (Robinson, DeMarche, & Wagle, 1960).

A number of agencies other than those ordinarily identified as psychiatric or psychological perform vital mental health services in a community. Public health services, for example, help alleviate the stress which comes from disease and poor health. Welfare agencies provide assistance for persons suffering from unemployment, disability, and lack of support. The schools, courts, churches, and other community institutions are also involved in the mental health effort.

Explicit mental health services may be provided by a number of workers and agencies. Among the individuals involved are physicians, psychiatrists, psychologists, social workers, and others. Among the agencies are family services, mental health clinics, child guidance centers, and psychiatric wards and outpatient services affiliated with or part of general hospitals.

A new and promising concept calls for the establishment of what has been called the "community mental health center." Such a center would provide a complete and coordinated program of services within the community. It would provide help for people of all ages and with all kinds of mental illness and adjustment problems. The goal of such a center would be to provide "total mental health services" to take care of the "total needs of the community" (Barton, 1964).

The community mental health center would not necessarily be a new facility nor would all its services be located under one roof. There is no intention to duplicate or replace existing resources. The goal is to improve established services, add to them where necessary, and coordinate the total operation (Glasscote, Sanders, Forstenzer, & Foley, 1964).

The movement toward the establishment of such centers was stimulated by legislation enacted by the 88th Congress. Federal matching funds are being made available to the states, and it is expected that 200 to 300 of these centers will be established in the next few years. To qualify for funds a center must provide five essential services, and five additional services are considered desirable. These are as follows:

Essential services:
1 Inpatient services
2 Outpatient services
3 Partial hospitalization services, including at least day care
4 Emergency services, provided twenty-four hours daily within at least one of the above services
5 Consultation and education services, available to community agencies and professional personnel

Desirable services:
1 Diagnostic services

2 Rehabilitative services, including vocational and educational programs
3 Precare and aftercare services in the community, including foster home placement, home visiting, and halfway houses
4 Training
5 Research and evaluation

SOME WORKERS IN IMPROVEMENT

Where do people go for help? Some of us may keep our problems pretty much to ourselves. (This may be one of our problems.) Some of us turn to relatives or friends for support and assistance. Sometimes, however, our problems are such that further help is necessary.

Where do people go for *professional* help? Of the 2,460 adults interviewed in a national survey, 345 reported that they had sought such help for a personal problem. Clergymen were most frequently consulted; they were turned to in 42 percent of the cases. Doctors were second, with 29 percent of the cases, and psychiatrists and psychologists were third, with 18 percent (Gurin, Veroff, & Feld, 1960) (see Table 10.1).

Generally speaking, there is a serious shortage of manpower in mental health professions. More workers need to be trained. Workers who are available need to be better distributed and utilized (Albee, 1959).

Many professions play roles in the improvement of adjustment and mental health. This section will describe the professions whose activities seem most central. And it will note the increasingly important part played by volunteers.

The Minister

Ministers are an important source of help for personal problems. Many people report that in times of stress they turn to prayer (McCann, 1962). It is not surprising that in times of stress they turn to their minister as well.

From the standpoint of numbers alone, ministers are an important mental health resource. It has been estimated that there are 350,000 ordained clergymen in the United States, the majority of whom serve parishes and congregations. There are more clergymen than all other mental health personnel combined, and they are found in many communities where no other personnel are available (Adler, 1965; Mc-Cann, 1962).

In addition to their availability, there are a number of other reasons why ministers are sought out for help. The troubled parishioner may already have a close relationship with his minister, and it is easier on that account to seek assistance. In going to a minister, the troubled person has less need to identify a problem as "mental." There are no intake procedures, no waiting lists, and no charge for services (Adler, 1965; McCann, 1962).

Ministers vary considerably in the amount of pastoral counseling they do. In a survey made of a random sample of 100 Protestant clergymen, it was found that an average of two or three hours per week was spent in counseling. In this sample, 7 percent of the ministers counseled from ten to twenty-two hours per week, 33 percent from two to nine hours per week, and 60 percent counseled less than two hours per week. As a group, the ministers who counseled more had more training in psychology and counseling (Nameche, 1958).

Seven categories of problems dominated the counseling activity. Marriage and family problems and concern with psychological distress were most common. Then, in order of frequency, were problems of youth behavior, illness and aging, alcoholism, religious and spiritual questions, and occupation. Actually, religious concerns made up only a small percentage of the problems (Nameche, 1958).

In order to help ministers in their mental health functions, many theological training programs include courses in psy-

Table 10.1 Where do people go for help? Of the 2,460 people interviewed in a national survey, 345 had sought professional help for a personal problem. Below are the sources of help and the percentage of time each source was sought. Since some respondents gave more than one response, the total comes to more than 100 percent.*

Source of Help	Percent
Clergyman	42
Doctor	29
Psychiatrist (or psychologist): private practitioner or not ascertained whether private or institutional	12
Psychiatrist (or psychologist) in clinic, hospital, other agency; mental hospital	6
Marriage counselor; marriage clinic	3
Other private practitioners or social agencies for handling psychological problems	10
Social service agencies for handling nonpsychological problems (e.g., financial problems)	3
Lawyer	6
Other	11

* From *Americans View Their Mental Health* by G. Gurin, J. Veroff and S. Feld, Basic Books, Inc., Publishers, New York, 1960. P. 307.

chology and counseling. Special programs in clinical pastoral education have been offered for theological students and clergymen seeking further training. These programs range from short-term academic courses to intensive training in a clinic, hospital, or some other mental health setting.

How ministers help persons with psychological problems is succinctly set forth in the following paragraphs:

> *Ministers are in a key position to intervene constructively in incipient difficulties, and many are skillful in being able to respond to a parishioner's demands, expectations and emotional turmoil in a manner that is corrective rather than disjunctive. Clergy enable many parishioners to gain relief by ventilating strong feelings, by unburdening themselves of guilt-laden thoughts and tension-producing conflicts, and by revealing socially unacceptable actions. The minister's acceptance and support is meaningful especially since he represents the authority of God and the church. He is often the one who can be most supportive as he brings the individual in need closer to the strengths inherent in religious practices, such as prayer, sacraments, etc.*
>
> *The clergyman may be an accepting listener. He may also take an active part in redirecting the parishioner's attention to pertinent issues, such as clarifying thoughts and feelings and supporting constructive steps in problem-solving. Providing emotional support, clarifying the difference between the reality of a situation and the counselee's special perception of that reality, and referral for more specialized treatment are all approaches that ministers may take in endeavoring to help parishioners resume healthy functioning (Adler, 1965; pp. 66–67).*

The Physician

As in the case of ministers, one reason that people turn to their physician for help with personal problems is that a relationship already exists. Furthermore, in time of stress, a person may not know for sure whether his problem is physical or otherwise, and it seems logical to consult a medical doctor. Moreover, seeing him is less formidable and threatening than going to a psychiatrist, psychologist, or some other specialist.

The family doctor can play a vital role in the prevention and alleviation of maladjustment and mental illness. He frequently is in contact with the family during its trying periods, as for example, following the birth of a mentally defective child, during a serious illness, and in time of death. Beyond his medical skill itself, the doctor's counsel and support can bolster the family's ability to bear up in its critical moments (Caplan, 1961).

A knowledge of psychology and psychiatry is essential for all physicians (Lief & Lief, 1963; Rosenbaum, 1963). In recent decades, there has been an increasing amount of psychiatric instruction in medical schools (Levine & Lederer, 1959). There is also an increasing number of postgraduate courses to keep general practitioners and other doctors abreast of latest developments in psychiatry and mental health.

Some physicians are well convinced of the value of psychiatric techniques. They make use of these techniques within the limit of their competence, and they make referral to other mental health personnel. Other physicians, however, are neither comfortable with nor convinced of the value of such approaches. They may minimize, ignore, or even ridicule psychological factors (Lief & Lief, 1963).

Early help or early referral by a physician may be the crucial factor in preventing the later hospitalization of a patient.

As programs in community mental health grow, the physician will have an even more vital role to play. He will be increasingly called upon to participate in patient after-care and other mental health programs (Lief & Lief, 1963).

Here is an example of the treatment of a troubled person by a physician. With the consultation of a psychiatrist, the medical resident who was not psychiatrically trained himself was able to be of help. The patient was a married woman, twenty-three years old, who entered the hospital with severe headaches, persistent hypertension (high blood pressure), and attacks of abdominal pain. She was a very dependent person, and, unable to accept the role of wife and mother, she and her children lived with her parents.

The current illness had started when her younger brother had returned from the Army and she had been forced to move from her mother's house into her own apartment to make room for him at her parents' home. From this situation, which was a repetition of the original traumatic experience (the birth of her younger brother), she developed intense hostility toward her mother and her siblings who were still living at home. These unexpressed feelings appeared to be associated with the severe attacks of headache and abdominal pain for which she was hospitalized.

After formulation of the psychodynamics in a conference with the psychiatric consultant, a therapeutic plan was proposed which was directed at meeting her frustrated dependency needs. This included occasional contacts with the psychiatric consultant, offers of material giving when indicated, and continued contacts with the medical resident. However, her presenting symptoms in combination with hypertension and severe spasm of the retinal arterioles aroused considerable anx-

iety in the medical resident who was following the case. The physician's anxiety was manifested by repetitive physical and laboratory examinations and frequent consultations. This affected the patient in two ways: first, it gave the symptoms attention-getting value, and second, it augmented the patient's anxiety, with a resulting increase in symptoms.

The psychiatric consultant continually reassured the medical resident that the patient was being handled properly, and, after a few months, the resident became more secure in dealing with her because he recognized that the symptoms were not evidence of malignant hypertension but that they recurred in direct relation to emotional and environmental problems. As a result of this knowledge, each time the patient suffered an exacerbation of symptoms the physician immediately inquired into her current life situation, with special emphasis on immediate difficulties with her husband, children, siblings, or mother. The patient was allowed to talk freely about such problems, and temporal relationships to the development of symptoms were discussed. This discussion, plus a rapid physical check-up, served to relieve both the patient's and physician's anxiety. With such therapy there was a remarkable diminution in both the frequency and severity of the "attacks." Although the blood pressure was unchanged, the patient became symptom-free and matured considerably, functioning more adequately as a mother and wife. When there was trouble she and her doctor had little difficulty in quickly discovering the precipitating factors (Rosenbaum, 1963, pp. 508–509).

The Psychiatrist

Physicians who specialize in the diagnosis and treatment of mental illness and adjustment problems are called *psychiatrists*. Some psychiatrists—a relatively small number compared with psychologists—are engaged in research. It has been estimated that there are about thirteen thousand physicians who devote themselves to the full-time practice of psychiatry (Blain, 1959).

In order to become a psychiatrist, a person must first complete a premedical and medical program, obtain the M.D. degree (doctor of medicine), and serve a medical internship. Then, generally speaking, he takes a psychiatric residency in which he receives additional course work and supervised experience, possibly in a variety of inpatient and outpatient settings.

Since the psychiatrist is first of all a physician, he is trained in the medical treatment of disease. He is qualified to employ such somatotherapies as shock treatment and drugs, and he is able to prescribe programs of hospitalization for his patients. Psychiatrists are also trained in psychotherapy.

In a recent study of psychiatrists in a Midwestern metropolitan community, it was found that the predominant pattern of treatment involved the use of drugs and shock treatment along with brief psychotherapy which was characterized by direct suggestions and persuasion. Their practice was primarily private and involved adult patients whose problems were of intermediate severity. Physical examinations or neurological examinations were not ordinarily performed (Malmquist, 1964).

Psychiatrists are found in a variety of settings. Many are in private practice. Many are on the staffs of clinics, hospitals, and other mental health facilities. Some psychiatrists serve as consultants to various mental health agencies, such as the juvenile court and family services. Commonly, a psychiatrist combines a number of different activities in his professional practice.

Psychiatric treatment takes so many forms and occurs in so many different settings that it would be impossible for any one case history to be considered representative. The following case, treated by a psychiatrist, involved a serious problem and was treated with both electroshock and psychotherapy:

This forty-nine-year-old married woman was referred to the psychiatrist by her own local physician. He had attempted for several weeks to deal with her complaints but had found that his therapy was not producing any improvement. The patient complained of a general loss of interest in her family and her friends. She said that she was becoming increasingly irritable and frequently suffered from crying spells. In addition to this she had a number of vague physical complaints for which no organic basis had been found by her local physician. She often suffered from headaches, constipation, and a general feeling of lassitude and weakness.

Upon questioning it developed that the patient's inability to sleep was a particularly bothersome symptom, and that much of her depression occurred during the early morning hours after a sleepless night. She had, on many occasions, entertained thoughts of suicide but had, at least at the time she was referred, not acted upon any of them. She felt that she was of no further use to her husband or to her two grown children, who had married and moved away. She was concerned about her general physical condition and also about her attractiveness, feeling that both were below par. She was no longer interested in pursuing the many social duties and obligations which she had in the past indulged in. She had resigned from most of the organizations to which she had previously belonged. She found herself no longer interested in her husband nor in his work. She could not even talk to him for any length of time without becoming irritable and critical of him. She was bitter about the fact that her married children visited her with decreasing fre-

quency and yet, when pressed, made it evident that she treated them in an uncordial manner whenever they did come to see her.

This patient's past history revealed that she had always been a rigid person with perfectionistic, meticulous standards. She had led a life which appeared on the surface to have been full, yet which contained no deep emotional values. She had had many friends, but none of them had been close or warm to her. She had always been an ambitious person striving for higher goals many of which she now felt she had never attained. She had spent a great deal of time and interest in her home and yet had chronically been displeased with the results. Although she initially attempted to paint her earlier life as having been satisfactory, happy, and contented, it soon became evident that she had never achieved any measure of pleasurable living. She had been a chronically worrisome person concerned about everything in the life of her husband, her children, and herself. She watched over her family and had carried this tendency to the point of domination.

When this woman found herself in the menopause and realized that she was beginning to grow older, she became increasingly bitter about not having attained many of her goals. She resented the fact that her children no longer paid her the attention which they had previously done. She resented the fact that her husband no longer found her as important as she thought he should. She began complaining of her physical symptoms, initially, and then made increased demands upon her husband and her children. She bitterly resented the fact that they did not respond as she wished to these excessive demands. As the situation continued she became increasingly depressed.

Three interviews, using a psychotherapeutic technique, did not result in any improvement and it was impossible to establish a useful relationship with this patient. Therefore, electroshock was recommended and the patient received a total of eight treatments. After approximately five she began to improve and by the end of eight her improvement had reached a more healthy pattern so that she was able to continue her psychotherapeutic interviews. Attempts were then made to help her re-establish her social activities and her interest in her children and grandchildren. She was also helped to understand how her previous life had been constricted, rigid, and lacking in joy. She was encouraged to make a more flexible adjustment and to appreciate the meaning and value of family and of friends. She gradually began to accept herself more thoroughly and to seek the companionship of others. She was seen in fifteen interviews over a period of several months. Her improvement was marked after electroshock and remained stabilized. After a follow-up of approximately four years, she suffered no relapse, as might well have occurred if she had not had the electroshock or had she had this treatment alone without any follow-up psychotherapy.[2]

The Psychoanalyst

Physicians who are trained to treat adjustment problems through the use of psychoanalytic methods are called *psychoanalysts*. Individuals planning to be psychoanalysts ordinarily must complete their medical program, including a year of internship and a year of psychiatric training before beginning their specialized training. (There are a few psychoanalysts who do not have medical degrees, and these are referred to as *lay* analysts in distinction to the majority who are identified as *medical* analysts.)

After completing his medical and psychiatric training, the prospective psychoanalyst must himself be psychoanalyzed. When this process is successfully accom-

[2] Reprinted from *Introduction to Psychiatry* by O. Spurgeon English and Stuart M. Finch. By Permission of W. W. Norton & Company, Inc. Copyright © 1954, 1957, 1964 by W. W. Norton & Company, Inc. Pp. 406–408 (1957 ed.).

plished, he is assigned several cases to psychoanalyze under close supervision. During this time he will also be taking various courses at a psychoanalytic institute. With the completion of his own analysis, his supervised analyses of others, and his course work, he becomes a fully qualified psychoanalyst. There are only about one thousand psychoanalysts in the United States.

In its classical form, psychoanalysis is an intensive, extensive, and expensive process. The patient may meet with his analyst an hour each day four or five days a week for perhaps a year or more. Analyses have gone on for three or four years or even longer periods. There are, however, some newer and briefer forms of psychoanalysis.

Today many psychotherapists make use of psychoanalytic concepts and techniques. Therefore, the therapeutic differences between a psychoanalyst (especially one using a modified approach) and a psychiatrist or psychologist (especially one who is psychoanalytically oriented) is not so great.

Psychoanalysis is not an easy process to describe. Most of us have some conception or misconception of psychoanalysis from seeing it portrayed or caricatured in motion pictures, television, novels, plays, cartoons, and dozens of jokes. Many people have the mistaken notion that to go to any psychiatrist or psychologist is to be psychoanalyzed.

The key method of psychoanalysis is free association. Other important aspects are resistance and interpretation, transference and countertransference, and abreaction, insight, and working through. Each of these is discussed in this description of psychoanalytic process:

Let me describe what psychoanalysis is actually like. The analyst usually begins by getting something of the personal biography of the patient, after the manner of a social worker's case history. The patient sits up and talks as he would to any physician. The analyst may have better interviewing methods, but there is little that is distinctive about the early sessions. There may be several sessions before the patient takes to the couch, before the typical free association method is used. Then the patient is taught to follow, as well as he is able, the basic rule: to say everything that enters his mind, without selection. This is much harder than it sounds, even for patients who are eager to co-operate with the analyst. As Fenichel puts it, "Even the patient who tries to adhere to the basic rule fails to tell many things because he considers them too unimportant, too stupid, too indiscreet, and so on. There are many who never learn to apply the basic rule because their fear of losing control is too great, and before they can give expression to anything they must examine it to see exactly what it is." . . . In fact, the whole lifetime has been spent learning to be tactful, to achieve self-control, to avoid outbursts of emotion, to do what is proper rather than what is impulsive. This all has to be unlearned for successful free association.

What free association aims at is the bringing to awareness of impulses and thoughts of which the person is not aware. Because these impulses are active, but out of awareness, they are called unconscious. It is necessary to break through resistances in order to bring them to awareness. The role of the psychoanalyst is, essentially, to help the patient break down these resistances, so that he may face his disguised motives and hidden thoughts frankly, and then come to grips in realistic manner with whatever problems or conflicts are then brought into view.

The activity of the analyst is directed skillfully at this task of helping the patient eliminate resistances. He does this in part by pointing out to the patient the conse-

quences of his resistances: the times of silence when his mind seems to go blank, forgetting what he intended to say, perhaps forgetting to show up at an appointment, drifting into superficial associations, or giving glib interpretations of his own. The analyst not only calls attention to signs of resistance, but he also interprets the patient's associations in such a way as to facilitate further associations.

Fenichel defines interpretation as "helping something unconscious to become conscious by naming it at the moment it is striving to break through." . . . If this is accepted, then the first interpretations are necessarily fairly "shallow" ones, the "deeper" interpretations waiting until the patient is ready for them.

The deeper interpretations are the ones we often think of in characterizing psychoanalysis, but very much of the time in an actual psychoanalysis is spent in rather matter-of-fact discussion of attitudes toward other people and toward oneself as they show themselves in daily life, without recourse to universal symbols, references to libidinal stages, and so on. Not all psychoanalysts agree on just how interpretations should be made, or when they should be made, and it is my guess that those who think they do agree may actually behave quite differently when conducting analyses of their patients. This is one reason why it is difficult to study psychoanalytic therapy, and a reason, also, why there are so many schisms within psychoanalytic societies.

Another aspect of the psychoanalytic therapy goes by the name of "transference." Transference refers to the tendency for the patient to make of the analyst an object of his motivational or emotional attachments. It is too simple to say that the patient falls in love with the analyst. Sometimes he makes of the analyst a loved parent, sometimes a hated parent; sometimes the analyst substitutes for a brother or sister, or for the boss at the office. The patient unconsciously assigns roles to the analyst of the important people in the patient's own life. Part of the task of the an-

alyst is to handle the transference. The word "handle" is easily spoken, but this handling of the transference is said to be the most difficult part of the analyst's art.

The psychoanalytic interview is a social one, an interpersonal one, with two people involved. The analyst is a person, too, and he reacts to the adoration and abuse of the patient he is analyzing. He is a good analyst to the extent that he understands himself well enough so that he preserves his role in the analytic situation, and does not himself become involved, as his patient is, in what is called countertransference, that is, using the patient as an outlet for his own emotions. If the patient's exploits become the occasion for the analyst's fantasy life, then the analyst gets preoccupied with his own free associations and cannot listen attentively to his patient. The discipline of learning to listen, and only to listen, is considered by Frieda Fromm-Reichman . . . to be the essence of the analyst's problem. . . .

Very often there is within the midst of psychoanalysis a state in which the patient is more disturbed than he was before entering treatment. Those unfriendly to psychoanalysis occasionally use this as an indication of its therapeutic ineffectiveness. . . . Two comments can be made here. First, what appears to others to be disturbance may not be "neurotic" at all. Some individuals are excessively kind to other people, at great cost to themselves. If they suddenly express their feelings more openly, they may become less pleasant to live with or to work with, because they can no longer be exploited. The troublesome child may be a healthier child than the child who is too "good." If a person changes, new social adjustments are required, and some that were in equilibrium now get out of focus. This is the first observation regarding apparent disturbance in the midst of analysis. The second comment is that the disturbance in the midst of analysis may be a genuinely neurotic one, an aggravation of the typical transference. That is, the substitution of the analyst for other figures emotionally important to the patient may produce an emotional crisis, in which the patient actually acts more irrationally than before treatment. If this crisis is well handled, the patient emerges the better for it. Although some analysts believe that such crises are inevitable in an analysis, other analysts attempt to ward them off by such devices as less frequent therapeutic sessions when transference problems become too hard to handle. . . . In any case, the fact that an aggravated transference neurosis may occur does not invalidate the therapeutic usefulness of psychoanalytic technique.

Three words often crop up in discussion of what is taking place as the patient improves. These are "abreaction," "insight," and "working through." "Abreaction" refers to a living again of an earlier emotion, in a kind of emotional catharsis —literally getting some of the dammed-up emotion out of the system. The therapeutic need is that described by the poet:

Home they brought her warrior dead.
She nor wept nor uttered cry.
All her maidens watching said:
"She must weep or she will die."
—Tennyson, The Princess

"Insight" refers to seeing clearly what motives are at work, what the nature of the problem is, so that instinctual conflicts, as psychoanalysts call them, are recognized for what they are. Insight is not limited to the recovery of dramatic incidents in early childhood that were later repressed. Sometimes such insights do occur, and sometimes they are associated with relief of symptoms. But neither a single flood of emotion in abreaction nor a single occasion of surprised insight relieves the patient of his symptoms. He requires, instead, the process of "working through," that is, facing again and again the same old conflicts and finding himself reacting in the same old ways to them, until eventually the slow processes of re-education manifest themselves and he reacts more nearly in accordance with the objective demands of the situation and less in accordance with distortions that his private needs create.

It is chiefly because the process of working through takes so long that psychoanalysis takes so long. The psychoanalyst often has the basic insights into the patient's problems quite early in treatment, but the patient is unready for them and could not understand the analyst if he were to insist upon confronting him with these interpretations. I have sometimes likened an analysis to the process of learning to play the piano. It is not enough to know what a good performance is and to wish to give one. The process has to be learned. The learner may know all about musical notation and may have manual skill and musical appreciation. But there is no short cut. Even with a good teacher the lessons must continue week after week before the player can achieve the kind of spontaneous performance he wishes to achieve. We do not begrudge this time, because we believe that the end is worth it. What the analyst is attempting to do is far more complex than what the piano teacher is attempting to do. The skilled management of a life is more difficult than the skilled management of a keyboard.[3]

The Nurse

Many workers serve as nurses in medical and psychiatric facilities. The largest percentage of these workers do not have full professional status but nevertheless perform a vital function in providing care, companionship, and social activity. These workers include the practical nurse, the ward attendant, and the psychiatric technician.

To have full status as a nurse, a person usually completes a three-year program at a training hospital (after which she is awarded a diploma) or a four-year or five-year college program (after which she is awarded a bachelor of science de-

[3] From E. R. Hilgard's Chapter, "Experimental approaches to psychoanalysis," in Psychoanalysis as Science, edited by E. Pumpian-Mindlin, Copyright © 1952 by California Institute of Technology, Basic Books, Inc., Publishers, New York. Pp. 25–29.

gree). Then she takes a state board examination and is registered to practice.

Every nurse receives some psychiatric training, but some complete an advanced program of education and training and are called *psychiatric nurses*. Such nurses work in hospitals and in a variety of outpatient services. The role and function of the psychiatric nurse varies widely from setting to setting.

Some of the work roles filled by the psychiatric nurse include mother figure, manager, teacher, socializing agent, and counselor or psychotherapeutic agent (Peplau, 1959). As a mother, the nurse may care for the patient's physical needs— bathing, dressing, and feeding him—or for his psychological needs—providing protection, support, discipline, and guidance. As a manager, the nurse arranges the patient's physical and social environment to facilitate improvement. As a teacher, the nurse orients the patient to the programs of the facility and provides him with information about health and hygiene. As a socializing agent, the nurse helps the patient develop and perfect social skills and the ability to relate to others. As a therapist, the nurse may provide service similar to that of a psychiatrist, or her work may be complimentary or supplementary to that of a psychiatrist (Miller & Sabshin, 1963).

The Occupational Therapist

An *occupational therapist* is a person who is trained to help people recover from illness through constructive activity—through being "occupied" in meaningful ways. Occupational therapy has been called "curing by doing." Through involvement in various creative, educational, physical, and recreational activities, the person is able to re-gain strength and skill as well as confidence and a sense of worth.

Occupational therapists work with people of all ages and with various kinds of illnesses and handicaps. For example, these therapists work with retarded and cerebral palsied children and help them learn to help themselves. Such therapists also work with adults who have been disabled by polio, stroke, or injury and help them recover or learn to live with their handicap.

Occupational therapists work in many different settings including general and mental hospitals, mental health clinics and centers, schools and workshops for handicapped or disabled children and adults, correctional institutions, homes for the aged, and so on. To become qualified as a worker in this area, a person first completes a four-year undergraduate program leading to the bachelor of science degree. Then, in order to qualify for professional registration, he must complete a clinical internship of nine or ten months.

All the occupational therapist's work is bound up with mental health since it involves helping people adjust to themselves and their environment. In addition to this, the occupational therapist plays a central role in the rehabilitation of the mentally ill.

Here are several brief illustrations of occupational therapy. For each of these hospitalized patients, the activity which was utilized allowed a meaningful contact with the therapist and a meaningful approach to improvement.

Karen, an 18-year-old girl, had been hospitalized for five years. She was a mute, autistic girl who spent most of her time sitting on the floor in the corner of the dayroom picking at her skin and twisting her hair. She was inaccessible to interview psychotherapy, and medication did not appreciably change her behavior.

The occupational therapist then began to make contact with this girl through food. Over a period of several weeks, she was given candy, chewing gum, soda, and milk. As she began to respond to this feeding, Karen was able to leave the ward with the occupational therapist and help to cook simple food for them to eat together. Ultimately the patient was able to talk during these experiences and later began to speak to her doctor when he would give her food and also in the dining room while she was eating. As the eating and cooking experiences continued in occupational therapy Karen began to assume more responsibility for both the planning and the cooking and was able to reach out to patients and staff by making candy and cookies for the ward. She was able to work with her psychotherapist and assisted in the hospital diet kitchen until her discharge.

Mrs. T. S., a 32-year-old woman, had been admitted to the hospital because of increased anger, which she could no longer control, hyperactivity, and suspiciousness. She had become completely overwhelmed by the demands of her two small children and was no longer able to care for them. Psychiatric interviews indicated that this patient had very strong dependency needs which were anxiety-provoking for her and which she denied to the extent that she was unable to form any really close relationship and ultimately became unable to give, even to her children. She was an aloof, critical, controlling, and hostile woman.

In occupational therapy it was suggested that she make a piece of jewelry for herself. Since the occupational therapist was unfamiliar with the particular craft process, it was arranged for them to work together from a book of instructions. Mrs. S. would read the directions aloud to the therapist, and they worked in this manner until the project was completed.

Emphasis on the activity and learning process made it possible for this patient to work with another person with much

less feeling of threat, and the use of the book of instructions provided a sense of both safe distance and control, which was necessary at this time. The success of their shared experience made it possible for the patient to feel more secure in this relationship and to begin to accept a more dependent relationship.[4]

The Psychologist

Psychologists of varying descriptions work in the field of mental health. There are, to cite some of the most common designations, school psychologists, consulting psychologists, counseling psychologists, and clinical psychologists. Regardless of their different designations and the somewhat different settings in which they may be found, there is considerable overlap both in their training and in the techniques they employ to evaluate and help the persons with whom they deal.

The clinical psychologist occupies a very central position in the mental health field. He is a psychologist who has received special training in the assessment and correction of adjustment problems. He is also specially trained in doing research in this area of psychology.

Most clinical psychologists have the Ph.D. degree (doctor of philosophy). In order to become a clinical psychologist, a person usually majors in psychology or some related science as an undergraduate. He then enters into three or more years of graduate study in psychology. He is also generally required to complete a one-year internship in a clinic or hospital, and some psychologists take further postdoctoral training.

Unlike most other persons in mental

4 Reprinted by permission of the publisher from *Occupational Therapy* by G. S. Fidler & J. W. Fidler. Copyright © 1963, The Macmillan Company. Pp. 88, 90.

health fields, clinical psychologists receive considerable training in psychological testing, and they are frequently called to assist in diagnosis and evaluation. Clinical psychologists are trained in psychotherapy; however, they are not medical doctors and do not perform somatotherapies. Clinical psychologists also receive intensive training in research, and much of the exploration in the field of mental health is carried on by them or with their assistance.

Like psychiatrists, with whom their work has considerable overlap, clinical psychologists are found in a number of different settings. Many work in clinics and hospitals. Many others work in colleges and universities where they may teach, counsel students, and do research. Psychologists are frequently members of the staffs of correctional and educational agencies. Many psychologists are in private practice, but ordinarily this is in addition to other assignments.

In the material which follows, two psychologists tell of their professional careers:

A Psychologist in a Child Guidance Clinic

One of the easiest things in the world is to look back and "misperceive" one's own motives. That is precisely what most persons probably do when asked how they "got into" the occupational field in which they find themselves in adult life. Nevertheless, I shall try.

Since I came from a minority group background with a feeling for the oppressed and from a childhood which constantly emphasized in discussion and practice the importance of people, it would not be unexpected that my interest should turn to medicine. But, fortunately or unfortunately, I was destined for bitter disillusionment when as a premed junior in college I was called into the office of

one of my science professors to be told that in his opinion, and in spite of the fact that I had "satisfactory" grades, I was not the "type" to become a physician and I ought to change majors immediately. Without this man's recommendation my chances for medical school were minimal. Another of my professors suggested that I try the business department, but here I was told that it was too late to start the program and that no one could take any business courses without the prerequisite full year introductory course in that field. As a possible help to me in my dilemma it was suggested that I take a battery of psychological tests. I shall never forget my interview giving me the "results" of these tests (and my confused, forced indecision certainly made me a ripe target for psychological instruments) and the summary statement of the person in charge of the testing, "Frankly, R., I don't see how you can succeed at anything."

This "advice" did several things: first, it made me angry; secondly, it increased my need for personal and academic support and for acceptance by someone; thirdly, it raised a big question in my mind regarding the efficacy of psychological tests. The anger made me work harder for grades and recognition than I ever had before; the need for support and confidence in myself and a statement by the speech professor suggesting confidence in me led me to take further courses in public speaking; the doubts about psychological tests remained as a gnawing problem to emerge at a later date.

Successful completion of college took me on to graduate school majoring in speech and with a growing interest in speech correction, in which I obtained a master's degree. Meanwhile interest in psychology was increasing, both in its application to speech correction and to other kinds of personal problems, especially those which involved communication and the understanding or acceptance of people's feelings. When World War II came, I was assigned to clinical work in an army hospital on the basis of my graduate courses in psychology. After the war, the

GI bill gave me a financial opportunity I had never had before to continue studying for a Ph.D.

My advanced work was not altogether the usual clinical training, being modified in the direction of its application to children's problems. This was largely a result of the support, interest, and thinking of another professor who stressed the importance of giving every child a "good start." In addition, it had been suggested, and accepted by me, that child clinical psychology was almost an open door for activity where it was unnecessary to cross swords with any other profession. When children are concerned, there is much less tendency to become jealous over professional proprieties.

Seldom have I regretted emerging, occupationally, as whatever I am. The work has not always been "satisfying" but the learning is continual. My interest in teaching has remained. Nearly every term I teach an evening course at a nearby state college. Undoubtedly, my choice of what I should teach—psychological diagnosis and psychological testing—has been influenced by my own unfortunate experience with psychological tests. The diagnostic interest remains and finds its outlet both in my regular work as a psychologist in a child clinic and also in private diagnostic work. My interest in the welfare of people finds its major satisfaction in therapeutic endeavor—in collaboration with other disciplines and the resources of the community—with children and their parents.

Thus, I now find myself leading the "full life" of diagnostic and therapeutic work in a child clinic, carrying on diagnostic work with both children and adults in private practice, teaching university extension courses in psychological diagnosis and testing, and having a growing interest in community interaction and cooperation in the field of mental health.[5]

5 From *Clinical Psychology* by Norman D. Sundberg and Leona E. Tyler. Copyright © 1962 by Meredith Publishing Company. Reprinted by permission of Appleton-Century-Crofts, Division of Meredith Publishing Company. Pp. 453–454.

A Clinician in a Large Government Hospital

My professional life at present is busy and varied. Besides working full-time for a government hospital, I teach at a medical school and have a private practice. The working hours in a week often total sixty, but I do not consider myself overworked— in fact, I consider myself fortunate to lead an interesting and stimulating life. What do I do at the hospital? As a supervisory psychologist, I work with psychology trainees in their testing and treatment activities. The ward I am assigned to has been experimenting with a night-hospital program for those patients still hospitalized but who work in the community during the day, and I have been made administrator of that program. Our ward has over 100 patients in a group therapy program—I am responsible for assigning patients to groups and arranging for supervisory conferences with hospital consultants on problems which arise in group handling. I am occasionally called on to lecture on the nature of mental illness to groups of hospital workers who are either regularly employed or are receiving training. My position with the government offers opportunities in testing, treatment, administration, training, lecturing, and carrying on research.

My duties in the medical school at present consist of lecturing to junior students once a week on the forms of mental illness and on personality theory. These duties have varied from time to time. I have worked in the out-patient psychiatric clinic and have assisted in departmental research projects. I find time for these activities during the day because my night-hospital duties require me to work at the hospital one evening a week.

The remainder of my working hours I devote to private practice of individual and group therapy. My patients come to me by referral from physicians and psychiatrists or from finding my name in the classified pages of the telephone book. Those whose condition is too serious for me to work with I refer to psychiatrists in the neighborhood. My approach is analytically ori-

ented and I attempt to set therapeutic goals which can be reached in one or two years.

Whence came my interest in psychology—and, specifically, clinical psychology? This is a difficult question to answer. I have always felt curiosity about people. At one time, in high school and while an undergraduate, this expressed itself as an interest in literature (I suppose for its portrayal of human experience in behavior and feeling) and this led me to consider seriously the career of teaching in English or the Humanities. However, during my sophomore and junior years, courses in psychology awakened my interest in the origins of human behavior, which has continued unabated ever since.

One of the reasons I find clinical psychology exciting is the fact that the final answers are not in. There are many basic questions in the areas of intelligence, perception, personality development, group dynamics, etc., etc. Thus I feel I am part of an expeditionary force on the outer frontier of human knowledge, and that I may be fortunate to be on the scene to share the thrill of discovery of what exists in the inner world of the mind. Clinical psychology is probably too unobstructed for those who feel secure only when they deal with closed systems—so I recommend it only to those who are challenged, not confused, by uncertainty.[6]

The Social Worker

Like psychologists, social workers in many different placements are concerned with the problem of mental health and illness. The situations with which social workers deal—poverty, unemployment, inadequate housing, broken homes, maladjusted individuals and families, illness, handicap, anti-

[6] From *Clinical Psychology* by Norman D. Sundberg and Leona E. Tyler. Copyright © 1962 by Meredith Publishing Company. Reprinted by permission of Appleton-Century-Crofts, Division of Meredith Publishing Company. P. 452.

social behavior, and so forth—are of central importance to mental health.

Social workers generally are employed with public and private agencies which carry out programs designed to improve the social welfare and mental health of certain individuals or groups of individuals. There are, for example, public assistance services, child and family services, medical care and health services, and mental health and psychiatric services.

Many social workers have only a bachelor's degree, but employment or advancement beyond an elementary level in certain placements is limited to those who have done graduate work. In order to achieve full professional status as a social worker, a person ordinarily majors in sociology, psychology, or some other social science in her undergraduate work (we say "her" because most social workers are women although increasing numbers of men are coming into the profession). Then she enters into a two-year graduate program at a school of social work. This program leads to the master of social work degree (M.S.W.). Some schools, however, award a certificate of proficiency upon completion of a one-year graduate program, and a few schools have doctoral programs leading to a doctor of philosophy degree (Ph.D.) or a doctor of social work degree (D.S.W.).

Some social workers, called "caseworkers," deal directly with individuals and families. They may help a person to deal with his environment and at the same time try to change the environment (or find a new environment) to better fit or accommodate the person. Case workers frequently work with a whole family, attempting to strengthen relationships in it, improve its medical and financial health, and its position in the community. Whether called case-work or psychotherapy, the activities of a social worker in helping a maladjusted person or marriage pair or whole family have a good deal in common with the procedures used by psychiatrists and psychologists.

Other social workers, called "group workers," employ group experiences to benefit both the individual and the larger society. Such workers may serve youth groups or participate in senior citizen programs. They may provide group services in correctional institutions, public housing projects, clinics, hospitals, and other mental health facilities.

A few social workers, called "community organization workers," work to improve the social welfare facilities of the entire community. They help the community identify its needs and work to fill these needs. They seek to coordinate and expand existing services and to involve a broad spectrum of professional people and lay people in programs of the community.

The following case illustrates the work of the social caseworker. The woman identified below as "Mrs. M" was a neglectful mother and homemaker. However, with the help and encouragement of the worker, she was able to deal more effectively with her problems.

The M family was referred to the agency because the children were chronically malnourished, poorly clothed, and generally neglected. Their home was badly deteriorated. Several windows were broken and both the interior and exterior of the house were very dirty. The father, aged forty, was an illiterate, alcoholic manual laborer who did not work steadily. The mother, aged thirty-three, was a poor housekeeper, and obese. They had been married for sixteen years. Most members of the community considered them "hopeless" and thought the mother uninterested in her children. The four children, who ranged in age from eight to fifteen years, were said to be mentally retarded and attended special classes at school.

During her first visit with Mrs. M, after spelling out the agency's concern for the children, the worker told Mrs. M that

---

Presentation 10.1 The broad spectrum of adjustment-related activities performed by social workers can be seen in this description of the principal areas of practice.

Public assistance workers *are employed largely by State and local government agencies on public welfare programs which extend financial assistance to needy persons such as the disabled, blind, or aged; unemployed persons; and dependent children. Their duties include determining their clients' needs and whether they are eligible for financial assistance; strengthening family ties; helping clients to become self-sufficient; explaining pertinent laws and requirements; and providing or arranging for other needed social services.*

Family service workers *in private agencies are primarily concerned with providing counseling services to families and individuals. They seek to strengthen family life, by improving interpersonal relationships, and to establish satisfactory relations between the family and the community.*

Child welfare workers *in government and voluntary agencies deal with the problems of children. They may find foster homes or institute legal action for the protection of neglected or mistreated children, arrange for homemaker service during the illness of a mother, arrange for adoptions or placements in specialized institutions, counsel youthful delinquents, or* advise parents on their children's problems.

School social workers or "visiting teachers" employed by school systems also help troubled children, including those who are excessively shy, aggressive, or withdrawn; failing in school subjects for no apparent reason; hungry or ill; or truants. Workers consult with parents, teachers, principals, doctors, truant officers, and other interested people. They frequently refer a child to other social work agencies in the community for help.

Medical social workers employed by hospitals, clinics, health agencies, rehabilitation centers, and public welfare agencies work directly with patients and their families, helping them meet problems accompanying illness, recovery, and rehabilitation. Usually these workers function as part of a medical team composed of doctors, nurses, and therapists.

Psychiatric social workers attend patients in mental hospitals or clinics. In clinical teams, composed of psychiatrists, psychologists, and other professional personnel, these workers help patients and their families to understand the nature of the illness, enlist the patients' aid in using the various kinds of help available, and guide the patients in their social adjustment to their homes and communities. In some organizations medical and psychiatric social workers are grouped together as "clinical social workers." Psychiatric social workers also participate in community mental health programs concerned with the prevention of mental illness and with the readjustment of mental patients to normal home and community living.

Social workers in rehabilitation services assist emotionally or physically disabled persons in adjusting to the demands of everyday living. As part of a rehabilitation team, which usually includes physical or occupational therapists, these social workers serve as a link with the community while patients are in the hospital and later help them adjust to home and community life.

Probation and parole officers and other correctional workers, who are employed primarily by Federal, State, county, and city governments, assist probationers, parolees, and juvenile offenders in their readjustment to society. They make investigations and submit reports to the courts concerning the activities of their clients. They also counsel their clients and may help them find jobs; keep a close watch on their clients' conduct; and direct them to other services in the community when possible. In addition, they frequently arrange for child placements or adoptions, provide marriage counseling, and collect court-ordered payments for support of families and children.

Social group workers are employed by a multitude of agencies—settlements and community centers; youth-serving groups; public housing developments; correctional institutions; resident and day centers for children, adolescents, or elderly people; and general and psychiatric clinics and hospitals. Group workers help individuals to develop their personalities and find satisfaction in life through group experiences in educational, recreational, or other activities. They may plan or direct group activities; or recruit, train, and supervise volunteer workers. Many administer departments and agencies which provide social group services.

Community organization workers plan welfare, health, and recreation services for the community; coordinate existing social services; develop volunteer leadership; and assist in fund raising for community social welfare activities. Usually these workers are employed by community chests, welfare councils, religious federations, health associations and federations, agencies which combine community planning and direct service, and by other professional groups in social work and related fields. Unlike other areas of social work, this field employs men in the majority. (Occupation Outlook Handbook, 1963–1964, pp. 258–259.)

she was there to help her deal with her problems. Mrs. M responded by saying her husband was her problem: because he drank so much, she did not have enough money to buy food; he kept most of his wages for himself and gave her only $10 or $15 a week. She also resented her mother-in-law's criticism of her way of rearing the children. She discussed the children's poor clothing and the fact that other children made fun of them. The family was in danger of being evicted, and Mrs. M said she hoped she could find a job to help pay the arrears of rent and the electricity and water bills. The worker told Mrs. M that she would visit her every week to help her straighten out her affairs.

During the next month Mrs. M was depressed. She complained about feeling ill and hopeless. She continued to discuss the reality problems facing the family, but she did not think the situation could ever be improved. The worker learned that Mrs. M's parents had brought her up strictly and that she had had very few friends as a child. She thought of herself as "not very bright" and she had married soon after quitting school in the tenth grade.

The worker encouraged Mrs. M to visit the school to discuss her children's problems with the teachers and praised her when she did so. She accompanied Mrs. M when she applied for emergency relief, and also took her shopping.

Some time later, Mrs. M found the strength necessary to make a court complaint against her husband for nonsupport, for the first time. The judge put him on probation and ordered him to give his wife most of his earnings. The worker continued to accompany Mrs. M when she went shopping and also helped her to make economical choices. Although Mrs. M doubted her ability to handle money, the worker helped her assume responsibility in this sphere.

In the tenth interview, the worker reported that Mrs. M was in a "fairly cheerful state." In the twelfth interview, she was in a happy mood. She said that the children were not fighting so much as they had previously, perhaps because they were no longer hungry. She also reported that her husband's behavior was much improved.

After four months of encouragement and warm support, the caseworker noted that Mrs. M had wallpapered one room and was planning to buy curtains and that the broken windows had all been replaced. Mrs. M was losing weight under the care of a physician. She purchased several new dresses for herself and was beginning to care more for her appearance. She also was learning how to wash and care for her children's hair. Mrs. M continued receiving supplementary financial assistance (Jacobucci, 1965, pp. 224–225).

Other Social Scientists

As mental health concerns go beyond narrow medical conceptions and emphasis shifts from the person to the person-in-the-environments, social scientists of many disciplines play greater and greater roles in mental health. Sociologists and cultural anthropologists have a good deal to tell us about societies and how they may be altered to achieve mental health goals. The terms "applied anthropology" and "applied sociology" as well as "clinical anthropology" and "clinical sociology" designate these areas of concern.

Applied sociologists have played key roles in the reshaping of large metropolitan areas. They have helped plan, conduct, and evaluate programs concerning juvenile delinquency and crime. They have helped improve educational and occupational conditions. They have participated in the renewal of old neighborhoods and the construction of new and better ones (Miller, 1965).

Anthropologists, sociologists and psychologists alike have provided important insights concerning the social and cultural factors in mental illness. Today there is considerable overlap in the research and applied activities of these groups of scientists. Other social scientists, such as economists, historians, and political scientists, are making contributions in this area.

The Counselor

In mental health, the terms "counseling" and "psychotherapy" are sometimes used interchangeably. However, counseling is more likely to be reserved for assistance that has to do with educational, vocational, or less severe personal problems, while psychotherapy characterizes assistance with problems of an intermediate or serious nature.

Many different workers are called counselors or provide counseling service of one kind or another. Some persons not in the field of mental health use this title, for example, life insurance counselors. Since the title "counselor" is not restricted by law, anyone can use this designation or similar ones, such as "marriage counselor," "personal problems counselor," and "family counselor." Therefore, it is necessary to use care in finding professional assistance.

The project dedicated to training lay persons as "mental health counselors" and "mental health aides" has already been mentioned. Below—briefly noted—are the activities of the psychological counselor, the rehabilitation counselor, and the school counselor.

The Psychological Counselor

Psychological counselors or counseling psychologists render some of the same kinds of assistance that clinical psychologists do. Counselors are generally more experienced in educational and vocational guidance than clinical psychologists and less experienced in dealing with personal problems of greater severity.

Counselors of this kind are found at various community agencies, clinics, and hospitals. Colleges and universities frequently have counseling centers or clinics where counseling and clinical psychologists are available to assist students with educational, vocational, and personal problems.

A master's degree (M.A.) or doctor's degree (Ph.D.) in psychology is the usual preparation for this kind of counseling. Like graduate programs in clinical psychology, counseling curricula include courses in evaluation, diagnosis, and counseling or psychotherapy.

The Rehabilitation Counselor

Rehabilitation counselors assist handicapped and disabled persons in obtaining suitable employment. These counselors may work with one kind or a variety of clients, including the deaf or blind, the mentally ill or retarded, the physically handicapped, alcoholics, and others. This work is done in close cooperation with physicians, psychiatrists, psychologists, and other professional persons who are involved in their cases as well as with actual and prospective employers.

The counselor's task includes evaluating the disabled person to determine the kind of work he can do, placing him, and helping him adjust in this placement. The counselor needs considerable ability to relate to others. He also needs considerable patience and persistence.

Some rehabilitation counselors have the master's degree (M.A.) earned in rehabilitation counseling programs or in related curricula in psychology, social work, or education. Some are graduates of doctoral programs in counseling or clinical psychology. Others have a bachelor's degree (B.A.) in addition to various kinds of work and training experience.

The School Counselor

School counselors provide counseling service for pupils in elementary and secondary schools. They also help modify school environments so that they become more suitable climates for learning.

School counselors help pupils directly; they also act as consultants, offering advice and suggestions to teachers and parents. Counselors help evaluate the interest and abilities of pupils and assist them in the selection of courses and in making employment or college plans. Counselors also arrange programs which supply the students with educational and vocational information.

School counselors generally are from teaching ranks. In fact, many of them teach or perform other duties in addition to their counseling activities. Most states issue certificates to school counselors if they have had a certain amount of experience and graduate work. Many school counselors have a master's degree.

The Volunteer

The problems of mental health and illness are being brought more and more into the community. And, as it should be, the community is being brought more and more into the problems of mental health and illness. The layman is being increasingly involved in this area as a volunteer worker and as a member of various organizations involved in mental health activities.

Local chapters of nationwide groups, such as the National Association for Mental Health, perform important tasks in the community. These organizations work to inform and arouse the community concerning the problems of mental health. They also attempt to ensure that proper facilities are available in the community for the evaluation, correction, and prevention of various kinds of problems.

Lay volunteers contribute their talents and energies in many different mental health settings. Their contributions provide an important addition to staff services. In mental hospitals, for example, these volunteers teach courses, crafts, and skills of various sorts. They also help conduct the recreational programs.

Lay volunteers may provide important sources of social stimulation and support for inpatients and outpatients. Some outpatient centers sponsor club and social activities involving both patients and volunteers, and some hospitals have established visitor or companion programs.

One interesting hospital companion program has involved college students and chronically ill mental patients. A program is set up in which each student is assigned a patient whom he then visits weekly throughout the academic year. Each student also participates in weekly meetings of the volunteers which are conducted by a member of the hospital staff. The program provides an important social relationship for the patients, many of whom have little contact with the outside world, and at the same time, helps the student achieve new insight into mental health and illness (Holzberg & Knapp, 1965; Holzberg, Whiting, & Lowy, 1964).

A pioneer volunteer program was initiated in 1954 at Metropolitan State Hospital by students at Harvard College and Radcliffe College. Since that time more than two thousand students have participated in the program. A variety of projects have been undertaken for both children and adult patients. Some of the projects have been group or ward activities and others have involved two-person (student-patient) relationships. Students working on the wards keep a diary or journal of their activities. Here are some excerpts from a diary of volunteer work and progress on an adult ward (E-3) during one school year:

10/9: Six of us altogether; we spent two hours in E-3 talking with the patients. Organized an art class which proved to be great success with many of the patients, who wish it to be continued. We asked to take patients to the courtyard, but were not allowed to because the male patients were already using it.

10/16: Five people out tonight; two took some patients bowling, and rest stayed on ward playing bingo, singing, doing jigsaw puzzles, drawing and talking. It would be hard to be too enthusiastic about the responsiveness on E-3 this evening, the patients greeted us eagerly and participated with remarkable interest and gusto in all activities..

The supervisor of the ward expressed delight at the success of this evening's work, and praised the activities. Especially pleasing to her (and to us) was the responsiveness of one who laughed and talked with enthusiasm for the first time in many months.

The only complaint was that we should come out earlier.

Next week one girl is going to bring equipment to give haircuts and another will bring her guitar.

We all enjoyed ourselves tonight, and many patients came up

to us afterwards and told us that they had had a good time.

10/30: Seven people out tonight; activities included piano and singing, checkers, puzzles, horse shoes, beanbags, and talking.

Sometimes in E-3 we can see the silhouettes of men from D-3 pressed against the door, as though they wanted to have a feeling of association or participation with our activity. So we decided to open the door, and see if they really were amenable to joining us for games, talking and other pastimes. As it happens, they weren't amenable last night. I think, though, they might be if we try a few more times.

11/10: Attended a group meeting with the resident doctor and the E-3 attendants. Both the other volunteers and myself participated actively in the discussions, all our comments were well received.

12/4: First time out after two week lapse for exams. Enthusiastic reception, with several breakthroughs to formerly uncommunicative or inactive patients.

12/18: Excellent results with lipstick applications and the lipstick to keep as a bingo prize. Established communication with a patient who has never spoken to us before; she accepted a lipstick application from another patient and seemed pleased at the compliments she drew.

2/26: I spoke to a group of patients tonight and asked them what they thought of the idea of putting on some sort of play. They seemed genuinely interested and made their own suggestions as to what kind of play they wanted—opinion ran high for a comedy, especially a light musical comedy.

Some of our volunteers came from Emerson College; they will approach the Theater Arts Dept. there for help in getting scripts.

3/17: Today we had our St. Patrick's Day party. It was highly successful. It was held on E-3, and all adjoining wards; the patients organized much of the party and this added greatly to its success.

This spreading of the volunteers into D-3 has done much for the male patients. Also, several of the women on E-3 who were at the party, commented on the dismal, drab appearance of the male ward and expressed a desire to help the men improve their surroundings. I think it might be a good project for us to paint and decorate the men's side.

3/19: We've gotten permission from Dr. McLaughlin to take girls onto C-3 and D-3 (male wards for the very sick patients) in the evenings, and the blessing of Mrs. Holmes to do sewing and crafts projects for the improvement of E-3 curtains, wastebaskets, and so forth.

Taking the women from E-3 onto the male wards for dancing is a joy to watch. This advance onto men's wards is of incalculable importance.

3/21: On E-3 we've started for the first time to aim directly at group dynamics—group activities that are united, and require patient interaction. It was not particularly easy tonight, for many of our "best" patients were at a party, elsewhere. But we did make a hard try at charades. The game was tough; the patients slow to catch on. Enthusiasm was only spotty. But the important point to note is that patients who at the onset withdrew from the group, and who refused flatly to participate, did ultimately take part—at first hesitantly, then more willing—in the game.

4/23: Banjo playing was highly successful last week. First part of the evening was used for the play-reading. Only three patients participated—the others claiming poor eyesight, etc., but they did quite well.

For the first time all year, Diana, the Greek-speaking patient stopped talking to herself and came over—completely voluntarily—to sit with the group.[7]

SUMMARY

New ideas concerning mental illness and new approaches in dealing with it have been reflected in treatment facilities. Mental hospitals have undergone three main changes. First, they have moved from being primarily custodial institutions toward being more therapeutic ones. Second, they have moved from relative isolation to a place in the community. Third, they have taken an increasing responsibility for changing the community to facilitate the recovery of troubled persons.

Partial-hospitalization programs—in effect, semihospitals—have been established for persons who need less than around-the-clock care but more than one or two or three hours a week of outpatient service. These programs include the day hospital, the night hospital, and the weekend hospital.

[7] Umbarger, C. C., Dalsimer, J. S., Morrison, A. P., & Breggin, P. R. College Students in a Mental Hospital. New York: Grune & Stratton, 1962. By permission. Pp. 26–28.

A number of other residential facilities have been established for persons who do not require intensive care. The residential or halfway house provides a home for persons who are not ready to become full members of their families or communities. The foster home, or family care program, provides a home for a person within a private family.

Other facilities include the sheltered workshop and the social club. The former is a resource for training people who have been disabled by injury or illness. The latter is an organization established for individuals who share common adjustment problems.

A new and promising facility is the community mental health center. Such centers are planned to provide a complete and coordinated program of services within a community. These centers would provide help for people of all ages and with all kinds of mental illness and adjustment problems.

Among the most important workers concerned with improving adjustment are ministers. There are more clergymen than all other mental health personnel combined, and they are frequently consulted by members of their congregation in times of trouble.

Physicians also play an important role in this area. People frequently turn to their family doctor in times of stress, and he can play a vital role in the prevention and alleviation of maladjustment and mental illness.

Psychiatrists are physicians who specialize in the diagnosis and treatment of mental illness and adjustment problems. Psychiatric treatment takes many different forms and occurs in many different settings. Some psychiatrists are in private practice; others are on the staffs of clinics, hospitals, and other mental health facilities.

Psychoanalysts, generally speaking, are physicians who have been trained to treat adjustment problems through the use of psychoanalytic methods. In its classical form, psychoanalysis is an intensive, extensive, and expensive process. There are, however, some newer and briefer forms of psychoanalysis.

Many workers serve as nurses in medical and psychiatric facilities. There are, for example, the practical nurse, the ward attendant, and the psychiatric technician. Psychiatric nurses combine both nursing and psychiatric training. Such nurses work in hospitals and in a variety of outpatient services.

An occupational therapist is a person who is trained to help people recover from illness through constructive activities, that is, through being occupied in meaningful ways. Occupational therapists work with people of all ages and with various kinds of illnesses and handicaps. By involving the person in creative, educational, physical, and recreational activities, the therapist helps him regain strength and skill as well as confidence and a sense of worth.

Psychologists of varying descriptions work in the field of mental health. The clinical psychologist occupies a very central position. He is trained in evaluating and changing behavior. He also is responsible for a good deal of research that is done in mental health and illness.

Social workers provide a wide range of services in mental illness. Some social workers, called caseworkers, deal directly with individuals and families. Others, called group workers, employ group experiences to benefit both the individual and the larger society. A few social workers, called organizational community workers, work to improve the social welfare facilities of the entire community.

In addition to these workers, many other people play a part in improvement processes. These include sociologists, anthropologists, and other social scientists, counselors of various kinds, and last but not least, lay volunteers.

REFERENCES

Adler, M. D. An analysis of role conflicts of the clergy in mental health work. *Journal of Pastoral Care,* 1965, **19**(2), 65–75.

Albee, G. W. *Mental Health Manpower Trends.* New York: Basic Books, 1959.

Barton, W. E. Introduction. In R. M. Glasscote, D. S. Saunders, H. M. Forstenzer, & A. R. Foley, *The Community Mental Health Center.* Washington, D.C.: Joint Information Service of the American Psychiatric Association and the National Association for Mental Health, 1964. Pp. xiii–xvi.

Blain, D. The organization of psychiatry in the United States. In S. Arieti (Ed.), *American Handbook of Psychiatry.* Vol. 2. New York: Basic Books, 1959. Pp. 1960–1982.

Caplan, G. *An Approach to Community Mental Health.* New York: Grune & Stratton, 1961.

English, O. S., & Finch, S. M. *Introduction to Psychiatry.* (2nd ed.) New York: Norton, 1957.

Fidler, G. S., & Fidler, J. W. *Occupational Therapy.* New York: Macmillan, 1963.

Glasscote, R., Sanders, D., Forstenzer, H. M., & Foley, A. R. *The Community Mental Health Center.* Washington, D.C.: Joint Information Service of the American Psychiatric Association and the National Association for Mental Health, 1964.

Greenblatt, M., & Levinson, D. Mental hospitals. In B. B. Wolman (Ed.), *Handbook of Clinical Psychology.* New York: McGraw-Hill, 1965. Pp. 1343–1359.

Gurin, G., Veroff, J., & Feld, S. *Americans View Their Mental Health.* New York: Basic Books, 1960.

Hilgard, E. R. Experimental approaches to psychoanalysis. In E. Pumpian-Mindlin (Ed.), *Psychoanalysis as Science.* New York: Basic Books, 1952. Pp. 3–45.

Holzberg, J. D., & Knapp, R. H. The social interaction of college students and chronically ill mental patients. *American Journal of Orthopsychiatry,* 1965, **35**(3), 487–492.

——, **Whiting, H. S., & Lowy, D. G.** Chronic patients and a college companion program. *Mental Hospital,* 1964, **15**(3), 152–158.

Jacobucci, L. Casework treatment of the neglectful mother. *Social Casework,* 1965, **46**(4), 221–226.

Kramer, B. M. *Day Hospital.* New York: Grune & Stratton, 1962.

Levine, M., & Lederer, H. D. Teaching of psychiatry in medical schools. In S. Arieti (Ed.), *American Handbook of Psychiatry.* Vol. 2. New York: Basic Books, 1959. Pp. 1923–1934.

Lief, V. F., & Lief, N. R. The general practitioner and psychiatric problems. In H. I. Lief, V. F. Lief, & N. R. Lief (Eds.), *The Psychological Basis of Medical Practice.* New York: Hoeber-Harper, 1963. Pp. 485–500.

McCann, R. V. *The Churches and Mental Health.* New York: Basic Books, 1962.

Malmquist, C. P. Psychiatry in a Midwestern metropolitan community. *Mental Hygiene,* 1964, **48,** 55–65.

Miller, A. A., & Sabshin, M. Psychotherapy in psychiatric hospitals. *Archives of General Psychiatry,* 1963, **9,** 53–63.

Miller, S. M. Prospects: The applied sociology of the center city. In Λ. W. Gouldner & S. M. Miller (Eds.), *Applied Sociology.* New York: Free Press, 1965. Pp. 441–456.

Moll, A. E. Psychiatric night treatment unit in a general hospital. *American Journal of Psychiatry,* 1957, **113,** 722–727.

Nameche, G. F. Pastoral counseling in Protestant churches. Part I. The minister as counselor. Unpublished manuscript, 1958. Cited by R. V. McCann, *The Churches and Mental Health.* New York: Basic Books, 1962. Pp. 76–80.

Occupational Outlook Handbook. U.S. Department of Labor, 1963–1964.

Olshansky, S. The transitional sheltered workshop: A survey. *Journal of Social Issues,* 1960, **16** (2), 33–39.

Padula, H. Foster homes for the mentally ill. *Mental Hygiene,* 1964, **48,** 366–371.

Peplau, H. E. Principles of psychiatric nursing. In S. Arieti (Ed.), *American Handbook of Psychiatry.* Vol. 2. New York: Basic Books, 1959. Pp. 1840–1856.

Robinson, R., DeMarche, D. F., & Wagle, M. K. *Community Resources in Mental Health.* New York: Basic Books, 1960.

Rosenbaum, M. Treatment of psychosomatic disorders. In H. I. Lief, V. F. Lief, & N. R. Lief (Eds.), *The Psychological Basis of Medical Practice.* New York: Hoeber-Harper, 1963. Pp. 501–509.

Rothwell, N. D., & Doniger, J. Halfway house and mental hospital: Some comparisons. *Psychiatry,* 1963, **26,** 281–288.

Sundberg, N. D., & Tyler, L. E. *Clinical Psychology.* New York: Appleton-Century-Crofts, 1962.

Umbarger, C. C., Dalsimer, J. S., Morrison, A. P., & Breggin, P. R. *College Students in a Mental Hospital.* New York: Grune & Stratton, 1962.

Vernallis, F. F., & Reinert, R. E. The weekend hospital. *Mental Hospitals,* May, 1963. Pp. 254–258.

Wechsler, H. The expatient organization: A survey. *Journal of Social Issues,* 1960, **16** (2), 47–53. (a)

———. Halfway houses for former mental patients: A survey. *Journal of Social Issues,* 1960, **16** (2), 20–26. (b)

PART FOUR

SOME
IMPORTANT
AREAS
OF ADJUSTMENT

CHAPTER ELEVEN

FAMILY ADJUSTMENT

Most of us spend most of our lives in a family. We begin our lives in a family setting, grow up in it, and then marry and begin a family of our own. Our living is family living.

Early family experience is of great importance in the formation of personality. Adult adjustment patterns are heavily influenced by childhood events. Even though a person may be far distant and a long time away from the home in which he grew up, he is probably not removed from its effects.

This chapter and the one that follows examine some aspects of family adjustment. This chapter defines family adjustment and describes some ways it has been studied. The following chapter presents some important patterns of parent-child relationships. You may find it helpful to relate these several discussions to your own family and to other families with which you are acquainted.

DEFINING FAMILY ADJUSTMENT

When we begin to talk about families and begin to evaluate them, we tend to use certain adjectives. We speak, for example, of families that are old and respectable. We speak of problem families and of families that are successful. Sometimes we simply speak of good families.

If we say that Mr. Such-and-Such comes from an "old" family, we probably mean that his family has a high and long-established position in the community. If, however, we refer to Mr. Such-and-Such's family as a "respectable" one, we more likely imply that it is neither well-to-do nor socially prominent, but that its members are proper and conventional in their behavior. "Poor *but* respectable" is a phrase that poor but respectable people tend to use in describing themselves.

When we speak of a family as "successful," we frequently refer to its improved socioeconomic status. Does the family get ahead? Does it raise its standard of living? Is it able to move to a better house in a better neighborhood? Are its children granted opportunities the parents never had? We can, of course, think of families which seem to be social and economic successes but which, in some sense, are "psychological" failures. And, conversely, we can think of families which have little position or wealth but are psychological successes.

If someone is speaking of a "problem family," the someone is apt to be a social worker, but it might also be a teacher, a policeman, or some other representative of one of the community's organizations. Problem families have a history of some combination of social, legal, economic, and health problems which have made them well known to the community's agencies. Probably, too, they come from "problem neighborhoods"—neighborhoods that have a number of problem families.

If someone speaks of a "good family," it might be difficult to guess exactly what is implied. Of course, he means that the family has certain qualities which are valued and thought desirable, but what one person values highly, another may value much less or not at all. One person, for example, may consider a wealthy or socially established family a good family while another might reserve this designation for families with other characteristics.

Suppose we make use of the adjective "adjusted" to describe a family. What might we mean? We frequently speak of individuals who are well adjusted and maladjusted, but it is less often that we think of a whole family in these terms. What would a well-adjusted family be like? What would constitute a maladjusted family?

The material that follows will introduce some possible definitions of family adjustment. The first defines family adjustment in terms of physical coherence. The second involves an overall assessment of the family's happiness. The third considers how well the family achieves certain tasks or performs certain functions. And the fourth estimates a family's adjustment from its ability to meet and deal with the problems it faces.

Family Adjustment as Coherence

This approach to a definition of family adjustment considers whether or not the family coheres or stays together. Does it continue to exist as a physical entity? Or does it disintegrate? Does one parent or the other desert the home? Do the parents separate or divorce? Do the children leave the home before they might be expected to?

One definition of the word "family" is that it is "a group of persons living together in one household" (English & English, 1958, p. 202). A family that continues a common physical existence meets this basic requirement. Its members would appear to show some ability to accommodate one another.

The definition is attractive for a number of reasons. It is simple. It can be fairly easily and objectively determined. And it states a seemingly basic criterion.

On the other hand, such a definition has limitations. These limitations stem from the definition's minimal nature. A family that simply coheres hardly seems to merit the adjective "adjusted." We would expect it to meet other criteria as well.

The coherence of the family may be due to necessity rather than choice. Young children are usually unable to leave their home whether they want to or not. Some adults remain in nearly intolerable home situations because they have no alternative; bad as it is, they may have no better place to go.

Family Adjustment as Happiness

Another approach to a definition of family adjustment considers the happiness of the various members of the family. Many of us equate adjustment with happiness. To us a well-adjusted family is a happy one, or to put it the other way around, a happy family is a well-adjusted one. Certainly, it

is difficult to think of an unhappy family as very well adjusted.

This definition, like the first one, has a number of limitations. What exactly is meant by "happiness"? This word means different things to different people. How can we know that a person who reports himself as "happy" is really happier than the one who reports that he is "unhappy"?

If we try to form an objective assessment by having observers rate a family on some happiness dimension, we run into other problems. Some individuals attempt to give the appearance of happiness whether they are happy or not. In the same way, some families place a great store on appearing happy or harmonious; they go to great lengths to conceal their problems from the neighborhood and the community, and their appearances then can be deceiving.

The general happiness of a family varies from time to time depending on many changing circumstances. Some families seem to express a wide range of feeling, with moments of high spirits and low spirits; others appear to be on a more even keel, showing few extremes of feeling. Furthermore, within a particular family, there are many interpersonal differences in happiness: some members may be relatively happy while others are much less so.

As part of a comprehensive investigation of subjects from 100 large families, each person was asked to rate the relative happiness of the home in which he or she had grown up. Specifically, they were asked whether the "general tone" of their family was "happy," "medium," or "unhappy." Of the group, 50 rated their families as "happy," 36 as "medium," and 14 as "unhappy."

The investigators looked for the factors that made for happy, unhappy, and medium-happy families. They concluded:

> In . . . happy families . . . the cultivation of family rituals, conscious efforts of parents to promote family group life, and especially administrative and managerial ability on the part of the mother, were revealed rather clearly as important factors in the development of happy large family living.
>
> A study of the unhappy large families emphasizes the importance of the father's misbehavior, such as drinking and vile temper; the mother's ineffectiveness; the disorganization that appears in immigrant families because of intergenerational conflicts; and the death of a parent, followed by the subsequent remarriage of the other parent, with additional "flocks" of children.
>
> The medium happy families were those where the basic family situation was sound, and the family would have been completely happy but for some disturbing factor. Such factors include economic pressure, domineering fathers, ineffective mothers, favoritism toward some one or more of the children, the antics of some one troublesome sibling, cultural differences between parents, and the feelings of shame about the size of the family (Bossard & Boll, 1956, pp. 104–105).

Family Adjustment as Task Achievement

A third way of defining a family's adjustment is in terms of its ability to fulfill certain functions or achieve certain tasks which are generally set for families. Duvall (1962) who employs this approach uses the term "successful" rather than "adjusted" to describe families who are able to accomplish a number of basic tasks as they occur throughout the family's life cycle.

The functions served by families have varied over the years, and they differ from culture to culture. Some of the historic activities of the family have been taken over by other institutions of the community. Still every family is called upon to fulfill certain essential functions.

In the American culture, the family is primarily responsible for the economic support, the psychological well-being, and the social conduct of its members. Parents are ordinarily held accountable for their children's welfare, but if the parents fail, various agencies of the community may move in to take a hand with the family's affairs or with the conduct of its individual members.

The family is called upon to serve both its own members and the larger society. It is charged with seeing that its members meet their individual needs. At the same time, it is called upon to shape and modify these needs so that its members can live harmoniously both within the family circle and in the community.

Families that achieve these economic, psychological, and social ends are considered adjusted or successful. Of course, no family is completely successful or unsuccessful. Each may perform some tasks relatively well and fulfill others poorly. And each family may be expected to have varying success throughout its life cycle; for example, some families seem to do better when the children are young and some when the children are older and more on their own.

Family Adjustment as Problem Solving

A fourth way of defining family adjustment considers the problems associated with the family. Some problems may be largely contained within the family circle itself;

Presentation 11.1 According to Duvall, a "successful" family is able to accomplish a number of tasks which occur during the family's life cycle. Here are the tasks that have been noted for each of the nine stages of the cycle.

FAMILY DEVELOPMENTAL TASKS

Beginning Families: Establishment Phase
1 Establishing a home base in a place to call their own
2 Establishing mutually satisfactory systems for getting and spending money
3 Establishing mutually acceptable patterns of who does what and who is accountable to whom
4 Establishing a continuity of mutually satisfying sex relationships
5 Establishing systems of intellectual and emotional communication
6 Establishing workable relationships with relatives
7 Establishing ways of interacting with friends, associates, and community organizations
8 Facing the possibility of children and planning for their coming
9 Establishing a workable philosophy of life as a couple

Beginning Families: Expectant Phase
1 Arranging for the physical care of the expected baby
2 Developing new patterns for getting and spending income
3 Revaluating procedures for determining who does what and where authority rests
4 Adapting patterns of sexual relationships to pregnancy
5 Expanding communication systems for present and anticipated emotional needs
6 Reorienting relationships with relatives
7 Adapting relationships with friends, associates, and community activities to the realities of pregnancy
8 Acquiring knowledge about and planning for the specifics of pregnancy, childbirth, and parenthood

9 Maintaining morale and a workable philosophy of life

Childbearing Families
1 Adapting housing arrangements for the life of the little child
2 Meeting the costs of family living at the childbearing stage
3 Reworking patterns of mutual responsibility and accountability
4 Re-establishing mutually satisfying sexual relationships
5 Refining intellectual and emotional communication systems for childbearing and rearing
6 Re-establishing working relationships with relatives
7 Fitting into community life as a young family
8 Planning for further children in the family
9 Reworking a suitable philosophy of life as a family

Families with Preschool Children
1 Supplying adequate space, facilities, and equipment for the expanding family
2 Meeting predictable and unexpected costs of family life with small children
3 Sharing responsibilities within the expanded family and between members of the growing family
4 Maintaining mutually satisfying sexual relationships and planning for future children
5 Creating and maintaining effective communication systems within the family
6 Cultivating the full potentials of relationships with relatives within the extended family
7 Tapping resources, serving needs, and enjoying contacts outside the family
8 Facing dilemmas and reworking philosophies of life in ever-changing challenges

Families with School Children
1 Providing for children's activity and parents' privacy
2 Keeping financially solvent
3 Cooperating to get things done
4 Continuing to satisfy each other as married partners

5 Effectively utilizing family communication systems
6 Feeling close to relatives in the larger family
7 Tying in with life outside the family
8 Testing and retesting family philosophies of life

Families with Teenagers
1 Providing facilities for widely different needs
2 Working out money matters in the family with teenagers
3 Sharing the tasks and responsibilities of family living
4 Putting the marriage relationship into focus
5 Keeping communication systems open
6 Maintaining contact with the extended family
7 Growing into the world as a family and as persons
8 Reworking and maintaining a philosophy of life

Families as Launching Centers
1 Rearranging physical facilities and resources
2 Meeting the costs as launching center families
3 Reallocating responsibilities among grown and growing children
4 Coming to terms with themselves as husband and wife
5 Maintaining open systems of communication within the family and between the family and others
6 Widening the family circle through release of young adult children and recruitment of new members by marriage
7 Reconciling conflicting loyalties and philosophies of life

Families in the Middle Years
1 Maintaining a pleasant and comfortable home
2 Assuring security for the later years
3 Carrying household responsibilities
4 Drawing closer together as a couple
5 Maintaining contact with grown children's families
6 Keeping in touch with brothers' and sisters' families and with aging parents
7 Participating in community life beyond the family
8 Reaffirming the values of life that have real meaning

Aging Families
1 Finding a satisfying home for the later years
2 Adjusting to retirement income
3 Establishing comfortable household routines
4 Nurturing each other as husband and wife
5 Facing bereavement and widowhood
6 Maintaining contact with children and grandchildren
7 Caring for elderly relatives
8 Keeping an interest in people outside the family
9 Finding meanings in life (Reprinted by permission from *Family Development* by Evelyn M. Duvall, published by J. B. Lippincott Company. Copyright © 1962, 1957 by J. B. Lippincott Company.)

---

these may be thought of as "family problems." Other problems spill over and affect the family's functioning in the neighborhood and community; families with problems of this kind are called "problem families."

Family Problems

Just as no individual is without frustrations and conflicts, no family is free of strife. And just as the individual struggles to deal with his problems, families struggle to work out solutions to the difficulties which face them.

Ackerman, a prominent worker in the area of family relationships, feels that it is possible to conceptualize a continuum of family problem-solving success and failure. Every family would fall somewhere along the continuum depending upon how well it was currently dealing with its problems. A family's position on the continuum would vary from time to time as it enjoyed increasing success or suffered accelerating failure with its problem-solving efforts.

Ackerman distinguishes a number of "levels" of problem solving which he feels are useful in family diagnosis. Actually these levels are points along the continuum that are useful in pegging a family's current adjustment and in plotting its movement toward success or failure. These points or levels are as follows:

1 *The family confronts, accurately defines, and achieves a realistic solution of its problems.*
2 *Though unable to achieve a realistic solution, the family can nevertheless contain the problem and control the potentially noxious effects, while giving itself a longer period within which to find a solution.*
3 *Unable to find an effective solution or to contain the destructive effects of the conflict, the family responds to the tension of failure with an "acting out" pattern of impulsive, ill-judged, self-defeating, harmful behavior. Sometimes the family as a group seeks a scapegoat, either within the family or outside. In this condition the family as family cannot long maintain its defenses.*
4 *With persistent failure at the preceding three levels, the family shows increasing signs of emotional disintegration, which in some circumstances may culminate in disorganization of family ties.*[1]

Hansen and Hill (1964) present a somewhat different approach to family problem solving. Their model of family-crisis behavior has a roller-coaster profile which moves through four stages: stress → disorganization → recovery → reorganization

[1] From *The Psychodynamics of Family Life,* Copyright © 1958 by Nathan N. Ackerman, Basic Books, Inc., Publishers, New York. Pp. 99–100.

(see Fig. 11.1). The first reaction to stress may be seemingly a lack of reaction, a numbness, or a defensive maneuver. As tension mounts and old patterns prove inadequate, the family becomes disorganized. Then, as new behaviors are instituted, the family begins to recover and then to reorganize.

This model seems to describe a good deal of family-crisis behavior. It has been found to fit, for example, the adjustment made by a group of families, each with an alcoholic father. Jackson (1956), who studied these families, noted seven rather than four phases of adjustment, but the overall patterning closely matched the roller-coaster profile.

The stress stage was made up of two phases. The first phase was characterized by attempts to deny or play down the importance of the drinking episodes. So that the strain on the marriage might be reduced, other problems were minimized as well, and each spouse attempted to be a model mate.

The second phase was characterized by attempts to eliminate the problem. Mounting alcoholism was matched by mounting efforts at control. Husband and wife became increasingly alienated from each other, and the family became increasingly alienated from the outside world in an attempt to reduce the visibility of the problem and avoid ostracism.

The third stage was marked by disorganization. Attempts to control and hide the problem became sporadic or were abandoned entirely. The family's goal was progressively reduced from permanent sobriety to any sobriety to simply reducing tension.

The fourth and fifth phases marked the recovery process. Not all families which

were studied went through the fourth and fifth phases, nor did all families progress beyond these phases. In the fourth phase the wife took over as head of the family. There was no further pretense about the husband's occupation of husband and father roles, and he was relegated to a child's status. This phase was still filled with tension because of the husband's drinking and the behavior associated with it.

The fifth phase was characterized by the wife's attempt to escape the problem by separation from the husband. Infidelity, violence, imprisonment, or desertion might have prompted this decision. The increasing realization that the family could do better without the alcoholic father as well as increasing assistance from community agencies sometimes bolstered the decision.

Finally there was a reorganization of the family either with the father if he regained sobriety (sixth phase) or without him if he attempted and failed or failed to attempt (seventh phase). A reshuffling of roles and patterns of activities occurred. Little by little, the family stabilized itself and resumed its place in the community.

Problem Families

Problem families—or multiproblem families as they are increasingly called—are families which fail to work out a harmonious interaction with the community. The members of these families may be in constant trouble with various agencies because of truancy, delinquency, or crime, poor hygiene or disease, economic privation, or general failure to observe the minimum standards of their community. These families may fail to cope with the basic problems of living, such as finding employment or support, maintaining a home, or feeding, clothing, and caring for their children. There may be desertion by a parent, excessive drinking, fighting, filth, promiscuity, or disorder.

Studies of multiproblem families indicate that they generally share a number of common characteristics.[2] Some of these pertain to the internal processes of the family and some to the interaction of the family with the community. The several sets, of course, are closely interwoven.

Within the multiproblem family, parent-child relationships are generally un-

[2] This discussion is largely based on a review by Schlesinger (1963).

Figure 11.1 How does a family react to crisis? A common reaction to acute stress is illustrated in the diagram. The adjustment proceeds in this way: stress → disorganization → recovery → reorganization. As the diagram indicates, a particular family may not regain its previous level of organization (From Hansen & Hill, 1964, p. 810).

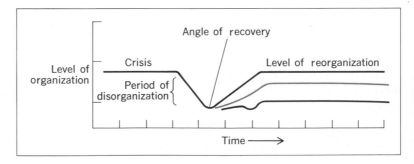

favorable and various members appear inadequate or incompetent to play usual family roles. The father may be unable to secure or keep a job and provide direction for the family. The mother may be unable to maintain a home and provide proper care for the children. The children may be unable to participate effectively in neighborhood or school activities.

In the community, the family may show exploiting, dependent, or generally incompetent behavior. There may be exploitation of the community through general imposition, petty theft, delinquency, or crime. There may be persistent dependence on the community agencies for support and guidance. Or there may be a failure to seek help or to respond to help when it is offered.

Some other characteristics associated with multiproblem families are large size and high mobility. Such families tend to contain a large number of children, and there is frequent moving about from one apartment or house to another, and frequently from one neighborhood or community to another.

Associated with high mobility is social isolation. The multiproblem family generally is not part of a kinship group. Nor

---

Presentation 11.2 What problems do families have? Some evidence concerning this question was gathered as part of a study by the United Presbyterian Church. Anonymously, 448 spouses from all over the United States completed a problem check list. Only one spouse was taken from a family; the average respondent was between thirty and forty years of age, lived in a city of around 100,000, and had two or three children. The responses of husbands and wives and college and noncollege respondents were analyzed separately, but there were few significant differences. The instructions to the respondents were as follow: "Most parents know of some things in their family which disturb them, things needing improvement. Remembering this questionnaire is anonymous, will you please check those items which you saw as a problem needing solution during the past year." Here are the problem items listed in the order of the frequency with which they were checked (not the order in which they were listed for the respondent):

Item	Percentage of Respondents Checking Item as Problem
1 TV and radio listening habits	46
2 Too little time spent together as a family	45
3 Recreation and leisure time, including visiting	40
4 How children are disciplined	35
5 Husband's job and its demands	22
6 Behavior of children	22
7 Lack of closeness between brothers and sisters	18
8 Amount of income	18
9 Health of family members	16
10 Children's achievement	16
11 Who does what among family responsibilities	16
12 Religious life and church participation of family	14
13 Tenseness and low morale in the family	12
14 How income is spent	10
15 Community as a place to live	10
16 Family's housing and furniture	9
17 Sex relations with mate	8
18 Family's community activity	7
19 Wife's work at home or outside home	7
20 Lack of closeness between husband and wife	7
21 Conflict of religious views in family	7
22 Family's action for community and world betterment	6
23 Friendships of family members	6
24 Other problems	5
25 Drinking by family members	4

(Brim, Fairchild, & Borgatta, 1961)

does it have close ties with neighboring families. It frequently appears to be alienated from its immediate as well as its larger environment.

One more characteristic should be noted. Multiproblem families often appear to be centered around the mother. The father may be inadequate or absent. There may never have been a father in anything more than a biological sense, or there may be a succession of "fathers." In such cases, the mother is nearly the sole source of support and direction.

STUDYING FAMILY ADJUSTMENT

Because of its great importance, the family has been much studied and written about. Many investigators have focused on the interaction between marriage partners and parental pairs. Many have been concerned about the interaction between parents and children. Some have been interested in the relationship between brothers and sisters. And a few have attempted to consider the family as a whole.

Studying Marital Pairs

Much has been written about dating, courtship, and marriage behavior. Among the main areas of research has been a concern with the ways in which spouses interact during the span of their relationship.

It is common knowledge that in a particular marital pair the pattern of interaction may change considerably from the engagement to the marriage period. During the engagement period, both parties may be on their best behavior. With marriage, a woman who overlooked or forgave her fiancé's shortcomings, may decide to

"help" her mate overcome them. And her husband may decide to reciprocate the "assistance" (Haley, 1963).

How much adjusting there is to do in early marriage is related to the amount of adjusting that was done before it. Young couples of old acquaintance—couples who have dated or been engaged for a relatively long period—have had a chance to try and test patterns of interaction. Research evidence indicates such couples have a greater chance for happiness in marriage.

In general, interaction in the first few weeks and months of marriage is rather intense, but it becomes less so with the passing years. A couple may become increasingly disengaged from each other and increasingly engaged in other activities. Children arrive and the wife may become more and more involved with them while the husband occupies himself with his career.

Many aspects of the marital interaction decline with increasing age. This is particularly true of sexual activity. In the earlier years of marriage, marital intercourse is frequent, averaging two or three times per week. With the passing years, intercourse becomes less frequent (Kinsey, Pomeroy, & Martin, 1948; Kinsey, Pomeroy, Martin, & Gebhard, 1953).

Inside the home, there may be less conversation and sharing of experience. In one study, it was noted that young couples related more closely to each other than did older ones. Young husbands would tell their wives about their daytime activities, and young wives would tell their troubles to their husbands, but older couples were much less likely to interact in this way (Blood & Wolfe, 1960).

Outside the home there may be less sharing of leisure-time pursuits. Evidence concerning this point was gathered in a follow-up study of couples who had been married for up to twenty years. The results indicated a sharp drop in the amount of mutual activities outside the home (Pineo, 1961).

Robert O. Blood, Jr. (1962), upon whose writing the present discussion draws, suggests that couples should set out to maintain (or recapture) their interaction. He notes the importance of both dialogue and doing things together. He recommends that spouses reserve time for themselves apart from general familial interaction, that romantic rituals be maintained, and that new activities be planned to relieve boredom and routine.

Studying Parental Pairs

Some authorities feel that the arrival of the first child presents more difficulty than the early months of marriage. Certainly for many couples, the advent of parenthood is a critical period which necessitates considerable readjustment. In a majority of the couples that have been studied in this regard, the coming of the first child was found to produce crises which were strong enough to be classified as extensive or severe. Although the couples, for the most part, made satisfactory recoveries, their relationship was considerably altered (Dyer, 1963; LeMasters, 1957).

Parenthood may serve either to strengthen or to weaken affectional bonds between a couple. The coming of children may give the marriage a deeper meaning and purpose, or it may put an intolerable strain on an already fragile relationship. Some couples are brought closer together by their children only to drift apart again when the children are grown and gone.

Other spouses, who have invested more and more of their affection in their children and who find themselves gradually estranged over the years, rediscover each other as their children begin to find lives of their own.

Ackerman (1958) writes, "A marital relationship is something beyond the sum of the personalities that make it up. The relationship itself tends to influence and change each partner and this in turn influences the relationship anew." He points out that some persons who seem well enough adjusted before they are married exhibit a number of problems afterward; conversely, some individuals who seem marginally adjusted before marriage achieve a better adjustment in marriage. He also notes that, although it is not the rule, "certain pairs of neurotic parents, despite distortions of individual personality, interact in such a way as to create emotionally healthy children. Other pairs, in which the man and woman are apparently healthy persons, produce disturbed children."

Not all authorities agree with Ackerman. For example, Baldwin and his associates (1945) hold that health in the parent is a prerequisite to health in the child. Some evidence on this contested point was provided by an intensive study of nine mentally healthy adolescents and their families. The parents were found to be quite varied in their quality of adjustment, and most of them, considered individually, were not so healthy as their offspring. Nevertheless, the marital relationships in these families were good ones, and sound environments were provided the children (Westley & Epstein, 1960).

The interaction of spouses will not be pursued further at this point. The next chapter will touch upon this area, and a later chapter on marriage will examine the matter in detail.

Studying Parent and Child

Researchers have been very concerned about studying the effect that particular patterns of parental attitudes and behavior have on children. Usually, however, the mother has been the focus of study because of her estimated importance and also because of her greater accessibility. Fathers, by contrast, have been largely disregarded. Only in recent years have studies focusing on the importance of the father begun to appear along with a few that have attempted to include both parents.

Do mothers have a greater effect on children than fathers? It is commonly assumed that the influence of the mother is greater. This assumption seems to be related to the idea that the early years of the child are of paramount importance, and during this time the child is usually in much closer contact with the mother than with the father.

Brim (1959), however, points out that actually very little is known about which parent has the greater influence. He maintains that a more meaningful question concerns the amount and kind of influence which each parent has in various areas of the child's continuing development. As a case in point, he refers to the process in which a boy learns the male role; he says, "In a child's learning how to behave as a man, it certainly could be argued that the role of the father in acting as model for his son equals or surpasses in importance the influence of the mother."

Research suggests some interesting differences which children perceive in mothers and fathers (Becker, 1964). In children's reports, mothers are usually pictured as more nurturant and loving while fathers are seen as stricter and more fear arousing. The same-sex parent is perceived as both more benevolent and more frustrating, and the opposite-sex parent as more likely to allow autonomy. Fathers are described as using more physical discipline (especially with boys), and mothers more psychological or nonphysical discipline (especially with girls).

Of course, many other environmental forces have an effect on the child, and these may serve to bolster, reduce, or modify the contribution of the parents. The child may be substantially affected by any or all of the family group, including brothers and sisters, grandparents, and other relatives. Neighborhood children and adults, schoolmates and teachers may also have considerable effect.

We have been speculating about the effects that parents (and others) have on children, but what effect do children have on parents? This question may startle us because we are so used to having it posed the other way around. It seems that we have a tendency to assume that the family involves a largely one-way interaction in which the parents are the influencers and the children are the influenced. But, as was already indicated, each family involves a complex network of interaction, with each member influencing and being influenced by each other.

Parents may respond differently to each of their children. One child may evoke greater parental affection or irritation than another. Despite his efforts to the contrary, a parent may find that he has developed a special attachment to one of his children or perhaps a definite antagonism toward one.

In considering this matter, one set of investigators notes how the personality of the parent can interact with the personality and characteristics of the child to produce a particular effect. They write:

The personality of the parent alone . . . is not sufficient for the understanding of any particular adult's adjustment to parenthood. The characteristics of the child are also important in determining the parental reaction to him. Is he ugly, misshapen, and repulsive, or is he well-formed, beautiful, and adorable? If he is advanced in his development he may be a source of pride to his parents, whereas if he doesn't get his teeth at the right age or walk as soon as the average, his parents may feel inferior about him. If he is mischievous he may drive his mother to distraction; if he is obedient and well-behaved, he will be a great satisfaction to some parents and a source of anxiety to others who would consider him spiritless and apathetic. All these personal traits will have an influence in determining the parent's attitude to the child (Baldwin, Kalhorn, & Breese, 1945, pp. 2–3).

The next chapter will examine some salient patterns of parent-child relationships. This area is complex and provocative, and research has provided some interesting insights and suggestions.

Studying Siblings

Children in the same family—siblings—generally spend a good deal of time in each other's company. In fact, during much of their childhood, siblings may spend more hours in interaction with each other than with their parents. And sibling interaction can be particularly intense and intimate. "Life among siblings," it has been said, "is like living in the nude psychologically speaking" (Bossard & Boll, 1960).

Despite the considerable importance of sibling relationships, relatively little research has been done in this area. A number of reasons have been suggested for this lack of pursuit. One reason is the overriding importance that has been placed on parent-child relationships and upon the earliest care and training experiences. Another reason is the greater difficulties in studying sibling groups than peer groups or parent-child pairs (Irish, 1964).

Siblings teach each other and learn from each other. They hammer out their patterns of adjustment in the give and take of family existence. There is constant sibling cooperation and rivalry, sharing and preempting, alliance and disalliance.

Siblings serve parental functions. They nurture and dominate each other. They may provide each other with affection, belonging, and a sense of security.

Siblings serve each other as role models. Younger sibs, in particular, may shape their behavior from the examples of older ones. Of course, the process can also work in reverse.

Sibling relationships appear to be influenced by several factors. The number of children in the family and their differences in age, sex, and personality—all are important considerations. Each child's relationship with his parents and with other important persons in the household must also be taken into account (see Table 11.1).

Sibling interactions are complicated processes, but here in brief are some hypotheses which have stemmed from the simplest sibships—the two-child family. Some evidence concerning these families suggests that a boy with an older sister (especially one close in age) may be somewhat less masculine than the younger boy of a two-boy pair. Other evidence from two-

Table 11.1 What role does a child play in a family? Here are eight personality roles which were identified in a study of large familes (six or more living children). The roles appeared to be assumed in some sequence, with each succeeding child electing a role which had not been preempted. Of course, not all roles appeared in each family, nor are such roles the exclusive property of large households.*

Role	Frequent Occupant	Brief Description by Sibling
The responsible one	Firstborn child, especially first daughter	
The popular one	Second born, or child following the responsible one	*Second son.* He is a good mixer. Gets along well with people. Is very likable. Is sweet to the rest of us to the point of being henpecked. *Second son.* He has developed the most normal personality of all of us. He is best liked by our parents and by the other children. *Second daughter.* The attractive one. Most popular one among all of us. Interested in the personal appearance of all of us. She would wash your hair and fix you up to go out if mother was busy. *Second son.* He was the one with the personality. He was much admired by all of us. *Second son.* Everybody likes him. He is very sociable. He gets along well with everyone. He is good looking and always knows the right thing to say and do and wear.
The socially ambitious one	Mostly daughters, third, fourth, or fifth born	*Daughter. Fifth born.* Social interests at the expense of all other things. Could always dig up a date. Was the life of the party. Was never left out of anything. Could turn her hand to many things and do them well. *Daughter. Third born.* She was the social butterfly of the family. The only one of the girls who had a debut. Instead of staying at home in the summer she must be off to summer camps. Had a wedding that knocked a hole in all of her brothers' pockets. *Daughter. Fifth born.* She wanted to be the social butterfly in the family. All she ever wanted to do was to primp and go out. But mama wouldn't stand for it. We all have to work, even the older boys washed their overalls when we were growing up.
The studious one	Son or daughter	*Daughter. Sixth born.* She was the smart one. She had a high IQ, and an excellent academic record. She was preoccupied with her books. *Son. Third born.* He was always very quiet and studious. A lover of books, with intellectual interests. *Son. Third born.* He was the scholarly one. He learned quickly. His interests were altogether intellectual. He was the first of the family to graduate from college. *Daughter. Second born.* She is the student of the family. Responsible, but yet lacking something, or what is not lacking manifesting itself in a curious way. She seems the sweet type but really is not. She has the least social grace of all the children.
The family isolate	Child separated by age or sex from the majority of siblings	*Son. Sixth born.* He always was uncooperative. He would not eat nor would he work. He was bright enough, but was at war with the world. He never worked out his adjustments until he got out of college, and he avoided his family until we got a car. *Son. Fourth born.* He was stubborn, bull-headed, dogmatic, with very set ideas. I was never quite sure

Table 11.1 (Continued)

Role	Frequent Occupant	Brief Description by Sibling
		that he believed what he said, or whether he just wanted to be ornery. *Son. Seventh born.* He always had to have his own way. He was stubborn and antisocial. He did not like school. He spent much time by himself. He seemed always to be in rebellion against his family and withdrew from it. He is a policeman now. *Son. Fifth born.* Always a lone wolf. Very independent. Feels less responsibility for the family than any other. He takes life very seriously.
The irresponsible one	Son or daughter	*Daughter. Firstborn.* Extremely irresponsible. She is our gadabout. The most immature of the whole family. Neither is her husband mature. She is definitely the flighty type. It is fortunate that her sister, a year younger, was a responsible person, for she left everything to this younger sister. *Son. Third born.* He is irresponsible and always was. A drifter. He was bright but it was a job to get him through school. He finally got to the university but was so irresponsible that father withdrew him after a year. *Daughter. Fourth born.* She was cowed and timid and irresponsible. It was all father's fault. He had a high temper, completely dominated the family. The older boys who might have given him a battle left home early to go to war.
The sickly one	Child with physical defect or chronic illness	*Daughter. Third born.* She was seriously ill for a time when she was a child and received a great amount of attention, which was soothing to her and which she has continued to demand ever since. She sulks frequently and complains and feels very sorry for herself. *Son. Fourth born.* We had very little that we were made to do. We didn't even make our own beds. My younger brother was sick a good deal of the time, and was always being protected, and urged to eat this and that. *Daughter. Fourth born.* She never liked to do housework. She was considered frail, so she never did as much as the rest of us. Mother treated her and one of the boys who once sprained his back very leniently. *Daughter. Second born.* She was a premature baby. As she grew older, she was nervous because of a thyroid condition. Her eyes were not good either. She never took an outside job, but stayed at home and helps mother.
The spoiled one	Last born or next to the last (if last born unexpected and resented by mother)	*Girl. Last born.* She was protected and babied and never expected to participate fully until most of the others left home. *Boy. Last born.* All the older children had to submit to his demands. He was known as the baby, and mother referred to him as the baby until her dying day. *Girl. Last born.* She was lazier than the rest of us and shirked all kinds of work. She loved to play and daydream, and because of her age was always petted and pampered and allowed to have her own way.

Table 11.1 (Continued)

Role	Frequent Occupant	Brief Description by Sibling
(The spoiled one)	[Last born or next to the last (if last born unexpected and resented by mother)]	*Girl. Last born.* She was the baby. Very much spoiled but with a pleasing personality. She got more than any of the others. Everyone babied and spoiled her. Mother gave in to her more than to the other children. She was cute, everybody recognized it, and she worked at it. She was the teacher's pet all through high school. *Son. Last born.* "The baby." The older siblings resented the parents' protectiveness toward him and consequently tried to control him more. The older children thought he was "spoiled," and it caused considerable conflict in the family. He continued to confide in me, but had no time for the others. He is sensitive but covers up by a care-free "I don't care" attitude.

* Adapted from Bossard, J. H. S., & Boll, E. S. Personality roles in the large family. *Child Development,* 1955, 26(1), 71–78. © 1955 by The Society for Research in Child Development, Inc.

child families suggests that a girl with an older brother may be more self-disparaging than one whose older sib is a girl (Altus, 1966; Koch, 1956).

Conjecture abounds concerning the behavior to be expected of the only child in a family, or the oldest child, or the youngest child. According to a number of investigators, only children have special problems in adjustment, but there is no agreement about what these problems are (Bossard & Boll, 1960). On one point, there is some consistent evidence: firstborn children tend to be relatively high in achievement motivation, and they also tend to be intellectually superior and more accomplished (Altus, 1966; Sampson, 1965). Other generalizations about the relationship of birth order to personality or adjustment patterns are more hazardous. Based on the available evidence, Sampson draws this picture of the firstborn and the later-born child (and he cautions that this should be treated as a general portrait, which in any particular family would be subject to many confounding factors):

The child firstborn occupies the center

stage in a drama whose participants include two rather inconsistent, somewhat anxious and confused actors, who nevertheless are proud of their product and wish him to obtain the skill and attributes which they lack and to attain heights which they long for but find themselves frustrated in reaching. They wish him to progress with lightning pace, yet often act in ways which only serve to increase his dependency on them. And the child himself, alone in this most confusing world, turns toward his parents, looming so large, so powerful, so distant, and uses them as his model for coping with the complexities he daily encounters.

One day, another is born. The stage now holds four; the play has suddenly been changed. More experienced parents, less confused by opening night jitters, more set in their stage movements, now work upon the second. From stardom on center stage to a lesser role . . . the fate of the child firstborn. Soon the second finds himself cast in more prominent parts, and learns rapidly to manipulate the stronger first by playing upon his own relatively less powerful position. And he, the second, finds a model, closer, manipulable, less powerful, to use to grasp the complexities of his own world. He has a ready antagonist and target, and thus suffers less from the pains of withhold-

ing aggressive attacks when his paths are thwarted. He finds himself less caught up in the future of his parents and less the victim of their oversolicitous actions, and thus finds a lesser conflict over dependency.

The second child grows up looking outward upon a world of peers and learns those skills required for coping with similars. The first child grows up looking inward, for without there lies a world of still powerful adults, a more difficult breed to handle, a breed requiring a different set of skills.

Together they grow up, each moving forward, but down a different path. For the first, still driven by the now internalized desires of his parents, education and intellectual pursuits and achievement become important. He turns towards the world of thought, leaving the world of people, and sociability, and play to the younger member of his family.

What seems like a reversal emerges at this point. The inner oriented firstborn turns outward to seek union and agreement with others when his world becomes difficult to handle or issues of choice arise. The outer oriented secondborn turns inward to seek isolation within himself when difficulties and decisions arise. The power and distance of his parents, not only give the first a reduced sense of personal autonomy, but also direct him more toward others as useful figures for providing structure, setting directions, and handling problems. On the other hand, the closer model which exists for the second not only permits him to develop a stronger sense of self-confidence, but also instructs him in the more autonomous manipulation of others; these turn him back upon his own skills when problems and issues of choice arise (Sampson, 1965, pp. 220–222).

Studying the Family as a Whole

If you were asked to describe your family, you would probably begin by describing your mother, father, or another member who seemed especially important. Or you might pick out a particular relationship—perhaps your relationship to your mother—and tell about that. If you continued long enough, every family member and a number of important relationships might be described. Still you might not have presented a very complete picture.

Like a ticking clock, a family is more than just a collection of parts. A family cannot be understood very fully by taking it apart and examining its individual members and their individual relationships. Insofar as possible, it is important to study the family as a whole and to retain the broadest possible focus and perspective.

Much of the research that has been done on family adjustment has concentrated on certain individuals of the family or on certain intrafamilial relationships. This is quite understandable because of the great difficulties that lie in the way of trying to make the whole family the unit for study. Understanding the individual— any one of us—is not easy. And understanding the family—made up as it is of a complex interaction of a number of individuals each of whom is complex in his own right—is exceedingly difficult (see Fig. 11.2).

Recent investigators, however, have stressed the importance of studying the family in broad perspective. They insist that as many familial elements as possible be scrutinized because each element affects every other element. No partial approach can tell the whole story about a family, and by omitting some crucial element, it may tell a misleading story (Spiegel & Bell, 1959).

Not only should the family be studied as a whole, it should be treated as a whole in order to help any one of its members.

This is especially true in the case of children, who are so responsive to everything happening in the family. It has been held that the problem behavior shown by a child is simply a reflection of the problems of the family group and that in order to help the child, the family as a group must be helped and changed (Ackerman & Lakos, 1959). This will be discussed further in the chapters on improving adjustment.

Figure 11.2 Some idea of the complexity of family adjustment can be gotten by considering how quickly the number of relationships grows as the family increases in size (Modified from *The Sociology of Child Development*, 3rd Ed., by J. H. S. Bossard and E. S. Boll (Harper & Row, 1960).

Persons	Relationships	Diagram
2	1	
3	3	
4	6	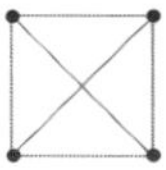
5	10	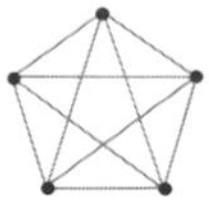
6	15	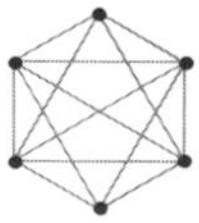
7	21	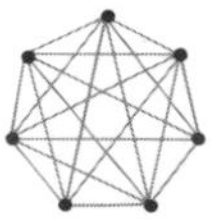
8	28	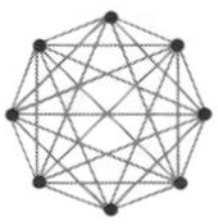

SOME FAMILY CONFLICTS

It would be hard to imagine a family without conflicts anymore than one could imagine a problemless individual. In fact, the material which follows presents some reasons why families are especially prone to conflicts. It will also consider some sorts of conflicts that families have and how they go about dealing with them.

Sources of Conflict

Families, as groups of individuals, share many of the problems that other groups have. However, a family has certain special properties which make it especially vulnerable to internal conflicts. Blood (1960) points out that these properties have to do with the family's compulsory nature, its intimacy and smallness, and its constant change.

Compulsion

If we affiliate with a group, it is because we think that the group will in some way help us meet our needs and reach our goals; if, instead, the group proves to be a source of frustration and conflict, we can abandon it. We do not, of course, in the same way "affiliate" with our families; we are born into them. And although parents do divorce or separate and children grow up and leave home, disaffiliation is not an easy process.

The involuntary and compulsory quality of the family, which, of course, can

Presentation 11.3 How can whole families be studied? One interesting method involves putting the whole family to work on a questionnaire concerning various aspects of the family. The ensuing discussion is taped, and arbitrarily selected segments are analyzed to throw light on the family interaction. Here is material from two contrasting families. In the total segments analyzed, Mr. and Mrs. Gaylord spoke to each other 73 times and to their child 23 times. The Bellingtons spoke to each other 4 times and to their child 76 times.

THE GAYLORDS

Introduction:

Eleven year old Mary Ann Gaylord is the only child in what is the second marriage for both parents. Both father and mother had lost their first spouses through death. Both first marriages had been childless. During the family interview with the Gaylords the parents mentioned many complaints about Mary Ann. For present purposes we will focus on just one aspect of the parents' problems with their child. Mrs. Gaylord was troubled and perplexed by Mary Ann's unhappiness. The girl "acts as though she is starved for attention," the mother said, although the parents are careful to include her in their activities. This problem of exclusion carried over to Mary Ann's relationships with her friends. The child explained that when she plays with just one friend she gets along well, but when the group expands to three people the others play together and exclude Mary Ann. With this paradox in mind—the child's feeling of exclusion despite the parents' efforts to include her in their activities—we will turn for clarification to a verbatim excerpt from the Gaylord's performance on the Family Questionnaire. The question under discussion is the seventeenth in the series: "What was the best time that each of you can remember? The worst time?"

Excerpt:

Father: *What did you enjoy the most? Going to Florida?*

Mary Ann: *Ohh, there are so many different things.*

Mother: *Well, it's all right with me as far as enjoyment . . .*

Father: *(breaking in) Picking out one particular one is kind of hard to do.*

Mother: *Yes, because of our trips out West there—they, each one had their own high points. . . .*

Father: *Yeah.*

Mary Ann: *(Makes an occasional sound indicating her wish to speak, but mother continues to talk.)*

Mother: *(continuing) and it would be hard to pick out which was the best. Last year was—just wonderful.*

Mary Ann: *I liked . . .*

Father: *(interrupting) Like I say, either the Arches or Yellowstone you know.*

Mother: *Well, there were so many things last year.*

Father: *Well, I—I. Actually, I think that I got the biggest kick out of it was the time—was the first time I took you out West. It was the first time we went out to Yellowstone.*

Mother: *(laughing) That snowstorm.*

Father: *(laughing) Yeah.*

Mother: *(continuing) And my first canyon?*

Father: *Yeah.*

Mother: *Well, that was a wonderful trip and, of course, it was all so new. But the subsequent trips have been just wonderful because I could anticipate . . .*

Father: *Yeah. Well, you knew what to look forward to. That time, I don't know, I know I got the biggest kick out of it because I was wondering how you were going to react, you know. And then seeing how your reaction was to the various things, the snowstorm and the canyons, and the mountains and Yellow-*

Presentation 11.3 (Continued)

	stone, itself, and all that sort of thing.
Mother:	Well, Annie, too, that year we went to Meadowlark. Annie and you spent all those days on the . . .
Mary Ann:	(interrupting) Ooooh, I'll never forget it. Oh, I liked that.
Mother:	(continuing) . . . on the horse. That was one of your favorites, too. Wasn't it?
Mary Ann:	(agreeing) Uh-huh.
Father:	How about the worst time?
Mother:	The worst time.
Father:	Well, I think my worst time was just prior to the time to Susan's death. My first wife's death. That couple of years there before she died. Boy, that was—I was ready to give up then.
Mother:	Well.
Father:	(continuing) I wouldn't want to go through that again. Of all the things I wouldn't want to do I think that was about the worst . . .
Mother:	(softly) Uh-huh.
Father:	(continuing) . . . in my own case.
Mother:	Well, as far as my case—I'd say that it was with my . . .
Mary Ann:	(breaking in) I thought you . . .
Mother:	(continuing) . . . was with my first husband and that year . . .
Mary Ann:	(starts to interrupt again)
Father:	Shh!
Mother:	. . . after his death. The uncertainty and . . .
Father:	From the time of his death and when the time that you and I got together.

Hypothesis:

In this excerpt the parents recalled their honeymoon trip before Mary Ann was born. They were focused on each other and for a while the child was forgotten.

The mother, rather guiltily, remembered her, and turned to her for a moment, but quickly the parents turned again to each other to discuss their worst time. The child twice attempted to break in, but was shushed by her father. Here the theme of "three's a crowd" was acted out. Earlier we had mentioned that Mary Ann had experienced the same exclusion in her play with other children. The parents, grateful to have found each other after the tragedies of their first marriages, acted as if they were still on a honeymoon, where a little girl could only be an intruder. Our hypothesis, briefly, was that Mary Ann felt left out of the family because she really was left out.

THE BELLINGTONS

Introduction:

Marjory Bellington, at six and one half years, is a bright and attractive child. Her parents had adopted her at 14 months of age and she is their only child. The Bellingtons came to the clinic because a school teacher had complained about Marjory's attention-seeking behavior. Although it seemed, at first, that the parents were angry at the teacher for her unjust criticism of Marjory and of their handling of the girl, it soon became clear in the family interview, that the parents too found Marjory to be a showoff. Her father said: "She wants to be the center all the time," and her mother wondered if she had spoiled the child, or if Marjory had been spoiled before they adopted her. The parents vacillated between denial of Marjory's problem and serious concern about it.

The following excerpt from the Bellingtons' performance on the Family Questionnaire helped to clarify Marjory's need to show off. In this excerpt the family discussed the questions: "Describe how one special holiday is celebrated by the family," and "What are the things that the family does on Sunday (or whenever everyone has a day off)?"

Presentation 11.3 (Continued)

Excerpt:

Mother: What do we do first on Easter morning?

Marjory: Morning? Well . . . we look and find the Easter basket?

Mother: Oh, no, huh-uh.

Marjory: First we go . . .

Mother: (interrupting) We go to church first!

Marjory: Yes.

Mother: And then who comes while we're in church?

Father: Come on over here, honey.

Marjory: The Easter bunny?

Father: Uh-huh.

Marjory: Does the Easter bunny come?

Mother: He sure does.

Father: The Easter bunny comes . . .

Mother: And he always hides your basket.

Father: (clears throat)

Marjory: Yes-s-s.

Mother: What are the things that the family usually does on Sunday or whenever everyone has a day off? What do we do on Sunday?

Marjory: Uh-we go to church . . .

Hypothesis:

The mother read the questions and addressed them to the child. When Marjory began to answer, the mother edited the child's responses. This process, with its intense focus on Marjory as spokesman for the family, continued throughout the procedure. Mother quizzed and father encouraged the child. Both parents centered their attention on her. We hypothesized that Marjory had to be a showoff because the parents made her the center of attention within the family (From Drechsler & Shapiro, 1963, pp. 368–372).

---

be a source of great security, is frequently a great irritation. Family members may find themselves locked into problem situations from which there is little relief or escape. Over the years petty grievances accumulate and are magnified out of all proportion.

Intimacy

The family is not only a compulsory organization; it is an intimate one as well. Our relationship with other groups is seldom so extensive or intensive as that with our family. Family members spend a considerable amount of time in contact with one another, and this contact is particularly sensitive and charged with emotion.

The closeness of contact, which can produce strong bonds and positive feelings between family members, may also lead to deep and violent negative feelings. As

Blood points out, the restraints and inhibitions that characterize interaction in the larger environment may be largely absent within the intimacy of the family circle. Anger, jealousy, and other emotions may erupt with considerable force to disrupt the functioning of the home.

Smallness

The family is not only compulsory in its membership and intimate in its interaction, but it is a relatively small group as well, particularly many modern American families. The smallness of the family contributes to its intimate nature and enhances its potential for conflict. Furthermore, the limited membership allows the lines of conflict to be sharply drawn.

In the one-child family, parents may compete with each other for the child's affection, or a pact may be drawn between two members with the third largely excluded. Two-child families may produce a sibling rivalry for the favored position. And three-child families may permit two children to ally against the third.

Change

The family is a constantly changing entity. It forms, expands, and contracts. It grows larger with the advent of every new child. It grows smaller as members die or depart.

The family's activities are also constantly changing. Young families with young children face different problems from those whose children are older, away in college, or busily forming their own families.

The family's socioeconomic status may change too. A family may rise in the world, or it may suffer reverses and need to retrench. Even if its income is fairly constant the changing demands of its members may make it feel rich and poor by turns.

Each member of the family is himself constantly changing. As he changes, the family changes with him. As Blood (1960) writes, "Every time a new child starts to crawl, to climb, to wander across the street, to go to school, to experience puberty, or to drive a car, the pattern of family living must be readjusted."

Because of this constant growth and change, a family cannot hope to effect an equilibrium. It cannot hope to arrive at a pattern of adjustment which will avoid conflict once and for all. But it can hope to learn to minimize its conflicts and deal effectively with those which do arise.

Kinds of Conflict

Some conflicts appear to arise because family members are not in agreement on the roles that each of them should play.

Other conflicts seem to stem from personality clashes among the members or from antagonistic value systems or differing philosophies of life.

Role Conflict

A *role* is the behavior associated with a particular position in a group. It is the way a person in this position is expected to behave or conduct himself. Within the family, for example, there are certain sorts of behavior associated with the role of father and the role of the mother. Children, too, are expected to behave in certain ways, and there are different sets of expectations based on sex, age, and number of children in the family.

Role expectations vary from culture to culture, from social class to social class, and from family to family. The expectations are generally not explicit or spelled out; they may not be easy to verbalize. Still they exist and they influence our behavior and the behavior of those around us.

Speaking of a particular person, you may say that he was just like a father to you. Or, perhaps, a person complains about his own father, lamenting that he was a father in name only. Both usages help substantiate the contention that there are definite sorts of behavior associated with the father role.

We expect a mother "to mother" her children, although other people may assume the mothering role as well. In the same way, we may chastise a child for assuming the role of an infant (Stop acting like a baby!) or for prematurely assuming the role of an adult (Aren't you getting too big for your britches?). If, when we are grown up, we are treated like children, we may become irritated or angry; we expect people to respect our status as adults.

Problems arise in the family when its members are not able to play their roles as they see fit or when they play their roles in ways contrary to the expectations of others. A husband who feels henpecked or a wife who is forced to be the bread-winner are examples of persons who are not able to play their roles as they wish. A mother who accuses her small son of being a bad boy and a small son who accuses his mother of being a bad mommy are in effect accusing each other of not playing their roles properly.

Some men expect to be the absolute rulers of their families. In the roles of husband and father, they may expect to be boss, to lay down the law, to wear the pants. But a man may find that his wife and children have other ideas on the subject. His wife may compete with him for power, or his children may openly or subtly resist his attempts to dominate them.

A woman may be reluctant to give up her role as a professional person to take on the roles of wife and mother. Her husband may resent her outside employment and insist that she give it up. Her children may constantly demand more time, attention, and perhaps more affection than she feels she can give.

Children, too, may fail to fill their family role as others in the home see it. A boy may be too mild mannered for his father or too wild mannered for his mother. As a young child he may be more dependent than his parents would like, while as an adolescent he may insist on more independence and autonomy than they feel he should have.

Ackerman observes that in the contemporary American family the roles of the father and mother are frequently unclear. There is confusion and competition about the division of responsibilities and duties. In the material which follows he draws a generalized picture of some of the role problems found in white, urban, middle-class families.

With the father absent much of the day, the mother assumes the dominant position in the home. The isolated pattern of living of the nuclear family group, cut off from the larger extensions of the family, focuses responsibility for family affairs sharply and exclusively on the mother. The father strives mightily to show success as a man. He pursues what has been called "the suicidal cult of manliness." To prove his merit, it is not enough to be a man; he must be a superman. In his daily work, he serves some giant industrial organization, or he is a lone wolf in the jungle warfare of modern competitive enterprise. The more he succeeds, the more he dreads failure. He brings his work worries home. Depleted by his exertions, he has little emotional stamina left over to give freely of his love to wife and children. From his wife, he seeks comfort and solace. He needs some mothering for himself and so competes with his children. He wants to be buttressed for the war of tomorrow, but he finds his wife absorbed in her own busy life. He feels deserted and alone and angry that his wife gives him so little understanding. She reproaches him for not taking a more responsible role in the family. She demands more consideration for herself and the children. For the difficulties with the children she feels guilty. But she denies this guilt and projects it to father. Father takes it. He thinks it must really be his fault. Though confused and angry, he appeases mother because of his need for her. He tries to be useful to win her favor. He washes dishes, minds the baby, becomes mother's "little helper." He submits to this role but silently begrudges his wife's dictates. He feels alien as parent, shut out of the relations of children and mother, or at least relegated to the far corner. In all this he feels self-conscious, unnatural, and somewhat lost.

The mother, in turn, pretends to a degree of strength and sureness she does not at all possess. Because she cannot feel safe in leaning on her husband's strength, she takes to herself the powers of regulating the family. She demonstrates her worth through imitating the stereotype of male strength. She tries to be omnipotent but succeeds only in being detached, impersonal, and alienated from the spontaneous sentiments of a mother. She strives intensely to do the right thing with the children but plagues herself with fear of making mistakes. Nonetheless, she pretends to know, acts strong, superior, and self-sufficient, and with this facade often deceives her husband. Fundamentally, however, she remains insecure and dependent, wanting mothering for herself, though she is loath to confess it.

Both parents therefore act unnatural. They are suspicious of any open show of emotion, which they regard as weakness. A free flow of emotion is felt to be dangerous, as if all emotion were equated with something bad and destructive. Therefore it must be curbed. Anxiety over loss of control is constant. Tender sentiment is avoided or, if expressed, is ignored; it spells weakness and the threat of loss of control. Thus the behavior of both parents becomes overcontrolled, unspontaneous, and reduced in vitality. Both parents are burdened with anxiety, guilt and doubt. They are afraid of life and have lost their zest for play and sense of adventure. They settle down to a stereotyped way of living, a safe, conforming routine. They strive to live up to the Jones's with all the external accoutrements of conventional success—a home, a new car, the latest gadgets.

In this family frame, there are, in the final showdown, only two possible roles: the role of the child, dependent, exposed, vulnerable; and the role of the superman, self-sufficient, infinitely strong and not needing anyone. Neither parent wants to be in the role of the defenseless child, exposed to attack. Each prefers the role of omnipotent master and the phantasy of

total immunity to hurt. The parents may in actual fact alternate these roles. An inevitable effect of this is to blur the essential, ineradicable differences which in nature should lead to a true joining and completion in one another. The striving for the position of omnipotent supremacy leads ultimately to a sense of aloneness and emotional deadness.[3]

Need Conflict

The members of the family are all individuals in their own right. Although there may be striking family resemblances and common family goals, each person has his own patterns of needs, acts, and goals—his own personality, so to speak. And as he struggles to meet his needs and reach his goals, he comes into conflict with other family members whose behavior is at cross-purposes with his own.

If a husband has very strong affiliation needs and his wife is a homebody, there can be continual arguments about how they should spend their leisure time. Or if the wife is ambitious and eager for the family to prosper and get ahead, and the husband is not much motivated to achieve, there may be incessant nagging and friction. A methodical, orderly husband who is married to a spontaneous, disorderly wife may be constantly vexed about the state of their house, while his wife is constantly bothered by her husband's great need to be exact, plan ahead, and leave nothing to chance.

Children, too, have their own patterns of response which may grate on the nerves of their parents or their siblings. A demanding, succorant child may make nearly intolerable demands of a mother who is very low in nurturance. Or a very warm,

[3] From *The Psychodynamics of Family Life*, Copyright © 1958 by Nathan N. Ackerman, Basic Books, Inc., Publishers, New York. Pp. 114–115.

nurturant mother may fight a losing battle to keep her children from getting out from under her wing. A dominant child may attempt to lord it over his siblings—and sometimes over his parents as well.

Value Conflict

When we speak of our system of values or our philosophy of life, we generally refer to the things in life that we think are important, to the goals that we think are worth working toward. Of course, people value different things. What one person feels is important and meaningful, another may regard as unimportant and without worth.

Within a family, value systems may vary from person to person, causing considerable tension and conflict. For one family member, perhaps, money is extremely important, and he tries to establish the acquisition of wealth as a prime family goal. Another member, perhaps, does not care about being rich or even well-to-do; he may feel that money should be kept in circulation, and his efforts to make the family outgo equal (or even exceed) its income may cause considerable consternation.

A wife may value appearances; well-kept kids in a well-kept house in a well-kept neighborhood may be of paramount importance to her. But her husband, perhaps, couldn't care less about kempt things, and he may refuse to tidy up or move up to better living, even though circumstances might permit such a change. He may scandalize his wife by running around in old clothes looking like a bum, while she irritates him by attempting to put on airs.

Children are frequently caught up in the crossfire of the conflicting value systems of their parents. The struggle may be out in the open or subtle and underground. In the end a child can be left confused and bewildered, cynical and pessimistic, and without a consistent and workable philosophy of life.

As children mature, they form their own value systems. They are influenced, to be sure, by their parents' philosophies, but they are also strongly moved by the values arising in their peer group and by other forces in their social environment. The rebellion of adolescents against domination by their parents and their parents' ideas is so common in our culture that it need not be elaborated here. Most of us will probably be enlisted in this battle more than once—first as an adolescent and then on the other side of the battle line as a parent.

Dealing with Conflict

As indicated earlier in this chapter, a family's ability to deal with its problems can be considered one measure of the family's adjustment. Families show a wide variety of approaches to conflicts, and within a particular family, efforts vary, depending on the nature of the problem at hand, the members who are mostly directly concerned, and many other factors. Some conflict behaviors which have been observed including blocking, restructuring, compromise, accommodation, mediation, and escape.

Blocking

Conflicting impulses within the individual serve to block him and prevent him from acting to meet his needs and reach his goals. In the same way, conflicting attitudes and behavior within the family block its members from proceeding on their goal-directed ways. Or, at least, these conflicts force the members to modify their actions.

The socialization process involves a good deal of frustration and blocking as parents prevent their children from behaving in certain ways and encourage them to act in others. In this process there are constant clashes between children and parents in which the former appear determined to do the things that the latter are determined will not be done. Sometimes, the clash comes between parents who have differing ideas about child rearing.

As the children in the family mature and become more skilled adversaries for their parents, the home can become a battleground of conflicting ideas, values, and philosophies, with each member of the family attempting to guide the family in certain directions while preventing it from moving in others. This battle is not necessarily a bloody or a destructive one, nor is it necessarily one in which there is victor and vanquished. It can be a set-to from which each member of the family and the family as a whole may benefit.

On the other hand, family conflicts can produce deadlocks, stalemates, and standoffs that serve as fairly permanent blockages to personal and familial development. Probably all of us are familiar with some family which has severe and intractable problems. It may have members who have never been able to communicate with each other. There may be enduring jealousies, bitterness, and misunderstanding.

Restructuring

Families are changing entities, and the problems they are occupied with also change. As families grow, they outgrow some of their problems and grow into others. Of course, certain problem themes may run through all of a family's existence, but even these cannot fail to be affected by the changes occurring in the members of the family and in the changing nature of the family itself.

Conflict situations in the family undergo constant restructuring. Forces within each member and between members wax and wane and in doing so alter the complexion of the conflict. In this way, "resolved" conflicts burst out again and "unresolvable" ones fade away and disappear.

Consider this example of restructuring. A son and his mother have a heated argument over whether or not he is to join a mountaineering expedition. Each attempts to persuade the other and change the other's perception of the matter. Perhaps the mother convinces the son to see and share her concern about the dangers involved. Maybe he prevails upon her until she weakens and gives in. If all else fails, the mother may redefine the situation from an equalitarian to an authoritarian one. She says, "No, and that's final!"

Of course, that may not be final. Perhaps the son begins a campaign to get his mother to reconsider her decision. Failing that, he can behave in ways calculated to make her less content about her action and maybe less likely to repeat it in a similar situation in the future.

The mountaineering incident may be just a battle in a larger and continuing war concerning the extent to which the mother will be successful in protecting (or overprotecting), nurturing, and dominating her son. Over the years the situation will be constantly restructured. As the boy grows older, he may become less vulnerable to his mother's power plays, and the warfare will enter a new phase. If so, the mother will need to adopt new tactics or abandon old expectations. It is possible, however, that the mother's previous actions may be sufficient to substantially retard or sabotage her son's efforts toward independence and autonomy.

Compromise

A good deal of family living is compromise, with each member making certain concessions for the sake of family harmony. Each member is called upon to adapt his own needs, acts, and goals to those of other members of the family and to the general welfare of the family itself. Of course, some members do more compromising and more adapting than others.

Some compromises are arrived at explicitly through some sort of family action. For example, an agreement can be reached in which a child is given a larger allowance (something he wanted) in exchange for taking over a larger portion of the household chores (something he didn't want). Or a wife agrees that her husband may golf Saturday mornings (something he insists on) if he absolutely devotes the rest of the weekend to his family (something he is not always careful about).

Most compromises, however, are not explicitly stated or explicitly arrived at. They come about in the everyday pull-and-tug and give-and-take of family interaction. They represent middle positions which members of the family do not find completely satisfying but not completely unsatisfying either.

Consider some examples. In one family, the father, who tends to be an authoritarian, attempts to soften his position in order to promote harmony in the household.

The children are granted more freedom than the father thinks is advisable but not so much as the mother feels would be optimal for their development. The family socializes more than the father prefers but not nearly so much as the mother and children would like.

In a second family both parents are considerably concerned about their adolescent son's rebellion. After trying to suppress it, with unfortunate effects, they seem to have arrived at a middle position. They grant him more freedom and autonomy than they are comfortable in allowing although it is less than he would like to have. They try to understand and make allowance for his choice of companions, his taste in music and dress, his rejection of the values they live by. Nobody is happy about the situation, but it is a tolerable one, and there is hope for happier days ahead.

Accommodation

One way of dealing with family problems is to not deal with them. There are some problems that we simply accept and learn to live with. We accommodate them. Or, to say it in yet another way, we tolerate them (Blood, 1960).

We accommodate some family problems because they may seem beyond our power to do much about. We put up with some family members because we despair of changing them. Sometimes, too, attempts to deal with a problem appear to be more trouble than it is worth, or the solution requires the cooperation of a member who refuses to cooperate or the forebearance of another who is unable to forebear.

Some family problems are accommodated because they are poorly understood.

Arising slowly over a long period, they may never have been pinpointed or brought into sharp focus. Some family members, for example, seem unable to get along with others. Almost any interaction leads to an argument or an antagonistic silence. These members may learn to tread lightly around each other without understanding very fully why they continually rub each other the wrong way.

Some family problems are accommodated because they are not constant vexations. They come and go, wax acute, then fade away. Realizing that things will get better, we ride them out. We learn to live through such problems, gritting our teeth and waiting for the better tomorrow.

Children, for example, pass through certain stages of development, some more tolerable to parents than others. In some families, children of age two provide some awful times, but by the next year things may be considerably happier on the home scene. (One film on young children is titled "The Terrible Two's and the Trusting Three's.")

Adults in the family too may have recurring problems which other members must accommodate. The father, perhaps, is nearly impossible to live with when his business is going badly. A mother has her periodic bouts with the bottle to which the other members of the family need to accommodate themselves; when the mother is "not feeling well," others in the family step in to take over her duties until she is able to do so herself.

Mediation

Generally speaking, most families attempt to keep their problems to themselves. There is some reluctance to admit that the problem is too difficult for the family to handle and that outside help may be needed. No matter how badly things may be within, a family may attempt to present the outward appearance of calm. But sometimes outside assistance may be necessary.

In family crisis, relatives, friends, and neighbors may serve as mediators. Sometimes they are turned to by a family member who is at his wit's end and desperate for some support and assistance. Sometimes they volunteer their own services, feeling that they know what should be done. Frequently, such mediators themselves are entangled in the family situation, and their services may be useless or worse than useless (Blood, 1960).

In many cities there are family agencies which are prepared to help families in trouble. In addition, there are psychologists, psychiatrists, and social workers at clinics and in private practice throughout the community who are able to help families with their problems. Frequently, ministers serve in the role of marriage counselors, and they may be one of the first persons whom a family thinks of and is willing to turn to in times of distress.

Professional mediators proceed in various ways. A couple or an entire family may be seen together in a series of counseling sessions, or the members of the family may be seen individually. Sometimes a combination of individual and group sessions is felt useful. The focus of the counseling may be on the family as a unit, or it may be on the adjustments of certain members if it is felt that these individuals are making a major contribution to the family's difficulties.

Escape

Family problems which cannot be solved or accommodated can sometimes be escaped. The escape may involve a psychological or physical process or a combination of both. The escape may be temporary or it may be permanent.

A family may seek escape from a problem area by refusing to recognize or face it. By common agreement, explicitly or implicitly arrived at, certain areas may be off-limits to discussion and exploration. For example, a husband and wife with considerably different political philosophies may learn to keep their opinions from each other. Or, perhaps, after a few years of marriage a couple finds it impossible to arrive at a satisfactory sexual adjustment, and sexual relations between them are abandoned.

Of course, such maneuvers may not be truly escapes since the problem—although unannounced—may remain to affect the family in various ways. A continued evasion of a serious problem may produce a family crisis. A temporary evasion, however, sometimes serves to allow a problem to be deferred to another time when members of the family may be better able to handle it.

Family members learn to escape interpersonal difficulties by avoiding each other and staying out of each other's way. A man who cannot seem to get along with his family may become completely occupied with his business. Children who have trouble getting along with their parents stay out of their parents' way, spend as much time as possible away from the home, leave it as soon as they are old enough, and return as little as possible. Some adults find that—despite good intentions—each time they return to visit their parents they begin acting like problem children again.

When the home situation becomes intolerable, parents sometimes escape from it through desertion. Legal separation and divorce also provide some escape for couples with seemingly impossible conflicts. However, such strategies may create as many problems as they relieve, especially as far as the children are concerned.

SUMMARY

Family adjustment can be defined in various ways. It may be defined in terms of simple physical coherence, of happiness, of the achievement of certain tasks, or of success in dealing with family problems.

In the study of family adjustment it is particularly valuable to observe the family as a whole. It is important to include as many elements of a family as possible because every element affects every other element, and partial approaches will not tell the whole story about a family; such an approach may, in fact, produce a misleading story. Because of the great complexity, however, researchers have generally focused on certain relationships, including those among marital pairs, parental pairs, parent-child pairs, and siblings.

Families share many of the problems of other groups. Families have, moreover, certain properties which make them especially vulnerable to internal conflicts.

These properties concern the family's compulsory nature, its intimacy and smallness, and its constantly changing nature.

Some family conflicts arise because its members are not in agreement on the role that each of them is to play. Other conflicts stem from personality clashes among the family members or from clashing value systems and differing philosophies of life.

Families show a wide variety of approaches to their conflicts, and within any one family, efforts will vary, depending upon the nature of the problem at hand, the members who are most directly concerned, and certain other factors. Some conflict behaviors which have been noted in families are blocking, restructuring, compromise, accommodation, mediation, and escape.

REFERENCES

Ackerman, N. W. *The Psychodynamics of Family Life.* New York: Basic Books, 1958.

——, **& Lakos, M. H.** The treatment of a child and family. In A. Burton (Ed.), *Case Studies in Counseling and Psychotherapy.* Englewood Cliffs, N.J.: Prentice-Hall, 1959. Pp. 56–72.

Altus, W. D. Birth order and its sequelae. *Science,* 1966, **151**(3706), 44–49.

Baldwin, A. L., Kalhorn, J., & Breese, F. H. Patterns of parent behavior. *Psychological Monographs,* 1945, **58**, No. 3 (Whole No. 268).

Becker, W. C. Consequences of different kinds of parental discipline. In M. L. Hoffman & L. W. Hoffman (Eds.), *Review of Child Development Research.* Vol. 1. New York: Russell Sage, 1964. Pp. 169–208.

Blood, R. O. Jr. Resolving family conflicts. *Conflict Resolution,* 1960, **4**, 209–219.

——. *Marriage.* New York: Free Press, 1962.

——, **& Wolfe, D. M.** *Husbands and Wives.* New York: Free Press, 1960.

Bossard, J. H. S., & Boll, E. S. Personality roles in the large family. *Child Development,* 1955, **26**(1), 71–78.

——, & ——. *The Large Family System.* Philadelphia: University of Pennsylvania Press, 1956.

——, & ——. *The Sociology of Child Development.* (3rd ed.) New York: Harper & Row, 1960.

Brim, O. G., Jr. *Education for Child Rearing.* New York: Russell Sage, 1959.

——, **Fairchild, F. W., & Borgatta, E. F.** Relations between family problems. *Marriage and Family Living,* 1961, **23**, 219–226.

Drechsler, R. J., & Shapiro, M. I. Two methods of analysis of family diagnostic data. *Family Process,* 1963, **2**(2), 367–379.

Duvall, E. M. *Family Development.* (2nd ed.) Philadelphia: Lippincott, 1962.

Dyer, E. D. Parenthood as crisis: A re-study. *Marriage and Family Living,* 1963, **25**, 196–201.

English, H. B., & English, A. C. *A Comprehensive Dictionary of Psychological and Psychoanalytical Terms.* New York: Longmans, 1958.

Haley, J. Marriage therapy. *Archives of General Psychiatry,* 1963, **8**, 213–234.

Hansen, D. A., & Hill, R. Families under stress. In H. T. Christensen (Ed.), *Handbook of Marriage and the Family.* Chicago: Rand McNally, 1964. Pp. 782–819.

Irish, D. P. Sibling interaction: A neglected aspect of family life research. *Social Forces,* 1964, **42**(3), 279–288.

Jackson, J. K. The adjustment of the family to alcoholism. *Marriage and Family Living,* 1956, **18**(4), 361–369.

Kinsey, A. C., Pomeroy, W. B., & Martin, C. E. *Sexual Behavior in the Human Male.* Philadelphia: Saunders, 1948.

———, ———, ———, & Gebhard, P. II. *Sexual Behavior in the Human Female.* Philadelphia: Saunders, 1953.

Koch, H. L. Sissiness and tomboyishness in relation to sibling characteristics. *Journal of Genetic Psychology,* 1956, **88**, 231–244.

LeMasters, E. E. Parenthood as crisis. *Marriage and Family Living,* 1957, **19**, 352–355.

Pineo, P. C. Disenchantment in the later years of marriage. *Marriage and Family Living,* 1961, **23**, 3–11.

Sampson, E. E. The study of ordinal position: Antecedents and outcomes. In B. Maher (Ed.), *Progress in Experimental Personality Research.* Vol. 2. New York: Academic, 1965. Pp. 175–228.

Schlesinger, B. *The Multi-problem Family.* Toronto, Canada: University of Toronto Press, 1963.

Spiegel, J. P., & Bell, N. W. The family of the psychiatric patient. In S. Arieti (Ed.), *American Handbook of Psychiatry.* Vol. 2. New York: Basic Books, 1959. Pp. 114–149.

Westley, W. A., & Epstein, N. B. Family structure and emotional health: A case study approach. *Marriage and Family Living,* 1960, **22**, 25–27.

CHAPTER TWELVE
FAMILY ADJUSTMENT, CONTINUED

Students of the family are very much interested in the interaction of parents and children. They are especially curious about the attitudes and behavior that parents express. And they have attempted to explore the causes and consequences of certain common actions.

Studies of parent-child interaction have been heavily criticized. The subjects chosen, the methods employed, and the conclusions drawn—all have come under fire. It has been suggested that investigations of the relationship between parent behavior and child behavior should include both parents (not just mothers as is usually the case), separate analyses for boys and girls (because of probable sex differences), and data gathered over a number of years (to accommodate changes in behavior through time). Few investigators, however, can boast even a near approach to such a design.

Because of the complexities of families and the limitations of the research that has been done on them, care needs to be taken in generalizing from existing studies. This chapter is based on some selected and representative investigations. It discusses four important patterns of parent-child relationships: acceptance-rejection, warmth-coldness, democracy-dictatorship, and permissiveness-restrictiveness.

ACCEPTANCE-REJECTION

A considerably studied and talked-about pattern of parent behavior is that concerning acceptance and rejection of the child. Although it is generally conceded that children need to be accepted, there is no agreement on what acceptance actually is. Rejection, too, is a complicated business and can be manifested in a number of ways.

Parent Behavior

One way of defining acceptance is in terms of the part that the child is allowed to play in the life of the parent. By this definition, the accepting parent is one who gives a good deal of himself to his child. The rejecting parent, by contrast, allows his child little or no close association.

This concept of acceptance has been employed by workers at the Fels Research Institute and is delineated in the scale shown in Figure 12.1. This is one of a number of scales devised by this organization. As was noted in the first chapter, the Institute has been engaged in a research program which followed the development of children from before birth to maturity. As part of the program, each home was periodically visited, and a number of ratings were made of the interaction between mother and child (Kagan & Moss, 1962).

A second way of defining acceptance is in terms of the conditions which are considered optimal to the child's development. By this definition, the accepting parent is one who provides a social and

Figure 12.1 One concept of acceptance is illustrated here in a rating scale modified from that used by the Fels Research Institute. The scale has six points. The accepting parent, one rated at the top of the scale, is highly devoted to his child; at this level, the lives of the parent and the child are completely bound up with each other. Below this extreme, there is provision for rating parents who accept and enjoy their children, but who also maintain their own activities and identities. Parents who openly resent and exclude their children from their lives fall at the lowest level of the scale (Modified from Champney, 1941. © 1941 by The Society for Research in Child Development, Inc.).

1   2   3   4   5   6
Devotion   Rejection

Identification of the six scale points is as follows:

1 Parent's behavior toward child connotes utter devotion and acceptance into his inner most self, without stint or suggestion of holding back in any phase of his life.

2 Parent clearly accepts child. Includes child in family councils, trips, affection, even when it is difficult or represents considerable sacrifice.

3 A "Charter member" of the family, but "kept in his place." Parent accepts child in general, but excludes him from certain phases of parent's life.

4 Tacit acceptance. Excludes child so frequently that to the child the rejection attitude may seem to predominate even though parent takes acceptance for granted.

5 Parent's predominant tendency is to avoid, repulse, and exclude the child, but without open rejection.

6 Child openly resented and rejected by parent. Never admitted to inner circle. Made to feel unwanted, ostracized.

physical environment which promotes the child's maturational and learning processes. The environment provided by the rejecting parent not only fails to contribute to the child's development, it burdens and impedes it.

This latter conception of acceptance has been developed by Porter. Interested in devising as clear and meaningful a definition as possible for his own research, Porter arrived at the following formulation:

Parental acceptance *may be defined as feelings and behavior on the part of the parents which are characterized by unconditional love for the child, a recognition of the child as a person with feelings who has a right and a need to express those feelings, a value for the unique make-up of the child and a recognition of the child's need to differentiate and separate himself from his parents in order that he may become an autonomous individual* (1954, p. 177).

Generally speaking, investigators have devoted more effort to defining rejection than acceptance, and usually, by exclusion, any behavior that is not by definition rejecting is regarded as accepting. In general, two separate patterns of rejection have been noted. One may be referred to as "passive rejection," the other as "active rejection."[1]

Passive rejection is characterized less by what is done than by what is not done. Passively rejecting parents neglect their children and ignore them as much as possible. These parents have their own lives, and they prevent their children from intruding into their affairs. Such parents are relatively unconcerned about their children's welfare, indifferent to their needs,

and sometimes they fail to provide their families with even the basic necessities of life. If possible, they may delegate the care of their children to other people.

The "ignoring" scale which follows provides a measure of maternal behavior which is similar to passive rejection. This is one of a number of scales which were devised to provide quantified data concerning the behavior shown by mothers while their young children were participating in a series of examinations. Each of the seven subquestions noted below was completed by an observer who checked a seven-point scale running from "not at all true" (scored 1) through "average" (scored 4) to "extremely true" (scored 7):

Does this mother ignore or reject her child?
1 Does she often comment on how much extra work or trouble the child is?
2 Does she tend to "leave the situation" during the examination as though she is glad the baby is in someone else's hands?
3 Would she be willing to have others assume most of the responsibility for the care of the child?
4 Does the mother seem to know very little about the child?
5 Does she tend to overlook the needs of the child?
6 Does she give the impression that the child is not necessarily her principal interest?
7 Does she fail to show much beyond polite interest in the child during the examination? (Schaefer, Bell, & Bayley, 1959, p. 94).

Active rejection is characterized by hostility and by dictatorial and repressive techniques. The child is hemmed in by rules and demands, many of them vague, arbitrary, and inconsistent. Rewards are few, and punishment is common. Penalties for

---

[1] A more detailed discussion of these patterns is presented by Baldwin, Kalhorn, and Breese (1945) and Wolberg (1944).

Presentation 12.1 Acceptance may be defined in terms of the conditions which are optimal to the child's development. Porter has provided a careful description of this concept of acceptance. He says:

An acceptant parent is one who:

A. Regards his child as a person with feelings and respects the child's right and need to express these feelings.
1. He does not become emotionally disturbed because the child expresses negative feelings. He realizes that such feelings need to be expressed for the maintenance of good mental health.
2. He makes a point of accepting and returning positive feelings.
3. He encourages freedom of emotional expression; shows the child that all feelings are understandable; that it is all right to have them; but at the same time helps the child find ways of expressing his feelings that do not produce guilt.
4. He keeps communication channels open.
5. He listens with an open mind to the child's side of a problem when there is conflict. He has a willingness to concede that he (the parent) is sometimes wrong.

B. Values the unique make-up of his child and does what he can to foster that uniqueness within the limits of healthy personal and social adjustment.
1. He allows the child to be different from every other child and feels all right about it.
2. He uses all cues he can to perceive the child's interests and feelings in trying to determine what kind of an individual his child is.
3. He does not attempt to modify greatly the child's basic constitutional structure, i.e., learnings are individualized in accordance with the potential of each child.

4. He accepts the child's limitations.
5. He refrains from evaluating the behavior and achievements of his child on the basis of a comparison with other children, but rather evaluates behavior in terms of his child's own growth patterns, interests, and values.
6. He helps the child make the most of his assets by providing opportunities which the child may accept or reject, even when these are not part of the parent's wishes for his child.
7. He helps the child find ways of feeling a sense of accomplishment in the activities in which he has talent and interest.

C. Recognizes the child's need to differentiate and separate himself from his parents; to become an autonomous individual.
1. He allows and encourages the child to become increasingly independent and does not resist growth toward independence.
2. He allows the child to identify with other people as he grows and develops and does not make the child feel "untrue" for such actions.
3. He encourages the child to assume responsibilities for himself and for others.
4. He lets the child carry some things out to conclusions even though he knows the child's course of action will lead him to disappointment.
5. He accepts that if a parent rears his child properly the child will become independent of his parent.
6. He recognizes that as the child becomes independent of his parents so the parent, too, must learn to become independent of the child.

D. Loves his child unconditionally.
1. He offers support and love at all times—shares his child's joys and sorrows; supports him in failures as well as successes.

2. He loves his child freely, never bargaining for love.
3. He lets the child know that he is loved—gives affection generously.
4. While he may dislike the deed, he is ever loving of the child who does it.
5. He likes to be with the child and enjoys the things they do together (Porter, 1954, pp. 176–177).

failure to please the parents are usually severe. There is a good deal of nagging, scolding, slapping, and spanking.

Child Behavior

What are the effects of acceptance and rejection on children? Although investigators have employed differing definitions, subjects, and methods, their findings have much in common.

Aggression

A number of investigators have concluded that parental acceptance tends to produce a friendly child, while parental rejection may create a hostile, aggressive one.[2] This is hardly astounding. The child who feels loved and accepted responds in kind to his parents and other people. The rejected child is sorely frustrated, and he frequently meets hostility with hostility.

The aggression shown by the rejected child is manifested in many ways and against a number of objects. Sometimes it is shown in outbreaks of sheer hostility. At other times it is more covert, making itself felt in antagonism and resentment. Resistance against adult direction and widespread nonconformity and noncompliance are also commonly seen.

This aggression finds many objects. In the home it is expressed against the parents in both open and concealed ways. In school it colors the child's relations with his teachers and other school authorities. In the community, aggressive acts bring the child into trouble with the juvenile authorities. In every area of living, children may be singled out as vulnerable objects for hostility, so that the rejected child may be truly alone and lacking in constructive relationships with his peers as well as with every other age group.

Abasement

Rejected children tend to show more aggression than accepted ones, and as a group they tend to show more abasement as well (Symonds, 1939; Wolberg, 1944). In many cases, their parents are highly punitive and not safe objects for aggression. Teachers, police, and other parent figures also cannot be assaulted with impunity. Aggression must frequently be expressed in subtle ways, and when it is sufficiently inhibited, it may be turned back upon the self.

Rejected children are neglected and punished, and they may be convinced that they are truly worthless and merit the treatment they receive. The hostile impulses that they sense in themselves and express may convince them further of their worthlessness. Guilt feelings arise, causing a need for punishment both from others and from themselves.

Rejected children generally suffer

[2] Representative studies include Baldwin, Kalhorn, and Breese (1945); Grant (1937); Newell (1934, 1936); Symonds (1939); Winstel (1951); and Wolberg (1944).

from self-devaluation. They feel unworthy, unloved, and inferior to others. It is important to note that a rejected child may manifest a high self-regard that serves as a front and cover for his true feelings. He boasts of what he is able to do and what he has done and what he will do. In his constant need to announce and to prove his worth to others and to himself, he demonstrates his underlying qualms.

Autonomy

The relationship of parental acceptance and rejection to autonomy is not simple. There is some evidence to suggest that rejected children tend to be more independent than other children. In some cases of rejection, however, the child demonstrates a heightened dependence upon the parent.

One set of investigators found that the children of mothers who showed "some" rejection were somewhat more dependent than the children of mothers who were not rejecting at all. We should add, however, that not many of the mothers in this particular study were found to be very rejecting. Where rejection is not great, and love and acceptance are available under some conditions, the child may solicit assurance of his acceptability and in the process appear more dependent (Sears, Maccoby, & Levin, 1957).

A number of investigators have noted that parental rejection may lead to accelerated independence. Since they have no one on whom they can or wish to rely, rejected children may be forced into an autonomous role. This precocious capacity for autonomy, independence, or self-reliance is sometimes held to be a "construc-

tive value" associated with rejection (Baldwin, Kalhorn, & Breese, 1945; Burgum, 1940). Unfortunately, this autonomy may represent a detachment from people; the rejected child may build a wall about himself to protect himself from painful interpersonal relationships and in doing so seal off affectional warmth as well (Wolberg, 1944).

General Findings

In general, accepted children demonstrate more highly valued personal characteristics than rejected children. Compared with rejected children, accepted youngsters are more cooperative, more friendly, and better socialized. They are more honest, dependable, and straightforward. They are better able to attend, concentrate, apply themselves, and persist at a task until it is done (Symonds, 1939).

Accepted children are more stable in their emotional reactions than rejected children. Accepted children are generally calm and happy, and their emotional expression is appropriate for their age and to the situation at hand. By contrast, rejected children tend to be emotionally unstable. They are restless, irritable, and given to wide swings in mood and infantile outbursts of temper (Symonds, 1939; Wolberg, 1944).

Rejected children have more difficulty in establishing satisfactory living routines. They demonstrate more "nervous" habits. They have more problems associated with eating, sleeping, and toilet training. These children have less control over their sexual impulses, and they show a precocious interest in heterosexual relations (Newell, 1934, 1936; Symonds, 1939; Wolberg, 1944).

Relevant Factors

Why are some parents accepting and loving, while others are rejecting? In any single case of rejection, many complex factors may be involved. However, a number of investigators have gathered evidence concerning accepting and rejecting parents that is seemingly consistent. As in other research of this kind, mothers have been more thoroughly studied than fathers, but in some of the studies both parents came under observation.[3]

The first finding has to do with the home backgrounds of the parents themselves. Accepting parents have been found to come from calm, happy, and generally well-adjusted homes in which discipline was reasonable and consistent. In many cases, rejecting parents come from broken, rejecting homes; they themselves were rejected children. They seem to be reenacting and passing along the same patterns of behavior that they were subjected to as children.

A second finding concerns the adjustment of the parents as individuals. Accepting parents demonstrate better personal adjustment. Rejecting parents tend to be immature and unstable, and they have more serious problems.

A third finding considers the interaction of the parents in the marriage relationship. In general, accepting parents are able to relate not only to each other, but to their children and other people as well. Rejecting spouses may bring defective patterns of adjustment into their marriages; the intimate relationships involved in family living more often compound than lessen their difficulties.

Rejecting Children

So far the discussion has concerned parents who accept or reject their children, but what about children who accept or reject their parents? This latter set of processes has been much less studied, but it is nevertheless important. One might expect to find a high degree of correlation between the several sets of behavior, with family members who accept or reject being accepted or rejected in return. However, there are many other factors that can enter the picture.

It has been noted, for example, that children are particularly rejecting when there are considerable differences between the two generations. This happens when rapid changes increase the distance between parents and children. It occurs in homes which attempt to preserve very different cultural patterns from those to which the children are being exposed in the community, as, for example, homes of immigrant parents or those transplanted from rural to urban settings (Bossard & Boll, 1960).

WARMTH-COLDNESS

Much of what was said about acceptance and rejection is true of warmth and coldness as well. It might be assumed that accepting parents are generally warm and that rejecting ones are generally cold. And some information concerning the effect of warmth and coldness comes from studies of institutional children who frequently ap-

---

[3] The studies on which this discussion is based include Figge (1931, 1932); Gleason (1931); Newell (1934, 1936); Porter (1955); Symonds (1939); and Wolberg (1944).

pear rejected as well as deprived of maternal warmth.

Nevertheless, researchers in this area have found warmth and coldness to be profitable concepts in themselves. They are narrower concepts, more exact and limited than acceptance and rejection. It may be difficult to imagine rejecting parents who are very warm or accepting ones who are very cold, but rejection may be masked with what appears to be affectional warmth, and even among parents who are generally conceded to be accepting there is a considerable range of affection.

Parent Behavior

The warmth or coldness of a home is usually described in terms of the affectional interplay between family members (see Fig. 12.2). Affection may be displayed in various ways. The infant may be held, cuddled, rocked, caressed, spoken and sung to. Older children may be embraced, kissed, and given verbal endearments. Affection for older or adult children may be expressed in subtle ways; considerable warmth may be revealed in a smile or a glance.

The child may experience warmth from any member of his family group. Ordinarily, however, the child's closest relationship is with his mother. In assessing the degree of warmth or coldness in a home, investigators almost without exception have focused on the interaction between mother and child. In fact, "mothering" is used synonymously with warmth; warm homes are those in which there is a good deal of mothering; in cold homes there is very little.

Investigators who have assessed maternal warmth have noted widely divergent patterns. Some mothers appear to be warm and affectionate. Others are cold and unfeeling. Between these two extremes, there are instances of every degree of warmth and coldness.

Figure 12.2 On this scale of affectionateness modified from that used by the Fels Research Institute, values range from a passionate, consuming warmth to hostile, icy coldness. Neither of the extreme ends of the scale might seem to indicate a favorable state of affairs. The term "warm" is generally used to refer to parents who express a considerable but not inordinate amount of affection, although there appears to be little to substantiate the sometimes expressed concern that "too much" warmth or affection will spoil a child. The term "cold" refers to the complete or nearly complete absence of affection (Modified from Champney, 1941 © 1941 by The Society for Research in Child Development, Inc.).

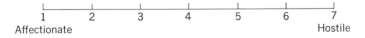

| | 1 | 2 | 3 | 4 | 5 | 6 | 7 | |
| Affectionate | | | | | | | | Hostile |

Identification of the seven points of this scale is as follows:
1 Passionate, consuming, intense, ardent, uncontrolled.

2 Affectionate, warm, fondling, loving, expressive.

3 Temperate, fond, attached, forgiving, kind.

4 Objective, inhibited, neutral, matter-of-fact.

5 Cool, aloof, distant, forbidding.

6 Avoiding, annoyed, irritated, bothered.

7 Hostile, rejecting, disliking, blaming, icy.

Sears, Maccoby, and Levin (1957) studied maternal warmth along with a number of other dimensions of child rearing. Information was secured through recorded interviews which were later transcribed and rated. Here, as an illustration, is part of the conversation between an interviewer (I) and a mother (M) who was rated "warm":

I: I am wondering if you could tell me a a little more about how you and Jane get along together—what sort of things do you enjoy with her?

M: Well, everything—I think it's because she's so sweet and we seem to get along famously.

I: If you were telling somebody about what she's like, what would you say? What do you like about her?

M: Everything—how very patient she is, and how understanding. She's very kind. Well, if I'm talking on the phone —sometimes the phone rings continuously here, and especially in the morning when I'm getting her breakfast, she's so good about it, she's so patient; and sometimes I'll tell the people on the phone "I'm getting my daughter's breakfast," and some people seem to ignore the fact that the baby should be taken care of.

I: In what ways do you get on each other's nerves?

M: We don't.

I: Not at all?

M: No, I don't think so. I can't think of anything that we do.

I: Do you show your affection toward each other quite a bit, or are you fairly reserved people, you and Jane?

M: Oh, no, we show our affections—we hug each other, and kiss, and play.

I: Do you find time to play with her just for your own pleasure nowadays?

M: Yes, I do.

I: Tell us about that.

M: Well, as soon as my work is done, if she's around, I'll call her and say,

"Come on, let's have some fun"; and we'll sit down and she'll sit on my lap, and sometimes I rock her back and forth, and kiss her. She likes to be kissed, she loves it, and I'll cuddle her, and she loves to be cuddled. Or I'll play a game with her.[4]

Here, by contrast, is part of an interview with a "cold" mother:

I: Have things been easier or pleasanter for you in any way since he's been in school?

M: Well, he's away, but the minute he comes home I wish the sessions were longer. While he's in school it's fine, but the minute he steps inside the door, trouble starts. He'll take something his sister is playing with, then the fight starts—oh, an argument starts, or something.

I: I'm wondering if you could describe the relationship between you and Bobby—what sort of things do you enjoy in him?

M: (Pause) He's naughty an awful lot, but I don't know whether I just take that as part of growing up, but I enjoy him. He talks too much sometimes.

I: In what ways do you get on each other's nerves?

M: Oh, guns, and the noise in the house get on my nerves most of the time. This constant run, run, run, you know, that shooting business. If I have the baby asleep—she's so finicky, if I do finally get her to sleep during the day —someone starts to cry or something else, and wakes her up, I usually get pretty ruffled. I think he starts to cry for no reason.

I: Do you show your affection toward each other quite a bit, or are you fairly reserved?

[4] From *Patterns of Child Rearing* by R. R. Sears, E. E. Maccoby and H. Levin. Copyright © 1957 by Harper & Row, Publishers, Inc. Reprinted by permission of Harper & Row, Publishers. P. 53.

M: *No—we—as much as I can. I, as a child, never kissed my parents, but I'll kiss him good night, or kiss him good-bye, something like that, hug him, that's about all. We're not over— not overdo it.*[5]

Child Behavior

What is the effect of affectional warmth on children? How much mothering does a child require? Some investigators have attempted to throw light on the problem by studying mother-child relationships in unbroken homes. Others have given a good deal of attention to situations in which mothering is sharply reduced or almost completely absent; they have studied children who have spent appreciable lengths of time in orphanages, hospitals, and other institutions in which normal patterns of mothering were disturbed.

Achievement

There is a good deal of evidence that sensory, social, and affectional stimulation plays a vital role in the development of young children (Yarrow, 1964). Warm mothers generally provide a good deal of this important stimulation. Babies who are inadequately mothered have been shown to be generally retarded in their overall development (Robertson, 1962).

Research on academic performance suggests that parental warmth may be an important ingredient in scholastic success. Generally speaking, students whose parents are warm and interested do better than those whose parents are lukewarm or neutral (Lavin, 1965). Children from warm homes may generalize positive feelings to

[5] From *Patterns of Child Rearing* by R. R. Sears, E. E. Maccoby and H. Levin. Copyright © 1957 by Harper & Row, Publishers, Inc. Reprinted by permission of Harper and Row, Publishers. P. 55.

teachers and scholastic activities. Children with cold or hostile parents may transfer unfavorable attitudes to the classroom; school relationships and accomplishment can suffer as a result.

Succorance

In one investigation of the practices of parents in dealing with preschool children, both the parent's affection for the child and the child's affection for the parent were considered. Interestingly enough, it was found that the children who received the least affection from their parents were the ones who made the most affectional overtures toward their parents. The investigator felt that these children were insecure about their status. In their actions they solicited needed affection and assurance (Lafore, 1945).

Sometimes we hear people worry about whether "too much" affection or warmth may spoil a child. Finney (1961), who searched for an answer to this question, concluded that there was no danger. Where a child appeared to be spoiled, that is, too dependent or self-centered or conscienceless, the ill effects were attributed to lack of firmness or to overprotection on the part of the mother. It was held that warmth itself lessened children's dependency behavior.

Aggression

Children who are raised in relatively affectionless environments prove to be more aggressive than children who have been raised in warmer ones. Bowlby (1952) in his review of the literature concerning institutionalized children found considerable evidence that such children were aggressive and poorly controlled. Sears and his associates (1957) studied children being raised in their own homes and found that maternal coldness was associated with high aggression.

It is interesting to consider the effect that parental warmth may have on children even when other family factors are far from optimal. Stein (1944) contrasted an over-inhibited group of children with another that was unsocialized and aggressive. She found that whatever its other faults, the home environment of the overinhibited group presented some evidence of warmth which, she speculated, caused the child to inhibit his hostility. By contrast, the home environment of the aggressive group was cold or indifferent.

General Findings

The evidence indicates that parental warmth is an essential ingredient of growth and development. Children from cold, affectionless environments suffer more problems than do those who have experienced greater warmth. This conclusion appears to hold true whether these children have been raised in institutions or in their own homes. Sears and his associates (1957) found that maternal coldness is associated with persistent bed-wetting, feeding problems, slow conscience development, emotional upset during severe toilet training, and, as we have previously noted, high aggression. Maternal warmth, on the other hand, appears to exert a widespread beneficial influence. In speculating about the reasons for this influence the authors state:

There is no clear evidence in our findings to explain why warmth should have such widespread influence. We can speculate, on the basis of our general theory of the learning process, about the possibility that it may play several roles. A warm mother spends more time with her child. She of-

fers him more rewards, technically speaking, and gives him more guidance. He develops stronger expectancies of her reciprocal affection, and thus is more highly motivated to learn how to behave as she wants him to. He becomes more susceptible to control by her, for he has more to gain and more to lose. It seems likely, too, that he gets proportionately more satisfaction and less frustration from his growing desire for affection.[6]

Finney (1961) concluded that maternal warmth and nurturance had an important positive influence on children. He found that nurturance lessened the child's pessimism, anxiety, passive hostility, and, as was already indicated, dependency. Furthermore, the mother's nurturance expedited the child's development of conscience.

Relevant Factors

Sears and his associates (1957) made a study of the factors which appeared to be associated with maternal warmth. In general, the mother's personal adjustment was found to be positively correlated with her ability to express warmth and affection. The higher the mother's self-esteem, esteem for her husband, and satisfaction with her general life situation, the greater the warmth she displayed in her relationships with her children.

The composition of the family also appeared to be related to maternal warmth. There seemed to be no difference in the amount of warmth demonstrated toward first, second, and third children. However, mothers were likely to be warmer toward a new child if his birth did not occur too soon after that of a sibling. For first chil-

[6] From *Patterns of Child Rearing* by R. R. Sears, E. E. Maccoby and H. Levin. Copyright © 1957 by Harper & Row, Publishers, Inc. Reprinted by permission of Harper & Row, Publishers. Pp. 483–484.

dren, the age of the mother seemed to be unrelated to the amount of warmth she exhibited; otherwise, older mothers proved to be warmer toward their children than did younger ones.

Levy (1955) has noted that there seems to be some lifelong consistency in the amount of maternal behavior that a woman shows. He points out that some women appear to be "natural-born" mothers while others innately seem to reject the maternal role. This led him to hypothesize that there might be important constitutional factors in maternal behavior, but so far the evidence for this is quite limited.

Schaefer and Bayley (1963) also found that mothers tend to be relatively consistent in the amount of love (or hostility) they show their children from infancy to preadolescence. By contrast, the amount of control that a mother exerts is not consistent over the same span. These investigators suggest that this may be attributed to the fact that while the child's need for control decreases with increasing maturity, his need for a warm and positive relationship remains constant and stable.

Several sets of investigators have found that middle-class mothers, as a group, are warmer toward their children than are lower-class or working mothers (Bayley & Schaefer, 1960; Sears, Maccoby & Levin, 1957). Other observers have noted that the American family seems to be getting warmer—that the present generation of parents is freer in expressing affection than earlier ones—and that this is especially true of the father, who appears to be less and less of a remote and authoritarian figure (Bronfenbrenner, 1961; Bronson, Katten, & Livson, 1959; Devereux, Bronfenbrenner, & Suci, 1963).

Warm and Cold Children

Warmth and coldness in parents and their possible effects on children have been discussed but what about these qualities in children and their effects on parents? Certainly they would seem to be important. However, as in the case of acceptance and rejection, these "reverse" processes have been much less studied.

Parents note considerable differences in the amounts of warmth expressed by their children. Some are warm and seek closeness; others are more matter-of-fact and detached. Of course, the amount of warmth varies considerably from time to time. The extravagant amounts of warmth (and coldness or hate) shown by the young child become considerably modified as the child grows older.

Ordinarily warmth is considered a desirable characteristic in children. When, for example, one parent has an unresponsive mate, he or she may look all the more for affection from the children of the family and be doubly frustrated if it is not forthcoming. But, depending on the particular needs of a parent, great warmth and affection expressed by a child can be a source of irritation or embarrassment as well as of satisfaction.

Presentation 12.2 How does socioeconomic status relate to parent-child patterns and mental health? Chilman reviewed the research evidence and found the patterns of very low income families in sharp contrast to patterns held conducive to the mental health of children. She concluded that the environments and child-rearing patterns of the poor should be simultaneously modified in order to reduce the high rates of mental illness found in this group.

Patterns More Characteristic of Families with Mentally Healthy Children	*Patterns More Characteristic of Very Low Income Families*
1. Respect for child as individual whose behavior is caused by a multiple of factors. Acceptance of own role in events that occur.	1. Misbehavior regarded as such in terms of concrete pragmatic outcomes; reasons for behavior not considered. Projection of blame on others.
2. Commitment to slow development of child from infancy to maturity; stresses and pressures of each stage accepted by parent because of perceived worth of ultimate goal of raising "happy," successful son or daughter.	2. Lack of goal commitment and of belief in long-range success; a main object for parent and child is to "keep out of trouble"; orientation toward fatalism, impulse gratification, and sense of alienation.
3. Relative sense of competence in handling child's behavior.	3. Sense of impotence in handling children's behavior, as well as in other areas.
4. Discipline chiefly verbal, mild, reasonable, consistent, based on needs of child and family and of society; more emphasis on rewarding good behavior than on punishing bad behavior.	4. Discipline harsh, inconsistent, physical, makes use of ridicule; based on whether child's behavior does or does not annoy parent.
5. Open, free, verbal communication between parent and child; control largely verbal.	5. Limited verbal communication; control largely physical.
6. Democratic rather than autocratic or laissez-faire methods of rearing, with both parents in equalitarian but not necessarily interchangeable roles. Companionship between parents and children.	6. Authoritarian rearing methods; mother chief child-care agent; father, when in home, mainly a punitive figure. Little support and acceptance of child as an individual.
7. Parents view selves as generally competent adults, and are generally satisfied with themselves and their situation.	7. Low parental self-esteem, sense of defeat.
8. Intimate, expressive, warm relationship between parent and child, allowing for gradually increasing independence. Sense of continuing responsibility.	8. Large families; more impulsive, narcissistic parent behavior. Orientation to "excitement." Abrupt, early yielding of independence.
9. Presence of father in home and lack of severe marital conflict.	9. Father out of home (under certain circumstances).
10. Free verbal communication about sex, acceptance of child's sex needs, channeling of sex drive through "healthy" psychological defenses, acceptance of slow growth toward impulse control and sex satisfaction in marriage; sex education by both father and mother.	10. Repressive, punitive attitude about sex, sex questioning, and experimentation. Sex viewed as exploitative relationship.
11. Acceptance of child's drive for aggression but channeling it into socially approved outlets.	11. Alternating encouragement and restriction of aggression, primarily related to consequences of aggression for parents.
12. In favor of new experiences; flexible.	12. Distrust of new experiences; rigid.
13. Happiness of parental marriage.	13. High rates of marital conflict and family breakdown (Slightly modified from Chilman, 1966, pp. 28–29).

DEMOCRACY-DICTATORSHIP

Democracy is an increasingly popular familial philosophy, but many homes remain strongly held dictatorships (see Fig. 12.3). It is not unusual to see one parent hold sway over the rest of the family, dictating to the children and to the other parent as well. Occasionally, too, a child may usurp power and through one tactic or another contrive to rule the rest of the family.

Parent Behavior

In the democratic home the child is given a voice in determining the policies of the family. Respect is shown for the child's ability to assist in his own direction and in the direction of the affairs of the family.

In the dictatorial home, policies are handed down by the parents without the consultation of the children. In intent, however, dictatorial policies may be benevolent as well as selfish.

A number of factors are associated with democracy in the home. In general, democratic homes provide a good deal of freedom. Requirements are relatively few and mild. Parental suggestions do not carry the weight of law; the child is free to consider and accept or reject them at his own discretion.

Democratic homes usually have well-formulated policies. Regulations and requirements are clearly spelled out and consistently followed. Furthermore, an attempt is made to justify these policies to the child. The reasons for suggestions, de-

Figure 12.3 Shown here is a somewhat modified form of the scale used by the Fels Research Institute to rate the democracy of the regulation and enforcement policy in a home. The top of the scale describes an adherence to democratic philosophy which may make excessive demands on the judgments of the children in the family; carried to this extent, there may be philosophy for philosophy's sake rather than for the sake of the family's welfare. The other end of the scale describes a home in which all the policies are dictated from above, and the children are never consulted (Modified from Champney, 1941. © 1941 by The Society for Research in Child Development, Inc.).

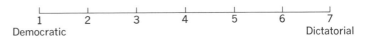

The seven points of the scale are identified as follows:

1 Endures much inconvenience and some risk to child's welfare in giving child large share in policy forming. Consults with child in formulating policies whenever possible.

2 Attempts to adjust policies to child's wishes wherever practicable. Often consults child.

3 Deliberately democratic in certain safe or trivial matters, but dictates when there is a sharp conflict between child's wishes and other essential requirements.

4 Neither democratic nor dictatorial, deliberately. Follows most practical or easiest course in most cases.

5 Tends to be rather dictatorial, but usually gives benevolent consideration to child's desires. Seldom consults child.

6 Dictatorial in most matters, but accedes to child's wishes occasionally when they do not conflict with own convenience or standards.

7 Dictates policies without regard to child's wishes. Never consults child when setting up regulations.

mands, and penalties are carefully explained.

Democratic homes tend to supply more intellectual stimulation. They generally encourage curiosity in the child and attempt to satisfy it by readily responding to his questions and search for knowledge. In addition, they provide a freedom for exploration and experimentation.

In democratic homes there is a close rapport between parents and children. The parents are knowledgeable about children; they understand their children's behavior. These homes are usually fairly affectionate, and the children in them are provided with a good deal of emotional support (Baldwin, 1948, 1949; Baldwin, Kalhorn, & Breese, 1945).

Child Behavior

This section will contrast the behavior of children raised in family democracies with that of children brought up in parental dictatorships.[7] Then the special section which follows will present several studies that contrast parent dictatorships with child dictatorships.

Achievement

Democratic homes are usually stimulating ones, and children from such homes are generally found to be accelerated in intellectual development. As a rule the children are curious, searching, and highly motivated for academic tasks. In their work they demonstrate a good deal of originality and constructiveness.

Dominance

Children from democratic homes generally

enjoy favored positions in the groups of which they are members. Their attempts to dominate others are relatively successful, and they tend to find positions of leadership. As leaders, they are assisted by their superior intellectual status as well as by their ability to relate to others. However, they are generally successful whether their leadership is domineering or friendly.

Deference

Although they successfully dominate their age-mates, children from democratic homes may show considerable deference as well. This is particularly true in their relationships with adults. Children from dictatorial homes may be submissive or rebellious or both of these patterns by turns, but children from democratic homes seem more genuinely compliant, more responsive to the opinions of others, and more sensitive to praise and blame.

Aggression

Children from democratic and dictatorial homes alike may demonstrate considerable aggression. In the democratic home there is usually greater tolerance for aggression, and this aggression may manifest itself in both constructive and hostile ways. In general, children from dictatorial homes show a greater tendency to quarrel and fight with other children in the school situation.

Affiliation

Children in democratic homes tend to form close relationships with members of their own families. By the time these children reach school age, they are able to relate well to other children and adults. In school they appear to be friendlier and more popu-

[7] This discussion is based on Baldwin (1948, 1949, 1955); Baldwin, Kalhorn, and Breese (1945); Lafore (1945); Mueller (1944); and Radke (1946).

lar than children from less democratic homes.

General Findings

Compared with other children, those from democratic homes are generally more stable in their emotional reactions. They express themselves well but in a modulated fashion. They are less excitable and demonstrate fewer reckless, uninhibited reactions. They are also less fearful than other children.

It has been pointed out, however, that even a genuinely democratic home may not provide the child with a good environment for development. For one thing, some democratic parents tend toward a cold scientific objectivity in dealing with their children. This family climate, sometimes called "cold democracy," may have a number of adverse effects on children (Baldwin, Kalhorn, & Breese, 1945; Bronfenbrenner, 1961).

To understand the effects of parental democracy (or any other dimension for that matter) we must consider it in relation to everything else that is happening in the home. Baldwin and his associates make this point in discussing a number of democratic homes which were studied at the Fels Research Institute. They write:

> Analysis of the cases falling in the democratic group makes it increasingly evident that neither a democratic philosophy nor democratic techniques applied in the training of the child can provide an automatically optimum environment. Parental goals are as important as the techniques used in attaining those goals, and healthy personalities in the parent are a prerequisite for a healthy child. Adequately applied, these techniques may facilitate the production of a child who is an independent human being, secure in his relationships, able to appraise himself and his environment, and capable of self-direction and attainment. But these goals of the democratic method can be defeated by the parent who warps the child's personality in some other way, the parent whose own misapplied devotion and confined viewpoint restrict the child's growth and freedom or the parent who, by his own withdrawal and detachment, makes the child insecure and uncertain in his goals and relationships (1945, pp. 51–52).

Relevant Factors

In general, democratic parents are superior in intellect to parents using mixed and autocratic practices. Democratic parents have higher intelligence quotients; they are more highly educated and more frequently have college educations. Therefore, the democratic household tends to be a more stimulating environment for children (Baldwin, 1949; Baldwin, Kalhorn, & Breese, 1945).

There is some evidence to suggest that in many instances parental dictatorships are wielded by one parent. This parent dictates not only to the children but to the other parent too. Mothers as well as fathers may assume dictatorship roles.

Symonds (1939) suggests that dominated children grow up to be dominating parents. In this way, dictatorial policy may be passed down from one generation to another. He cautiously states the hypothesis that ". . . a person adopts an attitude as a parent similar to the attitude held toward him by the parent of the same sex."

In general, however, the present generation of parents appears to be less dictatorial than the preceding one. And the trend toward greater democracy in the home appears to be continuing. Democracy is the most widely taught philosophy of family relations in our culture at the present time. It is encouraged by almost every worker in the field: psychologists, psychiatrists, social workers, teachers, pediatricians, and others.

Child Dictators

In the democratic home every member of the family is consulted to some extent in the making of policy. In the dictatorial home one or both parents usually formulate the policies. However, sometimes a child dominates the other members of the family.

Symonds (1939) studied twenty-eight matched pairs of children. The children of each pair were similar in all important respects except that one child was parent-*dominated* while the other was parent-*dominating*. Neither the dominated nor the dominating children had a monopoly on qualities which the investigator considered desirable. In each case certain desirable characteristics had been acquired at the cost of certain undesirable ones.

Dominated children tended to conform to adult expectations both at home and at school. They were polite, careful, and dependable. At the same time, they appeared to be quite sensitive and shy, and they had some difficulty in expressing themselves. Dominating children were more aggressive, disobedient, and irresponsible. At school they were disorderly and lacked ability to sustain interest and effort. However, these latter children demonstrated greater independence and self-confidence. They were outgoing and able to express themselves effectively.

Similar evidence was produced by Levy (1943) in his clinical study of a group of twenty children who were subjected to maternal overprotection. In eleven of the twenty cases, the child was found to be the dominant member of the mother-child relationship. To varying degrees in these cases the mother indulged the child and submitted to his demands. From this type of relationship the child emerged rebellious and aggressive; he was disobedient, impudent, and demonstrated his feelings in temper tantrums and tyrannical actions. Because he attempted to carry this behavior over to his playmates, he encountered considerable difficulty in social relationships.

In the remaining nine cases, the mother was the dominant member of the mother-child pair. She attempted to mold the child according to her own ideas by discouraging and punishing the child's independent efforts. This type of relationship appeared to produce a child that was dependent and submissive. At home he was conforming and obedient. Again there was difficulty in social relationships with playmates, this time because of a carry-over of home attitudes and behavior involving timidity and withdrawal.

PERMISSIVENESS-RESTRICTIVENESS

There are many reasons why the activities of children must be restricted in some degree. Most important, the safety of the child must be ensured. At the same time, the parent is concerned about the well-being of other objects, both animate and inanimate, that fill the household. The child must adjust his activities so that they assist rather than interfere with the activities of others. And as he develops, he is expected to display progressively more mature and adultlike behavior (Sears et al., 1957).

Parent Behavior

The dimension of restrictiveness-permissiveness refers to the extent to which the parents maintain standards of behavior to which the child is expected to conform. These standards refer to the do's and don't's of everyday living. In the restrictive family there may be many do's and don't's. By contrast, the permissive family allows the child considerable freedom of action (see Fig. 12.4).

In studying patterns of child rearing, Sears and his associates (1957) gave attention to the restrictions and demands that mothers placed on their children. A number of scales were devised to describe this behavior. At their restrictive end or

anchor point these scales identify or represent the following qualities of child-rearing behavior:

1 *High restrictions on play in the house and with furniture*
2 *High demands for good table manners*
3 *High restriction on making noise*
4 *High demands for being neat and orderly*
5 *Severe toilet training*
6 *High standards for strict obedience*
7 *Strong emphasis on doing well in school*
8 *Strict and rejective response to dependency*
9 *High use of physical punishment*
10 *Severe punishment for aggression toward parents*
11 *Low permissiveness for aggression toward parents*
12 *Low permissiveness for aggression among siblings*
13 *Low permissiveness for aggression to other children*

Figure 12.4 This is a modified form of the scale used to measure restrictiveness of regulations by the Fels Research Institute. The top of the scale describes highly restrictive parents; here the extreme number of do's and don't's seems unwarranted and crippling to the child. At the other end of the scale is a value identifying the family which scarcely limits the freedom of its children in any way; such a policy may be a manifestation of neglect rather than an expression of permissiveness as a policy (Modified from Champney, 1941. © 1941 by The Society for Research in Child Development, Inc.).

Identification of the six scale points is as follows:
1 Parent's standards for child's conduct are minutely restrictive beyond all reasonable interpretation of either child's welfare or family convenience.
2 Requirements are unnecessarily abundant and exacting, but usually aimed at practical ends rather than "pure discipline."
3 Restrictions are moderate and practical, but parent shows little concern for child's freedom as an end, slapping on requirements whenever they seem expedient.
4 Standards and regulations are somewhat liberal. Freedom is allowed in a few matters commonly subject ot regimentation.
5 Child is expected to conform to a few basic standards, but parent will endure considerable annoyance rather than unduly restrict child's freedom.
6 Standards are both scarce and mild, limiting child's freedom barely enough to avoid the police and the hospital.

14 *Low permissiveness for nudity or immodesty*

15 *Low permissiveness for masturbation*

16 *Low permissiveness for sex play with other children*[8]

It was found that mothers tended to be fairly consistent in the degree of permissiveness they displayed. Sears states, "If a mother was quite tolerant of her child's aggressive behavior, she was likely to be tolerant of his sexual behavior, too. And if she was permissive in those respects, the chances are she was not very strict about table manners, or noise, or neatness around the house. Likewise, she probably did not insist on rigid obedience to her every command" (p. 308).

Another set of investigators, however, found that, considered over the entire range of infancy and childhood and up to adolescence, a mother's controlling behavior may not be very consistent; she sometimes appears to offer her child less autonomy and sometimes more. They suggest that this may be due to the greater autonomy a child requires as he moves toward maturity, and that this is a dimension of behavior which may be quite amenable to change (Schaefer & Bayley, 1960, 1963).

Before considering the effect of permissiveness on children, we might give some attention to its effect on parents. Permissive parents experience more interference with their own activities and privacy than do restrictive parents. Permissive parents have more difficulty in controlling their children's activities even within the broad limits they impose. In one sense, more freedom for children means less freedom for parents (Blood, 1953b).

[8] From *Patterns of Child Rearing* by R. R. Sears, E. E. Maccoby and H. Levin. Copyright © 1957 by Harper & Row, Publishers, Inc. Reprinted by permission of Harper & Row, Publishers, P. 472.

Child Behavior

There is relatively little research information concerning the effects of permissiveness and strictness on children's behavior. Furthermore, some of the most carefully accumulated information reveals that permissiveness may have different effects, depending upon the sort of activity under consideration.

Aggression

Sears and his associates (1957) have noted that permissiveness tends to increase or lead to continuing aggression in children; homes that take a permissive attitude toward aggression produce children who are relatively more aggressive than homes that do not. Baldwin (1948) found that parents who exert considerable control may have children who are comparatively less aggressive and less disobedient, and less negativistic and quarrelsome as well.

Succorance

Sears's group studied the effect of permissiveness upon dependency as well as upon aggression. Although permissiveness for aggression leads to continuing aggression, permissiveness for dependent behavior appears to have no ascertainable effect. Even when dependency behavior is rewarded, dependency does not appear to increase. And, curiously enough, punishment for dependency serves to make children more dependent than ever.

General Findings

Reviewing the evidence of a number of studies, Becker (1964) concludes that both restrictiveness and permissiveness have their good and bad points. He writes:

Restrictiveness, while fostering well-controlled, socialized behavior, tends also to lead to fearful, dependent, and submissive behaviors, a dulling of intellectual striving and inhibited hostility. Permissiveness on the other hand, while fostering outgoing, sociable, assertive behaviors and intellectual striving, tends also to lead to less persistence and increased aggressiveness (p. 197).

The evidence suggests that there may be an optimum amount of control and that the child may suffer when there is too little or too much. And sometimes damage is done when control is inconsistent. In a study of juvenile delinquency, for example, it was noted that the delinquent group had been subjected to control that was too lax, erratic, or overly strict while the control

Table 12.1 An important way of shedding light on parent-child relationships is to examine the family backgrounds of children who are having trouble at home, in school, or in the larger society. Sheldon and Eleanor Glueck contrasted 500 delinquent boys with 500 who were comparable but nondelinquent. Many differences were found in the family backgrounds of the two groups. Compared with nondelinquents, delinquent boys were more frequently from broken and unstable homes; delinquents had experienced less acceptance and affection and, as the material below indicates, poorer patterns of discipline.*

	Parental Discipline			
	By Mothers of		By Fathers of	
Description	Delinquents	Nondelinquents	Delinquents	Nondelinquents
Lax	56.8%	11.7%	26.6%	17.9%
Overstrict	4.4	1.6	26.1	8.7
Erratic	34.6	21.1	41.6	17.9
Firm but kindly	4.2	65.6	5.7	55.5

* Modified from Glueck and Glueck (1950).

Table 12.2 What are the effects of various dimensions of parent behavior in combination? What happens when a parent is warm *and* permissive? What happens when he is warm *but* restrictive? Becker has tabulated the findings of some studies which have simultaneously explored the dimensions of warmth-hostility and permissiveness-restrictiveness. The warm-permissive parental condition appears to allow for a maximum amount of personal and social development.*

	Restrictive	Permissive
Warm	Submissive, dependent, polite, neat, obedient Minimal aggression Maximum rule enforcement, boys Dependent, not friendly, not creative Maximal compliance	Active, socially outgoing, creative, successfully aggressive Minimal rule enforcement, boys Facilitates adult role taking Minimal self-aggression, boys Independent, friendly, creative, low projective hostility
Hostile	"Neurotic" problems More quarreling and shyness with peers Socially withdrawn Low in adult role taking Maximal self-aggression, boys	Delinquency Noncompliance Maximal aggression

*Modified from Becker (1964, p. 198).

exerted on a nondelinquent control group was described as "firm but kindly" (Glueck & Glueck, 1950) (see Tables 12.1 and 12.2).

Relevant Factors

A number of investigators have been interested in the relationship between social class and patterns of parent-child interaction. Generally speaking, the results indicate that middle-class parents are more permissive than lower-class ones. However, the differences are not always large or significant, and there is some suggestion that the gap between the classes is narrowing (Caldwell, 1964).

It is not surprising that permissive and restrictive parents differ in their conceptions of the "good" child. Restrictive parents tend to take what has been called a traditional view; they prefer the child that is obedient, respectful, neat, helpful, and religious. Permissive parents take a "developmental" view; they identify the good child as one who is healthy, happy, loving, sociable, and eager to learn and grow (Blood, 1953a, 1953b).

During the past few decades the American home has become more democratic, and it appears to have become more permissive too (Caldwell, 1964). However, one writer has noted "a slowing up in the headlong rush toward greater permissiveness" correlated with a shift from adjustment to achievement as a prime goal of child rearing (Bronfenbrenner, 1958, 1961). There has also been a shifting of roles involving the father and the mother, with the father becoming more affectionate and less authoritarian while the mother has increasingly assumed more of the disciplinary role (Bronfenbrenner, 1961; Bronson et al., 1959).

SUMMARY

The interaction between parents and children has been considerably studied and written about. However, existing research has been open to a number of criticisms because of the subjects which have been used, the methods employed, and the conclusions drawn. Because of the complexities of families and the limitations of the research that has been done on them, care must be taken in attempting to generalize from existing studies.

One pattern of parent-child interaction which has received a good deal of attention is acceptance-rejection. Acceptance has been defined in various ways. For example, it has been defined as the amount of devotion that a parent shows and also as the extent to which a parent provides a home environment which is optimal for the child's development. Two sorts of rejection have been noted, one that is passive and another that is more active. Existing research indicates, among other important effects, that accepted children are better adjusted than rejected children. Compared with rejecting parents, more accepting parents generally appear to have more highly valued personal and marital qualities and more stable family backgrounds.

A second and related pattern is warmth-coldness. A number of effects in children have been held to be correlated with this dimension of parent behavior; in general, warmth appears to have a positive effect while coldness (especially in considerable degree) has a negative influence. Mothers are fairly consistent in the amounts of warmth they demonstrate over a period of time. The mother's personal and marital happiness seems to be positively related to her degree of warmth, and middle-class mothers as a group have been held to be warmer toward their children than are lower-class mothers. American parents seem to be becoming more openly affectionate over the years, and this may be especially true of the father, who appears to be less and less of a remote and authoritarian figure.

A third pattern of parent-child interaction is democracy-dictatorship. Democratic homes which have been studied appear to be relatively high in the amount of freedom they allow their children and in the amount of intellectual stimulation and emotional support they provide. Democratic policies in the home are generally believed to have a beneficial effect on chil-

dren, but other factors may modify or negate this effect. Dictatorial homes may be dominated by both parents, but such homes frequently seem to be under the control of only one parent, and occasionally a child usurps the position of power. American homes seem to be in the process of becoming more democratic.

A fourth pattern which has been studied is permissiveness-restrictiveness. There is some evidence that mothers of young children are consistent in the degree of permissiveness that they show, but considered over a number of years the amount of autonomy that a mother allows her children may vary. This pattern of interaction seems to have complex effects, and children can suffer from too much control as well as from too little. It appears that better-educated, middle-class mothers are not so controlling as are less-educated, lower-class ones. It has been suggested that the American home has been in the process of becoming more permissive over the past few decades, but that this trend may now be slowing down.

REFERENCES

Baldwin, A. L. Socialization and the parent-child relationship. *Child Development,* 1948, **19,** 127–136.

———. The effect of home environment on nursery school behavior. *Child Development,* 1949, **20,** 49–61.

———. *Behavior and Development in Childhood.* New York: Holt, 1955.

———, Kalhorn, J., & Breese, F. H. Patterns of parent behavior. *Psychological Monographs,* 1945, **58,** No. 3 (Whole No. 268).

Bayley, N., & Schaefer, E. S. Relationships between socioeconomic variables and the behavior of mothers toward young children. *The Journal of Genetic Psychology,* 1960, **96,** 61–77.

Becker, W. C. Consequences of different kinds of parental discipline. In M. L. Hoffman & L. W. Hoffman (Eds.), *Review of Child Development Research.* Vol. 1. New York: Russell Sage, 1964. Pp. 169–208.

Blood, R. O., Jr. A situational approach to the study of permissiveness in child-rearing. *American Sociological Review*, 1953, **18**, 84–87. (a)

————. Consequences of permissiveness for parents of young children. *Marriage and Family Living*, 1953, **15**, 209–212. (b)

Bossard, J. H. S., & Boll, E. S. *The Sociology of Child Development*. (3rd ed.) New York: Harper & Row, 1960.

Bowlby, J. Maternal care and mental health. *World Health Organization Monograph*, 1952, No. 2.

Bronfenbrenner, U. Socialization and social class through time and space. In E. E. Maccoby, T. M. Newcomb, and E. L. Hartley (Eds.), *Readings in Social Psychology*. New York: Holt, 1958. Pp. 400–425.

————. The changing American child: A speculative analysis. *Merrill-Palmer Quarterly*, 1961, **7**, 73–84.

Bronson, W. C., Katten, E. S., & Livson, N. Patterns of authority and affection in two generations. *Journal of Abnormal and Social Psychology*, 1959, **58**, 143–152.

Burgum, M. Constructive values associated with rejection. *American Journal of Orthopsychiatry*, 1940, **10**, 312–326.

Caldwell, B. M. The effects of infant care. In M. L. Hoffman & L. W. Hoffman (Eds.), *Review of Child Development Research*. New York: Russell Sage, 1964. Pp. 9–87.

Champney, H. The measurement of parent behavior. *Child Development*, 1941, **12**, 131–166.

Chilman, C. S. *Growing Up Poor*. Welfare Administration, U.S. Department of Health, Education, and Welfare, 1966.

Devereux, E. C., Jr., Bronfenbrenner, U., & Suci, G. J. Patterns of parent behavior in the United States of America and the Federal Republic of Germany: A cross-national comparison. *International Social Science Journal*, 1963, **14**, 488–506.

Figge, M. The etiology of maternal rejection: A study of certain aspects of the mother's life. *Smith College Studies in Social Work*, 1931, **1**, 407. (Abstract).

————. Some factors in the etiology of maternal rejection. *Smith College Studies in Social Work*, 1932, **2**, 237–260.

Finney, J. C. Some maternal influences on children's personality and character. *Genetic Psychology Monographs*, 1961, **63**, 199–278.

Gleason, M. C. A study of attitudes leading to the rejection of the child by the mother. *Smith College Studies in Social Work*, 1931, **1**, 407–408. (Abstract).

Glueck, S., & Glueck, E. *Unraveling Juvenile Delinquency*. Cambridge, Mass.: Commonwealth Fund: Harvard University Press, 1950.

Grant, E. I. Effect of certain factors in the home environment upon child behavior. Unpublished master's thesis, State University of Iowa, 1937. Cited by R. Updegraff, Recent approaches to the study of the preschool child. III. Influence of parental attitudes on child behavior. *Journal of Consulting Psychology*, 1939, **3**, 34–36.

Kagan, J., & Moss, H. A. *Birth to Maturity*. New York: Wiley, 1962.

Lafore, G. G. Practices of parents in dealing with preschool children. *Child Development Monographs*, 1945, No. 31.

Lavin, D. E. *The Prediction of Academic Performance*. New York: Russell Sage, 1965.

Levy, D. M. *Maternal Overprotection*. New York: Columbia, 1943.

————. Psychosomatic studies of some aspects of maternal behavior. In C. Kluckhohn & H. A. Murray (Eds.), *Personality in Nature, Society, and Culture*. (2nd ed.) New York: Knopf, 1955. Pp. 104–110.

Mueller, D. D. Parental domination as seen by a child guidance clinic. *Smith College Studies in Social Work*, 1944, **15**, 133–134. (Abstract).

Newell, H. W. The psycho-dynamics of maternal rejection. *The American Journal of Orthopsychiatry*, 1934, **4**, 387–401.

————. A further study of maternal rejection. *The American Journal of Ortho-psychiatry*, 1936, **6**, 576–589.

Porter, B. M. Measurement of parental acceptance of children. *Journal of Home Economics*, 1954, **46**, 176–182.

————. The relationship between marital adjustment and parental acceptance of children. *Journal of Home Economics*, 1955, **47**, 157–164.

Radke, M. J. The relation of parental authority to children's behavior and attitudes. *University of Minnesota Child Welfare Monographs*, 1946, No. 22.

Robertson, J. Mothering as an influence on early development. *Psychoanalytic Study of the Child*, 1962, **17**, 245–264.

Schaefer, E. S., & Bayley, N. Consistency of maternal behavior from infancy to pre-adolescence. *Journal of Abnormal and Social Psychology*, 1960, **61**, 1–6.

————, & ————. Maternal behavior, child behavior, and their intercorrelations from infancy through adolescence. *Monographs of the Society for Research in Child Development*, 1963, **28**, No. 3 (Serial No. 87).

————, Bell, R. Q., & ————. Development of a maternal behavior research instrument. *Journal of Genetic Psychology*, 1959, **95**, 83–104.

Sears, R. R., Maccoby, E. E., & Levin, H. *Patterns of Child Rearing*. New York: Harper & Row, 1957.

Stein, L. H. A study of over-inhibited and unsocialized-aggressive children. Part II. A quantitative analysis of background factors. *Smith College Studies in Social Work*, 1944, **15**, 124–125. (Abstract).

Symonds, P. M. *The Psychology of Parent-Child Relationships*. New York: Appleton-Century-Crofts, 1939.

Winstel, B. The use of a controlled play situation in determining certain effects of maternal attitudes on children. *Child Development*, 1951, **22**, 299–311.

Wolberg, L. R. The character structure of the rejected child. *The Nervous Child*, 1944, **3**, 74–88.

Yarrow, L. J. Separation from parents during early childhood. In M. L. Hoffman & L. W. Hoffman (Eds.), *Review of Child Development Research*. New York: Russell Sage, 1964. Pp. 89–136.

CHAPTER THIRTEEN

SCHOOL ADJUSTMENT

A large portion of childhood, adolescence, and young adulthood is spent in the classroom. School experiences during these important, formative years may have a widespread and lasting effect. Some of us have found the classroom stimulating and rewarding; others may have reacted with indifference, ambivalence, or open antagonism. All of us—regardless of our general reaction—probably have been influenced more deeply and in more ways than we realize.

This chapter is concerned with the school's part in the adjustment process. What is good school adjustment? What part does the teacher play in the adjustment process? And how much responsibility should schools assume for the pychological well-being of their pupils? For these—and a number of related questions—this chapter pursues some answers and insights.

DEFINING SCHOOL ADJUSTMENT

Teachers and parents frequently talk about a particular child's adjustment to school. They may say that the child is making a very good adjustment, perhaps better than in an earlier grade or a different school. Or, with considerable concern, they may note that the child seems unable to adjust.

What do we mean when we say that a child is making a good school adjustment? We may mean that he appears to be making satisfactory academic progress. Or that he is able to establish satisfactory relationships with his teachers and classmates. Or, perhaps, we are referring to a combination of both academic achievement and social adequacy.

School Adjustment as Academic Achievement

One way of defining school adjustment is to equate it with achievement. Whatever else a school may be called upon to do, it is expected to impart certain knowledge and skills to the student. By this definition, the student who achieves what he is expected to achieve is considered adjusted. The student who does not learn, who is held back in grade, or who drops out of school before graduation fails to meet these criteria of adjustment.

In one Midwestern city it was found that about 20 percent of the children failed one or more grades before they reached high school. In high school, with each subject graded independently, failures became increasingly frequent, and about one-fifth of the students dropped out of school during the ninth and tenth grades (Havig-

hurst, Bowman, Liddle, Matthews, & Pierce, 1962).

In practice, the achievement expected of a particular child is determined by a number of factors. One very important consideration is the average achievement of other children of his age and grade. A second important factor is the child's aptitude or learning potential.

Considering these two factors, a brilliant child who is doing only slightly better than average work would be making an unsatisfactory adjustment. At the same time, a child of very limited potential might be thought of as making a satisfactory adjustment if his achievement—even though below average—was commensurate with his ability.

School Adjustment as Social Adequacy

A second way of defining school adjustment is in terms of the relationships that a child forms with his teachers and fellow students. By this definition, a child who gets along with his classmates and his teachers is considered adjusted. A child who is unable to form satisfactory relationships— one who, for example, is aggressive and unruly or overly shy and withdrawing—is considered poorly adjusted.

In practice, this definition does not prove to be so simple. For one thing, classmates and teachers may differ in their ideas of acceptable or praiseworthy behavior. Lower-class children and middle-class teachers, for example, frequently do not share each other's standards or patterns of behavior.

Furthermore, as the material which follows indicates, the matter is made even more complicated by the varying views of adjustment taken by teachers, parents, guidance workers, school psychologists, and other authorities. There is, of course, little disagreement in identifying the very deviant child. But less clear-cut cases may be considered maladjusted by one worker but not by another.

School Adjustment as Academic Achievement *and* Social Adequacy

Academic achievement and social adjustment tend to be related in the elementary and secondary grades. Although schools are most directly concerned with the academic achievement of students, it is frequently noted that a child who is not achieving well has a number of personal problems—and that the child who has personal problems is not achieving well.

In one study of failing pupils it was found that the children tended to fall in several classifications, each of which showed a combination of academic and social factors. One category, made up mostly of boys, was characterized by poor learning ability and "aggressive social maladjustment." A second category, containing mostly girls, showed poor learning ability and "withdrawn maladjustment" (Havighurst et al., 1962).

Stringer, a psychiatric social worker employed in a school mental health program, has suggested that academic progress can serve as an index of mental health. And, for that matter, mental health could serve as an index of academic progress. She writes:

Mental health concern about children with

learning problems stems not only from the need to deal with teacher-concern about them, but also from clinical recognition that (1) children who start with only a learning difficulty tend to develop other disturbances in the wake of their accumulating failures in the learning task, and (2) children referred because of some other kind of disturbance tend to develop learning difficulties as their disturbance leads to inattention and disorganization (1959, p. 16).

Bower (1962) studied a large number of "emotionally handicapped" and non-handicapped children from 200 different classes. The two groups of children did not appear to differ significantly in intellectual ability or in socioeconomic background. However, the emotionally handicapped children did more poorly on standardized reading and achievement tests.

Bower found that the difference between his two groups increased with each succeeding grade level. The higher the grade the further behind the emotionally handicapped children were in academic achievement. The results suggested that nothing succeeds like academic success. Bower writes:

The relationship between achievement in the basic academic skills and school adjustment often becomes gyroscopic and mutually reinforcing. Those children who are able to be successful are rewarded, find wholesome satisfactions in what they are doing, are friendly to the school and its values, and are encouraged to invest more of themselves in their school activities. Conversely those who are not successful in academic activities find little reward in them, perceive themselves negatively, are perceived by their peers negatively, and are thereby unable to see the school or its activities in any constructive manner. The school to them be-

Presentation 13.1 The emotionally handicapped child. Many different terms have been employed to describe children with adjustment problems. "Emotionally disturbed," "personally maladjusted," and "socially maladjusted" have been frequently used. Bower prefers "emotionally handicapped" since he is especially interested in helping schools identify and help as early as possible those children who would otherwise be handicapped in their adjustment as adolescents and adults. He describes five qualities which characterize such children. As he notes, these characteristics are found in all children, but a child would be considered emotionally handicapped if one or more of them were true of him *to a marked extent* and *over a period of time*. These characteristics are as follows:

1 An inability to learn which cannot be explained by intellectual, sensory or health factors.

    An inability to learn is, perhaps, the single most significant characteristic of emotionally handicapped children in school. Such non learning may be manifested as an inability to profit from experience as well as inability to master skill subjects. The non learner seldom escapes recognition. Achievement tests often confirm what the teacher has long suspected. If all other major causative factors have been ruled out, emotional conflicts or resistances can be ruled in.

2 An inability to build or maintain satisfactory interpersonal relationships with peers and teachers.

    It isn't just getting along with others that is significant here. Satisfactory interpersonal relations refers to the ability to demonstrate sympathy and warmth toward others, the ability to stand alone when necessary, the ability to have close friends, the ability to be aggressively constructive, and the ability to enjoy working and playing with others as well as enjoying working and playing by oneself. In most instances, children who are unable to build or maintain satisfactory interpersonal relationships are most visible to their peers. Teachers are also able to identify many

such children after a period of observation.

3 Inappropriate types of behavior or feelings under normal conditions.

    Inappropriateness of behavior or feeling can be often sensed by the teacher and peer groups. "He acts funny," another child may say. The teacher may find some children reacting disproportionately to a simple command such as "Please take your seat." What is appropriate or inappropriate is best judged by the teacher using her professional training, her daily and long term observation of the child and her experience working and interacting with the appropriate behavior of large numbers of normal children.

4 A general, pervasive mood of unhappiness or depression.

    Children who are unhappy most of the time may demonstrate such feelings in expressive play, art work, written composition or in discussion periods. They seldom smile and usually lack a joie de vivre in their school work or social relationships. In the middle or upper grades a self-inventory is usually helpful in confirming suspicions about such feelings.

5 A tendency to develop physical symptoms, pains, or fears associated with personal or school problems.

    This tendency is often noted by the school nurse and parent. Illness may be continually associated with school pressures or develop when a child's confidence in himself is under stress. In some cases, such illnesses or fears may not be apparent to the teacher; peers, however, are often aware of children who are sick before or after tests or have headaches before recitations. Speech difficulties which may be the symptoms of emotional distress are usually most visible to the teacher and parent. (From Bower, E. M., *Early Identification of Emotionally Handicapped Children in School,* 1960. Courtesy of Charles C Thomas, Publisher, Springfield, Illinois. Pp. 8–10.)

comes an unfriendly, often persecuting institution with little opportunity for real satisfactions.[1]

THE PUPIL AND ADJUSTMENT

This section focuses on the adjustment of the pupil. Following sections will be concerned with the adjustment of teachers and with the place of adjustment and mental health programs in the school's curricula.

Maladjustment in Pupils

What is the extent of maladjustment among school children? Estimates vary depending upon who is being evaluated, who is doing the evaluating, and what definitions and procedures are employed. In several representative studies (see Table 13.1), it was estimated that 7 to 12 percent of the pupils were severely maladjusted; estimates of those who show moderate maladjustment varied from 20 to 42 percent (Mensh, Kantor, Domke, Gildea, & Glide-

[1] From *Readings on the Exceptional Child* edited by E. Philip Trapp and Philip Himelstein. Copyright © 1962, by Appleton-Century-Crofts, Inc. Reprinted by permission of Appleton-Century-Crofts, Division of Meredith Publishing Company. Pp. 613–614.

well, 1959; Rogers, 1942; Ullmann, 1952; Wickman, 1928).

Boys are much more likely to be considered maladjusted than girls (Beilin, 1959; L'Abate, 1960). Interestingly enough, this appears to be true no matter who is doing the evaluating. In one study teachers were found to identify four times more boys than girls as maladjusted. And classmates, even more than teachers, regarded boys as more maladjusted than girls (Ullmann, 1952).

According to the case files of four child guidance centers, boys were 2½ times more likely than girls to be referred as "problem children." As might be expected, it was found that the ratio varied, depending upon the particular problem category and age bracket. But with few exceptions, for each problem and age more boys than girls were sent to the centers for help (Gilbert, 1957).

Various reasons have been given to account for the higher maladjustment rates of boys. Ullmann (1952) suggests that boys are more likely to act out their problems than are girls, and, therefore, boys are more likely to be considered adjustment problems by teachers. Beilin and

Table 13.1 The incidence of maladjustment in pupils as indicated in four representative studies.

Study	Wickman, 1928	Rogers, 1942	Ullmann, 1952	Mensh et al., 1959
Subjects	870 elementary pupils	1,524 elementary pupils	810 ninth graders	827 third graders
Method	Teacher judgments	Multiple criteria including tests and peer and teacher judgments	Teacher judgments	Teacher and mental health worker judgments
Results				
Well adjusted	51%	58%	70%	72%
Moderate maladjustment	42	30	22	20
Severe maladjustment	7	12	8	8

Gilbert both feel that the difference in the amount of maladjustment is bound up with differences in expectations involving boys and girls. Beilin states:

> The reasons girls are considered better adjusted by teachers is that teachers have certain expectations of what good adjustment in school should be and the prescription for girls' adjustment is more consistent with these expectations than the prescription for boys' good adjustment . . . the teacher is concerned with getting what she is teaching "across," and behaviors which facilitate this are more likely to be valued. The behaviors of girls are of this kind.[2]

In a similar vein, Gilbert (1957) notes that boys are expected to be aggressive but are also expected to be not too aggressive. They are, as he says, expected to show "just so much aggression and no more" and it is the effort to maintain "just the right amount of aggression" that makes the adjustment process of the boy so difficult.

Studying Pupil Behavior

Teachers, clinicians, pupils, and parents do not fully agree on the relative importance of a number of children's problems. A teacher, for example, may be considerably upset by a particular bit of behavior about which a school counselor or psychologist may be relatively unconcerned. On the other hand, the psychologist may be alarmed by the adjustment of some pupil whom the teacher does not consider a

problem at all. Considering this difference in perceptions Stouffer writes:

> A mother will be quite disturbed about a particular behavioral manifestation of a child during the day and expect the same amount of concern on the part of the father when she describes the problem to him in the evening. Often to her amazement and confusion the father fails to share her sense of urgency or seems, to her, to be unaware of the problem's seriousness. The same situation often arises when parents and teachers, or parents and mental hygienists—psychologists, psychiatrists, and psychiatric social workers—attempt to discuss together behavior problems of children. Each is frequently puzzled and, at times, dumbfounded by the other's apparent or expressed attitude toward certain behavior problems of children which seems to be at variance with their own attitude. It would seem, then, that one could hypothesize that one of the obstacles to the mutual understanding and attack on the behavior problems of children on the part of the father and mother, and in turn, between parents, teachers, and mental hygienists is the difference of opinion between them as to the seriousness or undesirableness of certain behavior problems of children (1959, p. 11).

It is possible, of course, to dwell too much on the differences which occur between various evaluators. Some differences are to be expected, and a rather substantial core of agreement has also been noted. Furthermore, as will soon be shown, there appears to be a trend toward greater agreement.

In identifying maladjustment in children, we should, of course, secure as much information and as many different evaluations as possible. By contrasting the way a particular pupil sees himself with the

---

[2] From Beilin, H. Teachers' and clinicians' attitudes toward the behavior problems of children: A reappraisal. *Child Development*, 1959, **30**, 9–25. © 1959 by the Society for Research in Child Development, Inc. P. 18.

way that his peers, parents, teacher, and other school personnel see him, we arrive at the fullest understanding of the child.

Teacher versus Clinical Evaluation[3]

No study of pupil adjustment has been of more lasting importance than that published by Wickman in 1928. Wickman was interested in comparing the attitudes of teachers and mental hygienists or clinicians (psychiatrists, psychologists, psychiatric social workers, and teachers with backgrounds in social work) toward children's problems. He found a number of disparities in the ways these two groups regarded problem behavior in children.

From the material supplied by teachers who were asked to describe problem behavior, Wickman drew up a list of fifty behavior problems commonly found in school children. A large number of elementary teachers from schools in different communities rated the seriousness of each problem. These ratings were contrasted with those of thirty clinicians.

Wickman found that the teachers were more concerned about attacking or antisocial behavior, especially that which upset the classroom and interfered with school routines. Clinicians, on the other hand, were more concerned about withdrawing or asocial behavior. It was concluded that teachers should be helped to change their attitudes to conform to those held by the clinicians.

Wickman's study has been criticized on a number of grounds. For one thing, different instructions were used for the teachers and the clinicians. Teachers were asked to judge the *present* seriousness of each problem; the clinicians were asked

to focus more on *future* adjustment. Furthermore, the teachers were encouraged to respond rapidly, whereas the clinicians were allowed to respond at their own pace.

A second criticism has concerned the assumption that the clinicians were more correct in their attitudes than were the teachers. The clinicians, of course, had the benefit of special training and experience. However, little objective evidence exists to indicate that withdrawing children are especially prone to serious future maladjustment (Beilin, 1959). And the conclusion drawn from a review of a number of studies is that teachers, in general, are "valid observers and raters of children's emotional status" (Bower, 1960, p. 27).

A third criticism concerns the assumption that teachers should have the same frame of reference as the mental hygienists. Beilin points out that the roles of teachers and clinicians are necessarily different. The teacher is more "task-oriented," and the clinician is more "adjustment-oriented." Beilin writes:

> The teacher has a vital role in the socialization of the child. She is, after all, a culture carrier and to some extent a parental surrogate. Her own behaviors are significant in the child's development of self-control, character traits, values, and work habits. These functions are certainly as important as any. There is no question that the teacher needs to be aware of withdrawing and other undesirable personality characteristics. What is questioned is the need for the teacher to concern herself with them to the same extent and in the same way as the clinician.[4]

Since Wickman's study, a number of

[3] This discussion is largely based on Beilin (1959).

[4] From Beilin, H. Teachers' and clinicians' attitudes toward the behavior problems of children: A reappraisal. Child Development, 1959, 30, 9–25. © 1959 by the Society for Research in Child Development, Inc. P. 21.

similar investigations have been performed, some of which were specifically designed to eliminate the faulty procedures of the original investigation. These further studies suggest that the differences which were found by Wickman between teachers and clinicians were not just artifacts of his procedures, although perhaps the differences were not quite so great as he assumed. Over the years there is little to indicate that the clinicians have changed their position very much, but succeeding studies have indicated that teachers' attitudes are becoming increasingly like those of the clinicians. However, the teachers' attitudes are still different, and the difference is not unlike that reported by Wickman.

Parent Evaluation

How do parents' attitudes toward children's behavior problems compare with those of teachers and clinicians? In 1959 Stouffer published an investigation of the attitudes of 500 parents who he felt made up a fairly representative sample. He found that the attitudes of his parent group were very similar to those of the teachers measured by Wickman more than thirty years before! Summarizing his findings on parents' attitudes, Stouffer writes:

> It would appear that the problems which represent an objective type of behavior and which might be thought of as problems that outrage the parents' moral sensitivities and authority, frustrate their aspirations for the child's scholastic achievement, or threaten the tranquility and social status of the home through sibling friction and peer group non-acceptance are regarded as the most serious by the parents. Regarded as least serious are the inhibitive, repressive, inactive, personal problems of the children (1959, p. 15).

Fathers and mothers were measurably different in their attitudes toward certain problems. Interesting enough, compared with mothers, fathers did not rate any problem as more serious. The fathers, however, considered the following problems *less* serious: heterosexual activity, cheating, cruelty or bullying, truancy, obscenity, masturbation, domineering, profanity, enuresis, and smoking.

Comparing his parent group with teachers and clinicians, Stouffer concluded that the parents were much more in agreement with the teachers than with the clinicians. In general, parents seemed more concerned with overt, attacking, antisocial behavior, clinicians with covert, withdrawing, asocial behavior, while the teachers appeared to take an intermediate position.

Peer Evaluation

Children, of course, have value systems which differ from those of their parents and teachers. They have their own ideas of what sorts of behavior are serious or not serious, desirable or undesirable. In identifying children's problems and children with problems, researchers have increasingly considered it important to get the viewpoints of children themselves and to combine and contrast these data with the observations of teachers and with other information.

Peer judgments are of considerable value in the evaluation process. Summarizing the evidence, Bower states:

> Almost all studies of peer perception point to a strong relationship between emotional adjustment and peer judgments. Most, if not all, confirm the reciprocity of school adjustment and school success. The child who is most accepted by his peers gets the best grades, has the higher IQ, comes

from a higher socioeconomic level, and has fewer emotional problems. Conversely the child who is least accepted by his peers gets the poorest grades, has the lowest IQ, comes from a lower socioeconomic class and has more emotional problems.[5]

Teachers may gain new insights by comparing their own perceptions with those of their pupils. There are important differences in these several sets of perceptions (Bonney, 1947; Gronlund, 1959). This does not mean that one set or the other is incorrect. Each represents a different viewpoint and a different value system.

Bonney (1947) found that certain kinds of pupils were generally rated more highly and certain kinds less highly by teachers than by themselves. Teachers tended to rate the following more highly:

The individual who is outstanding in class or student body activities, but who lacks skill in interpersonal relationships (p. 139).
The individual who is courteous and responsive to teachers and who is more smooth and socially aggressive (in non-leadership behavior) than the average student, but who has some unfavorable personality traits which are not displayed in his relations with his teachers (p. 140).
The individual who has many desirable personality traits which are evident in his relations with his teachers, but who is socially inhibited (p. 141).
The individual who has many desirable personality traits, which are evident in his relations with his teachers, but who is regarded as an outsider by the majority of the students (p. 142).

In contrast, Bonney found that the following kinds of pupils tended to be less

[5] From Bower, E. M., Early Identification of Emotionally Handicapped Children in School, 1960. Courtesy of Charles C Thomas, Publisher, Springfield, Ill. P. 55.

highly rated by teachers than by the pupils themselves:

The individual who makes a poor response to the academic situation, who is not outstanding in any capacity, but who is skilled in inter-personal relationships within a particular clique or with only a few persons at a time (p. 143).
The individual who antagonizes his teachers, disregards their regulations, or offends their moral conceptions but who, nevertheless, is well liked by some students (p. 144).

One of the chief devices used to enable the teacher to see the classroom society as the pupils see it is the sociometric test. This test provides a way of determining the relationships among the individuals of a group, and such tests have been employed to study the social structure of different kinds of organizations. Used in the classroom, sociometric tests enable the teacher to determine the nature of the relationships among the pupils and to identify those who are popular or unpopular and accepted or rejected.

In the administration of sociometric tests in the classroom, the pupil is asked to name the members of his group whom he would choose to associate with in certain specified activities or situations. The pupil may also be asked to identify those members of his group whom he would like least to associate with, but this type of item may have an unfavorable effect on the group and is less commonly used (Northway, 1952). Presentation 13.2 lists some representative sociometric items.

After the choices of the members of the group have been tabulated, they can be depicted through the use of a sociogram. The teacher writes each pupil's name on a piece of paper and draws lines or arrows between the names indicating the direction of the choices. As the relationships between the pupils begin to be seen, the names can be rearranged so that mutual friends are placed together, and the social structure of the class is portrayed.

An illustrative sociogram is contained in Figure 13.1. The twenty-five children of this eighth-grade classroom were asked to name their three best friends and the three members of the class they liked the least. Only the positive nominations have been plotted.

Figure 13.1 Twenty-five children of an eighth-grade class were asked to name their three best friends and the three members of the class whom they liked least. The results have been plotted in the sociograph (a) and partially illustrated in the sociogram (b). In the sociograph the choices and rejections of each child can be seen by reading vertically down the columns. The symbol X denotes a positive nomination and O a negative one; for example, Charlie, No. 1, chose Tony, Jack, and John H. and rejected James, Maryann, and Henry. By reading horizontally across the rows you can see the reactions of other children to a particular child; for example, Charlie was chosen by Tony, Jack, Alex, John H., Ava, James, Maryann, and Pete, and rejected by Bob and Annette. Clusters of X's along the diagonal show the subgroupings in the class, and these can also be seen in the sociogram in which, for simplification, only the positive nominations are shown (From Clark & McGuire, 1952. © 1952 by the Society for Research in Child Development.).

Grade 8

		1 Charlie	2 Tony	3 Jack	4 Alex	5 John H.	6 Bob	7 Bill	8 Annette	9 Gail	10 Billie	11 Rose	12 Jane	13 Susan	14 Mary	15 Ellen	16 Betty	17 Emma	18 Ava	19 Joedel	20 Sue Ellen	21 John R.	22 James	23 Maryann	24 Henry	25 Pete
Charlie	1		X	X	X	X	O		O										X				X	X		X
Tony	2	X		X	X													O				X	X			X
Jack	3	X	X		X																					O
Alex	4	X	X																		O	O				
John H.	5	X																			O	O				
Bob	6							O	X		X	X						O		O						O
Bill	7		O						X	X		X						O				X				O
Annette	8									X	X		X	X	O					O		O	O			O
Gail	9								X	X	X		X							O						
Billie	10									X	X	X		X					O		X			X		
Rose	11								O	O			O	X					O							
Jane	12												X		X	X	X									
Susan	13											X	X		X	X										
Mary	14													X	X		X									
Ellen	15													X	X	X										
Betty	16											O	O					X	X	X		X		O	X	
Emma	17												O	O					X	O	X	X			X	
Ava	18							O				O						O	X	X		X		O		
Joedel	19			O				O				O		O	O	O	O	X		X				X		
Sue Ellen	20								O	O	O	O							X		X				X	
John R.	21		X																				X			X
James	22	O		O																	O	X				
Maryann	23	O	O				O			O	O		O	O	O			O		O	O					O
Henry	24	O	O	O	O				O									O			O	O				O
Pete	25																								O	

X = positive nomination O = negative nomination

Figure 13.1 (Continued)

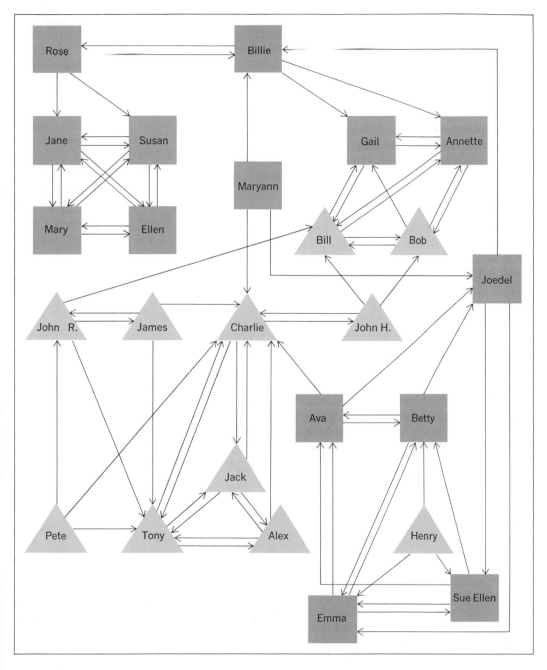

By studying the sociogram the teacher can assess and supplement her own information concerning the social structure of her classroom. Here is some of the information that the sociogram provides.

The Chosen   The individuals of the group who receive a relatively large number of choices can be termed *chosen.* In addition, these individuals may be the *leaders* of the group, but this is not necessarily the case (Lindzey & Borgatta, 1954). As might be expected, in the classroom depicted in the sociogram there is a strong tendency for boys and girls to choose members of their own sex. Charlie is the most popular choice; he is selected by six boys and two girls. None of the girls is designated to this extent, but a number of them are chosen four times.

The Unchosen   The individuals of the group who receive no choices can be termed *unchosen.* These individuals may be *rejected* as well as unchosen; that is, they may receive the negative nominations of the group. They may also be considered *isolated* if in addition to being unchosen by others they make no choices themselves. In the sociogram the three unchosens, Maryann, Pete, and Henry appear to be trying to bind themselves into the group in various ways. Maryann designates two girls plus Charlie, who is the most popular member of the group. Pete chooses Charlie and two other boys. Henry appears to be working his way into an environment of girls.

Bilateral Choices   Many of the members of the group will choose each other and these mutual or reciprocal selections may be termed *bilateral choices.* A number of

---

Presentation 13.2   Here are some representative sociometric items.

Nursery School and Kindergarten

(This is an individual test and presented orally.)

1   What do you like to play with in the garden? Whom do you like to do that with best? Second best? Third best?
2   What do you like to do in the playroom? Whom do you like to do that with best? Second best? Third best?
3   Whom do you like to sit beside in the music circle? Anyone else? Anyone else?

Grades 4 to 8

(This is a group test and presented in written form.)

1   When you are playing at recess which children in this classroom would you like best to play with you? 1st choice _____ 2nd choice _____ 3rd choice _____

2   When you are working on a project in your class which children would you like best to work with you? 1st choice _____ 2nd choice _____ 3rd choice _____
3   If you are having a party, which children from this classroom would you invite to it? 1st choice _____ 2nd choice _____ 3rd choice _____

High School

(This is a group test and presented in written form.)

1   Suppose you were to move to another classroom, which boys and girls from this classroom would you like best to go with you?
2   Suppose you were going away on a summer holiday, which children from this classroom would you like to go with you?
3   Suppose you were going on a class outing? Each car holds four people. Which children from this classroom would you like to have in your car? (Adapted from Northway, 1952, p. 4.)

examples of this type of selection can be seen in the sociogram. Most of these relationships involve members of the same sex, but reciprocal heterosexual relationships also occur. For example, Annette and Bob have reciprocated relationships with members of both sexes.

Unilateral Choices   Some of the members choose others of the group who do not reciprocate the choice, and these may be termed *unilateral choices.* Note in the illustration that none of the three girls who choose Joedel are designated by her in turn, and of the three girls whom Joedel chooses none reciprocates the action. Bob, by contrast, is involved in four relationships, two unilateral and two bilateral. All the relationships involving Ellen are reciprocated.

Cliques   A number of individuals who choose each other and exclude outsiders may be termed a *clique.* This self-contained subgroup may be a problem because of its limited integration in the larger grouping. In the sociogram Jane, Susan, Ellen, and Mary are depicted as a completely closed clique. Rose, who appears to be petitioning for membership in this subgroup, is not chosen by any of its members.

Self-evaluation

An important source of information about the pupil is, of course, the pupil himself. One problem in using self-reports is that the individual may not be able to describe himself very well. A second problem is that he may hold back information if he feels it will be to his advantage to do so.

Despite obvious shortcomings, self-report instruments have been widely used and found widely useful. These instruments are inexpensive, simple in design, and easy to administer. They provide important information about how the child views himself or, at least, how he wishes his world to view him. The information they supply can supplement and be validated against information from other sources.

An example of a self-report instrument upon which a good deal of research has been done is the Test Anxiety Scale for Children (Sarason, Davidson, Lighthall, & Waite, 1958b). It consists of thirty items describing a number of school situations which could be anxiety provoking. The items are read to the class, and each child

---

Presentation 13.3 Mental retardation and peer acceptance.

It has been estimated that about 3 percent of the population are mentally retarded. These are the persons who because of low intelligence are unable to meet the demands of their environment. There are many causes of mental retardation, including genetic or inherited factors, diseases, injuries, and severe environmental deprivation.

There has been some argument as to whether mildly retarded children make better adjustments in regular classrooms or in special groups by themselves. The studies which have been done so far are limited in number, design, and scope; their results are conflicting and must be interpreted with caution.

Generally, sociometric studies have shown that retarded children attending regular classes are less accepted and more rejected than other children. Retarded children in special classes appear to fare better. However, even in special classes there is a hierarchy of acceptance, with the least retarded at the top and the most retarded at the bottom (Dunn, 1963; Gardner, 1966).

responds by circling a "yes" or "no" on his answer sheet. Each time that he answers "yes" he is admitting that a particular situation has been the source of some unpleasantness for him. Here are some sample items:

When the teacher says that she is going to find out how much you have learned, does your heart begin to beat faster?

Do you sometimes dream at night that other boys and girls in your class can do things you cannot do?

Do you wish a lot of times that you didn't worry so much about tests?

A number of studies have compared children who have high anxiety scores with those who achieve low ones. Generally speaking, it has been found that high-anxious pupils are at a disadvantage, and this is particularly true for boys (Sarason, Davidson, Lighthall, Waite, & Ruebush, 1960). In one study, for example, children with high anxiety scores (especially the boys) proved to be less secure, less task-oriented, and less adequate academically than those whose scores were lower (Sarason, Davidson, Lighthall, & Waite, 1958a).

Girls, as a group, achieve higher anxiety scores than boys. This does not necessarily mean that girls are more anxious. Sarason and his associates hypothesize that the difference in anxiety test scores may be an artifact of the test items themselves and also that girls may be less defensive about admitting anxiety than boys. This hypothesis is a very interesting one; it suggests that boys are more anxious about being anxious or, at least, about showing their anxiety. In delineating this

hypothesis, Sarason and his associates write:

In our culture, at least, we expect and support the admissions of anxiety in girls to a degree and in ways different from boys. We react to anxiety in little girls in much the same way as in the case of the anxious woman, i.e., it is considered part of the "feminine character." It is in keeping with femininity to be anxious and, however troublesome this anxiety may be to others, it is not viewed as a derogation of a girl's or a woman's femininity. As important as how the relationship between anxiety and femininity is perceived in our culture are the ways in which we tend to handle its occurrence. Essentially, we react to anxiety in the girl by supporting her and allowing her to depend on others for the necessary reassurance and help. The net result is that she does not learn that she must or should hide anxiety from others.

The picture is rather different in the case of boys. Boys are viewed as little men who should already possess some of the essentials of masculinity. They should be active, brave, fearless, and stoical. In contrast to the girl, the boy is not expected to be clinging, dependent, and fearful. One of the most cruel forms of punishment which can be administered to a boy is to call him a "sissy," i.e., to be like a girl. Calling a girl a "tomboy" is not a form of punishment—it frequently is experienced by the girl as praise of a high order. A colleague has summarized what we are here saying as follows: "If your girl acts like a tomboy, it's cute. If your boy acts like a sissy, you're worried."

We realize that we have painted a black and white picture of the differences in cultural conceptions and reaction to the expression of anxiety in boys and girls. We have done so in order to emphasize the point that early in life boys and girls learn to have somewhat different attitudes toward the expression and admission of anxiety. The admission of anxiety by a girl tends not to be viewed by her as impairing or reflecting adversely on her femininity. In the case of a boy such an admission is experienced as a weakness in his masculine armor. It is these differences which, in our opinion, are reflected in the finding that girls obtain higher anxiety scores than do boys (1960, pp. 253–254).

Sarason found that teachers' ratings of anxiety in pupils were not close enough to the pupils' self-reports to be of any "practical significance." It was felt that teachers tended to underestimate the school anxieties of children who were doing adequate work. And it was suggested that academic achievement tends to be—but should not be—the only criterion of school adjustment.

THE TEACHER AND ADJUSTMENT

The adjustment patterns of teachers have been much less studied than those of their pupils. Glidewell notes, "Forty years ago the teacher was seen as a social agent, responsible to the community, dedicated to the transfer of the society's store of knowledge by lecture and drill, undistracted by emotionality" (1959, p. 60). In recent years, however, there has been a growing concern about the personal qualities of teachers and the effect of these qualities upon pupils.

Maladjustment in Teachers

A number of investigators have studied the extent of adjustment and maladjustment in teachers. Most of the studies were conducted some time ago, and all seem to suffer from limitations in scope and design. They also suffer from the fact that adjustment is no easier to define and measure in teachers than in pupils.

According to an estimate based on the available evidence, about 9 percent of the nation's teachers are seriously maladjusted. This would seem to indicate that teachers are no worse (or better) adjusted than people in other professions (Berlin, 1960; Kaplan, 1959). However, there is special concern about the adjustment of teachers because of the great influence they may have on children. Solomon states:

The schoolroom must be looked upon as a force secondary in importance only to the home in the development of human personality. Psychopathology which may have originated in the home can be crystallized or fortified in the school situation. A child with both stable parents and stable teachers is fortunate. Conversely, emotional problems are aggravated when a child with unstable parents is exposed to unstable teachers (1960, p. 79).

A teacher who according to some criterion suffers from maladjustment is not necessarily an ineffective or harmful one. For example, one psychiatrist studied five women teachers, each of whom had a number of phobic reactions, including a fear of teaching and of being in classroom situations. Despite their problems, all the women were considered excellent teachers. Three of them, in fact, were so outstanding in their teaching that they had received special consideration by their school boards (Monsour, 1961).

Furthermore, "problem teachers," like "problem pupils," are not necessarily problems in every school situation. It is frequently noted that a child who seems badly adjusted one year or in one classroom may appear to considerably better advantage another year or in another classroom. This seems true of teachers as well. In this connection, Berlin, who is a psychiatrist familiar with school problems, writes as follows:

> Eight years of psychiatric consultation with several school systems has convinced me that most problem teachers have resulted from certain pressures and practices which seem inherent in many school systems. I have rarely seen a teacher in consultation whose difficulties resulted only from her own personality problems. I have many times worked with teachers whose evident character disorders would seem to preclude their effectiveness as teachers, and yet with wise management and assistance from alert, intuitive administrators these disturbed teachers were doing good jobs in the classrooms. Other psychiatric consultants have confirmed my impressions that neurotic disturbances among teachers are not more frequent than those found in other professions that work with people. Problem teachers seem to result from the same juxtaposition of forces which make for neurotic disability in all human beings—namely, the severity of the stresses, their duration and the susceptibility or predisposition of the individual (1960, p. 80).

It has also been noted that problems which a child appears to develop at school and perhaps in connection with a particular teacher may be traceable to the child's home and family life. The classroom may trigger or precipitate a problem which has been building up in other areas. Sometimes the child displaces fear and anger stemming from relationships with parents onto teachers and other school authorities (Dombrose, 1955).

Studying Teacher Behavior

The teacher's needs, frustrations, conflicts, anxieties, and adjustment patterns will, of course, influence the teaching process and the classroom environment. And, as was indicated earlier, the school and classroom environments influence the teacher's adjustment. The studies which follow provide some insights into teacher behavior.

The Anderson Studies

Anderson and his associates made a number of studies of behavior in the classroom (Anderson & Brewer, 1945, 1946; Anderson, Brewer, & Reed, 1946). These investigators were interested in measuring the effect of one child's behavior on another as well as the impact of teachers' behavior on that of children in their classes. Observations were particularly directed toward two important types of contacts which were termed "dominative behavior" and "socially integrative behavior."

Dominative behavior involves attempts to make others conform to one's own patterns of action. It is an autocratic and rigid process in which an individual endeavors to make others behave in ways which are consistent with his own needs, activities, and goals. Dominative behavior in one person was found to induce similar behavior in others; therefore, this type of contact was said to put in motion a vicious circle of domination.

In dominating the classroom, teachers may stifle the spontaneity and initiative of their pupils. This is apparent in Anderson's report on a kindergarten group engaged in making May baskets:

> Terry had folded his basket on the lines which had been drawn on the material the

night before by the teacher. He had pasted the flaps as he had been instructed and had the handle fastened in place. The teacher had cut out of other paper a handful of diamond-shaped pieces which she had distributed four to a child. These were to serve as decorations to be pasted horizontally on the basket. As she walked about the room she noticed Terry pasting his diamond decoration vertically.

"Oh, oh, Terry," she said, "The decorations are to be pasted on lying down and not standing up."

"But I want to paste mine this way," said Terry.

"Well, that isn't the way they are supposed to go. Here now, just paste it this way." And she turned the diamond horizontally and pasted it before Terry seemed to know what had happened. She remained while Terry at her instructions pasted two more shapes horizontally. Then she turned away, leaving Terry to paste the fourth.

At the end of the period Terry had only three decorations on his basket. When the teacher inquired about his basket, Terry, pointing to the undecorated side of his basket, said that he did not want one there.

"Oh, but every basket should have four. Here is one your color. We'll just paste it on quickly." And with Terry speechless and transfixed she pasted it on quickly.

Mary Lou had observed that at her table several handles did not stick. "I guess I don't want a handle," she remarked to the boy seated next to her. She cut up the handle of her basket and pasted the pieces as decorations all over the basket. The teacher's remark to the fait accompli was, "Oh, you've spoiled yours, Mary Lou; yours is all messy and doesn't have a handle" (1943, p. 459).

Socially integrative behavior involves attempts to arrive at mutually satisfactory patterns of action. It is a democratic and flexible process in which individuals endeavor to arrive at common, harmonious needs, activities, and goals. Integrative behavior was found to promote further integrative behavior; therefore, this type of contact was said to put in motion a *growth circle* of cooperation and understanding.

Socially integrative behavior encourages spontaneity and initiative. Differences are freely expressed and then harmoniously adapted to the common welfare of the group. This process can be seen at work in the social interplay noted by Anderson in the following report:

In a second grade during singing period one of the children asked for the song about the organ-grinder and the monkey. Another child volunteered the page number. After the children had sung it, the teacher asked, "I wonder if you would like to play it (act it)?" There was general agreement. The boy who had asked for the song was to choose the organ-grinders. He designated three, who in turn chose their monkeys. Two monkeys had been chosen. James was hesitating, although several hands indicated that he could have a monkey.

"Why don't you choose, James?" the teacher asked.

James looked over the room again and said, "I want a little person and I want somebody who wants to be monkey." A hand shot up from a little girl who fitted James's specifications and she became the third monkey.

After the children had sung the song while the organ-grinders and their monkeys performed at the front of the room a child asked, "Don't they go down the street?"

"The organ man decides that," the teacher replied. The organ-grinders and the monkeys and the other children together seemed to decide it. The monkeys and the organ-grinders took positions at the head of aisles and the other children *began to reach with ostensible gestures into imaginary purses for imaginary pennies to drop into imaginary cups. They sang the song again and the teacher, adding her imaginary pennies remarked, "Well, I hope you enjoyed their song, and that the monkeys received lots of pennies" (1943, p. 460).*

Anderson and his associates were especially interested in determining the effects of teachers' dominative and integrative behavior on the classroom behavior of their pupils. Two second-grade teachers and their respective classes were the subjects of one investigation. These two groups of children were quite comparable in size, sex, socioeconomic status, and chronological and mental age. The teachers and the children were observed in usual classroom situations, and their behavior was recorded on specially designed observation blanks.

The results of the study showed the two teachers to be considerably different in their classroom contacts. One teacher was consistently more integrative in her contacts with children individually and as a group. The second teacher was consistently more dominative in both individual and group situations.

Significant differences were found in the classroom behavior of the two groups of pupils. The pupils of the dominative teacher showed more classroom behavior which was considered undesirable. The pupils of the integrative teacher were superior in a number of categories of behavior which were highly valued; for example, these pupils were more spontaneous and showed greater initiative.

A second investigator studied the same two teachers the following year in their contacts with new groups of children.

She found that the dominating teacher again demonstrated more dominative behavior while the integrating teacher continued to be highly integrative. This investigator also followed the two groups of second-grade children into the third grade where she found there was little tendency for their behavior patterns to persist from one year to the next. The undesirable classroom behavior of the children under the dominating teacher did not persist to the next year under a new and less dominating instructor.

The Symonds Study

Symonds was interested in determining the characteristics of teachers who were effective in promoting favorable attitudes in their pupils. He had a large number of intermediate (junior high) students rank their teachers on seven bases:

1 Which of your teachers makes the work most interesting?
2 Which of your teachers understands you best and likes you most?
3 Which of your teachers would you most like to have again next year?
4 Which of your teachers makes you most willing to study or to participate in the work of the class?
5 Which of your teachers helps you most to learn?
6 Which of your teachers would you feel most like consulting on some personal matter for guidance and counseling?
7 Which of your teachers most makes you want to continue to go through high school? (1955, p. 289.)

There was considerable halo effect in the rankings of the seven questions, indicating that the teachers who ranked high in one item tended to be high in all items and, conversely, that the teachers who ranked low in an item were low in the other items as well. In general, the pupils were in good agreement about who the most and least effective teachers were. Furthermore, the pupils' rankings correlated well with various ratings of the same teachers made by the principal of the school.

After the rankings were completed, the teachers from the top and the bottom of the list were observed in actual teaching situations. It was found that these two groups of teachers were essentially different in three characteristics: their liking for children, their feelings of security, and their personal organization.

Liking Children   The superior teachers demonstrated their liking for children in a number of ways. They were concerned about their students and knew their names, interests, and backgrounds. Their students were respected as individuals; questions were received attentively, requests were carefully considered, and the students were entrusted with various phases of the classwork. Each student's efforts, even when not completely successful, were accepted and appreciated. These teachers radiated warmth in their relationships with their students. They were pleasant, friendly, and genuinely affectionate toward all their students; they did not play favorites.

The inferior teachers clearly demonstrated a dislike for children. Sometimes they did not even know the names of their students or anything about their background. These teachers did not appear to respect their students; little attention was paid to their questions or requests. They were critical of their students and seemingly irritated by them. Sarcasm and ridicule were employed as methods of discipline, and the students were subjected to embarrassment and humiliation. These inferior teachers were generally cold and distant. However, they seemed to single out certain students who were given favored treatment and others who were specially marked for censure and criticism.

Feelings of Security   The superior teachers were secure and confident of their own abilities. On one hand, they were not afraid to be assertive and exercise firm control over their classes, and, on the other, they were able to be casual and informal, displaying a sense of humor, cracking a joke, and doing a little clowning. Their classes tended to be orderly, with discipline seldom appearing as a problem. These teachers were calm themselves and tended to communicate this calmness to their classes.

Inferior teachers felt insecure and inadequate in the classroom. They tended to be overassertive or underassertive. Characteristically, there was a lack of sustained control, with disorder and confusion mounting until the teachers lost their tempers, shouted at the students, or administered punishment. These teachers took themselves seriously and were unable to let down their guard to joke and laugh with their students. Inferior teachers took offense easily, interpreting irregularities as threats to their prestige.

Organization and Integration   The superior teachers gave the impression of better organization and integration. They arranged their work more effectively. Tasks were clearly defined, methods outlined, specific goals set, and the activities of the class went forward according to a time schedule. The superior teachers gave more of themselves to their teaching; they were interested in it and worked harder at it. Their students worked more efficiently, since they knew what was to be done and what standards of excellence were required.

The inferior teachers were disorganized and poorly integrated. Tasks, methods, and goals were not well defined, and the work of the class did not proceed according to a clear-cut timetable. These teachers looked upon their teaching duties as chores; receiving less satisfaction out of teaching, they put less of themselves into it. Their students worked less efficiently, since they were not always sure what was demanded of them or where they stood with their teacher.

The Ryans Studies

Ryans and his colleagues (1960) undertook a massive series of studies concerning the characteristics of teachers. One consequence of these studies was the identification of three major dimensions of teacher behavior which appeared to be highly important to teacher-pupil relations. These three dimensions of teacher behavior have been described as follows:

warm understanding friendly	versus	aloof egocentric restricted
responsible businesslike systematic	versus	evading unplanned slipshod
stimulating imaginative surgent	versus	dull routine

What are the correlates of warm, responsible, and stimulating classroom behaviors? An important goal of these studies was to find out as much as possible about teachers who were judged to be superior in the classroom. On the basis of his own studies and those of other investigators,

Ryans formed some generalizations concerning outstanding teachers.

First of all, outstanding teachers frequently have a background of teaching. There may be a history of teaching in their families or family support of teaching as a vocation. They may have early experiences in teaching and caring for children.

Second, outstanding teachers tend to be superior in intellectual ability, and they are generally above average in their own academic work. They also tend to have high interests in social service, in reading and literary matters, and in music and painting.

Third, outstanding teachers tend to be tolerant. They are generous in their appraisals of others. They have favorable attitudes toward pupils. They enjoy their relationship with pupils.

Fourth, outstanding teachers demonstrate good adjustment patterns. They are stable, friendly, and cooperative. They also participate widely in social and community affairs.

Ryans stresses that it is no simple matter to determine a teacher's effectiveness. There is no perfect agreement on how any set of objectives may best be realized. Consequently, there is not one set of teachers' qualities which is best in everyone's opinion or for every situation.

The characteristics of the pupil and the characteristics of the subject matter must also be considered. A particular teacher may do well in one situation but poorly in another. Ryans writes, "An aloof, rigorously academic teacher might be well suited to teach bright, academically minded, well-adjusted high school students, but he might be entirely unsuited to teach certain younger children vitally in need of sympathy and understanding above all else" (1960, p. 370).

Presentation 13.4 What is effective teacher behavior? More than five hundred "critical incidents" were reported by teaching supervisors, training teachers, school principals, teachers, student teachers, and education students. Each incident described a bit of teacher behavior which was critical to success or failure in a particular teaching situation. Here, generalized from the reports, is a list of effective and ineffective teacher behaviors.

Effective Behaviors	Ineffective Behaviors
1. Alert, appears enthusiastic.	1. Is apathetic, dull, appears bored.
2. Appears interested in pupils and classroom activities.	2. Appears uninterested in pupils and classroom activities.
3. Cheerful, optimistic.	3. Is depressed, pessimistic; appears unhappy.
4. Self-controlled, not easily upset.	4. Looses temper, is easily upset.
5. Likes fun, has a sense of humor.	5. Is overly serious, too occupied for humor.
6. Recognizes and admits own mistakes.	6. Is unaware of, or fails to admit, own mistakes.
7. Is fair, impartial, and objective in treatment of pupils.	7. Is unfair or partial in dealing with pupils.
8. Is patient.	8. Is impatient.
9. Shows understanding and sympathy in working with pupils.	9. Is short with pupils, uses sarcastic remarks, or in other ways shows lack of sympathy with pupils.
10. Is friendly and courteous in relations with pupils.	10. Is aloof and removed in relations with pupils.
11. Helps pupils with personal as well as educational problems.	11. Seems unaware of pupils' personal needs and problems.
12. Commends effort and gives praise for work well done.	12. Does not commend pupils, is disapproving, hypercritical.
13. Accepts pupils' efforts as sincere.	13. Is suspicious of pupil motives.
14. Anticipates reactions of others in social situations.	14. Does not anticipate reactions of others in social situations.
15. Encourages pupils to try to do their best.	15. Makes no effort to encourage pupils to try to do their best.
16. Classroom procedure is planned and well organized.	16. Procedure is without plan, disorganized.
17. Classroom procedure is flexible within over-all plan.	17. Shows extreme rigidity of procedure, inability to depart from plan.
18. Anticipates individual needs.	18. Fails to provide for individual differences and needs of pupils.
19. Stimulates pupils through interesting and original materials and techniques.	19. Uninteresting materials and teaching techniques used.
20. Conducts clear, practical demonstrations and explanations.	20. Demonstrations and explanations are not clear and are poorly conducted.
21. Is clear and thorough in giving directions.	21. Directions are incomplete, vague.
22. Encourages pupils to work through their own problems and evaluate their accomplishments.	22. Fails to give pupils opportunity to work out own problems or evaluate their own work.
23. Disciplines in quiet, dignified, and positive manner.	23. Reprimands at length, ridicules, resorts to cruel or meaningless forms of correction.
24. Gives help willingly.	24. Fails to give help or gives it grudgingly.
25. Foresees and attempts to resolve potential difficulties.	25. Is unable to foresee and resolve potential difficulties (Ryans, 1960, p. 82).

THE CURRICULUM AND ADJUSTMENT

There is considerable controversy concerning the amount of the schools' time and energies which should be expended in adjustment and mental health programs. Controversy or not, schools appear to be accepting more and more responsibility in this area. This section considers some positions which have been taken in this controversy and some current trends in school mental health programs.

Some Basic Positions

Attitudes concerning the place of adjustment and mental health in the curriculum vary widely. There are all shades of opinion and practice. This discussion presents the two most divergent positions, one holding that the curriculum should be limited to traditional subject matter and the other emphasizing the importance of adjustment in the school programming.

The Focus on Traditional Subject Matter

One position is that the curriculum should focus on the child's intellectual life. According to this position the purpose of schooling is to convey certain traditional areas of knowledge and skill. This approach to education has sometimes been called "traditional," "subject-centered," or "subject-matter-oriented."

The traditionalists themselves hold many different views toward adjustment or mental health. Some, for example, feel the student's adjustment will be benefited most if the school maintains its sights on intellectual achievement. Allinsmith and Goethals review the various defenses that have

been made of the traditional curriculum and summarize them in this way:

> *The defense of traditional curriculum in mental health terms suggests the following arguments: First, that a departure from it is destructive of the character development and personality integration which is thought to result from the intellectual rigor of the traditional curriculum; second, that attempts to deal with present-day solutions to living shortchange the student by not providing him with a background that would be useful for solving all kinds of problems; third, the best possible mental health position which the school should take, by default, is to accept traditional studies as "something that can be counted on in a changing world." There is the underlying suggestion that if the school departs from this, there is no alternative but to run helter-skelter after each new fad and fashion.*[6]

Other traditionalists are highly critical of the concepts of adjustment and mental health and of the attempts which have been made to spell them out in the schools. They point out that such concepts are difficult to define, and there is little agreement on the methods for achieving them. Furthermore, they note that energies given to such programs in the past have not always proved fruitful (Allinsmith & Goethals, 1962; Morse, 1961; Pearson, 1958).

A number of traditionalists are not critical of the concepts and goals of adjustment and mental health, but they believe that explicit programs are best kept out of the school. Some feel that emphasis on mental health in the schools has led the teacher to attempt to be both teacher and therapist even though these roles are

[6] From *The Role of Schools in Mental Health,* by Wesley Allinsmith and George W. Goethals, Basic Books, Inc., Publishers, New York, 1962. Pp. 15–16.

not always compatible. Others feel that the schools and teachers are already over-burdened and that other institutions and agencies in the community should accept this responsibility.

The Focus on Adjustment

A second position is that the curriculum should focus on the child's adjustment or mental health. This position holds that the child's present and future social adjustment is of direct concern to the school and that this concern should be reflected in the curriculum. This approach is sometimes called "student-centered" because it stresses adaptation of school programs to the abilities and needs of individual children. At the same time, it is also referred to as "group-centered" because it stresses the development of skills necessary for group living.

Like the traditionalists, those who emphasize the school's role in mental health vary widely in their attitudes and beliefs. Some value an emphasis on adjustment because they believe that it is so intertwined with academic achievement that both must be attended. Others value adjustment for its own sake and believe that it is as worthy a goal as intellectual attainment.

There is also considerable variety in the changes which are being called for in traditional school curricula. Some propose a modification of present programs to take account of principles being hammered out in mental health. Some would add discrete mental health courses or programs to the conventional school offerings. A few suggest a complete rethinking and overhaul of present curricula. The following section indicates the extent and direction of the changes occurring at this time.

Some Current Trends

This section considers two basic trends and six specific ones which are occurring in school mental health programs. The discussion is drawn directly from that of Hollister (1959), who has reviewed the programs of many schools and set forth goals and methods which appear to be common to many programs. As Hollister points out, some of these programs are the efforts of individual teachers, some are the joint product of a school or an entire school system, and some are the result of cooperation between school personnel and mental health workers from various agencies of the community.

Two General Trends

One of the general trends that Hollister identifies affects the entire field of mental health, but it has special impact on the classroom. The second general trend has directly affected mental health programs in the classroom.

1 In Mental Health: A New Emphasis on the Group In the past the forces producing maladjustment have been thought to be largely within the individual, and help was sought in one-to-one treatment programs analogous to medical care by a physician. In recent years adjustment problems have been increasingly considered problems of interpersonal relationships. Such problems arise from the social interaction within the groups in which the individual is involved, and they can be dealt with in these same social environments.

The child's primary groupings have been given special attention. His home and neighborhood, his peer group and school, are held to be primary determiners of adjustment patterns and adjustment problems. The school is seen as playing a central part in mental health, both as a force that can aggravate and create problems and as one that can ameliorate or solve them.

This changing emphasis has pointed up the important roles which can be played by teachers and other leaders in these primary groups. Furthermore, the shortage of trained mental health personnel makes it necessary that some of the responsibility be assumed by other personnel. With training, guidance, and support, teachers are increasingly assuming roles as intermediaries in mental health.

2 In the Classroom: A New Emphasis on the Individual   A second basic trend has concerned the individualization of education. Increasingly there is an attempt to form a deeper understanding of each child and to tailor his program insofar as may be possible to his particular needs. Specialists as well as teachers are being trained to assist in this process.

Guidance workers are being hired and guidance programs set up as part of this move toward individualization. Each child's assets and limitations are studied, and ways are sought to help him to capitalize on his assets and minimize his shortcomings. Each child is helped to find the most suitable immediate school environment and to prepare for his educational and vocational future.

Special educational programs for exceptional children have been on the rapid increase. Schools have given greater attention to the very bright and the mentally retarded child and to the physically handicapped or seriously maladjusted. Sometimes special provision is made for such children within the regular classroom, or special school facilities are developed.

Six Specific Trends

With the increasing emphasis on group experience in mental health and the growth of special education and guidance movements in the school system, Hollister notes the emergence of six specific trends. As Hollister points out, it is apparent that the teacher is being asked to be more and do more while at the same time being given more guidance and assistance than ever before.

1 Increased Use of Consultation Services   Rather than referring children to specialists for treatment, the teacher, where possible, works with the child and the problem in the classroom with the guidance of the specialist. As Hollister says, "The literature and practice in school mental health reflect a growing conviction that many of the minor behavior and learning problems encountered in school life are best managed in the classroom." Mental health specialists are less occupied in dealing with individual children than in helping the teacher deal with them.

2 Wider Interest in Evaluation   There is increasing and wider interest in the evaluation of students. Intellectual and personal characteristics as well as physical and mental health are surveyed in the evaluative process. There is more attention to setting goals and collecting data to determine if these goals are being reached. Psychologists, psychometrists, and other workers are being retained to help with the evaluation.

3 Wider Employment of Group Methods   Because of the special advantages which group settings may have and because of the many students which must be accommodated, teachers and other school personnel have been moving toward group methods of behavior guidance. Special classes for children with adjustment and other problems have been established, and counseling and therapy procedures as well as tutoring and educational and vocational guidance find group settings. Greater efforts are being made to understand and put to use the special features of group interactions.

4 Greater Psychological Sophistication of Teachers   Both in preservice and inservice training programs there has been increased effort to convey a thorough understanding of child development, personality, and adjustment. Teachers are being trained to recognize and understand children's problems and to deal with them or seek proper assistance. Teachers are also learning more about themselves and the influence they have on pupils' adjustment.

5 Greater Psychological Sophistication of Pupils   Pupils themselves are being taught to know and understand themselves. They are also being helped to understand others and to relate to them. School programs contain units on personal and social problems and on family relationships; psychological material of various sorts is being incorporated into the curriculum, and a number of high schools offer introductory courses in psychology.

6 Greater Emphasis on Teacher-Parent Cooperation   Parents are increasingly being brought into the education process. Parent-teacher associations have assumed a greater voice in the school's affairs. Parent conferences and parent visits to the classroom are regular features of many school programs, and home visits by teachers are growing in importance.

SUMMARY

One way of defining school adjustment is to equate it with academic achievement. Another way is to consider the relationships that the child forms with his teachers and fellow students. In practice, these two criteria of adjustment appear to be interrelated, so that children who do well academically tend to be socially adequate while those who have academic problems tend to have other problems as well.

Estimates of the amount of maladjustment vary. In some representative studies, 20 to 42 percent of the pupils have been found to be moderately maladjusted, and 7 to 12 percent have been identified as seriously maladjusted. Boys are much more likely to be considered maladjusted than

girls. This appears to be true no matter who is doing the evaluating.

Teachers, clinicians, parents, and children themselves do not fully agree on the relative importance of children's problems. In the past four decades or so, the attitudes of teachers have become increasingly more similar to those of the clinicians, but there are still important differences. In general, parents seem more concerned with overt, attacking, antisocial behavior, clinicians with covert, withdrawing, asocial behavior, while teachers appear to take an intermediate position.

Children have their own ideas about what sorts of behavior are desirable or undesirable. In the identification of children's problems and children with problems, it has been increasingly considered important to get the viewpoints of children toward themselves and toward the children around them. Compared and contrasted with adult impressions, peer and self data are invaluable to the evaluation process.

Teachers appear to be no worse (or better) adjusted than people in other professions. There is special concern about the adjustment of teachers because of their influence on children. However, teachers who by some criteria are maladjusted are not necessarily harmful or ineffective in the classroom.

A series of studies has indicated that dominative behavior on the part of the teacher stifled the spontaneity and initiative of pupils. Socially integrative behavior, by contrast, promoted these qualities. Each kind of behavior was held to be self-perpetuating, that is, it tended to cause similar behavior in others.

Effective teachers have been found to like children, to be secure and confident of their own abilities, and to show good organization and integration in their classroom activities. Inferior teachers show less liking for children, and they are more insecure and disorganized.

Three major dimensions of teacher classroom behavior are (1) warm, understanding, and friendly versus aloof, egocentric, and restricted; (2) responsible, businesslike, and systematic versus evading, unplanned, and slipshod; and (3) stimulating, imaginative, and surgent versus dull and routine. Outstanding teachers —those who are warm, responsible, and stimulating—tend to be from families who have offered support for teaching as a career. These teachers also tend to be intellectually superior, and they have broad interests, including participation in social and community affairs. They are stable, friendly, and tolerant of others, and they enjoy their relationships with pupils.

There is considerable controversy concerning the amount of the schools' time and energies (if any) which should be expended in adjustment and mental health programs. However, the schools appear to be moving more and more toward greater involvement. This movement seems to be related to the growing emphasis on the group as a force in the adjustment process and on the person in the group as an individual with individual needs and goals. Trends in school mental health programs include the increased use of consultation services, wider interest in the continuing evaluation of pupils, wider employment of group methods of behavior guidance, greater psychological sophistication of both teachers and pupils, and a greater emphasis on teacher-parent cooperation.

REFERENCES

Allinsmith, W., & Goethals, G. W. *The Role of Schools in Mental Health.* New York: Basic Books, 1962. (Joint Commission on Mental Illness and Health Monographs Series, No. 7).

Anderson, H. H. Domination and socially integrative behavior. In R. G. Barker, J. S.

Kounin, & H. F. Wright (Eds.), *Child Behavior and Development.* New York: McGraw-Hill, 1943. Pp. 459–483.

———, & Brewer, H. M. Studies of teachers' classroom personalities. I. Dominative and socially integrative behavior of kindergarten teachers. *Applied Psychology Monographs,* 1945, No. 6.

———, & Brewer, J. E. Studies of teachers' classroom personalities. II. Effects of teachers' dominative and integrative contacts on children's classroom behavior. *Applied Psychology Monographs,* 1946, No. 8.

———, ———, & Reed, M. F. Studies of teachers' classroom personalities. III. Follow-up studies of the effects of dominative and integrative contacts on children's behavior. *Applied Psychology Monographs,* 1946, No. 11.

Beilin, H. Teachers' and clinicians' attitudes toward the behavior problems of children: A reappraisal. *Child Development,* 1959, **30,** 9–25.

Berlin, I. N. From teachers' problems to problem teachers. In J. C. Solomon (Ed.), Neuroses of school teachers: A colloquy. *Mental Hygiene,* 1960, **44,** 79–90. Pp. 80–83.

Bonney, M. E. Sociometric study of agreement between teacher judgments and student choices. *Sociometry,* 1947, **10,** 133–146.

Bower, E. M. *Early Identification of Emotionally Handicapped Children in School.* Springfield, Ill.: Charles C Thomas, 1960.

———. Comparison of the characteristics of identified emotionally disturbed children with other children in classes. In E. P. Trapp & P. Himelstein (Eds.), *Readings on the Exceptional Child.* New York: Appleton-Century-Crofts, 1962. Pp. 610–28.

Clark, R. A., & McGuire, C. Sociographic analysis of sociometric valuations. *Child Development,* 1952, **23**(2), 129–140.

Dombrose, L. A. Do teachers cause neurotic conflict in children? *Mental Hygiene,* 1955, **39,** 99–110.

Dunn, L. M. Educable mentally retarded children. In L. M. Dunn (Ed.), *Exceptional Children in the Schools.* New York: Holt, 1963. Pp. 53–127.

Gardner, W. I. Social and emotional adjustment of mildly retarded children and adolescents: Critical review. *Exceptional Children,* 1966, **33**(2), 97–105.

Gilbert, G. M. A survey of "referral problems" in metropolitan child guidance centers. *Journal of Clinical Psychology,* 1957, **13,** 37–42.

Glidewell, J. C. Some possible forecasts of research on mental health in the classroom. *Journal of Social Issues,* 1959, **15,** 59–60.

Gronlund, N. E. *Sociometry in the Classroom.* New York: Harper & Row, 1959.

Havighurst, R. J., Bowman, P. H., Liddle, G. P., Matthews, C. V., & Pierce, J. V. *Growing Up in River City.* New York: Wiley, 1962.

Hollister, W. G. Current trends in mental health programming in the classroom. *Journal of Social Issues,* 1959, **15,** 50–58.

Kaplan, L. *Mental Health and Human Relations in Education.* New York: Harper & Row, 1959.

L'Abate, L. Personality correlates of manifest anxiety in children. *Journal of Consulting Psychology,* 1960, **24,** 342–348.

Lindzey, G., & Borgatta, E. F. Sociometric measurement. In G. Lindzey (Ed.), *Handbook of Social Psychology.* Vol. 1. Reading, Mass.: Addison-Wesley, 1954. Pp. 405–448.

Mensh, I. N., Kantor, M. B., Domke, H. R., Gildea, M. C.-L., & Glidewell, J. C. Children's behavior symptoms and their relationships to school adjustment, sex, and social class. *Journal of Social Issues,* 1959, **15,** 8–15.

Monsour, K. J. School phobia in teachers. *American Journal of Orthopsychiatry,* 1961, **31,** 347–354.

Morse, W. C. A research evaluation of an action approach to school mental health. 2. The mental hygiene dilemma in public education. *American Journal of Orthopsychiatry*, 1961, **31**, 324–331.

Northway, M. L. *A Primer of Sociometry*. Toronto, Canada: University of Toronto Press, 1952.

Pearson, G. H. J. The most effective help a psychiatrist can give to the teacher. In M. Krugman (Ed.), *Orthopsychiatry and the School*. New York: American Orthopsychiatric Association, 1958. Pp. 3–22.

Rogers, C. R. A study of the mental-health problems in three representative elementary schools. In T. C. Holz et al. (Eds.), *A Study of Health and Physical Education in Columbus Public Schools*. Columbus, Ohio: Ohio State University Press, 1942. Pp. 130–161.

Ryans, D. G. *Characteristics of Teachers*. Menasha, Wis.: Banta, 1960.

Sarason, S. B., Davidson, K. S., Lighthall, F. F., & Waite, R. R. Classroom observations of high and low anxious children. *Child Development*, 1958, **29**, 287–295 (a)

———, ———, ———, & ———. A test anxiety scale for children. *Child Development*, 1958, **29**, 105–113. (b)

———, ———, ———, ———, & Ruebush, B. K. *Anxiety in Elementary School Children*, New York: Wiley, 1960.

Solomon, J. C. Neuroses of school teachers: A colloquy. *Mental Hygiene*, 1960, **44**, 79–90.

Stouffer, G. A. W., Jr. The attitudes of parents toward certain behavior problems of children. *Teachers College Bulletin*, 1959, **5**(1), 11–22.

Stringer, L. A. Academic progress as an index of mental health. *Journal of Social Issues*, 1959, **15**, 16–29.

Symonds, P. M. Characteristics of the effective teacher based on pupil evaluations. *Journal of Experimental Education*, 1955, **23**, 289–310.

Ullmann, C. A. *Identification of Maladjusted School Children*. Washington, D. C.: Public Health Service, 1952. (Public Health Monograph No. 7).

Wickman, E. K. *Children's Behavior and Teachers' Attitudes*. Cambridge, Mass.: Commonwealth Fund: Harvard University Press, 1928.

CHAPTER FOURTEEN

COLLEGE ADJUSTMENT

For some of us, college years are a high point in our lives. We enjoy the intellectual stimulation, the social activities, and the promise of important things to come. Others of us find college more of a trick than a treat as we struggle with our academic, personal, and other problems.

Why are some students so well adjusted to college while others have such a struggle? And what is meant by good adjustment to college anyway? This chapter examines some definitions of college adjustment and considers some factors which influence intellect and personality during the college years.

DEFINING COLLEGE ADJUSTMENT

There is no doubt that college is a stressful experience for many students. A psychiatrist who is chief of the student health service at a large university has estimated that one out of every nine students becomes sufficiently disturbed during college to need major professional help, hospitalization, or leave. According to his estimates, 8 to 12 percent of college students are "severely troubled," and 10 to 15 percent are "mildly to moderately troubled" (Paulsen, 1964).

Some problems seem common to many college students and campuses. Difficulties in studying, in finding interest and purpose in college work, and in hitting upon a suitable vocational goal are frequent complaints of students. Many problems reported by college students, such as loneliness, unsureness of oneself, difficulty in forming relationships with members of the opposite sex, and conflicts with parents, are widely found in young adults whether in college or not.

Colleges vary widely in the environments they provide and in the characteristics of their students (Astin, 1965; Stern, 1962). How easily a student adjusts to college depends in part on the needs of the student and the extent to which the college facilitates satisfaction of these needs and also on the demands of the college and the extent to which the student can meet these demands. Students who wither or fail at

---

Presentation 14.1 Suicide and college adjustment. Suicide rates are higher among college students than among noncollege persons of the same age. It has been estimated that each year there are one to two suicides for every 10,000 students. It has been further estimated that there are about nine attempts at suicide for each success and about ten threats for each attempt (Suicide and student stress, 1966).

Why do students commit suicide? A careful study was made of student suicides at the University of California at Berkeley during a ten-year period. Some of the main findings were as follows:

1 Suicidal students could be significantly differentiated from their classmates on the variables of age, class standing, major subject, nationality, emotional condition, and academic achievement. Compared to the student population at large, the suicidal group was older, contained greater proportions of graduates, language majors, and foreign students, and gave more indications of emotional disturbance. In addition, the undergraduate suicides fared much better than their fellow students in matters of academic achievement.

2 Contrary to the popular belief that suicides frequently occur during final examinations week, time relationships indicated that the peak danger period for student suicides was the beginning (first 6 weeks), not the midterm, nor end of the semester.

3 Most of the students gave recurrent warnings of their suicidal intent. Many of them presented a similar prodromal pattern marked by anorexia, insomnia, and periods of despondency.

4 Major precipitating factors were: Worry over schoolwork, chronic concerns about physical health (sometimes of a decidedly bizarre nature), and difficulties with interpersonal relationships. This last category contained some students who had reacted to romantic rejections but, for the most part, comprised the emotionally withdrawn and socially isolated student (Seiden, 1966, p. 399).

one college may survive or prosper at another.

One student, for example, may enjoy the impersonality of a large campus; he quickly adjusts to the new environment and enjoys the autonomy it grants him. Another student, however, feels lost in the same environment; perhaps his instructors seem distant, bent on other concerns, and lacking an interest in the students. As a consequence, he may feel powerfully moved to abandon his college career.

What exactly is meant by adjusting to college? What is good college adjustment? There are a number of different ways of defining college adjustment. The simplest definition would be in terms of academic achievement. A more complex definition involves the idea of personal growth. And an even more complex approach would combine both academic achievement and personal growth.

College Adjustment as Academic Achievement

The simplest measure of college adjustment is academic achievement. By this definition, the student who is adjusted to college is one who makes adequate grades, passes his courses, and graduates. Conversely, the maladjusted student is one whose grades are unsatisfactory, whose course work is marginal or failing, and who drops out of school before graduation.

Many studies have been concerned with the factors associated with academic achievement. In these studies, academic achievement is typically defined in terms of grade-point average; usually the grade-point average of the first semester in college is used, although sometimes the aver-

ages of the first year or the entire four years are employed. Sometimes achievement is defined in terms of persistence, that is, the number of semesters the student remains in college. And, occasionally, achievement is simply considered in terms of whether or not the student is able to graduate in the usual number of years.

How many students pass, persist, and graduate? One investigator was able to locate thirty-five studies of dropout or attrition rates in American colleges and universities. Hundreds of institutions were involved and the time span was nearly fifty years. It was noted that, on the average, about 40 percent of the students graduated on schedule and about 20 percent more graduated from some college, sooner or later.

Dropout rates were found to be fairly constant over the past half century. There were, however, considerable differences in attrition from college to college; the range was from 12 to 82 percent. In general, private institutions showed somewhat lower attrition than those which were state-supported, and this was attributed in part to the latter's more liberal entrance policies (Summerskill, 1962).

Defining college adjustment as academic achievement has a number of advantages. Unlike other possible criteria, academic achievement is relatively simple and easy to measure. And unlike other criteria, academic achievement would be accepted by most of us as a central or basic purpose of education.

Many of us, however, would be unhappy with the use of academic achievement as the sole measure—or even the chief measure—of college adjustment or success. After all, college should be more than just a matter of grit, grades, and graduation. But it is in trying to determine what else college should be that some considerable difficulties are encountered.

College Adjustment as Personal Growth

A fuller definition of college adjustment involves the idea of personal growth. The first definition appears to pose the questions: What does a student need to know? Does he know it? This latter definition seems to ask a somewhat different set of questions: What should a student become? Does he become it? (Sanford, 1962)

Not everyone would agree that the second set of questions is fully in order. To many people, the purpose of education is to convey to the student a certain body of information and perhaps a certain set of skills. Other purposes, such as concern for the student's physical and mental well-being, are rejected or looked upon with suspicion. Such matters may be considered none of the school's business or, at best, a watering down of proper goals (Sanford, 1962).

Other individuals, however, including some who have made higher education their lifelong study, are dissatisfied with colleges and the experiences they provide. In this regard, Katz and Sanford (1965), two college authorities, note that undergraduate programs have not kept pace with the Peace Corps and other noncollege activities in providing young adults with opportunities to grow and develop. And their colleague, Mervin Freedman (1965), Dean of Undergraduate Education at Stanford University, writes of the "dulling effects" of socialization in college.

Most colleges would agree that they

should do more than just convey knowledge. Almost every college catalog sets forth a list of goals or purposes which specify the kind of growth it hopes to produce in its students. Typically, however, the goals are broadly stated, and it may be difficult to know exactly what changes are expected. Typically, too, there is little follow-up to see if this growth actually occurs.

College Adjustment as Achievement *and* Growth

The richest definition of college adjustment would involve both academic achievement and personal growth. This implies that a person should develop his intellectual potentialities and his other potentialities as well. And this raises some interesting points which are pursued briefly in the following material.

Academic and Nonacademic Achievement

One way to determine whether a student is developing his nonacademic potentialities is to appraise his accomplishments outside the classroom. How accomplished is he in art and music? How creative is he? How much leadership does he show?

Research in this area has not supported the notion that academic and nonacademic talent go hand in hand. The results of a number of investigations suggest that academic potential and academic achievement are, at best, only modestly related to nonacademic achievement. What goes on in the classroom proves not to be a very good index of what goes on outside (Holland & Richards, 1965).

These findings suggest that high grades are not a guarantee that the student is developing his full potential. Neither are modest grades proof that he is not developing at all. For the fullest appraisal of a student, both his curricular and his extracurricular activities should be taken into account.

Academic and Later Achievement

Another way of seeing how well potentialities are being realized is to appraise later accomplishments. To determine the effects of a college education, we should study alumni. However, it is difficult to determine whether a particular set of changes is due to college experience or to precollege or postcollege forces (Freedman, 1962).

There is a considerable amount of evidence concerning the relationship of college achievement to later achievement. Hoyt (1965) reviews forty-six studies which have been done in this area and concludes that these two kinds of achievement are not highly related—college grades generally show little correlation with measures of postcollege accomplishment. He notes that in this less-than-perfect world, the measures of adult accomplishment are "highly suspect criteria," and the fact that grades and postcollege success are at variance is not an indictment (or a vindication) of the former.

Hoyt suggests that, in present practice, grades are measures of the acquisition of knowledge, which is one—but only one—purpose of education. He recommends that other kinds of student growth and development be encouraged and rewarded. This could be accomplished by basing grades on multiple considerations or by substituting a "profile of student growth and development" for the usual grade records and transcripts.

ACADEMIC ACHIEVEMENT IN COLLEGE

A number of factors are associated with success and failure in college. These factors can be called "predictors," because a knowledge of them helps predict how well students will do in college.

There is a good deal that is not known about academic achievement, and prediction of it is far from perfect. Some students prove to be overachievers; they achieve more than would be predicted on the basis of what is known about them. Others are underachievers; they do more poorly than would be predicted.

This section considers some important predictors of college achievement. In studying these correlates of academic success, we may gain new insights into college experience and new ideas about making it better. (See Fig. 14.1.)

Past Achievement Factors

The best predictor of future academic achievement is past academic achievement. The best predictor of how well we are going to do *next year* is how well we do *this year*. And the best predictor of how well we do *this year* is our achievement *last year*.

This may come as a surprise since people have become so accustomed to depending on tests of one sort or another, but a moment's reflection should reveal why it is true. Achievement is the product of many complex forces in complex interaction. Although these forces would be difficult to ferret out, earlier achievement shows how they have operated in the past and provides the best guess about how they will operate in the future.

Research evidence indicates that high school grades (or graduating ranks) correlate more highly with achievement in college than any other factor which has been studied (Garrett, 1949; Lavin, 1965; Stein, 1963). One investigator who surveyed the problem of college attrition found that in ten of the eleven studies concerned with this problem, college dropouts generally received lower grades in high school than did students who remained in college to graduate (Summerskill, 1962).

Since college achievement is related to achievement in high school, it might be expected that high school achievement, in turn, would be related to earlier achievement. If so, success in the elementary grades would, to some extent, presage later success in college. One investigator found this to be true. His results indicated that achievement tests given as early as the fourth grade correlated significantly—although modestly—with success during the first year of college nearly a decade later (Scannell, 1960).

Although past and present achievement records are related, it is important to note that the relationship is far from perfect. *On the average,* students who are achieving well continue to do so, and poorer students continue to do poorly, *but many exceptions occur.*

Students with mediocre high school records have been seen to take hold and thrive in the new college environment. And students who have done poorly in their early college work may show dramatic improvement during their junior or senior or graduate years. Sometimes this improvement is related to greater maturity. Sometimes there is greater goal orientation due to interest in a certain program of studies or in preparation for a vocation.

Conversely, sometimes students with good high school records do poorly in college. The greater freedom and responsibility in the college environment, the separation from home, and many other changed educational and social conditions may make adjustment difficult.

Ability Factors

Ability refers to the capacity to learn. This, of course, is an important factor in academic success. Colleges commonly require applicants for admission to take some kind of test of ability.

Various kinds of tests have been devised to assess learning capacity. One way of classifying these tests is in terms of their "educational loading," that is, their dependence on previous schooling and school-learned materials.

Tests employing relatively high educational loadings are sometimes referred to as "academic achievement" tests. These

Figure 14.1 Who survives in college? This study used certain ability test scores as predictors to establish eight levels of academic success expectancy for freshmen entering the Chicago Undergraduate Division of the University of Illinois. These two charts show expectation for students who score at the top and bottom levels. For every 100 students at the top level, 84 are expected to be in good standing at the end of the first semester, 11 on probation (allowed another semester to raise their grades), 4 withdrawn without completing the semester, and 1 dropped for poor scholarship. At the bottom level, only 18 are expected to do satisfactory work the first semester, 22 are expected to be on probation, 23 withdrawn, and 37 dropped. By the end of the second semester, 72 of the top-expectancy students are expected to remain and be in good standing but only 12 in the bottom level are expected to enjoy this status (Eells, 1961).

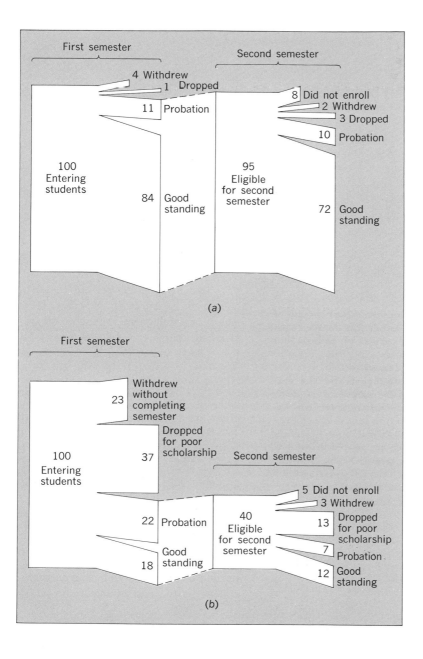

(a)

(b)

tests measure material that is taught in school. When such tests are used for the prediction of college success, it is assumed that students who are proficient in school-taught materials will continue to be so in the future.

Tests with relatively low educational loadings are sometimes called "academic aptitude" tests. These tests present the student with relatively novel tasks, comparatively free from the effects of previous schooling. In using such tests for prediction, one attempts to get at the student's basic potential (Cronbach, 1960).

As predictors of college success, achievement-type tests have proved gener-

ally superior to aptitude-type tests (Garrett, 1949). And there has been a shift toward achievement tests for predicting performance in college (Cronbach, 1960).

Evidence concerning the intellectual requirements of high school and college work has been brought together by Cronbach (1960). He estimates that the mean IQ of high school graduates is about 110 and that students of this intellectual level have about a 50-50 chance of graduating from college. The mean IQ of freshmen in a "typical four-year college" is about 115. The mean IQ of college graduates is 120, and of students receiving the Ph.D. degree, 130. (See Table 14.1.)

One investigator set out to see what happened to students of many different levels of intelligence who entered an accredited liberal arts college. The policy of the college was said to be "easy to enter, difficult to graduate." On the one hand, it admitted any high school graduate who had the usual course prerequisites; on the other, its achievement demands were high.

For the 187 students who were studied, intelligence quotients ranged from 78 to 154, with an average of 111. Of the students with IQs above 110, 65 percent graduated in the usual time. Of the students with IQs below 110, only 39 percent graduated in the usual time. And of the students with IQs below 100, only 25 percent graduated in the usual time; a sizable portion of the students in this category left college at the end of the first year (Marshall, 1943).

It has been suggested that persons of very superior ability may not perform better academically than those who are somewhat lower. Lavin writes that "after a certain level is reached, ability may no longer play a significant role in predicting

Table 14.1 What is the intellectual climate of a college freshman class? Of course, such climates vary from college to college, but here is some information concerning a group of 361 freshmen who were tested with the Wechsler Adult Intelligence Scale. The percentile ranks indicate the number of students who scored below a certain level; for example, 99 percent of the students achieved full-scale IQs below 135, but only 1 percent were below 96; 50 percent scored below 115, which constitutes the mean IQ for the group. Note the wide range of intellectual ability.*

Percentile Rank	Full-scale IQ
99	135
95	129
90	125
80	121
70	119
60	117
50	115
40	113
30	111
20	108
10	105
5	102
1	96

Number	=	361
Mean	=	115.2
Standard deviation	=	8.8
Range	=	91–145

* From Plant and Lynd (1959).

school performance, so that performance may then have to be accounted for through the use of nonintellective factors" (1965, p. 58). Such factors may include motivational patterns and other personality characteristics.

Motivational Factors

Many teachers, counselors, and research workers have been interested in the relationship between motivational factors and college success. Some of these workers have been concerned with the difference in college success between students who were "motivated" and those who were "unmotivated." Others have approached the problem more exactly, attempting to find what needs characterize successful and unsuccessful students.

Are unsuccessful students "unmotivated"? Students making higher grades have been found to study more hours per week than those doing more poorly (Bonner, 1957; Boyce, 1956; Diener, 1957; Wellington, 1956). Some evidence suggests that better students are more regular in class attendance and more active in class discussions (Knaak, 1957). They are also more goal-oriented, that is, directed toward more exact educational and vocational goals (Kerns, 1957; McQuary, 1954; Sherwood, 1957).

The extent of the motivational differences between successful and unsuccessful college students was demonstrated in an interesting series of experiments by Brown, Abeles, and Iscoe (1954). In the first experiment two groups of students equated for ability, but one on the dean's honor list and the other on scholastic probation, were sent letters asking them to cooperate in an investigation concerning study habits.

Those who did not respond were sent a second letter reemphasizing the need for their cooperation. Those who still had not responded were individually phoned and given definite appointments to appear at a specified time. It was found that four-fifths of the honor students appeared following the first request, and by the end of the experiment almost all of them had done so. By contrast, only one-eighth of the probation group appeared following the first request, and one-half failed to participate at all.

A second experiment took place in connection with a study of student attitudes. At the university concerned, every seventh male undergraduate listed on an alphabetical roster was sent a letter by the university president strongly urging participation. For those who failed to respond, a second letter, more strongly worded, was sent; this letter "ordered" the student "to report." Those who still failed to respond were contacted by phone and given special appointments. It was found that the students who responded after the first letter had significantly higher grades than those who needed to be phoned.

In the third experiment, students in an elementary educational psychology course were told that an examination would be taken directly from the objective questions in their workbook. Before the examination students who had answered the workbook questions (or at least pretended to do so) were allowed to check their answers against the instructor's key. It was found that more than half of the students who failed to use the key scored below 80 while only one-fifth of the key users did this poorly.

The experimenters concluded that motivational factors may be primary contributors toward poor scholarship. They found poorer students characterized by indecisiveness, a tendency to procrastinate, and, perhaps, an unwillingness to meet academic demands. Furthermore, these characteristics were seen to extend beyond the classroom.

One set of clinicians set out to discover as much as possible about five students who were doing failing work in college. The students were thoroughly studied through a series of clinical interviews and examinations. Lack of adequate motivation was found to be one of the chief reasons for the students' difficulties. The investigators concluded:

> Among the personal vulnerabilities which the students carried into the university situation, one of the most telling factors appears to be a lack of adequate motivation to engage in academic pursuits. Not one of our students had any real love of knowledge or respect for the products of scholarship. Nor did their cultural backgrounds imbue them with the value of intellectual growth and self-actualization. On the contrary, in every case, higher education was viewed in narrow, utilitarian terms—as a means of achieving vocational goals. Moreover, these vocational goals were, in themselves, largely founded on the sands of social prestige or financial security rather than on the granite of solid desire to perform the activities demanded by the particular vocation. Thus, our five subjects were characterized by a definite shallowness of motivation for the work they were expected to do at the university, and that which they would be called upon to do if they fulfilled their educational objectives. This lack of motivation appropriate to a university situation made it difficult for them to tolerate the tensions and demands which are an integral part of sustained intellectual effort (Sarnoff & Raphael, 1955, p. 370).

These studies and others show that motivational factors are important in college success and failure. In one sense, however, it is not correct to say that failing students are unmotivated. Such students may be motivated, but in ways which are inconsistent with success in a particular curriculum or in a particular college or in academic pursuits generally (Anderson, 1954; Summerskill, 1962).

In this connection, a number of investigators have attempted to determine the patterns of motivation which are related to academic success. What needs characterize students who do well in college? What needs are operating in those who do poorly or fail?

It might be hypothesized that students with high achievement needs tend to be more successful than those with lower achievement needs. The evidence in this area is not clear-cut, partly because the methods of measuring achievement motivation are so different (McClelland, 1958). However, where significant results have been found, they generally support the hypothesis (Lavin, 1965; Stein, 1963).

Some further evidence concerns affiliation needs. Several studies suggest that students who are high in affiliation may be generally less successful in their academic programs (Lavin, 1965). Such students seem to place friendship activities above scholarship (Gebhardt & Hoyt, 1958).

It may be possible to predict academic achievement more accurately from a combination of needs than from single needs alone. One set of investigators studied achievement and affiliation in a group of college women. The results were provocative.

It was found that students with high achievement needs tended to overachieve *only* when their best friends or affiliates tended in this direction; when their friends were low achievers, their own achievement tended to be average. Students with relatively low achievement needs made average achievements when their friends were high achievers, but when their friends' achievement was low, their own tended to be very low.

This investigation suggests how different needs and other factors may interact in academic processes. The need for achievement (or some other need) may be modified by the needs and values of the group with which one associates. Some groups may apply pressure on their members to achieve. Others may not reward such behavior; in fact, they may discourage achievement or emphasize motives which conflict with it (Applezweig, Moeller, & Burdick, 1956).

Other Personality Factors

Ability factors are much better predictors than motives and other nonintellective factors. One problem has been that investigators have generally pursued the person without considering the environment (Lavin, 1965). As we begin to take into account the student's personal characteristics *and* the characteristics of the academic and social situation, results should prove more promising.

Lavin (1965) reviews the evidence concerning the relationship of personality factors and academic performance. He concludes that the evidence is frequently inconsistent and that the relationships found are generally of a low order. Remembering

their tenuous nature, take note of his findings:

First, as indicated earlier, academic achievement is positively correlated with achievement motivation. Better students have higher achievement needs. They also have higher activity levels and higher endurance or persistence.

Second, academic performance is positively related to social maturity. Better students have greater social maturity and social presence. They are more responsible and more restrained in their social behavior.

Third, academic performance is positively associated with emotional stability. Better students are more stable and have higher morale. They are also less anxious about their studies and about taking tests.

Fourth, academic performance is related to cognitive or intellectual style. Better students tend to be more curious, original, and flexible. They enjoy thinking, and they participate in classroom activities more frequently and more effectively.

Fifth, academic achievement is related to independence. As noted earlier, better students are relatively low in affiliative needs. These students are less dependent on others and tend not to conform to group standards. They are intermediate in impulsivity—neither very impulsive nor very constricted.

Sixth, academic achievement is related to conformability. Better students have been found to be more orderly. They are also more docile and passive and more obedient in the classroom.

The fifth and sixth findings might seem inconsistent. Can both independence and conformability be related to higher grades? One possibility is that these students are relatively independent of their peer groups but relatively conforming to instructional pressures. Another possibility is that these several behaviors occur in different academic contexts. In this regard, Lavin notes that "expectations defining the student role may vary from one school to another and even from one department to another within a school, so that in some contexts independence is rewarded more highly than conformity, while in others the opposite is true" (p. 108).

Study Factors

College success requires study. But some students study and study and study without getting anywhere. Are study habits at fault, or is lack of success due to other reasons? And just what are effective study habits anyway?

Do better students have different study habits from poorer ones? A number of "study habit" tests have been devised, and a few have been found to have some value in the prediction of college achieve-

ment. These tests, however, are not simply made up of study habit items; they include motivational, adjustment, and other types of items as well. Close analysis has shown that the *other* categories of items predict college achievement better than do the study habit items (Brown & Holtzman, 1955; Carter, 1955).

Although our knowledge concerning the role of study habits in college success leaves something to be desired, there is some evidence which deserves examination. Moreover, workers in this area have a number of hypotheses concerning effective studying and learning. The material which follows briefly describes some study habits which have been held to characterize better students.

Study More

First, better students study more. The amount of studying that a student needs to do is, of course, related to his ability; some students grasp quickly what others absorb with difficulty (see Table 14.2).

Table 14.2   How much time do college students spend in study? And how do they occupy the rest of their time? Student interviewers collected information concerning 220 full-time undergraduate and graduate students at the University of Hawaii. Respondents were asked to estimate the number of hours they had spent on various activities during the preceding week ("a typical week late in the spring semester"). Although there was considerable variation, the average student appeared to be spending about 40 hours per week on his college work (about 20 hours in classes and laboratories and another 20 hours in preparation), and these findings were held to be similar to those reported for other campuses.*

Activity	Mean Hours	Range
Class (and lab)	20.0	3–50
Preparation	21.0	0–56
Sleep	49.9	28–84
Meals	11.5	1–32
Recreation	16.3	0–85
Travel	5.9	0–28
Miscellaneous	37.4	0–83
Of those reporting at least 1 hour:		
Paid employment	12.5	0–48
Cocurricular	4.5	0–26

* From Dole (1959).

Even so, the research evidence shows that grades are positively correlated with hours of study; on the average, students making higher grades study longer hours than those whose grades are lower (Bonner, 1957; Boyce, 1956; Diener, 1957; Wellington, 1956).

Study More Actively

Second, better students are assumed to study more actively. Before reading material, they survey it in order to see where they are going. After reading it, they review it to see where they have been and what they have absorbed. During the reading they stop to recite the material to themselves to enhance comprehension and retention (Robinson, 1961).

Better Scheduling

Third, it has been suggested that better students are more likely to schedule their studying. They may structure their days, apportioning certain times to certain tasks and setting certain hours aside for study. Their schedule, whether explicit or implicit, is organized to take advantage of the entire day—a one-hour period between classes is utilized as well as longer stretches of time.

Better Distribution of Studying

Fourth, better students are more likely to distribute their studying. Compared with poorer students, they are apt to study a certain amount every day rather than do all their studying just before a test. Furthermore, the amount of time given to any particular material is more likely to be distributed over a number of periods of study. Although cramming can be a useful supplement to studying, it is a poor substitute for studying. Most of the research evidence supports the conclusion that people learn best when they distribute their learning (Deese, 1958).

Better Surroundings

Fifth, better students are thought to study in more favorable surroundings. To a greater extent than less proficient students, they study in a particular place—frequently fairly secluded and away from social stimulation. Their desks are more likely to be free of distracting material and their study free of phonograph, radio, and television accompaniment.

Better Readers

Sixth, better students tend to read better. They read more words per minute, and they understand more of what they read. Although some students are slow but sure readers, while others are quick and careless, speed and accuracy generally go together. Better students read faster and more accurately (Bird & Bird, 1945).

Better Notetakers

Seventh, better students are believed to take better notes. Their notes are more likely to be selective. These students tend not to take down everything the lecturer says, but they get the important points. And their notes are more likely to be organized, and, when necessary, rewritten.

Teaching Factors

How much a student learns in college depends, in part, on how good he is at learning. But it also seems to depend on how good teachers are at teaching. Are some methods of teaching better than others? Are some sorts of teachers better than others?

Methods of Instruction

There are many different ways to teach and many different ideas about which way is best. Some of the issues have attracted more opinion than evidence. And determining the relative effectiveness of various teaching methods is a difficult task.

It is helpful to consider some points that McKeachie (1962), a leading authority on teaching methods, makes in this regard. Suppose that we want to determine which of two approaches is better. We take two classes, teach one by one method, one by the other, and compare the results. But it is not that simple.

The students of a new or unusual method may be excited and stimulated, and their enthusiasm may lead them to do well. On the other hand, a strange and novel approach may irritate them and make them resentful, and they may worry about their performance if they are being compared with students who are taught in a more conventional fashion.

If one professor teaches both methods, his own feelings and personal characteristics may prejudice the results. It would be better to get a number of instructors to participate and have them teach both methods, but this is very difficult to do.

Then there is the problem of trying to measure the results. Shall we simply try to determine the differences in the amount of information acquired under each method, or shall we attempt to get at less tangible effects? And if we are interested in how much information the students acquire, what sort of examinations should we administer? It is possible that students of a particular approach might do better on one kind of test than on another.

Research has not indicated that any particular method of teaching is clearly best for all situations. What method should be employed depends on educational goals and on the personalities of the students and the instructors involved. Furthermore, the selection of a particular method may be dictated or influenced by practical considerations.

If the objective is to communicate a good deal of information, straight lecturing may be superior to discussion. If the objective is to try to help students apply and develop the information, discussion or laboratory approaches may offer some advantages. Sometimes a combination of several methods presents a worthwhile solution to the problem of conflicting or multiple goals or to the conflict between what is desirable and what is possible.

Newer techniques—such as television, films, tapes, teaching machines, and programmed textbooks—all seem to be finding a place in modern education. McKeachie (1962) notes that the usefulness of these techniques has been found to vary "depending upon the objective, the characteristics of the students, and the excellence of their materials." And he adds, "Research at present reveals no danger that these devices will eliminate the need for face-to-face contacts between professors and students."

Some students will do best under one method, others under another. Wispé (1953) notes that "the best teaching method for some students is not the best teaching method for all students." And Stern (1962) adds, "The maximal success of the learning process may well depend on the optimal combination of teaching technique and student need."

It should also be noted that instructors have their own personal preferences concerning teaching methods. A particular instructor may show special competence in handling large lecture sections. Another may be at his best in leading smaller discussion groups or seminars. More will be said about instructors in the section which follows.

Characteristics of Instructors

How well a student learns depends partly on how well he is taught. Just as some students are better learners than others, instructors vary in teaching ability.

There is not very much evidence on the qualities that make for effective teaching. But some information can be gathered from students' reactions (see Fig. 14.2).

What characteristics do the best-liked teachers have? What characteristics do the most effective teachers have? In one very comprehensive study which questioned 775 college seniors and graduate students attending twenty-one teacher-training institutions throughout the nation, it was found that "best-liked" and "most effective" go together. Eighty-three percent of the students reported that the teacher they liked best was also the one they felt was most effective (Taylor, 1959).

Buxton (1956) has reviewed some of the literature concerning students' reactions to their instructors. He found five instructor traits that are generally valued highly by students. These are fairness, competence, enthusiasm, empathy, and intellectual leadership.

Fairness According to Buxton, students value the instructor who is fair in his assignments and grading. Although the teacher who demands little and grades liberally is not without his popularity, students appreciate and respect the instructor who sets fair goals and is rewarding when these goals are met. However, as Buxton points out, it is not enough for the instructor to *be* fair; he must also be *seen as fair*. He can accomplish this in a number of ways, for example, by "making perfectly plain how he arrives at the grades over which he expends so much conscientious worry" (1956, p. 295).

Competence Students appreciate the teacher who knows his subject matter and is able to teach it. And beyond this, the teacher should have faith in his own ability. Buxton says:

> The appearance of self-confidence is involved here; students become concerned if the instructor seems overly unsure of himself. Conversely, a willingness to admit an occasional error and correct it is regarded as human and desirable evidence that a fundamental self-confidence exists. Bluffing or covering up, if ever detected, is fatal to the student's attitude toward the instructor; inevitably he recognizes these as signs of incompetence (1956, p. 295).

Enthusiasm Students enjoy the instructor who is enthusiastic about his field. To be taught by an instructor who is thoroughly caught up by his own subject, who is intrigued and challenged by its problems, who is excited about its possibilities—this can be a highly stimulating experience. The enthusiastic instructor communicates his enthusiasm. Because of the instructor's own intense interest, many students find themselves interested in courses which they thought would be dull or boring.

Percent who agree

A good college teacher . . .

Men | Women

0   25   50   75   100

A good college teacher . . .	Men	Women
is someone who really knows his field.	99	99
is willing to discuss a student's career plans.	99	99
is someone who judges a student on his work and not on how he dresses or looks.	96	99
is someone who really makes students produce.	94	96
does not attempt to indoctrinate his students in a particular political, religious, or ideological belief.	94	94
is a person who can teach in an entertaining manner.	90	79
is active in campus activities.	85	77
is willing to discuss a student's personal problems.	80	73
is active in civic affairs.	76	70
is active in religious affairs.	57	47
permits students to take part in deciding the course objectives.	54	65
is someone who sticks to teaching and does not act as a "buddy" to students.	48	51
does not give a lot of reading assignments.	24	17
is willing to help students decide on how they should stand on things like politics and religion.	22	25
is someone who is willing to give the student a break when the student doesn't do his work.	14	26

Empathy Empathy is a highly regarded instructor trait. In this connection, empathy refers to the ability of the instructor to sense and understand the feelings and thought and actions of his students. The empathic instructor can put himself in the student's place and see problems as the student sees them. Buxton notes that ". . . the instructor's responses to the student must show that the student's world is adequately perceived by the instructor, else how can he deal with exactly those matters which the student needs to have clarified?" (1956, p. 296).

Intellectual Leadership Buxton points out that students have confidence in the instructor who is able to maintain intellectual leadership. To accomplish this the instructor must be superior in certain ways but not so superior that he frightens his students or is unable to form effective contact with them. He must provide a structure for the learning situation that defines the social interaction that is to occur and the intellectual goals that are to be reached.

An Overall View How can the various characteristics which make for effective teaching be summarized and understood? Actually the qualities that mark the superior instructor are very probably qualities that are highly regarded in every area of human endeavor. Buxton puts this very nicely when he says, "Perhaps one could put all of the traits discussed above into one general category of traits which in the classroom as elsewhere in social intercourse make for the appearance of maturity and

Figure 14.2 What is a good college teacher? Here are the responses of a large group of senior men and women at Michigan State University (Data from Lehmann & Dressel, 1963).

attractiveness, and thus for social effectiveness." And he adds, "This way of viewing instructor qualities helps to put in proper perspective the effect on teacher evaluation of such matters as dress, voice quality, rate of speech, and mannerisms. These, short of extremes producing annoyance, are evidently not fundamental" (1956, pp. 296–297).

PERSONAL GROWTH IN COLLEGE

College is a time of change and growth. How much do we change? How much do we grow? What part does college play in our development?

Recent research indicates that personal characteristics and capabilities are not so fixed by the time a student reaches college age as many people believe. Very important changes may occur during the college years (see Fig. 14.3).

The following discussion is in two parts. The first describes some intellectual changes which may occur. The second considers some other sorts of personality changes.[1]

Intellectual Changes

Contrary to widespread belief, not all of us reach our intellectual ceiling in our teens. There are wide individual differences in the rate at which our intellectual development takes place and in the time at which we begin to near our peak.

Research evidence indicates that brighter persons develop both faster *and* longer than those who are less gifted. This

---

[1] This discussion is largely based on Boyer and Michael (1965); Freedman (1965); and Webster, Freedman, and Heist (1962).

In what ways are you different now from what you were as a freshman?

Men   Women

	Percent more	Percent same	Percent less

Insight into the behavior of other people.
| Men | 85 | 13 | 2 |
| Women | 93 | 6 | 1 |

Confidence in my ability to deal with new problems.
| Men | 82 | 14 | 4 |
| Women | 83 | 13 | 4 |

Respect for the views and opinion of other people.
| Men | 80 | 17 | 3 |
| Women | 82 | 16 | 2 |

Responsibility for my own behavior.
| Men | 80 | 19 | 1 |
| Women | 80 | 19 | 1 |

Ability to change my views in the presence of facts.
| Men | 80 | 18 | 2 |
| Women | 78 | 20 | 2 |

Interest in world affairs.
| Men | 77 | 21 | 2 |
| Women | 77 | 20 | 3 |

Respect for views and opinions opposite to mine.
| Men | 76 | 20 | 4 |
| Women | 80 | 16 | 4 |

Awareness of my goals in life.
| Men | 75 | 16 | 9 |
| Women | 82 | 9 | 9 |

Interest in intellectual and cultural matters.
| Men | 73 | 23 | 4 |
| Women | 84 | 14 | 2 |

Ability to get along with other people.
| Men | 73 | 25 | 2 |
| Women | 73 | 25 | 2 |

Ability to adjust to conditions not to my liking.
| Men | 72 | 23 | 5 |
| Women | 73 | 22 | 5 |

Interest in scientific developments.
| Men | 70 | 23 | 6 |
| Women | 60 | 35 | 5 |

Interest in social issues.
| Men | 68 | 26 | 5 |
| Women | 72 | 23 | 5 |

In what ways are you different now from what you were as a freshman?

Men   Women

	Percent more	Percent same	Percent less
Feeling that a college should also stress a liberal-arts type of education.	67 / 68	24 / 25	9 / 7
Tolerance of people differing in race, creed, color, or religion.	66 / 73	27 / 23	7 / 4
Optimistic outlook for my future.	64 / 67	26 / 23	10 / 10
Ability to accept disappointment.	64 / 67	31 / 29	5 / 4
Desire to accept a job for the satisfaction it has to offer rather than the salary it pays.	61 / 63	30 / 26	9 / 11
Feeling that money is of primary importance.	61 / 58	30 / 35	9 / 7
Interest in political matters.	60 / 60	32 / 32	8 / 8
Feeling that a college education is necessary to succeed in the world.	60 / 59	27 / 27	13 / 14
Drive to get ahead as quickly as possible.	50 / 26	36 / 50	14 / 24
Tolerance of unconventional dress, behavior, and manners.	48 / 63	31 / 24	20 / 13
Optimistic outlook for future of civilization.	45 / 39	34 / 32	21 / 29
Respect for persons in positions of authority.	35 / 22	49 / 61	16 / 17
Respect for law.	34 / 26	55 / 67	11 / 7

(Values shown as Men / Women)

In what ways are you different now from what you were as a freshman?

Men   Women

	Percent more	Percent same	Percent less
Feeling of the necessity for religious faith for living in modern times. (Men)	32	38	30
(Women)	39	37	24
Feeling that a major aim of college is to prepare one for a vocation or profession. (Men)	32	31	37
(Women)	21	35	44
Dependence on class attendance for learning. (Men)	28	29	43
(Women)	27	33	40
Respect for rules and regulations. (Men)	28	49	23
(Women)	20	54	26
Pessimistic outlook for the future of civilization. (Men)	21	32	47
(Women)	27	31	42
Confusion as to what I want out of life. (Men)	21	23	56
(Women)	21	15	64
Commitment to a set of religious beliefs. (Men)	20	45	35
(Women)	24	43	33
Importance of grades as measures of achievement. (Men)	18	21	61
(Women)	11	23	66
Feeling that the quality of one's education depends on the institution rather than the individual. (Men)	13	24	63
(Women)	10	22	68
Attachment to a religious sect or denomination that I can believe in and defend. (Men)	12	51	37
(Women)	17	49	34
Acceptance of the Bible as a guide to modern living. (Men)	11	55	34
(Women)	13	57	30
Dependence on my age group for behavior patterns. (Men)	11	32	57
(Women)	10	26	64
Pessimistic outlook for my future. (Men)	8	24	68
(Women)	8	20	72

suggests that many students will continue to grow intellectually in college, and some students will grow markedly. The more brilliant or gifted a student is, the more he can expect to develop during the college years.

A study involving a group of students at Michigan State University indicated some of the intellectual changes which occur. During their college years, students showed significant increases in critical thinking ability. At the senior level, students were better able to define a problem, recognize the assumptions which were involved, select the pertinent information, formulate relevant hypotheses, and draw valid conclusions (Lehmann & Dressel, 1963).

In another study involving high-ability students, significant increases occurred in verbal and quantitative aptitude scores from the freshman to the senior year. The student's study program appeared to be an important influence. Students who were majoring in economics, chemistry, and mathematics showed more improvement in quantitative scores than verbal while students in the humanities reversed this pattern (Nichols, 1964).

Other Changes

Although the evidence is not perfectly consistent or dramatic, the results of a number of studies suggest a pattern of nonintellective changes which occur in college students. These changes largely concern the students' attitudes and values.

One change concerns independence and autonomy. Increased independence has

Figure 14.3 What changes occur in students during the college years? Here are the changes which a large group of seniors at Michigan State University perceived in themselves (Data from Lehmann & Dressel, 1963).

been called the "first and foremost" change which occurs during the college years (Freedman, 1965). Students become more autonomous, more rebellious, and more critical of authority.

A second change noted by a number of investigators doing research on college populations concerns dogmatism. The evidence indicates that students become less dogmatic during their college years. Specifically, they are less closed in their beliefs, more open-minded, and more receptive to new ideas.

A third change involves a rather complicated combination of attitudes called "authoritarianism." These attitudes are largely antidemocratic and anti-intellectual. Authoritarianism has been found to diminish in students in the course of their college years.

A fourth change concerns ethnocentrism. As they move through college, students become less prejudiced in their ethnic attitudes. They are less likely to resort to stereotypes in evaluating a person. They are more likely to consider the person as an individual.

A fifth change concerns attitudes toward civil liberties. Seniors have been found to be more tolerant and more permissive in their attitudes toward civil liberties than are freshmen. Seniors are also more committed to intellectual and academic freedom.

The evidence suggests that the amount of change varies considerably from student to student. Some students change a good deal, some but little. One set of investigators concluded that certain groups of students "so insulated themselves from some aspects of college life as to preclude many of the changes in attitudes and values normally considered desirable by most college communities" (Gottlieb & Hodgkins, 1963, p. 287).

Just as the amount of change varies from student to student, it varies also from college to college. Some colleges provoke change; others do not. For example, although the research on civil liberties shows a gain in tolerance during the college years, at some colleges the gain is considerable while at others it is quite small (McConnell, 1962).

Students grow in different ways. Heath (1964) made a close and continuing study of a group of Princeton students. He noted that different kinds of students were dependent on different kinds of experiences for growth. One type which he called "non-committers" (friendly, bland, and neutral) developed by becoming more lively and self-directed. A second type, "hustlers" (cold, driving, and ambitious), grew by becoming warmer, more flexible, and self-accepting. A third group, "plungers" (impulsive, changeable, and scattered) matured by becoming more settled, predictable, and comprehensible to others.

Research evidence suggests one more important point: the changes which occur in college are not necessarily the results of the college experience. Some of these changes may be generally expected of gifted adults whether or not they go to college. For some kinds of growth, the college experience may be a facilitator, speeding up changes which would occur anyway although at a somewhat slower pace.

SUMMARY

College adjustment can be defined in various ways. It can be defined most simply in terms of academic achievement and measured by the grades a student makes or by his ability to continue in college until he graduates. A second definition is in terms of the personal growth which is manifested in college and postcollege years. A more complex approach combines both academic achievement and personal growth.

A major emphasis of this chapter is on the factors which are associated with academic achievement in college. These factors can be called predictors because a knowledge of them helps predict how well students will do in college. Present knowledge of these factors is limited, and prediction of college success, although helpful, is far from perfect.

Past achievement factors make up the single best set of predictors. As a general rule, a student's high school record provides the best indication of his chances for success in college. However, there are many examples of students who blossom in college and do much better than would be expected and also of those who do much more poorly than would be assumed.

Ability factors bear an important relationship to college achievement. A certain minimum ability is necessary to college success, but this minimum varies from school to school and from curriculum to curriculum, some schools and curricula being more demanding than others. Academic ability tests vary in the extent of their educational loading, that is, in the extent of their dependence on previous schooling and school-learned materials. Tests relatively high in educational loading are sometimes referred to as academic achievement tests; those which are relatively low are called academic aptitude tests.

Motivational factors play a part in college success and failure. Poorer students may appear unmotivated, but it is possible to think of them as being motivated but in ways that are inconsistent with success in a particular curriculum or college, or in academic pursuits generally. Some evidence suggests that better students tend to have higher needs for achievement and lower needs for affiliation.

Generally speaking, motivational and other nonintellective personality factors have not proved to be very good predictors. This may be due to the fact that investigators have pursued personal characteristics independent of relevant environmental characteristics. There is some evidence suggesting that academic achievement may be positively correlated with achievement motivation, social maturity, emotional stability, originality and flexibility in thinking, and both independence and conformability.

Study factors are involved in college success, but the evidence in this area is not clear-cut. Compared with poorer students, better ones are assumed to study more. It has been suggested that they study more actively, schedule their time better, and distribute their studying rather than concentrating it. And they are believed to study in better surroundings and to be better readers and notetakers.

Success in college also depends on the effectiveness of instruction. Research has not indicated that any particular method of teaching is best for every occasion; the selection of a method for a particular situation depends on the educational objective and the characteristics of the students and instructors involved. Some instructor traits that are highly valued by students are fairness, competence, enthusiasm, empathy, and intellectual leadership.

A second major emphasis of the chapter was personal growth in college. Research evidence suggests that considerable intellectual and other kinds of growth occur during the college years.

Many students demonstrate growth in intellectual capacity during their late teens and twenties. Since very bright students grow both faster and longer, a good deal of additional potential may be realized during the college years. One ability that has been shown to increase is that involved in critical thinking.

Other changes occurring in college are increased independence and tolerance and decreased dogmatism, authoritarianism, and ethnocentrism. The amount of change varies markedly from student to student and from college to college. Some of the changes are not necessarily the results of college experience—they occur generally in gifted adults—but college may facilitate or accelerate the changes.

REFERENCES

Anderson, J. R. Do college students *lack* motivation? *Personnel and Guidance Journal,* 1954, **33,** 209–210.

Applezweig, M. H., Moeller, G., & Burdick, H. Multimotive prediction of academic success. *Psychological Reports,* 1956, **2,** 489–496.

Astin, A. W. *Who Goes Where to College?* Chicago: Science Research, 1965.

Bird, C., & Bird, D. M. *Learning More by Effective Study.* New York: Appleton-Century-Crofts, 1945.

Bonner, L. W. Factors associated with the academic achievement of freshmen students at a Southern agricultural college. Unpublished doctoral dissertation, Pennsylvania State University, 1956. (*Dissertation Abstracts,* 1957, **17,** 266–267).

Boyce, E. M. A comparative study of overachieving and underachieving college students on factors other than scholastic aptitude. Unpublished doctoral dissertation, University of Wisconsin, 1956. (*Dissertation Abstracts,* 1956, **16,** 2088–2089).

Boyer, E. L., & Michael, W. B. Outcomes of college. *Review of Educational Research,* 1965, **35**(4), 277–291.

Brown, W. F., Abeles, N., & Iscoe, I. Motivational differences between high and low scholarship students. *Journal of Educational Psychology,* 1954, **45,** 215–223.

———, & Holtzman, W. H. A study-attitudes questionnaire for predicting academic success. *Journal of Educational Psychology,* 1955, **46,** 75–84.

Buxton, C. E. *College Teaching: A Psychologist's View.* New York: Harcourt, Brace, 1956.

Carter, H. D. Development of a diagnostic scoring scheme for a study methods test. *California Journal of Educational Research,* 1955, **6,** 26–32.

Cronbach, L, J. *Essentials of Psychological Testing.* (2nd ed.) New York: Harper & Row, 1960.

Deese, J. *The Psychology of Learning.* (2nd ed.) New York: McGraw-Hill, 1958.

Diener, C. L. A comparison of overachieving and underachieving students at the University of Arkansas. Unpublished doctoral dissertation, University of Arkansas, 1957. (*Dissertation Abstracts,* 1957, **17,** 1962).

Dole, A. A. College students report on their use of time. *Personnel and Guidance Journal,* 1959, **37,** 633–637.

Eells, K. A vivid method of presenting chances for academic success. *Journal of Counseling Psychology,* 1961, **8**(4), 334–350.

Freedman, M. B. Studies of college alumni. In N. Sanford (Ed.), *The American College.* New York: Wiley, 1962. Pp. 847–886.

———. Personality growth in the college years. *College Board Review,* Spring, 1965. Pp. 25–32.

Garrett, H. F. A review and interpretation of investigations of factors related to scholastic success in colleges of arts and sciences and teachers colleges. *Journal of Experimental Education,* 1949, **18,** 91–138.

Gebhardt, G. G., & Hoyt, D. P. Personality needs of under- and over-achieving freshmen. *Journal of Applied Psychology,* 1958, **42,** 125–128.

Gottlieb, D., & Hodgkins, B. College student subcultures: Their structure and characteristics in relation to student attitude change. *The School Review,* Autumn, 1963. Pp. 266–289.

Heath, R. *The Reasonable Adventurer.* Pittsburgh, Pa.: University of Pittsburgh Press, 1964.

Holland, J. L., & Richards, J. M., Jr. Academic and nonacademic accomplishment: Correlated or uncorrelated? *Journal of Educational Psychology,* 1965, **56**(4), 165–174.

Hoyt, D. P. *The Relationship between College Grades and Adult Achievement: A Review of the Literature.* Iowa City, Iowa: American College Testing Program, 1965.

Katz, J., & Sanford, N. Causes of the student revolution. *Saturday Review,* Dec. 18, 1965. Pp. 64–66, 76f.

Kerns, B. L. A study of under-achieving and over-achieving first-semester college freshmen as revealed by the way in which they view the college situation and themselves as college students. Unpublished doctoral dissertation, University of Illinois, 1957. (*Dissertation Abstracts*, 1957, **17**, 2500).

Knaak, N. K. A study of the characteristics of academically successful and unsuccessful freshmen women who entered Northwestern University in the fall of 1954. Unpublished doctoral dissertation, Northwestern University, 1956. (*Dissertation Abstracts*, 1957, **17**, 304–305).

Lavin, D. E. *The Prediction of Academic Performance.* New York: Russell Sage, 1965.

Lehmann, I. J., & Dressel, P. L. *Changes in Critical Thinking Ability, Attitudes, and Values Associated with College Attendance.* East Lansing, Mich.: Michigan State University Press, 1963.

McClelland, D. C. Methods of measuring human motivation. In J. W. Atkinson (Ed.), *Motives in Fantasy, Action, and Society.* Princeton, N.J.: Van Nostrand, 1958. Pp. 7–42.

McConnell, T. R. Differences in student attitudes toward civil liberties. In R. L. Sutherland, W. H. Holtzman, E. A. Koile, & B. K. Smith (Eds.), *Personality Factors on the College Campus.* Austin, Tex.: Hogg Foundation for Mental Health, 1962. Pp. 29–42.

McKeachie, W. J. Procedures and techniques of teaching: A survey of experimental studies. In N. Sanford (Ed.), *The American College.* New York: Wiley, 1962. Pp. 312–364.

McQuary, J. P. Some differences between under- and over-achievers in college. *Educational Administration and Supervision*, 1954, **40**, 117–120.

Marshall, M. V. What intelligence quotient is necessary to success? *Journal of Higher Education*, 1943, **14**, 99–100.

Nichols, R. C. Effects of various college characteristics on student aptitude test scores. *Journal of Educational Psychology*, 1964, **55**, 45–54.

Paulsen, J. A. College students in trouble. *Atlantic*, July, 1964. Pp. 96–101.

Plant, W. T., & Lynd, C. A validity study and a college freshman norm group for the Wechsler Adult Intelligence Scale. *Personnel and Guidance Journal*, 1959, **37**, 578–580.

Robinson, F. P. *Effective Study.* (2nd ed.) New York: Harper & Row, 1961.

Sanford, N. Higher education as a field of study. In N. Sanford (Ed.), *The American College.* New York: Wiley, 1962. Pp. 31–73.

Sarnoff, I., & Raphael, T. Five failing college students. *American Journal of Orthopsychiatry*, 1955, **25**, 343–373.

Scannell, D. P. Prediction of college success from elementary and secondary school performance. *Journal of Educational Psychology*, 1960, **51**(3), 130–134.

Seiden, R. H. Campus tragedy: A study of student suicide. *Journal of Abnormal Psychology*, 1966, **71**(6), 389–399.

Sherwood, E. J. An investigation of the relationship between the academic achievement and goal-orientations of college students. Unpublished doctoral dissertation, Temple University, 1957. (*Dissertation Abstracts*, 1957, **17**, 2924).

Stein, M. I. *Personality Measures in Admissions.* New York: College Entrance Examination Board, 1963.

Stern, G. G. Environments for learning. In N. Sanford (Ed.), *The American College.* New York: Wiley, 1962. Pp. 690–730.

Suicide and student stress. *Moderator*, October, 1966. Pp. 8–15.

Summerskill, J. Dropouts from college. In N. Sanford (Ed.), *The American College.* New York: Wiley, 1962. Pp. 627–657.

Taylor, G. F. Characteristics of best-liked teacher, least-liked teacher and most effective teacher in teacher training institutions. Unpublished doctoral dissertation, University of Connecticut, 1959. (*Dissertation Abstracts,* 1959, **20,** 1233).

Webster, H., Freedman, M. B., & Heist, P. Personality changes in college students. In N. Sanford (Ed.), *The American College.* New York: Wiley, 1962. Pp. 811–846.

Wellington, J. A. Factors related to the academic success of resident freshman men at a Midwestern liberal arts college during the academic year 1952–53. Unpublished doctoral dissertation, Northwestern University, 1955. (*Dissertation Abstracts,* 1956, **16,** 69).

Wispé, L. G. Teaching methods research. *The American Psychologist,* 1953, **8,** 147–150.

CHAPTER FIFTEEN

VOCATIONAL ADJUSTMENT

Donald E. Super, whose research and writing are considerably drawn upon in this chapter, points out that the average person gives more of his adult life to work than to any other activity. To the daily eight hours or so actually spent at work must be added the time it takes to get there and back as well as that taken up by work-related activities (the noontime and nighttime meetings, the social life centered around work associates, and the extra work and work worry that occupy evenings and weekends at home).

Happiness or unhappiness in work bears an important relationship to general happiness and adjustment. "Occupations are our most time-consuming activities," says Anne Roe, a psychologist who has made the study of occupations *her* most time-consuming activity, "and it is in point of fact impossible to separate occupational satisfaction from satisfaction with life." And William C. Menninger speaks for his psychiatric colleagues when he notes, "The psychiatrist rarely sees a patient in whom, if there are pronounced symptoms of poor mental health, there are not also concomitant disturbances in his work life."

How can people be helped to achieve happiness and satisfaction in their work? In the last decade an increasing amount of attention has been given to finding answers to this question. This chapter will present some of the things which have been discovered.

DEFINING VOCATIONAL ADJUSTMENT

Work is an important part of life. Meeting an old friend, we wonder how he is getting along in his work. Has he found himself and taken hold? Has he been promoted? Is he satisfied with his job?

Our ideas about vocational adjustment are implicit in these questions. Like adjustment in other areas of our lives, vocational adjustment may be defined and measured in various ways. One can use objective criteria such as the amount of money and prestige or subjective criteria such as satisfaction and happiness (Super, 1957).

This discussion considers three definitions of vocational adjustment. The first is broad in approach and concerns the vocational implications of all behavior and every stage of the life span. The second is narrower and concerns job histories themselves. The third poses a question that is not so simple as it sounds: Are you satisfied with your job?

Vocational Adjustment as Vocational Maturity

If we have a friend who is unable to keep a job, or who continually moves from job to job, or whose vocational aspirations seem completely unrealistic to us, we may wonder when he is going to grow up. We imply that he is immature because most other people of his age have established themselves in a career. "Vocational maturity" is a concept that is useful in judging vocational adjustment, but before this idea can be discussed the concepts of "vocational behavior" and "vocational development" must be introduced.

Throughout life much of our activity is directly or indirectly related to our careers; this activity may be said to be *vocational behavior* (Super, 1957). Included as vocational behavior is the play of the small child as he pretends to be a cowboy, fireman, or doctor. When he becomes a little older his vocational behavior may include a paper route and an afterschool and Saturday job at the supermarket. The educational choices that he makes in high school and college are further examples of vocational behavior, as, of course, are his job-seeking and job-holding activities upon graduation.

The systematic changes in vocational behavior which occur with age may be said to constitute *vocational development* (Super, 1957). Certain kinds of vocational behavior are characteristic of each stage of life; as the individual grows and develops he outgrows some kinds of activity and grows into others. For example, young children may have fanciful notions of what they want to be when they grow up, but as they grow up their choices become more and more realistic.

Vocational maturity is a concept that has been introduced to indicate the degree or level of vocational development (Super, 1957). We may be said to be vocationally mature if our vocational behavior is appropriate for our chronological age, that is, if our vocational behavior has reached the level of development which is generally characteristic of our age peers. If our vocational behavior is less fully developed than our age warrants, we would be considered vocationally immature or maladjusted; if our vocational behavior is more advanced than is expected, we could be considered precocious, just as we would be if our physical, intellectual, or social behavior showed accelerated development.

In order to determine a person's vocational maturity, we need to have some way of comparing his vocational behavior with that which is characteristic of various ages. This can be done in a gross way by identifying certain vocational tasks which are associated with each stage of life and determining the extent to which the person has achieved these tasks. In a somewhat similar but more exact way, we could evaluate his maturity by establishing the dimensions along which vocational development appears to occur and setting up indexes of each dimension.

Tasks of Vocational Development

The concept of *developmental tasks* has been found useful in both education and psychology. As defined by Havighurst (1952), "A developmental task is a task which arises at or about a certain period in the life of the individual, successful achievement of which leads to his happiness and to success with later tasks, while failure leads to unhappiness in the individual, disapproval by the society, and difficulty with later tasks." For example, developmental tasks in infancy and early childhood include learning to walk and talk; in middle childhood, learning to read and write; in adolescence, achieving independence and preparing for a career; in early adulthood, marrying and establishing a family, and so on.[1]

Vocational developmental tasks are developmental tasks which are related to one's career (Super, Crites, Hummel, Moser, Overstreet, & Warnath, 1957). Some of these tasks pertain directly to the job,

[1] The concept of developmental tasks was introduced in the chapter on evaluating adjustment (see pp. 231–232).

Presentation 15.1 Outline of vocational developmental tasks in chronological order.

Preschool Child
1 Increasing ability for self-help
2 Identification with like-sexed parent
3 Increasing ability for self-direction

Elementary School Child
1 Ability to undertake cooperative enterprises
2 Choice of activities suited to one's abilities
3 Assumption of responsibility for one's acts
4 Performance of chores around the house

High School Adolescent
1 Further development of abilities and talents
2 Choice of high school or work

3 Choice of high school curriculum
4 Development of independence

Young Adult
1 Choice of college or work
2 Choice of college curriculum
3 Choice of suitable job
4 Development of skills on the job

Mature Adult
1 Stabilization in an occupation
2 Providing for future security
3 Finding appropriate avenues of advancement

Older Person
1 Gradual retirement
2 Finding suitable activities for skills to occupy time
3 Maintaining self-sufficiency insofar as possible (From Super, Crites, Hummel, Moser, Overstreet, & Warnath, 1957, p. 44, after Stratemeyer, Forkner, & McKim, 1947.)

for example, the choice of a job itself. Other vocational developmental tasks are only indirectly related; for example, learning to be an independent and responsible person, although not specifically vocational, is certainly important to vocational adjustment.

Presentation 15.1 outlines vocational developmental tasks occurring throughout the life span. As this chart indicates, the tasks which are set for the preschool and elementary child, although basic, are only indirectly related to the work that we do as adults. At later ages, the tasks become more directly related to job behavior.

Dimensions of Vocational Maturity

The concept of vocational maturity is a fairly recent one, and not very much is known about the dimensions which will be useful in elaborating it. Because of the differing sorts of vocational behaviors which fade in and out during development, the dimensions which appear appropriate to one stage or level are not likely to be useful at every other stage. For example, in adolescence much of a person's vocational behavior relates to choosing a career; later on he is more occupied with establishing himself and advancing in the career he has chosen.

Super and his associates (1957) have pioneered this area; since 1951 they have followed the vocational development of a group of males who were first observed in the eighth and ninth grades. As these subjects are studied, information is being gathered which is helpful in determining the dimensions of vocational maturity appropriate to various ages and stages of development. Five dimensions which have proved useful at the ninth-grade level (and which seem to have some general relevance

for adolescence and young adulthood) are concern with choice, acceptance of responsibility for choice and planning, specificity of information about the preferred occupation, specificity of planning for the preferred occupation, and use of resources in orientation. In scoring each dimension, the investigators sought and evaluated the answers to the following sorts of questions:

1 Concern with choice. How aware is the student of the necessity of choosing among various high school curricula, among courses of education or training after high school, and among various occupations? How aware is the student of the various factors that go into making a vocational choice, such as the nature of his own personal qualities and the nature of the job for which he is planning? How aware is the student of special factors which may upset his plans, such as the discontinuance of financial or psychological support, military service, changes in the labor market, and so on?

2 Acceptance of responsibility for choice and planning. Has the student accepted the responsibility for choosing a career? Has he accepted the responsibility for making educational plans leading to this career? Has he accepted the responsibility for making occupational plans?

3 Specificity of information about the preferred occupation. How much does the student know about the educational, training, economic, psychological, and physical requirements of the vocation he has selected? How much does he know about the duties involved in the occupation, the conditions of work, and the opportunities it affords?

4 Specificity of planning for the preferred occupation. Has the student taken steps

to obtain information for planning in high school, and how well formulated are these plans? Has he taken steps to obtain information for post-high school planning, and has he formulated such plans? Does he have alternative plans for high school and post-high school? Does he have plans for entering an occupation and advancing in it?

5 Use of resources in orientation. How much use has the student made of various resources, such as employment agencies, guidance counselors, teachers, people in an occupation, and so on, in getting himself oriented to the world of work? (Super, Overstreet, Morris, Dubin, & Heyde, 1960)

Vocational Adjustment as Orderly Progression

Are we able to get a job and keep it? The ability to do so might be considered one measure of vocational adjustment. Some of us move from job to job, trying one, then another, then another, in such a way that our friends may wonder if we will ever settle down.

Are we able to get ahead? Beyond establishing ourselves, we are expected to make some progress, to expand our business, to be promoted, to gain greater prestige, power, and responsibility, and to acquire more money, security, and other wanted things.

Orderly progression, that is, taking hold and moving ahead in a line of work is a widely shared index of vocational adjustment. Implied here is movement through a succession of related and increasingly valued or desirable jobs. The succession is a meaningful one with each job serving as a stepping-stone to the next.

This idea of orderly progression is based on Wilensky's concept of *career* which he defines as "a succession of related jobs arranged in a hierarchy of prestige, through which people move in an ordered (more or less predictable) sequence" (1961, p. 523). According to Wilensky, many individuals cannot look forward to having an orderly career. He writes:

> Most men . . . never experience the joys of a life plan because most work situations do not afford the necessary stable progression over the worklife. There is a good deal of chaos in modern labor markets, chaos intrinsic to urban-industrial society. Rapid technological change dilutes old skills, makes others obsolete and creates demand for new ones; a related decentralization of industry displaces millions, creating the paradox of depressed areas in prosperous economies; metropolitan deconcentration shifts the clientele of service establishments, sometimes smashing or restructuring careers; recurrent crises such as wars, depressions, recessions, coupled with the acceleration of fad and fashion in consumption, add a note of unpredictability to the whole. There are many familiar variations on the main theme: in industries such as construction, entertainment, maritime, and agricultural harvesting, the employment relationship is typically casual. In food processing and the needle trades, drastic seasonal curtailments are common (1961, pp. 523–524).

Wilensky found that disorderly careers were not limited to the "depressed, deprived, or marginal." Investigating the work histories of 678 lower middle-class and upper working-class men, he found only 30 percent had orderly careers. Adding in the lower working class with their even greater amount of work disorder, he concluded that the "vast majority of the labor force

. . . can expect a worklife of thoroughly-unpredictable ups and downs" (p. 526).

Mobility: Floundering or Exploration?

It has been estimated that the average worker will have twelve different jobs during his working life (Wilensky, 1961). A person may expect a good deal of mobility or moving about when he first enters the work market. He tries one job, then another and another, perhaps not staying in any job for very long. And, in his moving about, there may appear to be very little sequence or meaningful relationship between one job and another.

Floundering is a term that has been used to describe some early work experiences (Davidson & Anderson, 1937). This term captures what sometimes appears to be the aimless and meaningless quality of a person's efforts to get started in a career. He may move from job to job with no job related to any other and with no pattern or purpose emerging.

Exploration is a term that is sometimes used to describe the same processes, but it has very different connotations (Super, 1957). A person's early work history, while apparently aimless and meaningless, may be an important process of trial and error. As the individual moves from job to job, he is continually learning about himself, the world of work, and the pursuits in which his best hopes for a career lie.

Stability: Trapping or Taking Hold?

Some people establish themselves in a career with relatively little trial and error, and a few start off in a job which they keep the rest of their work life. A doctor or lawyer, for example, may establish a practice in a community immediately upon completing his professional training and remain in it until his death or retirement. Generally speaking, workers at higher occupational levels show more stability than those at lower levels (Form & Miller, 1949, 1962; Miller & Form, 1951; Roe, 1956).

A number of factors are influential in the stabilization process. As we become older, we become more settled, and we are less likely to move from job to job or place to place. We build up seniority, and we are unwilling to give up or jeopardize the greater security, pay, and privileges which seniority brings. We have increasing family responsibilities, and we and our families form ties with our neighborhood and community (Super, 1957).

Taking hold is a term in common usage and implies a stability which comes about when a worker and his job are suitably matched. The worker is able to perform the job, and the job meets the needs of the worker at least in some minimal fashion. Beyond this, the term implies a "settling" of the worker in the job—an increasing involvement in it and an increasing commitment to it.

Trapping, as a term, also denotes stability but for different reasons. It implies that a person is placed in a job which he cannot leave. This may come about when a person is unsuitably placed but has no better place to go, or it may be that he is unwilling to take the risk, bear the inconvenience, or sacrifice the perquisites that a change would entail. The more that a man has invested in his occupation, the more difficult it is for him to chuck it all and start over again in something new. Furthermore, there is the pressure of public opinion to keep him captive. Darley and

Hagenah write, "For an adult to make a *major* change in his employment history is extremely difficult, since we tend to view such an attempt as evidence of instability, or dubious past performance, or immaturity, or unreality" (1955, p. 13).

Vocational Adjustment as Job Satisfaction

How do you like your job? Why?

Asking a pair of questions like this would seem to be the easiest way of getting information about a man's vocational adjustment. Does he like his job? Is he satisfied? If so, why so? If not, why not?

Job satisfaction has been the most widely used measure of vocational adjustment. Hundreds of studies of job satisfaction have been performed. The amount of satisfaction and dissatisfaction among many different groups of workers has been determined through the use of interviews, questionnaires, and tests of various kinds. In addition, the kinds and causes of satisfaction and dissatisfaction have been explored.

Amount of Satisfaction

A review of many studies indicates that vocational satisfaction varies considerably from group to group. The percentage of dissatisfaction has ranged from a low of 0 percent to a high of 92 percent. The median amount of dissatisfaction is 13

percent, which indicates that, on the average, one worker in every eight is dissatisfied with his job (Robinson, Connors, & Whitacre, 1966).

"Taking into Consideration All the Things About Your Job, How Satisfied or Dissatisfied Are You with It?"

As part of a larger study of mental health, many employed men in various parts of the country were asked this question. Their answers were classified into one of six categories ranging from "very satisfied" and "satisfied" to "dissatisfied" and "very dissatisfied." If an answer was not very positive or very negative, it was classified as "neutral." If it contained both positive and negative elements, it was classified as "ambivalent." Since few men proved to be "very dissatisfied," this category was combined with the "dissatisfied" category in the presentation of results which appears in Table 15.1. As you can see, about 3 in every 4 men reported themselves to be satisfied or very satisfied, and the remainder were less content (Gurin, Veroff, & Feld, 1960).

"What Three Things or Activities in Your Life Do You Expect to Give You the Most Satisfaction?"

This was one of the questions asked in a national survey involving nearly three thousand male students at eleven universities. The students indicated that they looked

Table 15.1 "Taking into consideration all the things about your job, how satisfied or dissatisfied are you with it?" Here are the responses of 911 men employed in various kinds of occupations:*

Reply	Percentage
Very satisfied	28
Satisfied	49
Neutral and ambivalent	15
Dissatisfied and very dissatisfied	8

* Data from Gurin, Veroff, and Feld (1960, p. 146).

forward to obtaining a good deal of satisfaction from their work. Only family outranked work as an anticipated source of
satisfaction (Goldsen, Rosenberg, Williams,
& Suchman, 1960).

"What Was Your Major Field of Study in
College?"
"What If You Had It to Do Over Again?"

These were the sorts of questions which
were included in a survey of over nine
thousand men and women who had graduated from more than one thousand different American colleges. The average age of
the graduates was about thirty-seven, so
for the most part they had been out of college some time. In general, the graduates

Table 15.2
Question: "What type of work would you try
to get into if you could start all over again?"
Answer: "The same or similar work."*

Percentage of professional and lower white-collar
occupations who answered in this way:

Urban university professors	93%
Mathematicians	91
Physicists	89
Biologists	89
Chemists	86
Firm lawyers	85
School superintendents	85
Lawyers	83
Journalists (Washington correspondents)	82
Church university professors	77
Solo lawyers	75
Engineers	70
White-collar workers, age 21–29	46
White-collar workers, age 30–55	43

Percentage of working-class occupations who answered in this way:

Skilled printers	52%
Paper workers	52
Skilled auto workers	41
Skilled steelworkers	41
Textile workers	31
Blue-collar workers, age 30–55	24
Blue-collar workers, age 21–29	23
Unskilled steelworkers	21
Unskilled auto workers	16

* After Wilensky (1964, p. 137).

had few regrets about their college experience, and in looking back, three out of four
said that they were satisfied with their
major field in college. The percentage of
dissatisfaction varied, depending upon the
particular major, but in no field was there
a majority of malcontents (Havemann &
West, 1952).

"Exactly How Satisfied Are You with Your
Work?"

Another investigator set out to determine
the extent of vocational satisfaction among
a group of male graduates from the liberal
arts program of a large Midwestern university. Each graduate indicated his degree
of satisfaction with his job on a seven-
point continuum: (1) completely satisfied,
(2) well satisfied, (3) more satisfied than
dissatisfied, (4) equally satisfied and dissatisfied, (5) more dissatisfied than satis-
fied, (6) very dissatisfied, and (7) completely dissatisfied. It was found that the
large majority of the graduates were satisfied with their jobs. Out of the 229 graduates who responded, 175 (76.3 percent)
indicated that they were "completely satisfied" or "well satisfied"; only 3 (1.3 percent) indicated that they were "very dissatisfied" or "completely dissatisfied"
(Inlow, 1951).

Are we as satisfied with our jobs as
these studies seem to indicate? No, says
Wilensky (1964), after scrutiny of the evidence. For one thing the questions posed
in these studies are usually superficial and
unsophisticated. Then too, the answers are
probably less than candid because of the
reluctance of certain workers to admit their
plight or to be seen as gripers. Furthermore, the studies generally do not take

into account the workers who have no steady employment.

"What Type of Work Would You Try to Get into If You Could Start All Over Again?"

Wilensky found that indirect approaches such as that indicated by the above question produced less cheerful results. He found that given a chance to start over, a large percentage of the professional classes would go into a similar line of work, but less than one-half of a group of white-collar workers (small proprietors, managers, semiprofessionals, technicians, salesmen, clerks, and so on) and less than one-quarter of a sample of semiskilled blue-collar workers would want to be in the same line of work (see Table 15.2).

"If by Some Chance You Inherited Enough Money to Live Comfortably without Working, Do You Think You Would Work Anyway or Not?"

A sample of 401 employed men were asked this question by Morse and Weiss (1962), who reported that 80 percent of the men said they would continue to work, but only 9 percent said they enjoyed the work they were doing. They appeared to need to keep busy to avoid feeling bored and useless. As the investigators point out, the men seemed more deeply committed to working than to the particular work they were doing. Few workers wanted to quit working, but many, including those who reported themselves satisfied with their work, said that they would change to some other job if they could.

The further down one goes in the job hierarchy the less satisfaction one finds (Gurin et al., 1960). Simone Weil, for example, eloquently describes the brutalizing and demeaning effects of factory work. She captures the "barren monotony," the "exacting obedience," the "exhausting passivity," and the absence of meaning in the factory workers' daily routine. She says, "After a day thus spent, the workingman has but one plaint, a plaint that cannot reach the ears of men who have never known this condition, and which would not speak to them if it did: *I thought the day would never end*" (1962, p. 456).

Talking about his own work on an automobile assembly line, Swados reports feelings nearly identical with those of Weil. He writes:

> It came as something of a shock to discover that the one unifying force among all those men, so different from one another in ethnic background, educational attainment, and personal ambition, was hatred of their work. But if I was surprised to observe that among the men on the assembly line there was near unanimity of contempt for what they did and a shame at their inability to earn their livings in a better way, I was doubly surprised that my middle-class friends found it difficult to accept this. In more than one case they preferred to believe that I was reading my own preconceptions into what the men on the line had told me—or that, if I was not grinding my own axe, I was naively magnifying the traditional American occupational gripe into an out-of-proportion shame and loathing (1959, p. 13).

Swados goes on to make the larger point that many who are more highly placed than the workman have vocational lives which are filled with "boredom and frustration." However, these feelings are hidden because to admit them would be painful to self-esteem. Says he:

No one likes to be reminded that he is not in some way important as a contributing member of society. A restless young architect may very well tend to reject any picture which portrays the American mass-production worker as profoundly dissatisfied with his lot. While this architect may be regarded by his family and neighbors as a "professional man," he himself is all too sharply aware that he is doing nothing more than the most dull and deadening draftsman's work in a vault ranked with his similars, who know him to be nothing more than they are—all-but-anonymous units in the firm's labor force. In short, it is painful for him to be confronted with the evidence that the difference between him and the factory worker may be only one of degree. It is a pun that can hurt (1959, p. 14).

Goodman (1960) points out that there are not enough "worthy jobs" in our society for youths "to grow up toward." There seems to be agreement among a number of writers that the situation is getting worse not better (Goodman, 1960; Swados, 1959; Wrenn, 1964). Jobs for many people are becoming less and less satisfying, and, indeed, in the changing nature of things there is worry that for an increasing number of persons there will be no jobs at all.

Kinds of Satisfaction

Satisfactions which are inherent in work are said to be *intrinsic satisfactions* or *intrinsic rewards*. Work is intrinsically satisfying if it is enjoyed for its own sake. Some of us find our jobs so interesting and stimulating that we work at them harder and longer than we need to. We may keep at them even though another job offers the promise of more money or greater security or even though we might be able to quit or retire.

Extrinsic satisfactions are those which are extraneous to the nature of our work. They relate to the things the work provides, such as money, security, power, prestige, or pleasant working conditions. Such rewards are not specific to certain kinds of jobs; they may be found in a wide variety of occupations.

Jobs could be ranged along a continuum of satisfaction (Darley & Hagenah, 1955). At one end would be those jobs which offer their holders primarily extrinsic rewards; at the other end would be those with largely intrinsic satisfactions; the center would be reserved for jobs whose satisfactions were equally extrinsic and intrinsic.

For example, rated at the high extrinsic end might be an unskilled laborer who works because he has to and gets nothing out of his job but the money. Or there might be a person who is highly placed in a professional or managerial position but whose work is not gratifying, and who is unable or unwilling to sacrifice the money, security, or other things the position provides.

At the high intrinsic end, would be those people whose inherent involvement in their job transcends other considerations. Teaching is frequently mentioned as an example of an occupation which attracts people despite relatively modest financial reward. The ministry, too, is a vocation or calling in which satisfactions may be much more intrinsic than extrinsic.

Many of us have found or will find ourselves in the center of the continuum with jobs which provide some measure of both extrinsic and intrinsic reward. In fact, the selection of a job may necessitate a compromise between extrinsic and intrinsic satisfactions.

By and large, it is generally thought that workers at the upper rungs of the job hierarchy are more oriented toward intrinsic satisfactions, while those on the lower rungs are more occupied with extrinsic rewards. Part of the reason for this is that workers at the upper levels may be relatively certain of sufficient income and other extrinsic satisfactions while at the lower levels these things cannot be taken for granted (Wilensky, 1964).

For whatever reason, workers in higher-status occupations are more likely to mention intrinsic reasons as sources of job satisfaction than those who are in lower status. In one study it was found that 80 percent of a professional group of workers mentioned exclusively intrinsic reasons when they were asked concerning the sources of their job satisfactions, while only 29 percent of a group of unskilled workers did so. On the other hand, the unskilled workers made more exclusive mention of extrinsic reasons than the professionals (29 percent to 2 percent) and more mention of a combination of both extrinsic and intrinsic reasons (26 percent to 16 percent) (Gurin et al., 1960).

Actually we know very little about the role that intrinsic and extrinsic satisfactions play in vocational adjustment. Brender suggests a number of hypotheses to guide further exploration in this area. These hypotheses may be treated as guesses at relationships—guesses that are based on the best information that has been accumulated so far. Some of his most basic hypotheses follow:

1 *The more inclined the individual is to expect or demand extrinsic gratifications rather than intrinsic rewards from his work, the more likely he is to adapt himself with equal alacrity to a variety of different vocations and to experience equal satisfaction with most of them.*

2 *The more inclined the individual is to expect or demand intrinsic gratifications rather than extrinsic rewards from his work, the more likely he is to show himself adaptable only to a narrow range of occupations, or to a particular family of occupations, and the less apt is he to express satisfaction with any occupation not falling within the narrow range of his preference.*

3 *When both are satisfied in their occupational pursuits, the individual who receives intrinsic gratification from his work will experience more intense satisfaction than will the individual who seeks and obtains extrinsic gratification from his work.*

4 *When both are dissatisfied in their occupational pursuits, the individual who seeks but does not receive intrinsic reward from his work will experience stronger dissatisfaction than will the individual who seeks but does not receive adequate extrinsic gratification from his work.*

5 *Individuals suited by need and ability to enter higher level occupations will show themselves to be more inclined to seek intrinsic rewards from their work activities.*

6 *Individuals suited by need and ability to enter lower level occupations will show themselves more apt to seek extrinsic rewards from their work activities (1960, p. 100).*

SOME STAGES IN VOCATIONAL ADJUSTMENT

Vocational development, like life itself, is a continuous process. But just as life is separated into infancy, childhood, adolescence, and adulthood, so can vocational development be divided into certain stages or periods. Each stage is identified by some salient characteristics and each presents some salient problems of adjustment. The discussion which follows is drawn largely from the writings of Super and his associates (Super, 1957; Super et al., 1957).

Taking his lead from earlier writers on the subject, Super identifies five vocational life stages as follows: growth, exploration, establishment, maintenance, and retirement or decline.

Presentation 15.2 Vocational life stages.

---

1 Growth stage (Birth–14)
Self-concept develops through identification with key figures in family and in school; needs and fantasy are dominant early in this stage; interest and capacity become more important in this stage with increasing social participation and reality-testing. Sub-stages of the growth stage are:
Fantasy (4–10). Needs are dominant; role-playing in fantasy is important.
Interest (11–12). Likes are the major determinant of aspirations and activities.
Capacity (13–14). Abilities are given more weight, and job requirements (including training) are considered.

2 Exploration stage (Age 15–24)
Self-examination, role tryouts, and occupational exploration take place in school, leisure activities, and part-time work. Sub-stages of the exploration stage are:
Tentative (15–17). Needs, interests, capacities, values, and opportunities are all considered. Tentative choices are made and tried out in fantasy, discussion, courses, work, etc.
Transition (18–21). Reality considerations are given more weight as the youth enters labor market or professional training and attempts to implement a self-concept.
Trial (22–24). A seemingly appropriate field having been located, a beginning job in it is found and is tried out as a life work.

3 Establishment stage (Age 25–44)
Having found an appropriate field, effort is put forth to make a permanent place in it. There may be some trial early in

this stage, with consequent shifting, but establishment may begin without trial, especially in the professions. Sub-stages of the establishment stage are:
Trial (25–30). The field of work presumed to be suitable may prove unsatisfactory, resulting in one or two changes before the life work is found or before it becomes clear that the life work will be a succession of unrelated jobs.
Stabilization (31–44). As the career pattern becomes clear, effort is put forth to stabilize, to make a secure place, in the world of work. For most persons these are the creative years.

4 Maintenance stage (Age 45–64)
Having made a place in the world of work, the concern is now to hold it. Little new ground is broken, but there is continuation along established lines.

5 Decline stage (Age 65 on)
As physical and mental powers decline, work activity changes and in due course ceases. New roles must be developed; first that of selective participant and then that of observer rather than participant. Sub-stages of this stage are:
Deceleration (65–70). Sometimes at the time of official retirement, sometimes late in the maintenance stage, the pace of work slackens, duties are shifted, or the nature of the work is changed to suit declining capacities. Many men find part-time jobs to replace their full-time occupations.
Retirement (71 on). As with all the specified age limits, there are great variations from person to person. But, complete cessation of occupation comes for all in due course, to some easily and pleasantly, to others with difficulty and disappointment, and to some only with death (From Super et al., 1957, pp. 40–41).

Growth Stage

The first period of vocational life is called the "growth stage." Roughly speaking this stage includes infancy and childhood. It extends from the moment of conception through age fourteen.

The first stage of life is a time of great physical, intellectual, emotional, and social development. During this time the individual develops patterns of needs, interests, attitudes, and abilities which are crucial to later vocational adjustment.

It has been suggested that occupational preferences and choices bear an important relationship to early interpersonal experiences. Nachmann (1960), for example, studied a number of male students doing advanced work in law, dentistry, and social work and found characteristic differences in the childhood experiences of the three groups. Among other findings, she noted that the fathers of the dentistry and law students were generally strong, dominant, and very masculine figures; by contrast, the fathers of the social workers more often than not were weak and inadequate (or absent from the home) while the mother was the dominant and more adequate figure in the family.

Roe, whose writings have stimulated a good deal of interest in this area, has found the research evidence sparse and inconsistent. She suggests that exploration in this area is barely under way and, based on her own work and the work of others, has presented the following hypotheses for study:

Generally satisfactory early experience with interpersonal relations, both with parents and others—experience which is sufficiently warm and supportive, but neither stressful nor very intense—should, within adequately stimulating environments, permit individual development allowing free play to individual aptitudes within a wide range of culturally approved activities. This is as previously stated, but it may now be suggested that the resulting occupational focus might be upon technological or business activities for men, and upon homemaking, teaching, nursing, and other traditional pursuits for women.

Intense concentration on interpersonal experience in early childhood, if rewarding rather than stressful, should lead to attempts to repeat the pattern in later life. These attempts might or might not be primarily expressed vocationally, except in a negative sense—the individuals would avoid activities which did not involve a great deal of personal contact.

A limited childhood experience with interpersonal relations which are free of stress, neglect, or rejection may lead to later focus on non-personal interests. Stress in early relations, combined with some degree of affection, may lead to choice of activities which involve working with other persons in close relationship terms. The stress may be introduced because of the differing behavior of the two parents or the inconsistent behavior of one or both (1964, pp. 210–211).

Our attitudes toward work as adults are related to our early socialization experiences. Whether we learn to work and learn to like to work depends to an important extent on how we were introduced to the world of demands, obligations, and responsibilities as children. If our parents were dictatorial, we may build up patterns of resistance and defiance which continue into adulthood. Menninger writes, "Among adults, many who have much difficulty with their employers at work are very probably still using the pattern of fighting authority which they developed in childhood." And he adds that "the failure to work or work well may represent one way of expressing defiance" (1964, p. xiii).

Many of our activities in childhood form an introduction to the world of work. At home we are called upon to do chores, and, in one sense, school is a work assignment. As we grow older, we undertake jobs after school and on weekends.

At the same time, we are finding out about the work other people perform. We learn about our father's work and about any work our mother might perform outside the home. We also learn about the work activities of other fathers and mothers in the neighborhood. Stories, television, and movies supply a constant stream of ideas about people and the ways they make a living.

When we are very small, we play at work. We pretend that we are a cowboy, a doctor, or a storekeeper. We put on a play, put out a newspaper, or operate a lemonade stand. And many times we are asked, "What do you want to be when you grow up?" Our answers, if they were faithfully recorded, would form an interesting chronicle of our vocational development. As we become older, we become better informed about the world of work and more realistic about the part we will play in it.

Exploration Stage

The second period is called the "exploration stage." This phase of vocational life includes adolescence and young adulthood, extending from fifteen years of age through the twenty-fourth year.

It is during this period that the individual needs to decide whether to continue schooling or find a job. If he continues in school, he needs to determine what direction his education will take. If he drops out to find a job, he needs to decide what sort of work to look for.

This period is one of trial and error. It is also one of hope and discouragement. A person may move from job to job, struggling to find himself and to improve his lot and bring some purpose and pattern into his vocational life.

For some, the trial-and-error process goes on in an academic setting. A student may move from major to major or college to college, trying to find one into which he can fit and take root. He may alternate between college and the world of work, struggling with one, then abandoning it and trying the other.

All of life is exploration, but it is in the adolescent and early adulthood years that searching seems most intense. It is during this time that we are very much occupied with the process of forming an image of ourselves, and we are also forming images of various occupations.

Our self-image or self-concept is built up of all the ideas we have about ourselves. It is our personal answer to the question, Who am I?

At the same time questions about various occupations are being implicitly formed and implicitly answered: What kind of people are doctors? Lawyers? Merchants? How do they live? What do they do?

Many college students have little information about the actual hour-by-hour, day-by-day activities of the occupations for which they are preparing. This has been a matter of concern to a number of vocational psychologists and counselors. In one study, for example, undergraduates were asked to state specifically what they would do in the occupation for which they were preparing, and many were unable to do so. The students offered such hazy statements as: I will talk with people. I will deal with people. I will attend committee meetings. I will help people and answer the questions they bring to me. When the interviewers attempted to get more specific information, they found that the students expressed embarrassment, annoyance, and hostility (Beardslee & O'Dowd, 1962; O'Dowd & Beardslee, 1960).

While many students have little information about what people in various occupations *do*, they have quite definite ideas about what people in various occupations *are*. This was the conclusion of a study which assessed the occupational images held by a representative group of liberal arts students. The investigators made use of a research instrument which permitted the students to rate fifteen occupations on thirty-four different seven-point scales. Some examples of these scales are:

```
unsure__:__:__:__:__:__:__confident
sociable__:__:__:__:__:__:__unsociable
wealthy__:__:__:__:__:__:__not well-to-do
```

A large amount of agreement was found among the students concerning the kinds of people and the styles of life to be found in each occupation, so much so that the investigators were able to construct student images or stereotypes of each occupation. Here, are the students' images of the doctor, lawyer, college professor, scientist, engineer, schoolteacher, business executive, accountant, and artist:

Doctor. *The doctor is a culture hero for college students. He anchors the desirable end of a surprising number of scales. Indeed, the doctor's position on a scale, whether it be at an extreme end or in the*

middle, can be used as a reliable indicator of the ideal score on that scale. Medicine is rated by students as a calling that is richly rewarded by high social status, wealth, and success. The doctor is favored with high opportunity for advancement, and he derives great personal satisfaction from his work. Compared to men in most other occupations he can count on an unusually pretty wife and a very happy home life. The doctor is very much a realist. He approaches the world responsibly and with perseverance. He is outstandingly calm, confident, and self-sufficient; and his great stability, caution, and rationality are balanced by his adaptability. The doctor is seen as very much oriented to people. Although it appears that this attitude may be partially a professional concern, still he is thoughtful and unselfish; he gives of himself to others. The doctor's cheerfulness and optimism fit well with this unfailing orientation to other people. His high intelligence appears to be more a correlate of his strong, active, masterful qualities than a sign of the highest intellectual culture. There are no undesirable traits attributed to the doctor. All students recognize the remarkable personal and social attractiveness of the doctor's role.*

Lawyer. *The image of the lawyer has many characteristics that are also attributed to the doctor, but the doctor is usually rated more favorably on traits that they have in common. The lawyer possesses high social status, success, and wealth. He has considerable opportunity to advance in his job, and he is outstandingly powerful in public affairs. The lawyer is viewed as an outgoing, sociable person who likes to be with people and is at ease in the company of others. The lawyer shares with the doctor realistic, persevering, forceful, strong, and active qualities. He is a person who is effective in the world of objects, events, and people. These characteristics are qualified, however, by a high degree of hardness and self-assertiveness. There is more than a hint of a selfish, manipulative attitude* in the lawyer that is wholly lacking in the doctor image. The lawyer is perceived as having high intelligence and good taste. He rates a pretty wife, but his home life is not seen as particularly happy. The lawyer, like the doctor, is without negative properties, but on many more scales than the doctor he earns values that come in the middle of the distribution of means from the 15 occupations. The lawyer image combines most of the rewards promised by the medical profession and possesses many of the same desirable personal properties, while providing somewhat more scope for less service-oriented, less unselfish ambitions. Of particular prominence in the case of the lawyer is the stress placed on sociability and access to public power.

College Professor. . . . A dominant feature of the image is the great stress on intellectual competence accompanied by sensitivity to artistic or aesthetic experience. The professor is seen as an individualist with colorful, interesting, exciting qualities coupled with a degree of rashness, changeability, emotional difficulties, and lack of adaptability. It is quite likely that he is interesting because of his emotional, unpredictable nature. In spite of these characteristics and a high score on radicalism, he is granted considerable power in public affairs. Students rate the professor as very valuable, and they see his role as a source of great personal satisfaction. On the debit side, the professor is described as not well-to-do and lacking in opportunity for advancement. He does not equal the independent professionals in either social or worldly competence. Whereas the doctor and lawyer are stable and dependable, he is changeable and unpredictable. His intellectual qualities are the primary asset of the college professor. . . .

Scientist. Two strong impressions are conveyed by this profile. First, the scientist is characterized by high intelligence dissociated from artistic concerns and sensitivities. This cool intelligence is linked with strong individualism in personal and political realms. Second, there is a clear lack of interest in people on the part of the scientist. He anchors the undesirable end of scale scores on sociability for all the occupations studied. A good deal of control is implied by the description of the scientist as self-sufficient, rational, persevering, and emotionally stable. He has power in public affairs, but he is rated only moderately responsible and quite radical. This suggests that uncertainty about the motives and trustworthiness of the scientist noted in younger people by other investigators lingers on in college students. The personal life of the scientist is thought to be quite shallow, his wife is not pretty, and his home life is not very happy. He is rewarded by great personal satisfaction, considerable success, and reasonable opportunity for advancement. He enjoys moderate wealth and social status. In summary, the scientist is a cool, controlled intellectual. He is competent in organizing the world of things, but disdainful of the world of people. Although more richly rewarded than the college professor, the scientist contrasts strikingly with him in aesthetic sensibilities and social skills. . . .

Engineer. Engineering is a less colorful profession for liberal arts students when compared with the alternatives already mentioned. The image of the engineer is most easily understood when juxtaposed with that of the scientist, with whom the engineer has many features in common. The engineer is rated generally intelligent but not nearly so powerful in this regard as the scientist. On the other hand, although he is no social lion, he is considerably more socially adept than the scientist. The engineer is quite successful and reasonably wealthy, but he gains less satisfaction from his work than the scientist derives from pure research. Finally, the engineer is more conservative, and more likely to be a conformist than the scientist. Except for these important differences, the engineer is almost identical with the scientist.

School Teacher. In every classification of occupations according to social status the school teacher is located in the second or third tier among the professions. But school teaching accounts for the occupational preferences and choices of a substantial percentage of college graduates. The school-teacher image is dominated by the depressed economic state of the profession. The teacher scores conspicuously low in wealth, social status, and opportunity for advancement. He has little power in public affairs, and he cannot even command an attractive wife although he can count on a happy home life—just the opposite of the lawyer's situation. The teacher is considered intelligent, sensitive, and, like the professor, interested in art but to a lesser degree. Furthermore, he is attentive to people and unselfish in his relations with them. In this regard he has an orientation toward service somewhat like the doctor's. Finally, the teacher is seen as lacking in confidence and in hard, assertive properties. . . .

Business Executive. The avoidance of business occupations by freshmen liberal arts students is at first glance surprising when the image is studied. The business executive is extremely high in social status, wealth, and success. He has power in public affairs, ample opportunity to advance himself, and even a very pretty wife. He is classified as very conservative, but when his conservatism is paired with his good taste, a picture of quiet elegance emerges. He possesses the sociability earlier noted in the lawyer, accompanied by a confident, assertive, masculine manner. He is also rated strong and active, responsible and persevering. Thus far the sketch coincides with that of the highly favored lawyer. But the business executive lacks both the high intelligence and the hard, rational properties that make the lawyer a most formidable figure. The executive is even less service-oriented than the lawyer; he is in fact a selfish individual. Finally, the business executive is believed to possess a component of excitability and emotional instability,

which probably relates to the popular belief about his tendency to suffer from peptic ulcers. The business executive has both weaknesses and personal problems that offset to some degree his wealth and status. It has also been pointed out that the road to this role is not so clear or so predictable for most college students as that which leads through the professional schools into the high-status occupations.

Accountant. This occupation represents a lower-status business activity, perhaps comparable in some ways to the status of school teaching among the professions. The image that surrounds the field is remarkably negative. If the doctor is the occupational hero, the accountant is the antihero of the occupational world. He is low in status, not well-to-do, and unsuccessful. He has little power in public affairs, not much opportunity for advancement, and his job is lowest of all the occupations studied in providing personal satisfaction. He is a conformist, with a minimum of social skills, limited intelligence, and inadequate personal and aesthetic sensibilities. He is rated as passive, weak, soft, shallow, cold, submissive, unsure of himself, and evasive in meeting life. His positive characteristics of caution, stability, conservatism, and calmness rest upon a shaky emotional interior. They probably refer most directly to his control of a limited area of occupational specialization. Students have a rather specific model in mind when they produce this wretched portrait. He is apparently something of a Victorian bookkeeper, chained to a desk and a ledger, from which he has no inclination to depart for traffic with the world or contact with man. Given this description there is some doubt as to whether, according to undergraduate liberal arts students, the accountant is alive.

Artist. This calling is for many young people either a positive or negative reference point in their thinking about career alternatives. On a number of scales the artist anchors the end opposite that marked by the doctor. The artist's notable sensitivity to matters of aesthetic impor-

tance is associated with a variety of traits reflecting violent emotions and impulsive expression. For example, he is intuitive, rash, changeable, excitable, attention-demanding, and at the same time, deep, interesting, and colorful. His outstanding individualism and radicalism accompany a group of traits indicating irresponsibility and unwillingness to contribute to society in a disciplined way. The artist is uninterested in people and evidently unsuccessful with them. His moods tend to be dark, depressed, and pessimistic. The only reward that he can expect for his work is a high sense of satisfaction. Neither wealth, nor status, nor any other marks of the rich, full life are associated with the artist. A blind labeling of the role might easily describe this profile as applicable to a teenager in the throes of adolescent problems (Beardslee & O'Dowd, 1962, pp. 614–617).

Erikson notes that it is in adolescence and young adulthood that the person struggles to establish an identity. And, he says, "In general it is primarily the inability to settle on an occupational identity which disturbs young people" (1959, p. 92). Certainly the choice of an occupation and the establishment of a firm sense of who we are constitute crucial tasks of the exploration stage. What we think we are influences what we try to become, and what we see ourselves becoming influences what we think we are.

Establishment Stage

The third period of vocational life is termed the "establishment stage." This period begins at about the age of twenty-five and continues through the forty-fourth year. It takes in a substantial portion of adulthood.

This time of life is an establishment stage in a number of respects. The voca-

tional career begins to stabilize and find some consistent patterning and direction, and many persons marry, establish a home, begin a family, and find a place in the community. It is an establishment of a whole way of living as well as a way of earning a living.

During this period there is an integration of work, family, and social life. An important work problem will have repercussions at home, just as an important marital problem or some other salient family difficulty will affect vocational functioning. Counselors are alert to this interaction among problem areas and to the necessity of considering the individual in broad perspective even though his problem appears to be a more limited one. Thompson emphasizes this point and illustrates it with the following case:

For example, a 35 year-old Army reservist came to our counseling center, uncertain as to whether to remain in the service, making it a life career, or whether to look for a civilian job at the end of his current term of enlistment. Ostensibly his problem was one of vocational choice but it soon became apparent that any occupational decision had to take into account his own self-concept, his attitude toward his wife, her attitude toward being an "army wife," his expectations for their children. The interaction of home life and work life was direct and immediate and the two were inextricably interwoven. Although the focus of counseling was on the career problem, the areas explored covered the total life situation of the client (1964, p. 227).

The establishment stage is characterized by both stability and mobility. There is stability in the sense that the person hits upon a particular field or line of work in which he may remain. There is mobility in the sense that in order to develop his career, he may move from position to position.

The establishment stage is one in which the person attempts to root himself and find some measure of security in work. Some interesting information concerning the attainment of occupational security has been provided by Form and Miller (1949, 1951, 1962) who studied the work histories of a large group of men. An attempt was made to determine the patterning which occurred in these work histories, and it proved useful to distinguish three stages of evolvement which were termed the initial work period, the trial work period, and the stable work period.

The *initial work period* includes the part-time and temporary work experiences of adolescence and young adulthood while formal education is being completed. It is during this time that we decide whether to continue through high school and then through college or to drop out and enter the world of work on a full-time and permanent basis. Included in this work period are the jobs which we hold before and after school, on weekends, and during summer. Full-time jobs are included in this period too if they are temporary and stop-gap measures.

The *trial work period* includes full-time but relatively short-term positions once the person enters the regular labor market. These positions may last just a few days or up to three years or so. This is a transitional period in which one moves from school to work and then perhaps from job to job. Some of us skip this period completely; we move directly from school or college to a job which we hold for the rest of our career. Others may never get

much beyond this period, moving from position to position and never staying in any job very long.

The *stable work period* includes full-time work positions which are permanent or relatively so, lasting three years or more. After a time the worker establishes certain ties with his work position and work community and is less likely to quit even though he may not be satisfied.

In their study of work histories, Form and Miller found fourteen main patterns or sequences of work periods, seven reflecting secure patterns and seven reflecting insecure patterns. These were:

Secure Patterns
1 *Stable*
2 *Initial—stable—trial—stable*
3 *Stable—trial—stable*
4 *Initial—stable*
5 *Initial—trial—stable*
6 *Initial—trial—stable—trial—stable*
7 *Trial—stable*

Insecure Patterns
8 *Trial—stable—trial*
9 *Initial—trial—stable—trial*
10 *Initial—trial*
11 *Trial*
12 *Stable—trial*
13 *Initial—stable—trial*
14 *Trial—trial—trial—trial*[2]

In general, white-collar workers were found to have more secure patterns while blue-collar workers led less secure work lives. There was one exception: skilled workers and foremen were more secure than clerks and kindred workers. The ranking of occupational levels in terms of years

[2] From Form, W. H., & Miller, D. C. Occupational career pattern as a sociological instrument. *American Journal of Sociology*, 1949, 54(4), 317–329. By permission of The University of Chicago Press.

spent in secure patterns (most secure to least secure) was as follows: (1) professional and semiprofessional workers; (2) proprietors, managers, and officials; (3) skilled workers and foremen; (4) clerks and kindred workers; (5) semiskilled workers and operatives; (6) domestic and personal workers; and (7) unskilled workers and laborers.

Certain patterns were found to characterize each occupational level. Here are some conclusions set forth by the investigators:

1 . . . *Professional workers start their initial work on many different levels but soon move to the professional level without much intervening experience in other occupations. Once they become professionals, only a few risk trying other jobs. Those that do usually have trial jobs in the proprietary and/or managerial occupations.*

2 *The proprietors, managers, and officials show histories of much vertical mobility in the initial and trial periods, but also show stability in the stable period of their work lives.*

3 *Clerical workers exhibit some vertical movement before reaching the clerical level but little movement thereafter. Only four of the twenty-two patterns indicate a rise into the managerial class, and these were but brief excursions.*

4 *The patterns for the skilled workers and foremen indicate that their work origins are largely in unskilled and semiskilled labor. When they become skilled workers and foremen, they achieve a high degree of stability.*

5 *The semiskilled workers display some vertical movement, for many of them have had early jobs as personal and domestic service workers. Mobility above the semiskilled level, once it is attained, is rather infrequent.*

6 *The immobility of the unskilled and domestic worker is pronounced. Many*

of them began their work lives in domestic and personal service jobs. Some moved to the unskilled labor classification and there remained; the others never budged from their original classification as domestic and personal service workers. Both groups experienced many trial jobs and achieved only fleeting security.[3]

Maintenance Stage

The fourth period is called the "maintenance stage." This period begins with the end of the establishment phase and continues until the usual time of retirement. Roughly speaking, it takes in the age period of forty-five to sixty-five.

As the term "maintenance" implies, this period is one in which old patterns are continued rather than new ones established. A person can become set in his vocational ways; vocational movement follows lines which have been already set down. He becomes set in other ways as well. He evolves a style of life which is peculiarly his own and which may be particularly resistant to change.

"From the point of view of adjustment and happiness," writes Super (1957, p. 148), "the maintenance stage is one of fruition or frustration." We may be enjoying the fruits of our labors, or we may be increasingly aware of failure to achieve what we had hoped to achieve and of the increasing likelihood that we will never achieve it. For many of us, it is a bittersweet period, not good enough, but not so bad either, and we grow to accept the compromise. "After all," one may ask, "what is a man to do?"

Older men tend to be slightly more

[3] From Form, W. H., & Miller, D. C. Occupational career pattern as a sociological instrument. *American Journal of Sociology,* 1949, 54(4), 317–329. By permission of The University of Chicago Press.

satisfied with their jobs than are younger men according to the nationwide survey conducted by Gurin, Veroff, and Feld. More than half of the youngest group (twenty-one to thirty-four years of age) expressed a desire for another kind of work, whereas only one-quarter of the oldest group (fifty-five years and over) did so. Younger workers made more frequent mention of work problems, and these problems were different from those noted by older workers.

The younger men more often mention problems indicative of the unsettled nature of their work choice—problems in vocational choice, dissatisfaction with a job that is not need-satisfying, problems in meeting the demands of a job. The older workers, on the other hand, more often refer to problems that do not reflect on the work itself or on the particular choice they have made . . . they speak of such things as failures in health, dissatisfaction with certain extrinsic aspects of a job, problems that arose because of external factors (such as losing a job when the company closed) (1960, pp. 170–171).

For some of us, to call this stage of our vocational lives "maintenance" may be a gross misnomer. We may not yet have found ourselves, our position may be precariously held, or we may have been moved up and out of an area of competence into one for which we may have uncertain qualifications. Thompson identifies a number of kinds of problems which bring workers for "mid-career counseling" during this stage of their vocational lives:

An opportunity may have arisen for promotion to an executive level position, requiring a change from a professional or technical role to one of administration and bringing with it adjustment to a different mode of life and drawing on a different set of values. Or the slowing down of rate of advancement in the occupation may cause a vague dissatisfaction which raises doubts as to whether he really belongs in that type of work. Or the reaching of a career plateau sooner than expected or below the level of aspiration is threatening to the individual's self-concept. Or his technical skills have become obsolete, requiring either re-training or change in occupation (1964, p. 228).

Even those who are apparently settled into an occupation may find this stage a deceptively effortful time. In this rapidly changing world, just to maintain our relative position (to hold our own) we may need new vocational knowledge, skills, and tactics (Super, 1957). The doctor and dentist need to keep up with the latest scientific discoveries and techniques. The machinist, mechanic, technician, and technologist find it necessary to reschool themselves. The independent grocer may have to change his methods of merchandising and competition to keep up with the chain supermarket, and the chain supermarket may have to change its methods to keep up with the changing community.

Retirement Stage

The final period of vocational life is called the "retirement" or "decline" stage. This stage begins at age sixty-five, which for many people is the age of retirement from work. It has been estimated that about half of the male population above sixty-five is retired (Super, 1957).

Retirement and decline, of course, have very different connotations. To some, retirement is decline, and they decline to retire; if they retire, it is because they have to. Others look forward to the time when they can retire, change the pace of living, and turn attention and energies into other activities; if they continue to work, it is because they must.

All of life can be thought of as an aging process, but it is at the point of retirement that many of us begin to think of ourselves as old. We begin to feel our years and show our age. Some, of course, seem old at forty and decrepit at fifty while others appear young at sixty and seventy. Occupations, too, "age" at different rates. At thirty, an athlete may be getting old for his occupation, while at the same age a medical doctor may have just completed his training in a field of specialization and be ready to hang out his shingle.

All of life involves change, but the change in status from employee to retiree is one that is especially clear-cut and impactful (Streib, Thompson, & Suchman, 1958). For many workers retirement is a point of crisis. From their study of a group of aging men, Reichard, Livson, and Petersen concluded that the act of retiring itself posed more difficulties than the period which followed. They write:

> The real aging crisis for the men we studied occurred in late middle rather than in old age—particularly at critical transitions in age status such as retirement. Dramatizing the fact of aging, retirement can abruptly disrupt a man's self-image, causing him to see himself as old. However, anxiety over retirement and over aging in general was less prevalent among our older respondents, most of whom were already retired and had come to accept themselves as old. There was evidence that retirement was most stressful for our respondents just before it took place (1962, pp. 168–169).

Some of us shift to retirement status gradually so that the changeover is not such a discrete and critical one. Perhaps we move from a full-time job to a part-time one, or we get to the office later in the mornings and leave earlier in the afternoons. We may begin to restrict other activities as well, perhaps substituting less strenuous or demanding ones. Retirement becomes a time of slowing down, cutting out, and tapering off (Super, 1957).

Researchers have challenged some of the generally shared images which people have about aging and retirement. "Popularly it is assumed that retirement leads to a decline in physical well-being," write Thompson and Streib (1958), "for everyone knows of at least one person whose health deteriorated or who died suspiciously soon after retiring." It is true, of course, that people in poor health tend to retire. However, studying a large group of males, some of whom had retired and some of whom had continued to be employed, these investigators found that retirement itself did not lead to a decline in health. In fact, there was some suggestion that the health of retirees tended to improve while that of nonretirees tended to decline!

Using interview techniques and psychological tests, Reichard, Livson, and Petersen made an intensive study of eighty-seven men between the ages of fifty-five and eighty-four. About half of these men were retired, and their occupations had been largely in skilled or semiskilled occupations. It was found that the adjustment of many of the older men had actually improved in their later years. Here is the case study of a man who made a successful transition to retirement:

Mr. A is an example of a man who found freedom and enjoyment in retirement. "This is the best life I ever had. . . . It's an easy life. You don't have to worry about anything. You can just poke around; sleep when you're sleepy; eat when you're hungry."

However, Mr. A was far from inactive. His interests were extensive and stimulating. While his career had been reasonably successful, his work had never been essential to his self-esteem; he had always looked to outside activities for his major satisfactions. Retirement freed him from the burdensome need of earning a living, allowing him to devote himself to hobbies he had always pursued.

Mr. A was a 70-year-old man who had voluntarily retired 3 years before from his last job as a janitor in a bakery. He was a cheerful optimist with a sociable, playful manner. Married and living with his wife, he had three children, a daughter in the Middle West, an unmarried son at home, and another living nearby. He visited his three grandchildren every week. In good health, his financial position was marginal. Though he owned his own home, he had almost no savings. His 50 dollars monthly income from Social Security was supplemented by taking in a roomer, by odd jobs, and by his wife who earned extra money occasionally as a dressmaker. At one time he had applied to the state for financial assistance to the aged but had been ineligible. However, he was unworried about his economic future and did not feel handicapped by his low income.

Mr. A was enthusiastic about his hobbies, most of which reflected long-term interests. In addition to remodeling his home, he repaired furniture for friends, constructed model sailboats, "knick-knacks," and supplemented his income by repairing violins. He had a lively interest in music and played the violin. (His mother, a singer, had encouraged his musical development.) American-born of Swedish immigrants, he had always had strong ties with local Swedish groups. He attended numerous social events and kept up a vigorous correspondence with relatives and friends.

During most of his working life, Mr. A owned and operated a dairy farm in the Middle West. However, he had always had outside activities. For 6 years, he was assessor for the Federal Land Bank and was also employed for 4 years by the federal government as a consultant to farmers on soil conservation. He was on directors' boards of cooperative creameries. Although he enjoyed some aspects of farming, particularly raising livestock, he found it arduous. His main satisfactions came from administrative and community activities. In this he closely resembled his father, a farmer and minister whose clerical duties frequently took him away from home.

When he was 60 years old, Mr. A sold his farm and moved to California. His sons had entered military service, and he could no longer manage the farm by himself. However, he was glad to be free of his agricultural responsibilities. "I think the happiest time of my life was when I left the farm and came here. . . . I was all through with farming. Life would go easier now."

After he came to California, he worked for 7 years as a night watchman and janitor for various firms. Emotionally, however, his actual retirement occurred when he sold his farm. He continued to work because he needed the money, and he finally retired altogether because he felt his work was too difficult and dangerous for his health.

Why did Mr. A adjust so well to retirement? His work had never comprised his sense of identity. Having always found his major satisfactions in community service, carpentry, music, and social relationships, he was able to continue these after retirement. Thus, retirement neither threatened his image of himself nor cut down on his satisfactions.

Mr. A was able to enjoy his passive and sensual needs. Having previously accepted responsibility, he now welcomed freedom from hard work and the opportunity for play.

Mr. A's ties with a closely knit social group with strong traditions such as the Swedish community probably helped him to adjust to retirement. He faced neither social isolation nor the need to establish new social ties.

Satisfied with his past accomplishments, Mr. A felt he had achieved his goals and could enjoy retirement without regretting lost opportunity or past failure. "My part looks pretty nice. My part is all done," he said (Livson, 1962, pp. 85–87).

SOME FACTORS IN VOCATIONAL ADJUSTMENT

Many factors play a part in vocational adjustment. However, not very much is known about most of these factors, either their individual effects or the ways they interact with other factors to influence career patterns (Super et al., 1957). Whatever else may be involved, choice of an occupation depends on opportunities, interests, motive or personality patterns, and abilities.

The Availability Factor: What Is There to Do?

How many jobs are there to select from? A dictionary of occupations put out by the U.S. Department of Labor in 1949 defined over twenty-two thousand jobs. Today there is a greater variety of occupations than ever before.

Roe (1956), a chief investigator in this area, has been interested in devising a meaningful way of classifying occupations and in establishing some of the characteristics associated with each classifica-

tion. She has brought together and reviewed the results of many pertinent studies. As Roe points out, the findings to date are more suggestive than conclusive, but they provide many interesting speculations and possibilities for future research.

In organizing the findings, Roe arranged occupations into a dual classification of *groups* and *levels*. The groups are distinguished from one another according to the primary focus of activity that each has. Within each group there are six levels of skill and responsibility (see Table 15.3).

Service Occupations

The first group which is called *service* includes all those occupations primarily concerned with attending to the personal needs and welfare of others. Included here are guidance, social, and welfare occupations as well as domestic and protective services.

The outstanding characteristic of this group is an interest in interpersonal relationships. This interest is both nurturant and succorant. The service group is concerned about social and religious matters and comparatively unconcerned about intellectual and artistic ones.

Business Contact Occupations

The second group is called *business contact* and includes all those occupations involving persuasive selling in a direct person-to-person relationship. Included here are promoters, auctioneers, dealers and salesmen involved in the sale of automobiles, stocks and bonds, insurance, real estate, and similar items.

Like the service group, this group is interested in interpersonal relationships. But unlike the preceding group, its interest is exploitive instead of nurturant. The business contact group is high in dominance, and, as might be expected, interested in persuasive matters. Like the service group, it is low in intellectual and aesthetic interests.

Organization Occupations

The third group is called *organization* and includes all those occupations primarily concerned with the organization and functioning of government and private enterprise. Included here are the executives and white-collar workers of government, business, and industry.

Interestingly enough, this group is fairly average in personality characteristics. At the upper levels it appears to be high in dominance and in persuasive interests. Clerical aptitudes are a factor in many of the occupations of this group, but artistic, mechanical, and scientific interests are generally absent.

Technology Occupations

The fourth group is called *technology* and includes all the modern industrial occupations. Included here are the applied scientists, engineers, craftsmen, and others who are concerned with producing, maintaining, and transporting various commodities and utilities.

This group was found to be object-oriented rather than people-oriented; its interest in personal relationships is quite low. Mechanical interest and aptitude are higher in this group than in any other. In the upper levels there are marked intellectual interests, but they are of a distinctly nonverbal sort. Artistic interests are low.

Outdoor Occupations

The fifth group is called *outdoor* and includes occupations in animal husbandry, farming, fisheries, forestry, mining, and similar employment. As the name implies, most of the activities of this group take place in the open and involve a considerable amount of physical activity.

Not very much information is available on this group. Many of the people in outdoor occupations appear to be following in their fathers' footsteps. There is a good deal of mechanical interest and aptitude, but not so much as in the technology group. Artistic and intellectual interests are quite low.

Science Occupations

The sixth group is called *science* and includes all those occupations concerned with scientific research and its application in nontechnological fields. It includes scientists on college faculties and in other positions as well as physicians, dentists, pharmacists, nurses, and allied personnel.

This group is high in intellectual interests and abilities. In much of this group there appears to be an orientation away from people; however, a few occupational categories tend to be high in social interest, and practitioners and teachers usually require some facility in interpersonal relations. The group is generally not very high in artistic interests, and clerical and mechanical interests are not particularly relevant.

General Cultural Occupations

The seventh group is called *general cultural* and includes those occupations chiefly concerned with preserving and transmitting the general cultural heritage. Included here are occupations in journalism, law, the ministry, and also educators who are more concerned with administration and teaching than with subject matter.

Table 15.3 Roe suggests a two-dimension classification of occupations. One dimension concerns the focus of activity, the other the level of activity. Altogether this scheme of classification provides forty-eight cells or categories. This table provides some examples of occupations which fit in the various cells. There are some cells in which no occupations fall because of the nature of the activity involved.*

Level	Group			
	I. Service	II. Business Contact	III. Organization	IV. Technology
1. Professional & managerial (1)	Personal therapists Social work supervisors Counselors	Promoters	United States President and Cabinet officers Industrial tycoons International bankers	Inventive geniuses Consulting or chief engineers Ships' commanders
2. Professional & managerial (2)	Social workers Occupational therapists Probation, truant officers (with training)	Promoters Public relations counselors	Certified public accountants Business and government executives Union officials Brokers, average	Applied scientists Factory managers Ships' officers Engineers
3. Semiprofessional and small business	YMCA officials Detectives, police sergeants Welfare workers City inspectors	Salesmen: auto, bond, insurance, etc. Dealers, retail and wholesale Confidence men	Accountants, average Employment managers Owners, catering, dry cleaning, etc.	Aviators Contractors Foremen Radio operators
4. Skilled	Barbers Chefs Practical nurses Policemen	Auctioneers Buyers House canvassers Interviewers, poll	Cashiers Clerks, credit, express, etc. Foremen, warehouse Sales clerks	Blacksmiths Electricians Foremen Mechanics, average
5. Semiskilled	Taxi drivers General houseworkers Waiters City firemen	Peddlers	Clerks, file, stock, etc. Notaries Runners Typists	Bulldozer operators Deliverymen Smelter workers Truck drivers
6. Unskilled	Chambermaids Hospital attendants Elevator operators Watchmen		Messenger boys	Helpers Laborers Wrappers Yardmen

| | Group | | | |
Level	V. Outdoor	VI. Science	VII. General Cultural	VIII. Arts and Entertainment
1. Professional & managerial (1)	Consulting specialists	Research scientists University, college faculties Medical specialists Museum curators	Supreme Court justices University, college faculties Prophets Scholars	Creative artists Performers, great Teachers, university equivalent Museum curators
2. Professional & managerial (2)	Applied scientists Landowners and operators, large Landscape architects	Scientists, semi-independent Nurses Pharmacists Veterinarians	Editors Teachers, high school and elementary	Athletes Art critics Designers Music arrangers
3. Semiprofessional and small business	County agents Farm owners Forest rangers Fish, game wardens	Technicians, medical, X-ray, museum Weather observers Chiropractors	Justices of the peace Radio announcers Reporters Librarians	Ad writers Designers Interior decorators Showmen
4. Skilled	Laboratory testers, dairy products, etc. Miners Oil well drillers	Technical assistants	Law clerks	Advertising artists Decorators, window, etc. Photographers Racing car drivers
5. Semiskilled	Gardeners Farm tenants Teamsters, cow-punchers Miner's helpers	Veterinary hospital attendants		Illustrators, greeting cards Showcard writers Stagehands
6. Unskilled	Dairy hands Farm laborers Lumberjacks	Nontechnical helpers in scientific organizations		

* Modified from Roe (1956, p. 151).

Verbal abilities clearly predominate over nonverbal abilities in this group. It tends to be fairly low in dominance, although it is more so than the service group. Intellectual interests are quite strong, and for a few members of the group artistic interests may be important.

Arts and Entertainment Occupations

The eighth group is called *arts and entertainment* and includes occupations in athletics, fine arts, music, dancing, and public entertainers of various sorts. Included in this group are both those who create and those who perform, although, of course, many people in this group are involved in both functions.

As would be expected, this group manifests special artistic and physical abilities. It also shows relatively more adjustment problems than other groups. Intellectual interests are not particularly strong, and level for level, compared with other groups, fewer intellectual demands may be made on members of this group.

The Interest Factor: What Would You Like to Do?

By the time an individual reaches late adolescence or adulthood he probably has been interested in a number of vocations. He may have abandoned the possibility of entering some occupations—not because of a lack of interest—but because they involved too much training and uncertainty or too little prestige and income or for a number of other reasons. He may seriously consider some seemingly less interesting occupations because of the special opportunities and rewards they present.

Interest, as this term is used in voca-tional psychology, simply refers to the like or dislike of certain activities, things, or people. Other things being equal, a person is more likely to be successful if he is doing what he likes to do. Of course, interest alone does not ensure success in a vocation.

As we begin to plan our future, some of us are fairly sure of our interest in certain occupations. For example, we may find that we like psychology and decide that we would like to teach it at a college or practice it in a clinic. Others who are not certain about an occupation have some general interests that serve as clues. If, for example, one likes to be with people, he may look for an occupation that involves a good many of them.

But some of us may be in the dark. We may be unenthusiastic about the occupations with which we are most familiar. And although we do have some general interests, it may be very difficult for us to imagine how these can be of any assistance in earning a living.

If a person went to a counselor for help in choosing a vocation, the counselor might administer a battery of tests. Possibly included would be a test of interest. As a matter of fact, a lot of information concerning vocational interest has been gathered through the use of such tests. Two of the most important and widely used tests of this sort are the Strong Vocational Interest Blank and the Kuder Preference Record (Vocational).

Strong Vocational Interest Blank

The Strong Vocational Interest Blank is designed to show how an individual's interests agree with those of successful men or women in many different occupations. People who are employed in a particular occupation tend to share certain interests. They have certain likes and dislikes that characterize their occupational group and differentiate it from other groups. Under lying this test is the assumption that your chances for vocational happiness will be enhanced if you choose an occupation whose members have interests like your own (see Fig. 15.1).

If you were taking the Strong, you would note that it has 400 items divided into various categories. These categories include items concerning occupational title, activities, school subjects, amusements, and so on. Usually you are required to indicate whether you like, dislike, or are indifferent to the item. Sometimes you are asked to compare several items and indicate a preference.

When you received the results of the test, you would note that they had been plotted on a specially designed profile form. This form lists many different occupations and shows how your interests conform to those of successful workers in each occupation. And since the occupations are grouped according to similarity of interest, you could see whether your interests were concentrated in a single group or spread out among different ones.

The Strong has been especially useful in the vocational guidance of college students. Research has shown that interests as measured by this test tend to be quite stable by the time one reaches late adolescence or early adulthood. It has also been shown that persons who choose occupations congruent with their Strong profiles tend to stay in these occupations; those who choose noncongruent occupations tend to shift away, often to occupations more in line with their test profiles (Tyler, 1962, 1964).

Kuder Preference Record (Vocational)

The Kuder Preference Record (Vocational) is designed to measure interests somewhat differently from the Strong. The Kuder attempts to identify the types of activity that you like. Once your pattern of preference has been established, you can be directed into occupations that involve or are related to these preferred activities (see Fig. 15.2).

In taking the Kuder you are confronted with 160 groups of activities. In each group you are concerned with comparing three activities. You are asked to decide which of the three you like most and least.

The results of the Kuder are plotted on a profile form that indicates ten areas of interest. These areas are designated as outdoor, mechanical, computational, scientific, persuasive, artistic, literary, musical, social service, and clerical. In this way, you can get an idea of the general occupational areas in which your interests lie. In addition, the Kuder suggests certain specific occupations that might be advisable.

Like the Strong, the Kuder measures interests—not abilities. There may be a considerable discrepancy between what a person is *interested in* and what he is *capable of.*

Considerable caution must be used in interpreting the Kuder, the Strong, and other vocational tests. Generally speaking, testing is only one part of a larger process of vocational exploration which is undertaken with a counselor or guidance worker. The counselor or guidance worker decides what tests (if any) will be useful in this exploration process and what meaning the results of such tests have for the individual.

Figure 15.1 The Strong Vocational Interest Blank. A person's scores on the Strong Vocational Interest Blank are plotted on a profile form. There are separate forms for men and women. On each form the occupational scales are grouped according to their similarity, and special attention is given to the patterns of scores among groups. The shaded area of each scale indicates an average range for people in general. Scores which achieve an A rating indicate that the person's interests are similar to individuals who are successfully employed in an occupation. C ratings indicate interests unlike those of members of the occupation. B+, B, and B— ratings indicate intermediate amounts of shared interests. Here is a case study of the person whose scores are plotted on the accompanying profile form:

This 18-year-old college student sought counseling near the end of his freshman year to determine whether "I should continue with or change my major," which was engineering. He was maintaining about a C average but complained of being bored by the courses.

In high school his favorite subjects had been mathematics and science, his principal avocation music (he was an accomplished pianist). His mother was a free-lance writer, his father an artistic person who had been variously engaged in interior decorating and window display work.

On the College Entrance Examination Board, using national norms, he ranked 27th percentile on the verbal test and at the 90th percentile on mathematics aptitude. On a test of mechanical comprehension, he ranked at the 60th percentile of engineering freshmen; on a test of spatial visualization, at the 93rd percentile. On an art judgment test, he scored on the 54th percentile of art students. On the Minnesota Multiphasic Personality Inventory, he had a peak of 76 on masculinity-femininity, suggesting more "feminine" interests and attitudes than usual, especially for engineering students.

His profile on the Strong Vocational Interest Blank . . . yielded high scores scattered through several groups. He showed very strong resemblance to engineers and chemists, architects, physicians, and musicians. In discussing the results, the counselor pointed out that though engineering seemed compatible with his interests and aptitudes, perhaps it might conflict with some of his values and personality traits. The client observed that engineering "isn't very creative" and that he found many fellow engineering students rather unexciting personalities. He inquired about physics as a possible major and was advised that his profile gave little reason to suppose it would be better for him than engineering. The counselor suggested that he consider architecture and provided him with occupational information in this field.

In his evaluation of the SVIB profile, the counselor judged that the high scores in artist, architect, and musician represented some creative-artistic element in the client's make-up and felt that the MF [masculinity-femininity] scores on both the SVIB and MMPI tended to support this interpretation. The client had had excellent exposure to music and had rejected it as a career. Neither had he shown any willingness to pursue the biological sciences. The counselor felt that architecture might fulfill his creative-artistic needs while calling upon his engineering background, his superior mathematical aptitude, and his talent for spatial visualization. The client tried courses in architecture, liked them, and transferred to that department. He received his bachelor's degree in pre-architecture with a superior record despite his mediocre scholastic aptitude score. He was offered an apprenticeship with an architect of international reputation on the basis of some sample work and was thoroughly pleased with his vocational decision (Reprinted from *Manual for Strong Vocational Interest Blanks for Men and Women* by Edward K. Strong, Jr., revised by David P. Campbell, with the permission of the publishers, Stanford University Press. © 1959, 1966 by the Board of Trustees of the Leland Stanford Junior University).

PROFILE – STRONG VOCATIONAL INTEREST BLANK FOR MEN

FOR USE WITH SVIB FORM T399 OR T399R, HAND-SCORED ANSWER SHEET, AND HAND-SCORING STENCILS

Group	Scale	Plus Score	Minus Score	Raw Score	Std. Score	LETTER RATINGS AND STANDARD SCORES
I	Dentist					
	Osteopath					
	Veterinarian					
	Physician					
	Psychiatrist					
	Psychologist					
	Biologist					
II	Architect					
	Mathematician					
	Physicist					
	Chemist					
	Engineer					
III	Production Mgr.					
	Army Officer					
	Air Force Officer					
IV	Carpenter					
	Forest Service Man					
	Farmer					
	Math–Science Teacher					
	Printer					
	Policeman					
V	Personnel Director					
	Public Administrator					
	Rehabilitation Counselor					
	YMCA Secretary					
	Social Worker					
	Social Science Teacher					
	School Superintendent					
	Minister					
VI	Librarian					
	Artist					
	Musician Performer					
	Music Teacher					
VII	CPA Owner					
VIII	Senior CPA					
	Accountant					
	Office Worker					
	Purchasing Agent					
	Banker					
	Pharmacist					
	Mortician					
IX	Sales Manager					
	Real Estate Salesman					
	Life Insurance Salesman					
X	Advertising Man					
	Lawyer					
	Author–Journalist					
XI	Pres., Mfg. Concern					

Nonoccupational Scales

SL: _____ +1 _____ −1   raw   standard   OL: _____ +1 _____ −1   raw   standard   MF: _____ +1 _____ −1   raw   standard   AACH: _____ +1 _____ −1   raw   standard   NUMBER

Stanford University Press   Stanford, California

0		1		2		3		4		5		6		7		8		9	
OUTDOOR		MECHANICAL		COMPUTATIONAL		SCIENTIFIC		PERSUASIVE		ARTISTIC		LITERARY		MUSICAL		SOCIAL SERVICE		CLERICAL	
M	F	M	F	M	F	M	F	M	F	M	F	M	F	M	F	M	F	M	F

PERCENTILES (left scale): 90, 80, 70, 60, 50, 40, 30, 20, 10

PERCENTILES (right scale): 90, 80, 70, 60, 50, 40, 30, 20, 10

The Motivational Factor: What Do You Need to Do?

Motivational factors or patterns would seem to play an important role in the determination of a career. Some vocational writers and researchers use the term "personality" to denote essentially the same patterns. In the present discussion the two terms are used interchangeably.

Figure 15.2 The Kuder Preference Record (Vocational). A person's scores on the Kuder Preference Record (Vocational) are plotted on a profile sheet. Separate columns are used for the scores of males and females. Scores above the top dashed line (the 75th percentile) are considered high and indicative of a definite liking for the activities of the area. Scores below the bottom dashed line (25th percentile) are considered low and indicative of a dislike for the activities concerned. Scores between the two lines indicate an average interest.

On this profile sheet the scores of a young college woman are plotted. The student was twenty years old, a junior, and majoring in sociology. In high school she tentatively planned to become a teacher, but in college she had been considering the possibility of becoming an occupational therapist. Her patterning of high scores in the artistic and social service areas showed that her interests were highly consistent with the latter choice. Interestingly enough, she had taken the Kuder previously in the eleventh grade, and her earlier profile was available. It also showed high artistic and social service interests although not as high as on the second testing. In addition, the earlier profile indicated relatively high mechanical, computational, and clerical scores; these were lower on the second profile although she was working her way through college as a clerk-typist and research assistant. (Scales reprinted from Profile Sheet for the Kuder Preference Record Vocational. Copyright 1950, by G. Frederic Kuder. Reprinted by permission of the publisher, Science Research Associates, Inc., Chicago, Illinois.)

There is considerable overlap between the things measured by interest tests and tests of motives or personality. The things you are interested in are the things you need to do, and the things you need to do are the things you are interested in. Personality, however, is a much broader concept than interest and subsumes many more personal qualities. In fact, in some discussions of vocational adjustment, "personality" is used as a remainder bin designed to include any factor which is not treated independently. For example, Tyler writes, "For convenience . . . in this discussion we will simply say that we lump together under 'personality' all those characteristics of a person that do not fall in the abilities or interests categories—his needs, drives, motives, and defense mechanisms, his habitual way of relating to people, and his general character traits" (1964, p. 187).

How important are motivational factors in vocational adjustment? For example, are there certain occupations in which dominance patterning is an asset? Or a liability? How about deference? Or affiliation? Or autonomy?

The answers to these important questions are not easily obtained. For one thing, workers in the areas of motivation and personality employ many different systems of concepts and ideas. Second, the tests which have been devised to measure motives and personality are poorly validated. Third, little is known about the patterns of motives and personality which make for successful adjustment in specific occupations (Tyler, 1964).

A number of important studies concerning the role of motivational or personality factors in vocational adjustment have been brought together and reviewed by Super (1957). He was interested in determining the extent to which these factors were related to vocational preference, entry, success, and satisfaction, and he found that the relationships were not very significant.

Super felt that part of the reason for the low relationships was the considerable variety of activity found in almost any vocation; consequently, people of many different motivational patterns may be accommodated. Consider, for example, the field of psychology. There are jobs in research, application, and teaching. These jobs may be performed in schools and colleges, clinics and hospitals, business and industry. Once in the field, a psychologist may move about until he has found a compatible setting.

To illustrate further, a psychologist with high dominance needs may be able to head a department in a school or hospital. Another with low needs of this sort may avoid leadership positions. A psychologist with high affiliation needs may find an environment in which there are many people. A psychologist with high autonomy needs may seek positions which allow him to work independently, perhaps in research. Certainly, there is room in psychology for people of very different motivational patterns.

Table 15.4 What need or personality patterns are found in various occupational groups? There is some evidence that the people in specific jobs tend to be different in personality from those in others; however, relatively little is known about this matter and what is known suggests that the relationship of personality factors to occupation may be quite complicated.

Some evidence concerning this area has been provided by Gray, who used the Edwards Personal Preference Schedule to measure the need patterns of male groups of secondary teachers, accountants, and mechanical engineers. Interestingly enough, no important differences were found between the need patterns of accountants and mechanical engineers. However, the teachers differed significantly from each of the other two groups. Compared with the teachers, the accountants showed significantly higher needs for achievement, dominance, endurance, and exhibition, and significantly lower needs for affiliation, intraception, nurturance, deference, and abasement. Compared with the teachers, the engineers showed significantly higher needs for achievement, dominance, endurance, and order, and significantly lower needs for affiliation, intraception, nurturance, and succorance.* (These needs are defined in the Glossary, and most of them are discussed in Chapter 2.)

Need	Edwards Personal Preference Schedule Mean Scores		
	Teachers	Accountants	Engineers
Achievement	15.22	18.42	19.14
Deference	13.44	11.62	12.44
Order	11.82	12.72	13.58
Exhibition	12.98	14.70	13.64
Autonomy	13.20	13.94	14.36
Affiliation	15.22	13.58	12.14
Intraception	17.90	13.48	11.90
Succorance	10.22	8.82	8.36
Dominance	16.66	19.40	19.04
Abasement	13.16	11.58	12.80
Nurturance	15.68	11.86	12.34
Change	14.18	13.72	14.10
Endurance	13.86	19.02	17.78
Heterosexuality	12.96	15.52	14.18
Aggression	12.80	14.00	13.78

* Data from Gray (1963).

However, for a specific job, it may be possible to determine certain patterns of motivation which characterize the occupants (see Table 15.4) or differentiate those who are successful or satisfied from those who are not. Super suggests that for certain occupations it is possible to draw "a picture of the typical personality." However, he adds that such "personality sketches are not sufficiently clear-cut to provide a scientific basis for occupational choice. . . ."

A good deal of research is being done in this area, and a good deal more is needed. What are we likely to find? This is Super's conclusion:

> It seems possible that, if occupations are sufficiently narrowly and precisely defined, for example in terms of functional specialties within an occupation, significant personality differences in occupational groups may be found. Perhaps some will be found which are so highly structured that only individuals with certain traits are successful or satisfied in them, whereas others will be found in which there is so little structure that individuals with greatly varying personality patterns can find satisfaction in them, each structuring the occupation in his own way. There is some indication that this may be the case (1957, p. 241).

The Ability Factor: What Are You Able to Do?

In some areas of interest there may be few opportunities. And some jobs that interest a person may be beyond his doing or learning to do. *Ability* is a term that is used in various ways, but in this discussion it includes present knowledge and skills (proficiency) and the potential for acquiring further knowledge and skills (aptitude).[4]

[4] Ability is also discussed in connection with college achievement (pp. 400–403).

General Ability

General ability refers to the capacity to learn many types of material and acquire many types of skills. General ability is frequently referred to as mental ability or intelligence.

Many of the most sought-after occupations involve complex learning tasks and require considerable intelligence. Other occupations make less intellectual demand, and in some simple occupations, too much intelligence can actually be a handicap since in them the very bright person may feel uninterested and bored.

How much intelligence is required in various vocations? One way of finding out would be to administer an intelligence battery to a number of people in many different types of work. This would be expensive and difficult to do, but similar information is available from the testing program of the military forces during World War II.

Harrell and Harrell (1945) report on the Army General Classification Test scores and civilian occupations of over 18,782 white enlisted men in the Army Air Forces. Although this sample is not fully representative of the general population, it permits some idea of the relationship between intelligence and occupation.

When the test results were arranged in broad occupational groupings, the professional occupations, on the average, were found to have the highest IQs. Managerial and semiprofessional occupations also ranked high. Sales, clerical, and skilled occupations had intermediate or average scores. The lowest scores were made by the semiskilled, personal service, and agricultural occupations (Christensen, 1946) (see Table 15.5).

It is important to note the considerable range of scores within each occupa-

Table 15.5 Grouped in major occupational categories, here are the Army General Classification Test Scores of 18,782 white enlisted men who were in the Army Air Forces Air Service Command during World War II.*

Classification	Mean Score
Professional	122.9
Managerial	118.8
Semiprofessional	117.6
Sales	112.1
Clerical	104.4
Skilled	101.7
Semiskilled	99.6
Personal service	98.7
Agricultural	92.0

* Data from Christensen (1946, p. 100).

tion and the overlapping of scores between occupations. For example, accountants, the top occupation, ranged in IQ from 94 to 157. The bottom occupation, the teamsters, ranged from 46 to 145.

It should also be noted that even in the very lowest occupations, some of the individuals scored higher than the mean for the very highest. However, on the other hand, none of the men in the top occupations scored as low as the mean for the very lowest ones. The investigators conclude, "Evidently a certain minimum of intelligence is required for any one of many occupations and a man must have that much intelligence in order to function in that occupation, but a man may have high intelligence and be found in a lowly occupation because he lacks other qualifications than intelligence" (Harrell & Harrell, 1945, p. 239).

When the test results were considered for individual occupations, considerable differences in mean scores were found. The occupations ranged from accountant, lawyer, engineer, public relations specialist, and auditor, who all achieved mean IQs over 125, to lumberjack, farmer, farmhand, miner, and teamster, whose mean IQs were under 95 (Harrell & Harrell, 1945) (see Table 15.6).

Special Ability

Even the most intelligent or able person finds some things difficult to do. Even the person of modest general ability may have some areas of competence. In considering vocational adjustment, we must take into account *special abilities*. This term refers to the capacity to learn certain specific types of material and perform certain specific tasks.

Much attention has been paid to the role of special ability factors in vocational adjustment. A number of special abilities have been described, and various tests have been devised to measure them. The relationship between the possession of such abilities and success in various learning programs and job placements has been the subject of many studies.

Generally speaking, the results of these investigations have not been encouraging, and there is lessening enthusiasm about the contribution which ability or aptitude tests can make to the prediction of vocational success (Thorndike, 1963; Tyler, 1962, 1964). Some sorts of aptitude tests have proved useful, for example, those measuring clerical, mechanical, and academic aptitude. On the other hand, tests of musical and artistic talent appear to measure only a small part of whatever it is that makes for success in these fields, and attempts to construct useful tests of teaching aptitude or sales aptitude (to mention just two) have been largely unrewarding (Tyler, 1964).

Many aptitude tests are actually batteries or groups of individual tests. Some of these batteries are specially designed or specially assembled for specific vocations; for example, there are measures of medical, legal, and engineering aptitude. Such bat-

Table 15.6 Here are the Army General Classification Test Scores and civilian occupations of 18,782 white enlisted men who were in the Army Air Forces Air Service Command during World War II.*

Occupation	Mean Score	Range	Occupation	Mean Score	Range
Accountant	128.1	94–157	Machinist	110.1	38–153
Lawyer	127.6	96–157	Foreman	109.8	60–151
Engineer	126.6	100–151	Watchmaker	109.8	68–147
Public relations man	126.0	100–149	Airplane mechanic	109.3	66–147
Auditor	125.9	98–151	Sales clerk	109.2	42–149
Chemist	124.8	102–153	Electrician	109.0	64–149
Reporter	124.5	100–157	Lathe operator	108.5	64–147
Chief Clerk	124.2	88–153	Receiving & shipping checker	107.6	52–151
Teacher	122.8	76–155	Sheet metal worker	107.5	62–153
Draftsman	122.0	74–155	Lineman, power and tel & tel	107.1	70–133
Stenographer	121.0	66–151	Assembler	106.3	48–145
Pharmacist	120.5	76–149	Mechanic	106.3	60–155
Tabulating machine operator	120.1	80–151	Machine operator	104.8	42–151
Bookkeeper	120.0	70–157	Auto serviceman	104.2	30–141
Manager, sales	119.0	90–137	Riveter	104.1	50–141
Purchasing agent	118.7	82–153	Cabinetmaker	103.5	66–127
Manager, production	118.1	82–153	Upholsterer	103.3	68–131
Photographer	117.6	66–147	Butcher	102.9	42–147
Clerk, general	117.5	68–155	Plumber	102.7	56–139
Clerk-typist	116.8	80–147	Bartender	102.2	56–137
Manager, miscellaneous	116.0	60–151	Carpenter, construction	102.1	42–147
Installer-repairman, tel & tel	115.8	76–149	Pipe fitter	101.9	56–139
Cashier	115.8	80–145	Welder	101.8	48–147
Instrument repairman	115.5	82–141	Auto mechanic	101.3	48–151
Radio repairman	115.3	56–151	Molder	101.1	48–137
Printer, job pressman, lithographic pressman	115.1	60–149	Chauffeur	100.8	46–143
Salesman	115.1	60–153	Tractor driver	99.5	42–147
Artist	114.9	82–139	Painter, general	98.3	38–147
Manager, retail store	114.0	52–151	Crane hoist operator	97.9	58–147
Laboratory assistant	113.4	76–147	Cook and baker	97.2	20–147
Tool maker	112.5	76–143	Weaver	97.0	50–135
Inspector	112.3	54–147	Truck driver	96.2	16–149
Stock clerk	111.8	54–151	Laborer	95.8	26–145
Receiving & shipping clerk	111.3	58–155	Barber	95.3	42–141
			Lumberjack	94.7	46–137
Musician	110.9	56–147	Farmer	92.7	24–147
			Farmhand	91.4	24–141
			Miner	90.6	42–139
			Teamster	87.7	46–145

* Data from Harrell and Harrell (1945, pp. 231–232).

teries are frequently used for the selection of students for a particular professional school or for a set of such schools, and their use is carefully restricted. These batteries are usually administered to the student when he is nearing or at the end of his preprofessional training, and they tend to be high-level achievement tests, intelligence tests employing a special professional vocabulary, or assortments and modifications of various kinds of individual aptitude tests (Roe, 1964; Super & Crites, 1962).

Some aptitude batteries have been designed to be used in planning for a wide variety of occupations. These batteries include tests measuring aptitudes which are involved in many different kinds of work. By considering the aptitudes and the combinations of aptitudes which a person has, a counselor may get some idea of the direction in which the individual's vocational explorations should be made.

Probably the most promising standard battery is the General Aptitude Test Battery (GATB) which was developed by the United States Employment Service (United States Employment Service, 1962). This battery is administered and used by state employment services to guide older adolescents and adults toward jobs for which they may be best suited. The GATB is especially useful for directing workers who are below the professional level and who are heading for skilled and semiskilled occupations.

The GATB requires about two hours to take. It is made up of twelve tests which together measure nine aptitudes or factors. These factors are named and described as follows:

G—General learning ability or intelligence:

Ability to understand instructions and underlying principles. To reason and make judgments.

V—Verbal aptitude: Ability to understand meanings of words and ideas associated with them, and to use them effectively. To comprehend language, to understand relationships between words, and to understand meanings of whole sentences and paragraphs. To present information or ideas clearly.

N—Numerical aptitude: Ability to perform arithmetic operations quickly and accurately.

S—Spatial aptitude: Ability to comprehend forms in space and understand relationship of plane and solid objects.

P—Form perception: Ability to perceive pertinent detail in objects or in pictorial or graphic material. To make visual comparisons and discriminations and see slight differences in shapes and shadings of figures and widths and lengths of lines.

Q—Clerical perception: Ability to perceive pertinent detail in verbal or tabular material. To observe differences in copy, to proofread words and numbers, and to avoid perceptual errors in arithmetic computation.

K—Motor coordination: Ability to coordinate eyes and hands or fingers rapidly and accurately in making precise movements with speed. To make a movement response accurately and quickly.

F—Finger dexterity: Ability to move the fingers, and manipulate small objects with the fingers, rapidly or accurately.

M—Manual dexterity: Ability to move the hands easily and skillfully. To work with the hands in placing and turning motions.[5]

A second standardized battery which has been useful in vocational guidance is the Differential Aptitude Tests (DAT) (Bennett, Seashore, & Wesman, 1947, 1952,

[5] Descriptions modified from "Guide to the Use of the General Aptitude Test Battery," Section III, published by the United States Employment Service, October, 1962.

1959). This battery is designed to be used with students in the eighth through the twelfth grades. The battery is made up of eight tests, each measuring one aptitude; two of the tests taken together provide a ninth measure. The tests themselves require slightly more than three hours of working time, but including time for passing out materials, giving directions, and so forth, four to six hours may be required altogether.

The individual tests of the battery and the aptitudes they measure are described as follows:

Verbal Reasoning: Ability to reason with words, to understand and use concepts expressed in words. Important in academic courses; also in jobs requiring much written or oral communication and jobs involving high levels of authority and responsibility.

Numerical Ability: Ability to reason with numbers, to deal intelligently with quantitative materials and ideas. Generally important in school work—but especially for such fields as mathematics, chemistry, physics, and engineering. Useful in such jobs as bookkeeper, engineer, laboratory technician, statistician, shipping clerk, carpenter, navigator, etc.

VR + NA (Verbal plus Numerical): General scholastic aptitude—ability to learn from books and lectures, to master school subjects. Indicative also of potential for jobs of more than ordinary responsibility. This score is the equivalent in meaning of "mental ability" scores on most traditional group tests of "intelligence."

Abstract Reasoning: A non-verbal, non-numerical measure of reasoning power. Ability to see relationships among things—objects, patterns, diagrams, or designs—rather than among words and numbers. Useful in shop, drafting, and laboratory work—also in mathematics,

in electrical or mechanical trouble-shooting, in computer programming, etc.

Clerical Speed and Accuracy: Quickness and accuracy in perceiving and marking simple letter and number combinations. Important in paper work in school, and in offices, laboratories, stores, warehouses, or wherever records are made or filed or checked. Sometimes a low score on CSA for a generally able person may indicate great emphasis on correctness rather than genuine lack of ability to work rapidly.

Mechanical Reasoning: Comprehension of mechanical principles and devices, and of the laws of everyday physics. Courses in the physical sciences, technical studies, or manual training shop are easier for those who score high in MR, as are mechanical repair work and a wide variety of factory and engineering jobs.

Space Relations: Ability to visualize, to "think in three dimensions" or picture mentally the shape, size, and position of objects when shown only a picture or pattern. Drafting, shop courses, some kinds of mathematics and some kinds of art or design courses are among those demanding this sense. It is needed by carpenters, architects, machinists, engineers, dentists, dress designers, and others whose work requires them to visualize solid forms or spaces.

Language Usage: Spelling: An important skill in school and college work as in many jobs. Among other things this score is one of the best predictors of the ease and speed with which one can learn typing and shorthand. When this score and/or the Grammar score (see next paragraph) are very much lower than the Verbal Reasoning score, extra study or tutoring may help improve language skills so that the student is less likely to be handicapped by lack of competence in the mechanics of English.

Language Usage: Grammar: A measure of how well one can distinguish between correct and improper grammar, punctu-

ation, and wording of sentences. An excellent predictor of grades in most high school and college courses. While such careers as writing and teaching require especially well-developed language skills, nearly all kinds of work requiring college-level education demand a considerable competence in this area.[6]

SUMMARY

Vocational adjustment may be defined in various ways. First, it can be equated with vocational maturity. In this framework a person is considered adjusted if his vocational behavior is as well developed as that of the average individual of his age. Development itself can be measured in terms of certain crucial vocational tasks or along certain pertinent dimensions.

Second, vocational adjustment may be defined as orderly progression—a movement through a succession of related and increasingly desirable jobs. This process involves both mobility and stability. As a person moves from job to job, he may seem to be floundering and moving aimlessly about, or he may appear to be gaining a good deal from his explorations. Increasing stability may represent a settling-in and taking-hold process, or it may be a process of trapping in which one is locked into an unsuitable position.

A third way of defining vocational adjustment is in terms of satisfaction. The amount of satisfaction workers report varies widely and depends upon the subjects and research methods employed. Work satisfactions are of two sorts: intrinsic satisfactions are those which arise out of the inherent nature of the job; extrinsic satisfaction are those which are extraneous to the nature of the work. Generally speaking, workers higher up in the job hierarchy report more satisfaction and more intrinsic satisfaction than those in the lower rungs.

Vocational development is a continuous and lifelong process, but it can be divided into five stages. The first or growth stage includes infancy and childhood years; this is the time when patterns of needs, interests, attitudes, and abilities crucial to later vocational adjustment are formed. The second period is called the exploration stage and includes adolescence and early adulthood; during this period a person is heavily occupied with forming images of himself and the vocational world and making basic decisions about a career. The third period or establishment stage includes the young adulthood years; during this time one is busy establishing a career, a home and family, and a place in the community. The fourth period is called the maintenance stage and takes in the remainder of adulthood up until the age of retirement; during this time the person becomes more set in his ways and less likely to break new ground. The fifth and final period is called the retirement or decline stage and includes the adjustment necessitated by changing vocational status and aging.

Many factors play a part in the determination of careers. For one thing, career patterns depend upon the job market.

More than twenty-two thousand different jobs have been identified, and it has been suggested that these may be classified by group (or focus) and by levels within each group. The groupings which have been used in this two-way classification system are service, business contact, organization, technology, outdoor, science, general cultural, and arts and entertainment. Six levels have been proposed, including two professional and managerial levels, a semiprofessional and a small business level, and skilled, semiskilled, and unskilled levels.

Interest is a second important determinant of career patterns. Other things being equal, a person is more likely to be satisfied with his job if he is doing what he likes to do. Two vocational interest tests which are widely used and which have provided a good deal of information about the role of interest in vocational adjustment are the Strong Vocational Interest Blank and the Kuder Preference Record (Vocational).

Motivational or personality factors are assumed to make up a third important set of determinants. The relationship between such factors and vocational choice, success, and happiness is not well known as yet, and because of the wide variety of work placements, an occupation may accommodate many different sorts of people. The more narrowly a job is defined, the more likely it is that certain motive or personality patterns will be found associated with that job.

Ability is a fourth important determinant of career patterns. A certain minimum of general ability or intelligence is required for the successful pursuit of an occupation, and workers in the higher rungs of the job hierarchy are brighter on the average than those at the lower levels, although there is a considerable amount of intellectual overlap. In addition, certain special abilities appear to be involved in the learning and performance of many jobs. Two widely used and useful tests of special ability are the General Aptitude Test Battery and the Differential Aptitude Tests.

REFERENCES

Beardslee, D. C., & O'Dowd, D. D. Students and the occupational world. In N. Sanford (Ed.), *The American College.* New York: Wiley, 1962. Pp. 597–626.

Bennett, G. K., Seashore, H. G., & Wesman, A. G. *Differential Aptitude Tests.* New York: Psychological Corporation, 1947, 1952, 1959.

——, ——, & ——. *Differential Aptitude Tests: Individual Report Form.* New York: Psychological Corporation, 1961, 1963.

Brender, M. Toward a psychodynamic system of occupational classification. *Journal of Counseling Psychology,* 1960, **7**(2), 96–100.

Christensen, T. E. Dictionary classification of the A.G.C.T. scores for selected civilian occupations. *Occupations* (now *Personnel and Guidance Journal*), 1946, **25**(2), 97–101.

Darley, J. G., & Hagenah, T. *Vocational Interest Measurement.* Minneapolis: University of Minnesota Press, 1955.

Davidson, P. E., & Anderson, H. D. *Occupational Mobility in an American Community.* Stanford, Calif.: Stanford, 1937.

Erikson, E. H. Growth and crises of the healthy personality. *Psychological Issues,* 1959, **1**(1), 50–100.

Form, W. H., & Miller, D. C. Occupational career pattern as a sociological instrument. *American Journal of Sociology,* 1949, **54**(4), 317–329.

———, & ———. Occupational career pattern as a sociological instrument. In S. Nosow & W. H. Form (Eds.), *Man, Work, and Society.* New York: Basic Books, 1962. Pp. 287–297.

Goldsen, R. K., Rosenberg, M., Williams, R. M., Jr., & Suchman, E. A. *What College Students Think.* Princeton, N.J.: Van Nostrand, 1960.

Goodman, P. Youth in the organized society. *Commentary,* 1960, **29**(2), 95–107 (February, 1960).

Gray, J. T. Needs and values in three occupations. *Personnel and Guidance Journal,* 1963, **42**, 238–244.

Gurin, G., Veroff, J., & Feld, S. *Americans View Their Mental Health.* New York: Basic Books, 1960.

Harrell, T. W., & Harrell, M. S. Army general classification test scores for civilian occupations. *Educational and Psychological Measurement,* 1945, **5**(3), 229–239.

Havemann, E., & West, P. S. *They Went to College.* New York: Harcourt, Brace, 1952.

Havighurst, R. J. *Developmental Tasks and Education.* (2nd ed.) New York: McKay, 1952.

Inlow, G. M. Job satisfaction of liberal arts graduates. *Journal of Applied Psychology,* 1951, **35**, 175–181.

Kuder, G. F. *Kuder Preference Record (Vocational).* Chicago: Science Research, 1939, 1951.

Livson, F. Adjustment to retirement. In S. Reichard, F. Livson, & P. G. Petersen, *Aging and Personality.* New York: Wiley, 1962. Pp. 71–92.

Menninger, W. C. The meaning of work in Western society. In H. Borow (Ed.), *Man in a World at Work.* Boston: Houghton Mifflin, 1964. Pp. xiii–xvii.

Miller, D. C., & Form, W. H. *Industrial Sociology.* New York: Harper & Row, 1951.

Morse, N. C., & Weiss, R. S. The function and meaning of work and the job. In S. Nosow & W. H. Form (Eds.), *Man, Work, and Society.* New York: Basic Books, 1962. Pp. 29–35.

Nachmann, B. Childhood experience and vocational choice in law, dentistry, and social work. *Journal of Counseling Psychology,* 1960, **7**(4), 243–250.

O'Dowd, D. D., & Beardslee, D. C. *College Student Images of a Selected Group of Professions and Occupations.* Cooperative Research Project No. 562(8142), U.S. Office of Education. Middletown, Conn.: Wesleyan University, 1960.

Reichard, S., Livson, F., Petersen, P. G. *Aging and Personality.* New York: Wiley, 1962.

Robinson, H. A., Connors, R. P., & Whitacre, G. H. Job satisfaction researches of 1964–65. *Personnel and Guidance Journal,* 1966, **45**(4), 371–379.

Roe, A. *The Psychology of Occupations.* New York: Wiley, 1956.

———. Personality structure and occupational behavior. In H. Borow (Ed.), *Man in a World of Work.* Boston: Houghton Mifflin, 1964. Pp. 196–214.

Stratemeyer, F. B., Forkner, H. L., & McKim, M. G. *Developing a Curriculum for Modern Living.* New York: Bureau of Publications, Teachers College, Columbia University, 1947.

Streib, G. F., Thompson, W. E., & Suchman, E. A. The Cornell study of occupational retirement. *Journal of Social Issues,* 1958, **14**(2), 3–17.

Strong, E. K., Jr. *Strong Vocational Interest Blank.* Palo Alto, Calif.: Consulting Psychologists Press, 1927, 1947, 1951.

———, & Campbell, D. P. *Manual for Strong Vocational Interest Blanks.* Stanford, Calif.: Stanford, 1966.

Super, D. E. *The Psychology of Careers.* New York: Harper & Row, 1957.

Super, D. E., & Crites, J. O. *Appraising Vocational Fitness.* (2nd ed.) New York: Harper & Row, 1962.

———, ———, **Hummel, R. C., Moser, H. P., Overstreet, P. L., & Warnath, C. F.** *Vocational Development: A Framework for Research.* New York: Bureau of Publications, Teachers College, Columbia University, 1957.

———, **Overstreet, P. L., Morris, C. N., Dubin, W., & Heyde, M. B.** *The Vocational Maturity of Ninth-grade Boys.* New York: Bureau of Publications, Teachers College, Columbia University, 1960.

Swados, H. Work as a public issue. *Saturday Review,* Dec. 12, 1959. Pp. 13–15, 45.

Thompson, A. S. Counseling and the ages of man. *Journal of Counseling Psychology,* 1964, **11**(3), 221–229.

Thompson, W. E., & Streib, G. F. Situational determinants: Health and economic deprivation in retirement. *Journal of Social Issues,* 1958, **14**(2), 18–34.

Thorndike, R. L. The prediction of vocational success. *Vocational Guidance Quarterly,* 1963, **11**(3), 179–187.

Tyler, L. E. Research on instruments used by counselors in vocational guidance. *Journal of Counseling Psychology,* 1962, **9**(2), 99–105.

———. Work and individual differences. In H. Borow (Ed.), *Man in a World at Work.* Boston: Houghton Mifflin, 1964. Pp. 174–195.

United States Employment Service. *Dictionary of occupational titles.* Vol. 1. *Definitions of Titles.* U.S. Department of Labor, 1949.

United States Employment Service. *Guide to the Use of the General Aptitude Test Battery.* U.S. Department of Labor, October, 1962.

Weil, S. Factory work. In S. Nosow & W. H. Form (Eds.), *Man, Work, and Society.* New York: Basic Books, 1962. Pp. 452–457.

Wilensky, H. L. Orderly careers and social participation. *American Sociological Review,* 1961, **26**(4), 521–539.

———. Varieties of work experience. In H. Borow (Ed.), *Man in a World at Work.* Boston: Houghton Mifflin, 1964. Pp. 125–154.

Wrenn, C. G. Human values and work in American life. In H. Borow (Ed.), *Man in a World at Work.* Boston: Houghton Mifflin, 1964. Pp. 24–44.

CHAPTER SIXTEEN

MARRIAGE ADJUSTMENT

We fall in love, marry, and adjust. How much adjusting will we have to do?

Some couples appear to have an easy time of it. Others seem to be in crisis nearly all the time. And about one out of every three or four marriages ends in divorce. Why?

What is good marriage adjustment? What can we tell in advance about our chances for success in marriage? What is poor marriage adjustment? How can we work to make it better? These are some of the questions which this chapter will ask and try to answer.

DEFINING MARRIAGE ADJUSTMENT

How is marriage adjustment defined? Permanence is frequently used as a definition. Another common definition is happiness. And for a fuller, richer definition, one might use both permanence and happiness and maybe a number of other criteria as well.

Marriage Adjustment as Permanence

"Until death do you part," read the marriage vows. Most people think of marriage as a permanent venture. And society and circumstance place a number of obstacles in the path of spouses who begin to think otherwise.

As a definition or criterion of marriage adjustment, permanence has certain advantages. First of all, it states an essential. A divorce, no matter how friendly, marks the end and failure of a marriage.

Second, permanence is relatively easy to measure. Marriage, annulment, legal separation, and divorce are matters of record and common knowledge. Desertion, especially by a now-you-see-him-now-you-don't spouse, is a more complex matter. Generally speaking, however, this criterion is not difficult to apply.

Permanence is frequently used by researchers as a gross measure of marriage adjustment. For example, one investigator (Jacobson, 1952), who was interested in the influence of attitudes on marriage, contrasted the ideas of married and divorced couples toward marriage roles. (As he hypothesized, married couples proved to be more similar in their attitudes than the divorced spouses were.)

On the other hand, permanence as a definition of marriage adjustment is open to criticism. For one thing, most of us expect more of a marriage than mere durability. Some marriages persist and are persistently unhappy.

Reviewing their practice, a pair of psychiatrists readily identified a number of "durable incompatible marriages." These consisted of couples who had been in unholy deadlock for twenty years or more. In describing these marriages, the psychiatrists write, "In spite of their harrowing experiences with each other, the couples we saw remained married. A tacit agreement seemed to exist between them that their threats of divorce and separations were not to be taken literally, as possible solutions to their problems, but rather represented additional weapons or, in some cases, relief from the strain of their long continued encounters" (Houston & Forman, 1961, p. 6).

A second criticism of using permanence in evaluating marital adjustment is that it attributes no measure of success to an abandoned marriage. Some permanent marriages leave much to be desired, and by some standards might be considered failures. And some impermanent marriages must be credited with at least partial success. Although a marriage finally ends in divorce, it may have been quite a workable one for a number of years and in a number of ways (Bernard, 1964).

How permanent are American marriages? In 1963 there were about 1,600,000 marriages and 400,000 divorces. Trends in divorce change, but it has been estimated that at current rates the average marriage has about three chances in ten of winding up in the divorce courts, assuming that both spouses live forty years after taking their vows (Divorce rate half-truth, 1963).

Over the past one hundred years, more and more marriages have ended in divorce. Some idea of the huge upswing can be gained from comparing the number of *existing* marriages which end in divorce in selected years. For the year 1860, for example, the ratio of divorces to existing marriages was only slightly more than 1 per 1,000. For 1965, the predicted ratio of divorces to existing marriages was about 9 or 10 per 1,000 (Jacobson & Jacobson, 1959).

Although the divorce rate has risen sharply in the last century, the rate today is not so high as during World War II. In 1946, when the divorce rate reached its all-time peak, about 18 out of every 1,000 existing marriages dissolved. Today the rate is only about half that large.

Marriage Adjustment as Happiness

"And they lived happily ever after" is the ending to more than one fairy-tale romance. Alas, we mortals live our lives in the real world. Still, most married people appear to be happily married.

Although it is being discussed second, happiness is probably the first thing one thinks of in considering a marriage. "What is their chance for happiness?" we wonder in estimating the future of an engaged couple. And later on, if we ask how they have been getting along since they were married, the answer is likely to come back in terms of happiness or unhappiness.

Since happiness is such a familiar and widely agreed-upon criterion of marriage adjustment, many researchers make some assessment of happiness in their studies of marriage. Sometimes spouses are asked to rate the happiness of their own marriage. Sometimes an outsider—a close relative or someone else in a position to know—is asked to make an evaluation.

Use of happiness as a criterion of adjustment in marriage is not without objection. Happiness is such a subjective thing. Suppose a spouse says his marriage is *very* happy. How *very* happy is *very* happy? And is he *really* very happy? Is he being honest with us? Is he being honest with himself? (Burgess, Locke, & Thomes, 1963).

For all its limitations, this definition is a useful one. First of all, raters seem to have little difficulty in rating the happiness of a marriage. Second, different raters—husbands and wives or insiders and outsiders—show fairly good agreement in their evaluations. And, third, happiness as a criterion correlates well with other measures of marriage adjustment (Burgess et al., 1963).

How happy are American marriages? According to figures assembled by a number of investigators over the past thirty years, marriages in this country are relatively happy. In seven major studies which were published between 1932 and 1962, 65 to 84 percent of the spouses or couples were considered happy in their marriages (see Table 16.1).

Happiness statistics, of course, depend upon the procedures which happiness statisticians follow. For example, such statistics depend upon *whom* you ask. They also depend upon *how* you ask.

If an investigation were confined to spouses in marriage counseling or in the divorce courts, happiness figures might be close to zero. Studies of couples who have been married for a few years can paint relatively rosy pictures because divorce has served to eliminate some of the least happy pairs (Landis & Landis, 1963). The higher the subjects are in education and socioeconomic class, the happier the marriage ratings, and the fact that lower-class couples are less well represented in marriage studies doubtless makes the picture brighter than it otherwise would be (Gurin, Veroff, & Feld, 1960; Komarovsky, 1964).

It is possible that the simple questions used by investigators to assess marriage happiness have produced answers which are less than candid. Practically all spouses rate their marriages as average or above in happiness. Where are the less than average spouses? Surely, not all divorced. There is some indication that more probing procedures will produce less favorable pictures of marriage adjustment (Komarovsky, 1964).

How happy must a marriage be? How unhappy can it become and still survive? Even a relatively unhappy marriage may have much to recommend it. Such a marriage—although far from perfect—may be the best of the various alternatives available to the several persons involved. Although not the best imaginable situation, it may be the best possible one (Bernard, 1964).

We will not find perfect happiness in marriage any more than we find it before marriage or—considering those who divorce—after marriage. Practically all of us marry and most of us stay married. If we unmarry, we remarry. There seems to be no doubt that most adults consider marriage the happiest (or, at least, the least unhappy) of the available alternatives.

A Multiple Definition

When couples marry, we wish them a long *and* happy life together, and there are obvious advantages to using both criteria in evaluating a marriage. And, the more one thinks about it, the more one may think of other criteria as well.

Researchers who are interested in

Table 16.1   Some studies of marriage happiness.

Investigators	Subjects	Procedures	Very Happy or Happy	Medium or Average	Unhappy or Very Unhappy
			Ratings, percent		
Lang, 1932 (Cited by Bossard & Boll, 1955)	8,263 couples	Rated by friends and acquaintances	65	19	16
Terman, 1938	792 couples	Self-ratings	84	11	5
Burgess & Cottrell, 1939	526 couples	Self-ratings	63	15	22
Landis, 1946	409 couples	Self-ratings	83	16	1
Bossard & Boll, 1955	440 persons	Rated by brother or sister	71	15	14
Gurin, Veroff, & Feld, 1960	1,872 persons	Self-ratings	68	29	3
Landis, 1962	2,640 couples	Rated by college-age children	74	21	5

marriage evaluation commonly use a number of criteria (Bowerman, 1964). The usual practice is to decide on the criteria which are to be used, devise a number of questionnaire items to measure each one, and incorporate these items in a marriage-adjustment test. Some of the criteria which have been used are noted below; each forms a definition or, at least, a part definition of marriage adjustment.

Satisfaction

A marriage pair might be considered adjusted if they express satisfaction with each other and with their marriage. This criterion is not very different from happiness, but it has been used by a number of investigators. Burgess and Wallin (1953), for example, included this criterion with seven others which together formed their definition of marriage success. They were interested both in measuring *general satisfaction* which they described as "an over-all feeling of contentment with the marriage and one's mate" and *specific satisfactions and dissatisfactions* "which include a hundred and one commendations, and appreciations, or resentments and complaints about personality characteristics, habits, and behavior of one's marriage partner" (p. 487).

Consensus

How much does a couple agree and disagree? Ability to reach a consensus has been used as a measure of marriage adjustment. Some investigators have been interested in the amount of congruency in the spouses' philosophies of life or value systems. Do they agree on what is and what is not important (Burgess & Wallin, 1953; Farber, 1957)? There has also been interest in measuring the amount of agreement and disagreement in specific areas of marriage, such as finances, recreation, religion, friends, and relationship with in-laws (Locke & Williamson, 1958).

Companionship

Couples report that companionship is one of their chief sources of gratification in marriage (Burgess & Wallin, 1953; Burgess et al., 1963). Consequently, it is held to be a useful index of marriage adjustment. In measuring companionship, investigators seek answers to a number of related questions: How much affection does the couple demonstrate? Do they talk to each other and confide in each other? Do they share each other's feelings? Do they understand each other's views? Do they do things together? (Burgess et al., 1963)

Sex Behavior

A number of investigators have included measures of sex adjustment or satisfaction in their evaluation of marriage success. Sex is an important aspect of marriage, it is frequently a troublesome one, and a couple's sexual adjustment may provide important clues to the rest of the marital interaction (Burgess et al., 1963). Sex adjustment is generally measured by determining the satisfaction that each spouse has found in the couple's sex relations and whether or not intercourse is as frequent as each wishes.

PREDICTING MARRIAGE ADJUSTMENT

Why do some marriages last while others end up in the divorce courts? Why do some marriages provide so much satisfaction while others are filled with unhappiness? And is it possible to tell beforehand whether a marriage will be lasting and happy?

Many times we hear people predict success or failure for a couple who are approaching marriage. We probably have done some predicting ourselves. One couple, we may feel, were made for each other, and their marriage, we predict, is bound to be a happy one. Another couple, we fear, will never be happy together because they are too different or too much alike or too immature or for a number of other reasons.

Social scientists, of course, are interested in prediction, but they have not been highly successful in their attempts to predict. Natural scientists are better predictors. (Even though marriages are reputed to be made in heaven, celestial eclipses are easier to predict than marital ones.)

After reviewing the evidence, Kirkpatrick, a student of marriage for many years, concluded that there was "no very complete or unanimous verdict by science on what makes for happiness in marriage" (1963, p. 384). A factor which one investigator finds significant, another may not. The discussion which follows will focus on those factors which at this time appear most significantly related to marriage adjustment (see Table 16.2).

Background Factors

No set of factors seems more important than that having to do with family background. Those of us who remember our

Table 16.2   Premarital factors found to be associated with marriage adjustment.*

Factor	Number of Studies Reporting
1. Acquaintance: well, or over 6 months	6
2. Adaptability: good general adjustment	4
3. Age at marriage: 20 or older for women, 22 or older for men	7
4. Age differential: man older or the same age as woman	6
5. Attachment to father: close	4
6. Attachment to mother: close	4
7. Church attendance: 2 to 4 times a month	4
8. Church membership	4
9. Conflict with father: none or very little	5
10. Conflict with mother: none or very little	5
11. Discipline: not harsh	4
12. Educational level: some college or college graduate	6
13. Engagement: 9 months or longer	4
14. Friends before marriage: many friends	4
15. Happiness of childhood: happy or very happy	4
16. Happiness of parents' marriage: happy or very happy	7
17. Married by: clergyman	4
18. Mental ability: equal	4
19. Occupation: professional	4
20. Organizations: member of some	4
21. Parents' attitude toward mate: approval	6
22. Savings: some	4
23. Sex instruction: adequate	4
24. Sex, source of information: parents	4
25. Sex relations, premarital: none or only with future spouse	8
26. Sunday school attendance: some and beyond childhood	5

* From Burgess, Locke, and Thomes (1963, pp. 318–319) (slightly modified).

childhood as warm and happy are likely to report our marriage as happy too. Of course, some of us may be "set" to take a bright or dim view of things, and this could make the connection between early and later events seem greater than it really is.

Parents' Marriage Happiness

Happiness seems to run in families. A number of investigators have noted that those who recall and report their parents as happily married are more likely to report themselves as happily married too. If one's parents were unhappy, personal chances for marriage happiness are not so great (Burgess et al., 1963; Kirkpatrick, 1963).

Divorce appears to run in families too. Persons from homes broken by divorce have a higher divorce rate than those who came from unbroken homes. When a large group of college students reported the marital status of their grandparents, parents, and uncles and aunts, it was found that if both sets of grandparents stayed married, the ratio of divorce to nondivorce in the next generation was only 1 to 6.8; with one set of grandparents divorced, the ratio rose to 1 to 4.2; and with both sets of grandparents divorced, the ratio was 1 to 2.6 (Landis, 1956). And information produced in a later survey of a large and heterogeneous urban population led to the conclusion that "divorce, separation, and desertion by the parents more than doubles the probability that the children will also become divorced or separated" (Langner & Michael, 1963, p. 164).

Childhood Happiness

Happiness seems to run in lifetimes. At least, those of us who remember our childhood as happy are more likely to think of our marriage as happy and successful too. An unhappy childhood seems to lessen the chances for happiness later on (Burgess et al., 1963; Kirkpatrick, 1963).

Of course, if our parents were not happy in their marriage and if our home was broken by divorce, it is less likely that we found childhood a happy time. Divorce can be a traumatic event, bringing radically changed living conditions, painful reassessments of parents, and difficult redefinitions of relationships. Still, some children whose homes were particularly tense and conflict-ridden places, find greater personal happiness following their parents' divorce (Landis, 1960b).

Attachment to Parents

There appears to be a significant relationship between attachment to parents and success in marriage. The closer we are to our parents (both in childhood and adulthood), the closer we are to our mates. Those of us who report warm attachments to parents also identify our marriages as happier and more successful (Burgess et al., 1963; Kirkpatrick, 1963).

There also appears to be an interesting relationship between our closeness to our parents and *their* happiness in marriage. The happier we rate our parents' marriage, the closer we feel our relationship was to them. However, close attachments to mothers tend to be reported regardless of the success of the parental marriage, while close relationships with fathers tend to be reported only if the parents' marriage was happy (Landis, 1962; Wallin & Vollmer, 1953).

Why?

Why should our family backgrounds loom so large in our own marriages? Our childhoods are of salient importance in every stage and area of our lives. Happy, successful parents provide us with good models for identification and furnish us with calm secure environments in which to learn and grow. Healthy patterns of interaction built up in our home environment serve us well as we move out into the neighborhood, the school, and the larger world.

In a study involving college students it was found that students whose parents had happy marriages were more confident in their heterosexual relationships than students who were from unhappy homes. The former group of students saw themselves as more acceptable and attractive to others. They also had more active dating histories in junior high school, senior high school, and college (Landis, 1963).

In childhood and adolescence, we are continuously observing and participating in the interaction between our mother and father. Over the years we build up a set of attitudes and ideas about marriage (see Case Studies 16.1 and 16.2). If our parents' marriage is viewed as a happy one, it is likely that marriage will be considered a desirable and reachable goal for ourselves. However, if our parents' relationship was filled with discord, we are more likely to view marriage with alarm and caution (Landis, 1963; Langner & Michael, 1963; Wallin, 1954).

Bill R.'s present marriage is going on the rocks. He has been in various kinds of trouble since his father "drank himself to death." His parents separated about a year before that, having quarreled frequently. He was in his early teens at the time, and can't remember feeling anything about his father.

Now Bill's own marriage is going on the rocks. He and Jane had never been very sociable people. They only went out visiting seven times during eleven years of marriage. He was often given to crying spells of depression during which Jane comforted him. This behavior would alternate with periods when he would humiliate her verbally, and occasionally hit her. After he took up with another woman, Jane walked out on him. Now he is worried over the results of this separation on his child, and fears that it will all end in divorce. "My daughter is on her way to becoming neurotic—she'll develop problems just like mine if I'm not straightened out." His work is suffering. He feels he is going downhill, and that it's irreversible.

Bill senses that his fear of rejection has prompted him to withdraw from his wife and his child before they withdraw from him. This is the same defense he used when his parents separated, and when his father died. His bitter early experience with a broken home seems to have laid the groundwork for his own marital difficulties. He has had no model of stable family life as a guide. In fact, he has in part modeled his own marriage on his parents' marriage, which foundered when he was only a little older than his daughter now is.[1]

Case study 16.1   The influence of family background on marriage attitudes. (This material, edited and condensed, was written by a young woman, nineteen years old.)

My attitude toward marriage today is far different from what it was ten years ago. About a decade ago, I wanted to be strictly a career woman and an old maid. I believed marriage produced nothing but unhappiness and strife. Of course, I was rather young at the time to know about marriage, or even understand much about it, but my early experiences made a deep imprint upon my thinking. I had some definite ideas about the trials and tribulations of marriage and had no

[1] Reprinted with permission of the publisher from *Life Stress and Mental Health.* By T. S. Langner and S. T. Michael. Copyright © 1963 by The Free Press, a Corporation. P. 166.

inkling that I could be mistaken. When I was three, I remember getting up several times in the middle of the night to hear noises and the sound of my parents' voices as they engaged in heated arguments. My father used to drink a great deal and used to come home drunk, to the distress of my mother. Sometimes he even used to strike her, and she would then come to bed crying. Somehow, I sensed the deep chasm between them. He died when I was four, and I felt lonesome, but also relieved since it was no longer necessary for me to close my eyes and ears to shut out the loud bickerings and "ugly" sounds. As I grew up, I felt, What's the sense of being married if fathers hit mothers and make life miserable for them? Also, I wondered why my father would leave us so that my poor hard-working mother would have to bring four children up by herself, for I saw my mother suffer for five long years. Then and there, I vowed that I would never be married and go through all the suffering she went through and lead an unhappy life. When I remembered the past, the idea that marriage would be an undesirable activity obsessed me. This is the attitude I bore when my mother remarried ten years ago.

Before their marriage, I begged and cried to keep my mother from remarrying. My new father was a widower without children. I thought that he would be just like my natural father and that he would bring suffering to my mother and us children. My sisters and brothers took to him immediately, but I was rather hostile. Sometimes when my parents used to argue in our presence, I used to feel "hate" for him, and memories flowed back as I felt sure he would strike her at any moment. How many times I was surprised when he didn't lift his arm, and in a few minutes they were talking peacefully!

With the passing of time, I saw this marriage grow into a deep and loving one. There was true devotion between my parents, and I was perplexed. Why, my new father never hit my mother, never came home drunk, and never argued much. They worked together in neighborhood and church activities. They confided in each other and helped each other out. Despite their work, they didn't fail to take us out and show us a good time. Yes, as time went by, they became closer and closer, and we all became a happier family.

Now it was my time to think and wonder if my views about marriage were correct. I was seeing two marriages, both in my eyes, extreme cases. What to do? One day I finally asked my mother about her two marriages and told her how puzzled I was, as I felt all marriages were bad. My mother told me firmly that my attitude was completely wrong. Perhaps her first marriage was not very successful, but my father was not bad. He had his faults, like everyone else, but many things were due to her own faults. She said everyone has fights in marriage, but that doesn't mean that they are unhappy. My mother pointed out that her present marriage was probably so successful because she had learned from her past mistakes.

After several similar conversations and through my own observations, my attitude changed. My negative feelings toward marriage were changed into ambivalence, and then into positive feelings. I had seen and experienced two marriages. I saw the first one in a different light, and I appreciated the second one even more. My wish for the future is that I can be as good and wise a wife as my mother is.

Case study 16.2 The influence of family background on marriage attitudes. (This material, edited and condensed, was written by a man, twenty-two years old.)

My fiancée doesn't know it yet, but I'm afraid of getting married. It may sound ludicrous when put down on paper—as indeed most emotional problems seem ludicrous to those reading about them—but I'm afraid of getting married to such an extent that whenever my fiancée suggests I set a definite date for our marriage, I utilize every ounce of my intellectual faculties to evade the issue. I look forward to having a home and family of my own, and I am positive after a year or so of assimilating and weighing the facts that I love my fiancée as much as is possible; yet I still cannot take the final plunge into matrimony. My reason or adult mind tells me to go ahead, but my emotions somehow cannot seem to agree with my reason. I find myself yearning to get married and edging away from it at the same time, and because I experience these positive and negative feelings concomitly, I don't move in any direction at all, but remain riveted to my bachelor status. If this keeps up I might not get married at all.

I suppose my conflict stems from my experience with my parents' marriage. Although they are more happily married now, I can remember when their marriage wasn't so successful. My father used to drink quite heavily, and would come home drunk almost every night. He would spend all the paycheck on liquor, so my mother had a difficult time making ends meet. When she chided him for drinking to the extent of neglecting his family, it inevitably initiated a heated argument between the two, which often left them surly for the remainder of the day. My mother felt bitter toward my father, for she picked on him often, telling him that she was ashamed of his drunkenness. My father would get angry with her and hit her. Often they would go for days without speaking a word to one another after an argument. Once my parents argued so violently that my mother packed some of her belongings and moved out of the house for two weeks. There were six children in our family—two boys and four girls—and I often heard my mother tell my sisters to be extremely careful whom they married, for if they were unfortunate enough to pick the wrong man, they would regret it for the rest of their lives. She said that one spent one's happiest days while single.

When I think back on my parents' marriage, I can remember only these arguments and battles, a houseful of children, and the reek of alcohol. My mother naturally had the hardest lot to bear in the household, and after putting up with my father's drunkenness through the years, and being brought with child so very often, her disposition began to sour quite definitely. She became cranky, faultfinding, and nervous. She would complain and nag about the smallest trifle. She never called attention to our misconduct in a quiet and calm voice, but shrilly yelled her grievances at us, jumping from one grievance to another till she'd be yelling and grumbling for hours. Her schedule was heavy with work, so she never had much time to devote to us, but expected us to be model children who never made any extra work for her. Whenever a toy was left on the floor, or the sink dirtied, we never heard the end of it.

I guess I grew up thinking of all marriages in terms of my parents' marriage, and even if I know that this is definitely untrue, that all marriages are different according to the individuals concerned, somehow I cannot seem to shake off this attitude. I begin to experience symptoms of anxiety whenever I am cornered into setting a definite date for my marriage. I find myself fabricating excuses for not getting married. There's the vague feeling at the back of my mind that the girl puts her best foot forward while you're dating and courting her, but the minute you marry her, she will suddenly drop all her pretenses and show her true colors—her fangs will protrude, saliva will drip, she will become quite a monster, etc. Though my parents' marriage is better now, I somehow cannot seem to shake the feeling that all marriages are doomed to be unhappy and sorrowful. So while I do want to get married, I cannot bring myself to take the final plunge.

Engagement Factors

Acquaintanceship and engagement provide a second important set of factors. The information from a number of studies suggests that engagements should be long rather than short, temperate rather than tempestuous, and, in addition, merit the approval of parents and friends.

Length of Acquaintanceship and Engagement

Common sense and research evidence agree: long acquaintanceships and long engagements are good omens. Those of us who know each other well are more likely to contract successful marriages than those who marry on brief acquaintance. Generally speaking, the longer and better the acquaintanceship, the better the chances for happiness in marriage (Burgess et al., 1963; Kirkpatrick, 1963).

Adjustment during Acquaintanceship and Engagement

Of course, acquaintanceships and engagements should be harmonious as well as lengthy. Those who make a successful adjustment before marriage are more likely to continue this adjustment after marriage (Burgess et al., 1963; Kirkpatrick, 1963). Marriage vows are sacred, but they are not magical; unsolved premarital problems remain to confront us after the wedding.

Approval by Parents and Friends

If parents approve of our marriage, chances for success are higher than if they disapprove. If friends approve, this is also a good sign. And if both parents and friends approve, the outlook is particularly favorable (Kirkpatrick, 1963).

Why?

Why are acquaintanceship and engagement factors of such importance? Dating and engagement activities serve vital premarital functions. Dating permits us to associate with a wide variety of possible mates and to pick and choose among them. Serious dating—going steady or courting—provides us with the opportunity to see whether we are paired with a person whose needs, attitudes, and values are compatible with our own. Engagement offers a final assessment period before the serious step of marriage.

Long periods of acquaintanceship and engagement give us the time we need to explore our relationship. We need time to know and interact with each other in many different situations and under many different conditions. We need time to differ and time enough to see if we can deal with our differences. We need time to grow into the relationship or time to grow out of it.

When parents and friends approve of our marriage, we are reassured that the decision is a wise one. Their knowledge of us and their greater detachment from the situation make their views well worth considering. And—if a person's family and friendship groupings are important to him —he will have a more difficult time if his spouse doesn't fit in.

Other Factors

Other factors associated with marriage adjustment and maladjustment include age, culture, religion, education, personality, and sex experience.

Age

Teen-age marriages have a relatively high rate of failure, and, generally speaking, marriages between persons in their twenties or late twenties are more hopeful than those of younger couples. It is also considered a good sign if the couple is of approximately the same age or if the man is slightly older (Burgess et al., 1963; Kirkpatrick, 1963).

Culture

Divorce and happiness rates vary from class to class and from subculture to subculture. In general, lower-class marriages are less happy than middle-class ones (Komarovsky, 1964). Marriages of people from considerably different backgrounds require more working at and have lower success rates (Barnett, 1963; Burgess et al., 1963; Cheng & Yamamura, 1957; Kirkpatrick, 1963).

Spouses in such marriages are more likely to have conflicting attitudes and values, and the couple may encounter ostracism and discrimination (Barnett, 1963). Still, each marriage and category of marriage must be considered on its own merits. In a study of marriage and divorce in Hawaii, for example, it was found that outmarriages involving Filipino-American women and Caucasian men had lower divorce rates than either Filipino or Caucasian inmarriages (Cheng & Yamamura, 1957).

Religion

Religiousness has been found to be positively correlated with marriage adjustment (Burgess et al., 1963; Kirkpatrick, 1963). In one study involving a large number of college students of varying faiths, the parental divorce rate in the nonreligious families was four times that of the devout ones (Landis, 1960a). Similarity in religious preference is also associated with marriage adjustment (Blood & Wolfe, 1960; Kirkpatrick, 1963; Levinger, 1965). Companionship, for example, is greater in couples who have a common interest in religion (Blood & Wolfe, 1960), and same-faith marriages are generally more durable than those of mixed faiths (Landis, 1949).

Education

Educational level is related to marriage adjustment. Marriages involving college graduates, for example, have lower divorce rates than those between couples who have gone no further than high school (Burgess et al., 1963; Kirkpatrick, 1963; Landis & Landis, 1963), and marriages between high school graduates are generally happier than those involving less-educated couples (Komarovsky, 1964). There is a little evidence that similar amounts of education are a favorable sign (Kirkpatrick, 1963); if there is a discrepancy in the amount of education between the spouses, it is probably better that this be in favor of the husband (Levinger, 1965).

Personality

Certain personality characteristics have been held to be positively associated with success in marriage. Adaptability, according to several investigators, is related to marriage success. Conventionality, that is, conventional behavior and values, has been found to be correlated with marriage happiness and cohesiveness. Sociability, as shown by number of friends and participation in social organizations before marriage, has also been found to be a good omen for later marital adjustment (Burgess et al., 1963). Of course, much depends upon the compatibility of the couple's needs, and this will be considered shortly.

Sex Experience

Those who report that they received frank and full sex information from parents also tend to report more successful marriage adjustments. A number of investigators have been interested in the relationship between premarital intercourse and later adjustment in marriage. Generally speaking, persons reporting little or no intercourse before marriage report better marital adjustment, but the relationships have been low and, when the intercourse has been restricted to one's future spouse, nearly negligible (Burgess et al., 1963; Kirkpatrick, 1963).

UNDERSTANDING MARRIAGE ADJUSTMENT

What factors are involved in marital adjustment and maladjustment? One useful focus is on the marriage needs of the couple. Are their needs compatible? Are they met? A second useful focus is on the images that each spouse has of himself and his mate and other people who may be involved in the marriage interaction. Does each spouse see himself as his mate sees him? And how do the spouses see themselves—in a happy or unhappy light? A third useful focus is on the roles which the spouses expect to play in marriage and the roles they actually find themselves playing. How much discrepancy is there between expectation and actuality? And what do the spouses do about it?

Need Factors

Our goal-seeking behavior involves people. People are our goals, and people help us reach our goals. We need people to love and to be loved by. We need people whom we can nurture or who will nurture us and whom we can dominate or defer to.

We form close ties with people who help us meet our needs. We feel affection for such people. We like them. We love them. And, under certain conditions, we fall in love with them.

Love, according to Winch (1963), a prominent theoretician in the field of marriage, is firmly rooted in needs. No romanticist, he writes that love is the positive emotion which one person feels for a second person who (1) meets certain highly important needs of the first and/or (2) manifests (or seems to manifest) certain personal qualities highly valued by the first. Since these personal qualities are, in a sense, "needed" ones, the entire definition of love is based on need and need satisfaction.

Some supporting evidence for this approach was obtained in a study of engaged and newly married persons. Each was asked to describe his major needs and to indicate the extent to which these needs had been satisfied by his mate and by other persons. The very large majority of respondents reported that their mates had satisfied their needs more completely than anyone else; very few reported that some person other than their mate had satisfied their needs better (Strauss, 1947).

It has been pointed out that a person does not look to his mate to meet all his needs—just those needs which are specific to marriage (Tharp, 1963b). For example, although we are rather deferent in many situations, we may expect to be dominant in our marriage. And although we are not generally very succorant, we may very much want a home filled with warmth and nurturance.

Sources of Conflict

Problems arise in a marriage when the need patterns of the spouses are incompatible or when they become so with the passing years.

Incompatible Need Patterns   We look for a mate who shows some promise of meeting our marriage needs. It may be a person who has some needs which are very much like our own. For example, if our sex needs are high, we will be better off married to a person who shares our sex interest and drive. If we have a high need for achievement, a spouse who understands, shares, and abets our ambitions will make for a happy alliance.

On the other hand, we require a person who has some need patterns which complement rather than duplicate our own (Winch, 1963). For example, if we want to be the undisputed boss of the household, we are better off married to a person who enjoys our authority and leadership. If we are a very nurturant person, we will appreciate a spouse who likes to be mothered or babied.

Conflict occurs when the need patterns of the spouses are not compatible. It may be because need patterns which ought to be similar are not. When one spouse is ambitious and the other is not or when one seeks excitement and change and the other prefers the familiar, there will be some adjusting to do. Even when spouses appear to share general need patterns, problems arise because of the specific bits of behavior which each prefers; for example, most people need a certain amount of order in their homes and their lives, but a couple may have very different ideas on what *must* be orderly and what just does not matter.

Conflict also occurs when need patterns which ought to be different prove to be the same. Sometimes a battle rages over who will be boss. Who gets crowned when both spouses want to be king? Or who takes the responsibility when two dependent individuals marry? And what happens when two aggressive, hostile people pair?

Changing Need Patterns People grow and change. Sometimes they grow together. Probably we have had occasion to remark on how similar a particular couple have

become since they married. And the couple themselves may be astounded to find that they have the same thoughts and sometimes even say the same things at the same time.

Sometimes the couple grow apart. As they grow older, as the husband becomes captive to a job, as the wife becomes increasingly occupied with her family, each may change without knowing it. A man who depended upon his wife's emotional and financial support while he was completing his education may become increasingly independent of her as he becomes established in his occupation, and this may be a source of considerable unhappiness to his mate. Or perhaps it is the other way around: a husband finds to his considerable frustration that his wife's attention and affection are being increasingly removed from him to his expanding family.

Winch reports that need patterns are likely to change with changing socioeconomic status. And, says he, "Modifications in need-patterns seem particularly evident in people who emerge from humble origins to positions of fame and eminence" (1963, p. 675). He writes:

Such seems to have been the story of the marriage of Sinclair Lewis and Grace Hegger as reported in the caustic accounts of both: his Dodsworth, and her Half a Loaf and With Love from Gracie. At the time of their meeting Sinclair Lewis admired Grace Hegger's cosmopolitanism. She states that in their early relationship he tended to regard her as a Princess of Faraway and himself as a sort of court jester. Her idea of a man who could sweep her off her feet had been a decorated and haughty ambassador. This sounds like an idealized version of her father, a traveled and sophisticated art dealer. Then why did she marry the awkward, homely, *"penniless publisher's editor with one un-accepted novel"? "I married him because he touched my heart and delighted my brain." And at another point: ". . . no other man had ever made me feel so tenderly possessive." In her fictional account of their relationship she indicates that her wedding day was less thrilling than the day she won her major promotion at Vogue magazine. She points out that from Mr. Wrenn to Dodsworth Lewis's heroes "either married ladies" or made efforts to adjust themselves to the social standards of the ladies they admired. In other words, both Lewis and his heroes were attracted to women of higher social status who observed social amenities rather unknown to the men. Moreover, she observes that the "resentments and personal inadequacies" of Sam Dodsworth "were really those of Sinclair Lewis."*

Their final parting was apparently initiated by Lewis. According to Grace Hegger his statement was to the effect that he loved her more than anyone else but that she had become "extraordinarily bullying," that she had deprived him of "self government," and that he wished no more to ask her permission, to await her plans, or to resent her orders. Lewis was perpetually animated by wanderlust, and his wife began to wish to sink roots. She feels that probably she imposed this need for security and routine on her restless husband, and that her importuning undoubtedly "made him even more restless and eager to escape." She concludes her account of their relationship by observing that through it "he experienced an interval of domestic security indispensable to his development, though in the later years he called it tyranny" (1958, pp. 302–303).

Sex Factors

For most adults, sexual intercourse with one's spouse is the chief mode of sexual expression. Before we marry, our sex needs may be frustrated or inadequately met, but marriage provides an approved and convenient way of satisfying sex desires. Consequently, sex is an important part of marriage.

A number of researchers have found that sexual adjustment and marriage adjustment tend to go together (Burgess & Wallin, 1953; Komarovsky, 1964; Terman, 1938). Those who make good sexual adjustments in marriage tend to adjust in other marital areas as well. Or it can be put the other way around, those who make a good general adjustment to marriage tend to make a good sexual adjustment too.

But which way around is it? Can sexual satisfaction or dissatisfaction override other considerations to create a successful or unsuccessful marriage? Can other considerations override sexual adjustment? Although sex is an important factor, it is only one of a number of factors involved in marriage. The various factors are so interwoven that it is difficult to separate and measure the contribution of each.

Where the remainder of the marriage interaction is satisfactory and where other needs are adequately met, it is likely that the sex relationship will also be a good one. But where there are conflicts in other areas, with accompanying tension and hostility, the sex relationship is likely to suffer as well (Burgess & Wallin, 1953). Still, it should be noted that some very unhappy couples have been found to have excellent sexual adjustments while other couples appear happily married despite their maladjusted sex life (Komarovsky, 1964).

Sources of Conflict

Some of the most important sources of sex conflict in a marriage concern spouse differences in sex attitudes, needs, arousability, and satisfaction.

Differences in Sex Attitudes   Early sex activities may be frustrated and punished, and children can develop the attitude that sex is bad or hazardous. Since parents may be especially concerned about their daughters and go to great lengths to ensure their "good" conduct, strong negative attitudes toward sex may be built up in young women.

Less-inhibited and with a wider experience, the male may not understand the fears of his wife, her hesitancy in the sexual situation, or her inability to release herself completely. Inexpert himself in such matters, he may give his wife a first impression of sexual intercourse which serves to vali-

Figure 16.1 "Before marriage was your general attitude toward sex one of disgust and aversion, indifference, interest and pleasant anticipation, or eager, passionate longing?"

This item was included in a questionnaire administered to 598 couples. Their answers provide information concerning some differences in premarital sex attitudes of husbands and wives. Attitudes of husbands were considerably more favorable than those of wives. About one female in every four regarded sex with disgust and aversion or indifference (From *Engagement and Marriage* by Ernest W. Burgess and Paul Wallin. Copyright, 1953, by Ernest W. Burgess and Paul Wallin. Published by J. B. Lippincott Company).

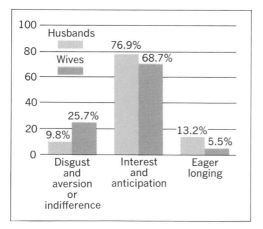

date her worst assumptions. Consequently, this lack of appreciation for each other's attitudes may prevent successful sex adjustment (see Fig. 16.1).

The following excerpts are taken from interviews with wives who have been married three to five years. The excerpts provide examples of a wide variety of attitudes toward sex. They range from the highly negative to the strongly positive, from rejection and aversion through resignation to great affirmation.

Wife: I do not feel I've achieved good sex adjustment. I have orgasm sometimes. I I am by no means warm and do not particularly enjoy it and am just as glad not to be bothered by it. There seems to be something bestial about it. I would prefer marriage without it.

Wife: I did find the sex adjustment rather difficult. I did not like the physical aspects. It seemed animal-like. I don't care especially for sex relations. I wouldn't miss sex if it was removed from marriage.

Wife: My husband desires intercourse much more frequently but has never made an issue of it. It doesn't make me unhappy. It's just that I still don't feel very happy about it, but perhaps it's more or less necessary. I have more or less resigned myself to it. At times my attitude makes him unhappy. I feel resigned to it and can't plan on it. There are some things we have to put up with and to me that is one of them. I've never thought of it as anything but a necessary evil. Somehow it seems to me distasteful. I'd just as soon do without it. I'd be just as happy.

Wife: Sex relations were distasteful to begin with. That lasted about a year. I don't know what happened, but I became adjusted. I wasn't sure whether I was in love with my husband, a few months after that I felt definitely in love. We never quarrelled; perhaps the sexual side of marriage got me down. I now have orgasm all of the time. But you could take sex out of marriage and it wouldn't make any difference to me. It doesn't bother me one way or the other. You might call me cold-blooded, I guess.

Wife: *Although I seldom have a very strong sex desire I feel that the closeness of sex relations—a relation you have with nobody else—is a bond and a very strong one. It's like if a man is unfaithful to his wife; it's not the physical relation that matters so much but that the close bond is gone. The thing you have with no one else is gone.*

Wife: *The sexual adjustment was not difficult with me. It has been a very satisfactory comfortable relationship. It is important, but important chiefly as an outlet for tensions, for so many things you can't express to each other except through liking each other that way.*

Wife: *It would make quite a bit of difference to me if sex were taken out of marriage. I think it is the only way, the only complete way of demonstrating your affection for a person and I would feel pretty deprived if I could not express my affection for my husband in that way, because I would feel that any other expression would be inadequate.*

Wife: *Sex is very important. It gives a feeling of unity that cannot be achieved otherwise. It is the completion of love and it is more than physical.*

Wife: *I think sexual intercourse is the bulwark of marriage and that marriage gains significance through the sexual act. It is hard to think of marriage without sex relations.*[2]

Differences in Sex Needs   Differences in the strength of sex need may be a source of difficulty in marriage. There is some evidence to indicate that in the early years of marriage husbands tend to be more passionate and desire intercourse more frequently than their wives. Furthermore,

wives are more likely than husbands to refuse to have intercourse when their spouses desire it (Burgess & Wallin, 1953) (see Fig. 16.2).

In young couples, the husband may want frequent intercourse at the time that his wife is just freeing herself from her inhibitions and developing responsiveness. Over the years, however, the sex desires of the female in marriage tend to develop while those of the male may decline due to aging, or earlier disagreements, or, especially in the more highly educated male, to extramarital relations. Consequently, in the early years of marriage, the male expresses a desire for more and the female

Figure 16.2 "About how many times *per month* would you prefer to have sexual intercourse?"

Here are the responses of 577 husbands and 562 wives who were married three to five years. An indicated, husbands desired more intercourse than wives. More husbands than wives report a preference for sex relations nine or more times monthly, while more wives than husbands would prefer to limit intercourse to four times a month or less (From *Engagement and Marriage* by Ernest W. Burgess and Paul Wallin. Copyright, 1953, by Ernest W. Burgess and Paul Wallin. Published by J. B. Lippincott Company).

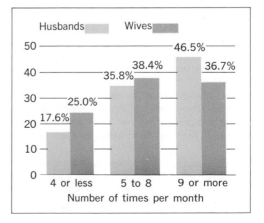

[2] From *Engagement and Marriage* by Ernest W. Burgess and Paul Wallin. Copyright, 1953, by Ernest W. Burgess and Paul Wallin. Published by J. B. Lippincott Company. Pp. 683–687 passim.

for less intercourse than that sought by the spouse. But in the later years of marriage many wives report a desire for more intercourse than that desired by their husbands (Kinsey, Pomeroy, Martin, & Gebhard, 1953).

Here are two excerpts from interviews with husbands who have had to compromise their sex drive:

Husband: One of the biggest adjustments we had to make was in sex urge. Naturally we had to compromise. I would not put that as a difficult adjustment to make. I think I have a great deal more sex drive than my wife and that involved compromising, if you want to call it that. That was mainly in frequency of sexual intercourse.

   Husband: At all times since we began to have intercourse I have had the desire for more frequent intercourse. She enjoys it as much as I when she wants it, but she wants it less frequently. I have developed the only sane and sensible attitude possible. I don't importune her for intercourse when I know she doesn't want it.[3]

And here, to present the other side of the story, are brief accounts of sexual maladjustment caused by the greater sex needs of the wife. (In both cases, the marriages were considered generally successful.)

An attractive 23-year-old high school graduate, married for five years and a mother of three infants, spoke sadly about the declining interest of her 26-year-old husband in sexual relations: "You have to go and sit on his lap before he would show any affection. A couple of weeks or more pass before he takes any notice of me. I don't want to wait long enough to find out." She talked to him and he said, "Well, that's just the way I am." The young wife is resigned: "He is just not that much of a lover."

   In another case, two young high school graduates, married for three years and parents of one child, describe themselves as extremely happy. But the husband often comes home so tired that he can hardly wait to get to sleep. She doesn't "have the heart to ask him to make love when he needs his rest." They talked about this and he said that, being around the house all day, she "worked up a lot of energy," and that they "must do something about it," but so far they have found no solution.[4]

Differences in Sex Arousal   Some of the reported differences in sex drive and satisfaction between males and females may actually be attributable to differences in sex arousal. Responding to psychological as well as physiological stimuli, the male is more easily aroused than the female, and he reaches orgasm more quickly. Kinsey states, "For perhaps three-quarters of all males, orgasm is reached within two minutes after the initiation of the sexual relation, and for a not inconsiderable number of males the climax may be reached within less than a minute or even within ten or twenty seconds after coital entrance" (Kinsey, Pomeroy, & Martin, 1948, p. 580).

   The speed of the female in reaching orgasm in masturbation is almost equal to that of the male, and her slower response in intercourse is not due to any innate incapacity. However, in intercourse the female is less aroused by psychological stimuli than the male and does not make the same anticipatory response. She is primarily dependent upon continuous physical

[3] From Engagement and Marriage by Ernest W. Burgess and Paul Wallin. Copyright, 1953, by Ernest W. Burgess and Paul Wallin. Published by J. B. Lippincott Company. Pp. 667–668 passim.

[4] From Blue-Collar Marriage by Mirra Komarovsky. © Copyright 1964 by Random House Inc. Reprinted by permission. P. 87.

stimulation, and when for any reason physical contact is interrupted, the buildup of her response must begin again (Kinsey et al., 1953).

Because of the difference in sex arousal, a number of authorities have emphasized the necessity of proper timing in intercourse. It is important that the male recognize the discrepancy in readiness and that he delay his own response until his wife has been sufficiently prepared. Commonly, there should be a good deal of foreplay with a slow but continual buildup until the female's response begins to approach that of her spouse.

The difference in the speed of sex arousal between males and females frequently causes conflict in marriage (Kinsey et al., 1948). Terman (1938) reported on the unsatisfactory aspects of sexual intercourse checked by 300 happily married and 150 unhappily married husbands and wives. Two of the most frequent complaints of both unhappy and happy wives concerned the facts that their husbands did not pet enough before beginning intercourse and that their husbands ejaculated too quickly. Furthermore, it is noteworthy that about 39 per cent of the unhappy wives made the first complaint as compared with only 23 percent of the happy ones, and 42 percent of the unhappy wives made the second complaint compared with only 9 percent of those who were happy.

The following excerpts from interviews with young wives illustrate the problem caused by differences in the rate of sex arousal (and, in several cases, indicate some resolutions which have been reached):

Wife: *My husband is faster than I am usually, so I don't get orgasm. The fact that he desires intercourse so often is one of the difficulties in our marriage. If that would be satisfactory there would not be any difficulty at all. I feel tired and irritable and don't desire intercourse and then, too, for the reason that I am not always as satisfied as he. It becomes a circle.*

Wife: *The greatest problem was that at first I didn't get aroused easily or get any special feeling in intercourse. I worried about this until I found my friends were the same way. This has improved. I now have orgasm about once every five times. At first this feeling came very seldom, then gradually more. I'm hard to arouse.*

Wife: *I don't have orgasm all the time. When I don't there's no frustration. I have it 75 per cent of the time. My husband desires intercourse more frequently, but I've never refused him. He is very affectionate and this is a greater source of satisfaction than the sheer sensation itself. I'm slower in reaching an orgasm, but he's patient. I'm not like some women that can't tolerate their husbands, but I can take it or leave it. Intercourse is a beautiful thing if it can create a child in the image of yourself and husband.*

Wife: *There was some pain at the start and that's all. I think I have an excellent husband because I have known so many girls that turned frigid after marriage because their husbands were impatient. The fact that my husband is so considerate makes living together so much easier. If I feel my husband wants physical satisfaction I go through it because I think it is the least I can do for him. He is very thoughtful and I almost always have orgasm.*[5]

Differences in Sex Satisfaction   Husbands report greater relief of sexual desire from intercourse, and they are more likely to achieve orgasm than wives. However, husbands have been found to be less satisfied

[5] From *Engagement and Marriage* by Ernest W. Burgess and Paul Wallin. Copyright, 1953, by Ernest W. Burgess and Paul Wallin. Published by J. B. Lippincott Company. Pp. 683–686, passim.

with marital sex relations, and they are more likely to complain about such relations (Burgess & Wallin, 1953; Terman, 1938). Although these findings appear to be contradictory, it has been suggested that wives are more content because they expect less satisfaction and are content with less; husbands expect more satisfaction and are critical if this satisfaction is not forthcoming (Burgess & Wallin, 1953).

Although orgasm cannot be considered the sole index of satisfaction in intercourse, it can serve as a specific measure. Kinsey and his associates (1953) found that, on the average, the females they studied reached orgasm in marital coitus about three-fourths of the time. However, orgasm was related to the length of marriage, so that up to a certain point at least, the female experiences increasing satisfaction in intercourse. The findings were as follow:

Year of Marriage	Percent of Coitus Resulting in Orgasm
First	63
Fifth	71
Tenth	77
Fifteenth	81
Twentieth	85

Here are some excerpts from interviews with husbands who express concern about satisfaction differences in their marriage:

Husband: *I have a sense of guilt when I have relations with her and feel she does not enjoy them as much as I do. The fact that she's not getting orgasm takes the pleasure of intercourse away from me.*

Husband: *I'm much more conscious than my wife of the fact that I want intercourse more than she. It worries me in a way because a lot more satisfaction is achieved by me than by her. I wonder if males are exactly square about the whole thing.*

Husband: *I wouldn't say my wife dislikes intercourse. She likes it, but it is the after effects that come because she does not get anything out of it. It makes me feel bad that she doesn't. Otherwise it would be complete, if she would get something out of it.*

Husband: *I would prefer her sex desire to be stronger. We don't have any trouble. The only trouble that ever comes up is for her not to have orgasm. I don't know whether it's her fault or mine but it is not very satisfying to me either when I know she is not satisfied. I don't enjoy it either and I can always tell.*

Husband: *My wife gets a lot more out of intercourse now than she did before. I feel much better about it now that she gets satisfaction too.*[6]

Self Factors

A person's perception of himself, his spouse, and of other people bears an important relationship to his marriage happiness. The perceptions of happy spouses and of unhappy spouses tend to be quite different.

First of all, two earlier definitions should be recalled.[7] The *subjective self* is the person's private view of himself; it is what he thinks himself to be. The *ideal self* is the self he would like to be; it is what he would like to become.

There is some evidence that those who are successfully married have fairly congruent subjective and ideal selves. That is, they see themselves as not too different from what they want to be. On the other hand, less successfully married persons

[6] From *Engagement and Marriage* by Ernest W. Burgess and Paul Wallin. Copyright, 1953, by Ernest W. Burgess and Paul Wallin. Published by J. B. Lippincott Co. P. 671.
[7] See pp. 217–219.

show a greater discrepancy between these several self-concepts (Eastman, 1958; Luckey, 1960a).

Interestingly enough, the husband's self-other concepts appear more important to the success of a marriage than are the wife's. It has been found that in happy marriages the husband tends to see himself in about the same way that his wife sees him. Furthermore, in such marriages the husband tends to see himself in much the same way as he sees his father. And, to add more of interest, the wife tends to see her husband in much the same way that she sees *her* father (Luckey, 1960a, 1960b, 1961). After reviewing the evidence, one researcher writes, "It seems, therefore, that the maximally happy marital situation can be described as follows: husband and wife agree that he is as *he* wishes to be, namely, like his father, and as *she* wishes him to be, namely, like her's" (Tharp, 1963b, pp. 101–102).

In a study of eighty couples (see Fig. 16.3) it was found that satisfied spouses took a happy view of their mates; unsatisfied spouses took a dim one. Happy spouses saw their mates as having positive, moderate qualities while unhappy spouses attributed negative, extreme, or intense qualities to their mates. For example, happily married persons described their mates as responsible, conventional, generous, cooperative, and neither very modest nor very managerial. On the other hand, unhappily married persons saw their mates as blunt, aggressive, distrustful, and either too passive or too dictatorial (Luckey, 1964).

Sources of Conflict

Some of marriage's stormy weather is brewed by spouses who are unable to accept themselves (or others) and by spouses who do not see themselves as their mates see them.

Discrepancy between Subjective Self and Ideal Self   People who accept themselves are more likely to be accepting of others. And people who accept themselves are more likely to accept their spouses and report that they are happily married (Luckey, 1960a).

Why should this be so? Are people more happy in marriage because they accept themselves? Or do they accept themselves (and each other) because they are happy in marriage? Self-acceptance and marital happiness seem thoroughly interwoven, each having an effect on the other, and both, in turn, are influenced by early experiences (Eastman, 1958). Happy childhoods make for greater happiness with oneself and others and greater happiness in marriage.

Self-rejection can be a two-edged sword. Sometimes a self-rejecting person may strike out at himself; sometimes at others. Nothing he does may be good enough to please himself, and nothing others do may be good enough either.

If a person falls far below his ideal, he may look for a mate who will compensate for his deficiencies. He will want his mate to have the qualities he lacks or have other qualities to make up for them. In this predicament, he may never find a mate to suit him or, if he does, overexpectations and demands will place a heavy burden on his spouse.

Discrepancy between Subjective Self and Self as Seen by Spouse   It has been hypothesized that in happy marriages each spouse tends to see himself as his spouse sees him (Luckey, 1960b; Mangus, 1957a, 1957b). Our behavior depends to some

Descriptive phrases (arranged by general category)

<table>
<tr><td>More used by unhappy spouses</td><td></td></tr>
<tr><td>More used by happy spouses</td><td></td></tr>
<tr><td>No difference</td><td></td></tr>
</table>

I. Managerial-Autocratic

1. Well thought of; often admired	H	
2. Makes a good impression; respected by others	H	
3. Able to give orders, good leader	H	
4. Forceful; likes responsibility	ND	
5. Always giving advice; tries to be too successful		U
6. Acts important; expects everyone to admire him		U
7. Bossy; manages others		U
8. Dominating; dictatorial		U

II. Competitive-Exploitive

9. Self-respecting; self-confident	H	
10. Independent; self-reliant and assertive	H	
11. Able to take care of self; businesslike	ND	
12. Can be indifferent to others; likes to compete	ND	
13. Boastful; somewhat snobbish		U
14. Proud and self-satisfied; egotistical and conceited	ND	
15. Thinks only of self; selfish		U
16. Shrewd and calculating; cold and unfeeling		U

III. Blunt-Aggressive

17. Can be strict; hard-boiled when necessary	ND	
18. Firm but just; stern but fair	H	
19. Can be frank and honest; irritable	ND	
20. Critical of others; straightforward, direct	ND	

<table>
<tr><td>More used by unhappy spouses</td><td></td></tr>
<tr><td>More used by happy spouses</td><td></td></tr>
<tr><td>No difference</td><td></td></tr>
</table>

21. Impatient with others' mistakes; sarcastic		U
22. Self-seeking; cruel and unkind		U
23. Outspoken; frequently angry		U
24. Often unfriendly; hardhearted		U

IV. Skeptical-Distrusting

25. Can complain if necessary; resents being bossed	ND	
26. Often gloomy; skeptical		U
27. Able to doubt others; hard to impress	ND	
28. Frequently disappointed; touchy, easily hurt		U
29. Bitter; resentful		U
30. Complaining; rebels against everything		U
31. Jealous; stubborn		U
32. Slow to forgive; distrusts everybody		U

V. Modest-Self-Effacing

33. Able to criticize self; easily embarrassed	H	
34. Apologetic; lacks self-confidence	ND	
35. Can be obedient; easily led	H	
36. Usually gives in; modest	ND	
37. Self-punishing; timid		U
38. Shy; always ashamed of self		U
39. Passive; unaggressive; obeys too willingly		U
40. Meek; spineless	ND	

extent on how we see ourselves and our environment. Spouses who agree in their perceptions are in better communication. They understand each other, know what to expect of each other, and are able to mesh their behavior (Luckey, 1960b).

It is especially important that the member of the couple who has to do the more adjusting see the other as the other sees himself. Luckey, who intensively studied the topic, says that ". . . if it is the wife who does the adjusting, it is to the benefit of the relationship if she knows what she's adjusting to! If she sees the husband as he sees himself, she is better able to make adjustments which bring more satisfaction to the marriage" (1960b, pp. 156–157).

Unhappy couples are frequently characterized by mutual disparagement. Each partner depreciates the other. At the same time, a spouse (perhaps in self-defense) may overappreciate himself or herself. As a result, there is considerable discrepancy between the self-other perceptions of the spouses.

Role Factors[8]

A *role* is the behavior associated with a particular position in a group. It is sometimes helpful to make a further distinction between role expectation and role percep-

[8] This discussion was stimulated by and borrows from several papers of Mangus (1957a, 1957b) and Tharp (1963a, 1963b).

Figure 16.3 How do happily married and unhappily married spouses describe their mates? Eighty married couples rated their own marriage satisfaction and described their spouses by checking descriptive phrases on a list. Here are the phrases along with indications of those more used by each group of spouses in describing their mates (Modified from Luckey, 1964).

tion. A *role expectation* is the behavior which society or a particular person expects or hopes will be associated with a particular position. A *role perception* is the behavior which is perceived or seen to occur.

Society's role expectations change from generation to generation. Traditionally, the husband and wife have played quite different roles in marriage. These days the roles are not so exactly divided. More women have become breadwinners and decision makers. More men participate in housekeeping and children-raising activities.

An individual's role expectations may vary considerably from those generally held by society (W. G. Dyer, 1962). Whatever they are, by the time he reaches adolescence and adulthood, he has some definite expectations about the roles of husband and wife. These expectations may be explicit and spelled-out or they may be implicit and not well understood. Still, they exert a powerful influence on dating, courtship, and marriage behavior.

Many of us look forward to marriage. Some of us do not. The ideas we have about ourselves and about marriage may make us apprehensive or, at best, ambivalent about assuming marriage roles.

Sources of Conflict

Role discrepancies are a source of considerable trouble in marriage. Spouses differ in what they expect of themselves. And they differ in what they perceive in themselves.

Discrepancy between Role Expectations What do the spouses expect of themselves in marriage? What do they expect of each other? Do they agree on the role a wife should play? Do they agree on the role a husband should play? Shared role expectations are associated with harmony and happiness in marriage.

Some couples prove to have very different role expectations. The wife, perhaps, decides that she would like to continue working and delay having children at least for awhile. To her husband, this may be unthinkable. To him, the purpose of marriage is to raise a family, and, says he, "A wife's place is in the home!"

The husband, perhaps, looks forward to getting the special treatment that his mother accorded his father. He sits and waits to be waited on. His wife is incredulous. In *her* family, everybody pitched in and her dad was the best cook and housekeeper in the bunch. "Wait on yourself," she says. "I'm not your slave."

Here is an interviewer's account of role-expectation conflict in a couple who have been married seven years and who have three children. The husband is a taxi driver, the wife works part time, and the marriage is a generally happy one despite differences in expectation.

"He doesn't want me to work at all," said the wife. Her husband nodded. "He's against it, but I got to do it because we got to have enough money to eat and dress and it isn't just the rent and the food we have to have. It's to keep on going and to get places. He works harder than most people and I work real hard too. But we still have to have more money coming in. We want to have another baby in a year or two and we have to save up for that too. We want to start him in his business and not be stuck this way for the rest of our lives. But he doesn't like me to work at all. He thinks kids should have their own mothers around. He thinks nobody can love them the way we can. He ain't proud about my working like some men are, no sirree. It's just that he thinks the kids really need us." At that

the husband said firmly: "That's right. It's just like she says. If I can get the work the way I've been doing, you'll never have to go out and work again." "But, hon, I like to go out and do some work sometimes. It's nice for a change, and I like to think I'm bringing in some money too. We could buy our house sooner and get you set up sooner if we could just get some more money quicker." "If you feel that way about it," said the man, "We'll borrow money." But the wife countered that she doesn't believe in borrowing if they can possibly make it themselves. She was then told by her husband that their plan to use his friend's capital was after all a form of borrowing.[9]

Discrepancy between Role Perceptions How do the spouses perceive each other? What roles do they see themselves playing? What qualities do they see in themselves? Shared role perceptions, like shared role expectations, are associated with marriage success.

Some couples seem to agree on nothing. Their role expectations are different, and their role perceptions are at variance too. However, it is possible for a couple to share role expectations (likely, the society's stereotypes), but disagree on whether or not these roles are being enacted.

For example, the couple agree that the husband should be the provider and that the wife's place is in the home. And he is, says he, a good provider; they have a nice home and a nice car. What more does she want? There's a mortgage, she reminds him, and no money in the bank and practically no insurance, and what if something should happen?

Or the couple agree that since both work in order to pay off the mortgage sooner, both ought to pitch in around the

[9] From *Blue-Collar Marriage* by Mirra Komarovsky. © Copyright 1964 by Random House Inc. Reprinted by permission. Pp. 71–72.

house. But she accuses him of not being very helpful. He is, he says, he does everything he can. Besides nothing he does seems to please her.

Consider the following illustration of role-perception conflict provided by a couple who were involved both in a marriage research project and divorce proceedings:

> In this instance the wife, who had initiated divorce proceedings, sees herself as being just about all that a wife is expected to be. She describes herself as cooperative almost to a fault, as affectionate and understanding, and otherwise exhibiting the qualities considered appropriate to a wife in her community. Her husband sees her in quite a different image. He describes her as self-seeking, impatient with his mistakes, frequently angry, always proud, independent, and self-satisfied.
>
> Such interpersonal discrepancies are greatly magnified when the husband's self-description is compared with his wife's description of him. He pictures himself as a fairly well balanced spouse. He sees himself as being overgenerous to his wife and highly responsible as a mate. The picture he presents of himself is most incompatible with that presented by the wife. She perceives him as essentially an aggressive, blunt, competitive, skeptical, and distrustful mate. She sees him as bossy and dominating; as egotistical, conceited, and boastful; as a shrewd and calculating person who thinks mostly of himself. In her view he is sarcastic and impatient, jealous, stubborn, and unforgiving. In fact she sees him not only as possessing qualities that disqualify him for the role of husband but also as lacking nearly all qualities of warmth, love, generosity, and responsibility that she considers are required in a mate (Mangus, 1957b, pp. 206–207).

Discrepancy between Role Expectation and Role Perception What does a spouse expect and what does he perceive in the mate he marries? And what does he expect and what does he perceive in himself? Are his role expectations fulfilled or frustrated? Harmony in marriage is generally associated with congruence in role perceptions and role expectations.

Of course, it is possible that a spouse perceives what he expects to perceive. If he expects the worse and finds it (or thinks he does), this sort of congruence will not be associated with marriage happiness. And it is also possible that a particular couple's qualms about marriage roles may prove groundless, and the resulting discrepancy between the expected and the perceived may be a happy surprise.

Here again is the divorcing couple of the research project. They show a considerable amount of incongruence in role perceptions and role expectations. Especially striking is the disparity between what the wife expects of her husband and what she sees in him.

> She expects a husband to be warm, loving, cooperative, with only the normal or appropriate qualities of dominance, aggressiveness, and hostility. She sees her mate as essentially a hateful, blunt, exploitative person with both active and passive hostilities. She sees him as a role-frustrating rather than as a role-fulfilling partner. On the other hand she sees herself as conforming rather closely to her role expectations for a wife.
>
> Turning to the husband, he sees his spouse as failing to conform to his expectations of a wife. To him she is not as distrustful as he expects a wife to be. At the same time he sees her as lacking in expected qualities of cooperation, love, and affection. It seems that the husband wants the wife to be two incompatible women, a role she evidently cannot fulfill.
>
> When this man's self description is compared with his role expectations of a husband, discrepancies again appear.

He sees himself as being notably less cooperative and loving than he thinks a husband should be. Also he sees himself as lacking in qualities of dominance in his relations with his wife (Mangus, 1957a, p. 260).

ACHIEVING MARRIAGE ADJUSTMENT

When can a couple expect to achieve a satisfactory adjustment in marriage? Who makes the greater effort? And how are the adjustments made? These are the questions which will be asked and answered in this section.

When?

How long does it take to achieve satisfactory adjustment in marriage? This was a question posed by Landis, a pioneer in marriage research. The spouses he studied were mostly parents of college students, and they had been married on an average of twenty years. Each spouse rated the happiness of the marriage and indicated the extent of adjustment and the time taken to achieve adjustment in each of the following areas: sex relations, spending the family income, social activities, in-law relationships, religious activities, and mutual friends.

Since the spouses responded independently, it was possible to see how well a couple agreed on their marriage adjustment. Most of them agreed pretty well. Only about one couple in ten showed disagreement. It was found that more time was required to achieve adjustment in sexual relations than in any other area. Only about half of the couples felt that there had

been a satisfactory sexual adjustment from the beginning. The average time required to work out a satisfactory adjustment was six years, but one couple in eight reported that a satisfactory adjustment had never been reached.

The second most difficult area of adjustment involved spending the family income; this proved to be nearly as bothersome as sex relations. Next in difficulty were social activities and in-law relationships, where about two out of every three couples reported that they had achieved a satisfactory adjustment from the beginning. Religious activities and mutual friends appeared to present the least difficulty, with about three out of every four couples agreeing that adjustment in this area had been satisfactory from the beginning (Landis, 1946).

How long does it take to achieve satisfactory adjustment in marriage? On second thought, one might question the question. It seems to imply that once a couple have reached a happy state of affairs there will be no more adjusting to do. But states of affairs, happy and unhappy, have a way of changing. In a sense, a couple never "achieve" marriage adjustment; they have to keep achieving it. Marriages take working at, some more than others, and more at some times than at other times.

What happens to marriage adjustment as the years go by? Many of the most precarious marriages are weeded out by divorce in the first few years. Even so, a number of researchers have noted a general tendency for marriages to decline in happiness and satisfaction with the passing years (Blood & Wolfe, 1960; Hobart, 1958; Pineo, 1961).

Some couples become increasingly disenchanted. The romance and excitement of the early months and years of marriage fade. The novel becomes the familiar. High hopes (some hopelessly high) and great expectations (some gratuitously great) go unrealized, adding to the dissatisfaction (Blood, 1962).

The disenchantment may be accompanied by the couple's disengagement from each other. Intercourse, sexual and otherwise, declines. There is less sharing of leisure-time activities (Pineo, 1961). He goes off to play poker with the boys, and she gets together with the girls for a hen session. Even in the home, there may be less conversation and interaction between the couple. The activity becomes centered more and more around the children so that the spouses are less husband and wife than mother and father (Blood, 1962).

For some couples, the first few years of marriage are a critical time. In one group of college couples who had been married for about two years it was found that one-fifth of the spouses had already considered separation (Landis & Landis, 1963). In a similar group of couples who had been married about three years, one-third of the husbands and wives reported that they had considered separation (Johannis, 1956).

For many couples, the arrival of the first child is a crisis situation, necessitating assumption of new roles and major changes in living routines. Better-adjusted, better-prepared couples experience less crisis, but most couples find this time a difficult one. Marriage twosomes are less complicated than family trios; trios sometimes become triangles with one spouse or the other feeling neglected or left out, and the marriage relationship suffers (E. D. Dyer, 1963; LeMasters, 1957).

The middle years bring crises for some marriages and spouses. This period seems especially crucial for wives. Their homemaking role declines as children grow up and depart (Bossard & Boll, 1955). At that point, a wife's happiness may depend on how much taste and talent she has for participating in activities outside the home (Rose, 1955).

The middle-year crises for husbands are frequently related to job fortunes. Marital strain occurs when a man who has achieved a considerable measure of success and prominence finds that his wife has not kept up with him and cannot gear her activities to his. Other men, who feel themselves to be vocational failures, let their unhappiness spill into their homelife; more than this, they may make their wives and families scapegoats for their lack of accomplishment (Bossard & Boll, 1955).

For some couples, however, the postparental years are golden ones. Enjoying the pleasures of grandparenthood without the responsibilities of parenthood, less tied down to business, home, and chores, they can indulge themselves and renew acquaintance. There may be more time and more money and more mobility. When spouses in their postparental years are interviewed, they generally present a favorable view of their circumstances (Deutscher, 1964).

Who?

Who Has Made the Greater Adjustment in Marriage?

This was a question which Burgess and Wallin (1953) asked of the husbands and wives they studied. In very few cases did it appear that the husband had made the major effort. Frequently, there was agreement that the endeavor for satisfactory adjustment was equally shared. In the preponderance of cases, however, husbands and wives felt that it was the wife who had made the greater effort.

When You and Your Husband Differ About Something, Do You Usually Give in and Do It Your Husband's Way, or Does He Usually Come Around to Your Point of View?

A large sample of Detroit wives who were asked this question said that they gave in more than their husbands did. The wives gave in 34 percent of the time and the husbands 24 percent. The rest of the time the matter was apparently subjected to conversation and compromise (Blood & Wolfe, 1960).

The evidence seems to show that wives are more accommodating than husbands. Still it depends on what area of the marriage is under consideration. In religious conflicts, for example, the wife may stand pat, and the husband will have to accept the situation and reconcile himself to it.

In a family, some areas may be disputed or shared while others are allotted to the husband or to the wife, with each supreme in his or her own bailiwick. In the study of Detroit families, for example, it was found that the husband made the decisions about *his* work and the car, the wife about *her* work and the food, while the rest of the decisions were jointly arrived at (Blood & Wolfe, 1960).

Interestingly enough, although wives generally have the more conciliatory role, the success of a marriage may be more dependent upon the husband's behavior. Much of the research seems to indicate that his role is the key role. Wives give and give in a good deal in marriage, but the ability of husbands to play their role well and give in at least a little may make the crucial difference between marriage suc-

cess or failure (Farber, 1957; Tharp, 1963b).

How?

How do couples approach their problems? How do they deal with marital frustrations and conflict? How do they deal with each other?

It has been suggested that explicit problem solving in marriage can involve a number of steps. First of all, we recognize the problem, admit that it exists, and agree to work on it. Second, the problem is thought out and talked out; brought to light and analyzed, the problem may seem quite different from before. Third, we consider various courses of action, evaluate each course, and then select and implement the best (Blood, 1962).

Most problem solving in marriage is not so explicit. Many couples have little insight into their problems and little ability to pursue their solutions so directly. Whether identified or not, our problems exist. Whether directly or indirectly, we work on them, and they work on us. Some patterns which occur (and which were introduced in earlier chapters) include blocking, restructuring, compromise, accommodation, mediation, and escape.

Blocking

Conflicting impulses within the individual serve to block him and keep him from reaching his goals. In the same way, spouses in conflict keep each other from meeting their marriage needs and playing the marriage roles which they wish to play.

Some couples prefer not to approach their problems at all. Or perhaps they are unable to do so because they are unable to communicate with each other. In fact, this may be the larger problem from which all their other problems stem (see Case Study 16.3).

Case study 16.3 Lack of communication as a marriage problem. (This material, edited and condensed, was written by a woman, thirty-four years old.)

Before I was married, I knew that my future husband was not the talkative type. He talked an average amount, and I didn't realize that there was a possibility he would talk even less in a few years or that it would ever become a problem of adjustment on my part. Even if I had been absolutely sure this was to happen, it probably would not have made any difference. He had and still has more than enough good points to outweigh any criticisms I may make against him.

My adjustment to marriage was relatively easy. We seemed to agree on most things and disagreements did not end in bitter quarrels but were resolved in one way or another. During these first years of my marriage I waited eagerly for my husband to come home. I was interested in what he had done and was ready to tell him all the events of my day. If nothing important had happened to him, he at least listened to me and added a "yes," "no" or "uh huh" now and then. Many times these few remarks were all that kept the conversation from being a monologue. This state of affairs continued for several years, but gradually his remarks became more infrequent, and finally the time arrived when I felt that I was talking to myself.

As the years passed there was a decrease in the events I found interesting enough to remember and to relate to my husband. This is when my husband's lack of participation became a real problem. I still felt the need of conversation with my husband but did not have either the energy or the inclination to carry on a monologue as I had often done in the past. It was a problem I could not resolve. "Talk to me" became almost a joke in our home, at least to my husband, and a much-repeated phrase when we engaged in discussion with other couples who were experiencing the same difficulty.

Talking this situation over with my husband and others has brought out logical explanations. My husband, who has spent a hard day at work, wants to rest and relax when he gets home in the evening. He has spent a good part of eight hours in verbal communication with others and is now ready to read or garden. I can understand my husband's feelings, but after spending all day around the house by myself I am ready for conversation, regardless of the subject, and feel that my husband should make an effort to help me fulfill this need. I have beaten my head against the wall in anger and have gotten nowhere. Now that I am attending school it has subsided in importance. I am so occupied with school work in the evenings that I do not have time to miss the conversations I used to expect my husband to participate in. It is also probably true that I am fulfilling that need at school and when I am home I feel much the same way as my husband does after a day's work. Even so, there are still times when I feel in the mood for conversation and become upset because I cannot reconcile myself to the fact that my husband does not want to talk. I think I am learning to live with this situation but do not think I will ever completely adjust to it. There is also the possibility that it will again present a real problem some time in the future. School cannot go on forever and if I decide to stay home instead of working I will again find this problem very important. (I want to add that television has been a boon to wives whose husbands are nonconversationalists.)

Sometimes only one of the spouses is incommunicado. A wife may complain that her husband won't talk to her about the couple's problems. "What is there to talk about?" her husband replies, retreating behind his newspaper. And, of course, when the situation is not to one's disliking, refusal to recognize a problem may be an important bit of strategy.

Sometimes a particular problem may be taboo. It may be too painful or threatening to admit, much less discuss. A couple's sex adjustment, for example, may be extremely unsatisfactory, and yet neither member may be able to bring himself to broach the matter and try to find a solution.

How much of the marriage occasions blocking? Of course, if too many of the couple's needs go unmet, a marriage is hardly likely to be happy, and it may not last (Landis, 1946). Problems in one area may spill over to affect other areas. Marriage workers talk about "tremendous trifles"—conflicts of seemingly no importance which get blown up out of all proportion and serve to influence the entire marriage interaction.

Restructuring

The structure of the marriage and its problems constantly change. Some problems fade away with time. Others escalate and assume great importance. New problems emerge.

Some of the problems which occupy a newly married couple are outgrown. Living together, loving together, take practice. Playing a new role takes practice too. Released from her earlier inhibitions, a wife may become a more eager sex partner while with patience and experience her husband becomes a more proficient one. She learns to cook, and his morale goes up. He gets a raise, and the household no longer teeters on the edge of bankruptcy (Bernard, 1964).

Need patterns change. After a considerable amount of sex frustration, his sex needs may wane or find extramarital solutions. The nurturance which has welled up

in her and was rejected by him may be lavished on her increasing family.

Roles are altered. He may be a poor husband but a good father. She may find fulfillment in the role of mother to the exclusion of that of wife.

Power within the family shifts. He suffers business reverses, causing a deterioration of his prestige and influence in the family. She gets a job and assumes new power or new autonomy in the marriage.

Marriage partners attempt to restructure their relationship to fit their own needs, goals, and roles. This can be a mutual and mutually beneficial process. Or it can be war (hot or cold) as each persuades and threatens, rewards and punishes, withdraws, thrusts, parries, and counterattacks. Each attempts to force the marriage to his own mold and pattern.

Compromise

Much of living involves compromise, and marriage is no exception. Few spouses dare demand everything they want. Even a spouse who is seemingly in an undisputed position of power learns to give in some of the time to keep pressures below the boiling point. Even a spouse who wields little power gets his back up occasionally and exacts a few demands.

Compromises in marriage take a number of forms. Some compromises involve an alternation of concessions. Sometimes one spouse gives in, sometimes the other. A spouse may consider it good strategy to ostentatiously give in on many small controversies to win a concession on an issue that seems more important.

Some issues allow a couple to meet each other halfway or, at least, partway. A couple compounded of a pinchpenny and a spendthrift, a loner and a joiner, or a slob and an antislob may be able to assume a middle course of spending, joining, or order. To mollify her meticulous husband, a wife can make an effort to keep the house tidier than she thinks it needs to be, and her husband can make an effort not to notice that her efforts are less than perfectly successful.

Other compromises involve a division of the marriage territory. Each spouse reigns supreme in certain areas. The wife's territory, for example, may begin at the front door. The house is hers, and she has the final say on how the furniture in the living room is to be arranged and rearranged. The yard is his, including the de-

cision to tear out the hedge and replace it with a redwood fence that is guaranteed never to need trimming.

Accommodation

"For better for worse, for richer for poorer" are the conditions we agree to in marriage. Sometimes things turn out for worse and for poorer and with little apparent remedy. With skill, we learn to recognize and work on the solvable problems. With patience, we learn to accept and live with the others: we accommodate them.

After we are married, we may find our religious differences more bothersome than we thought. Perhaps our views are vexingly incompatible, but because they are

Presentation 16.1 Brainwashing in marriage. How do we adjust in marriage? Sometimes we attempt to "adjust" each other, to change each other, or restructure the marriage interaction so that it is more to our liking. Bernard, who has made a comprehensive study of marriage adjustment, notes that brain washing is a technique used by some spouses to achieve this goal.

Brainwashing is a subtle use of the carrot-and-stick method of manipulating responses. For maximum effectiveness, it requires isolation of the subject, removing him or her from competing stimuli. It requires alternate punishment and reward in a way that creates willingness to accept control as an alternative to the anxiety of uncertainty. It seems to work best when carried out in a spirit of ostensible friendliness. The best-known applications of brainwashing techniques were those used by communists in prisoner-of-war camps; but in less sophisticated ways they are commonly used in everyday life, even in marriage. The husband manages to cut his wife off from contacts with her family or friends so that his definition of any situation cannot be counteracted by

theirs. To the outsider, the spouse seems to be in thrall. "He has her hypnotized." "She doesn't dare to call her soul her own." The taming of the shrew, Kate, by Petruchio, as described by Shakespeare, is an illustration of change by brainwashing using the conditioned response. A wife might, similarly, make certain behavior on the part of her husband so painful that he would cease to indulge in it in order to avoid the punishment she inflicted; we say he is "henpecked." Either spouse may be so conditioned in the direction of compatibility with the other. The punishments may take many forms: weeping, sex refusal, beating, coldness, withdrawal, money deprivation, brawling, or what have you. Whatever it is, the spouse comes in time to prefer to concede whatever is under issue rather than endure the punishment, and finally the very anticipation of the punishment is enough to make him avoid the situation. A change has been effected; the difference has been removed. The entire cost has been borne by one of the partners. The resulting relationship may or may not be stable (Bernard, 1954, p. 693).

deeply rooted in each of us, they are not likely to change, nor is a compromise conceivable. There is nothing to do but make the best of a bad situation.

A person may find his in-laws hard to get along with. If he had a choice, he would not have picked them, but there they are, and their ties with his spouse may be close. Furthermore, he may share a house or neighborhood with them and be dependent upon them for assistance. There may be nothing to do but accept them. (At least, he says out of hearing range, he can choose his friends.)

A wife may be very unhappy with the working conditions imposed by her husband's job. Perhaps it keeps him away from home much of the time and prevents him from playing the roles of husband and father as she expected they would be played. Yet her husband is deeply committed to his work; it is hardly thinkable that he would change vocations, and she must think about changing her expectations and accommodating the situation.

Mediation

Where do people go with their marriage problems? Some of course, go nowhere. A couple may not even discuss their problems with each other. This, as was already indicated, may itself be their biggest problem.

Problems which seem too great for the marital pair may be taken outside the marriage. It has been noted that many wives have a confidant—someone whom they can tell their troubles to. Frequently the confidant is their mother or sister. Husbands, by contrast, are less likely to confide their marital troubles to someone (Komarovsky, 1964).

According to a national survey, marriage problems are the chief reason that people seek professional help, and clergymen are the chief helpers they seek out. Physicians are the second most used resource (Gurin et al., 1960). Many of us, of course, have continuing relationships with our ministers and doctors, and it is no surprise that we take our troubles to them (Blood, 1962).

Social workers, psychologists, and psychiatrists—all are called upon to help people with their marriage problems. Marriage counseling is a growing specialization, and a number of universities provide training in this area (Leslie, 1964). However, there are still relatively few marriage counselors, as such.

Many communities have agencies or clinics which provide help for people with marriage and family problems. The Family Service Association of America, for example, has about 300 member agencies which work with marital problems. The Planned Parenthood Federation of America has approximately 250 local branches which provide a wide range of educational and counseling services (Leslie, 1964).

Some cities have family courts which include staffs of social workers and other professional personnel. Couples who are seeking divorce are provided with counseling. An attempt is made to help the couple work out their problems and reconcile their differences.

Escape

There are many strategems for "escaping" marriage problems. We may deny they exist by not thinking about them or talking about them. With vigor, perhaps, we direct our attention and energies elsewhere.

If the marriage is filled with unresolved problems, spouses may try to escape from the marriage itself. They can attempt this by minimizing the marriage interaction. A pair may focus on other areas—the husband on his job, the wife on her children or other interests outside the home.

Finally, if nothing else works, there is the escape provided by separation or divorce. Such a "solution" sometimes seems to solve little and provide little escape. The spouse remarries only to find his old problems still with him—still waiting to be solved—and with greater maturity and understanding he may be able to solve them.

SUMMARY

How can marriage adjustment be defined? Two frequently used definitions are permanence and happiness; a marriage may be considered a success if it persists and if it brings happiness to the people involved in it. Other measures of marriage adjustment include the general satisfaction of the marriage pair, their consensus or ability to agree, the amount of companionship they provide each other, and the satisfactoriness of their sex relations.

How can marriage adjustment be predicted? Among the factors which are most significantly related to later marriage adjustment are those having to do with childhood. Those who remember childhood as a happy time, who had close and warm attachments to parents, and whose parents were permanently and happily married are more likely to report their own marriage as successful.

Behavior during engagement provides another basis for the prediction of marriage adjustment. Research evidence suggests that it is auspicious if an engagement is long rather than short, if it is temperate rather than tempestuous, and if it merits the approval of parents and friends. Other signs favorable for marriage adjustment concern age (couples in their twenties have a lower rate of marriage failure than teenage pairs), culture (higher-class and culturally homogeneous couples tend to have a happier and easier time), religion (same-faith and practicing-faith couples tend to be better adjusted and more permanently married), education (marriages involving college graduates have lower divorce rates than couples who have gone no further than high school), personality (adaptability, conventionality, and sociability are considered good signs), and sex experience (successfully married couples are more likely to have had frank and full sex information as children).

How can marriage adjustment be understood? One useful focus is the marriage needs of the couple. Conflict arises when the need patterns of the spouses are incompatible or when they become increasingly so with the passing years. The sex need is of special importance; problems occur when there are crucial differences in a couple's sex needs, attitudes, arousability, and satisfaction.

A second useful focus concerns the view that each person takes of himself, his spouse, and other people. Happily married individuals tend to take a more favorable view of their mates; they accept themselves and other people too. Such spouses tend to see themselves as they are seen by their mates; this harmony in perception makes for better communication and interaction.

A third useful focus is on the roles which spouses expect to play and which they perceive themselves as playing. Conflicts arise when husbands and wives differ in their role expectations or in their role perceptions. Another source of friction exists when a spouse discovers that his role expectations are frustrated and unfulfilled.

In a sense, a couple never achieve a satisfactory marriage adjustment; they have to keep achieving it. There is a general tendency for marriages to decline in happiness and satisfaction with the passing years. For some couples, the first few years of marriage are a critical time. For many, the arrival of the first child is a time of great crisis and readjustment. The middle years necessitate major changes in many marriage patterns; children grow up and de-

part from the home and spouses are called upon to reevaluate and redefine their marriage roles.

Generally speaking, wives appear to do more accommodating than husbands. Of course, who is called upon to make the greater effort or concession depends to some extent on the matter under consideration. In some areas the husband may be boss; in others, the wife may make the decisions.

Explicit problem solving in marriage involves recognition and analysis of the problem and selection and implementation of a course of action; however, most marriage problem solving is not so explicit. Among the patterns of behavior which are observed in marriage conflicts are blocking, restructuring, compromise, accommodation, mediation, and escape.

REFERENCES

Barnett, L. D. Research on international and interracial marriages. *Marriage and Family Living,* 1963, **25**(1), 105–107.

Bernard, J. The adjustments of married mates. In H. T. Christensen (Ed.), *Handbook of Marriage and the Family.* Chicago: Rand McNally, 1964. Pp. 675–739.

Blood, R. O., Jr. *Marriage.* New York: Free Press, 1962.

———, & Wolfe, D. M. *Husbands and Wives: The Dynamics of Married Living.* New York: Free Press, 1960.

Bossard, J. H. S., & Boll, E. S. Marital unhappiness in the life cycle. *Marriage and Family Living,* 1955, **17**(1), 10–14.

Bowerman, C. E. Prediction studies. In H. T. Christensen (Ed.), *Handbook of Marriage and the Family.* Chicago: Rand McNally, 1964. Pp. 215–246.

Burgess, E. W., & Cottrell, L. S. *Predicting Success or Failure in Marriage.* Englewood Cliffs, N.J.: Prentice-Hall, 1939.

———, Locke, H. J., & Thomes, M. M. *The Family.* (3rd ed.) New York: American Book, 1963.

———, & Wallin, P. *Engagement and Marriage.* Philadelphia: Lippincott, 1953.

Cheng, C. K., & Yamamura, D. S. Interracial marriage and divorce in Hawaii. *Social Forces,* 1957, **36**(1), 77–84.

Deutscher, I. The quality of postparental life: Definitions of the situation. *Journal of Marriage and the Family,* 1964, **26**(1), 52–59.

Divorce rate half-truth. *Science News Letter,* 1963, **84**(10), 157. (Sept. 7, 1963).

Dyer, E. D. Parenthood as crisis: A re-study. *Marriage and Family Living,* 1963, **25**(2), 196–201.

Dyer, W. G. Analyzing marital adjustment using role theory. *Marriage and Family Living,* 1962, **24**(4), 371–375.

Eastman, D. Self acceptance and marital happiness. *Journal of Consulting Psychology,* 1958, **22**(2), 95–99.

Farber, B. An index of marital integration. *Sociometry,* 1957, **20**, 117–134.

Gurin, G., Veroff, J., & Feld, S. *Americans View Their Mental Health.* New York: Basic Books, 1960.

Hobart, C. W. Some effects of romanticism during courtship on marriage role opinions. *Sociology and Social Research,* 1958, **42**, 336–343.

Houston, M., & Forman, R. B. The durable incompatible marriage. Unpublished manuscript, 1961.

Jacobson, A. H. Conflict of attitudes toward the roles of the husband and wife in marriage. *American Sociological Review,* 1952, **17**(2), 146–150.

Jacobson, P. H., & Jacobson, P. F. *American Marriage and Divorce.* New York: Holt, 1959.

Johannis, T. B., Jr. The marital adjustment of a sample of married college students. *The Coordinator,* 1956, **4**(4), 24–31.

Kinsey, A. C., Pomeroy, W. B., & Martin, C. E. *Sexual Behavior in the Human Male.* Philadelphia: Saunders, 1948.

———, ———, ———, & Gebhard, P. H. *Sexual Behavior in the Human Female.* Philadelphia: Saunders, 1953.

Kirkpatrick, C. *The Family as Process and Institution.* (2nd ed.) New York: Ronald, 1963.

Komarovsky, M. *Blue-collar Marriage.* New York: Random House, 1964.

Landis, J. T. Length of time required to achieve adjustment in marriage. *American Sociological Review,* 1946, **11**(6), 666–677.

———. Marriages of mixed and non-mixed religious faith. *American Sociological Review,* 1949, **14**(3), 401–407.

———. The pattern of divorce in three generations. *Social Forces,* 1956, **34**(3), 213–216.

———. Religiousness, family relationships, and family values in Protestant, Catholic, and Jewish families. *Marriage and Family Living,* 1960, **22**(4), 341–347. (a)

———. The trauma of children when parents divorce. *Marriage and Family Living,* 1960, **21**, 7–13. (b)

———. A re-examination of the role of the father as an index of family integration. *Marriage and Family Living,* 1962, **24**(2), 122–128.

———. Dating maturation of children from happy and unhappy marriages. *Marriage and Family Living,* 1963, **25**(3), 351–353.

———, & Landis, M. G. *Building a Successful Marriage.* (4th ed.) Englewood Cliffs, N.J.: Prentice-Hall, 1963.

Lang, R. O. The rating of happiness in marriage. Unpublished master's thesis, University of Illinois, 1932. Cited by J. H. S. Bossard & E. S. Boll, in Marital unhappiness in the life cycle. *Marriage and Family Living,* 1955, **17**(1), 10–14.

Langner, T. S., & Michael, S. T. *Life Stress and Mental Health.* New York: Free Press, 1963.

LeMasters, E. E. Parenthood as crisis. *Marriage and Family Living,* 1957, **19**(4), 352–355.

Leslie, G. R. The field of marriage counseling. In H. T. Christensen (Ed.), *Handbook of Marriage and the Family.* Chicago: Rand McNally, 1964. Pp. 912–943.

Levinger, G. Marital cohesiveness and dissolution: An integrative review. *Journal of Marriage and the Family,* 1965, **27**(1), 19–28.

Locke, H. J., & Williamson, R. C. Marital adjustment: A factor analysis study. *American Sociological Review,* 1958, **23**(5), 562–569.

Luckey, E. B. Implications for marriage counseling of self perceptions and spouse perceptions. *Journal of Counseling Psychology,* 1960, **7**(1), 3–9. (a)

———. Marital satisfaction and congruent self-spouse concepts. *Social Forces,* 1960, **39**(2), 153–157. (b)

———. Perceptual congruence of self and family concepts as related to marital interaction. *Sociometry,* 1961, **24**(3), 234–250.

———. Marital satisfaction and personality correlates of spouse. *Journal of Marriage and the Family,* 1964, **26**(2), 217–220.

Mangus, A. R. Family impacts on mental health. *Marriage and Family Living,* 1957, **19**(3), 256–262. (a)

———. Role theory and marriage counseling. *Social Forces,* 1957, **35**(3), 200–209. (b)

Pineo, P. C. Disenchantment in the later years of marriage. *Marriage and Family Living,* 1961, **23**, 3–11.

Rose, A. M. Factors associated with the life satisfaction of middle-class, middle-aged persons. *Marriage and Family Living,* 1955, **17**(1), 15–19.

Strauss, A. Personality needs and marital choice. *Social Forces,* 1947, **25**, 332–339.

Terman, L. M. *Psychological Factors in Marital Happiness.* New York: McGraw-Hill, 1938.

Tharp, R. G. Dimensions of marriage roles. *Marriage and Family Living,* 1963, **25**(4), 389–404. (a)

———. Psychological patterning in marriage. *Psychological Bulletin,* 1963, **60**(2), 97–117. (b)

Wallin, P. Marital happiness of parents and their children's attitude toward marriage. *American Sociological Review,* 1954, **19**, 20–23.

———, **& Vollmer, H. M.** Marital happiness of parents and their children's attitudes to them. *American Sociological Review,* 1953, **18**, 424–431.

Winch, R. F. *Mate Selection: A Study of Complementary Needs.* New York: Harper & Row, 1958.

———. *The Modern Family.* New York: Holt, 1963.

GLOSSARY

abasement need The need to admit inadequacy, accept blame, and suffer punishment.

ability The capacity to learn and perform. Includes aptitude and achievement (which see).

academic achievement Proficiency in school-taught material.

academic achievement test Instrument measuring proficiency in school-taught material.

academic aptitude Potential for acquiring proficiency in school-taught material.

academic aptitude test Instrument measuring potential for acquiring proficiency in school-taught material.

acceptance As parental behavior, giving a good deal of oneself to a child or providing conditions optimal to the child's development.

accident-prone Highly susceptible to accidents.

accommodation Acting conformably; putting up with problems or difficult situations.

achievement The capacity to perform; accomplishment. Also see ability, aptitude.

achievement need The need to overcome obstacles, accomplish difficult things, and surpass others.

act The behavior prompted by a need and directed toward a goal.

act conflict Competition among several modes of meeting a need and reaching a goal. Also see need conflict, goal conflict.

act frustration Frustration due to the inefficacy of a particular act. Also see need frustration, goal frustration.

activation level Extent of arousal or tension. Same as level of activation.

active rejection As parental behavior, rejection of a child which is characterized by hostility and dictatorial and repressive techniques. Also see rejection, passive rejection.

acute anxiety Anxiety which is sharp, intense, and sudden in onset. Also see chronic anxiety.

adjustment A person's interaction with his environment.

adjustment by ailment As a defense, the non-insightful use of illness, imaginary or real, as a way of averting anxiety.

adjustment mechanism Synonym for defense (which see).

affect expression A person's state of feeling.

affiliation need The need to associate with, cooperate with, and form friendships with others.

age role The behavior associated with a particular age.

age specific Occurring at or characteristic of a certain age or period of development.

aggression need The need to overpower opposition and to criticize, attack, and punish others.

Alcoholics Anonymous An association of alcoholics formed to help the members abstain from drinking.

alternating In conflict, achieving several incompatible alternatives or expressing several incompatible impulses in turn.

anorexia Lack of appetite or desire for food.

anthropologist A specialist in anthropology.

anthropology The science that deals with the origin and development of mankind.

anxiety A state of arousal caused by threat to well-being.

anxiety attack A sudden burst of anxiety that rapidly mounts to a peak and then fades away.

approach-approach conflict Simultaneous attraction to several incompatible courses of action.

approach-avoidance conflict Simultaneous attraction to and repulsion for a course of action.

aptitude The capacity to learn; potential. Also see ability, achievement.

arousal A condition of tension, unrest, or uneasiness.

arts and entertainment occupation In the classification of occupations, those in athletics, fine arts, music, dancing, and public entertainers of various sorts.

authoritarianism Disposition toward a hierarchy of authority or power with unquestioning submission to those higher and unremitting domination of those lower.

autonomic nervous system A division of the nervous system which controls internal bodily changes during emotion or stress.

autonomy need The need to be free and independent.

avoidance-avoidance conflict Simultaneous repulsion for several courses of action, but to escape one, another must be carried out.

bilateral choice As indicated by a sociometric test, members of a group who show a mutual or reciprocal preference or attraction.

blocking In conflict, frustration of or interference with goal-directed behavior because of a competition between alternatives or persons.

bound anxiety Synonym for situational anxiety (which see).

business contact occupation In the classification of occupations, all of those which involve persuasive selling in a direct person-to-person relationship.

cardiovascular psychophysiologic reaction Psychophysiologic reaction affecting the heart or blood vessels.

caseworker A social worker who deals directly with individuals and families.

catharsis The open expression or release of pent-up thoughts and feelings.

change need The need to do new and different things; to try new patterns of behavior, meet new people, go to new places.

characterological anxiety Synonym for general anxiety (which see).

chlorpromazine A commonly used tranquilizing drug.

chosen As indicated by a sociometric test, individuals of a group for whom many members express preference.

chronic anxiety Anxiety which has persisted over a long period of time. Also see acute anxiety.

civil liberties Personal freedoms which are guaranteed by law.

clinical psychologist A psychologist who specializes in the evaluation and correction of adjustment problems as well as in research in this area.

clique A small number of individuals who form a closed group; on a sociometric test a subgroup that shows high attraction only to each other.

coherence As a definition of family adjustment, staying together, continuing to exist as a physical unit or entity.

coldness As parental behavior, offering little or no affection to a child. Also see warmth.

community mental health center A facility or group of facilities which provide a complete and coordinated program of mental health services in a community.

community organization worker A social worker who works to improve the social welfare facilities of the community.

compensation As a defense, substitution of achievement in one area to make up for failure in another.

compromising In conflict, choosing a course of action which combines features of various alternatives.

conflict Competition among several patterns of behavior.

conquering-hero fantasy Daydreams in which the person gains satisfaction from imagining that he is the acclaimed or accomplished master of some situation. Also see suffering-hero fantasy.

conscience A person's ideas of right and wrong which influence his behavior. Also see superego.

conscious With awareness.

conscious anxiety Anxiety in open awareness; anxiety that is not controlled or defended against. Also see unconscious anxiety.

conscious motivation Motivation of which the person is aware.

contact with the environment Ability to see the world as others do; accurate perception of the environment.

continuous reinforcement Reinforcement in which a particular response is always followed by reward. Also see partial reinforcement.

counseling Giving information, advice, or help.

counselor A specialist in counseling; one who gives assistance with educational, vocational, or personal problems.

daydream Fanciful and pleasing train of

thoughts with a definite theme. Also see reverie.

day hospital A hospital program in which the patient participates during the day and returns to his home at night. Also see night hospital, weekend hospital.

defense A pattern of behavior employed for protection against anxiety.

defense mechanism Same as defense (which see).

deference need The need to admire, follow, and be guided by others.

delayed reinforcement Reinforcement in which reward occurs some time after the response. Also see immediate reinforcement.

democracy As parental behavior, giving children a voice in determining family policies and activities. Also see dictatorship.

denial As a defense, refusing to admit some threatening external reality.

developmental crisis A conflict between positive and negative qualities which confronts a person at a particular stage of development and whose favorable resolution is important to good adjustment or mental health (Erikson).

developmental task An achievement expected of a person at a particular stage of development which is critical to further achievement and happiness (Havighurst).

dictatorship As parental behavior, giving children no voice in determining family policies and activities. Also see democracy.

discrimination Distinguishing between situations in which a particular response is and is not successful.

displacement As a defense, the shift of a thought, feeling, or action from one person or situation to another less threatening one.

dogmatism Unfounded positiveness about one's beliefs and ideas; closed to other ideas.

dominance need The need to influence, direct, and control the behavior of others.

dominative behavior Efforts to make others behave in ways consistent with one's own needs, acts, and goals (Anderson). Also see socially integrative behavior.

dramatic therapy Psychotherapy which makes use of the enactment of roles and incidents. Includes role playing and psychodrama (which see).

drug therapy Changing adjustment patterns through the use of drugs.

dynamic Changing; not fixed; causing change. Also see static.

educational loading Dependence on previous schooling and school-learned materials.

effectiveness in the environment The ability to relate to others and be productive.

ego In psychoanalysis, the problem-solving portion of the personality. Also see id, superego.

ego defense mechanism Same as defense (which see).

electing In conflict, decisively choosing one alternative and excluding other alternatives.

empathy Sensing and understanding the thoughts and feelings of another.

endurance need The need to stick to a problem, keep at a job, or work toward a goal until one is successful.

environment Everything external to the person with which he is in some relation.

escaping In conflict, slipping away from a number of unattractive alternatives.

establishment stage In vocational adjustment or development, the third period beginning at about the age of twenty-five and continuing through the forty-fourth year.

ethnocentrism The tendency to consider one's own group superior and the standard by which all other groups are to be judged.

exhausted response method Facilitation of an unacceptable response while withholding reward so that it may be extinguished more rapidly.

exhibition need The need to attract attention to oneself and to make an impression on others.

exploration In vocational adjustment, purposeful trial-and-error movement from job to job, especially early in one's career. Also see floundering.

exploration stage In vocational adjustment or development, the second period, including adolescence and young adulthood.

extended family A set of parents, their children, and other relatives. See nuclear family.

extinction The weakening of a response.

extrapunitive As a response to frustration, blaming others. Also see intropunitive, impunitive.

extrinsic satisfaction Satisfaction extraneous to the nature of the work or activity. Also see intrinsic satisfaction.

family therapy Group psychotherapy involving two or more members of a family who are seen simultaneously.

fantasy As a defense, finding satisfaction in imaginary constructions such as make-believe play, reveries, and daydreams.

fixation As a defense, continuation of a pattern of behavior which has become immature or inappropriate.

floundering In vocational adjustment, aimless and meaningless movement from job to job, especially early in one's career. Also see exploration.

foster home A private household or family in which a nonfamily member is placed.

free-floating anxiety Synonym for general anxiety (which see).

frigidity Inability of the female to enjoy sexual intercourse. Also see impotence.

frustration Interference with goal-directed behavior.

frustration threshold The level or point of frustration above which conduct or demeanor is adversely affected.

frustration tolerance The ability to withstand frustration.

gastrointestinal psychophysiologic reaction Psychophysiologic reaction affecting the digestive system.

general ability The capacity to learn and perform many types of material; mental ability or intelligence. Also see special ability.

general anxiety Anxiety that pervades the activities of the individual. Also see situational anxiety.

general cultural occupation In the classification of occupations, those chiefly concerned with preserving and transmitting the general cultural heritage.

generalization Transfer of a response from one stimulus or situation to similar ones.

generativity Commitment to the new generation and to the future (Erikson).

goal The end toward which behavior is directed. Also see positive goal and negative goal.

goal conflict Competition among several goals. Also see need conflict, act conflict.

goal frustration Frustration due to the inaccessibility or unavailability of a particular goal. Also see need frustration, act frustration.

good adjustment Valued or desirable patterns of behavior or personal characteristics. Almost synonymous with mental health except that adjustment is more environment-oriented and more dynamic in connotation while mental health is more personal, static, and implies a physical or medical condition. Also see maladjustment.

group therapy Psychotherapy in which two or more persons are seen simultaneously.

group worker A social worker who uses group activities to benefit the individual and the larger society.

growth stage In vocational adjustment or development, the first period, including infancy and childhood.

happiness An overall sense of well-being.

harmony An overall balance between personal and environmental demands.

heredity Characteristics which are biologically transmitted from parent to offspring.

heterosexuality Sexual interest or behavior directed toward a person of the opposite sex. See sex need, homosexuality.

homosexuality Sexual interest or behavior directed toward a person of the same sex. See sex need, heterosexuality.

hustler A person who is cold, driving, and ambitious (Heath). Also see noncommitter, plunger.

hydrotherapy Use of prolonged baths and wet packs in the treatment of mental illness.

id In psychoanalysis, the primitive pleasure-seeking portion of the personality. Also see ego, superego.

idealism principle In psychoanalysis, demand by the superego for perfection or the ideal (Arkoff). Also see pleasure principle, reality principle.

ideal self The self which the person would like to be.

identification As a general term, establishment of a oneness with another person, group, or object. As a defense, protecting oneself against anxiety by drawing upon the valued qualities of other persons or things with which one has established a oneness.

identity The qualities which distinguish a person.

immediate reinforcement Reinforcement in which reward coincides with or immediately follows a particular response. Also see delayed reinforcement.

impossible response method Extinguishing a response by making it impossible or at least extremely difficult for the response to occur.

impotence Inability of the male to have sexual intercourse. Also see frigidity.

impunitive As a response to frustration, withholding or not employing blame. Also see extrapunitive, intropunitive.

incompatible alternative method An extinction procedure involving the alteration of a situation so that a strong acceptable response which is antagonistic to the unacceptable response is called forth.

increasing stimulus method An extinction procedure in which the stimulus for an unacceptable response is introduced at a strength insufficient to elicit this response; then it is gradually increased until considerable amounts of stimulation can be presented without triggering the unacceptable response.

independence of the environment The ability to be autonomous and not bound by group patterns.

initial work period A part of the establishment stage of vocational adjustment or development, including the part-time and temporary work experiences of adolescence and young adulthood while formal education is being completed. Also see trial work period, stable work period.

insanity A condition in which the person is not legally responsible or accountable for his actions. Also see sanity.

insight Self-understanding.

insomnia Inability to sleep.

integration Unity and consistency in personality and behavior. Synonym for personal integration.

interaction Mutual bearing or influence.

interest In vocational adjustment, like or dislike of certain activities, things, or people.

intraception need The need to analyze and understand one's own feelings, thoughts, and actions as well as those of other people.

intrinsic satisfaction Satisfaction which arises out of the inherent nature of the work or activity. Also see extrinsic satisfaction.

intropunitive As a response to frustration, blaming oneself. Also see extrapunitive, impunitive.

irrational anxiety Synonym for nonobjective anxiety (which see).

isolated As indicated by a sociometric test, an individual of a group who is not chosen or preferred by others and who makes no choices or indicates no preferences himself.

learning Relatively enduring change in behavior which results from past experience.

level of activation Extent of arousal or tension. Same as activation level.

lying As a defense, the deliberate use of falsehood to prevent threat to one's well-being.

maintenance stage In vocational adjustment or development, the fourth period, including the years from forty-five to sixty-five.

maladjustment Undesirable or poorly regarded patterns of behavior or personal characteristics. Shares meaning with mental illness, but maladjustment is more environment-oriented and dynamic in implication while mental illness is more personal, static, and pejorative. Synonym for poor adjustment. Also see good adjustment.

malingering As a defense, removal of a threat by feigning illness.

masturbation Stimulation of the genitals by means other than intercourse.

mediation Use of an intermediary or outside party in dealing with a problem.

mental health Valued patterns of behavior or personal characteristics. Almost synonymous with good adjustment except that adjustment is more environment-oriented and dynamic in connotation while mental health is more personal, static, and implies a physical or medical condition. Mental health is sometimes reserved to designate *very* desirable personal characteristics. Also see mental illness.

mental hospital A hospital for the custody and treatment of serious adjustment problems and mental illnesses.

mental illness Very undesirable or poorly regarded patterns of behavior or personal characteristics. Shares meaning with maladjustment, but maladjustment is environment-oriented and has dynamic implications while mental illness is more personal, static, and pejorative. In the medical approach, mental illness is considered a disease analogous to physical disease; in the psychosocial approach, mental illness is considered the result of certain learning experiences. Also see mental health.

motivation   A general term referring to need-pushed and goal-pulled behavior. Also see motive.

motive   A pattern of need-pushed and goal-pulled behavior. Also see motivation.

motor expression   The muscular activity of the body.

multiple approach conflict   Confrontation by a number of attractive alternatives only one of which can be elected.

multiple approach-avoidance conflict   Confrontation by a number of alternatives each of which has attractive and unattractive features.

multiple avoidance conflict   Confrontation by a number of unattractive alternatives one of which must be elected.

multiproblem family   Synonym for problem family (which see).

need   A condition that prompts action.

need conflict   The competition of several needs or the simultaneous operation of impulses to express and inhibit a single need. Also see act conflict, goal conflict.

need frustration   Frustration of a particular need. Also see act frustration, goal frustration.

negative goal   Something which repels the individual; something he acts to avoid. Also see positive goal.

negative identity   An identity based on generally repudiated or undesirable attributes. Also see positive identity.

negative reinforcement   Weakening a response through the use of a negative reinforcer or punishment. Also see positive reinforcement.

negative reinforcer   Something which strengthens a response when it is withdrawn. Also see positive reinforcer.

nervous breakdown   A term loosely applied to various conditions in which the person is acutely incapacitated by his anxieties, frustrations, and conflicts.

neurosis   Intermediately deviant and undesirable personal characteristics and behavior patterns. Also see normality, psychosis.

neurotic anxiety   Synonym for nonobjective anxiety (which see).

night hospital   A hospital program in which the person participates during the evening and nighttime but pursues his regular activities during the day.

noncommitter   A person who is friendly, bland, and neutral (Heath). Also see hustler, plunger.

nonobjective anxiety   Anxiety not commensurate with the threat involved in a situation or if the threat is vague or unknown. Also see objective anxiety.

norm   A usual, general, or average value.

normal   To conform to a norm or usual value; to be average.

normal anxiety   Synonym for objective anxiety (which see).

normality   Average or typical characteristics or patterns of behavior. Also see neurosis, psychosis.

nuclear family   A set of parents and their children, but not including other relatives. See extended family.

nurturance need   The need to sympathize with, assist, and protect others.

objective anxiety   Anxiety commensurate with the threat posed by a situation. Also see nonobjective anxiety.

objective self   Other people's views of a person.

occupational therapist   A specialist in helping people recover from illness through constructive activity—through being "occupied" in meaningful ways.

orderly progression   As a definition of vocational adjustment, movement through a succession of related and increasingly desirable jobs.

order need   The need to be neat, precise, systematic, and well organized.

organization occupation   In the classification of occupations, those which are primarily concerned with the organization and functioning of government and private enterprise.

orgasm   Sexual climax.

outdoor occupation   In the classification of occupations, those including animal husbandry, farming, fisheries, forestry, mining, and similar employment.

overcompensation   As a defense, turning an area of weakness into one of great strength.

parasympathetic nervous system   A subdivision of the autonomic nervous system which is in charge during quiescent and vegetative activities. Also see sympathetic nervous system.

partial reinforcement   Reinforcement in which reward sometimes but not always follows the response. Also see continuous reinforcement.

passive rejection As parental behavior, rejection characterized by indifference, disregard, and neglect. Also see rejection, active rejection.

permissiveness As parental behavior, allowing children considerable freedom of action. Also see restrictiveness.

personal growth The realization of one's potentialities.

personal integration Unity and consistency in personality and behavior. Synonym for integration.

personality The qualities which characterize a person.

personal maturity The realization of age-specific goals.

play therapy Changing adjustment patterns through play activities.

pleasure principle In psychoanalysis, demand by the id for immediate gratification. Also see idealism principle, reality principle.

plunger A person who is impulsive, changeable, and scattered (Heath). Also see non-committer, hustler.

poor adjustment Synonym for maladjustment (which see).

positive goal Something which attracts the individual; something he acts to get. Also see negative goal.

positive identity An identity based on generally valued or desirable attributes. Also see negative identity.

positive reinforcement Strengthening a response through the use of a positive reinforcer or reward. Also see negative reinforcement.

positive reinforcer Something which strengthens a response when it is presented. Also see negative reinforcer.

primary prevention In dealing with mental illness, programs designed to ward off mental illness by reducing the conditions which produce it. Also see secondary prevention, tertiary prevention.

primary reinforcement The strengthening of a response by a primary reinforcer. Also see secondary reinforcement.

primary reinforcer A goal object whose reward value does not have to be learned. Also see secondary reinforcer.

problem family A family which fails to work out a harmonious interaction with the community; a family in constant trouble with community agencies. Also called multiproblem family.

problem solving As a definition of family adjustment, ability to deal effectively with family problems.

prodromal Pertaining to an early indication or warning sign of a disease or disorder.

projection As a defense, attributing one's own negative qualities to others.

psychiatric nurse A nurse who is specially trained to assist with patients who have serious adjustment problems or mental illness.

psychiatrist A physician who specializes in the diagnosis and treatment of mental illness and adjustment problems.

psychoanalysis A theory of personality and a method of psychotherapy devised by Sigmund Freud.

psychoanalyst A person who is specially trained to treat adjustment problems through the use of psychoanalytic methods.

psychodrama Dramatic therapy in which persons act out or improvise roles in a theater setting.

psychological counselor A person trained in giving educational and vocational guidance and in helping with more common kinds of personal problems.

psychologist A specialist in the science of behavior.

psychology The science of behavior.

psychophysiologic reaction Physiological disorder which is due to a state of chronic and exaggerated emotion. Also called psychosomatic disorder.

psychosis Very deviant and undesirable personal characteristics and behavior patterns which may be qualitatively as well as quantitatively different from normality and neurosis (which see).

psychosomatic disorder Physiological disorder which is due to a state of chronic and exaggerated emotion. Also called psychophysiologic reaction.

psychosurgery Treatment of mental illness through surgical operations performed on the brain.

psychotherapy Changing adjustment patterns through psychological means.

rational anxiety Synonym for objective anxiety (which see).

rationalization As a defense and without conscious intent, explaining circumstances in personally and socially acceptable ways.

reaction formation As a defense, inhibiting, masking, or overcoming threatening impulses by emphasizing opposite ones.

realistic anxiety Synonym for objective anxiety (which see).

reality principle In psychoanalysis, demand by the ego that the requirements of the external environment or reality be taken into account in resolving the conflicting pressures of id and superego. Also see idealism principle, pleasure principle.

reciprocal inhibition As a general term, mutual interference or blocking. In behavior change or psychotherapy, same as incompatible alternative method (which see).

regression As a defense, return to a pattern of behavior which has become immature or inappropriate.

rehabilitation counselor A counselor who assists handicapped and disabled persons in obtaining suitable employment.

reinforcement The strengthening of a response.

rejected As indicated by a sociometric test, individuals of a group who are spurned or repudiated.

rejection As parental behavior, giving little of oneself to a child or failing to provide conditions optimal to the child's development. Also see active rejection, passive rejection.

repression As a defense, automatic inhibition of threatening stimuli.

residential facility In the treatment of adjustment problems and mental illness, a protective and supportive dwelling place. Includes residential house and foster home (which see).

residential house A protective and supportive boardinghouse for persons with adjustment problems and mental illness.

respiratory psychophysiologic reaction Psychophysiologic reaction affecting the breathing apparatus.

restrictiveness As parental behavior, putting considerable constraints on a child's actions.

restructuring In conflict, resolution of the situation through changing perception.

retirement stage In vocational adjustment or development, the fifth and final period, beginning at age sixty-five.

reverie Fanciful and pleasing train of thoughts or sequence of images with no very definite theme. Also see daydream.

rewarded alternative method Extinguishing an unacceptable response by withholding reward but simultaneously rewarding an acceptable alternative.

role The behavior associated with a particular position in a group.

role expectation The behavior which society or a particular person expects or hopes will be associated with a particular position. Also see role perception.

role perception The way a particular person is perceived or seen to carry out a particular role. Also see role expectation.

role playing Dramatic therapy in which the person acts out the behavior of a certain individual in a particular situation.

sanity A condition in which the person is legally responsible and accountable for his actions.

schizophrenia A psychosis characterized by markedly deviant patterns of feeling, thinking, and acting.

school counselor A counselor who helps pupils in elementary and secondary schools and who offers advice and suggestions to teachers and parents.

science occupation In the classification of occupations, those concerned with scientific research and its application in nontechnological fields.

secondary prevention In dealing with mental illness, programs designed to lower the rate of mental illness by preventing mild or moderate conditions from dragging on and worsening. Also see primary prevention, tertiary prevention.

secondary reinforcement The strengthening of a response by a secondary reinforcer. Also see primary reinforcement.

secondary reinforcer A goal object whose reward value is learned. Also see primary reinforcer.

self-acceptance A positive image of oneself.

self-actualization The fulfillment of one's potentialities.

self-disclosure A willingness to let oneself be known to others.

self-esteem A pride in oneself.

self-identity A sharp, stable image of oneself.

self-insight A knowledge or understanding of oneself.

semihospital Partial hospitalization programs; programs for persons who require less than around-the-clock care.

service occupation In the classification of occupations, those which are primarily concerned with attending to the personal needs and welfare of others.

sex need The need to think about, associate with, fall in love with, and have sexual relations with members of the opposite sex (heterosexuality) or the same sex (homosexuality).

sex role The behavior associated with a particular sex.

sheltered workshop A workshop in which disabled or handicapped persons can be trained in work attitudes, habits, and skills.

shock therapy Changing adjustment patterns through the use of electric current or chemical agents which induce sudden and profound changes in bodily functioning.

sib, sibling A brother or sister.

situational anxiety Anxiety that occurs only under certain circumstances. Also see general anxiety.

situation specific Occurring in or characteristic of a particular situation.

skin psychophysiologic reaction Psychophysiologic reaction affecting the skin.

social club In improving adjustment, an organization of individuals who share common adjustment problems.

social competence Relating satisfactorily to others.

socialization The process of acquiring patterns of behavior prescribed or valued by an organized group or society.

socially integrative behavior Efforts to arrive at mutually satisfactory patterns of behavior (Anderson). Also see dominative behavior.

social self The way a person thinks he looks to others.

social work A profession devoted to improving the environment and behavior of disadvantaged and maladjusted persons.

social worker A specialist in social work.

sociogram A diagram depicting relationships among members of a group.

sociograph A graph on which sociometric test results are plotted.

sociologist A specialist in sociology.

sociology The science of group behavior and social organizations.

sociometric test A measure of preference, acceptance, and rejection within a social group.

sociometry The quantitative study of relationships within a group especially through the use of sociometric tests or techniques.

sociotherapy Various techniques designed to change the adjustment or mental health of an individual by altering his environment.

somatotherapy Medical and surgical techniques which are designed to change a person's adjustment by altering his physical being.

special ability The capacity to learn and perform a certain type of material. Also see general ability.

stable work period A part of the establishment stage of vocational adjustment, including full-time work positions which are permanent or relatively so, lasting three years or more. Also see initial work period, trial work period.

state A condition involving the entire organism.

static Fixed; not changing. Also see dynamic.

stress The state of a person in a threatening or difficult situation. Used interchangeably with anxiety.

stressor A condition which is potentially threatening or difficult.

stuttering A speech disorder characterized by blocking, prolongation, and repetition of word sounds.

subjective self The person's private view of himself.

sublimation As a defense, expression of a frustrated motive in socially sanctioned ways.

succorance need The need to seek sympathy, assistance, and protection from others.

suffering-hero fantasy Daydream in which the person gains satisfaction from imagining that he is the heart-rending or pity-evoking victim of some situation. Also see conquering-hero fantasy.

superego In psychoanalysis, the perfection-seeking portion of the personality; conscience. Also see id, ego.

suppression As a defense, deliberate inhibition of threatening stimuli.

sympathetic nervous system A subdivision of the autonomic nervous system which is in charge during excitement and emergency. Also see parasympathetic nervous system.

systematic desensitization In behavior change or psychotherapy, same as the increasing stimulus method (which see).

taking hold Job stability which comes about when a worker and his job are suitably matched. Also see trapping.

task achievement As a definition of family adjustment, ability to fulfill certain functions or achieve certain tasks which are generally set for families.

technology occupation In the classification of occupations, a category including all the modern industrial occupations.

tertiary prevention In dealing with mental illness, programs designed to avert the residual effects or aftereffects of mental illness. Also see primary prevention, secondary prevention.

threat Anticipation of pain or danger or serious interference with goal-seeking activities.

tranquilizer A drug used to calm and relax a person and make him less anxious, agitated, excited, or aggressive.

trapping Job stability which comes about because the worker has no better job to go to or is unwilling to take the risk, bear the inconvenience, or sacrifice the perquisites a change would entail. Also see taking hold.

trial work period A part of the establishment stage of vocational adjustment, including full-time but relatively short-term positions once the person enters the regular labor market. Also see initial work period, stable work period.

unchosen As indicated by a sociometric test, individuals of a group for whom no members express preference or attraction.

unconscious Without awareness.

unconscious anxiety Anxiety that is not in awareness; anxiety that is adequately controlled or defended against. Also see conscious anxiety.

unconscious motivation Motivation of which the person is unaware.

undoing As a defense, making amends or atoning for guilt-producing thoughts, feelings, and actions.

unilateral choice As indicated by a sociometric test, an unreciprocated choice, preference, or attraction of one group member for another.

unrealistic anxiety Synonym for nonobjective anxiety (which see).

unrewarded response method Extinction of an unwanted response by withholding reward or reinforcement.

visceral expression Physiological changes occurring within the body.

vocational behavior Activity which is directly or indirectly related to one's career.

vocational development Systematic changes in vocational behavior which occur with age.

vocational developmental task A developmental task which is related to one's career.

vocational maturity A concept introduced to indicate the degree or level of vocational development: one is said to be vocationally mature if his vocational behavior is appropriate for his chronological age, that is, if his vocational behavior has reached the level of development which is generally characteristic of his age peers.

warmth As parental behavior, lavishing affection on children. Also see coldness.

weekend hospital A hospital program in which the person participates during the weekend but pursues his regular activities and routines during the rest of the week. Also see day hospital, night hospital.

withheld stimulus method An extinction procedure in which a stimulus is prevented from occurring so that an unacceptable response which is linked to it is not elicited.

SUBJECT INDEX